EXXON

Joseph A. Pratt with William E. Hale

EXXON

TRANSFORMING ENERGY, 1973–2005

DOLPH BRISCOE CENTER FOR AMERICAN HISTORY
The University of Texas at Austin
Austin, Texas
2013

For Henrietta Larson

CONTENTS

ix   FOREWORD

xiii   PREFACE
Oil and ExxonMobil

1   INTRODUCTION
TRANSFORMATION
From Exxon to ExxonMobil

23   CHAPTER ONE
DOWNSIDE UP
The Rise of Producer Power after 1973

69   CHAPTER TWO
UNDER SIEGE
Political Challenges in Consuming Nations

111   CHAPTER THREE
COLDER AND DEEPER
The Search for Non-OPEC Oil and Gas

167   CHAPTER FOUR
OUT OF OIL
*Diversification and Divestment in an
Era of Oil Price Swings*

215   CHAPTER FIVE
REVIVAL
*Organizational Innovations after the
Oil Bust of 1986*

260   CHAPTER SIX
EXXON VALDEZ
Responding to Environmental Disasters

310   CHAPTER SEVEN
NEW FRONTIERS
Beyond Traditional Political Risks

362   CHAPTER EIGHT
UPGRADING DOWNSTREAM
Operational Excellence in Refining and Chemicals

421   CHAPTER NINE
MEGAMERGER
Integrating Exxon and Mobil

477   EPILOGUE
TRANSFORMATION
From the Past to the Future

503   NOTES

570   APPENDIX A
The ExxonMobil Historical Collection at the
Dolph Briscoe Center for American History

573   APPENDIX B
Interviews

577   APPENDIX C
ExxonMobil Directors and Officers,
December 1975–June 2012

594   APPENDIX D
ExxonMobil Operating Statistics, 1975–2009

609   INDEX

FOREWORD

This history of the Exxon Corporation covering the final years of the last century is a byproduct of a decision ExxonMobil made in 2003 to donate its massive historical collection to the Dolph Briscoe Center for American History at the University of Texas at Austin. The Briscoe Center is a research unit of the university that includes an archive, library, and three museums. By far the largest energy industry history collection at the Briscoe Center, the ExxonMobil Historical Collection documents the long history of the corporation, focusing on the activities and functions of four major corporate entities—Standard Oil Company, Mobil Corporation, Exxon Corporation, and Exxon Mobil Corporation—as well as various predecessor, affiliate, and subsidiary companies, notably Texas-based Humble Oil & Refining Company and Magnolia Petroleum Company.

Bill Hale, at that time senior advisor in ExxonMobil's Public Affairs Department, proposed this book project to me in October 2003 at the event officially announcing ExxonMobil's gift of its historical collection to the Briscoe Center. Bill reminded me that Exxon had sponsored a series of company histories that scholars have hailed as invaluable sources for the history of the petroleum industry. Bill suggested that the Briscoe Center was the logical institution to manage a project to research, write, and publish the fifth volume of Exxon's corporate history covering the years 1975 until 2000. Bill also believed that ExxonMobil would consider funding such a project.

I had a special interest in Bill's proposal because the Briscoe Center initiates and manages research projects based on the center's archival holdings. Past programs have included extensive oral history projects to document the history of the titanic legal battle in the 1980s between Pennzoil and Texaco over ownership of the Getty Oil Company and to document the institutional history of the Texas Independent Producers and Royalties Owners organization (TIPRO), as well as the editing and publication of the memoir of Texas governor Ross Sterling, one of the founders of the Humble Oil & Refining Company. A project to document the history of the Exxon Corporation from 1975 until 2000 would follow an already well-established program path. Despite my enthusiasm for the project, however, I realized that it would take several months for the center to absorb the vast collection before we could tackle a project of such importance. I asked Bill to give us some time and then we would look more closely at the possibilities.

Several months later, in February 2005, Truman Bell, senior program officer at ExxonMobil, called me to ask if the Briscoe Center would now be in a position to take on the next volume in the corporate history. Truman said that Bill Hale had convinced Kenneth P. Cohen, ExxonMobil's vice president for public and government affairs, of the importance of this project. Cohen had, in turn, received approval from Rex W. Tillerson, the newly appointed ExxonMobil Chairman and CEO. By this time, our staff had established adequate control over the ExxonMobil Historical Collection, so I informed Truman Bell that we were ready and eager to move forward. He asked me to submit a proposal and a budget to the ExxonMobil Foundation.

ExxonMobil approved the Briscoe Center's proposal and generous funding, which not only included support for the research, writing, and publishing of the fifth volume, but also support for additional cataloging and digitalization to make the ExxonMobil Historical Collection more accessible as a resource for the project.

With funding from ExxonMobil in hand, it was obvious that the most important decision I faced was to select the historian who would research and write the book. The first and only person to come to my mind was Joe Pratt, University of Houston professor of history and management and former chairman of that institution's Department of History. Joe was an obvious choice. He is a highly regarded scholar who has written several historical studies of the energy industry. I also was aware of Joe's keen personal interest in Exxon's history. I was delighted that Joe agreed to be the author. I also asked Bill Hale, who had recently retired from ExxonMobil, to join the research team. Because of Bill's contacts within the company and his firsthand knowledge of the period under study, I was confident that he would provide significant research support to Pratt and help facilitate the overall project.

Joe Pratt and Bill Hale have made a great team and now we have an outstanding book, which extends the history of Exxon and its predecessors to more than 125 years, the longest in-depth account of a private company in existence. It is my hope that this work will not only become the definitive academic account of Exxon's operation at the end of the twentieth century, but that it will also inspire further research efforts in the ExxonMobil Historical Collection.

DON CARLETON, PH.D.
Executive Director
Dolph Briscoe Center for American History
University of Texas at Austin

OIL AND EXXONMOBIL

The world demands oil, natural gas, and chemicals, and ExxonMobil supplies them. Since its creation in 1882, the company has invested hundreds of billions of dollars in the technology and infrastructure needed to produce these products, helping make the petroleum industry a mainstay of the global economy. ExxonMobil has refined oil into gasoline, jet fuel, and diesel fuel, facilitating the movement of people and products in an increasingly global economy. The company's growing supplies of natural gas have provided a relatively clean-burning industrial fuel for markets ranging from large factories to electric power plants while also supplying fuels for home heating and cooking. In the post–World War II era, petroleum-based chemicals have revolutionized entire sectors of the world economy by creating inexpensive and durable products for a variety of uses, including automobile tires, containers, and casings for computers. ExxonMobil has been an important part of the fast-growing oil, natural gas, and chemical industries that have developed these products and created jobs for people around the world.

While doing so, ExxonMobil also has been among the most criticized corporations in the United States. Its size and power have made it a ready symbol of Big Oil. At times, critics have blamed the company for degrading the environment, subverting democracy, raising gasoline prices, making excess profits, encouraging war in the Middle East, creating oil shortages by holding back supplies, blocking the development of alternative energies, and numerous other offenses. In producing nations, ExxonMobil and Big Oil have been blamed for transferring wealth to already-prosperous countries, exploiting workers, failing to pay fair taxes, and infecting local economies with the oil curse.

The company's image of itself has differed sharply from its public image. Those who have run ExxonMobil have been engineers, not buccaneers. Their company has been conservatively managed—steady, financially disciplined, and systematic in its decision making. It has been a highly profitable enterprise throughout most of its 130-year history, a fact that investors have accepted as a measure of success in a capitalist economy. Those comfortable with U.S.-style capitalism seem inclined to grant the company the benefit of the doubt; critics seem prepared to believe the worst about it.

My own point of view toward both oil and ExxonMobil has been shaped by my thirty-five years of teaching both history and business courses that emphasize a long-term perspective on the evolution of the petroleum industry. I have taught and written about numerous oil-related topics, including the histories of the Oil, Chemical and Atomic Workers (the once-powerful AFL-CIO union in the oil industry), the American Petroleum Institute (the dominant oil industry trade association), the Department of Energy, the National Petroleum Council (an industry-sponsored advisory committee to the U.S. Department of Energy), and oil- and natural-gas-related companies, including Amoco Corporation, Texas Eastern Corporation, and Brown and Root's offshore division. I have studied oil pollution and offshore oil development as well. I have taught an array of petroleum-related courses at the University of California in the business school and the Energy and Natural Resources Group, the History Department at Texas A&M University, and the History Department and the Bauer College of Business at the University of Houston, where I regularly teach courses on global energy.

The business professor in me admires the company's record of efficient operations. Financial discipline, managerial talent, and technological and organizational innovativeness have enabled it to maintain leadership in a vital industry for 130 years. It remains today one of the world's largest privately owned (that is, non-state-owned) oil companies as measured by market value, sales, profitability, oil and natural gas production, and refining capacity. Its record of sustained success has few parallels in American business history. That said, the historian in me is well aware of the dark side of the company's past. The discovery and development of oil has been a curse instead of a blessing for some regions around the world. Oil production and refining and the manufacture of chemicals are inherently dangerous undertakings, and workers have often paid a high price during accidents. Before the 1960s, Exxon and its industry long neglected oil pollution and waste. In the late twentieth century, growing concern about the impact of the burning of fossil fuels on climate change has placed the public spotlight on the company and the coal and oil industries as a whole. Its relationships with governments and its treatment of labor in foreign producing nations have generated intense criticism. Its difficulties in addressing such public concerns have contributed to its image as a powerful, uncaring corporate giant.

The historian and the business strategy professor do, however, share important common ground: the analysis of change over time. All of us, including big oil companies, learn from our failures as well as our successes. ExxonMobil has experienced its share of both. Its long history stretches from the time of kerosene lamps to the era of jet travel, from the days of finding oil by searching for surface indications to the days of three-dimensional seismic scanning, which uses powerful computers to create images of oil deep underground. Its learning curve was particularly steep in the years covered by this book, 1973–2005, when the company adapted to new realities confronting it at every turn.

ExxonMobil has had strong incentives to change in the recent past. As it has become less powerful with the increase in power of major oil-producing nations, it has learned to better accommodate the interests of other institutions and groups. As its projects have grown larger, requiring decades to complete and operate in order to earn long-term returns on the capital invested, it has learned the value of good corporate citizenship in staying the course in producing nations. The company has witnessed the rise of strong national oil companies with giant reserves, preferential access to national markets, and growing expertise, and it has learned to work with them and their governments as partners, seeking ways to satisfy mutual, long-term interests. ExxonMobil has remained among the most profitable concerns in the history of modern capitalism by showing flexibility when faced with the need to adapt to changing conditions.

My academic career has shaped my opinions about the oil industry, but so has the rest of my life. I grew up in the refinery town of Port Neches, Texas, a part of the large refining-chemical complex near Beaumont and Port Arthur, Texas. Many members of my family and my wife's family have worked in oil refineries or petrochemical plants. I worked as a laborer for more than a year in chemical plants and on pipelines to help pay my way through college. I earned my undergraduate degree from Rice University in Houston, which has greatly benefited from the philanthropic contributions of oilmen. Most of my academic career has been spent at Texas A&M and the University of Houston (UH), which have strong ties to the energy industries. The chaired position I have enjoyed at UH since 1986 was endowed in part by Hugh Roy Cullen, an independent oilman whose support helped transform UH into a major university.

Like my father and many of his generation who moved from poor farming communities in the interior of Texas and Louisiana to industrial jobs in the oil and chemical industries along the Gulf Coast, I believe strongly that these industries have presented significant opportunities for upward mobility. A university professor whose father had a seventh-grade education and worked more than twenty-five years as a fireman in a petrochemical plant could hardly believe otherwise. Hard as it might be for those from different economic backgrounds and from other regions to understand, in the place and time I have lived most of my life, the benefits of oil-led development have far exceeded the costs.

This book does not present a tally of those benefits and costs. Instead, it presents a long-term perspective on the company's adaptation to far-reaching changes in its competitive environment. This was no easy job for a company as large and geographically dispersed as ExxonMobil. Four previous volumes covering Exxon's history from 1882 through 1975 and a companion volume on Humble Oil & Refining have been written with the cooperation of the company over the last sixty-five years. These books have produced about 4,300 pages of detailed information about all aspects of its operations. I admire the work of those who wrote the previous volumes; I have favorably reviewed several of them over my long academic career, and I have used them regularly in my teaching and research. Taken together, the books constitute a sort of encyclopedia of Exxon, providing a comprehensive reference work on this historically important company.

This volume does not claim to be comprehensive; it focuses on what I and my collaborator, William Hale, consider the key changes that transformed the company in a volatile and demanding era. We did this with the express purpose of writing a shorter, more analytical book than the earlier Exxon volumes. That was easier said than done. Once our research began, the extraordinary scale, scope, and complexity of the company's business stunned me, despite my forty years of studying the oil industry and my previous experience in writing a history of what, at the time, I had considered a big oil company, the Amoco Corporation. This book devotes much space to changes "upstream"—the exploration for and production of oil and natural gas—but it does not try to cover every area in which the company searched for oil. Instead, our book provides details about areas and events that seem of particular importance in Exxon's evolution, stressing those that illustrate important themes in its history. We include less coverage of downstream activities, with limited discussion of petroleum refining and chemicals and very little treatment of marketing and transportation.

The book also slights an array of social and political issues of broad interest to many inside and outside the industry, including the transformation of the workplace by automation, especially in the refineries and petrochemical plants; the process of creating a more diverse and global workforce that includes growing numbers of people from nations outside the United States and Europe; and the changing position of women in the company and the oil industry as a whole. We have given considerable emphasis to the growing power of major producing nations over their own resources, but we have not presented detailed analysis of the internal politics that accompanied that change.

We have emphasized strategic decision making on issues vital to the company—and to those who produce and consume petroleum and its products. The world of global oil has been a chaotic place in the years since the energy crisis of 1973, and we have sought to capture both the tone and the process of change in an important international company as it sorted through the chaos and adapted to the new realities that emerged in that era. As it responded to sweeping changes in global markets, its decisions reflected a deeply held corporate culture that rested on the key operating values of engineering efficiency and financial discipline.

Our primary sources shaped our work. They included material from the company's records, including detailed minutes from the deliberations of the corporate management committee, which had final approval over all major decisions for most of the years covered in this volume. We had excellent materials on the major projects undertaken by the company. We conducted almost 120 interviews with more than eighty key decision makers, who at times allowed us access to their personal records. Searches of media from around the world gave us a somewhat broader context, as did the extensive published literature on the history of global petroleum and petrochemicals.

We have tried to take the reader into a black box not often opened to the outside world—the decision-making process within a major oil company. We have included instances in which the company succeeded and failed, with an eye for the ways that it tried to learn from such failures. The result is primarily an extended case study of management and technological change examined in the context of the history of the international petroleum industry. This is the focus we chose six years ago and have held to over the life of the project. We acknowledge that the focus of other historians would have been different, and we hope that future researchers will find value in the records generated by our work, which will be deposited in the ExxonMobil Historical Collection at the Dolph Briscoe Center for American History at the University of Texas at Austin.

This book must, of course, stand on its own merits, not on the authors' intentions. It is unlikely to please either the most fervent supporters or the harshest critics of Exxon, for each reader's perspective will shape his or her response. We ask you to read our book for what it is: a historical perspective from inside one of the most powerful corporations in the world as it responds to the closely related cluster of energy, environmental, and economic challenges that will have a profound impact on the future of the modern world.

I have been assisted in the research and writing of this volume by William E. Hale, who was a history major as an undergraduate at the University of Wisconsin and later earned a degree from Princeton University. Bill worked first for the U.S. government and then joined Exxon Corporation in New York. Over the course of nearly three decades with Exxon, he worked for the company's U.S. division, its international headquarters company, and the corporation's Public Affairs Department. Before his retirement from ExxonMobil, he was the principal speechwriter for senior managers and contributed to many of ExxonMobil's public communications.

This project was enthusiastically supported by Kenneth P. Cohen, ExxonMobil's vice president for public and government affairs, who was instrumental in persuading ExxonMobil's chairman and CEO, Rex W. Tillerson, to endorse the project. The authors thank these two men for their support, including facilitating our access to people and records.

We also were assisted in our work on this volume by many other people at ExxonMobil. Of particular value were the twelve interviews with Lee R. Raymond, the eleven interviews with Harry J. Longwell, the very lengthy interviews and subsequent written comments provided by Rene Dahan, and a daylong interview with Clifton Garvin. These executives provided invaluable insight into the management of Exxon and ExxonMobil during this tumultuous period.

A variety of others within ExxonMobil provided important help. Frank Risch and Jack F. Bennett were central to our understanding of the company's innovative financial initiatives. The late Mel Harrison offered useful insights into events in Libya and Alaska; Otto Harrison provided good material on the cleanup of the *Exxon Valdez* oil spill; and Edwin J. Hess gave detailed information on the environmental and safety initiatives within the company after the *Valdez* accident. Frank B. Sprow helped with the company's research efforts as well as its environmental and safety undertakings. John E. Seddelmeyer and Charles W. Matthews provided useful perspectives on the company's legal issues, particularly those surrounding the *Exxon Valdez* accident. André Madec helped us piece together the Chad pipeline story. Samuel J. Vastola and Steven

Stamas gave insightful assessments of the culture of the company and how it approached problems. Jon L. Thompson was a central figure in the modification of the company's exploration strategy, and his recollections were invaluable. The senior executives Edward G. Galante, Don D. Humphreys, K. Terry Koonce, Stuart R. McGill, the late J. Steven Simon, and Robert E. Wilhelm were also especially helpful. Internal publications of Exxon proved quite useful; we owe a special debt to the authors of numerous articles in *The Lamp*, the corporation's major in-house magazine, particularly Mike Long.

This book was a project of the Dolph Briscoe Center for American History at the University of Texas at Austin. To its director, Don Carleton, goes much of the credit for providing organizational leadership for this project, for selecting its authors, and for managing the completion of the book. His periodic assessments of the project's progress and the quality of its output were very helpful. Holly Taylor, Erin Purdy, Matthew Darby, and David Zepeda at the Briscoe Center played important roles in the research, writing, and editing of this book.

Louis Galambos, my friend, coauthor, and often-ignored dissertation director at Johns Hopkins University, helped us at a critical point in this project. The best editor I have ever had, Lou gave the manuscript a "hard read" when it was nearing completion. During one long summer day in Baltimore spent sitting across his dining room table and going through his comments page by page, I understood more about the major themes of the book than I had taught myself in my previous four years of research, interviewing, and writing. Long may he edit.

I am fortunate to work with a great "EUE" group of faculty members and graduate students at the University of Houston in the closely related fields of energy, urban, and environmental history. I have different sets of valued colleagues in the Global Energy Management Institute in the Bauer College of Business and the Energy and Management and Policy Group (an interdisciplinary group on campus whose activities I coordinate). In the long journey to the completion of this book, I benefited from the insights offered by Gunnar Nerheim, Stephen Arbogast, Ty Priest, Marty Melosi, Kairn Klieman, Kathy Brosnan, Jimmy Schafer, Jason Theriot, David Raley, Julie Cohn, Joe Stromberg, Jeff Womack, Mark Young,

Tomiko Meeks, and Tom McKinney. I also appreciate the help provided by excellent research assistants, including the last four people on the list above plus Joseph Abel and Kate Pratt.

The dedication to Henrietta Larson reflects her impact on the Exxon history project and on my own career. Professor Larson helped organize and manage the Business History Foundation at the Harvard Business School, where she was the first tenured female professor. The foundation took on the job of writing the original three volumes of the history of Standard Oil (New Jersey). In addition, the project published an excellent stand-alone history of Humble Oil & Refining Company, as well as a volume entitled *Standard Oil Company (New Jersey) in World War II*. The fourth volume of Exxon's history was written through a cooperative agreement with Tulane University. This current volume, number five in the series, was written under two agreements, one between the Dolph Briscoe Center for American History at the University of Texas and ExxonMobil, and a second between the Briscoe Center and the authors.

One of the enduring achievements of the Business History Foundation was the creation of a model contract between the professional business historians who wrote the histories and the corporation. The contract included safeguards for the independence of the historians, who had editorial control of the manuscripts and access to the records and people of the company. The company had the right to review the manuscript and make suggestions for corrections or changes, but the authors retained the final authority to accept or reject those suggestions. Our project followed that model contract. Funding for research and writing came from ExxonMobil through the Briscoe Center. I thank Professor Larson and the others who operated the Business History Foundation for their model contract.

I thank Henrietta also for her kind encouragement early in my training as a historian. The first historical paper I delivered during graduate school was at the Business History Conference in 1974 in Wilmington, Delaware. My paper was a graduate student's take on the "political naïveté" of the treatment of Venezuelan politics in the 1920s and 1930s included in the third volume of the Standard Oil (New Jersey) history, which Henrietta had coauthored. My presentation focused on the plundering of Venezuela by Standard Oil, acting in cahoots with the nation's evil dictator.

After the session, a pleasant older woman came up to the table where I sat, introduced herself as Professor Larson, made a few short comments, and asked for a copy of the paper. A week or so later, the copy came back to me in the mail, filled with detailed handwritten critiques of my comments. These were written on cut-up pieces of lined paper and stapled to the passages in my essay to which they referred, making the original paper much thicker than it had been. Apparently, I had missed a bit of the complexity of the early history of Venezuelan oil. By later mail arrived a box filled with the three then-published volumes of the Jersey Standard histories and the Humble Oil companion volume. They were neatly signed in a precise handwriting: "To Joe Pratt, a young historian who faces great challenges and opportunities in the study of business and economic history, with the best wishes of a pioneer in the fields, Henrietta M. Larson."

Professor Larson politely and constructively checked in on my progress as a historian until she died in 1983 at age eighty-eight. As I finish this volume, I would relish the opportunity to talk with her again about "political naïveté" in her book and the "great challenges" of this new volume, which includes two sections on Venezuela. My guess is that she would be pleasantly surprised by my "mature" views on political economy and somewhat disappointed that this volume lacks the detail and comprehensiveness of her own works on Jersey Standard's history. She would, no doubt, be pleased by my use of her volumes to check facts for this book. The dedication is my message across time, thanking her again for the books she sent me more than thirty-five years ago. Her encouragement during and after our meeting in Wilmington led finally, almost inevitably, to my work on this volume on the history of John D. Rockefeller's company—now known as ExxonMobil.

JOE PRATT
Houston, Texas
December 2012

EXXON

TRANSFORMATION

FROM EXXON TO EXXONMOBIL

I n 1973, Exxon was the largest and most profitable of the "Seven Sisters" (Exxon, Mobil, Standard Oil of California, Texaco, Gulf Oil, Royal Dutch Shell, and British Petroleum). These major international oil companies dominated the petroleum industry of the free world.[1] From 1973 to 1983, the control of oil shifted dramatically toward the producing nations and their national oil companies.[2] The immediate impact of this change on Exxon was that nationalization in Venezuela, Saudi Arabia, and Libya dramatically reduced its global production of oil. This era of upheaval in the major oil-producing nations has continued into the early twenty-first century; in 2005, only four of the original Seven Sisters remained: the newly merged ExxonMobil, Chevron (formerly Standard Oil of California, which had acquired both Texaco and Gulf), Shell, and British Petroleum (now known simply as BP). These giant "megamajors" remained important parts of the global petroleum industry, but they held far smaller reserves than the national oil companies such as Saudi Aramco of Saudi Arabia, the National Iranian Oil Company, or Petróleos de Venezuela, SA (PDVSA). Despite far-reaching changes in global oil since the early 1970s, however, one thing was the same: ExxonMobil remained the largest and most profitable of the international oil companies.

This book examines how the company adapted and continued to prosper in an era marked by the growing power of the major producing nations. It analyzes Exxon's strategic choices in the years from 1973 through the completion of the Exxon-Mobil merger, which was announced in 1998, approved by regulators in 1999, and largely completed through the integration of the two companies by about 2005. This book uses detailed case studies of key decisions and events to examine how Exxon's leaders used their company's traditional strengths in engineering, finance, technology, and organizational innovation to adapt to an evolving and demanding competitive environment.[3] But Exxon also developed new strengths after 1973. It improved its ability to manage risk in international politics, becoming more diplomatic in its dealings with the governments of the major oil-producing nations. It learned to manage economic and technical risks while working within networks of other oil companies, and government agencies. The merger of Exxon and Mobil accelerated and consolidated ongoing changes within the two companies, producing a unified organization bound together by Exxon's distinctive corporate culture. This book tells the story of that transformation.

DRIVERS OF CHANGE

For a quarter of a century after 1945, Standard Oil Company (New Jersey), renamed Exxon Corporation in 1972, prospered by taking advantage of a growing global demand for oil, access to abundant supplies of relatively inexpensive oil from Venezuela and the Middle East, and a generally permissive regulatory environment. In an era that saw no sharp changes in oil prices, the company enjoyed steady growth in a relatively stable business environment. Events in the 1970s undermined these postwar arrangements, clearing the way for the emergence of a new global order in international oil.

The energy and environmental crises of the late 1960s and early 1970s brought into sharper focus three fundamental drivers of change that converged after 1973: the coming of producer power, the return of sharp swings in oil prices, and the enforcement of environmental regulations much stricter than those that had been in force. These powerful forces altered conditions abruptly and fundamentally, forcing the international oil companies to make long-term strategic adjustments.

The coming of producer power was the defining event of the 1970s. One stark statistic from Exxon captures the heart of the matter. In 1973, the company produced about 6.7 million barrels of crude per day, but by 1986 it was producing only 1.8 million, a 73 percent drop.[4] The international oil companies and the major producing nations had struggled over control of the revenues from oil and gas production since at least the 1930s, with the international oil companies retaining the upper hand in managing both the price of oil and the quantities produced in each nation. Producer power became a reality after 1973 as the Organization of Petroleum Exporting Countries (OPEC), whose membership came from the ranks of the largest oil-exporting countries in the world, asserted control over oil prices and national production rates. Established in 1960, OPEC asserted new powers in the early 1970s as its member nations individually and collectively pushed for greater oil revenues.

History shifted into high gear in the rush of events after October 6, 1973, when the invasion of Israeli-occupied territory by Egypt and Syria sparked a major conflict in which the United States emerged as the primary supporter of Israel. The Arab members of OPEC unsheathed the "oil weapon," namely, an embargo on oil shipments to the United States and other supporters of Israel. The embargo had unforeseen consequences. After the withdrawal of oil from world markets with limited surplus capacity, oil prices rapidly quadrupled; the resulting increased oil revenues and shared sense of triumph greatly strengthened OPEC's power to influence oil prices by managing the amount of oil exported by its members.[5]

Flush with new power, the governments of most major producing nations hastened to nationalize the properties of foreign oil companies and then to create or strengthen national oil companies.[6] This clearly established their power to control their national oil reserves. It also reduced the traditional power of the international oil companies in areas that contained most of the world's proved reserves of oil. The speed of this historic about-face stunned even members of OPEC. The oil world settled down for a brief period after the whirlwind of change in the early 1970s. Yet before a new economic equilibrium could be established in the

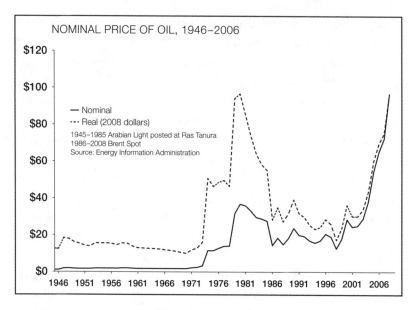

FIGURE I.1: Source: *United States Energy Information Administration*

international petroleum industry, another crisis sparked a second round of adjustments. The Iranian revolution of 1979 led to another sharp disruption in global oil supplies, one that temporarily doubled the spot market price of oil and fed a frenzy of unsustainable drilling in the early 1980s, which was followed by a devastating oil bust in 1986.

The bust reminded all involved in the industry that even producer power had limits in a world of sharp and unpredictable swings in oil prices. The relative stability in the price of oil in the twenty-five years after World War II (figure I.1) had created attitudes and habits of mind that proved difficult to adjust when the swings in the price of oil resumed with a vengeance in the decades after 1973. The oil industry rode the roller coaster of oil prices steeply upward until 1983, when it reached the peak of this first climb, hovered for a moment, and then plunged almost straight back down in 1986. Exxon, which took great pride in its long-term energy outlook, found that extreme oil-price volatility made long-range planning almost impossible. The modern oil industry involves large, long-term investments in massive projects. These investments often take many years to begin to return profits, and sharp drops in oil prices can quickly turn once-promising projects into disasters. High oil prices also fuel inflation, undermining financial planning for the construction of large projects. Extreme swings in oil prices since 1973 have been the bane of energy planners, investors, and policy makers alike.

Exxon also faced intense political challenges in a number of consuming nations.[7] Environmental regulations had particularly deep and far-reaching impacts on the oil industry. As the largest and most visible oil company, Exxon often found itself at the center of debates about the trade-offs between the supply and use of energy, on the one hand, and the protection of environmental quality on the other. Several waves of new environmental laws around the world required the company to invest substantial amounts of time and money in completing environmental impact statements, meeting stricter standards for cleaner air and water, implementing new safeguards for the disposal of toxic waste, phasing out leaded gasoline, and producing cleaner-burning gasoline.[8] The new wave of environmental regulations that crested in the 1970s in the United States and other developed nations forced all energy producers and users to begin to view energy and the environment as two sides of the same coin. These laws gave governmental agencies unprecedented powers to shape corporate decision making on investments and technology.

From 1973 through the 1980s, these challenges—producer power, cycles of boom and bust in oil prices, and environmental regulation—staggered Exxon and the rest of the industry. To regain its balance, the company drew on strengths it had built over more than a century of operations. One major strength was a strong corporate culture that stressed the core operating principles of financial discipline, the systematic control of costs, organizational innovation, and technical leadership. Another included core competencies in oil, natural gas, and chemicals, and a global network of facilities and markets for these closely related industries. As it adapted these strengths to help it navigate the changing global market, the company had to address several long-standing weaknesses as well. Chief among these was the decline of U.S oil production and the company's increasingly outdated bureaucratic decision-making structure, which slowed its response to opportunities. Few oil companies faced the crises of the era after 1973 with greater resources than Exxon. None had more to lose.

JOHN D. ROCKEFELLER'S COMPANY

Exxon's distinctive corporate culture influenced its responses to the demands of the new era in oil. Those who led the company could call on operating values deeply embedded in its history and corporate culture. Many of these core values had been built into the company in the late nineteenth century by John D. Rockefeller as he created Standard Oil, which set the standard for both high quality and low prices in oil products in the late nineteenth century. Obviously, much changed in the petroleum industry in the century after Rockefeller created the world's first modern oil company, but Standard Oil's DNA continued to shape ExxonMobil into the twenty-first century, especially in its commitment to efficient internal operations.

Controlling costs was an obsession with Rockefeller, who was a book-keeper by training but a cost accountant by nature. When he entered the oil industry in the early 1860s, he noted, "Many of the brightest [busi-nessmen] . . . did not actually know when they were making money on a certain operation and when they were losing. . . . We knew how much we made and where we gained or lost."[9] Strict financial controls provided the foundation on which Standard Oil grew. The "Great John D." kept close track of his capital and worked hard to determine where it could be put to the best use. He cut costs habitually, for he recognized that in a contin-uous-process industry, a penny saved through improvements in manufac-turing processes was a penny saved again and again, hour after hour, day after day, year after year. His strict, systematic enforcement of cost controls helped make Standard Oil the low-cost producer in its industry. Embod-ied in his crusade to cut costs was the assumption that operational excel-lence and reliably good products were the sources of long-term strength. The combination of low costs and budgetary discipline in good times gave the company the resources to take advantage of opportunities presented by distressed competitors in hard times. Buying properties at the bottom of the business cycle was a key source of long-term competitive advantage for Standard Oil.

In his sustained effort to make his company the industry leader, Rock-efeller focused sharply on petroleum: "We devoted ourselves exclusively to the oil business and its products. The company never went into outside ventures, but kept to the enormous task of perfecting its own organization."[10] This "enormous task" required finding a path to orderly expansion amid the chaos of the early years of the oil industry. Rockefeller's passion for efficiency made him acutely aware of problems arising from the organization of the industry in its early years. He had begun his oil career in refining, but came to realize that he could not adequately protect his growing investment in that sector if other companies controlled the related businesses of oil production, transportation, and marketing. Accordingly, he embarked upon his most enduring contribution to the development of the modern oil industry—vertical integration. This foundational structural innovation defined the organization of major oil companies for almost a century by combining production, refining, transportation, and marketing into a unified organization.[11]

By reducing operational risks and dramatically lowering costs, vertical integration allowed Standard Oil to build or buy larger, more efficient refineries. As Rockefeller later recalled, "We proceeded to buy the largest and best refining concerns and centralize the administration of them with a view to securing greater economy and efficiency."[12] After the fact, professional economists gave the name "economies of scale" to the results of this process, which lowered unit costs and created tremendous competitive advantages that the company used to dominate all phases of the U.S. petroleum industry by the turn of the twentieth century. Rockefeller also pioneered the creation of the trust, which he used as a holding company to coordinate the efficient operations of his company as it grew in scale and geographic scope in the late nineteenth century.

A final enduring corporate value originally instilled by Rockefeller was technical leadership. In building the first modern oil company, Rockefeller examined all aspects of its operations systematically, looking for ways to make efficient use of people, capital, and equipment.[13] He pushed best practices throughout his far-flung organization. The drive to eliminate waste in the refining process led Standard Oil to search for ways to increase the types of refined products distilled from each barrel of crude. This encouraged Rockefeller to hire the first professional chemist employed by the refining industry, who was asked to develop a process to make commercial products from sulfur-laden crude, which could not be refined with traditional technology. This was one of the first instances in oil-industry history when new technology allowed "unconventional" crude, not previously marketable, to be transformed into a product that could be economically refined and sold. Standard "spared no expense in utilizing the best and most efficient method of manufacture" and did not hesitate "to sacrifice old machinery and old plants for new and better ones."[14] The company also stayed at the cutting edge of pipeline and tanker technology, either through its own research or by purchasing the work of others. New technology fostered growth while also driving down the cost of refined goods.

In Rockefeller's era, the recruitment and promotion of managers was simple and practical. As a ruthless competitor that used all methods available to dominate the oil industry in an era noted for its cutthroat competition, the company put to the test those who ran competing companies. Those who impressed Rockefeller as he put them out of business often joined his company. Once inside Standard Oil, they were given considerable leeway in a decision-making system whose long-term strategy was centralized in the hands of a few top executives, but whose operational authority was decentralized among the components of the company's growing global enterprise. They also joined a dedicated and tight-knit team of managers who were highly motivated to succeed in a very demanding environment and possessed ample resources to win most of the battles they chose to fight.

With few laws to restrain him, Rockefeller made his own rules and zealously enforced them with his company's economic power. He demanded and received rebates on posted railroad rates and drawbacks on those of his competitors, which meant that a portion of the rates they paid went to Standard Oil without their knowledge. He made use of industrial spies and undermined competitors with what would later be defined as predatory pricing. Long after Standard had won near-monopoly control in oil, laws passed partly in response to its abuses outlawed many of those practices. But changes in the law did not remove the outrage engendered by Standard Oil's earlier behavior.

Although others in the industry voiced indignation at the competitive power of the "Standard Oil gang," they also at times voiced grudging respect for the ruthless efficiency and single-minded purpose of those who ran the company.[15] Testifying before the U.S. Congress, the railroad leader William Vanderbilt said of the company's leaders: "I never came into contact with any class of men as smart and able as they are in their business. . . . You can't keep such men down. . . . They will be on top all the time."[16] For their part, Standard's managers believed strongly that they had built the best-run oil company in the world, and they relished the chance to prove their superiority in the marketplace. Viewing the cutthroat competition of the late nineteenth century as a fight to the death between "us" and "them," they remained highly confident of the ultimate outcome. Their strong tribal sense remained an important part of Standard's corporate culture. Others in the oil industry and the general public often interpreted the company's supreme confidence as arrogance. In Rockefeller's era, the public's negative opinion of Standard Oil coalesced into support for the breakup of the company under the nation's antitrust laws, exemplified by the Sherman Antitrust Act of 1890.

At the turn of the twentieth century, the historian and muckraker Ida Tarbell recognized Standard Oil's "legitimate greatness" in building an efficient organization, but strongly condemned its behavior as excessive, unnecessary, and unethical.[17] President Theodore Roosevelt referred to Standard Oil in his campaigns as a symbol of a "malefactor of great wealth" and a "bad trust." The muckraker Henry Demarest Lloyd captured its reputation for political corruption in memorable language: "The Standard had done everything to the Pennsylvania legislature except refine it."[18] In an era of newspaper-circulation wars, the *New York World*, a part of the Pulitzer chain, did not exhibit prize-winning standards of objectivity when writing about Standard: "There has been no outrage too colossal, no petty meanness too contemptible for these freebooters to engage in. From hounding and driving prosperous business men to beggary and suicide, to holding up and plundering widows and orphans . . . all this has entered into the exploits of this organized gang of commercial bandits."[19] More than the company's hard-edged competitive practices fed this fear and loathing. Many Americans worried that its near monopoly spelled the end of traditional free markets and perhaps even the end of American democracy. Others found it a readily available, potent symbol around which to organize support for political reform. Some simply found Rockefeller to be a compelling villain.

In response to this avalanche of criticism the "Great John D." offered

simple advice to his compatriots: "Let the world wag." The efficient production of useful products would answer the critics. From within the
company, political leaders were viewed as opportunistic and insincere;
the public seemed ignorant, or at least economically illiterate.[20] Accustomed to the logic of engineering and efficiency, Standard's executives
appeared baffled by the public's outrage. Failing to take seriously the rhetoric and symbolism of democratic politics, Rockefeller and others underestimated the political risks from antitrust. The dissolution decree by the
U.S. Supreme Court in 1911 hammered home the cost of their insularity,
as well as their need to look beyond their disdain for politicians in order
to avoid being blinded to the potential impacts of political change.[21]

Rockefeller thus left a dual legacy within Standard Oil. While creating a model of efficient operation, he also created an enduring image of
the evils of "Big Oil." The company's extraordinary economic and engineering successes provided a sharp contrast with its difficulties in dealing
with political and societal demands. Its internal image as the best-run oil
company remained in conflict with its public image as the most hated and
feared one.

Is it possible that Exxon remained "John D. Rockefeller's company" on
the eve of the energy crisis in 1973, seventy years after he had retired from
active management of the company? Did his spirited approach to business still influence the management of Exxon? Or as his critics might have
put it, did his ghost still haunt the company's efforts to gain greater public
acceptance? Interviews with nearly 120 current and former Exxon executives conducted during the research for this book brought numerous comments about Rockefeller's emphasis on cost cutting and efficient operations, as well as his competitive zeal. It makes sense that employees in a
company with a long record of success would embrace the memory and
image of its founder, especially if he is widely viewed as a major figure in
business history. But it is likely that Rockefeller's approach to operations,
not his image, was his enduring contribution to the offspring of Standard
Oil, and that Exxon's managers in the late twentieth century embraced
that approach when confronted by very difficult challenges somewhat
similar to those that had confronted Rockefeller a century earlier.

Much obviously has changed at ExxonMobil and in the world of
oil since the formative years of Rockefeller's leadership, but interesting

parallels remain between the oil industry of the late nineteenth century and that of the late twentieth. All three major drivers of change in the 1970s had parallels in the 1870s–1890s. The last step in attaining near-monopoly control of the American oil industry for Rockefeller was his effort to more tightly control production, and he never quite succeeded, because major new oil fields were drilled outside his strongholds in Pennsylvania, Ohio, and West Virginia. Large oil discoveries in the western and southwestern United States after 1900 gave rise to new competitors and led quickly to discoveries in other nations, notably Mexico and Venezuela. The return of oil-price swings in the late twentieth century put Exxon's managers in the situation Rockefeller had faced for most of his career, when business cycles brought severe ups and downs in general market conditions. Strict environmental regulations were certainly not a problem for Standard Oil and its competitors in the age of Rockefeller, when widespread oil pollution and waste was the norm.[22] But the enforcement of strong antitrust laws had effects somewhat parallel to those of environmental regulations almost a century later.

The industry's wild ride in the high-price era of 1970s followed by the price bust of the mid-1980s forced Exxon executives to confront challenges similar to those faced by Rockefeller a century earlier. They ultimately responded, as he had, by going back to fundamentals that applied as well in 1986 as in 1886—stick to core businesses, cut costs, practice financial discipline, stay on the leading edge of technology, and use organizational innovations to improve overall performance. Like Rockefeller, the leaders of the transformation of Exxon in the years from the oil bust through the merger with Mobil had to respond creatively to challenges brought by geographic expansion, high political risks, and the impact of unpredictable oil-price swings on potential investments. New communication technologies permitted the centralized decision-making structure to stay efficient, in ways similar in many respects to the system of management established and enforced by Rockefeller a century earlier. And like him, they focused on return on investment and long-term profitability as the best measures of success.

Taken as a whole, the corporate culture within Exxon in the late twentieth century reflected the historical strengths of the oldest and most successful of the major international oil companies. Steady growth in the mid-twentieth century had created a very large corporation that at times buried these core values under layers of management, but they proved durable and adaptable. Their practical effects could be seen in the strong company inherited by Exxon's management as it entered the new era after 1973.

INHERITED STRENGTHS

As the company entered the 1970s, it had impressive strengths, including a very effective system of personnel recruitment, training, and advancement. Exxon used its Compensation and Executive Development Committee to make regular, systematic, and extensive performance reviews. The CEO chaired the corporate-level committee, which directly reviewed 200 senior managers and oversaw the progress of 400 other positions. Each level of management down the hierarchy had similar committees. At all levels, employees were rank-ordered through rigorous and ongoing reviews. Those who came up short received counseling and training aimed at improving their performance. Those who came out on top could expect raises, promotions, and rotation to positions that would broaden their experience and increase their responsibilities. This merit system generated intense competition for advancement, which helped create a productive work environment and great loyalty in those who succeeded.

This approach regularly developed talented and experienced cohorts of managers. As promising executives moved up the ladder, they gained experience with varied aspects of the company's far-flung operations. At young ages, many future leaders within Exxon found themselves working as executive assistants to those running the company. They also regularly worked with others who were moving up the corporate hierarchy. By the time they neared the top ranks of the company's management, they usually had led large regional companies within Exxon. They also had worked closely with many of the other people who converged at the top of the company from their cohort. This common experience over decades produced a unified vision of the company and shared trust with other leaders.

The company believed strongly in developing leadership from within, primarily from the ranks of its engineers and scientists. Though it drew employees from a range of backgrounds, the company had particular success hiring upwardly mobile young engineers who came from less-than-privileged backgrounds and who had the incentive and the ambition to work hard as members of strong teams of specialists. Well into the 1960s, these recruits were almost exclusively white males from North America, and they often came from small towns and state universities. Many of these overachievers flourished in Exxon's merit-based personnel system, which rewarded hard work over long periods and seldom recruited outsiders from other companies or people with "connections."[23]

Those who reached the top level of the corporate ladder inherited a layered system of managerial authority that had evolved from the committee-based system developed in John D. Rockefeller's era to bind together the original Standard Oil Trust. The CEO's office in Rockefeller Center in New York City sat atop a pyramid of power that reached down into the company's sprawling operations around the world through a series of interconnected management committees. In the mid-1970s, the corporate management committee consisted of a small group of high-ranking executives who also served as inside directors on the company's board of directors. The CEO and chairman of the board, positions usually held by the same person, served as the chair of this committee, which met several times a week to review contracts, major projects, and financial matters. Each February, the management committee reviewed detailed reports of the financial and operating performance of each of the company's major units. Then, in the late fall, it reviewed four-year investment plans and capital budgets from those units.

These plans became the company's road maps for the future. After a reorganization in 1966, the company was organized as ten wholly owned divisions or affiliated companies and one 70 percent–owned affiliate, Imperial Oil Limited of Canada, which reported directly to headquarters. This new, regionally organized management structure replaced an unwieldy system of forty global affiliates, including a variety of companies that were active in a single nation but had reported directly to corporate headquarters. After the company changed its name to Exxon Corporation in 1972, the regionally organized companies included Esso Middle East, Exxon Company USA, Esso Eastern, Esso Europe, Esso Inter-America, and Imperial. Functional affiliates included Exxon Chemical Company, Exxon International Company, Esso Exploration, Exxon Enterprises, and Exxon Research and Engineering. Preparation of the annual performance reviews and four-year plans for the corporate management committee required a great deal of detailed analysis by management groups in the affiliates and the regional companies. In this work, as well as in the preparation of detailed information about upcoming major projects, the regional companies could draw on the insights of specialists within the nations in their region.

After such plans had worked their way up to the corporate level, the heads of the regional companies journeyed to Rockefeller Center to seek the approval of headquarters. There, the members of the corporate management committee drew on their own experience, along with detailed studies prepared by staff members in New York, to decide the fate of project proposals or four-year plans. An additional level of financial scrutiny came from a separate Investment Advisory Committee made up of other top Exxon executives. If all went well in New York, the heads of the regional companies returned to their own headquarters around the world with commitments for the capital their projects needed. This lengthy, painstaking review was used to vet all major expenditures at several levels. It generally produced a document in which the corporate management committee stated that it had "no objections" to the plans as finally approved.

The board of directors participated in these reviews indirectly through its inside directors, each of whom served as "contact executive" for one or more of the regional and affiliated companies. The board, which by the late 1970s had a majority of outside directors, met quarterly to consider key issues raised by the company's operations. Then, in December of each year, it reviewed the company's long-term investment plans and capital budget, which had been put together from analogous plans submitted by the regional companies.[24]

Even a short review of the company's management system in the early 1970s suggests an increasingly bureaucratic organization. This was the reality of a giant, century-old, global organization. The CEO and his corporate staff put in place and enforced financial controls and executive development; within the broad guidelines regularly set and enforced in New York, however, the regional companies had much discretion to carry out their operations. Indeed, a close examination of the corporate management records from this era suggests that in important ways, requests from the regional companies to corporate headquarters strongly shaped the company's long-term strategy. Corporate management seemed to focus more on evaluating plans submitted by the regions than on directly planning the future of the company as a whole.[25]

Those who became top corporate managers inherited a company that could afford to be conservative and slow moving, given the extraordinary resources accumulated by their predecessors. The company had the technical and research capabilities to develop new producing regions or technologies, as well as the financial strength to wait for others to develop new opportunities and then buy its way in. As the company entered the 1970s, one key measure of its strength was its solid production of crude oil in major producing areas throughout the free world. In 1970, Standard Oil produced about 15 percent of the free world's total daily demand of approximately 40 million barrels of crude oil and natural gas liquids. The company enjoyed balanced production from the United States, Canada, Venezuela, and Libya and had inviting prospects in the North Sea and Australia.[26] By 1973, its worldwide refineries were processing an average of more than 5.8 million barrels of crude oil a day. Its total revenues of $28.5 billion came primarily from the sale of refined oil products and natural gas, but chemicals provided growing sales, which surpassed $1.6 billion that year. Its earnings, or net income, in 1973 reached $2.44 billion. Such statistics made Exxon the largest oil company in the world and the widely recognized "king" of the international petroleum industry.

Venezuela, where Creole Petroleum Corporation had been Exxon's most profitable source of oil and revenues for much of the post–World War II era, had begun to decline as a source of oil for Exxon in the 1960s. By that time, the company was depending more for increased oil production on Saudi Arabia, Iran, and Libya. Viewed in retrospect, this was "easy oil," that is, oil produced from giant fields at much lower costs than it could be produced in harsher and more demanding environments. Initially, terms of access to easy oil were also favorable to the international oil companies, but the Middle Eastern producers steadily learned to extract greater taxes and royalties after World War II. Even before the energy crises of the 1970s, change was in the air in the major producing regions.

In areas of the world with more stable and predictable political environments, Exxon had great historical strengths in oil production but pessimistic assumptions about future expansion. This was particularly true in the United States, long the company's primary source of crude oil. Humble Oil & Refining Company (renamed Exxon Company USA in 1972), the Houston-based subsidiary that managed Exxon's petroleum operations in the southwestern United States, produced more than one million barrels of oil a day in the early 1970s. But by then, its production in the lower forty-eight states had peaked, and its development of prom-ising reserves on Alaska's North Slope had been delayed by regulatory challenges. At the same time, Imperial Oil produced more than 250,000 barrels of oil a day, with prospects for additional sources in the Arctic and in the oil sands regions of Alberta. Prospects in the North Sea were begin-ning to look quite promising, as were fields in Australia's Bass Strait.

Counterbalancing uncertainties about the future of oil production was the company's strong global presence in petroleum refining, market-ing, and transportation. In 1973, Exxon remained the largest oil-refining company in the world. It was a leading refiner in Europe as well as in the United States, and its sales of refined products in other regions were expanding. It owned and developed vast quantities of natural gas, which played a growing role as a feedstock for petrochemical products and as a source of heat and power in its refineries and petrochemical plants. Even at low prevailing regulated prices, Exxon's worldwide sales of 9.3 billion cubic feet (BCF) of natural gas a day in 1973 provided significant revenue. (5.3 BCF equals 1 million barrels of oil.)

Exxon's basic strengths had always been in oil and natural gas. But early in the twentieth century, it had successfully diversified into another closely related business, the production of petrochemicals. In 1920, its major refineries began making isopropyl alcohol from waste gases produced dur-ing refining, and the manufacture of other new chemical products grew in subsequent decades. During World War II, the company's chemical pro-duction shifted to butyl rubber and additives for fuels, in support of the Allied war effort. Chemical production continued to expand in the refin-eries during the postwar boom, and in the mid-1960s, a separate chemical company was created. By the early 1970s, Exxon Chemical was poised to expand its production of basic chemicals that were sold to manufac-turers of intermediate and final products. As Exxon Chemical extracted additional value from the corporation's raw materials, it produced profits that had the potential to balance ups and downs in the oil and natural gas industry. Petrochemical production and refining shared similar technologies and often the same physical locations.

INHERITED WEAKNESSES

The embargo in 1973–1974 revealed a key weakness inherited from the post–World War II era by decision makers at Exxon and its competitors. Those who went to work in the oil industry after the war and moved up corporate hierarchies in the next quarter century made up one of the few generations of oil executives in history whose primary management experience came during an era of relative oil-price stability and steady economic growth. This meant that they had little experience with price volatility and few planning tools to help them cope with it. From 1945 to 1973, oil executives could set long-term strategies and make long-term investments with confidence that the price of oil would stay within a predictable range of about $2 to $3 a barrel. By extending trend lines from the post–World War II era into the future, planners at Exxon and other companies assumed that they could accurately project the long-term price of oil and thus the investment climate for their companies.

They were dead wrong. In the 1970s, these prices unexpectedly soared, reaching a then-staggering range of $30–$35 a barrel before plunging to less than $10 a barrel in the mid-1980s. Planners inside Exxon—as in other oil companies and governments—predicted neither of these dramatic swings in prices. Effective long-term strategy became a victim of the company's inability to predict the direction, much less the intensity, of such changes in the price of its basic commodity.

Exxon's increasingly unwieldy and inefficient administrative structure also posed problems in the early 1970s. A management structure that had served the company well in the boom years for oil after World War II began to show the effects of decades of expansion and the addition of layers of bureaucratic decision making. As the company entered the 1970s, a number of key executives realized that its management system had become sluggish and slow to react to market changes. The traditional influence of several of the largest regional companies reflected the economic realities of earlier times. Humble Oil, Imperial Oil, and Creole Petroleum had enjoyed privileged positions within Standard of New Jersey in the decades after World War II. The decline of their relative share of oil production and thus of their traditional standing within the company created organizational tensions, which in turn impeded the adaptation of a more global approach to business by the corporation as a whole.

Some of these organizational tensions could be dampened by the company's financial strengths, but fundamental strategic adaptations proved difficult to accomplish. Corporate strategy was muddled because of the influence of the regional companies on the planning process. The best example of this haphazardness was the lack of a system for prioritizing prospective oil and natural gas exploration prospects around the world. The corporate management committee tended to allocate capital for such projects according to their priority within each of the regional companies. This approach impeded the efficient reallocation of resources, since it did not take into account the rise and fall in importance of the regional companies or their potential for growth. Indeed, the company's history hampered it fundamentally: an organization with a long record of success was slow to recognize that dramatically changed circumstances might require new approaches to management.

STRATEGIC AND STRUCTURAL RESPONSES TO THE NEW ORDER IN OIL

The company's transformation from 1973 to 2005 went forward in two distinct eras: the period of high oil prices from 1973 into the mid-1980s, and the era of relatively low oil prices from the mid-1980s through the years immediately after the turn of the century. The beginning of the high-price era coincided with the end of the tenure of J. Kenneth Jamieson, who was president of Standard of New Jersey (1965–1969), chairman of Exxon (1969–1975), and CEO (1972–1975). High oil prices continued for much of the tenure of Clifton C. Garvin Jr., who served as chairman and CEO (1975–1986). In the low-price era that followed, Lawrence G. Rawl (1986–1993) and Lee R. Raymond (1993–2005) each served as chairman and CEO. The pivotal year for the company's transformation was 1986, when a very sharp downturn in oil prices forced Exxon to make fundamental changes in its organization and operations. This book is organized around those two eras, with chapters focused on important problems that the company had to deal with in each.

The energy crises in 1973 and 1979 shaped Garvin's years as CEO. As discussed in chapter 1, "Downside Up," Garvin played an important role in working through the aftermath of the expropriation of Exxon's properties in the Middle East and Venezuela. In Saudi Arabia and Venezuela, nationalization became a bargaining process in which Exxon and the two governments sought a mutually acceptable transfer of ownership, a process that some labeled "capitalist nationalization." In Iran and Libya, on the other hand, nationalization came amid the assertion of power by Islamic nationalists, and Exxon had very little bargaining power. In all four nations, Exxon lost control of vast reserves that had been critically important in its planning for the future.

Garvin took a strong public role in the major consuming nations as an advocate for the oil industry in the tumultuous political debates about energy and environmental policies. Chapter 2, "Under Siege," discusses the political difficulties facing Exxon and its competitors in those years and the barrage of proposals to break up the oil companies that followed. It also uses the construction of the Trans-Alaska Pipeline System and the removal of lead from gasoline as case studies of the impact of environmental regulations on Exxon.

Chapter 3, "Colder and Deeper," examines Exxon's most significant strategic response to the changed conditions in the global petroleum industry during Garvin's years—the acceleration of its search for non-OPEC oil in Alaska, the North Sea, Australia, and Malaysia. This search encouraged significant technological advances and led to the addition of substantial new reserves. It did not, however, offset the staggering losses from nationalization. The shortage of crude available to Exxon and other major international companies, combined with the very high oil prices that prevailed in the late 1970s and early 1980s, convinced many that petroleum was a dying industry.

Making strategy amid the chaos of the 1970s was no easy matter for Garvin and his team of managers. A basic planning assumption of the era was that oil prices would continue to rise, but that Exxon would not have sufficient investment opportunities in oil and natural gas to maintain its long-term profitability. A logical response seemed to be diversification beyond oil and gas. As described in chapter 4, "Out of Oil," Exxon moved into a number of energy-related areas such as oil-shale and nuclear-fuel processing, as well as other businesses with no direct ties to energy. These initiatives failed, teaching Exxon often-painful lessons about diversification into businesses outside its historical expertise. The gradual decline of the price of oil after the early 1980s forced the divestment of most of the businesses acquired through diversification, and Exxon began to refocus on its core businesses in Garvin's final years as CEO.[27]

Garvin's retirement in 1986 came on the heels of one of the most precipitous drops in oil prices in the twentieth century. To his successor, Larry Rawl, fell the demanding task of responding to the harsh challenges brought by the low oil prices that persisted into the late 1990s. Organizational innovation—as discussed in chapter 5, "Revival"—became the watchword of Rawl's years as CEO. He reorganized the critically important areas of exploration and production. Changes begun under Rawl culminated in the coming of global functional organization in these areas and later in the corporation as a whole.

One defining event in Rawl's tenure would affect the company's public image for decades to come. As recounted in chapter 6, "*Exxon Valdez*," a series of avoidable mistakes resulted in a major tanker accident in Prince William Sound in southern Alaska in March 1989. This was the worst nightmare for an oil company—a major environmental disaster with its name attached to it.[28] During the spill and the cleanup, Exxon faced harsh public criticism, which it had little success in deflecting. But it made a determined effort to minimize the possibility of future accidents with the creation of an internal self-regulatory system known as the Operations Integrity Management System.

In 1993, Rawl handed the reins of authority to Lee Raymond, who served as chairman and CEO until 2005. An analytical, forceful presence, Raymond presided over the most profitable era in Exxon's modern history. During Raymond's years as CEO, Exxon pursued important new exploration and production projects around the world, including many in regions with extreme political risks. Chapter 7, "New Frontiers," presents case studies of such projects in Russia, Venezuela, Chad, and Angola.

As examined in chapter 8, "Upgrading Downstream," Raymond encouraged fundamental changes in the company's operations in refining and petrochemicals. He helped guide Exxon toward a greater involvement in the high-growth economies of Asia while also consolidating the refining business and coordinating operations of major refineries and chemical plants. By sharpening Exxon's focus on strict financial controls and engineering efficiency, he led the company to a sterling record of financial performance during a period of low oil prices.

Raymond conceived the merger with Mobil and led its planning and implementation. This is the focus of chapter 9, "Megamerger." This union accelerated a process that had begun in earnest in the early 1980s.[29] The pursuit of larger scales of operation and greater profitability had been an important part of the company's strategy from its beginning. By choosing a merger partner that proved to be a good fit, acquiring it at a relatively low price, and combining the two companies in a well-engineered consolidation, Exxon emerged as ExxonMobil—the prototype of the super-major international petroleum company.[30] The merger was announced in 1998 and approved by regulators in 1999, but we chose to end the book in 2005 in order to discuss how the two companies integrated their operations.

Taken as a whole, the years covered in this book, 1973–2005, present a story of Exxon's adjustment to new global conditions under Cliff Garvin, the company's revival under Larry Rawl, and the completion of its transformation under Lee Raymond. In retrospect, it is not surprising that Exxon, like the other international oil companies, only with difficulty understood the pace and direction of change during the first decade of the energy crises. The company's revival came in response to very hard times, which convinced its top management to emphasize traditional values and to refocus on its core businesses of oil, natural gas, and chemicals. The Exxon that emerged exhibited an innovative global organizational structure that sought economies of scale, financial discipline, and technical leadership throughout its operations. The successful consolidation of two giant oil companies provides a distinctive climax to a long period of organizational change. ExxonMobil retained the basic corporate culture and core operating values that had been embedded by John D. Rockefeller in both parties to the merger. In its global operations, management structure, and technology, however, the company had changed as much from 1973 to 2005 as it had from 1911, with the breakup of Standard Oil, to 1973.

CHAPTER ONE

DOWNSIDE UP

THE RISE OF PRODUCER POWER AFTER 1973

A s Cliff Garvin sought to negotiate with OPEC and major producing nations in the Middle East in the years after 1973 on matters ranging from nationalization to crude-oil contracts, Jack Clarke, an Exxon lawyer, was often at his side. Clarke sorted through the legal ramifications of the ongoing changes while also representing the company in high-level talks with producers. Recounting the frustration of negotiating from weakness in those years, he recalled an observation made by one of his predecessors, Howard Page, who had handled similar talks from the 1950s through the early 1970s. Page noted the crucial difference after 1973: "In my day, when I was negotiating, I at least had the appearance of having a gun. You fellows don't have anything." Historically, Exxon had been one of the most powerful organizations in the international petroleum industry. After the world of oil turned downside up in the 1970s, however, major producing nations increasingly asserted control over their own oil. While acknowledging this difficult situation, Clarke was a realist about the inevitability of producer power: "If Venezuelans were running the oil business in Texas, how long do you think we would like them to do that? . . . It's only natural for people to want to take it over."[1]

Although Exxon could not turn back the tide of producer power, its great strengths helped it adapt to changing conditions in its industry. Its well-developed organizational abilities ensured that it would retain an important position in the international order in oil that emerged after the energy crisis. It used state-of-the-art technology to find, produce, and refine oil. It had access to global markets and capital, and its vertically integrated operations around the world were run with sophisticated management systems. These strengths had enabled Exxon and other international oil companies to connect the oil supplies of the major producing nations with the demand for oil in the major consuming nations. Exxon continued to perform this central function after the 1970s, although the chaos of the era left much uncertainty about how long it could do so.

The company's immediate task in the early 1970s was to manage the process of nationalization—to the extent it could be managed. Exxon had long experience with political risks, but the growing strength of the producer nations meant that it had to become more adept at the kind of corporate diplomacy required when negotiating from a position of weakness. In the case studies examined in this chapter, the company faced two versions of nationalization. Venezuela and Saudi Arabia used what has been called "capitalist nationalization," in which governments and companies agree to compensation for expropriated properties and adjust existing contracts so as to maintain a working relationship. In contrast, Iran and Libya turned to "revolutionary nationalization," in which new regimes seize power, abrogate agreements reached by previous rulers, take the company's properties, and force it out with the threat of violence. In each case, the outcome was essentially the same: the producing nations took control of their own oil.

Much of the burden of managing this change fell to Garvin, whose career reflected that of many of the managers who advanced within the company. He grew up in the Washington, D.C., area, the son of an executive with Safeway Stores. After graduating with a chemical engineering degree from Virginia Polytechnic Institute in 1943, he entered officer training as a combat engineer. After serving two years in the Pacific theater, he returned to Virginia Polytechnic, earned a master's degree in chemical engineering, and took a job at Jersey Standard's major refinery at Baton Rouge, Louisiana. While working his way up to the position of operating engineer, he greatly benefited from the management training provided by

Cliff Garvin and Howard Kauffmann. ExxonMobil Historical Collection, Dolph Briscoe Center for American History, di_06250.

Henry Voorhess, a Cajun plant manager who used the Baton Rouge refinery as a laboratory in which to train generations of young managers. From there, Garvin began the circuit of numerous transfers that awaited those in the company who showed promise. He spent several stays in New York assisting top managers, rotated through various positions within Humble, rose to become president of the newly created Exxon Chemical Company, and became a director of the corporation and a member of its management committee in 1968.[2]

As president of Exxon between 1972 and 1975, Garvin was given responsibility for the "portfolio for the Middle East" by CEO J. Kenneth Jamieson. This included chairing regular meetings of a group of senior executives from Exxon, Standard of California, Texaco, and Mobil, the four American companies that jointly owned Aramco, the only major oil company in Saudi Arabia at the time. In this position, he worked closely with the Saudi oil minister, Zaki Yamani, as well as with officials from other OPEC nations. As he continued to grapple with changes in the Middle East in his years as chairman and CEO, he came to rely heavily on advice from Jack Clarke, who moved through the company's legal departments in New York and Venezuela to become "Middle East representative," based in New York and London. Clarke became a director and the vice chairman of the Investment Advisory Committee in 1976, and he remained an advisor to top management into the twenty-first century.[3] Clarke, Garvin, other Exxon corporate managers, and those in charge of the regional offices responsible for Venezuela and the Middle East had their hands full in the 1970s.

VENEZUELA: CREOLE'S NATIONALIZATION THROUGH THE REVERSION OF LEASES

Venezuela had been important to Exxon since the 1920s, when the company entered what was then a new producing nation under the control of the dictator General Juan Vicente Gómez (who governed 1908–1935). In its early years in Venezuela, the company profited from a close relationship with Gómez and his family and friends; one ready symbol of the standing of Exxon in its early dealings with the Venezuelan government is that in 1922 its lawyers helped draft the nation's original petroleum law. In 1938, the government of nearby Mexico expropriated the properties of Exxon and other foreign oil companies after they opposed all manner of government oil policies. Chastened by losses in Mexico, the company became more flexible in its subsequent dealings with Venezuela's government and its oil workers. The company agreed to a demand in 1943 of the liberal Acción Democrática party for a fifty-fifty profit-sharing agreement, and this division of oil revenues gradually became the global norm.[4] Creole, the company's primary affiliate in Venezuela, also put in place a program of "welfare capitalism," including worker pensions, vacations, recognition of unions, higher wages and benefits, and technical training for increasing numbers of local workers. By accepting the Venezuelan government's demands for a better deal on oil revenues, the company retained control over both the amount of petroleum produced and its price until the 1970s. This policy paid substantial rewards in the post–World War II era, making Creole "the principle source of crude production and the company's most profitable operation until the mid-1960s."[5]

From the 1920s onward, oil came to dominate the Venezuelan economy. Many Venezuelans hoped that oil-fueled prosperity might lead to a higher standard of living and perhaps even a more open political system. Political demands grew for more oil revenues, more national control over oil, and a more equitable distribution of oil wealth. Petroleum remained a lightning rod in national politics from the 1940s into the 1970s as the nation moved haltingly toward a more democratic political system. Rómulo Betancourt, one of the founders of Acción Democrática and its "revolution of 1943," captured the essence of resource nationalism in the title of his influential book *Venezuela's Oil* (1976). After passage of the petroleum law in 1943 that required a fifty-fifty division of oil revenues, the Acción Democrática came to power in 1945 and put the law into practice. After losing control of the government in a military coup in 1948, the party returned to power in the 1960s and 1970s and led the way toward the nationalization of Venezuelan oil.[6]

Creole, the largest oil company in Venezuela, was the most obvious target of nationalist sentiment. By 1974, it was producing approximately 1.5 million barrels per day (b/d) of oil out of total national production of about 3.3 million b/d.[7] Along with the other international oil companies in Venezuela—notably Shell, Gulf, and Texaco—Exxon faced serious problems. Some were geological. The companies in Venezuela had access to lower-cost, higher-quality crude oil in the younger, larger fields of the Middle East, putting Venezuela at a distinct price disadvantage on the global market. Other problems were political. Opposition to foreign oil companies had been a staple of Venezuelan politics for almost forty years. Indeed, Creole's most pressing problem in 1973 was the product of one such historical challenge. The petroleum law of 1943 contained provisions for the recognition of existing and often-disputed leases, thereby establishing a large number of new forty-year leases set to expire beginning in 1983. In 1971, the Venezuelan government passed a law of reversion that stipulated that as the old leases expired, the production sites, along with all property on them, would revert back to the nation, with limited compensation. The reversion clock was ticking as Exxon sought ways to retain a strong position in Venezuela, one of its most important sources of oil imports for the giant U.S. market.[8]

In the presidential election of December 1973, the early reversion of the 1943 leases became the main topic of debate. Creole's management kept close tabs on the campaign and reported its observations to Exxon's New York headquarters. The position on reversion of the Acción Democrática candidate, Carlos Andrés Pérez, was simply that Venezuela must take control of its own oil. In his winning campaign and later as president, Pérez took a reformist stance, seeking a middle way between the military dictatorships of Venezuela's past and the radical Cuban model of communism. He recognized the need for cooperation with foreign oil companies, at least in a transitional period after the reversion of the leases. This approach reflected the nation's recent, rough experience of nationalizing its iron industry, as well as the fear that Venezuela was not yet ready to manage its own oil industry without the technical assistance and access to markets provided by the international oil companies.

Reporting to the corporate management committee in May 1973, the president of Creole, Robert Dolph, summarized Exxon's options as follows: "There is a need to negotiate a broad realization of the relationship between the Company and the Venezuelan Government, both with regard to existing conditions and the development of new source areas. The first step is felt to be a pre-requisite for [Creole's] corporate survival until 1983, and the second as a necessary adjunct to possible extension of corporate life beyond 1983."[9] Conciliatory steps became increasingly difficult because of new governmental dictates on price, volume of exports, and the leases—a set of issues that presented "major uncertainties beyond [Creole's] control."[10] Yet despite acknowledging that the process of change was largely beyond Creole's control, its executives reported, "Even if early reversion does take place, Creole is optimistic that new long-term relations may evolve between Venezuela and the corporation, which would allow the corporation to continue to provide important services to the Venezuelan nation on a mutually satisfactory and profitable basis."[11] This response reflected Creole's primary goals: to retain access to Venezuelan crude for as long as possible and to receive fair compensation for its properties in the event of nationalization.

Robert Dolph, president of Esso Middle East, 1980.
ExxonMobil Historical Collection, di_06136.

Events after the embargo by the Arab nations in OPEC created tensions between the international oil companies, the U.S. government, and the Venezuelan government. As Exxon scurried to make up shortages caused by the embargo, Venezuelan oil was critically important to both the company and consumers in the United States. In response to U.S. criticism in November 1973 that Venezuela was not doing enough to make up this lost supply, Creole's president told the *New York Times*: "Venezuela is going all-out now. There is nothing left to give."[12] After the election of Pérez the next month, Dolph reassured Exxon's corporate management committee that the new president's administration would not curb crude oil production while Venezuela's "traditional customers are having crude supply difficulties."[13]

Pérez moved quickly toward nationalization. In his inaugural address, in March 1974, he proclaimed that the early takeover of foreign oil operations and assets in Venezuela was a "certainty." He announced a two-year deadline to arrive at a national consensus on the early reversion of the 1943 leases, but called for a "coolheaded approach," which would "fulfill the old aspiration of our people, that our oil will be Venezuelan."[14] To help build this consensus, Pérez in May 1974 appointed a Reversion Commission, made up of more than thirty prominent Venezuelans, to study the issues raised by reversion and recommend government policy. According to Creole officials, when the commission at times had threatened to get "out of hand, the administration had maintained control." They reported that after an early draft of the nationalization law seemed too radical for the administration, it "apparently" sought "to moderate the proposal."[15]

Early reversion was now an accepted reality, not a matter of speculation. In 1973, the government had given control over gasoline service stations and other local markets to CVP (Corporación Venezolana del Petróleo), a national oil company created in 1960 to help collect information but now asked to manage the transition to Venezuelan control. In April 1974, Creole reported that the foreign companies had been "arbitrarily assigned, by decree, supply and distribution obligations to CVP at very low prices" in order to provide oil products to subsidize Venezuelan development.[16] Subsidies for domestic energy were a traditional policy of national oil companies such as PEMEX (Petróleos Mexicanos) in Mexico, and the content of this government policy came as no surprise. But the tone of this edict was hardly coolheaded.

In response, Creole of necessity chose diplomacy over indignation. It lacked the leverage to do otherwise. When the government called for a drastic reduction of natural-gas flaring, Creole launched a "very aggressive program to install additional gas compression capacity" designed to "raise Creole's gas utilization in Lake Maracaibo to essentially 100 percent."[17] When the government announced its desire to cut back production in order to conserve reserves, Creole accelerated its efforts to save oil by making its operations more efficient. When Exxon purchased the outstanding 5 percent of Creole's shares in June 1975, a company spokes-man commented that the "move would give Creole more flexibility to draw on Exxon for the services and assistance that might be needed in developing and fulfilling the company's new role in Venezuela."[18] At every step on the path toward early reversion, the growing political pressures for nationalization and the harsh realities of a seller's market for oil lim-ited Exxon's options. Creole's president, Robert Dolph, acknowledged the obvious: "We couldn't win. . . . The actual nationalization gave us little room to maneuver."[19] Instead of taking a hard line that would certainly be doomed to fail, the company focused on its goal of retaining a productive, profitable, long-term presence in Venezuela.

Howard Kauffmann, the president of Exxon Corporation during the nationalization, recalled the reality of the negotiations: "We did not have any leverage. . . . We recognized that they had the right to nationalize that property. All we wanted [them] to do was pay us a fair price for it, and we wanted to continue to be a customer of theirs. . . . They always said they were going to pay us fairly—fairly as defined by them. . . . It was something that made you irritable, made your blood boil occasionally . . . [but] we realized that losing your temper or showing any animosity was not going to get you anywhere. . . . We came out with good commercial contacts with respect to our need for crude oil, and we left a few pennies on the table."[20]

As part of the transition, the government placed "observers" in each of the international oil companies as the bill for early reversion made its way through the political process. Opponents of the administration had sought "the installation in each company of government interveners . . . with substantial powers." Such officials could have monitored the foreign companies' operations to ensure that they continued to run their facili-ties and their finances in a "normal way" during the transition to nation-alization. Instead, the observers had little effective power to intervene. Creole announced that the observer assigned to it, retired General Rafael Alfonzo Ravard, was a man of "impeccable credentials" who could use his time at Creole to "get a feel" for some of the problems and complexities of running the company. In internal correspondence to their superiors in New York City, Creole officials acknowledged that the appointment of observers came in response to growing political pressure from opposition political parties. Creole hoped, however, to "make positive use of this new development by establishing, through our observer, an important and meaningful communication link with the government."[21]

Legislation passed in July 1975 called for the early reversion of the 1943 leases on January 1, 1976, and announced the framework for the newly organized Venezuelan oil industry. Six months earlier, the president of Creole had sent a discouraging letter to New York, decrying the company's lack of input into political decision making on this key issue. He noted that Creole's personnel had taken part in "many technical discussions underway at government request, between their representatives and industry professionals concerning refining, computing, technology, research, etc." But the Reversion Commission included no representatives of the major foreign oil companies. And when the Venezuelan president and the commission held a mass meeting with 400 industry employees and "listened attentively" to their presentations, executives were shunned. Creole's president complained of neglect: "No high level discussions between industry and government have taken place in over half a year."[22]

The law asserted control over the nation's oil, but despite fierce political opposition, it also acknowledged that Venezuela was not yet ready to manage the industry without assistance from the international oil companies. To facilitate a smooth transition to national ownership, the new law grouped all existing Venezuelan oil companies into four companies, Lagoven (built around Creole), Maraven (built around the holdings of Shell), Meneven (built around the holdings of Gulf Oil), and a fourth company named Corproven (created out of CVP). Smaller companies were folded into these four.

This approach sought to retain as much as possible of the organization, the Venezuelan personnel, and the expertise of the nationalized companies. Sitting on top of the four competitors was the newly created Petróleos de Venezuela, SA, a holding company that quickly became known by its initials, PDVSA. To allow the government to control exports, export permits went only to Corproven, Lagoven, and Maraven. PDVSA, which was headed by General Ravard, initially exercised oversight of the operating companies. In the following decades, it evolved into a strong national oil company.[23] This organizational framework was originally encouraging to Creole, since the structure embodied well-developed ties between Creole and Venezuelans in charge of one of the four major new companies. This seemed to pave the way for future cooperation.

These ties would not much matter to Exxon, however, unless it retained access to large quantities of crude while also earning a reasonable profit on the technical, marketing, and managerial services it contracted to provide to the new companies. The reversion law allowed the foreign oil companies to sign "two-year renewable technical assistance contracts—to include marketing—with the government in order to continue providing essential support services after nationalization." The international oil companies and the government vigorously negotiated all aspects of those contracts, which took the place of the direct ownership of oil that Creole had enjoyed under the old lease system. The contracts specified payments of ten to twenty cents per barrel of oil for different services; such small sums quickly added up when a company was processing a million barrels a day. Creole and the government bargained hard on pricing and production: the first had to be flexible enough to reflect changes in global markets, and the second needed to be acceptable both to Exxon, which was crude short, and the government, which sought to limit exports. Only days after the official nationalization on January 1, 1976, Exxon signed a contract with the government to purchase an annual average of 965,000 b/d of crude, at least temporarily fulfilling its major strategic objective in Venezuela—continued access to large, relatively secure supplies of crude at market prices.[24]

The attainment of Creole's second strategic objective, fair compensation for its nationalized properties, proved more difficult. The Venezuelan government awarded about $1 billion in total compensation to all nationalized oil companies, with Creole receiving about half of that sum. As called for in the law, compensation reflected the net book value of the companies, on which taxes had been based, rather than the total amount invested by the companies, which they estimated to be approximately $5 billion. The reversion law gave the foreign companies only sixty days to accept the government's compensation offer. Although dissatisfied with the deal, Creole and the other major U.S. companies lacked the power to negotiate a better one, and so they "accepted [it] at the last minute." Payments were made in government bonds, not in oil, with all properties to be turned over to the government by January 1, 1976.[25]

A minor irritant at the time of reversion, however, quickly ballooned into a major dispute, suggesting that future cooperation between Exxon and the Venezuelan government would not be easy. Only months after the deal had apparently been done, the Venezuelan government filed suit against Creole for disputed taxes from 1970. The sum involved was $231 million, almost half of the compensation payment. To Exxon, the sum in question was not as important as the principle involved. The company had accepted the government's offer in part because it included the promise of fair and timely compensation. In this context, the tax claims appeared to be an end run around an agreement negotiated in good faith, and the company fought long and hard to resolve the resulting dispute. Indeed, in September 1978, the president of Esso Inter-America, Exxon's holding company for South America, warned: "Failure to reach equitable settlement of the outstanding nationalization issues could result in [the] phasing out of our Venezuelan activities." Tensions over the unresolved tax dispute festered for years. In the early 1980s, Lee Raymond, in his position as president of Esso Inter-America, reported to corporate management on the seemingly intractable dispute: "The key issue in Venezuela remains the settlement of the income tax . . . claims. The timing and scope of the eventual resolution of these claims continue to be ill-defined." In the mid-1980s, the company cut the knot. Robert Wilhelm, a high-ranking Exxon executive, was concerned about the $275 million contingency still being carried in the company's annual report pending the resolution of this dispute. Wilhelm recalled his advice to Cliff Garvin: "The best deal we are going to get is to call it even. And Cliff just swallowed hard and said, 'I don't like it, but okay.'" In September 1986, a deal was reached to write off this contingency. The end game for the reversion process foreshadowed things to come in Venezuela, where long-term investment opportunities beckoned the company even as unfavorable governmental policies pushed it away.[26]

Despite the dispute over back taxes, Exxon sought to put itself in a position to bid on new Venezuelan projects in the future. It showed special interest in two expensive and ambitious projects, the Cristobal Colon LNG (liquefied natural gas) project and the very heavy oil of the Orinoco Basin. Yet as talks about these multibillion-dollar projects moved forward, the softening of oil prices in the early 1980s made them more risky.

Both had long-term potential for becoming great prospects if and when oil and gas prices rebounded, but the combination of economic and political risks made them uninviting. In the short term, Exxon was fortunate to get away from both of them before the oil-price collapse of the mid-1980s.

In the 1970s, Exxon worked with the Venezuelan government to move the nation as smoothly as possible toward state ownership of petroleum. Despite intense political pressure to use the process of nationalization to demonize and punish the foreign oil companies, the government chose instead to accept their assistance and then to move gradually toward more independence in operations. Having no better option, Exxon cooperated with the government and then with PDVSA during the transition years, to the benefit of Venezuela and world consumers of petroleum.

As discussed below in chapter 7, the issues raised by the nationalization of Creole in the 1970s reemerged after the international oil companies reentered Venezuela in the 1990s. Twenty years after nationalization, the central question remained: could the international oil companies and the major producing nations find mutual, sustainable self-interest in the new world of producer-controlled oil?

The same question faced the major producing nations in the Middle East in the years after 1973, and Exxon's management sought insights from the company's experience in Venezuela that might prove useful in other nations. The most obvious difference between Venezuela and the major producers in the Middle East was the state of the oil fields in each region. Venezuela's major producing properties were older and in decline, and Exxon estimated that "producing and investment costs [in Venezuela] are now [in 1974] three to four times as high as in the Middle East." The higher cost of production was somewhat offset by the "greater, although still limiting, resource availability of technical and managerial talent" in Venezuela. In addition, the nation's long history with the international oil companies had produced "more sophisticated legal and tax codes." A "very strong legislative branch which must approve any new arrangement" meant that public opinion could shape political choices. In short, Venezuela's political system, unlike the authoritarian systems in the Middle East, had slowly become more democratic and thus more open to "a strong national sentiment, kindled by politicians of all shades, towards nationalization and Venezuelan control of the oil industry."[27]

These significant differences might have shaped different outcomes in the two regions except for two powerful similarities that marked the turmoil of the 1970s: a strong nationalistic urge to take control of valuable national resources from foreign oil companies and the shared experience of the extraordinary wealth brought about by OPEC's dramatic assertion of control over oil prices after 1973.

In the Middle East as in Venezuela, Exxon thus faced governments motivated by resource nationalism and emboldened by the success of OPEC. Exxon had strong incentives to do whatever it could to defend its interests in this region, which included a fully owned affiliate in Libya, a 30 percent interest in Aramco, a 7 percent interest in the dominant consortium in Iran, and a 12 percent interest in the Iraq Petroleum Company. In addition, it had smaller affiliates working in Qatar, Abu Dhabi, and Lebanon. In 1972 *BusinessWeek* reported that the region contained almost 70 percent of Exxon's proved reserves worldwide. The company's own published estimates placed its daily production in 1972 in Saudi Arabia at more than 1.73 million b/d, in Iran at 320,000, and in Libya at more than 300,000, with additional oil from Iraq, Abu Dhabi, and Qatar. The Middle East supplied almost half of the company's total global production of 6.2 million b/d in 1972.[28] These figures suggest that during its sustained growth after World War II, the company had become perilously dependent on oil from a region that was becoming increasingly volatile. In the long term, it could not halt nationalization in the region, but it fought hard to try to soften its short-term impact.

SAUDI ARABIA: CAPITALIST NATIONALIZATION IN SLOW MOTION

The largest producer in the Middle East was Saudi Arabia, where, after 1948, Exxon held a 30 percent interest in Aramco—the most important consortium in the history of the petroleum industry. It was a force in the global oil industry because of its access to Saudi Arabia's reserves, which were far and away the largest in the world. The four partners, Standard Oil of California, Texaco, Exxon, and Mobil, were all American companies, and each individually ranked among the largest international oil companies. In the years before 1973, Aramco produced as much as 15 percent of the world's oil, making it the center of global oil production. Its decisions had far-reaching ramifications for Exxon and for U.S. foreign policy. With political power in the country tightly held by the House of Saud, Aramco made a determined effort to keep in good standing with the royal family by developing oil in ways that enriched the nation but minimized disruptions to its traditional way of life.

In the post–World War II era, Aramco pursued a strategy of accommodation in Saudi Arabia, much as Creole did in Venezuela. In 1950 the company put in place the fifty-fifty profit-sharing policy pioneered by the Venezuelan government. It gradually expanded training programs, allowing more Saudis to become involved in its technical operations. In addition, Aramco took steps to limit its impact on Saudi culture by housing most of its workforce in enclaves of American-style suburbs largely segregated from Saudi society. As it sweetened the pot for the Saudis, however, Aramco maintained tight control of decision making. An executive committee made up of officials from the four member companies made key decisions by coordinating the policies of Aramco with their companies' own goals. Other consortia made up of the largest international oil companies dominated the oil industries of Iran, Iraq, and Kuwait, where they exercised significant control over pricing and production. They magnified this power by negotiating only with individual countries, not with groups of nations.[29]

To comply with American antitrust laws, Aramco's partners (who technically were shareholders in the company) used management procedures that minimized the access of the partners to financial and planning information submitted by each in the process of planning Aramco's operations. Inevitably, tensions grew between the four partners, which at times had different needs within Aramco. Traditionally, Standard of California, which had limited marketing outlets, favored holding down Saudi production; Exxon and Mobil tended to favor higher production; Texaco generally held a position in between. In the years after 1973, of course, the growing shortage of petroleum pushed the partners toward a common view of the need to expand production when possible.[30]

The dynamics of decision making changed quickly with the coming of producer power. By 1974, for example, Aramco's board consisted of two executives from each American partner, three Saudi government representatives, and seven officers from Aramco itself. These officers and many on the technical staff of the company came from the four partners, but Saudis came to fill more of these technical slots over time. After 1972, when the government had demanded and received 25 percent participation within Aramco, it became in effect the fifth partner, often with quite different needs from those of the other four. Frank Jungers, Aramco's CEO in 1974, explained the change this way: if the oil companies' interests were different from one another, the interests of the government were "different more so."[31] As representatives of the government of a nation with a small population and immense oil reserves, the Saudi members of Aramco and the nation's oil ministers took a long view of oil policy. This often meant a willingness to forgo short-term profits and growth in order to maximize the long-term benefits from oil. Within OPEC, the Saudis often sought to limit oil-price increases to avoid damaging the global economy and to constrain the rise of alternatives to oil, which influenced their views on the best strategies for Aramco. After 1972, an even more fundamental difference in mind-set created tensions within Aramco: the original partners focused on ways to retain access to Saudi crude, while the newest partner, the Saudi government, focused on taking 100 percent ownership in Aramco.

The president of Esso Middle East, Charles J. Hedlund, discussed the resulting difficulties in a report to the Exxon Management Committee in October 1973: "The new role of the Saudi Government as part-owner of Aramco is bringing about a substantial shift in the role of the Aramco management," including the direct participation of the government in such things as approval of the company's budgets. But he also noted a "more subtle shift" within the company:

> In the past, Aramco's management has scrupulously maintained a neutral position with respect to matters involving disagreement among its four owners. Application of the same principle today by its five owners tends to make it impossible for Aramco's management to exercise even an advisory role in matters involving disputes with the government.

The change had far-reaching implications:

In varying degrees, depending on the corporate structural arrangement in each area, we can expect this same effect in other operating areas. To deal with this developing situation, we must find new ways to exercise our continuing management responsibility over these operations.[32]

In particular, Exxon's traditional emphasis on strict budgetary controls faced serious challenges in a management system responsive to the needs of four oil companies and the Saudi government.

Hedlund made these observations on October 2, 1973, four days before the outbreak of the Yom Kippur War, which accelerated the pace of change in the Middle Eastern oil industry. The report provides a useful snapshot of Exxon's perceptions of the growing challenges it faced in the region just before the energy crisis of 1973–1974. It began with a simple statement: "The business environment in our region continues to lack stability," which presented very difficult "challenges for forward planning." First on the list was the "erosion of contract sanctity."[33] Exxon had long championed the strict enforcement of contracts as the foundation of the international petroleum industry. By the early 1970s, however, unilateral revisions of contracts by producer governments eager to move as rapidly as possible toward full nationalization had become the industry norm.

The other major challenge facing Esso Middle East was the growing tension between Israel and the Arab nations in the region. As events later in the week confirmed, that conflict was of pressing concern to the Aramco partners because of the increasingly militant tone of King Faisal of Saudi Arabia in his demands for what he considered a more evenhanded U.S. policy toward Israel and the Arab countries. As tensions grew in the early 1970s, the king at times delivered strong private "lectures" on the topic to the Aramco partners, with warnings that it was becoming "extremely difficult" to resist pressures from other Arab nations to curtail oil experts to the United States.[34] Exxon and its Aramco partners were put in an impossible position. In the post–World War II era, the U.S. State Department's foreign policy in the Middle East centered on unconditional support of Israel. For much of the same period, the nation's unofficial oil policy—largely implemented by U.S.-based oil companies with the tacit support of the U.S. government—was the protection of U.S. access to Middle

Eastern crude, with special emphasis on blocking the expansion of Soviet influence in the Middle East. As growing tensions between Israel and the Arab states brought those two positions into collision, American oil companies found themselves as major oil producers in Arab states that were in conflict with the key U.S. ally in the region.

A range of challenges directly related to Aramco's operations faced planners at Exxon. These included the desire of the Saudi government to sharply reduce the flaring of natural gas, the growing imposition of governmental controls on production, threats to Exxon's future acquisition of crude, and the long-range development of refining capacity in the Persian Gulf. On some of these issues, Exxon's short-term interests did not align with those of the Saudi government. The company wanted to accelerate the growth of Aramco's production, while the government sought to slow the pace of expansion. The Aramco partners came to a compromise on the best methods to reduce gas flaring, with the government approving their plans to use previously flared gas for projects shown to make economic sense.[35] In pursuit of Aramco's objective "to establish a working relationship on gas that could benefit both parties," the companies and the government successfully reached an arrangement in which, from Exxon's perspective, "there has been no recent pressure [as of October 1973] by SAG [the Saudi Arabian Government] for uneconomic gas conservation steps."

The "Summary of Results Expected" of Hedlund's report made it clear why Exxon needed to find ways to address these challenges. Its base-case analysis for the five years after 1972 projected the near doubling of Exxon's portion of Saudi crude between 1972 and 1977, with steady expansion yielding about 3.2 million b/d to Exxon from Aramco by 1977. Total Exxon production from Saudi Arabia, Libya, Iran, Iraq, Abu Dhabi, and Qatar, plus relatively small purchases of Middle Eastern oil from other international oil companies, was projected to be 5.25 million b/d by 1977, up from actual production of 3.4 million b/d in 1972. Earnings were projected to be $807 million in 1977 (at 50 cents a barrel), as compared with the $306 million earned in 1972 (at 32 cents a barrel).[36] These figures illustrated the scale of production and profits available in the Middle East, even at the low prices that prevailed before the oil-price spike in 1973–1974.

In retrospect, the projections of the report proved wildly optimistic. The Yom Kippur War shattered the assumptions and the time frame underlying its projections. Yet one conclusion remained the same: Exxon could not abandon the Middle East. Despite rising oil nationalism, its only realistic choice was to negotiate the best terms possible and then stay, despite the extreme political risks and formidable planning challenges.

For Aramco and Exxon, one key point of engagement with the Saudi Arabian government, as well as with OPEC, was Zaki Yamani, the Saudi minister of petroleum and natural resources and its leading envoy to OPEC from 1962 to 1986. Although not a member of the royal family, Yamani became a force within the international oil industry through his intellect, his knowledge of oil, and his standing as the oil minister of the nation with the largest oil reserves. He took a long view of the management of the kingdom's oil reserves, making him the leading advocate in OPEC for a strategy of restraint in oil pricing.[37]

As both the strategist for Saudi Arabian oil development and the face of OPEC, Yamani held great power over Exxon and its partners in Aramco, and the company took pains to prepare for its meetings with him. An internal memorandum from Esso Middle East to Exxon's headquarters in late May 1974 included a copy of the "terms of reference for meeting with Yamani in early June 1974." The bulk of the message discussed the terms under which Aramco and the Saudis might agree to increase Saudi "participation" in Aramco from 25 percent to 60 percent. The last item noted that the "documentation of a new agreement with Yamani may be in the form of a letter signed or received by Yamani." This suggests a Middle Eastern variant of the "handshake deal" so common in the lore of the Texas oil industry. In this case, however, the handshake covered the value of 35 percent of the largest oil company in the world, which at prevailing oil prices held proved reserves valued at 2 trillion to 3 trillion dollars.[38]

Yamani brought a passion to his work that reflected his basic starting point on Saudi oil policy: "I don't care who brings the oil to the surface in Saudi Arabia. It is still ours."[39] He became deeply involved in the affairs of Aramco, and his activities in a variety of official positions, including (as Saudi oil minister) member of the board of directors, shaped the company's evolution. In 1963, he became chairman of Petromin, the Saudi government agency created to manage energy and minerals within the kingdom. As one of the primary architects of the OPEC oil embargo in the winter of 1973, he helped radically alter the bargaining process through which the producing nations gained higher prices, levied higher taxes, and, ultimately, assumed ownership and control of their reserves. As oil prices rose in the 1970s, he sought to restrain them in order to avert a global recession and slow the rise of alternate sources to oil. Then, as chair of OPEC's long-term strategy committee, he established the agenda for debate within OPEC on the setting of oil prices through production controls.

All this was a tough juggling act, but Yamani was up to the task. The *New York Times* depicted him as coming "to embody Arab oil power." *U.S. News & World Report* voiced the same sentiments more bluntly: "For more than two decades, Ahmed Zaki Yamani's commands boosted or battered personal pocketbooks and national economies around the world."[40]

Yamani's counterpart within Exxon was Cliff Garvin. The two men shared similar backgrounds. Neither was born to privilege. Yamani had been born in Mecca, where his father was a respected Islamic scholar. As was the norm for those who succeeded within Exxon, Garvin had a degree in chemical engineering. Yamani's primary academic training, in the law, proved quite useful in the place and time in which he worked. He graduated from New York University and the Harvard Law School. Both had been identified early in their careers as promising talents and had moved relatively quickly to the top of their organizations. After thirty years of experience in many phases of Exxon's diversified operations, Garvin became CEO at fifty-four. Yamani, who was ten years younger than Garvin, had advanced even more rapidly. As one of a small group of English-speaking, Western-educated Saudis with understanding of the legal and financial sides of the petroleum industry, Yamani held a variety of Saudi government positions in finance and law before coming to the attention of the royal family. He became a favorite of Crown Prince Faisal in the early 1960s and took over the key position of head of the ministry of petroleum in 1962 at only thirty-two years of age. In the 1970s, Yamani and Garvin led two of the most powerful organizations in the global oil industry.

As the two worked together within Aramco and in Exxon's dealings with OPEC, they became friends. They were an odd couple. Yamani was a night owl who wrote poetry in Arabic when he was not shaping the world oil economy. Garvin had the orderly habits of an engineer, with bird watching and golf as his primary leisure activities. They shared a deep understanding of the oil industry, but from quite different perspectives. Garvin's point of view flowed naturally from his temperament, training, and long career in the largest international oil company. Yamani acknowledged that Exxon had been an agent of change within Saudi Arabia, encouraging technical training for Saudis while creating national wealth and opportunities for the country. But he expressed anger at the tone and procedures used by Aramco before the 1970s, when the American companies held tight control, carrying out mandates from their headquarters with little input from the Saudis. Yamani had forced his way into the inner sanctum of Aramco, first as a powerful member of OPEC and then as the voice of Saudi Arabia in the era of participation and nationalization. Garvin had great respect for Yamani even when he strongly disagreed with his policies. Years later, he recalled his fondness for Yamani and his family, including even the telephone calls in the middle of the night from Yamani, who lost track of time differences around the world.[41] Garvin did not, however, remember fondly Yamani's leadership in the nationalization of Aramco.

In contrast to nationalizations of Exxon's operations in other parts of the world in the 1970s, the process unfolded in slow motion in Saudi Arabia. The Esso Middle East report of October 2, 1973, noted the completion the year before of an agreement for 25 percent participation by the governments of Saudi Arabia, Kuwait, Qatar, and Abu Dhabi in Exxon's operations in each country. It projected that these countries would move to 51 percent participation by 1982, a schedule proposed by OPEC as the basis of a general agreement that might bring a measure of stability to Middle Eastern oil. By the summer of 1974, however, Exxon and its partners already had agreed in principle to 60 percent participation by those countries, with the agreement retroactive to January 1, 1974. Yet as Exxon and Aramco contemplated the prospect of a quick movement to 100 percent participation, negotiations stalled.

It was becoming clear that Yamani and the Saudi government did not agree with Aramco's timetable for the completion of nationalization. By October 1974, the top managers at Esso Middle East lamented the failure to establish "a firmly structured solution for Aramco as the key determinant of the form of new long-term arrangements providing a more stable business environment." They concluded that "the transitional phase will continue into 1975 and that our other deals [in the Middle East] may be vulnerable to further leap-frogging as a result of a Saudi settlement."[42] Earlier in the year, a story in the *New York Times Magazine* had reported that Yamani opposed immediate nationalization of all the major oil companies in the Middle East. He pointed out that the countries lacked "the know-how, the skilled labor, and, above all, the world markets controlled by the big companies, and would be walking into a disaster area if they nationalized before they were ready and organized to produce, market, and sell."[43]

Amid the uncertainties arising from partial nationalization, Exxon sought ways to improve its chances of maintaining a strong position in Saudi Arabia over the long term. One promising avenue appeared to be participation in joint ventures with Saudi Arabian companies in a variety of government-sponsored projects aimed at industrializing the country. In the summer of 1974, Exxon signed an agreement with Petromin to study a range of joint-venture projects in such areas as the expansion of Saudi refining capacity and the construction of petrochemical plants. One attraction of these deals was the promise of access to Saudi crude, an enticement so appealing that Exxon proved willing to consider such deals even when they did not meet the company's normally stringent guidelines for return on investment.[44]

Esso Middle East's strategy in Saudi Arabia and the Middle East as a whole included a range of general objectives: retaining access to long-term crude supplies; improving contacts and relations with producer-nation governments; diversifying supply sources in order to minimize the consequences of political risks associated with any particular nation; and limiting investments in "high capital intensive projects" in countries with uncertain investment climates. At the top of the list of "overall objectives and challenges" was to "resolve the Saudi '100 percent' demand in a form which will preserve an acceptable level of profitability and crude supply without affecting adversely other areas."[45]

This became a central task of Exxon's management in 1975. The week after becoming CEO, Cliff Garvin journeyed to Saudi Arabia to meet with

oil companies." On the plus side, the growing technical complexity of operations required to maintain maturing fields boded well for Exxon, since the resulting technical demands would "provide the incentive for most countries to maintain service arrangements and, in some cases, crude sales contracts with the companies for some time to come." Despite trends in the region since 1973, the company did not rule out the possibility of "renewed producing government interest in having the private oil companies invest in oil operations."[58]

In September 1978, Esso Middle East voiced concern that political influences might sway governments on such key issues as the setting of production rates for each member nation when determining the total production of OPEC. It lamented its lack of managerial control over investment and operating efficiency, and it noted the "divergent driving forces of the participants in our joint venture" as the individual international oil companies sought to balance their commitments throughout the Middle East. Of special concern to Exxon's top officials in the Middle East were "increasingly violent disruptions in Iran," which threatened "the stability of the Shah's regime." Although they expected such tensions to continue "for some time to come," they predicted that "while occasional upsets are likely, we believe that the need for stability is recognized by the more powerful countries and that they will try to avoid major conflict in the area." Overall, the short-term possibilities for profitable operations appeared favorable, although Exxon expected "to see a continuing but gradually decreasing role for the privately owned international oil companies in the region."[59]

IRAN AND FUNDAMENTALIST NATIONALIZATION

Three months later, all bets were off. When revolutionary forces overthrew the existing regime in Iran, the second-largest producer in the Middle East, new uncertainties over oil prices and the future of Iran shook global oil markets. Before the revolution, Exxon had a relatively small holding in the Iranian consortium that dominated oil production there. Indeed, the company's contingency planning in 1978 even included a reappraisal of "the value of our interest in Iran in light of its potential for unfavorable impact on interests elsewhere." Yet the report did not advocate withdrawal. Instead, it projected that "new arrangements will be finally agreed upon in Saudi Arabia and Iran and we will then undertake to fully implement them. . . . The most critical task will be providing our share of the required manpower, management, and technical service."[60] In short, only months before the overthrow of the shah, Exxon foresaw a future in Iran shaped by the completion of ongoing talks with him in a framework that had evolved over more than a quarter of a century of give-and-take with a familiar cast of characters and issues.

The shah, Mohammad Reza Pahlavi, had ruled during Exxon's entire history in Iran. For more than forty years after the discovery of oil in Persia by British Petroleum (previously called the Anglo-Persian Oil Company and then the Anglo-Iranian Oil Company), that company had enjoyed a dominant position in the region that became Iran. A growing wave of resource nationalism in Iran peaked in the early 1950s, when a revolutionary government took control and asserted authority over the nation's oil reserves. During its brief time in office, this government created the National Iranian Oil Company (NIOC), the first independent national oil company in the Middle East. The independence of the company was short-lived, however, since the United States and Britain aided a coup against the revolutionary government and returned to power the shah, whose father, founder of the Pahlavi dynasty, had been deposed during World War II.[61] NIOC remained, but the international oil companies returned in 1954 with the organization of the Iranian Oil Participants (IOP), a consortium that included American companies for the first time in Iran. BP held 40 percent of the consortium, with the remainder spread broadly among a variety of French, British, Dutch, and American companies, including Exxon, which held a 7 percent share.

Under the Consortium Agreement, signed in 1954 by the IOP and Iran, the nation retained ownership of its oil reserves while granting the members of the consortium control over the operation of much of the oil industry. The agreement also gave IOP the right to purchase the oil it produced at favorable prices for twenty-five years, with an option for the consortium to extend the agreement for fifteen more years.[62] A historian of BP, James Bamberg, has described this agreement as conceding "only the principle of nationalization without the substance of effective national control," since it left effective control of most of the nation's oil in the hands of the foreign consortium.[63] State-owned NIOC managed only a portion of the domestic market. The government of Iran received 50 percent of the profits of the consortium, as calculated by the IOP.

After 1954, the shah sought to assert greater control over Iran's oil. He was in a race with history to use oil revenues to modernize Iran before religious and economic tensions within the nation overwhelmed his regime. Iran's large population, about 70 million people, meant that the shah faced a much more difficult challenge than the Saudi royal family, which ruled a much less populous nation. Oil-fueled growth produced prosperity for a minority of Iranians fairly quickly, but development that improved the lives of most Iranians would take longer. In this sense, the shah confronted the same difficulties as generations of Venezuelan leaders, who had sought to "sow the petroleum" in order to diversify their economy and thereby bring prosperity to a broad segment of the population. With rising expectations in Iran that oil would improve living conditions, reaping proved harder than sowing. Competing uses of revenue, including social services, military spending, and the lavish lifestyles of the nation's elite, tended to reduce funds available for development. The shah and his ministers remained price hawks, demanding higher oil prices within OPEC, and production hawks, demanding larger exports from the consortium, even if this required "preferential lifting" of Iranian oil at the expense of other producing nations.[64]

During most of the shah's rule (1954–1978), Iran's increasing control of its oil had been a negotiated process. By the 1970s, the shah held much greater power to dictate terms. He used this power to demand higher prices for his oil and preferential treatment from foreign oil companies. His power reflected more than Iran's vast reserves of oil and natural gas. He carved out a special relationship with a series of American presidents by serving as a counterweight to the strong anti-Israeli sentiment in Saudi Arabia and other Arab states. Although Iran and Saudi Arabia both enjoyed strong financial and military ties to the United States, they were bitter rivals within the region and within OPEC, and they vied for economic and political leadership in the Middle East.[65]

The shah was determined that his arrangement with the international oil companies would remain equal to or better than that of Saudi Arabia. Thus, after Aramco agreed to the House of Saud's request for 25 percent participation in 1972, Iran reopened the 1954 agreement with the IOP. Representatives of the IOP entered into these "negotiations" only to find, instead, that they faced a series of nonnegotiable demands by the shah. In January 1973, a team of negotiators from the IOP put forward a proposal for a ten-year agreement with the creation of a fifty-fifty partnership for the production and export of oil.[66] But this proposal was "barely given a hearing by the Shah and rejected out of hand." He forcefully reminded the IOP negotiators of their lack of power to resist his will, making it clear that he would accept one of two alternatives: "Either a long term purchase/sale contract with Iran assuming 100% control of operations immediately, or alternatively, the Consortium could continue its present Agreement until 1979 (subject to equalization of the financial benefits of Participation) whereafter the Agreement would terminate and the Consortium Members would take [a] place in line with other customers for the purchase of Iranian oil." The shah warned that he would "announce these alternatives during a speech he planned to make in the near future to the [Iranian] National Congress."[67]

According to a report from Esso Middle East to Exxon's headquarters, "around January 19, letters from President Nixon and Sir Douglas-Home [the British foreign secretary] were delivered to the Shah." The letters "referred to past contacts with H.I.M. [His Imperial Majesty], to the desirability of continuing good relations and urged moderation in the Shah's upcoming speech." Ignoring these letters, the shah included in his speech to the National Congress "the alternatives put before the Team on January 14 and 15."[68]

The IOP's negotiating team recognized that the shah held the power to dictate terms: "The Shah wants a new agreement . . . throwing off the yoke of the past, so as to, in his mind, establish the desired political posture essential to preserving his leadership role throughout the region and thereby establishing the stability and security so essential in long term arrangements." Yet they feared that to "abandon the rights inherent in the old Agreement will lead to demands for rewriting the old concession agreements throughout the OPEC world." They warned that the shah's proposal would, in effect, "take over all operations and facilities without just compensation." This would have an "impact on participation" while also setting a "horrible principle for all types of foreign investments the world around." The members feared that a complete takeover by the National Iranian Oil Company would reduce their roles to "mere purchasers of crude and products." They also voiced concerns that "Iran will receive economic benefits in excess of those which will accrue to the countries signatory to the General Agreement [a set of general contract terms accepted by numerous producers on the Arabian peninsula]. This, of course, will place the General Agreement in jeopardy."[69]

Despite these grave misgivings, the consortium accepted the basic demands of the shah as an amendment to the 1954 agreement. This sales and purchase agreement gave the IOP the right to purchase all oil it produced in defined regions of Iran, with the exception of oil needed for the country's own growing requirements and oil set aside for export sales by NIOC. The agreement granted the members of the consortium a twenty-year contract to purchase much of the petroleum produced in Iran. Its complex rules for establishing the price of oil gave Iran considerable leeway to alter the price without rewriting the agreement.[70]

The shah could now claim the lead in the race to nationalization in the Middle Eastern oil industry. In one important respect, this was true. The National Iranian Oil Company had grown and gained experience in the years since its creation in 1954. It had managed domestic operations within Iran, and now it would be an overseer of sorts of the consortium, which had created the Oil Service Company of Iran to act as operator under the direction and control of NIOC. In theory, Iran's national oil company stood to gain managerial and technical experience in this new role, but in practice, its power over Iran's oil remained limited for several more decades.

This much-heralded agreement turned out to be only another case of "leapfrogging" in the Middle East, since other producers quickly demanded additional concessions from the international oil companies. In response, during the years between the signing of the agreement in 1973 and the Iranian Revolution in 1978–1979, the shah regularly "reinterpreted" the terms of the agreement as he sought to keep Iran's deal equal to the new ones cut by its neighbors. After Saudi Arabia and its neighbors won sixty-forty participation in 1974, the Iranian government and the consortium had great difficulty agreeing on revisions to the existing contract. Stalled, both sides simply began to circumvent provisions in the existing agreement that no longer suited their needs.[71] The waning years of the shah were not easy for the consortium.

Yet in separate negotiations, Exxon bid on new concessions in Iran while also agreeing to collaborate with NIOC on research on petroleum processes and procedures and on petrochemicals.[72] These agreements signaled Exxon's intent to build a stronger presence in Iran. In April 1978, Exxon Research and Engineering (ER&E) contracted with the NIOC to conduct studies in the United States on technical processes to be used in a new refinery being constructed by the company. In September 1978, the two sides reached agreement on further cooperative research, with four Exxon researchers carrying out projects in NIOC's facilities in Tehran on gasoline product quality, automotive emissions, and other refining-related matters. These two agreements produced fees for services of about $4 million. This was not a large sum for Exxon, but the projects demonstrated the company's resolve to maintain a lasting relationship with the Iranian government.[73]

This continuing relationship between Exxon and the shah remained profitable for both parties. By 1978, Iran was exporting about 4.5 million b/d out of total oil production of about 5.5 million b/d. Exxon received more than 300,000 b/d of much-needed crude oil from its relatively small share of the consortium's production.[74] The shah received billions of dollars in oil revenues to finance both industrialization and the SAVAK, a secret police force organized with the help of the CIA, capable of holding down public discontent. Iran also remained a favored regional client for U.S. foreign aid and for purchases of advanced U.S. weapons systems.

Domestic discontent continued to grow, however, and the shah was driven from power. A strike in and around the Oil Service Company facilities in December 1978 became increasingly violent, with one Exxon supervisor barely escaping the blast from a bomb thrown into his car. Soon after, protestors gunned down another Oil Service Company employee as he sought to enter the facility. His death convinced the consortium to withdraw all its workers as quickly as possible. It was unclear whether the withdrawal would be permanent.

The case of the ER&E researchers illustrates the tensions of the time. On December 4, 1978, the head of research for NIOC suggested that "the Exxon Research personnel should stay away from the NIOC Laboratory because of civil disturbance." He raised the possibility that the researchers might have to "temporarily leave Iran." Within two weeks, the researchers had departed for Rome, where they continued work on the Iranian projects while waiting to see whether they would return to Tehran.

They never did. With the departure of the almost 1,200 consortium workers, the Iranian oil fields shut down, interrupting oil exports and plunging global oil markets into chaos. Exxon and the other members of the consortium became spectators, watching from outside Iran as a series of fast-moving events gave birth to a new Iranian oil industry. As conditions spiraled out of his control, the shah left Iran in January 1979 for medical treatment, and his opponents asserted authority. The shah did not return; he had lost his race with history. The planning report for 1980 for Esso Middle East commented on the fallout from the shah's departure as follows: "The challenges of achieving massive development while preserving cultural and social traditions with adequate participation by the full population are enormous. Accordingly, upheavals and revolutions may occur in other countries."[75] For the moment, however, the company had its hands full with the revolution in Iran.

When a new Iranian government came to power, it broke patterns established by the shah on many issues, including oil policies. Officials from Exxon and the other members of the Iranian consortium had to bridge epoch-defining discontinuities in the Iranian oil industry. Faced with a new cast of characters, a new set of problems, and a new urgency to act, they proved powerless as the revolutionary government moved quickly to expel them. The consortium received little effective support from the U.S. government, whose influence in Iran disintegrated with the departure of the shah.

In late 1979, events took a turn that led the U.S. government to impose a ban on U.S. companies dealing with Iran. Growing tensions between the new Islamic revolutionary government in Iran and the Western powers, particularly the United States, exploded in November 1979 with the storming of the U.S. Embassy in Tehran and the taking of sixty-three American hostages. With the freezing of Iranian assets in parts of the West, a long legal march began as an international tribunal sorted out competing claims from Iran and companies whose properties had been expropriated in the revolution. Before the smoke cleared in Tehran, oil prices had more than doubled from their level in mid-1978. Against this backdrop of turmoil and strife, Iraq invaded Iran in December 1980, marking the beginning of an eight-year war that further reduced oil exports, adding to the uncertainty in the region and in global oil markets.[76]

Exxon's relatively brief time in Iran had ended with the company forced out by revolutionary violence and the new Islamic regime. U.S. government sanctions blocked the company's return. Just before the Iranian Revolution, Exxon's leaders in the Middle East had contemplated withdrawal from Iran. They feared that the company's relatively small share of oil production there might not be worth the management effort required to stay. By 1981, no doubt, that road not taken looked very good to Exxon.

REVOLUTIONARY NATIONALIZATION IN LIBYA

The North African nation of Libya, which also came under the management of Esso Middle East, played an important part in the changes in the Arab world in the 1970s, and it ultimately took a path to nationalization somewhat similar to that of Iran. In both countries, Exxon entered under one regime and then found itself vulnerable after the overthrow of that regime. The company also confronted what came to be known as a "fundamentalist Muslim" government, and the gulf between a worldview based on science and one based on absolutist religion proved difficult to bridge. An added barrier to cooperation was intense anti-Americanism in Libya, as in Iran after 1978. Exxon never quite overcame these barriers, especially after the ascent to power of Muammar el-Qaddafi in 1969. One distinctive feature of nationalization in Libya was that Exxon operated a first-generation LNG plant there. The presence of this facility altered somewhat the process by which the government nationalized its properties.[77]

Exxon was among the earliest of the major international oil companies to explore for oil in Libya. In 1959, it discovered the nation's first major oil field, the Zelten (later renamed Nasser) field. Exxon completed Libya's first significant trunk line, a hundred-mile-long pipeline to transport oil from the Zelten field to the coast at Marsa el-Brega, from which it shipped the first exports of crude oil from Libya. By the late 1960s, Exxon was producing about 700,000 b/d in Libya. Operating as an independent

The vast liquefaction plant, part of the larger LNG facility at Marsa el-Brega, Libya, ca. 1970. ExxonMobil Historical Collection, di_08132.

company, not as a member of a consortium, it accounted for roughly half of the nation's crude-oil exports.[78]

As a relative latecomer to the oil industry, Libya could survey existing conditions in nearby producing nations before choosing its course. Instead of trying to oversee a consortium of major international companies, as had been done by the governments of Saudi Arabia, Iran, and Iraq, the Libyan government created a highly competitive concession system that attracted many different oil companies from around the world. Independent oil producers from the United States proved more vulnerable to government pressure than did the larger international oil companies. Libya used leverage over the smaller companies to secure increased oil revenues and greater control over foreign companies. King Idris, who ruled Libya from its establishment in 1949 until his overthrow in a coup in 1969, put in place these original concession agreements in the 1950s. He also led the nation into OPEC in 1962. He pressured Exxon to build a refinery at Marsa el-Brega that would help supply Libya's growing domestic consumption, and in 1968 he created the Libyan National Oil Company to help manage the nation's reserves. Qaddafi's revolutionary government could build on the foundation laid by King Idris while taking advantage of the vulnerabilities of the smaller foreign oil companies within the competitive system designed by the king.[79]

In the year after taking office, Qaddafi confiscated Exxon's distribution system for gasoline within Libya, giving the properties to the Libyan National Oil Company. Along with numerous other foreign oil companies, Exxon then lost substantial production to partial nationalization in the early 1970s. All the while, Libya remained a price hawk within OPEC. Its ability to extract higher prices from its divided oil industry encouraged the leapfrogging of oil prices in the Middle East, which exerted strong upward pressure on prices in the years leading up to the energy crisis of 1973.[80]

Determined to win better agreements from the international oil companies than other producing nations in the 1970s, Qaddafi substituted production-sharing agreements for existing concessions. The companies argued long and hard—and futilely—for an agreement in Libya along the lines of that struck with the Saudis. As happened regularly in the Middle East in the 1970s, the companies quickly found that they were in no position to negotiate. Instead, the Libyan government rejected their proposals out of hand, settling the matter by decree in September 1973. The decree gave Libya ownership of 51 percent of all of the hydrocarbons of the six international companies involved (Exxon, Atlantic Richfield, Mobil, Royal Dutch Shell, Standard of California, and Texaco). It also created three-member committees to manage each company, with two members, including the chair, appointed by the government. It forbade resignations by any employee of the companies without approval of the management committees, and it established a separate committee, appointed by the government, to set compensation levels. Libyan officials put an exclamation point in the decree with the provision that anyone who violated its terms could be punished by fines or imprisonment.[81]

In 1976, the president of Esso Middle East reported back to the Exxon Management Committee: "We have been concerned for some time with the corporate structure we have in Libya. Government action, which has imposed upon Esso Libya a management committee chaired by a government-appointed Libyan national, exposes us to potentially costly business risks." Under this form of partial nationalization, as in Saudi Arabia in the

1970s, Exxon could be required to provide 49 percent of the investment capital for projects that were important to the government, but were not necessarily in Exxon's self-interest. It had lost effective control of both its investments and its operations, causing great practical and philosophical concerns for the company's management, which wondered whether the company could "continue to function in the Middle East."[82]

Yet almost immediately after posing this question, the company's leaders in Esso Middle East asserted: "Exxon cannot divorce its long range future from the future of the Middle East, and, although you are well aware of the potential instability in the area, we would be remiss in not pointing out some of our major concerns." Chief among these was that the region "is a powder keg" that might be set off by a superpower confrontation in the region, by the "persistent issue of the Israeli presence in the Arab world which has defied resolution for 28 years," or by "inter-Arab . . . factional and ideological disputes which have been brewing and are beginning to surface."[83] The symbol in Libya of these growing tensions was Colonel Qaddafi, who wooed the Soviet Union in his search for support, sponsored terrorists in the region in the ongoing war on Israel and its allies, and made life miserable for Exxon executives who hoped to retain long-term access to his nation's abundant oil.

Before Qaddafi took power, Exxon had, as mentioned, made a substantial investment in a state-of-the-art LNG plant at Marsa el-Brega.[84] The Zelten field, which the company had discovered, held large amounts of associated natural gas. Initially, this gas was flared to allow for oil production from the field. But in the early 1960s, a task force within Exxon studied options for getting it to market. Concluding that a pipeline to Europe was not economically feasible, it recommended the building of an LNG system—a relatively new and expensive technology for transporting natural gas to markets that could not be reached by pipeline. In the late 1960s, the company moved forward on the construction of a large, ambitious project whose final price reached about $350 million, making it, at the time, one of the most expensive projects in Exxon's history.[85]

The project transported via pipeline ample natural gas from the Zelten field to the Libyan coast. At the end of the pipeline stood the heart of the project, the Marsa el-Brega liquefaction plant, which froze natural gas at -290 degrees Fahrenheit, creating a liquid approximately 600 times denser than natural gas. The LNG was then stored in large, specially constructed tanks on-site while awaiting shipment in specially designed and constructed tankers across the Mediterranean to markets in Italy and Spain. Demand for natural gas was growing in Europe, and customers stood ready to experiment with LNG if the price was right. The tankers added considerable expense, and the primary customers in Italy and Spain signed long-term contracts with Exxon and agreed to build the four LNG tankers required. The maximum projected capacity of the liquefaction plant was about 325 million cubic feet per day, the equivalent in heating content of approximately 80,000 b/d of oil.[86]

Throughout the 1970s, Exxon struggled to forge some sort of working accommodation with the Qaddafi government (to find a satisfactorily high price for gas) and with the company's European customers (to find a price not so high as to be unworkable) that would allow the LNG facility to continue to operate (at a reasonable profit for the company). The fact that in 1973 the Libyan government excluded the company's LNG project from its hard-line negotiations on the ownership and price of crude oil suggested that it recognized the substantial long-term benefits that might flow from the production and sale of LNG. Although small by the standards of modern LNG facilities, the Libyan LNG operation was path-breaking for its time. Upon its completion in 1970, it was among the largest such facilities in the world. It promised to demonstrate the economic and technical potential of a new approach to creating markets for the vast supplies of "stranded" natural gas being discovered around the world, that is, gas too remote to reach existing markets through pipelines. This was a risky proposition, but companies that led the way stood to reap extraordinary rewards. The ingredients for success included a giant supply of natural gas, customers with a strong demand for natural gas and a willingness to gamble on a new product, and a company with the financial and technical resources to develop a new technology and put together an effective partnership of industrial producer, consumer, and producing nation.[87]

In Libya, forging a partnership with the government proved to be the most difficult task for Exxon. The company planned and built its LNG facility under the administration of King Idris. After the contracts were signed and the plant was nearing completion, however, Qaddafi came to power. Exxon and its LNG customers had used the prevailing price

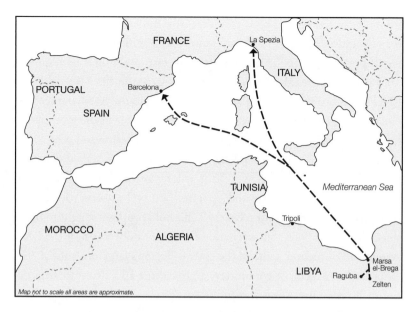

MAP 1.1: Source: *Esso Middle East, "Frozen Energy from Libya to Europe,"*
ExxonMobil Historical Collection, box 2.207.2/G199.

of natural gas in planning the system in the late 1960s.[88] In light of the
price increases of the early 1970s, Qaddafi wanted a higher take for Libya.
He was in a strong position to get what he wanted, since Exxon and its
customers had hundreds of millions of dollars in sunk costs that could
not be recovered until the LNG began flowing. The first round quickly
went to Qaddafi, who demanded and received an increased payment from
Exxon. Then, as the price of oil surged forward, Libya joined other producing nations in attempting to tie the price of natural gas to that of oil.
The producing nations never quite accomplished this goal, in large part
because gas, unlike oil, was not sold in global markets. They did, however,
receive steadily higher prices for natural gas in the 1970s because of strong
demand for the fuel.

Exxon went through several rounds of painful renegotiations of its
existing long-term contracts with both the Libyan government and its
European customers. In the summer of 1974, Esso Libya and Esso Middle East reported to corporate headquarters in New York City that they
intended to inform the Libyan government that "conditions resulting

from official actions and policies of that Government prevent the satisfactory operation of said LNG plant," and that a "fundamental restructuring of present ownership and contractual relations" might be required. They proposed the sale of a 51–60 percent interest in the Marsa el-Brega LNG facility to the Libyan government. Doing so might encourage "the Government's involvement as a responsible co-owner in the joint operations," essentially shifting Libya's role from outside critic and rent seeker to partner. Under its proposal, Exxon would continue to staff and operate the facility "at full cost recovery" for as long as the company remained in Libya. It would manage and operate the LNG tankers too "during their charter life at full cost recovery." This bold proposal sought to break through the deadlock that prevented the smooth operation of the LNG system and to recover some of the costs of Exxon's large investment. The corporate management committee approved the effort to start negotiations with the Libyan government.[89]

The Libyan government was not, however, convinced of the wisdom of buying half ownership in an expensive project over which it already exercised effective control. After rejecting this proposal, the government demanded "a substantial price increase" for LNG, which already was roughly four times the price agreed to by the European customers in their original contracts in 1969, only five years earlier. Not surprisingly, those customers refused to accept the new price, and the company "shut down the plant to avoid the high contingent liabilities to Exxon."[90]

Negotiations between Libya and Exxon then took a different path. In December 1975, Esso Middle East reported that it had "reached agreement, subject to appropriate confirmation by both parties," with the Libyan Government for a plan "whereby Esso Libya would anticipate realizing . . . profit after tax for its gas plant operations" in the range of $10 million to $20 million a year in 1976 and beyond, along with a "profit improvement of $5 million for 1975." This profit would result from the operation of the government-controlled "market" for natural gas in Libya. The government promised to reduce "overall taxes paid by Esso Libya to the Libyan Government to enable Esso Libya to realize the profit levels indicated."[91] Although never carried out, this proposed agreement showed that the Libyan government valued the continued operation of the LNG plant.

By the late 1970s, the company and the government could find no common ground. As their negotiations over the fate of Exxon's properties in Libya continued, violence against foreign companies grew. The fervor of Islamic fundamentalism and nationalism after the Iranian Revolution focused criticism throughout the Middle East on the operations of Western companies and their governments. In November 1979, demonstrators burned the American embassy in Tripoli. In the aftermath, "expatriate dependents of Esso Libya and most other foreign oil companies were temporarily evacuated in mid-December 1979 for about a month." Esso Middle East painted a bleak picture of conditions in Libya in its annual report back to headquarters in 1980: "The Libyan environment remains very difficult.... Qadhafi may be able to remain in power for some time to come, in which event the government will remain radical, socialistic, and anti-western." Despite this, the company continued to plan for business there, even assuming in its forecasts, as it had done throughout the decade, that the government would ultimately become a 51 percent partner with Esso Libya in its LNG operations. Esso Libya's strategy included the goal of protecting "Exxon's access to Libyan crude oil for as long as possible" and also of obtaining "additional gas supplies to meet future requirements for the LNG plant feed."[92]

Exxon's future in Libya did not last much longer. Tensions between Esso Libya and the government increased in 1981 as positions hardened and the tone of discussion worsened. Meanwhile, the newly elected U.S. president, Ronald Reagan, and his administration took a hard line in diplomatic relations between the two nations. Indeed, intelligence reports in Washington of Qaddafi's support for terrorist groups around the world helped persuade President Reagan to close Libya's U.S. embassy in May 1981. Then, in the summer of 1981, the U.S. Sixth Fleet held a series of maneuvers in the Gulf of Sidra off the Libyan coast, seemingly inviting a response from Qaddafi. When it came, American jets shot down two Libyan planes. The assassination of Egypt's Anwar Sadat, a U.S. ally in the region, and reports of a Libyan plan to assassinate Reagan further heightened tensions.[93]

On the ground in Libya, conditions became intolerable for Exxon. Esso Middle East's report to headquarters in the fall of 1981 told of the country's preparations for war, such as the stockpiling of Soviet arms.

The report examined the implications for oil companies of the increased production of oil for the military, and the drain of technically trained individuals from the oil companies to staff the military. In addition, "harassment of our employees, occupation of company housing at Marsa el-Brega by security forces, and general tensions have escalated over the past few months." As a result, the report continued, "our main objectives in Libya are to assure the safety of our employees and to obtain improvement in Exxon's earnings and cash flow from existing oil, gas plant, and refinery operations." Despite this bleak portrayal of conditions in Libya, the report made projections about Exxon's operations in Libya for the rest of the 1980s.[94]

The end came quickly for Esso Libya. In November 1981, Exxon ordered the withdrawal of its employees from Libya. Negotiations led by Mel Harrison at Exxon resulted in an agreement calling for Libya to pay the company "close to the book value of [its] assets." On December 1, 1981 the government quickly turned over the company's properties to the Libyan National Oil Company to operate. At the time, Exxon's crude production in Libya had dropped to an estimated 40,000 b/d out of a total Libyan production estimated by the U.S. Department of Energy at about 700,000 b/d, or roughly the production of Exxon alone in Libya the late 1960s. In the United States, newspapers speculated that Exxon and other American oil companies had been pressured to leave by the Reagan administration.[95] Any such high-level diplomatic intrigue was not necessary to explain Exxon's withdrawal. Company personnel were in danger, and the costs and political risks were simply too high. Cliff Garvin explained the company's 1981 withdrawal from Libya simply and convincingly: "Qaddafi came into power, and we all had a crack at trying to talk to him over the years. Exxon was big in Libya and found a lot of oil, but when he got to the heyday of his managing the country with his attitudes and all, he told us to get out, and we got out. We left a lot of oil in place in Libya."[96]

This was also true in Iran, and the company's departure from both Iran and Libya in the early 1980s left a gaping hole in its production in the Middle East and in its long-term strategy for retaining access to the oil in that region. By 1981, it was clear that Saudi Arabia, despite its slow movement toward full nationalization, remained the linchpin of Exxon's oil supply in the Middle East and worldwide. Writing back to headquarters in 1979, the head of Esso Middle East noted that Saudi Arabia remained the company's "major source of earnings and Exxon's largest single source of crude oil." He pointed out that although "the company currently provides numerous contributions to the Saudis," it still needed to "strengthen our interdependence with Saudi Arabia." The best strategy for retaining a strong presence in the kingdom included "not only increasing the support activities" provided to Aramco, "but also increasing Exxon's direct presence." This could be done by investing in oil-related activities such as petrochemicals, natural gas, and refining, even though the company faced "limitations on the availability of personnel" and the prospect of below-average returns on some of those investments. It was also understood that Saudi Arabia would eventually take over more of its own industries and that other large oil and chemical companies from around the world were eager to participate in joint ventures with the Saudis. Exxon faced an uncertain future in Saudi Arabia, but at least it had emerged from the turmoil of the 1970s with a foothold in the kingdom, which is more than it had done in Iran and Libya.[97]

In response to its problems in the major producing nations in the Middle East, the company aggressively explored its options in smaller, less-developed oil provinces in the region. Abu Dhabi, which allowed ownership of reserves by foreign companies, was a favorite of Exxon's management. The company also developed oil and natural gas fields in Egypt, which historically had not been a major petroleum-producing nation. In those years, it also unsuccessfully attempted to gain a position in the giant gas fields of Qatar. Iraq, where Exxon held a relatively minor position within a consortium of producers, remained a source of frustration as it, too, asserted greater control over its oil under the regime of Saddam Hussein. These other nations held promise, but as Exxon entered the 1980s, they did not have the capacity to replace the reserves it had lost through nationalization.

Exxon left a lot of oil in place around the world in the post-1973 wave of nationalizations. Despite the differences between the "capitalist nationalizations" in Saudi Arabia and Venezuela and the "revolutionary nationalizations" in Iran and Libya, the result in all four nations was roughly the same. Exxon lost direct control over oil in those countries, and it retained access to crude only for as long as it remained in the good graces of the governments and their national oil companies. As discussed in chapter 7, the company briefly reentered Venezuela in the 1990s only to see its fortunes reversed with the coming to power of Hugo Chávez in 1998. It played a stronger role in Saudi Arabia, where it retained access to large volumes of oil through purchase while participating in joint ventures with national companies to help industrialize the kingdom. The 1998 merger with Mobil, a company that also had maintained a substantial presence in Saudi Arabia, consolidated the holdings of the two former partners in Aramco. In 2001, ExxonMobil reported that the merged company was both the largest private investor in Saudi Arabia, with more than $11 billion in capital projects, and the largest foreign purchaser of crude oil and other hydrocarbons from Saudi Aramco. ExxonMobil also reported a variety of joint ventures with Saudi companies involving refineries and petrochemical complexes.[98] The story line was much shorter in both Iran and Libya, where the company was expelled and then prevented by U.S. government sanctions from doing business.

One common theme of Exxon's experience in all four nations was its loss of control in the face of "major uncertainties." The rush of events after 1973 caught even experienced managers off guard, exposing the limitations of using traditional assumptions and trends to plan for the future. Again and again, the company's managers in the major producing nations greatly underestimated how quickly they could lose control of crude oil production and pricing. Company planners did not foresee the dramatic price increases of 1973–1974 and 1978–1979, and they repeatedly overshot the mark in projecting future oil supplies from the major producing nations. Even after the rise of OPEC, the wave of nationalizations, and the quadrupling of oil prices, they continued to downplay the likelihood of sharp breaks with the past. Old attitudes and planning assumptions, much less the habit of power, did not die quickly or easily. As fundamental changes continued at breathtaking speed in the decade after 1973, Exxon executives struggled to reassert some measure of control, despite the lack of real weapons in their negotiating arsenal.

As they did so, they had to take into consideration the growing power of the national oil companies. These national oil companies had different histories and powers, but they became much stronger during the nationalizations of the 1970s. The Iranian National Oil Company had been created in the early 1950s, but it became a powerful force in the global petroleum industry after the expropriations following the Iranian Revolution. Venezuela constructed PDVSA around the properties and organizational structures of the international oil companies nationalized in 1975, and the company had evolved by the 1990s into what the *Financial Times* called a "rare case of well-oiled efficiency." Saudi Aramco, the national oil company that emerged in 1988, came of age as a partner in Aramco during the long nationalization process of the 1970s and 1980s before subsequently becoming one of the world's leading oil companies. Saudi Aramco, the Iranian National Oil Company, and PDVSA steadily evolved into competitors and joint-venture partners with the international oil companies that had dominated the industry before 1973. With control over many of the largest oil reserves in the world, these and other national oil companies embodied the new balance of power in the global petroleum industry.[99]

A symbol of the difficult transition to this new era was the falling-out of Cliff Garvin and Sheikh Yamani over the nationalization of Exxon's holdings in Saudi Arabia. Garvin later recalled being present in 1986 when Yamani learned from a television newscast that the king of Saudi Arabia had fired him after a dispute over policy. Yamani moved to London, where he organized a think tank on petroleum-related issues. Several years later, he asked Garvin to join his board, but his old friend had to refuse because he had already accepted a position on the board of Saudi Aramco. The two never spoke again, and Garvin remained on the board of Saudi Aramco until his retirement.[100]

Exxon prospered as the king of the old order in global oil before 1973. But when that order was overthrown by producer power, the company was forced to adapt to new realities in the OPEC nations, accepting its status as a contractor, not a king. In response to the loss of its historical control of large volumes of oil in Venezuela and the Middle East, Exxon pursued strategic options outside those regions, including searching aggressively for non-OPEC oil in areas with the potential to become major new sources of crude, and looking outside the petroleum industry for profitable investments. And as Exxon sought to adapt to the new realities in the international petroleum industry, it also had to cope with strong political challenges in the United States and western Europe.

CHAPTER TWO

UNDER SIEGE

POLITICAL CHALLENGES IN CONSUMING NATIONS

As oil-producing countries around the world asserted power, consumers felt threatened and angry. In the United States and other major consuming nations, the sharp increases in oil prices after 1973 and then again after 1978 fed political movements to regulate and punish "Big Oil." Exxon, the biggest of the big, sought to defend itself by opposing what it considered bad public policy. Yet the heated anti-oil sentiment of the era limited its options. In 1979, the company's Public Affairs Department opposed Exxon USA's proposal to create a political action committee to support political candidates who opposed public policies such as the breakup of the major oil companies: "Given this environment, and the anger now being directed at the industry because of gas lines and higher prices, an Exxon announcement of a political action committee will give industry's critics a handle with which to attack Exxon and its role in politics. Even more reasonable observers are likely to be troubled and react critically."[1] In essence, the public was so skeptical of Big Oil that Exxon risked further undermining its public image by defending itself.

Much was on the line for the company in the politics of the era. In the years immediately after the embargo of 1973–1974, far-reaching public-policy initiatives sought to control oil prices, restructure the oil industry, and restrict its profits. Throughout the 1970s, political debates on national energy policy focused primarily on finding alternatives to oil and natural gas, usually through subsidies to competing sources of energy. Alongside these initiatives remained the most significant energy-related issue of the late twentieth century—defining a new balance between the demand for more energy and the demand for improved environmental quality. In an era of intense political passions, public policies in the closely related areas of energy, the environment, and the economy were not so much debated as fought to the finish.[2]

Exxon had a variety of political weapons in its arsenal. Its top executives frequently presented the company's point of view to a variety of public audiences and to politicians and regulators at the local, state, and national levels. Cliff Garvin became a leading spokesman not just for Exxon but also for the oil industry as a whole. Company representatives ranging from public affairs specialists to refinery managers carried the company's message to local audiences around the nation.[3] Exxon also employed professional public affairs specialists, lobbyists, and lawyers and armed them with excellent detailed data about its operations. In cooperation with the American Petroleum Institute (API) and other trade associations, company representatives voiced the industry's position to Congress, the White House, state and local governments, and the general public. Exxon employees also made significant contributions to the research and writing of industry-wide reports under the auspices of the National Petroleum Council (NPC)—an advisory committee to the secretary of the interior and, after 1977, to the secretary of energy.[4] The public image of Big Oil stressed the political power of the major oil companies, but in this era of very high gasoline prices and great skepticism about the activities of big oil companies, Exxon remained on the defensive. At times, it helped block legislative challenges to its traditional operating autonomy, but it won few outright political victories in the 1970s.

Exxon's public image plagued the company, and Cliff Garvin spent considerable time defending the company in presentations as CEO and as chairman of the Business Roundtable (an association of CEOs of leading corporations). Despite the uphill fight he faced, he was philosophical about public suspicion of Exxon and the other major oil companies: "The American is a funny person. He worships the result of things that are big, economies of scale, mass production, but he hates anything that is big and powerful, and the oil industry is seen as the biggest and most powerful industry." [5] Garvin spoke often of the need for Exxon to regain the public's trust and yet of the inevitability that the company would continue to be singled out for criticism in light of its size and profitability.[6] He knew that while many in the oil industry conceded that Exxon was the best-run oil company, it remained the most hated one by many in the public.

Exxon employees found such public criticism difficult to reconcile with their view of their company. Speaking to an audience at the Georgia Institute of Technology in November 1975, Exxon senior vice president Roy Baze spoke for many at Exxon when he scoffed at critics who "see something sinister" about the size and profitability of major oil companies. After outlining the contributions of Exxon and other oil companies to the national economy, he concluded that the nation "must recognize that energy problems stem not from the size and structure of its oil industry but rather from years of counterproductive national energy policies." Solutions would come from competition in existing markets, not from "piling one layer of regulation upon another."[7] Such comments embodied a clash of worldviews between Exxon and its critics that could not be easily reconciled in the bruising political battles of the day.

ANTI-OIL POLICIES IN AN ERA OF HIGH OIL PRICES

Higher gasoline prices and long lines at service stations in the immediate aftermath of the Organization of Arab Petroleum Exporting Companies embargo in the winter of 1973–1974 stunned American consumers. Long accustomed to cheap, abundant oil, they turned to the government for answers. Who was to blame? What could be done? Exxon and other international oil companies offered one answer: the economics of oil had changed fundamentally with the growth in global demand, the rise of producer power, and the coming of OPEC-led pricing. Critics in the United States responded with a much different answer: Big Oil had manipulated markets to push oil prices to unreasonable heights, far beyond the stable, low prices during the twenty-five years after World War II. In the ensuing political disputes over oil pricing and oil company profits, the new economics of global oil clashed repeatedly with the old politics of oil.

As political pressures on Exxon mounted, in January 1974 the corporation's management committee conducted a review of national tax and price policies. "It is now clear," the review stated, that "the petroleum industry will be faced immediately with many legislative tax proposals" designed to "prevent oil companies from realizing windfall profits which may result from an energy shortage." The political environment is "highly charged and hostile to the oil industry," and things were only going to get worse: "This environment will likely deteriorate further as the public reacts to shortages . . . incidents of price gouging . . . and announcements of most major oil companies that they received record profits in 1973." Likely results included the continuation of price controls, an excess-profits tax, and the elimination of the oil-depletion allowance and other tax breaks for the industry. The review cautioned that "in the current situation, it is believed that strong opposition to change will not be in the industry's best interest," since "open advocacy by the industry of any specific tax or price legislation would create negative reactions."[8] Tough political times were at hand.

The immediate concern in the winter of 1973–1974 was the shortage of adequate supplies of gasoline. Exxon and other international oil companies used whatever flexibility they could find to manage the impact of shortages by adjusting global patterns of distribution. For its part, the U.S. government rationed gasoline by limiting access to individual consumers according to their license plate numbers; it also imposed a mandatory speed limit of fifty-five miles an hour in order to improve gas mileage. In the private sector and in governmental energy use, fuel switching and measures to use oil more efficiently had some near-term impact. The easing of the embargo by the Arab members of OPEC in the spring of 1974 allowed government planners and industrial users of energy to begin to focus on long-term conservation.

Price controls on oil proved more enduring. Before the energy crisis, President Nixon had responded to rising inflation by implementing general price controls for oil and most other commodities. These price controls became the point of departure for public policy when the oil-price spike after 1973 threatened to worsen inflation. Passed in the immediate aftermath of the 1973–1974 embargo, the regulation of domestic oil prices at levels significantly lower than the new world prices became one of the most controversial economic-energy policies of the era, and one of the most complex to implement.

U.S. voters generally accepted the argument that the quadrupling of international oil prices did not justify similar increases in domestic oil prices. The oil had been found and developed before the coming of OPEC pricing. What possible justification was there for allowing oil companies to charge almost four times more than they had two years earlier simply because OPEC had learned how to raise the price of sources of oil beyond the regulatory control of the U.S. government? The economics of inflation and the politics of oil made oil price controls almost inevitable, but the reality that international, not domestic, forces shaped prices in the new political economy of oil doomed them to failure.[9]

Controls on domestic prices in the United States, a major producer and consumer of oil, could not help distorting the ongoing global adjustments to the new economics of oil. Domestic oil still accounted for almost 65 percent of U.S. consumption in 1973, or about 22 percent of world consumption. Keeping prices of domestic oil below those in world markets encouraged the growth of demand for U.S. oil when new supplies were becoming difficult to find—and when public policy should have been trying to dampen demand. At the same time, lower revenues for companies selling oil at controlled prices meant less capital to invest in the quest for new sources of energy.

Price controls specific to oil emerged in 1973 and remained throughout the 1970s. The newly created Federal Energy Administration (FEA) enforced an increasingly complex set of laws that mandated both oil price controls and an allocation program among different types of oil companies affected by the regulations. The system as it evolved became almost too complicated to describe, much less to administer. The controls began in the second half of 1973 with the creation of two tiers: a price for "old" oil found and produced before May 15, 1973, and a higher price allowed for categories of "new" oil developed after that date. Price controls on domestic oil at a time when international oil prices were rising sharply introduced problems of equity, since Exxon and other companies with access to large amounts of domestic crude now enjoyed a significant cost advantage over companies more dependent on international oil. Under the Buy-Sell Program, a mandatory allocation plan put into effect in November 1973,

Exxon and others had to sell significant amounts of domestic production at reduced prices to other companies, usually smaller refiners. Exxon also was required to make direct payments to small refiners in order to lower their cost for non-price-controlled crude oil. Designed in theory to help companies put at a competitive disadvantage by the much higher price of international oil compared to regulated domestic oil, the allocation system evolved into an entitlement program inevitably marked by intense interest-group lobbying by those who most benefited from it.[10]

As had been the case historically on a variety of political issues important to domestic oil companies, Exxon and the other international oil companies had little political leverage on this issue. One thorough history of oil-price controls and the allocation system concludes that a politically strong coalition of independent refiners, gasoline retailers, and distributors of home-heating oil strongly supported the continuation of the allocation and entitlement subsidy system, and "against this coalition, the contrary advice of Exxon, Texaco, and the other international majors had little impact."[11] Randall Meyer, who became president of Exxon Company USA in 1976, aptly summarized the company's general problems with price controls and the allocation program in this era: they "plagued us for a number of years . . . greatly complicating doing business" and also "ended up with us sending huge checks every month to our competitors."[12]

Exxon opposed oil price controls as an unnecessary and destructive intrusion by government in the market for oil. Of course, the global market for oil was hardly a free market, since governments of the major producing nations organized in OPEC shaped world prices in these years. Exxon joined many observers in the 1970s in criticizing the price-control system in the United States on the grounds that it was cumbersome and extraordinarily inefficient. Even without the added burden of administering an unwieldy allocation and entitlement system, price controls proved extremely difficult to manage. They placed government deeply into the business of creating and administering a market for oil based on the location and timing of the production of each of the approximately seventeen million b/d of crude purchased in the nation. Additional layers of complexity resulted as government regulators created new tiers of oil based on whether the barrels in question came from categories of domestic oil that seemed to promise new supplies, such as heavy oil and oil produced from certain forms of tertiary recovery. Such inherent problems made oil-price controls the most difficult and controversial task attempted by government in response to the energy crisis. It was a regulatory nightmare deeply resented by many in the oil industry as wrongheaded, inefficient, and doomed to fail. If Exxon remained the symbol of the power of Big Oil in this era, price controls became the new symbol of the inefficiency and counterproductive policies of Big Government.

Despite the dislocations caused by oil-price controls in domestic markets, they proved hard to dismantle. The Ford administration strongly favored decontrol, but Congress extended the controls as part of the comprehensive Energy Policy and Conservation Act of 1975, with the provision that they would end in 1989 or two years later, at the discretion of the president.[13] When the second sharp spike in oil prices after the fall of the shah greatly enlarged the gap between domestic and international prices, deregulation became a hot-button issue in American politics, and a political consensus emerged about the need for the deregulation of oil prices. Allowing domestic oil prices to rise to the level of international prices, then higher than $30 a barrel, however, would create an estimated $200 billion in revenue for the U.S. government, the oil companies, or some combination of the two. After several years of debate, Congress passed a deregulation act in early 1980, near the end of President Carter's term. It contained a complex plan to tax at steadily declining rates the giant revenues generated as domestic oil prices gradually rose to world prices, with government and the oil industry sharing the proceeds.[14]

Harsh arguments about these "windfall profits" put a sharp edge on political debates about oil policies in the late 1970s. This debate vanished quickly in the early 1980s, when rapid drops in oil prices greatly reduced the revenues previously projected from deregulation. U.S. and world oil prices came together again in the mid-1980s as international prices plunged from more than $30 a barrel to less than $10 in an extremely volatile global market.[15] The much-anticipated windfall from deregulated oil prices thus accrued primarily to consumers, whose thirst for cheap oil had helped create the energy crisis to begin with. High oil prices shaped the politics of oil in the 1970s, and the return of low prices in the 1980s removed oil-related issues from the top of the political agenda.

Before crashing to earth in the 1980s, high oil prices returned antitrust to the political forefront, and Exxon became a prime target. In July 1973, the Federal Trade Commission (FTC) filed a much-ballyhooed antitrust case against Exxon and other large American oil companies. The breakup of the companies was one possible remedy for their alleged restraint of trade. This "Exxon Case" received considerable publicity and had to be taken seriously by the companies targeted, but it gradually moved out of the public spotlight before being dismissed by the courts in 1986.[16]

The other work of antitrust officials was the enforcement of the per se rules set forth in the Clayton Act of 1914, which explicitly forbade offenses such as price fixing. At the state level, charges of price fixing became a common response to public outrage over the high profits reported by the major oil companies in the early years of the energy crisis. Exxon settled several of these out of court without admitting guilt. But when the company felt strongly that it had done nothing illegal, its lawyers fought to the finish. It remained confident that its legal resources were second to none and that its reputation as a company willing to fight instead of settle would deter future lawsuits. For example, in a 1977 case filed by the City of Long Beach, California, against several oil companies, Exxon stayed in court for seventeen years before winning a jury verdict that it had not conspired with six other oil companies active on the West Coast to fix oil prices in the years 1971–1977. The other companies had settled early on for a total of about $320 million. An Exxon spokesman explained the company's view of its vindication: "This case is an example of a lawsuit that should never have been filed. . . . We are pleased by the verdict, but it is extremely unfortunate that the case went this far."[17]

U.S. antitrust laws had been designed in an earlier era to address problems of near monopoly and abuse of market power domestically. The new economics of oil undermined the effectiveness of traditional U.S. antitrust policies in the oil industry. OPEC had been organized by the major producing nations to constrain trade and fix prices, and for a time it did so, but U.S. laws could not reach outside the nation's borders to counteract the actions of sovereign countries. In addition, antitrust actions that reduced the size or economic power of the largest American companies threatened to limit their capacity to compete in international markets. In the 1970s, however, the U.S. political system continued to focus on the competitive power of major oil companies in domestic markets. Instead of fashioning new policies to address competition in a global market shaped by producer power, Congress sought to strengthen traditional antitrust laws in an effort to bring the major oil companies to heel.

One early move in this direction was the drive toward "vertical divestment" of oil companies by limiting their operations to only one major part of the oil industry. Thus, Exxon, which had invented vertical integration in oil in the late nineteenth century, would be forced to become either a producer or a refiner or a transporter, and to divest itself of the other functions. Although the political appeal of vertical divestiture was strong, the economic logic was dubious. "Breaking up the oil companies" offered the chance for critics to attack Exxon and other large petroleum companies with the big stick of antitrust. Supporters of vertical divestment argued that it would reduce Big Oil's economic and political power and encourage new competition.

Exxon strongly disputed the arguments of those who favored what the oil industry labeled "dismemberment." In Exxon's view, vertical divestiture was a solution for a problem that did not exist. Cliff Garvin and other top Exxon executives stressed the value of vertical integration, which for almost a century had allowed the major oil companies to capture efficiencies from the scale and scope of their operations. Citing statistics drawn from governmental and industry sources, spokesmen for the company and professional economists from outside the company argued convincingly that competition in the oil industry was thriving in domestic and international markets. This was not, they stressed, 1911. In contrast to the near monopoly of Standard Oil Company (New Jersey) at the time of its dissolution, Exxon in 1973 accounted for only about 11 percent of domestic production and approximately 9 percent of domestic refining capacity.[18]

Professional economists stressed the potentially high costs of breaking up Big Oil. At a time of great uncertainty in the global oil industry, vertical divestiture might create higher oil prices, weaken global competition, slow economic recovery, and depress a vital sector of the stock market. Exxon spokesmen called vertical divestiture "economic malpractice."[19] This was no time for experimentation with the fundamental structure of an industry that had been the mainstay of the nation's energy supply for most of the twentieth century. The political fever finally broke, and government officials backed away from the matter. There were too many other energy-related challenges in the 1970s to bet the ranch on a policy that offered more political than economic benefits and posed significant long-term economic risks.

As the political sentiment for vertical divestment waned in the mid-1970s, a more intense political debate emerged over horizontal divestment. This policy sought to extend the coverage of existing antitrust laws to a relatively recent development, the diversification of oil and natural gas companies into other sources of energy. Structural regulation would be used to block such diversification and to force major oil companies to divest themselves of any holdings in energy sources other than petroleum. This policy assumed that governmental action was needed to prevent Big Oil from squelching the development of alternatives to oil. It strongly appealed to public fears of the power of Big Oil and to popular beliefs that the major oil companies would protect their own interests at the expense of the broader national interest. In 1975, the U.S. Senate came within eight votes of passing a law calling for horizontal divestiture, and by early 1976 some thirty bills containing some form of divestiture awaited congressional action. With the political tide running against the major oil companies, horizontal divestiture seemed to have a chance of becoming law.[20]

Exxon joined the rest of the industry in a determined effort to stop horizontal divestiture. With a touch of hyperbole, the *Wall Street Journal* reported that "oilmen" viewed this policy as "the greatest threat to their industry since the breakup of John D. Rockefeller's Standard Oil Trust in 1911."[21] The stakes were high for Exxon, which had substantial investments in fuels other than oil and natural gas. Cliff Garvin denounced horizontal divestment as an "utterly misguided" policy that would slow energy development. "The U.S. would be the loser," he argued. The major oil companies had the money, the highly trained workforces, the experience in designing and completing big projects, and the management talent to hasten the growth of alternatives to oil.[22] Garvin felt strongly that they should be allowed to do so and thereby make the nation less dependent on oil imported from unstable regions.

As political sentiment for horizontal divestiture grew during the early years of the Carter administration, Exxon responded with a comprehensive communication program entitled "Response to Attack on Industrial Structure." This program emphasized the competitiveness of the oil industry and the possible impact of horizontal divestiture on energy development. As was generally the case with Exxon, communication to internal audiences—employees, annuitants, and shareholders—was one important focus of the campaign. But the company also reached out through its own public affairs departments, the API, the Business Round-table, and other business-oriented organizations to a broader audience. It was by no means clear that a wide-ranging communication campaign could change political opinion, but the company nonetheless distributed data supporting its arguments to government, universities, customers, and the general public. Included were visits by representatives of the company to media outlets in seventy cities, television appearances, speeches by top executives at major venues, interviews with national magazines, and media briefings in New York and Washington, D.C.[23]

A principal part of this campaign was a brochure entitled *Competition in the Petroleum Industry*, which contained the testimony of several Exxon executives before Congress in the years 1973–1975. Page after page of detailed testimony made the case that the regulation of the industrial structure of the petroleum industry was unnecessary to foster competition and potentially destructive to the nation's energy future. The testimony in January 1975 of W. T. (Bill) Slick Jr.—a senior vice president of Exxon Company USA and a specialist in public affairs—before the Senate Judiciary Subcommittee on Antitrust and Monopoly strongly opposed the Industrial Reorganization Act then before Congress. Slick examined the concentration ratios in all areas of the oil industry, the lack of concentration in the energy industries as a whole, oil industry performance, the ease of entry into petroleum, and other traditional economic measures of competition. As justification for the oil industry's need for profits, he quoted the estimate of a senior economist at Chase Manhattan Bank that the energy industry worldwide would require $1.35 trillion in investment capital from 1970 to 1985. He concluded that the evidence proved that "the energy industry is both competitive and efficient."[24]

Senate testimony by Exxon USA president Randall Meyer in December 1973 advocated a key role for oil companies in developing alternatives to oil. Focusing on Exxon's growing involvement in coal production and the processing of uranium, Meyer argued that its activities had increased competition in both of those industries while also providing much needed growth in each. With battle flags flying, Meyer charged that "some people react by attacking the petroleum industry rather than the root problems which have led to the energy crisis." He argued that most such attacks were "based on irrelevant economic theories, erroneous and incomplete facts, plus naïve assumptions" about the operations of the oil industry. He then lamented that "at a time when the nation's energy situation is entering such a critical phase," such attacks would "divert the government's attention from the truly monumental job that needs to be done."[25]

Perhaps more persuasive for those still sitting on the fence were media accounts containing the views of people on both sides of the issue. A *Wall Street Journal* article headlined "Oil Firms Fear Moves to Bar Their Owning Other Energy Sources" caught the essence of the debate over horizontal divestiture in the early years of the Carter administration. The article quoted numerous congressmen and agency heads. It noted that Interior Secretary Cecil Andrus "sees dangers that big energy companies may control the pace of development and pricing of all energy types." The head of the Federal Energy Administration, John O'Leary, mirrored this view: "I'd rather see tough coal and uranium industries rather than one big homogeneous energy industry." Representative Morris Udall (D-Arizona) voiced fears that the oil companies "might well conclude that their overall profits would be maximized by keeping oil prices high and by restricting the production of coal." To counter these fears and charges, Bill Slick summarized the simple economics of his company's investments in other energy sources: "They were good business opportunities. . . . It's in the best interests of the country to encourage anyone who can get in and develop them [new energy technologies]." Unexpected support for Big Oil's position came from a representative of the coal industry, who noted that coal could not attract the capital needed for development without oil companies' investments. For this reason, "dismantling the coal industry as it has evolved over the past five years would be a misguided effort."[26]

In addition to arguments about existing energy sources, the *Journal* article offered a short exchange on the future of solar energy. Exxon had made a relatively small investment in solar, and it reported in an advertisement that this form of renewable energy might become a major energy source "in the next century." This prediction reflected the company's financial and technical analysis of the probable price and availability

Exxon-manufactured solar panels on a Connecticut home, 1978.
ExxonMobil Historical Collection, di_06234.

of solar energy as it grew from a very small percentage of the nation's energy mix to a more important, but still minor, source of energy. Several solar advocates in Congress, including Senator Gary Hart (D-Colorado), took offense at Exxon's ad and wrote a letter to the company, complaining that it was "misinforming the public" with "pessimistic projections" that suggested that Exxon might keep solar "under wraps" until "fossil-fuel markets are exhausted." Slick labeled such charges "preposterous and irresponsible." This exchange captured the central problem with the "debates" on energy policy of the era: because each side started from a different set of assumptions, real dialogue was blocked.[27]

President Carter's enthusiasm for horizontal divestment waned as he focused on passing a comprehensive energy policy based on conservation, and the divestment argument faded from political debate. As discussed in chapter 4, in the mid-1980s, economic pressure from lower oil prices convinced Exxon and many other large oil companies to sell their holdings in energy industries other than oil and gas. But before that time, Exxon spent considerable time and money fighting proposals to break up the oil companies or limit their activities in other energy industries. The opposition of the company and the rest of the oil industry helped block the passage of both vertical and horizontal divestiture.

EXXON AND ENERGY POLICY

As political support for divestiture waned, Congress and executive agencies considered energy policies to encourage the expansion of alternatives to oil. Exxon, however, had limited input into these discussions. The company remained on the defensive. It had earlier failed to block the end of the oil-depletion allowance for larger companies under the 1975 Tax Reform Act. It had struggled unsuccessfully to sway the government from its lengthy experiment with oil-price controls. Meanwhile, the federal government, a range of interest groups representing other forms of energy, and environmentalists who favored renewable energy supported a variety of proposals for developing alternatives to oil, including nuclear power, coal, synthetic fuels from coal, oil shale, solar power, wind power, and conservation. Exxon was one of many competing voices in the loud and raucous political struggles over energy policy; it was, however, far from the dominant voice.

To say that Exxon did not shape the nation's energy policy in these years is not necessarily to say that any other company, industry, or interest group had effective control over the process. From 1973 to 1986, Presidents Nixon, Ford, Carter, and Reagan put forward different energy plans. In general, all favored the addition of as much energy as possible from all alternatives to oil, but each placed his own political twist on the idea of "everything except oil and gas as fast as possible." Subsidies were the order of the era, with each new package of energy policies containing tax breaks or other policies to promote one of the alternatives to oil. Inevitably, interest groups sought to win subsidies or to block them for competitors.

Fragmented by federalism, checks and balances at all levels, and intensely partisan politics, the political process in the United States had great difficulty in producing coherent public policies on major issues such as energy. Indeed, what had passed for "energy policy" before the 1970s had been a variety of ad hoc, piecemeal policies to promote or regulate individual types of fuel. A key departure after the crisis in 1973 and 1974 was the effort to create a comprehensive framework for a unified energy policy based on the assumption that the nation needed to develop domestic alternatives to imported oil. Gasoline lines and much higher oil prices convinced Presidents Nixon, Ford, Carter, and Reagan of the need to respond to public anger by doing something to make things better. President Nixon took the lead with his announcement of Project Independence in late 1973. Its implausible goal of complete independence of the United States from all forms of imported energy by 1980 made cynics of those who understood the nation's energy supply. The next three presidents all sought energy independence, but their different proposals to reach that elusive goal added confusion to the debates, as did voters' lack of knowledge about energy. The confusion plagued voters, elected officials, and oil executives alike. The world of international oil had turned downside up, challenging the American assumption that cheap, abundant oil was a birthright and leaving much uncertainty and anxiety about what would come next. A comprehensive energy policy proved elusive, in part because the concept "energy" encompassed many different types of fuel. In addition, severe oil-price swings in the 1970s and 1980s undermined long-term planning by government or business. To make matters worse, the U.S. government lacked the institutional capacity and the political will to coordinate policies in response to the two major crises of the era—energy supply and environmental quality.[28]

The major energy-related acts passed during this era reflected these realities. The Energy Policy and Conservation Act of 1975, for example, contained so many initiatives and sprawled out in so many directions at once that it quickly became known as the "Omnibus Energy Act."

To attract enough votes to pass, it presented something for everyone: the Strategic Petroleum Reserve, the first automotive Corporate Average Fuel Economy (CAFE) standards, subsidies for renewable energy, support for coal, the extension of oil-price controls, and assorted other policies. The major energy acts passed in 1978 phased in deregulation of natural gas, and prohibited the use of natural gas in newly constructed electricity-generating plants. In 1980 came legislation imposing the windfall-profits tax and implementing a system of subsidies for the development of synthetic fuels. Several of these policies, notably the strategic reserve and the CAFE standards, proved durable and had lasting impacts. But taken as a whole, the incoherent policies of this era did not provide an overarching plan to improve the nation's energy future.[29]

In contrast to the government, Exxon had clear and relatively simple prescriptions for national energy policy. Its CEO, Cliff Garvin, enunciated these principles in a series of speeches; articles in the *Lamp*, Exxon's shareholder magazine; and communications to shareholders in annual reports. He began by asserting that "we must really buckle down to the job of conserving energy . . . As a second step, we in the petroleum industry have to be sure that we are doing our best to find new oil and gas." The government could pave the way by allowing easier access to public lands. "As a third step," Garvin continued, "the United States should be doing all it can to speed the development of alternative energy sources." Of particular interest to Garvin and Exxon were two sources favored by the company and many others in that era—coal and nuclear power.[30] A fourth important principle of an effective energy policy was the need "to think hard about the proper balance between the environment and energy development" and to minimize "the regulatory and judicial delays that now impede new investments."[31] Taken as a whole, Garvin's view of energy policy clearly mirrored Exxon's business strategy. It provided an incentive-based set of policies for an energy future in which oil and gas played an important but diminishing role. Unlike politicians, Garvin did not, of course, have to guide his "capitalist energy policy" through a Congress handcuffed by partisanship and devoid of strong leadership on those issues.

For Garvin, as for most Americans in the 1970s, the development of alternative energies was central to energy policy. But "alternative energies"

meant different things to different people. Did the nation need alternatives just to oil imported from OPEC nations, or to all imported oil? How
could the advanced technology and infrastructure needed for renewables
and other alternatives to oil be developed quickly? Other than in the
case of the early development of nuclear power and regional development projects like the Tennessee Valley Authority, the United States had
little history of federal government ownership of energy. It did have a
long tradition of promoting essential industries, such as transcontinental
railroads, and promotion through subsidies was a favored form of energy
policy during this era, in areas ranging from making homes more energy
efficient to the development of solar power and synthetic fuels. Speaking
as Exxon's CEO, Garvin acknowledged that the government might have
to go beyond subsidies. He voiced serious doubts that "the private sector
will be able to finance the development of these fuels in the necessary
time frame," adding that "energy can no longer be left exclusively to the
private sector" and "there is a big role for government." Yet government
and business both proved fickle in an era of extreme swings in oil prices,
which greatly affected the future prospects of alternatives to oil. When
the oil-price bust hit in the mid-1980s, cheap oil quickly trumped expensive alternatives requiring long-term investments by oil companies and
government subsidies.[32]

Unlike most government policy makers, Garvin mentioned the need
to find more oil and gas. But even at Exxon, natural gas was largely forgotten in the debates over alternatives to oil. Before the OPEC embargo, the
natural gas industry had become a problem child in the family of fuels.
U.S. price regulation from the 1930s into the 1970s had kept American
natural gas prices relatively low. This had encouraged the expansion of a
national grid of pipelines and the growing use of natural gas. But by the
late 1960s, these regulations also had helped create a shortage of natural gas, and a hard-fought battle over deregulation in the 1970s finally
resulted in the Natural Gas Policy Act of 1978, which contained a series
of compromises that pleased few on any side of the issue. The "phased
deregulation" called for in the act introduced a long period of uncertainty
in the industry, and few in the late 1970s were optimistic about the future
of natural gas.[33]

The pessimists included Garvin and many others in the petroleum industry. Garvin favored the deregulation of natural gas prices, which was finally passed in 1978, but he remained pessimistic: "Natural gas offers little hope as an alternative energy source; the share of energy it supplies is expected to decline, especially in the United States where production from existing reserves is declining."[34] The Powerplant and Industrial Fuel Use Act of 1978 embodied this consensus by banning the use of natural gas in newly constructed electricity-generating plants. The view of natural gas as a premium fuel too scarce to be wasted for "inferior uses" such as boiler fuel plagued the petroleum industry in this period. At the same time, it gave a brief boost to nuclear power as a replacement for natural gas and coal in the generation of electricity.[35]

More vexing for petroleum company executives was the short shrift given to oil in the debates over energy policy. One alternative to buying oil from politically volatile nations was the development of new reserves in friendlier, non-OPEC nations. Another alternative was, of course, increased exploration for domestic oil. In response to the growing realization that American production was declining, Exxon used enhanced-recovery techniques to increase production from existing fields, new technology to find new reserves, and energy-efficient methods to conserve oil. On the important issue of the long-term role of oil in the world energy supply, Garvin reminded government officials and voters alike that "oil will continue be the largest supplier of the world's energy for many years to come."[36]

This conclusion did not find favor with critics of the oil industry, but Garvin encouraged policy makers to adapt to the reality that the transition to other fuels would take a generation or two: "The most important step in this direction would be the elimination of price controls that prevent market forces from bringing energy supply and demand into balance."[37] Restricted access to public lands for oil and natural gas exploration further hampered the growth of domestic petroleum supplies, as did the strict enforcement of environmental regulations, which slowed the construction of major energy projects such as the Trans-Alaska Pipeline System. The symbol of the government's dismissal of oil as a fuel of the past was its elimination of traditional industry tax breaks such as the oil-depletion allowance as alternatives to oil were receiving new subsidies.

One form of alternative energy emphasized in Exxon's operations was conservation, or the efficient use of energy. Conservation was an alternative to oil, in that every barrel of oil saved was one less barrel that had to be produced. It was also renewable in that once a method of saving oil was identified and implemented, it produced savings again and again. Unlike many of the proposals for alternative fuels in the various energy policy acts of the 1970s, conservation did not require extensive governmental incentives or subsidies. The high price of energy gave all large users of oil and natural gas strong incentives to do the same work with less energy. Exxon's well-developed research capabilities hastened its efforts to find ways to make money by saving energy.[38]

Conservation at Exxon and many other large industrial consumers of energy yielded substantial savings for the companies while lowering the nation's energy use without reducing its industrial output.[39] Conservation experts noted that almost one-third of the nation's energy use was for industrial purposes and that seven industries consumed the bulk of this energy. Exxon was active in two of these industries, petroleum refining and chemicals. Because the giant scale of its plants meant that energy costs directly affected the bottom line in ways too expensive to ignore, Exxon did not need government incentives to become more fuel efficient; the high price of oil provided all the incentive it needed.

U.S. domestic use of energy and the use of gasoline as the primary transportation fuel presented a different situation. Individual energy consumers did not have the same strong motivation to conserve as did large industrial consumers. Garvin argued that "it is up to government to find a way to get people to conserve."[40] For its part in the difficult task of increasing a conservation ethic in people's energy use for residential and transportation purposes, Exxon reached out in various ways around the world to inform consumers of practical ways to save energy in their homes and in transportation.[41] For industrial and residential consumers alike, Garvin felt strongly that conservation and increased energy production "are both imperatives."[42]

Larry Rawl, Exxon's president at the time, put a punctuation mark on Garvin's comments. Noting that conservation was necessary and that Exxon had increased energy efficiency in its refineries by 20 percent and in oil production by 15 percent between 1972 and 1977, Rawl reminded an interviewer that the United States would still need more energy in the future. He then concluded with a series of predictions: "You can't save yourself into prosperity.... Between now [1977] and 1990, we're going to have to build 145 more nuclear plants; boost coal production to 1.5 billion tons a year, more than double that of today; get going on synthetic oil and gas from coal and shale; and find enough oil and gas in new fields to supply us with about 7 million barrels a day." In response, the interviewer asked whether people should take his call for conservation seriously and start buying less energy, and if so, didn't that "contradict the company's basic interests?" Rawl replied: "The last thing we want is another shortage. We didn't cause the last shortage in 1973–1974, but people think we did. And the political and public opinion problems stemming from that time are still haunting us." He concluded: "I want my country to survive and prosper. I know that if it does, Exxon will survive and prosper."[43]

Because of its size and visibility, Exxon could not avoid criticism in a time of dislocations in its basic industries—oil, natural gas, and chemicals. It found few allies in government in its quest for better conditions for exploration and the production of new oil and natural gas supplies. In an area over which it had clear control, its internal crusade for energy efficiency, its actions proved quite productive. This was the kind of long-term incremental change that could gradually alter patterns of energy use. The price of oil, not government policy, drove this change.

BALANCE OR GRIDLOCK IN ENERGY AND ENVIRONMENTAL POLICIES

In the decade after 1973, the closely related demands for more domestic energy and a cleaner environment clashed again and again. Oil companies often found themselves in the eye of the resulting regulatory storm, attempting to respond to often-competing societal demands. A wave of new environmental regulations starting in 1969 created far-reaching new requirements that affected all major activities of Exxon. The new laws also gave government much greater authority than before to define and enforce environmental controls. In the early years of increased concern for the environment, conflict, not cooperation, shaped the relationship between business and government. Both the lines of authority and the content of decisions regarding what to do and how to do it were fought out in the legislative arena, in the courts, and in day-to-day confrontations between government officials and corporate managers.

The strong environmental regulations of the era marked a sharp increase in government's influence over corporate decisions in areas traditionally considered the domain of management. Within the oil industry, major new environmental requirements affected daily operations, planning, the choice of technologies, investment patterns, and the focus of research and development. As Exxon sought to adapt to the far-reaching changes wrought by structural changes in the global oil economy, it also had to absorb an array of new demands placed on its operations by more stringent environmental regulations. Highly publicized political battles over the content of new laws mandating cleaner air and water and safer petroleum products were only the beginning. Once the laws were passed, companies such as Exxon had to marshal the resources to develop and put in place technology to meet the new legal requirements while continuing the quest to find new energy supplies.

THE TRANS-ALASKA PIPELINE SYSTEM: TRANSPORTATION

Exxon's first and most significant encounter with the new realities of environmental regulations came in the building of the Trans-Alaska Pipeline System (TAPS). The expensive and technically demanding project involved building a large-diameter pipeline 800 miles from the giant Prudhoe Bay oil field on the North Slope of Alaska across mountain ranges, major rivers, and earthquake-prone fault zones to the ice-free port of Valdez in southern Alaska. Randall Meyer, who oversaw the management of the project as an executive at Exxon USA, later called it "momentous" and compared it in scope and importance to the digging of the Panama Canal.[44]

There was one big difference, however: the Panama Canal had not required an environmental impact statement (EIS). Passed as part of the landmark National Environmental Planning Act of 1969, the EIS fundamentally altered traditional planning for construction in America. The intent of the law was clear and reasonable: before a federal government agency could issue a permit for an activity that might have a major environmental impact, the developers had to submit a planning document that discussed the possible environmental effects, steps that could be taken to mitigate them, and alternatives for achieving the same goals with less damage to the environment. The process was subject to review by the Council on Environmental Quality, and decisions could be appealed in the courts. The permit process was open to public comments by affected parties, and a final EIS had to include discussion of problems and issues raised by governmental agencies, private organizations, and individuals. Hailed as the largest private construction project in the history of the world, the Alaska pipeline was one of the first major projects subject to the new EIS process, which played itself out in a four-year-long flurry of detailed submittals, hearings, court cases, and appeals.[45]

Exxon was part of a group of eleven oil companies that owned a portion of the giant Prudhoe Bay oil field. It also became a member of Alyeska, the eight-company consortium that built and operated the pipeline. The company had begun oil exploration in Alaska in 1957, and it hit the jackpot eleven years later with an exploratory well drilled with the Atlantic Richfield Company at Prudhoe Bay. When the massive size of the field became apparent, the companies started examining their options for producing the oil and delivering it to markets. After considering a range of options that included sending oil tankers through the Northwest Passage and laying a pipeline through Canada, they chose to build a pipeline from the North Slope eight hundred miles to Valdez, Alaska.[46]

Planning for the project quickly moved forward. The companies examined the difficulties they faced with a keen awareness that the sooner the line could be built and filled with oil, the sooner they could begin to recoup their high costs. If initial plans had to be adjusted, this could be done as construction moved forward, with experienced construction specialists in the field making any needed changes in design or construction techniques. In the summer of 1968, survey teams walked the probable route to Valdez, marking the line's intended position. As they worked, a team of engineers put together what came to be called the "Gold Book," the original feasibility study, which included a cost estimate of $900 million for a pipeline built almost entirely underground and having a capacity of 500,000 b/d.[47] The three major partners—Exxon, BP, and ARCO—submitted the feasibility study and then answered follow-up questions about the possible environmental impact of the pipeline from the Department of the Interior, which had to approve projects on public lands. In June 1969, the companies requested approval of the project by the following month, if possible. As they waited for approval, the eight companies involved formed the Alyeska Pipeline Service Company to build the line, with Humble (Exxon) holding a 20 percent share. Edward Patton, an experienced pipeline specialist at Humble Oil who became the original president (and later the CEO) of Alyeska, estimated that it would take about three years to build the pipeline once permits were granted.[48]

His estimate did not, however, account for the complexities and delays raised by the environmental impact statement required by the National Environmental Planning Act, which went into effect on January 1, 1970. As Humble and the other members of Alyeska quickly discovered, a new day in construction had dawned. The legal meaning of the new law remained open to dispute, and the process of defining it inevitably led to frequent challenges in the courts. Secretary of the Interior Rogers Morton weaved his way through a variety of political forces in an effort to move the permit toward acceptance. Unfortunately for Alyeska, the political fallout from an oil spill off the coast of Santa Barbara, California, in 1969 ensured that government officials would be closely scrutinized as they implemented the EIS requirement. The sentiment that produced the first Earth Day in May 1970 also guaranteed that passionate environmentalists would enter the fray to save Alaska's wilderness from the potential damage done by the construction of the pipeline. Some of them would be lawyers adept at using legal challenges to delay the project. From 1970 through 1974, the story of the Alaska pipeline was one of hearings, lawsuits, delays, and growing tensions.

Months and then years passed with no sense of when the regulatory and legal gridlock would end and construction could begin. Edward Patton estimated in March 1971 that the delays were costing the pipeline partners $90 million a year on a project in which they had already invested $1.5 billion. Meanwhile, inflation continued to drive up costs. By September 1973, the new estimate for the total cost of the pipeline had risen from $900 million to $4.1 billion for a line whose capacity had been expanded from 500,000 to 1.2 million b/d.[49]

The frustration of the oil industry was clear in the reporting of the industry's leading trade publication, the *Oil and Gas Journal*. Under the telling title "The Environmental Craze: Will It Strangle Energy?" came the warning that "the greatest discovery in the history of the U.S. will lie unexploited for years because of this impasse." The article identified the National Environmental Planning Act as the single most important factor in impeding the development of oil on public lands, and it lamented that the Alaska pipeline was its "most celebrated victim." In a sentence that revealed much about the oil industry's perception of the situation, the author concluded, "There is as yet little indication that the environmental lion is ready to lay down with the energy lamb in the political arena." If anyone had missed the general point, it was repeated as the title to an accompanying editorial: "Environmentalists Forcing Energy Crisis on Nation." [50]

Growing shortages of natural gas and oil reinforced this message over the next two years. By the middle of 1973, the politics of energy and the environment had changed enough to allow for the passage of federal legislation specifically authorizing construction of the pipeline. The showdown in the Senate came in the summer of 1973, when Vice President Spiro Agnew cast the tie-breaking vote after the Senate voted 49–49 to pass an amendment to the proposed Trans-Alaska Pipeline Authorization Act mandating that the pipeline and the associated haul road were not subject to any additional challenges under the National Environmental Planning Act. Although critics feared that this vote gutted the law, the reality was less dramatic. This was a significant, but onetime, exemption for a vital energy-related project that had already undergone extensive reviews. The Alaska pipeline was not an ordinary project that would be used to justify numerous other exemptions. It was a much-studied project that promised to supply as much as 25 percent of the nation's domestic oil. After the oil embargo had further strengthened political sentiment in favor of domestic energy development, the final authorization act was passed and signed into law in November 1973.[51] Looking back on this series of events, one Exxon engineer who worked on the project concluded, "The only reason we have an oil pipeline today is because there was an Arab embargo."[52]

This exemption came with strings attached. The act gave the government a strong role in monitoring the line's construction and required Alyeska to reimburse government agencies for this surveillance. The act

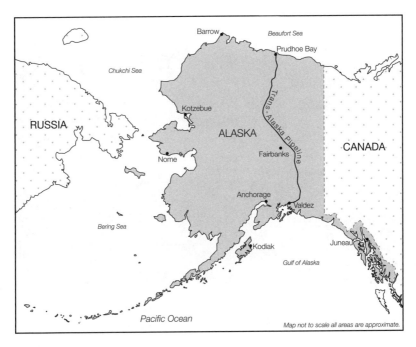

MAP 2.1: Source: *ExxonMobil,* 2005 Financial and Operating Review, *p. 47.*

established an oil-spill liability fund to be maintained during construction and for as long as the pipeline operated. It also gave the Department of the Interior authority to extend its jurisdiction past the territorial waters of the United States in order to regulate the possible dumping of oil-contaminated ballast at sea. The measure gave the government additional powers to regulate construction practices. Such powers, for example, authorized the government to monitor the quality of welds on the pipeline and required Alyeska to replace much-publicized defective welds.[53]

The delay in construction from 1969 to 1974 created a breathing space that allowed planners to step back and examine more closely the unique challenges of working in the Arctic. The man in charge of much of the Alaska operation for Exxon, Mel Harrison, acknowledged that "because of the delays, of course, there were some pluses . . . because we learned a lot more about the permafrost and problems of operating in the Arctic."[54] About 75 percent of the pipeline passed through permafrost, that is, ground permanently frozen. Shipping oil as hot as 160 degrees Fahrenheit

Trans-Alaska Pipeline System (TAPS) under construction, ca. 1976.
ExxonMobil Historical Collection, di_08137.

through a buried pipeline could cause serious long-term damage to the terrain and to the pipeline by thawing the permafrost. The possibility of significant settling as ice and ground thawed and then thrust upward as it refroze became an important focus for pipeline designers. The most practical protection against damage from such extreme movements was to build the pipeline aboveground in areas with fragile permafrost. When the line had to be buried to protect it against avalanches or to make way for highways or animal crossings, special insulation was installed around the underground pipe. In particularly sensitive areas, designers called for ground-refrigeration systems in addition to insulation. Additional leeway to absorb movement of the pipeline caused by extreme temperature changes came in the form of the zigzag pattern of construction that allowed the line to expand and contract in response to extreme temperatures without rupturing.[55] The greater understanding of Arctic conditions reached during the long delay in construction produced a safer pipeline that has less impact on the environment.

The oil industry as a whole, however, did not offer much praise for the government's overall management of the Trans-Alaska Pipeline. In its view, the four-year delay meant that its two million barrels of domestic oil a day were not available to reduce the impact of the energy crisis from 1973 (the original projected date of completion) until August 1977, when the first tanker filled with North Slope oil sailed from the terminal at Valdez. By then, the price of the pipeline had grown to approximately $8 billion as inflation, design changes, and environmental safeguards greatly increased the original cost estimates.

Garvin summarized his view in comments on the occasion of the opening of the pipeline: "We at Exxon recognize that the Trans-Alaska Pipeline that went into operation in 1977 is a stronger, safer pipeline than that originally proposed in 1969. And we have learned a great deal about environmental safeguards in that time." Garvin could not, however, resist qualifying his statement by citing the "years of delay with accompanying astronomical rises in cost."[56] The battle over the construction of the pipeline ended in a partial victory for the oil industry, but the new rules under the National Environmental Planning Act ensured that the industry would never regain the traditional autonomy over siting and design that it had enjoyed before 1970.

UNLEADED GASOLINE: REFINING

The early 1970s saw the passage of far-reaching legislation to clean up U.S. air and water. The laws mandated basic changes in industrial operations and transportation, posing great challenges and costs to Exxon, especially to the refining and petrochemical plants that produced the end products sold by the major oil companies. The Clean Air Act Amendments of 1970 and the Clean Water Amendments of 1972 touched all industries, but the petroleum industry absorbed especially high costs in complying with the much stricter standards for air and water quality. Part of that price was in dollars, part was in opportunity costs, particularly for investment forgone and for research conducted on control processes rather than production. But another significant cost from the point of view of many in the petroleum industry was the growth of governmental involvement in areas traditionally considered the preserve of business.

An Exxon "environmental conservation coordinator" summed up the "positive realism" of the company's "environmental objectives" as follows: "They are based on the desire of our top management to do whatever is

reasonable and feasible, within the constraints of technology and economics, to make our products and worldwide operations environmentally sound."[57] "Reasonable and feasible" were, of course, in the eye of the
beholder and might have been expanded to include "flexible" and "backed
by good science" in the company's view of the content of the Clean Air
Act Amendments of 1970. The law's "ambient air standards" for the
nation required sharp reductions in pollutants, mandating their removal
on a tight timetable with potentially severe restrictions being imposed on
regions that did not meet the deadlines. The law also required substantial
reductions in harmful emissions from automobiles on a timetable set by
the government, with the automobile and oil industries subject to stiff
penalties if the timetables were not met.

The comments of one of the law's chief advocates in Congress, Senator
Edmund Muskie (D-Maine), highlighted the political sentiment underlying the passage of the act: "The first responsibility of Congress is not
the making of technology or economic judgments—or even what is or
appears to be technologically feasible. Our responsibility is to establish
what the public interest requires to protect the health of persons. This
may mean that people and industries will be asked to do what seems
impossible at the present time. But if health is to be protected, these challenges must be met."[58] This was the epitome of "command and control"
regulation, in which government mandates a standard and a timetable
for compliance and expects industry to comply or face stiff fines—and
damn the expense.

As the largest U.S. refiner and an owner of substantial chemical operations, Exxon (Standard Oil [New Jersey] before 1973) faced high costs in
complying with the Clean Air Act of 1970. The American system required
industry to shoulder the costs of compliance, which might then be passed
on to consumers. The company felt that the strict new ambient-air standards could not be attained within the time limits set by government.
It also felt that the nation was headed in the wrong direction in reducing
auto emissions through the quick fix of adding catalytic converters to car
exhaust systems.

The fate of leaded gasoline became a central part of the debate over auto
emissions. Lead in other forms had been linked to serious health problems
since at least the early twentieth century.[59] In the early 1920s, the Ethyl

Corporation, originally a joint venture with Jersey Standard, General Motors, and DuPont, had developed tetraethyl lead (TEL), which was used in most gasoline starting in the 1920s to raise octane ratings. After a flurry of early opposition from doctors and other concerned citizens, TEL was used without great controversy for the next fifty years. Although the immediate justification in the early 1970s for lead removal was its harmful effects on catalytic converters, which would be rendered ineffective by leaded gasoline, regulators also pointed to the potential health hazards of airborne lead from gasoline.

The company was not immediately persuaded. On this and similar issues, it argued that more convincing scientific information was needed before concluding that leaded gasoline posed a significant health hazard. Critics might scoff that the company was simply following its bottom line, but it was also holding to one of its core values: the belief in the primacy of science and research. Although the dangers of lead in other forms had been the subject of scrutiny by doctors for much of the twentieth century, leaded gasoline had been little studied in post–World War II America. One of Exxon's researchers summarized the company's stance as follows: "Some reductions of lead have already been made even though the available medical evidence is not convincing that lead from auto emissions is detrimental to public health. Fuller reductions will be costly and will require substantial capital investment. Unless lead removal shows some tangible beneficial effect, then, this use of capital, which might better be applied elsewhere, would seem to be the antithesis of conservation."[60] The American Petroleum Institute was much more forceful in its condemnation of claims made by the Environmental Protection Agency (EPA; the agency was created in 1970) of possible health hazards from leaded gas. According to the *Oil and Gas Journal* in July 1972, the "API specifically lambasted the suggestion that lead contamination from auto exhausts poses a threat to children who eat urban dust. 'There is still not a shred of evidence to support this hypothesis.'"[61]

During this period, Exxon and the API held the same general stance on the health impacts of leaded gasoline: the science was inconclusive and the price was too high to justify lead removal on the basis of possible harm to human health. Yet scientific research was not static. As the debate on TEL removal went forward in the 1970s, new scientific studies used improved means for analyzing the amount and the impact of lead in the human body. Gradually, a consensus emerged that leaded gasoline did pose dangers to human health, especially to children living in densely populated urban areas with high volumes of traffic. Yet Exxon remained unconvinced regarding the science for a number of years. Looking back with the benefit of hindsight at the dispute, Robert Wilhelm, a longtime Exxon refining executive (and later senior vice president and board member), concluded that on the lead issue "the company was actually proved wrong." He theorized that "an underappreciation of the external environment and the impact it had on the company was an important part of some of the things that happened in the seventies and the early eighties."[62] Myron Harrison, a physician who joined Exxon in 1999 as a senior medical advisor in the Safety, Health and Environment Department, was not a party to the lead debates of the 1970s. But in considering those controversies he concluded, "We stayed too long defending lead. The science did change. . . . Sometimes we can be stubborn." He also noted that once the company became convinced of the health risks of leaded gasoline, it put in a "huge amount of time and effort working with the World Bank to remove lead from gasoline in places around the world where we did not have to," notably Africa.[63]

The scientific research on lead removal was not yet conclusive in the mid-1970s, however, and the debate on the subject in those years remained primarily driven by the time line for meeting auto-emissions standards, not by health concerns. In the early 1970s, the EPA established a timetable for the gradual removal of lead from gasoline so that older cars could continue to operate on leaded gas while the growing fleet of new cars would have ample supplies of unleaded. Despite historical tensions between the auto and oil industries on the best way to control exhaust emissions, they closed ranks on the immediate question of a practical schedule for lead removal. They argued strongly and persistently for delays so that they could pull together the catalytic-converter technology needed to clean the air quickly and the unleaded gasoline required by this new emission-control device.

The EPA was unconvinced. Asserting authority that had not been available to environmental regulators in the past, it initially refused to give ground to two industries that seemed to have forfeited their seats at the table for the debates on auto emissions by failing to address this problem in the years after World War II. The oil industry returned again and again to the theme of the need to slow down the process and allow industry more time to absorb this new regulatory demand. Oil spokesmen stressed also the need to moderate environmental demands in light of the energy crisis. M. A. (Mike) Wright, the chairman of Exxon USA, concisely stated the industry's position in May 1973: "Either U. S. petroleum demand will have to be restrained artificially or certain environmental quality restrictions will have to be reduced temporarily. We simply will not be able to have both ample supplies of petroleum products and current air quality regulations."[64] The industry stepped up such statements after the energy crisis, but the EPA remained immovable.

Then in 1975, a bombshell exploded in the ongoing negotiations when scientists reported that the operation of the new catalytic converter might cause serious environmental problems from its heightened emissions of sulfates. Sulfur standards had yet to be set, but the announcement raised concerns that the catalytic converter might have to be abandoned. Russell Train, the EPA administrator, even speculated that the decision to push the catalytic converter might have been a mistake. This revelation undermined the confidence of industry and citizens alike in the EPA's capacity to implement the auto-emissions control program. It called forth a new round of complaints about the high price of the program, the unrealistic deadlines, and the heavy-handed approach taken by the EPA. Texaco led the charge with an impassioned plea that serious reductions in the sulfur content of unleaded gasoline would cost the oil industry seven billion to ten billion dollars in additional expenditures and would result in a four-to-five-cent increase in a gallon of gas.[65]

Frederick Dennstedt, the vice president of refining for Exxon USA, testified before Congress on the sulfate dilemma soon after Train's announcement. He argued that Exxon would have to invest $270 million to remove sulfur from gasoline in its refineries, that the increased costs for consumers would be one or one and a half cents a gallon, and that the new processes would increase oil consumption in refineries by as much as 7 percent. He called for more time to conduct research on both the financial costs and the health benefits of sulfur removal, arguing that the nation "just can't afford to expend its limited resources of skilled manpower, raw materials, and money in hastily conceived or inefficient actions." He reminded the committee that the oil industry had already "spent one potful of money in capital investment in the refinery industry to make cleaner fuels," and suggested that a four-to-five-year moratorium on sulfate regulations would give industry time to study the problem and develop additional technology for emissions controls. He concluded with the hope "that in that time . . . noncatalyst technology to satisfactorily control emissions could be developed."[66]

Mounting evidence that the automobile industry could not meet the original EPA deadline to produce new cars that ran on unleaded gas added a desperate tone to the debate on both sides. In a political game of chicken over extending the deadline, the EPA and Congress finally backed away in 1976, granting carmakers a one-year extension.[67] That short delay was not enough to encourage further research on "noncatalyst technology." By then, the regulatory process had become locked into catalytic converters as the central, long-term technological solution to the control of auto emissions.

The high cost of compliance remained a source of persistent conflict between the EPA and the oil industry. All involved acknowledged the substantial costs of getting the lead out. Throughout the 1970s, oil companies, the API, and other industry organizations asserted that lead removal would cost refiners billions of dollars, primarily to pay for the new refining processes needed to boost octane ratings in the absence of lead. The EPA consistently countered those industry arguments with lower cost estimates. The EPA's annual report to Congress in 1979 reported total expenditures by the oil industry in 1977 of $1.46 billion for new equipment to control air and water pollution, and more than $2 billion in added operating costs to meet environmental mandates. The figures were higher than those for any other industry.[68] Such expenditures year after year had a substantial impact on investment patterns as U.S. refineries struggled to make profits in the new regime of high oil prices.

Money was far from the only cost to Exxon. The company had a long tradition of strict financial controls, and it resisted the reduction of its autonomy over its investments in the refining process, including pollution controls. Both environmental and health and safety regulations greatly expanded the governmental presence in the refineries. Funds committed to comply with the new regulations might have been used for other purposes, and the company assumed that inefficient management by regulators added to the expense of meeting societal demands for cleaner air and water.

Governmental mandates for the type of gasoline to produce and the type of equipment to use to meet air-quality standards flew in the face of Exxon's confidence in its engineering and technical prowess. The company had a long tradition of excellence in downstream research aimed at producing more and better kinds of gasoline, and in its view the new demand for cleaner-burning fuels, no matter how important, drew funds away from this research. In addition, the management of its basic refining operations suffered what the *Oil and Gas Journal* had called in 1972 "a flood of uncertainties" amid the new and demanding regulatory requirements of the era.[69] As its refineries juggled the changing mix of unleaded and leaded gasoline production, they also faced the often-chaotic demands of the allocation program under price controls. And the political strength of the environmental movement, particularly its opposition to new refineries, made it difficult to construct new facilities on the East Coast to serve the area's large markets for refined products.

In short, the demands on the industry from government and the public fundamentally altered the landscape of decision making in the refining industry. One insider in 1974 captured the confusion of the era: "In the past, refiners could have gotten an inkling of the future by appraising the economic climate, looking at what the auto industry was going to push in the way of new models and their octane needs, and then applying some historic driving habits of American motorists. All these guideposts are virtually worthless now."[70] The U.S. refining industry confronted a new era in which the old rules no longer applied to its basic product, gasoline. It had to learn as quickly as possible what the new rules would be over the long term and to absorb them into its decision-making process. Doing so was particularly difficult in an era when the EPA itself was a new and unpredictable part of a decision-making process undergoing rapid change.

During this period, lead reduction was controversial in most of the major industrial nations, not just the United States, and—as with many new environmental mandates—differences in timing and in the process of change required globally active companies to adapt to each national approach. In general, for example, western European nations moved more slowly than the United States in banning lead in gasoline, choosing instead to give individual nations the discretion to reduce the amount of lead allowable so that it was within a range set by the European Economic Community (forerunner of the European Union), effective January 1981. This meant that Exxon faced different demands in different nations. In response, it scheduled timetables for improvements in its refineries that would ensure the production of the unleaded gasoline as needed around the world. Its "octane strategy" stressed two tiers of refining investments: a first tier focused on investments to improve production at existing units, and a second tier of much larger investments to construct new equipment capable of producing much larger quantities of unleaded gasoline. The first-tier investments went forward in $20 million to $100 million increments at refineries around the world. Thus, in May 1974, when headquarters in New York approved substantial funding for alterations to the company's German refineries to reduce the lead in gasoline produced there—the country had mandated that lower lead levels be achieved by January 1, 1976—Exxon's Investment Advisory Committee labeled the expense "a non-discretionary investment required to maintain participation in the German motor gasoline market."[71]

In the United States, the implementation of ambient-air standards called for in the Clean Air Act Amendments of 1970 mirrored that of the process for removing lead from gasoline. Many cities and industries found the strict new standards and the demand for quick compliance to be unrealistic. Representatives of the refining and chemical industries quickly joined others in calling for delays in the cutoff dates for adhering to the new standards. Amid growing evidence that most regions could not or would not meet the original 1975 deadline, the EPA granted a two-year extension of the target date. In December 1976, the API petitioned the EPA for a broad review and revision of the air-quality standards put forward under the act. Citing the language of the law that required the EPA to develop standards based on the latest scientific knowledge concerning the effects of pollutants on public health and welfare, the institute argued that this had not been done. The EPA rejected the petition, responding that "any changes the agency might make most likely will toughen rather than relax air quality standards."[72]

The tone of the "debates" over air standards suggested both the high stakes and the growing frustration of people on each side of the issue. In November 1976, the EPA's administrator, Russell Train, waved a red cape in the face of industry when he proclaimed, "The time has come for business leadership to abandon the fundamentalist, knee-jerk resistance against any form of government control." He challenged business leaders to "recognize the genuine merit of environmental values and the public insistence that those values be protected values." This had to anger many business leaders who recognized the need for improved environmental quality but criticized what they considered the political posturing of those who wrote the laws and the poor management of the regulations by the EPA. Industry spokesmen responded in kind. An editorial in the *Oil and Gas Journal*, for example, argued, "The top executive of a large petrochemical company was right on the mark when he said, 'We can't afford legislation written by technological illiterates.'"[73] This could not have sat well with scientists hard at work on pollution-related public health issues in the public sector and in universities and research institutes.

The high costs of compliance remained at the forefront of industry complaints. Expenditures for new investments, increased operating costs, and the additional energy needed to make some of the necessary changes in manufacturing processes mounted quickly. By 1976, the Manufacturing Chemists' Association estimated that U.S. chemical companies had spent more than $2 billion for pollution control, with that figure likely to reach $4.6 billion through 1977. It also claimed that "the energy used to reduce pollution amounts to 7.3 percent of the industry's total energy consumption." Even the EPA projected in 1976 that the petroleum industry's costs to meet air and water cleanup regulations between 1974 and 1983 would absorb approximately 25 percent of its total capital expenditures. This spending inevitably cut into budgets for all other functions.[74]

HONDO: OFFSHORE SITING AND OPERATIONS

The figures cited above give some sense of the long-term financial cost of complying with the wave of environmental regulations passed in the 1970s. They do not, however, suggest the added managerial and regulatory costs of adapting the process of technological innovation to the new demands of an era of increased regulation. Exxon's Hondo project offshore Santa Barbara, California, was perhaps an extreme case of life under the newly strict environmental regulatory regime, but a brief look at this project indicates the delays and frustrations encountered in trying to bring a promising new oil- and natural-gas-producing platform onstream in the 1970s.

Work on the project was slowed for more than a decade by a combination of the EIS process, questions about compliance with the Clean Air Act amendments, intense opposition from local environmentalists, and jurisdictional disputes among federal agencies and between federal, state, and local officials. By 1969, Exxon had defined the broad outlines of the Hondo field; it then purchased leases in the region and drilled exploratory wells that showed great promise in an area that proved to contain very large reserves, later estimated at 500 million barrels. In 1970, Humble (Exxon) joined Chevron and Shell, which also had made discoveries in the area, in putting forward a proposal to operate their holdings as a unit, with Humble as the operator—an efficient system of production that gained the approval of the U.S. Geological Survey. After these years of rapid progress, however, the company encountered increasingly determined resistance from regulators and environmentalists in the region. Galvanized by Union Oil's Santa Barbara oil spill in 1969, environmentalists built well-organized public interest groups that became highly effective in mobilizing opposition to offshore drilling.[75]

Over the next decade, the company fought battle after battle while trying to obtain the permits and approvals needed to build and operate an offshore producing platform and related onshore treating and transportation facilities. The project required the first EIS drafted for a project on the Outer Continental Shelf, where governmental jurisdiction over environmental issues had not yet been clearly established. The Department of the Interior, which manages federal offshore lands, drafted the EIS and, after three and a half years of studies and public hearings, it was approved. Hearings on the site of the planned onshore receiving and processing plant in Santa Barbara County were hostile, with local citizens, activist groups such as Get Oil Out, or GOO, and public officials strongly opposed to its construction. Meanwhile, the company had begun the process of gaining a permit for a planned natural gas pipeline to Los Angeles from the Federal Power Commission, which exercised regulatory authority over natural gas.

The story of the permitting process for the Hondo project is almost too convoluted to summarize. From the early 1970s into the early 1980s, Exxon found itself pushed and pulled, approved and rejected, by government agencies at the local, state, and national levels with authority over the Outer Continental Shelf and over offshore and onshore activities. Resolution of several of the disputes came only after lengthy detours into the courts.

For the Hondo project, Exxon initially planned to build an onshore processing plant to remove water from the crude before shipping it to markets in tankers. Objections to this approach, however, resulted in the state asking Exxon to process the oil onshore and build an onshore pipeline to transfer the processed oil to Los Angeles refineries. Exxon believed this would be unworkable given the many jurisdictions that would have to approve the pipeline. After numerous contentious public meetings over potential environmental impacts and the final rejection, and after prolonged delays of its original plans by local authorities, Exxon decided to develop an offshore treating facility that could receive oil from the platforms, process it, and then load it onto tankers. This approach placed the processing and loading facilities in federal waters, where the California Coastal Commission lacked regulatory authority; it was approved by the Department of the Interior. After it operated for a few years, California agreed to allow Exxon to process the oil onshore if it would decommission the offshore treating and loading operation. Exxon agreed, and the controversy finally subsided, but not before creating highly contentious attitudes among all parties involved.

Throughout this episode, public concern about Exxon's operations in the Santa Barbara Channel led to often bitter battles between the company and local and state regulators. Tom Quinn, a "special assistant to the governor of California" and the chairman of the powerful California Air Resources Board, explained to Exxon officials in 1976 that "substantial controversy still exists" over the company's plans for Hondo and that "unless rapid progress is made, the State and Exxon appear headed toward an adversary relationship." The threatening tone of the letter suggested that the state would block the project if Exxon did not cooperate by accepting the state's terms. In a carefully worded reply, Howard Kauffmann, Exxon Corporation's president, expressed his distress at Quinn's assessment of the project, outlined the various options being considered by Exxon, and calmly agreed with Quinn that "the State's interest and Exxon's are not incompatible."[76]

Although state and local authorities remained involved in the permitting process, federal authorities moved to the forefront of the disputes surrounding Hondo. To take control of the final stages of the process, the EPA asserted its authority under the Clean Air Act to regulate compliance with air-quality standards, including emissions from Exxon's offshore platform. In a battle that foreshadowed future tensions over offshore siting and regulation, as well as over oil-spill responses, the company asserted that the Department of the Interior had authority over air quality on projects on the Outer Continental Shelf, and the courts ultimately agreed. "Regardless of the jurisdiction," Exxon announced, "air quality studies indicate that air emissions from the Hondo project will not adversely affect onshore air quality."[77] By late 1979, an Exxon publication reported that the company had "slogged its way" through the regulatory process with three major environmental impact studies, twenty-one major public hearings, ten major governmental approvals, fifty-one consultant studies, twelve lawsuits, and a county-wide referendum in Santa Barbara County." But with almost $400 million invested in the project to develop Hondo and the remainder of Exxon's Santa Ynez Unit—projected to include two other major platforms, along with Hondo, and an onshore oil- and gas-processing plant—no oil had yet been produced.[78] Oil production did not begin until 1981. Exxon's frustrating twelve-year journey from the discovery of the Hondo field in 1969 to first production said much about the limited future of oil production offshore California.

Indeed, the "battle of Hondo" offered a glimpse into the future of offshore drilling on the Outer Continental Shelf around much of the United States. Exxon's efforts to build two more platforms in its Santa Ynez Unit after the completion of Hondo were met by determined opposition from environmentalists, and the company worked for six years to obtain some 400 major permits in the 1980s before it could begin construction. During this interval, opponents of offshore drilling turned to Congress to win a moratorium on new leasing offshore California. Congressional allies embedded the moratorium in the annual Department of the Interior Appropriations Act. The annual renewal of the moratorium thus

Hondo platform under construction in yard, 1977.
ExxonMobil Historical Collection, di_06212.

became a political prerequisite for the approval of the department's budget. Other regions followed this approach, and the moratorium spread to include most of the United States, including New England, the Georges Bank (between Cape Cod and Nova Scotia), the mid-Atlantic, the Pacific Northwest, much of Alaska, and a portion of the eastern Gulf of Mexico off Florida. Supporters justified this approach by pointing out the potential harm from offshore drilling to industries such as fishing and tourism and to public health. In 1990, President George H.W. Bush put in place a ten-year moratorium on drilling offshore California, Florida, and New England. Only along the Texas and Louisiana Gulf Coast, where oil and natural gas were major industries, did widespread offshore leasing continue.[79] Far more than concerted actions against individual projects such as Hondo, this broad moratorium shaped the evolution of offshore development in the United States after the early 1980s.

This ordeal and others made the company keenly aware of the impact of new environmental regulations on drilling. Exxon USA concluded in 1980: "These may cause few dramatic major project delays, such as the Hondo project, but they do place heavy demands on investment and contingency planning, and on manpower and technology utilization."[80] In 1980, this adaptation process was far from over. Historically, Exxon and the oil industry as a whole had enjoyed considerable discretion in deciding what level of pollution was acceptable and what sort of controls should be used.[81] The hard-fought environmental conflicts of the 1970s were only the beginning of long-term efforts to create a new accommodation between business and government in what would remain a vital issue for both. The technologically intensive quest for oil in deeper waters and harsher environments around the world would inevitably heighten political conflicts over the often-competing societal demands for more energy and improved environmental quality. Refining and petrochemical production would be required to continually adapt to new standards for cleaner production and cleaner products. The siting of major facilities would require increasingly complex advanced environmental planning. The environmental revolution, which picked up steam in the 1960s and 1970s, fundamentally altered important aspects of the operations of major oil companies such as Exxon.

As a global corporation, the company did not judge the U.S. system in a vacuum. It had experience in other nations that took quite different approaches to managing the long-term trade-offs between energy and the environment. In early 1973, those in charge of Exxon's refineries in Japan, for example, observed firsthand how a cooperative, government-led planning system managed the competing demands of energy supply, environmental quality, and economic growth. The government of Japan, a nation with almost no domestically produced energy, asserted much stronger and direct control over issues that affected energy supply.

In the early 1970s, the Japanese government responded to the coming of the energy crisis and the growing demand for pollution control with a coordinated effort to reduce the nation's dependence on fuel oil. It took measures to increase the supplies of other fuels, especially LNG and uranium. At the same time, the government took steps to sharply reduce the amount of sulfur in fuel oil by requiring refiners, including Exxon, to make expensive changes in the refining process. To further reduce air pollution in heavily populated regions, the nation's planning agency, the Ministry of International Trade and Industry (MITI), explored the option of guiding those interested in expanding refining capacity to remote areas of Japan or overseas. To reward the Japanese refining industry for its cooperation, MITI sought ways to guarantee that those companies would continue to achieve acceptable returns "despite increased requirements for pollution abatement."[82] Such a comprehensive set of policies coordinating energy, environmental, and economic concerns allowed Exxon to consider a range of planning options for its Japanese affiliate, with confidence in the government's commitment to maintain a cooperative partnership with business interests.

MITI's approach, however, also raised difficulties for Exxon. Its rules were designed to promote an indigenous Japanese oil industry, and at times it discriminated against foreign companies. Exxon's Japanese affiliates struggled for many years to make money in Japan as a result of this discrimination, and a number of non-Japanese oil companies closed up shop there. In Japan, as in other nations around the world, Exxon had to learn to adapt to an often-difficult regulatory environment in order to retain access to an expanding market for refined products.

In Europe, Exxon operated in political economies more closely resembling that of the United States. There, governments long concerned with their fragile dependence on Middle Eastern oil mustered the political will to push gasoline taxes to levels sufficient to encourage conservation. They also subsidized effective mass transit and adopted stricter environmental regulations. The entire world was coming to grips with the dual challenge of energy and environment; as a global company, Exxon had to learn to manage political risks associated with environmental challenges while also efficiently absorbing into its operations the varied regulations it encountered at every turn.[83]

From inside Exxon looking out, the U.S. government performed poorly during an admittedly difficult period of transition in both energy and environmental policies. Exxon, on the other hand, looked for an effective set of long-term policies that would safeguard national energy security—and enable the company to remain profitable in the long term. Company spokesmen conceded that strong environmental regulations markedly reduced many sources of pollution, but the cost in money, confusion, and corporate autonomy seemed excessive to the engineers who ran Exxon. The company consistently called for more "balanced" energy and environmental policies. Exxon's definition of balance was not, however, the order of the day. Indeed, the political turmoil of the period brought with it a basic recalibration of a historical balance that had favored the production of cheap and abundant energy supplies over the quest for improved environmental quality. From the 1960s onward, environmental regulations became much more demanding, challenging oil companies to learn to run greener operations while continuing to find new sources of oil and producing refined products.

Overall, Exxon and the oil industry as a whole spent much of the 1970s and early 1980s pushing back against what they considered unreasonable political attacks and policies such as price controls and divestiture bills that hampered their ability to operate efficiently. Industry leaders often had great difficulty finding an effective voice to defend their industry; the exaggerated rhetoric they often used probably fed the public's skepticism. Although Exxon tried to assert its views more effectively in political debates, it succeeded better at efficiently adapting its operations to the demands embodied in a wave of new environmental regulations. As it did so, Exxon pursued an internal energy policy based on conservation; investments in alternatives to oil; lobbying for what it considered balanced environmental laws that recognized the need for energy development; and exploration for more oil and natural gas, especially in non-OPEC nations.

CHAPTER THREE

COLDER AND DEEPER

THE SEARCH FOR NON-OPEC OIL AND GAS

C liff Garvin clearly stated Exxon's energy strategy in his introduction to the company's annual report for 1975, his first year as CEO. After acknowledging the importance of retaining access to the vast crude reserves recently nationalized by Saudi Arabia and Venezuela, Garvin informed the company's shareholders that "Exxon is directing its efforts to other parts of the world which offer good prospects for new energy sources," with a focus on the United States, Canada, the North Sea, and Australia. He explained that "many of these potential reserves are located in technically challenging areas such as the deep waters beyond the continental shelf or in the far reaches of the Arctic." Developing such reserves would reduce the political uncertainties that had plagued the company's operations in the OPEC nations, but the production of non-OPEC oil would require "major commitments of capital and long lead times . . . and the oil and gas ultimately produced will be very costly compared to the energy supplies developed in the past."[1] The era of easy—and inexpensive—OPEC oil had ended.

The new era tested Exxon in colder, deeper, and harsher conditions. To succeed, the company had to develop new technical, financial, and managerial capabilities. The stakes were higher, since projects grew larger and more expensive, and to hedge financial and technical risks, Exxon increasingly worked in joint ventures with other companies. Indeed, as good opportunities outside the OPEC nations pulled the industry into deeper offshore waters, the company benefited from the efforts of an off-shore fraternity made up of thousands of companies around the world. They provided specialized services including the construction of platforms, the provision of helicopter transportation, and research on technology to improve all aspects of the technologically advanced systems needed in regions such as the North Sea. In the boom years after 1973, Exxon learned a great deal about the technical and managerial demands of frontier regions—and more than it wanted to know about the difficulties of finding new reserves to replace those nationalized in Venezuela and the Middle East.

The search for non-OPEC oil called forth fundamental adjustments within Exxon. Morris Foster, whose career in production spanned from the 1960s into the twenty-first century, recounted the differences before and after the early 1970s: "Up until we got into the Prudhoes and the North Seas and Malaysia and the Bass Strait [in Australia], what we'd primarily done [outside Venezuela and the Middle East] was develop onshore and relatively small stuff," much of which was in the United States. "We weren't developing billion-barrel fields . . . [or] in the case of Prudhoe, fifteen billion barrels. We hadn't done that. We were not prepared from an organizational standpoint, we weren't prepared from a procedures and processes standpoint, and we weren't prepared with the experience." A generation of managers had to learn by doing, often at great personal sacrifice: "We made it happen by sleeping on desks . . . fighting the big war."[2] The effort to replace the easy oil lost to nationalizations in the OPEC nations took Exxon around the world into a series of demanding, large-scale projects that taught it skills it would need to prosper in the years after 1973.

THE CHALLENGES OF THE ARCTIC
ON ALASKA'S NORTH SLOPE

Production of oil in the United States peaked in 1970. As the largest producer of oil in the United States, Exxon fought the decline of domestic production, intensifying its search for new domestic fields and for ways to maximize production from existing fields. As mentioned in the last chapter, the oil field discovered at Prudhoe Bay on Alaska's North Slope in 1968 was the largest in the United States, making it a top priority for Exxon, one of the four major partners in the joint venture that developed the field. By 1986, Prudhoe Bay had become far and away Exxon's largest producer of oil. The field also held vast supplies of natural gas, raising the tantalizing prospect of substantial profits if a way could be found to transport the gas to markets. The Arctic environment of northern Alaska posed great challenges for Exxon and its partners, and the companies responded with innovations that helped open other Arctic regions to development.

Prudhoe Bay was a major project for Exxon and for the nation as a whole. The early estimates of more than ten billion barrels of recoverable oil represented about 30 percent of total U.S. oil reserves in 1977. Its more than thirty-five trillion cubic feet of natural gas amounted to about 12 percent of the known gas reserves in the United States. This single giant field promised to provide about 20 percent of the domestic oil supply when it reached its maximum productive capacity of two million barrels per day. Exxon's share, about 400,000 barrels per day, with additional supplies anticipated from expected nearby discoveries, was critically important to the company at a time when its access to reserves in OPEC nations had been severely limited by nationalization.

Harry J. Longwell—later a senior vice president of Exxon—recalled the importance of Prudhoe Bay for the company: "Because of its size and significance . . . it was an oil-field boom . . . like East Texas and Titusville and places in California . . . but just an order of magnitude larger scale in terms of the number of people, dollars being spent, [and] production . . . generated."[3] Longwell understood the long-term importance to his career and those of other Exxon engineers in this once-in-a-lifetime project. Prudhoe Bay became a training ground for future company leaders, a testing ground for Arctic technology, and a case study of the value of efficient management of large projects.

The company had been involved in Alaska at least indirectly since the early twentieth century when John D. Rockefeller helped finance the "Anglo-American Polar Expedition" to explore the North Slope of Alaska. One member of this expedition, Earnest de Koven Leffingwell, remained in northern Alaska for seven years studying the terrain and mapping the region's geographical features. When he returned to Washington, D.C., in 1914, he compiled a geological paper ultimately published in 1919. It contained the first accurate chart of the northern coast of Alaska, including a description of the Sadlerochit formation, a gray sandstone outcropping that marked the general location of the Prudhoe Bay field.[4] Humble Oil & Refining (Exxon USA) explored in southern Alaska in the late 1950s and early 1960s, but with only limited success. But company geologists took a growing interest in the oil and gas potential of the North Slope. As rumors began to surface in the early 1960s that the State of Alaska might be planning a North Slope lease sale, Humble's Exploration Department began searching for an opportunity to establish a foothold in the area. That opportunity came courtesy of the California-based Richfield Oil Company, which had conducted seismic studies and held leases on federal tracts on the North Slope. In 1964, the well-capitalized Humble and the smaller Richfield formed a joint venture to explore the North Slope. The venture conducted seismic mapping before the pivotal state lease sale in July 1965, in which Richfield-Humble successfully bid on more than half of the 104 tracts offered. After Atlantic Refining merged with Richfield in 1966, the new joint venture between Atlantic Richfield (ARCO) and Humble moved forward with drilling on its new state leases. In 1968, ARCO-Humble announced it had drilled the discovery well and a confirmation well for what would become the giant Prudhoe Bay field. At about the same time, a joint venture formed in 1969 between BP and Standard Oil of Ohio (Sohio) drilled a successful well in the same general area.[5]

This certainly was not easy oil. Managerial and technical challenges abound in the Arctic, and Exxon took important roles in the management of production, the division of oil and gas among the companies that owned portions of the field, maximization of production through operational efficiency and enhanced oil recovery, and the search for additional fields on the North Slope. In all these tasks, the company operated as one of the four major companies in two major joint ventures (which had begun with eight companies). Here, as in the construction of the Alaska pipeline, the company learned much about Arctic conditions, earthquakes, enhanced oil recovery, and working under close government oversight. Management experience gained over the life cycle of this giant,

*View of Prudhoe Bay field on the flat tundra of Alaska's North Slope shows
some of the hundreds of producing wells and the pipeline that transports
crude oil and natural gas to the central processing and separation facilities,
ca. 1988. ExxonMobil Historical Collection, di_08130.*

complex field contributed greatly to the company's future success in other
big projects around the world.

Early discussions about the management of the Prudhoe Bay field were
described by Longwell as the "most complex, drawn out negotiations
between the two major partnerships." Longwell continued, "We've got
this huge discovery, billions of barrels of oil . . . by far the largest thing ever
found in North America. You have this consortium of companies trying
to pull this thing together." Unified management of the entire field, or
"unitization," was needed for efficient production, but the self-interest of
the two major partners diverged widely. BP-Sohio held about 60 percent
of the oil rim and a much smaller portion of the gas cap; ARCO-Exxon
had only 40 percent of the oil rim, but approximately 80 percent of the
gas cap. As the Alaska pipeline moved slowly through the permitting process from 1969 to 1973, and then as construction moved forward from
1974 to 1977, discussions about how to manage the field stalled. Those
who owned primarily oil would soon have a market for their production,

but Exxon and others that owned mostly natural gas would not. There was also an ongoing debate about the value to be placed on natural gas that could be reinjected into the field to maintain the pressure needed for the efficient production of oil.[6]

Mel Harrison, one of Exxon's negotiators, called the long negotiations over unitization "a technical nightmare that originally I said could not be done," but "it looked like it was required, so we set about writing an agreement that defined all that was to be done." As the Alaska pipeline moved toward completion in 1977, pressure to come to an agreement increased and negotiations intensified. Exxon brought to the table a team of twenty or so specialists armed with technical and legal knowledge of the value of the reinjected gas. It also compiled thorough studies of the potential markets for the estimated 35 trillion cubic feet of gas at Prudhoe Bay, although its value was difficult to determine in the absence of ready access to markets. Mark Albers, who led the renegotiation of this agreement for Exxon more than twenty years later, found that the companies had "never been able to bridge the gap" between their differing views on the value of the oil and the gas produced from the Prudhoe Bay field.[7] Despite reaching no definitive resolution of this key issue, the companies involved finally agreed in March 1977 to a complicated compromise that essentially made BP-Sohio the operator of half of the field and ARCO-Exxon operator of the other half. Exxon accepted this arrangement while acknowledging that it was not ideal, since true unitization would have produced more efficient long-term management of the field.

As early as 1971, a study group including the members of the Prudhoe Bay joint ventures had conducted a $12 million study on the feasibility of building a natural gas pipeline from the North Slope to Winnipeg, in southern Manitoba, Canada. Throughout the construction of the Alaska pipeline, the discussion of options for transporting Arctic natural gas continued.[8] Several options emerged. The most appealing to Exxon was a gas pipeline from Alaska through Canada. Other options included the construction of an "all-Alaska" gas pipeline along the existing right-of-way of the Trans-Alaska Pipeline to a massive gas-liquefaction plant at Valdez, as well as the conversion of the natural gas to liquid methanol. All those were high-cost, high-risk options. The default option was to continue to reinject the natural gas while also using it to supply the fuel needed for the oil operations at Prudhoe Bay.[9]

Construction of a natural gas pipeline connecting Prudhoe Bay to the existing North American gas-pipeline grid would be technologically demanding, but financial risks outweighed technical ones. Construction costs were thought at the time to be more than three times those of the Trans-Alaska Pipeline. In addition, ongoing political debates about the deregulation of natural gas in the United States presented great uncertainties about the future of natural gas prices, which would have to remain high in order to justify the costs of the pipeline. Despite the risks, Exxon remained confident that a natural gas pipeline from Prudhoe Bay through Canada would be built. In its annual reports and its communications with stakeholders in the early 1970s, Exxon regularly provided updates on planning for a project called the Alaska Natural Gas Transportation System, or ANGTS. The prevailing assumption was that a pipeline for natural gas would be constructed after the completion of the Trans-Alaska Pipeline, with a projected start-up date in the period 1982–1984.[10]

During the late 1970s, debates over the route and ownership of the natural gas pipeline became more visible as competing interests began to battle over the relative merits of different pipeline routes. Who would provide the financing? Would Exxon and other gas producers hold partial ownership of the line? Who would pay for the massive gas-processing plants needed to prepare Prudhoe Bay gas for shipment? Could the line be built without extensive damage to the environment and the sort of social dislocation caused by the mass migration of workers during the construction of the Trans-Alaska Pipeline? Randall Meyer recalled "trying to encourage the company to get into what is now called the midterm": "I was trying to get them [Exxon's corporate management] into the pipeline business for gas . . . But they didn't feel like they wanted to because it was still regulated."[11]

With the completion of the oil pipeline in 1977, planning for the gas pipeline picked up as rival groups sought the favor of Canadian and U.S. elected officials and regulators. National interests of course entered the discussions. In 1977, the related questions of ownership and route reached the highest political levels in the United States and Canada as President

Jimmy Carter sent Congress his decision on which group should build the line, and the National Energy Board of Canada eliminated the group favored by Exxon for "environmental and socio-economic reasons."[12]

Yet Exxon USA nonetheless pushed on. In its 1979 budget planning report to the corporate management committee, Exxon USA included for the first time expenditures for a gas-treatment unit at Prudhoe Bay, reporting that "strategies and plans are being developed to assist completion of the Alaska segment of the gas pipeline." In the same year, a company report on supplemental gas supplies concluded: "Alaska gas is the most reliable and risk-free supplemental supply available. Reserve potential is large, significant volumes are proven, the source is domestic, and the technology is available to produce and deliver the gas to market. . . . In 1990, Alaskan gas is forecast to supply 4 percent (0.8 trillion cf) of total U.S. gas requirement." In 1979, Exxon USA signed twenty-year sales contracts for its entire share of the natural gas at Prudhoe Bay.[13]

The gas pipeline seemed on the way to construction after the extreme oil-price spike following the disruption of Iranian exports in 1979. This reminder of the vulnerability of oil imports and the profits produced by much higher oil prices encouraged oil companies to embrace big projects, including increased Arctic exploration, synthetic fuels, and the gas pipeline, which now carried an estimated price tag of more than $30 billion for both the pipeline and the gas-processing plant at Prudhoe Bay. The renewed sense of urgency for the development of domestic alternatives to imported oil, however, raised new concerns at Exxon. Its base plan for natural gas in 1980 started with the assumption that the gas pipeline would be built without financial assistance from the producers and that it would be in operation in the fall of 1986. But in its 1980 budget report, Exxon USA explored the implications of different contingencies on its plans for the sale of Arctic gas: "The assumption is that Alaska Northwest [a consortium organized to build the gas pipeline] and the producers fail to reach agreement on a financial package for construction of the ANGTS as presently contemplated. This could result in proposals for federal government legislation directing that ANGTS be built, owned, and operated by the U.S. government." To provide other options, the company prepared studies of alternative financing for the gas pipeline and reexamined the use of liquefaction and gas-to-liquid technologies. Uncertainties over the high price and financing meant that "completion of the entire ANGTS project remains in doubt."[14]

Exxon USA's budget plan for 1981 nonetheless put forward detailed plans for ANGTS. The Alaskan section of the line would be forty-eight inches in diameter, the same as TAPS. Its initial capacity would be 2 billion to 2.5 billion cubic feet per day (bcf/d), which could be expanded to 3.2 bcf/d with the addition of pumping stations. Structural design was well underway, as was financial planning. The owners of the natural gas and those of the proposed pipeline company had worked out a financing proposal that gave the gas producers ownership of 30 percent of the gas-processing plant and the pipeline, and this proposal was presented "to the financial community in June 1981." The projected start-up for the line had been moved to late 1987. A concluding section of the budget plan discussed contingencies: "The ability of the ANGTS [Alaska Natural Gas Transportation System] sponsors to finance the project within the private sector continues uncertain for several reasons. The willingness of the Administration and Congress to permit the government or consumers to accept some role to assure completion of the project to whatever extent required by potential lenders remains the key to private financing." The company's earlier concern that government might decide to own and operate the line seemed "unlikely under the Reagan Administration."[15]

The next year brought growing concerns of a glut of natural gas supplies and the softening of oil prices. One bad omen for North Slope natural gas was Exxon USA's announcement that the "large gas accumulation" from its newly discovered northern Alaska field at Point Thomson would not be added to its reserve figures from 1982 to 1985 "because of the major differences between oil and gas development on the North Slope." While voicing determination that "an important upstream goal is to achieve a 1991 startup of ANGTS and the Prudhoe Gas Project," the company conceded that "the overall viability of the ANGTS project remains to be proven."[16] Judgment day came in February 1983. Citing "uncertainties as to pipeline economics," Exxon USA announced the decision "to defer startup for up to two years." Although studies suggested that "ANGTS still appears to be the most economic alternative for transportation of Alaska gas" in the long term, "gas marketability questions" raised concerns about the cost of Alaska natural gas compared with other sources in the early years of the project. That report was already outdated by November 1983, when worsening economic conditions forced Exxon USA to acknowledge that the gas pipeline project fared poorly in comparison with other proposed investments. The company's conclusion marked the beginning of the end for the project: "In a low cost environment, we feel this project would be deferred beyond the Plan period. ANGTS start up is projected in 1993 in the Plan."[17]

Almost thirty years later, the project remains on the drawing board. Looking back in 2007 amid renewed proposals for the construction of a natural gas pipeline from the North Slope, Harry Longwell gave the simplest explanation for the decision in 1983 to "defer" work on the project: "It's never been economical."[18] A window of opportunity had opened for the Trans-Alaska Pipeline in 1973 with the sudden rise in oil prices and the intense concern over national energy security. That pipeline made it through before falling oil prices slammed the window shut. For a brief moment after the completion of the oil pipeline and the second oil price spike, the gas pipeline seemed likely to be built. But it was doomed by the collapse of oil prices and growing uncertainties about the supply and price of natural gas as phased deregulation began. Thirty billion dollars was, after all, a substantial sum to invest in building an extraordinarily long pipeline over an environmentally fragile route in order to carry natural gas from Prudhoe Bay to markets with access to less expensive supplies of gas. Like so many giant projects planned by Exxon and other large petroleum companies in the heady days after the oil-price spike in the late 1970s, the gas pipeline fell victim to the combination of rising construction costs and a growing realization that energy prices were headed down.

With the gas pipeline sidelined, the debate on the proper evaluation of the reinjected gas from the field intensified. As the years passed and large amounts of oil continued to flow from Prudhoe Bay, this gas became increasingly important in maintaining high levels of oil production. To compensate Exxon and other gas producers, the partners at Prudhoe Bay reapportioned the oil, giving Exxon an additional 17,000 b/d.

As talks about the overall organization of the field continued, the partners focused on the more efficient operations of the Trans-Alaska Pipeline, the use of enhanced recovery to increase long-term production, and the discovery of new fields on the North Slope to fill the pipeline as the original field became depleted. In 1977, Exxon appropriated $89 million as its share of support for increasing the capacity of the line to two million barrels a day, with expansion to begin in 1978. In an early effort to enhance the efficiency of the pipeline, Exxon joined others in encouraging the development and use of an "anti-drag agent" to improve the flow of oil.[19]

From the early days of production at Prudhoe Bay, Exxon and its partners made large investments in technology to expand the amount of oil recovered from the giant field. The oil industry had a long history of enhanced recovery, and the scale of the Prudhoe Bay field gave the companies there a strong incentive to find ways to expand production beyond the original estimate of ten billion barrels. In 1979 and 1980, Exxon joined its partners at Prudhoe Bay in equipping the six existing gas-separation facilities there with new low-pressure separators. According to reservoir simulation studies, the resulting reduction in system pressure "would increase ultimate recovery by 1.1 billion barrels (200 million barrels Exxon net)."[20] In 1980, Exxon USA gained approval from corporate management to add $256 million of funding for Exxon's share of the $1.2 billion investment needed by the partners for "the engineering, fabrication, and installation of wells and facilities capable of treating and injecting one million b/d of produced water into the Sadlerochit formation . . . in order to maintain pressure and improve ultimate reservoir recovery." Since a majority of this water was produced with oil flow from the formation, reinjecting it reduced the cost of disposal of the water by other means. The Investment Advisory Committee agreed that this investment had "excellent economic and conservation justification."[21] Engineering efficiency was a hallmark of Exxon's corporate culture, and such projects reinforced its image as a master at maximizing long-term profits through technical proficiency.

The next year, Exxon USA was back with a proposal for a more limited, tertiary recovery project involving the flooding of a region in the ARCO-Exxon section of the field with miscible gas, that is, natural gas and natural gas liquids alternately mixed with water. Among the benefits for Exxon would be additional oil production, the generation of data to evaluate the prospects for a larger project later, and tax benefits by taking advantage of a lower federal tax rate for oil produced through tertiary recovery.[22] Enhanced oil-recovery projects steadily increased the

amount of oil recovered from the Prudhoe Bay field. By 2000, the estimate of its recoverable reserves had grown from about ten billion barrels
to as much as thirteen billion barrels. Because of the enormous size of the
field, this 30 percent expansion in production was equivalent to discovering and developing three giant, one-billion-barrel fields in other regions.
This development dramatically illustrated a quiet, ongoing revolution
that steadily expanded the supply of petroleum through innovations in
enhanced recovery.

As the application of new technology, enhanced-recovery techniques
borrowed from other oil fields, and increases in operating efficiency
allowed the Prudhoe Bay consortium to "milk" additional oil, the companies also pushed to discover new oil fields in the region. The existence
of the Trans-Alaska Pipeline meant that production from oil fields found
nearby could be transported at a relatively small additional cost.

Exxon and its partners at Prudhoe Bay were far from alone in searching for additional oil on the North Slope. After the oil-price spike in 1979,
enthusiasm about Alaska swept through the oil industry. A much-publicized report by the National Petroleum Council in 1981 concluded that
approximately 24 billion barrels of oil and 109 trillion cubic feet of natural gas—a total of 44 billion barrels of oil and oil-equivalent natural gas
(the combined measure is in barrels of oil equivalent, or BOE; one BOE is
the amount of energy released by burning one barrel of oil)—was potentially recoverable from the U.S. Arctic, with a 1 percent probability that
the figure might be as high as 99 billion BOE. A year later, a *BusinessWeek*
cover article, "The Great Arctic Energy Rush: Far from OPEC's Grasp,
170 Billion bbl. of Oil May Lie Waiting," quoted "an Exxon exploration
executive" as saying that "the Arctic is the future of the oil industry." The
breathless tone of the entire article captured the industry's excitement
over Alaska.[23] This was not a new sentiment within Exxon USA, which,
in its 1979 budget proposal, had included requests for "investments for
frontier oil and gas including expenditures to explore and develop the
assumed Beaufort and Bering Sea discoveries and the marine and pipeline
expenditures required to move the crude to refining centers." That budget
plan included "$1.4 billion in 1979 dollars for terminals, collection pipe-
lines, and six additional tankers for frontiers."[24]

The peak of this Alaska enthusiasm was the frenzied bidding in the

A model of the Beaufort Sea ice island exploration platform, 1983.
ExxonMobil Historical Collection, di_06109.

fall of 1982 for leases offshore Alaska. Oil companies bid more than $2 billion, convinced that large discoveries waited in the Arctic. Sohio paid $227 million for the right to drill on the Mukluk tract in the Beaufort Sea, where seismic evidence of very promising structures tantalized major oil companies. Results did not, however, fulfill the expectations of the early 1980s, and many of the promising structures identified by geoscientists, including the Mukluk prospects, did not yield commercial quantities of oil. A spokesman for Sohio summed up the resulting frustration of oil explorers with an often-repeated explanation of the company's failure on its Mukluk lease: "We were simply 30 million years too late." Oil probably once held in the promising geological structure had long since migrated away.[25] The failure to find commercial oil deposits in the much-ballyhooed Mukluk area shook the confidence of the oil industry with a sobering reminder: success was not certain, no matter how much money was spent or how good the seismic results looked.

As a major owner of the Prudhoe Bay field and a 20 percent owner of the Trans-Alaska Pipeline, Exxon joined in the enthusiasm for onshore and offshore exploration around the North Slope. It had several distinct advantages over those without a foothold in the area. The Prudhoe Bay facilities provided a headquarters from which to find and develop new fields in a region with almost no other infrastructure. The pipeline would transport any oil discovered near the bay. And in the drilling that immediately followed the discovery wells for the Sadlerochit formation, numerous other, smaller fields nearby had been identified and leased by the partners. Several of these satellite fields—including Lisburne, Endicott, Kuparak River, and Niakuk—proved to be substantial.[26]

The partners at Prudhoe Bay paired up in several combinations to develop nearby fields. Exxon and ARCO were partners on several projects, with British Petroleum and Sohio joining them on several others. The first big project for Exxon and ARCO was the Lisburne structure, originally discovered in 1968 underneath the original North Slope field. This new field held an estimated three billion barrels of oil, making it "one of the largest undeveloped reserves in Exxon USA's inventory of opportunities" in the early 1980s. Its structure made it difficult to develop, however, and the original estimate that only about 12 percent of its reserves could be recovered gave pause. After several years of technical study, the companies moved ahead with development in 1984, with initial production scheduled for 1987. Production ultimately rose to about 100,000 barrels a day.[27] This was a promising, early success in the push to find reserves that could take up the slack in filling the Trans-Alaska Pipeline when the original Prudhoe Bay field began to lose production in the late 1980s.

Offshore, the development of oil in the extreme conditions of the Beaufort Sea required innovative and expensive technology. Traces of oil had been found in the late 1960s about ten miles offshore, northeast of Prudhoe Bay. Exxon purchased leases in the area in 1969 and 1982, and it became a 21 percent partner in a new field discovered nearby. Amoco and Union Oil were also joint-venture partners in what became in 1987 the first field to produce oil in the Beaufort Sea. Exxon Production Research Company (EPR), Exxon Research and Engineering Company, and Imperial Oil joined in the development of the technology to produce oil from the Endicott field. The partnership constructed two connected gravel islands in the Beaufort Sea to serve as locations for a permanent producing plant. An aboveground pipeline built on a gravel causeway connected the islands to a large processing plant at Prudhoe Bay. Initial estimates of development costs came in at $2.2 billion. According to the leader of Exxon's production engineering group in Alaska, however, "Good engineering and good project management, along with favorable market conditions, brought the cost down to $1.1 billion." A sharp focus on cost containment was becoming more and more important with the weakening of oil prices in the mid-1980s. Saving more than a billion dollars in development costs enhanced the long-term profitability of a field with estimated recoverable reserves of 350 million barrels of crude.[28]

Exxon and its partners developed several other large fields in the vicinity of Prudhoe Bay. An increasingly sophisticated geological understanding of the region came in the late 1980s and early 1990s when Exxon used more powerful computers and more advanced programs to reexamine all geological data previously collected from the region. The result was the discovery of what Exxon called the largest domestic discovery in the decade before 1993, the Point McIntyre field, on the eastern shore of Prudhoe Bay. Because of the lack of surface indications of oil, this field had been hiding in plain sight since 1968. But in the 1980s, advanced computer analysis produced new insights into the impact of permafrost on seismic mapping, leading to the discovery of an estimated 340 million barrels of recoverable oil at Point McIntyre. Advanced drilling technology helped develop the field efficiently, and the processing of its oil and natural gas liquids at the nearby Lisburne Processing Center lowered the costs of preparing this oil for its four-to-five-day trip down the Trans-Alaska Pipeline to Valdez for tanker shipment to markets.[29]

Beyond the neighborhood of Prudhoe Bay, Exxon joined most other major oil companies in searching for oil in the Beaufort Sea, the Chukchi Sea, and the Bering Sea. Before the oil-price bust of the mid-1980s, optimism reigned. Even after oil prices plummeted, Exxon and others continued to explore leases acquired in better times. More money was lost than commercial oil was found, but one benefit of this era of exploration was the development of new technologies for exploration and production in the extreme Arctic conditions. This was a technical area in which only the Soviets in Siberia and the Canadians, including those in the Exxon affiliate Imperial Oil, had much previous experience.

EPR cooperated with Imperial Oil to develop new technologies for Arctic exploration and production. A necessary starting point was the gathering and analysis of basic data on the thickness, extent, and movement of ice. Exxon collected such data via satellite photography, observations from ships in the region's waters, aerial photography, and the tried-and-true, traditional work of expeditions by scientists. The industry had limited experience in designing offshore drilling rigs and production platforms that could withstand collisions with large ice floes. The traditional strategy of using drillships and semisubmersibles (large, platform-like floating vessels supported primarily on structures similar to pontoons submerged below the sea surface) in the summer months did not work in many Arctic areas, where the summer was too short to provide adequate time for drilling. One innovative response was the use of mammoth concrete island drilling systems. Built at other locations and towed to a site during the summer months, the systems used specially designed machines to spray water around the structure, creating barriers of ice to protect it from collisions with floes. When their work was completed, the concrete islands could be towed elsewhere.

Unlike drilling systems used to find oil, platforms used to produce oil had to operate year-round in fixed locations. One approach used man-made islands of gravel, as at the Endicott field, but shipping vast amounts gravel from faraway locations could be prohibitively expensive, and the gravel could not be easily recovered for reuse at other locations. Concrete islands were a possible answer, as were conical platforms, whose shape reduced the exposure of the legs to the direct force of ice floes.[30]

As Exxon searched for new Alaskan oil fields, it continued to protect its interests at Prudhoe Bay. In approving BP's purchase of ARCO in April 2000, regulatory authorities required the merged company to divest itself of ARCO's holdings on the North Slope in order to avoid potential antitrust violations. After Phillips Petroleum (now ConocoPhillips) purchased ARCO's interests, Exxon demanded the renegotiation of the long-standing agreement on the valuation of oil and gas and the distribution of shares to each company in the consortium. Mark Albers, one of a new generation of Exxon production engineers in Alaska, led the Exxon group in the resulting renegotiations. Throughout the process, he consulted on objectives and developed tactics with Harry Longwell and others with detailed, historically informed knowledge of the central issues involved in the original negotiations. Albers succeeded in winning a new agreement that gave all owners a proportional share in oil and natural gas while creating a unitized field with a single operator, BP. Exxon came out very well, trading a 44 percent ownership of the gas cap and a 22 percent interest in the oil rim for a 36 percent interest in the combined oil and natural gas—just on the eve of a period of extreme increases in oil prices.[31]

Prudhoe Bay was good to the company in many ways. Most obviously, it provided a large, long-term boost to Exxon's oil production at a critical time in the company's history. It also forced Exxon to develop project-management skills that proved useful in big projects in frontier regions around the world. Harry Longwell pointed to the importance of the company's experience in Alaska: it provided "a model, a life-cycle" project—a big, important project in which several generations of Exxon executives and scientists took a very large field from discovery, through pipeline construction, through development, and into decline.[32] The cycle included dealing with intense public scrutiny and opposition, both during the long delay in permitting and after the *Exxon Valdez* oil spill. The company's research centers mobilized to develop new technology that could be used in other regions with Arctic conditions or earthquakes. Exxon's management learned to grapple with the return of a phenomenon not much seen in the post–World War II era: unpredicted swings in oil prices. And Prudhoe Bay gave the company a proving ground for learning to work on big projects in a consortium, a type of relationship Exxon would experience more frequently as it became more active in big oil and gas projects in frontier regions around the world. Moreover, the company had to meet strict environmental standards in Arctic conditions while working under the scrutiny of an array of regulatory agencies from all levels of government. In short, from beginning to end, the experience forced the company to become more proficient at managing the financial and technical demands of giant projects in frontier regions such as the North Sea, Sakhalin Island (off the east coast of Russia), and West Africa.

DEEPER: OFFSHORE AROUND THE WORLD

The most promising oil frontiers were offshore. Since World War II, the industry had moved gradually out into the ocean in search of new oil supplies, with most of the action coming in the Gulf of Mexico off Louisiana and Texas. In 1970, "deep water" meant about 300 feet, which was the water depth of the deepest offshore production at the time. By the early 1980s, higher oil prices and a wave of technological innovations redefined "deep water," pushing offshore production to depths exceeding 1,000 feet. By 2000, planning was under way for production in 5,000 feet of water. The push into ever-deeper water in ever more demanding conditions produced a succession of major projects for Exxon. In the 1970s and 1980s, this search led the company from the Gulf of Mexico to Southern California; to the North Sea, Australia, and Malaysia; and then back to deeper waters in the Gulf of Mexico and off California. Fields in new regions and at greater depths presented different technical, managerial, and political challenges. The cumulative knowledge gained by the company around the world could be carried into new projects, including those in deeper waters in familiar regions.[33] In completing the technically demanding projects of this era, Exxon developed much-needed equity oil (that is, oil that it owned) to replace nationalized OPEC oil.

CALIFORNIA: HONDO

Until the late 1960s, drilling deeper meant drilling farther out into the Gulf of Mexico, but that changed quickly for Humble in 1968 when the company discovered oil at a very promising site in the Santa Barbara Channel in California. To reach those fields, Humble had to almost triple its previous water-depth record from the Gulf of Mexico, and the company christened the first field with the Spanish word for "deep," "hondo." (The numerous regulatory hurdles that slowed development of Hondo are described in chapter 2.) To work in the Santa Barbara Channel, the company adapted and extended technology brought from the Gulf of Mexico, but it still faced major technical challenges.

Humble brought to the task of drilling in deeper water a wealth of experience from more than thirty years of work in and around the Gulf of Mexico. The company made its first foray into the Gulf in the late 1930s,

Hondo oil production platform, Santa Barbara Channel, California, 1978.
ExxonMobil Historical Collection, di_08138.

when it used piers extending out into shallow water to develop a prospect off High Island, Texas. During the first boom in activity farther offshore in the Gulf after World War II, Humble was one of the early companies to build a large permanent platform to explore for oil, and it also made technical contributions to the improvement of one of the leading systems of oil production in the shallow areas of the Gulf of Mexico—the tender-assisted platform. In the 1950s and 1960s, Humble developed the Grand Isle field off Louisiana, using platforms attached to the ocean floor with piles and installed at sea with large, specialized "launch" barges. Movement into the deeper areas of the Gulf came step-by-step as companies identified promising prospects in depths beyond existing platforms, then extended existing technologies to drill exploratory wells, build and install appropriate production platforms, and construct pipelines to shore. These activities ultimately involved the coordinated efforts of an offshore fraternity made up of many different oil companies, drilling companies, fabricators, and oil tool and service companies that shared a common objective: deeper.[34]

The most striking difference at Hondo was the size of the platform needed to operate in deep water off California, and the Hondo platform represented a giant step for both the company and the offshore industry as a whole. Test drilling in the Santa Barbara Channel as early as 1965 brought a celebratory headline in the *Oil and Gas Journal*: "Humble Test Cracks 600-ft Deepwater Mark off California."[35] In 1976, an article in the *New York Times* headlined "Exxon Nears Completion of Deepest Offshore Rig" described the 1,163-foot platform by comparing it to "the 1,250-foot Empire State Building." It further noted that the 850 feet of water from the ocean floor to sea level was much greater than the existing drilling record for the Gulf of Mexico (375 feet) or the North Sea (475 feet). Of course, such depth records were short-lived in that era of offshore expansion. The *New York Times* article concluded, "The new rig is the tallest to be built to date, but Shell Oil Company is now building one in more than 1,000 feet of water in the Gulf of Mexico. And oilmen say that offshore technology probably won't stop there."[36] Oilmen also knew that fixed platforms attached to the ocean floor were rapidly reaching the limits of their effectiveness, and that Hondo, as well as Shell's new platform, would become relics of an outmoded technology as the industry developed more economical and flexible ways to move beyond 1,000 feet.

Design problems limited the use of fixed platforms in very deep water. As rigid metal platforms stretched into the ocean, their capacity to withstand the impact of waves declined. John Bardgette, the Exxon engineer who directed the Hondo project, noted that the structure had been designed to move "back and forth, in a normal sea, about 6 to 12 inches, the same way the Empire State Building is designed to move a little in the wind."[37] But there were limits to such accommodations, and the industry had already begun the search for refinements that would allow other types of production platforms to be installed in water depths beyond 1,000 feet.

Length and weight also limited the depth at which fixed metal platforms could be installed. Hondo was a 12,000-ton steel structure more than 1,100 feet long. Existing barges were too small to transport it from the fabrication yard to the installation site, and existing cranes had trouble lifting its weight. Exxon overcame this problem by constructing and transporting the platform in two pieces and then mating the two in the ocean. Such an innovation held obvious risks. Experienced offshore engineers were nervous about the launching of standard-size platforms, which involved sliding a large, expensive metal structure off a barge in the middle of the ocean and then using huge floating cranes to guide it as it sank to the bottom of the sea. The idea of being the first offshore crew to put together in the open sea a 7,000-ton structure and another weighing 5,000 tons, which together cost about $70 million, must have caused many sleepless nights.[38] The operations required to install Hondo had been developed in the Gulf of Mexico, but all of them had to be significantly adapted for use in the deeper water and on the sharper slope of the continental shelf off California.

Whereas platforms in the Gulf of Mexico had to be designed to withstand the power of hurricane-driven waves and winds, the California coast was subject to another type of natural disaster: earthquakes.[39] The Santa Barbara Channel had a history of earthquakes, including numerous small quakes, two (in 1925 and 1941) that measured magnitude 6 on the Richter scale, and several in nearby regions of magnitude 7. These strong quakes severely damaged the city of Santa Barbara and some of the region's onshore oil facilities. To design a platform for the channel that incorporated the best possible protections against the strongest earthquake that could be predicted for the area, Exxon engineers consulted with specialists from the California Institute of Technology. In addition to the cutoff valves on the ocean floor traditionally used by the industry to stop the flow of oil into the ocean in the event of major damage to the platform, the design also included a system of shutoff valves for compressors on the platform, which would be activated in the event of excessive vibrations of the platform. Along with the other thirteen platforms operating in the Santa Barbara Channel in 1978, the Hondo platform reported "strong motion" for about twenty seconds during a 5.1 magnitude earthquake centered in the channel, but it suffered no damage.[40]

Another major adaptation of the technology used in the Gulf of Mexico came about in response to the strong opposition of environmentalists to Exxon's original plans for Hondo. The continental shelf off California slopes steeply, so deep water is in sight of the beautiful beaches that make tourism an important regional industry and give the region its identity as an upscale place to live and work. The much-publicized Santa Barbara oil spill in 1969 greatly intensified scrutiny of oil-industry activity in the

Santa Barbara Channel. When plans for an onshore oil-processing facility at Las Flores Canyon, west of the city of Santa Barbara, stalled the Hondo project, Exxon responded by expanding an existing technology to meet a need specific to its Santa Ynez Unit, a large block off Santa Barbara that grew to include the Hondo, Harmony, and Heritage platforms. Specialized tankers moored near production platforms had been used at other fields for the temporary storage and processing of oil. As mentioned earlier, Exxon also used an offshore storage and treating vessel to remove hydrogen sulfide from the oil produced by Hondo and to treat some of the natural gas produced so that it could be used to generate the electricity required by both the vessel and the platform. The vessel, named the *Exxon Santa Ynez*, was a 50,000-deadweight ton tanker converted into a specialized vessel that could store more than 200,000 barrels of oil. An innovative single-anchor leg mooring system kept the vessel tethered to the ocean floor while allowing it to move freely about its mooring. The vessel also served as a link extending from Hondo, transferring oil, gas, water, and electric power to the pipelines. The *Exxon Santa Ynez* borrowed from concepts initially developed in the late 1940s and early 1950s in the Gulf of Mexico, where small platforms used tender vessels moored nearby for a variety of functions. Its use foreshadowed a technological future when giant floating production, storage, and offloading vessels would be used to develop deepwater fields.

Exxon faced considerable technological and political risks off California. Yet the oil industry had good reason to believe that the potential for production there made it an important domestic prospect. The coastal region of Southern California had been producing substantial amounts of oil since the late nineteenth century, when major onshore fields that extended out into the Pacific Ocean were tapped from long piers built out into the water. The company extended existing technology for use in a new environment. Although the political challenges proved frustrating, they forced the company to enter what was becoming a new frontier in the oil industry—the management of large projects under stricter environmental laws and in the face of determined opposition from public interest groups. Technical and political knowledge gained by Exxon on the Hondo project quickly proved useful as it tackled other projects around the world.

MALAYSIA: A NEW PATH

As illustrated in Alaska and California, Exxon's search for domestic oil encountered constraints in the form of stricter environmental regulations, but the company confronted more serious challenges from foreign governments. As it searched for non-OPEC oil around the world in the 1970s, Exxon learned that all producer nations expected to exert control over their own reserves and prices much as OPEC did. They expected to be senior partners with international oil companies in developing oil and gas while pursuing their national interests, which included the training of local workers, technicians, and managers.

For Exxon, a prime example of the new realities of international oil came in Malaysia. Standard Oil had begun marketing products in Malaysia in 1897, and as throughout Asia, long familiarity with Standard Oil and the Esso brand opened doors for Exxon. In the late 1960s, the company's early exploration offshore in the Malay basin in the South China Sea uncovered promising prospects. Production began under what was then a standard leasing contract, which gave the government a bit more than 50 percent of oil profits.[41] After the OPEC revolution, however, the government of Malaysia demanded a new contract, one providing it with much higher oil revenues. In addition, it created Petronas, a national oil company with significant power over all phases of the domestic oil industry and mandatory participation in production in oil projects in Malaysia. Richard Kruizenga moved within Exxon from Australia to Malaysia just in time to confront the new demands: "We got into a fight with the Malaysian government over the terms of the agreement. They tried to change them all just as we were getting going. That was just sort of the world of the seventies."[42]

From 1974 through 1976, negotiations ground to a standstill. Exxon considered walking away, but instead accepted far-reaching changes to its original contract.[43] In December 1976, Esso Eastern reported to the Exxon Management Committee that it had signed "three contracts with Petronas . . . for the exploration and development of petroleum." Those contracts replaced three earlier ones signed in 1965 and 1968, "which were required to be restructured by government demand." The new contracts were production-sharing contracts with terms very favorable to Petronas

An oil platform in the Lawit gas field off the coast of Malaysia, 1997.
Exxon Mobil Corporation.

and the Malaysian government. By one Exxon estimate, those contracts and future ones claimed as much as 88 percent of the revenues from oil production for the government and its national oil company. The new arrangement meant that Exxon had to adjust to being a contractor under a production-sharing contract, "an unfamiliar and difficult experience" for the company.[44] The explanation for agreeing to retreat from a bedrock principle of the company—the sanctity of contracts—was simple: "Although Exxon has just emerged from a very difficult period of negotiations, Malaysia, relative to other developing countries, is expected to continue to offer an attractive business environment."[45]

And it did. Under its new relationship with the government, Exxon prospered in the coming decades as it found and developed a steady stream of new oil and natural gas deposits in the South China Sea 100–200 miles offshore of Peninsular Malaysia. According to one former president of Esso Malaysia Production Inc. (EMPI), a key to the company's success was "the level of understanding and mutual respect that has been established between Esso and Petronas."[46] Another former president stated that over time, "Petronas became more sophisticated, and they have a reputation now as the best national oil company in the world."[47] In the early 1990s, a president of Petronas expressed his opinion of the benefits of working with Exxon: "Working with major oil companies has enabled our people to gain knowledge and achieve transfer of technology . . . that helps us go forward in the development of our own oil and gas resources . . . and will assist Petronas in mastering petroleum technology sufficiently to offer its services elsewhere in the world."[48] In general, the two companies maintained a mutually beneficial partnership.

It was often more difficult to maintain good relations with the Malaysian government. In its determination to ensure that oil-led development benefited the nation as a whole, the government made numerous demands on the company. In the mid-1980s, it encouraged Exxon and Petronas to create a new industrial center in a sparsely populated region on the east coast of Peninsular Malaysia. The center would place workers and supply facilities nearer to the primary offshore fields while stimulating growth in the region. The town of Terengganu steadily grew into an important hub of economic activity.[49] In addition, the government convinced Exxon to build a small refinery in Malaysia to reduce the nation's dependence on refined products from Singapore. It put forward plans to enlist the company's aid in supplying natural gas to internal markets and developing the infrastructure needed to export gas by pipeline and later as LNG.

Along with most other major producing nations, Malaysia encouraged international oil companies to foster the growth of local contractors and to train local workers for jobs in the industry. A president of EMPI in the mid-1970s remembered, "We set up all kinds of schools for them. But we also sent a lot of our [Malaysian] geologists and engineers, accountants, lawyers back to the U.S. and into other affiliates for training."[50] The company recruited Malaysians who had gone abroad for their educations to return to work in their home country. Recruitment took place within a government-mandated system to ensure balanced hiring from the country's many ethnicities. By the 1990s, the company's workforce was about 97 percent Malaysian. In addition, a growing number of well-trained Malaysians went on to work in Exxon's global operations.[51]

Exxon understood that national policies "from time to time may not be exactly aligned with our interests." In those cases it adopted an approach that it came to call "relentlessly reasonable." The flexibility of production-sharing contracts allowed some matters to be resolved by adjusting the terms for different projects. For example, because Exxon and Petronas shared costs and production, they often could find ways to satisfy both companies' self-interests as national oil production grew to more than 600,000 barrels a day by the 1990s.[52] Cooperation with the government was possible because of a long tradition of compromise in which each side recognized the long-term value of the relationship. Obviously, life had been easier for international oil companies before the 1970s, when they still held most of the cards. But in Malaysia Exxon found a new path toward a durable partnership with a government and its national oil company that produced much needed oil for the company.

GRONINGEN: DOORWAY TO THE NORTH SEA AND NATURAL GAS

Exxon's predecessor, Standard Oil (New Jersey), took its first steps toward the North Sea long before beginning to produce oil there. The company had been involved in marketing in Europe since the late nineteenth century, and it built a string of European refineries in the twentieth century. But the event that brought the company to the banks of the North Sea was the discovery in 1959 of the giant Groningen field in the northern part of the Netherlands, which proved to be one of the largest natural gas fields in the world. Exxon's joint development of Groningen with Royal Dutch Shell made the company a major producer in Europe.

The partnership between the two dominant international oil companies, Jersey Standard and Shell, had its roots in a seemingly minor agreement made before World War II. In the late 1930s, both companies were interested in exploring for oil and gas in Cuba and the Netherlands. Though not seen as major prospects, these areas seemed promising. To avoid duplication, they agreed to enter into what could be called an engagement of convenience: Jersey would explore Cuba, and Shell would explore the Netherlands. If either found commercial oil or gas deposits, it would invite the other in as an equal partner, in effect moving from an engagement to a marriage of convenience. Letters of agreement were exchanged in the 1930s. World War II then intervened, changing the face of Europe and submerging all considerations of oil development on the Continent.[53]

Royal Dutch Shell resumed exploration in the Netherlands after the war and began plans for the development of what was the first economically viable field there. When news of those events reached the United States, one of the men at Jersey who had been involved in the Cuba–Netherlands negotiations reminded his superiors of the agreement. Presented with the original letter of agreement, Shell honored its prewar commitment. A history of Jersey Standard reports that the deputy coordinator of production at the company called this "one of the greatest ethical demonstrations he had ever witnessed."[54] Royal Dutch Shell's history makes clear that the company was hardly pleased by Jersey's assertion of an ownership interest in discoveries in the Netherlands, reporting that the group's managing directors concluded: "Jersey's argument boils down to their coming in where they think we have got something and staying out where this seems to suit them better. However, all this is now water under the bridge and I still think we must abide by our decision to accept Jersey as a partner with the most possible grace."[55] To manage their new fifty-fifty joint venture, in 1947 the two companies created Nederlandse Aardolie Maatschappij, B.V. (NAM), with Shell as the operator.

Tests at Groningen gradually revealed that the field contained reserves of 100 trillion cubic feet—large enough to make natural gas a major source of energy for a large part of Europe. The government and the two companies agreed to a division of revenues from the field and established a set of institutions to transform the energy mix in the Netherlands and develop natural gas exports. This institutional framework, which came to be called the *Gasgebouw* (gas structure), formed the basis, in the words of a recent history, of a "long and very successful public-private partnership." As part of a coherent natural gas policy, the Dutch government oversaw NAM in a framework within which the companies could plan long-term production from Groningen. Established and managed for half a century without a formal contract or piece of governing legislation, the collaborative arrangement has at times been controversial, but the long-term results have been impressive.[56]

The government used the natural gas from Groningen to transform the basic energy supply of the Netherlands and, in the process, the national economy. The Dutch government pushed the rapid substitution of natural gas for other fuels in homes as well as in industry. It joined with the

NAM partners in planning and building a growing gas-distribution network and advertised the benefits of natural gas. When the 1973 embargo
cut oil exports to the Netherlands as well as the United States, the Dutch
government turned to Groningen's ample supplies of natural gas. In the
longer run, the government pursued a comprehensive energy policy that
included conservation, energy efficiency, and reductions of exports of
natural gas to free it for domestic use.[57]

Efficiency meant more than reducing energy waste by consumers. It
also meant the efficient long-term development of the Groningen field.
Here, Jersey and Shell played a leading role in ensuring the recovery of
as much as possible of the field's natural gas. In combination with other
factors, such as changes in technologies for transporting natural gas,
which steadily expanded gas markets, the Groningen experience helped
alter Jersey's outlook on natural gas, long seen as a byproduct of oil to be
sold as quickly as possible. Groningen also marked a turning point in the
evolution of Jersey Standard/Exxon from an oil company to an oil and
gas company.

Groningen became a very important part of the company's global
portfolio. Indeed, in 1985, more than a quarter century after its discovery,
Groningen ranked second in production among fields in which Exxon
had an interest, trailing only Prudhoe Bay. Moreover, its production of
271,000 barrels of oil equivalent per day for Exxon made Groningen
a critically important contributor to the company's efforts to find and
develop non-OPEC oil and gas. In 2009, at the fiftieth anniversary of the
field's discovery, Groningen remained a significant producer, with expectations that it would continue to produce natural gas on a lesser scale for
decades to come.[58] In giving the company a major presence on the shore
of the North Sea, Groningen also facilitated Exxon's entry into a frontier
region that proved to be the center of the 1970s and early 1980s oil boom.

THE CHALLENGES OF THE NORTH SEA

The development of the Groningen field gave Jersey and Shell strong incentives to explore for natural gas and oil in the shallow waters of the North
Sea off the Netherlands. Even before the ratification of an international
treaty for the division of national rights to the North Sea, the companies

joined together and completed four dry holes before suspending operations in anticipation of the early rounds of leasing by Norway and the United Kingdom. After extensive negotiations under the oversight of the United Nations, the countries surrounding the North Sea finally agreed to a division of territorial rights in May 1964, opening the way for expanded oil and gas exploration. Some remained skeptical, but discoveries of natural gas and, later, oil came in the next six years. Then, with the sharp spike in oil prices after 1973, the rush was on. Norway was particularly fortunate in the North Sea boundary division. In the words of Fredrik Hagemann, the early director general of the Norwegian Petroleum Directorate, "had the border been drawn some tens of miles further east, Norway would have had no part in North Sea oil and gas resources at all."[59]

Oil companies faced harsh environmental challenges in this new frontier region. The *Oil and Gas Journal* summarized the situation in 1967: "Bad weather, for which the North Sea is notorious, affects every offshore operation: survey, diving, mooring, installation, pipelining, and communications, and bad weather can develop rapidly with little warning. Over the sea as a whole, there are fewer than 2% of calms throughout the year."[60] The offshore industry had made great strides in forecasting and tracking the paths of hurricanes in the Gulf of Mexico and in developing the capacity to evacuate platforms there with helicopters when a hurricane threatened, but the giant storms in the North Sea could deliver 100-foot waves and 120-mile-per-hour winds with little warning. The severity and unpredictability of these storms meant that workers had to stay on the platforms and ride them out, and this required much stronger platforms and equipment than those used in the Gulf. Boulders covered portions of the hard bottom of the North Sea, making equipment and procedures developed in the Gulf of Mexico ineffective for installing platforms and laying pipe. The combination of relatively deep water and very harsh conditions presented unprecedented problems.[61] Adding to the physical and technical challenges of the region was that of producer power, which became evident to Exxon by the mid-1970s. Once OPEC had shattered the assumptions of the post–World War II petroleum industry, non-OPEC producer nations successfully pushed for greater control of their oil and natural gas, too.

THE BRITISH SECTOR:
A JOINT VENTURE OF GIANTS

Although Jersey entered the North Sea in search of natural gas, it came to play significant roles in both oil and gas, in both the British and Norwegian sectors. The first five years of North Sea exploration found natural gas but no commercial oil. This changed dramatically in 1970 with the discovery by Phillips Petroleum of the large Ekofisk field in the Norwegian sector. Exploration quickly intensified, and a succession of major discoveries followed. Jersey/Exxon, partnered with Shell, emerged with a partial interest in several of the major finds in the UK sector, including the Brent, Cormorant, and Fulmar fields. It also held an interest in Norway's giant Statfjord field and full ownership of the Odin field. The company was active as well in numerous other fields and in several large pipeline projects. From the Esso Europe offices in London, the company managed this array of investments in the booming North Sea.

Royal Dutch Shell remained Exxon's partner in the British sector of the North Sea, creating what one high-level executive at Exxon called "clearly, the most important relationship that we had." But in spite of their shared success, the two had distinctively different corporate cultures—"as opposite as they could be," from Exxon's point of view.[62] In some ways, those differences reflected geography and history: Shell was European; Exxon, American. Shell had grown up within a tradition of strong central governments that at times believed in nationalization and direct governmental involvement in vital industries such as petroleum. Exxon reflected the American political reality of a weaker and more decentralized government that generally believed in free markets. Exxon veterans recalled that Shell was "looking for an easier path, a less controversial path, particularly in dealing with the governments—well, let's accede to what they want to do here and maintain good relations; it won't cost us as much down the road.... And of course our approach was ... [that] we deal with the principles of the issue. We're not going to make any trade-offs for the future; hold the ground."[63] To executives who came of age in Exxon's system of regional companies, which were run with firm direction from the top, Exxon seemed "structured and disciplined," while Shell appeared "not very well coordinated."[64] Their counterparts at Shell no doubt saw the flip side of the coin. Exxon's approach to business appeared rigid, with little room for flexible responses to such things as governmental policies. The financial discipline so valued at Exxon could be seen as an obsession with quantitative measures of profitability. The company's more centralized approach to management was foreign to those who had made their careers in the sprawling, decentralized global empire that was Royal Dutch Shell.

Differences in corporate culture affected specific problems encountered by the partners. In the North Sea, as at Groningen, Shell served as the operator. This meant that Exxon was a full partner financially, but a junior partner managerially. Exxon kept close tabs on the financial options open to the partnership. Its responses to the performance of Shell as operator often created tensions, especially on the delicate matter of cost overruns.

In the case of the Brent and Cormorant platforms, for example, Exxon's internal memos in 1976 complained that prior cost estimates had been understated, "with budget additions sought routinely by Shell, the Operator." Concerns that "the performance of certain U.K. contractors could lead to slippage in the completion" of two other platforms in the same region were heightened when "these schedule uncertainties were confirmed by the Operator in the annual program discussions with Esso." Worse yet, Shell's new cost estimates resulted in "Esso's share [of costs] being substantially increased," leading Exxon to push for "an intensive effort . . . to define a realistic cost and schedule" for future developments in those fields. This led "Esso, with Shell's participation," to lead "a probe into the construction situation," which produced "an independent assessment of the outlook for current projects." Such vigilance and insistence on financial discipline could be expected from Exxon on a project with an estimated cost to the company of \$2.6 billion.[65] Nevertheless, "the Operator" no doubt tired of such scrutiny, given that cost overruns and construction delays were the norm in the 1970s in the difficult conditions in the North Sea.[66]

Despite the fact that Shell was more or less a "home team" with strong ties to the UK, the Shell-Exxon joint venture encountered frequent problems with the British government. Although the UK and the major oil companies in the North Sea shared the general goal of rapid and profitable development of the region, they had quite different views about the

The Shell/Esso Brent Spar oil storage buoy in the North Sea, 1975.
ExxonMobil Historical Collection, di_06104.

best way to move forward. Britain's postwar economic decline colored its response to the opportunities presented by North Sea oil. A writer for the *Economist* suggested in 1975 that North Sea oil might be "God's last chance for Britain." The comment reflected a growing sense that "the lag of virility and adaptability of British business" was causing it to trail other nations in taking advantage of the windfall from North Sea oil. Particularly galling was the rapid progress being made by "tiny Norway" in asserting control over its oil industry and in attracting increasing investment in oil-related manufacturing and supply services.[67]

A Conservative government had pursued a market-based energy policy in the early years of development in the British sector, but the return of Labour Party control in 1974 brought a sharp shift toward a government-formulated industrial policy that sought to assert greater control over oil and to use it to help build up the nation's industries. The government sought from the oil industry higher taxes on North Sea oil, increased control through the creation of a national oil company, and cooperation with the industry in creating oil-related jobs in Britain. Self-sufficiency in oil was an important goal, and high gasoline prices encouraged consumers to conserve. The British government encouraged the use of natural gas to replace portions of coal and coal gas in the nation's energy mix.[68]

The first chapter of this history went relatively smoothly. Following the discovery of natural gas in 1965 in the British sector, the private companies involved agreed to work exclusively through the British Gas Council, the national gas company, to bring the gas reserves to British markets. This enabled the nation to join the natural gas revolution that had taken hold on the Continent with the development of the Groningen field.

Such alignment of public and private goals proved much harder to attain in the case of oil. Following the discovery of giant oil reserves in the UK sector in the early 1970s, the Tory government put in place a program of market-led development that used generous tax laws to encourage the private companies in the North Sea to bring the oil to market as quickly as possible. The tone of governmental policies changed dramatically in 1974, however, with the ascent of Labour, which favored public ownership of and control over substantial parts of the economy and saw the emerging oil industry as an obvious target for stricter governmental controls. The Labour program included both public direction and public ownership, and Exxon opposed it. At the heart of Labour's approach was partial nationalization of North Sea oil combined with a series of proposals aimed at capturing more of the benefits of North Sea industrialization for Britain. In practice, this meant that the major oil companies were expected to expand refining facilities in Britain and that the government would take steps to ensure that British fabrication yards captured more of the offshore platform and equipment business.

Conflict over governmental policy came in response to the growing tax rates imposed on the oil companies and the debates over public ownership. From 1970 to 1986, Exxon's internal discussions of the business climate in Europe returned again and again to complaints about the rising "take" of the North Sea governments. Exxon opposed increased taxes, citing its need for billions of dollars to build and operate platforms in the region. As the cost of operating in the North Sea skyrocketed, Exxon and other companies protested that additional tax hikes threatened their capacity to earn a fair profit in the region. In 1975, Exxon and other oil companies even threatened a sort of strike of capital, announcing plans to reduce further investments in light of proposals by both the British and Norwegian governments that would push the effective tax rate to roughly 75 percent of the companies' North Sea revenues.[69]

In Britain, such issues became intertwined in a decade-long political debate about the partial nationalization of North Sea oil. The British government came late to the issue, trailing Norway in both the timing and the design of a national oil company. Labour's approach in 1975 was for the government to negotiate agreements with the oil companies for the transfer to a newly created British National Oil Company (BNOC) of 51 percent of the participation in projects already underway in the British sector, including—in theory—such giant ongoing projects as BP's Forties field and Shell-Exxon's Brent field. Not surprisingly, Exxon strongly resisted.

Negotiations centered on a plan to have the government take 51 percent but then make it available for the company to repurchase through a complex "buy-back formula." This might "establish BNOC's title to half the oil" produced while preserving the ongoing operations of the companies. In this way, 51 percent participation by the government would become the accepted norm. The British energy secretary had previously made it clear that "companies who have thrown in the towel over participation will be given a favourable nod in the next round of licensing." The government also suggested that future favors would come to companies that made investments in oil-related industries in the UK. When Exxon and Shell resisted the government's initial entreaties, the British energy secretary summoned their CEOs to two meetings. He made clear to Cliff Garvin of Exxon and Michael Pocock of Shell that only companies agreeing in principle to 51 percent participation by BNOC would be allowed to bid on more blocks in future licensing rounds.[70]

Exxon did not approve, and it "noisily if politely bowed out of the sixth round" of licensing in the UK sector in 1978. Shell, Chevron, and Conoco participated in the bid round, but restricted their bids. Exxon pointedly refused the "request" to build additional refining capacity in Britain, standing by its resolve to avoid investments that seemed uneconomic.[71] In this case, Exxon's views prevailed. In the face of determined oil company resistance, the government dropped the idea of 51 percent participation for BNOC in existing projects. Although 51 percent participation by the national company was included in licensing requirements in the late

1970s, the provision quickly came under attack with the return in 1979 of a Conservative government under the leadership of Prime Minister Margaret Thatcher, who favored privatization. Thatcher curtailed BNOC's powers in 1979 and abolished it altogether in 1985, splitting off its business functions into Britoil. The episode reinforced Exxon's reputation as a determined, profit-driven company that would aggressively resist what it considered wrongheaded public policies.[72]

NORWAY: EXXON AND SOCIAL DEMOCRACY

In contrast to its experience in the UK, Exxon's relationship with the Norwegian government, while at times combative, was characterized by an orderly process more in keeping with the company's approach to business. Norway had a sturdy, diverse economy managed by a strong government with broad political support from its relatively small population of about four million. Rather than cashing in its oil wealth as quickly as possible, Norway proceeded slowly with oil-led development, seeking to minimize the potential long-term costs of economic dependence on petroleum. The Norwegian government recognized that it needed the international oil companies in the early stages in developing its oil, but it plotted a course toward "Norwegianization." Exxon and others might complain about such "oil nationalism," but it was a predictable approach that reflected a political consensus in Norway, which had a tradition of governmental involvement in vital sectors of the economy.

Viewed from afar, the path chosen by the Norwegian government appeared more threatening to the oil companies than that taken by Great Britain, but a distinct difference in tone and process made the Norwegian approach easier for Exxon to accept. The rules were known, and the government generally had the power, the national support, and the skilled public officials to enforce them consistently. In this sense, Exxon faced a government whose commitment to efficiency and profits for the nation resembled, in spirit, Exxon's approach to business.

In a social democracy defined by its large public expenditures and comprehensive social safety net, high taxes were a fact of life. In its 1979 planning report to the Exxon Corporation in 1979, Esso Europe acknowledged that "we expect increased national and international government surveillance and involvement in our business. . . . In all countries where we have major producing interests there will continue to be serious risks of increases in government take." The company noted that its responses had to be "tailored to the circumstances in each country." Its strategy for Norway was to stay the course, since the government would "continue at a carefully controlled pace in awarding new licenses." Despite the fact that "licensing terms are expected to require increased Norwegian, and particularly Statoil [the Norwegian national oil company], participation, Norwegian company operatorships, and industrial cooperation," Esso Europe planned to "participate to the maximum extent possible in new license awards." By 1980, Exxon was second only to Statoil in the number of licenses held in Norwegian waters. This fact reflected both the extraordinary opportunities in the Norwegian sector of the North Sea and the growing sense within the company that future returns in Norway and the North Sea in general "should be adequate for an efficient, disciplined, technically advanced company."[73]

Instead of requesting that companies build additional refining capacity or train local workers, as the British had done, the Norwegians required them to do so in licenses. The government gave the companies discretion within clear guidelines to meet such requirements. One Exxon executive remembers the reality of bidding in Norway: "They wanted to know, what can you give us training wise. And so every time we bid on a block, one heavy, heavy part . . . was sending Norwegians to our research lab and even sending our Norwegians to MIT or Princeton or some school where they wanted that kind of technology." In 1979, for example, when Exxon discussed its plans to participate in a Norwegian licensing round, it noted that bidding would require the company to submit a "list of potential research and development projects totaling $3.5 million to be undertaken in Norway" in cooperation with Norwegian companies. Also included was a stipulation that the company "would identify opportunities for their future involvement in business activities in Norway and would pursue such opportunities as are judged consistent with [Exxon's] . . . long range business objectives in Norway, are economically attractive as separate business ventures and would permit financial involvement by a Norwegian company." In Britain, Exxon resisted the government's entreaties to build refineries. In contrast, it responded to Norway's proposal by asking for "immediate and concentrated efforts" from within the corporation to identify the best possible projects or ventures to meet this requirement.[74]

Norway's success in "absorbing" oil-led industrialization also reflected the existing strengths of its economy and its educational system. In Norway, Exxon found a high-quality workforce that was "very technically astute" and could be "gotten up the curve extremely fast."[75] By slowing the pace of oil development, the Norwegian government also had a measure of success in preventing the extreme booms and busts in oil that hampered so many new oil producers after the return of oil-price swings in the early 1970s. By the mid-1970s, Norwegian companies had established a growing presence in oil-related construction businesses for rigs, specialized ships, and innovative concrete production platforms, enjoying success that the *Economist* characterized as "a record to shame every British shipbuilder."[76]

Despite reluctance voiced within the company, Exxon also agreed to the direct involvement of the Norwegian government in basic decisions about the construction and operation of projects. When the government directed that a major pipeline come ashore in Norway instead of other, more economical locations, Esso Europe backed the recommendation in its proposal to the corporate management committee in 1981: "While the pipeline route including the landfall in Norway is far from ideal, it was dictated by the Norwegian government so that natural gas liquids would be available for future petrochemical production." Participation in the venture, according to the author, would help the company secure present and future gas reserves in the Norwegian sector while also maintaining "good relationships with Statoil and the Norwegian government by contributing to the realization of energy related projects meeting the country's objectives and aspirations."[77] The year before, Esso Europe had explained to the corporate management committee that "development of some discoveries in Norway may be arbitrarily delayed so that the government production and activity level targets will not be exceeded."[78] Amid unpredictable cost increases and daunting technical and financial risks around the world, a steady approach to development, largely unaffected by political partisanship, must have been welcomed by even those oil companies that objected to aspects of the government's oil policies.

The sturdy institutional framework created to manage the Norwegian oil industry was one important reason for the stability and relative success of Norway's North Sea policies. Its management was nationalistic, yet evenhanded enough to ensure the continued involvement of the international oil companies. Once again, the key was the tone as well as the content of policy. The Norwegian government took a consistent, long-term approach to oil policy within strong institutions somewhat insulated from the pressures of day-to-day politics. At the forefront of these institutions stood the Norwegian Petroleum Directorate (NPD), created in 1972 to oversee the development of Norway's North Sea petroleum industry. The first director-general of the NPD, Fredrik Hagemann, acknowledged that in the early years, "There is no doubt but that we were totally dependent on the foreign oil companies to get the ball rolling in the North Sea." Initially, "American companies," including Exxon, the holder of production license number 001, "dominated the picture," but the Norwegian government steadily pursued the goal of building a strong industry under governmental control with growing Norwegian participation. The directorate grew stronger over time, becoming deeply involved in all aspects of North Sea development in its sector. Hagemann recalled that "right from the start, it [the NPD] focused on high standards," attracting many of the best professionals in the oil industry and successfully retaining outstanding experts for extended periods of time. The NPD remains directly involved in such activities as collecting and selling seismic-survey data and collecting, by law, 25 percent of core samples taken from the seabed.[79]

Statoil, the primary national oil company in Norway, originally served as the government's agent in the oil fields. After its creation in 1972, Statoil moved early and decisively into the oil fields in the Norwegian sector, avoiding the uncertainty and controversy that later haunted the BNOC in the British sector. Its participation in all fields was simply part of the deal that international oil companies made with Norway for the right to produce oil. Though initially more an observer than a participant, Statoil owned, by law, a substantial share in most of the major oil fields in Norway. In the 1973 agreement between the government and private companies to develop the giant Statfjord field, the government established the clear precedent that Statoil would have a 50 percent share in the field, the chance to participate in production, the right to take over as operator of the field in ten years, and the promise that the private companies would assist Statoil in developing "expertise and capacity."[80] Under such agreements, Statoil had a ringside seat in the 1970s at two of the most expensive and technically demanding projects in the world: the Statfjord and Beryl fields. As it observed, Statoil learned much from the major international oil companies.

Highly motivated by personal and national ambitions, Statoil's technical and managerial personnel learned quickly, and the company steadily moved toward the commercialization of fields in the 1980s and 1990s, and then toward partial privatization and international activities in the twenty-first century. In the mid-1980s, the Norwegian government responded to fears that Statoil's success and the growing importance of oil in Norway's economy could give the company too much political power. Norway moved to correct this situation and to push Statoil back toward a more strictly commercial posture by creating the State's Direct Financial Interest (SDFI), which reclaimed a portion of Statoil's holdings for direct ownership by the state, giving the Norwegian government a partial stake in the nation's North Sea oil fields and direct participation in both the profits and the risks of their operations.

Exxon and the other international oil companies had no choice but to learn to work within Norway's legal and institutional framework. Statoil's substantial holdings in Norwegian oil fields gradually funded a larger role for the company in local exploration and production, and it quickly grew into both a sturdy partner with, and a formidable competitor of, the international oil companies. As time passed, Exxon began to develop a growing respect for the Norwegian company. Howard Kauffmann, who worked in Norway before becoming the president of Exxon Corporation under Cliff Garvin, described the company's association with Statoil: "They understood the need to have good technology, reputable people conducting those operations, so it was easy to get along.... Now, we did not give away proprietary information, but we did cooperate with them. We tried to get their engineers into schools that would be beneficial for them and to attend industry associations that would be useful to them."[81] In 1976, the managing director of Statoil acknowledged the value of that collaboration: "We know from experience that Exxon is one of the companies with very important technological know-how, especially in deepwater drilling. We've had a close relationship with Esso at Statfjord and in other areas.

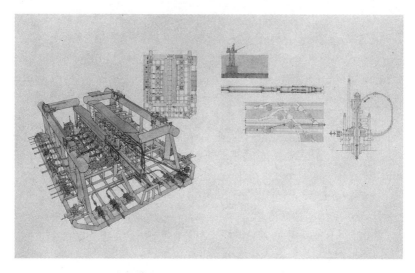

*Schematic of Underwater Manifold Center (UMC) for Cormorant Field
in the North Sea, 1992. ExxonMobil Historical Collection, di_06252.*

We feel there is every reason to continue to cooperate with them."[82] Given
the technological challenges of the North Sea, both Statoil and the Norwegian government well understood the benefits of Exxon's continued
participation.

In addition to Statfjord, which straddled the boundary between Norway and the UK, the Brent and Cormorant fields, located near Statfjord but in the British sector, were the company's largest producers in
the North Sea in this era. Both Brent and Statfjord had recoverable oil
reserves of about two billion barrels. At Brent, as in all of Exxon's projects
off Great Britain, it was an equal partner with Royal Dutch Shell, which
served as operator. At Statfjord, Exxon held a relatively small share (8.55
percent) of a massive operation with Statoil (44.34 percent) and seven
other oil companies, including Mobil (the operator, with 12.82 percent),
Conoco, Shell, Chevron, BP, and Enterprise Oil.[83] Both Brent and Statfjord had nearby satellite fields. The most prominent of these were the
Cormorant fields, which were economically viable because they could
use much of the infrastructure created for Brent. Lower in the British
sector of the North Sea was the 550-million-barrel Fulmar field, which
Exxon and Shell jointly developed using traditional steel platforms. These

platforms became important points for the collection of natural gas for shipment to St. Fergus, Scotland. Odin was a relatively small gas field off southern Norway; Exxon held a 100 percent interest at Odin, but it experienced considerable difficulties in developing the field. The company was involved in many other fields in the North Sea (see map 3.1), but these five shaped its early experience in the region, collectively contributing more than 400,000 barrels of oil equivalent each day to the company's total production in 1985.[84]

THE COLD NORTH SEA: A HOTHOUSE OF TECHNOLOGICAL CHANGES

The head of the Production Department for Esso Europe in 1975 admitted, "Our experience in the Gulf of Mexico and other offshore areas didn't really prepare us for the North Sea."[85] Again and again, equipment, procedures, and platforms originally designed for the Gulf of Mexico had to be significantly modified to withstand the North Sea's harsh conditions. Exxon discovered this on one of its first platforms at Odin. An engineer detailed some of the difficulties: "The North Sea's wave heights . . . are the highest in the world; they're over a hundred feet sometimes, which is amazing. They found that the weldings weren't holding and . . . we had to shut down production and spend a bunch of money to redo all the damn welds on the thing."[86] In addition to unprecedented wave stress on offshore structures, the region's unpredictable weather did not allow the luxury of an orderly, timely evacuation in the event of sudden storms.

Flush with cash from high oil prices from 1973 until the mid-1980s bust, and spurred to move fast by surging inflation, oil companies used the North Sea as a laboratory for technological innovation, at times justifying expensive improvements as investments in the long-term knowledge needed for the conquest of deeper waters in general. In the 1970s and early 1980s, the demanding north-central North Sea, which contained the Brent, Cormorant, and Statfjord fields, witnessed an extraordinary transformation in platform design. Different companies followed starkly different approaches for the development of fields in roughly the same area and conditions. As each sought the most efficient platform for use in this tough section of the North Sea, the companies collectively advanced the technological frontier for deepwater oil production around the world.

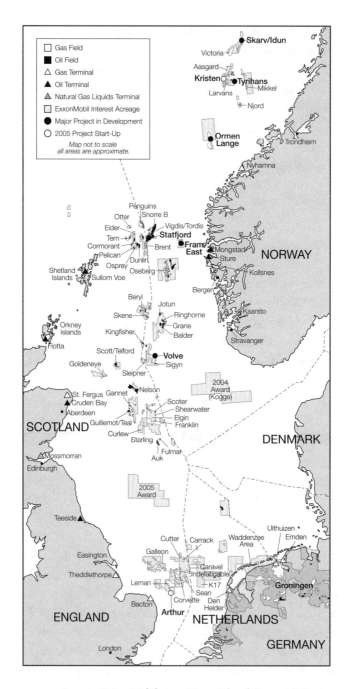

MAP 3.1: Source: *ExxonMobil*, 2005 Financial and Operating Review, *p. 47, ExxonMobil Historical Collection.*

In a classic *Scientific American* article of 1982, Fred S. Ellers captured the excitement of the era with his subtitle: "Creating structures that can withstand 100-foot waves in waters 600 feet deep calls for audacious engineering and heavy capital expense."[87] The article compares four major offshore projects being built at the same time but using quite different designs for their production platforms. In the British sector at the Magnus field, BP oversaw the fabrication and installation of what amounted to a "super" Gulf of Mexico steel jacket. Across the way in the Statfjord and Brent fields appeared concrete deepwater (Condeep) structures, platforms made of concrete and fabricated and assembled in the protected fjords of Norway. In the smaller Hutton field (UK), Conoco had embarked on the first installation of what promised to be a pathbreaking technology, the tension-leg platform. At the same time in the Gulf of Mexico, Exxon focused on the development of a "guyed tower" designed for wells deeper than 1,000 feet. These four projects were not the only innovations of the era. Exxon, for example, was designing two platforms for the Santa Ynez Unit that would be taller and more advanced than Hondo. Never before had the industry seen such a burst of advances in platform design. Big projects backed by a wave of creative thinking and extraordinary research and development stretched the bounds of existing technology.

Ellers concluded that "scores of technological advances" at the time meant that "the rate of change has far exceeded anything previously known in the petroleum industry."[88] Companies had to test the limits of traditional technology while also risking the use of new, unproven methods. Exxon and the other major companies in the North Sea remained at the forefront of this effort. By the late 1970s, it was clear to all that the steel-jacket platform, the workhorse of the past, was being superseded. In the North Sea, the combination of deeper water and stronger wave forces required longer, heavier legs and massive platforms that could not be easily transported and installed at production sites with existing barges and cranes. At Hondo, Exxon had found a creative response to the problem of installing giant metal platforms by building the platform in two sections and then assembling them on-site in the ocean. For the Magnus field, BP designed a platform that floated on its side by using two very large corner legs equipped with buoyancy compartments. At the installation site, the legs were flooded, the platform was lowered, and piles were driven

The Brent offshore platform in a rough North Sea storm, 1994.
ExxonMobil Historical Collection, di_06244.

to attach it to the seafloor. Then, as had been the custom in the Gulf of Mexico, the topsides, or decks, were lifted into place and installed on top of the platform—no easy task in 611 feet of water in the stormy North Sea. The Magnus platform eventually came in at a hefty cost estimated at $2.6 billion, which worked out to almost $22,000 for each barrel of daily production capacity.[89]

In comparison, Statfjord B, a Condeep structure placed in 471 feet of water, cost "only" $1.8 billion, or $12,000 per barrel a day of production capacity. Such numbers demanded the attention of any company committed to remaining in the North Sea. These recently developed concrete-gravity structures marked a radical departure in platform design. Giant, steel-reinforced concrete storage tanks capable of holding as much as one million barrels of oil served as the base. Towers reached up from the base as far as needed for the water depth where the platform would be sited, and the very large topsides could be installed on top of the concrete towers while the structure remained protected in a fjord. This meant that the entire structure could be towed out upright, avoiding the stress of launching very long metal platforms. This design also eliminated the demanding, expensive process of driving piles through the legs of metal platforms and into the seafloor. Instead, the extremely heavy concrete platforms could be lowered to the ocean floor by flooding and remain fixed by their weight. Statfjord B, for example, contained almost 900,000 tons of concrete and steel reinforcement. Although relatively expensive to construct because of this bulk, the concrete platforms often more than made up the cost difference with other types of platforms in installation cost savings. As a bonus, the tow-outs were among the most spectacular events in the oil industry, with spectators stunned by the sight of such giant structures moving out to sea.[90]

Norway led the way in designing, constructing, and installing concrete platforms, which became the norm throughout the Norwegian sector of the North Sea. In the nearby British sector, by contrast, the Brent platforms were both steel and concrete. This difference reflected in part the oil companies' desire to please the Norwegian government by using Norwegian contractors. But concrete platforms were also attractive because of the high-quality standards of skilled Norwegian contractors and the abundance of deep and protected water for construction provided by the Norwegian fjords.

Because of the difficulty of adapting this new design to other parts of the world and the clear leadership of Norwegian contractors, Exxon had only a small part in the design and construction of concrete structures in the North Sea, and the company was never a big booster of such platforms. One of its executives in the North Sea recalled that Exxon "led Shell away from that [concrete] in the choice of platform type for the North Cormorant field near Brent."[91] When it had the power to choose, Exxon chose modified versions of the steel jackets it had grown up with in the Gulf of Mexico and off California. Its preference could be at least partly explained by the company's early experiences with concrete platforms at Brent B and Statfjord B, which were plagued by extremely high cost overruns and delays.[92] Ultimately, concrete-gravity platforms, while an important part of North Sea infrastructure, had less lasting impact on the global offshore industry than other innovations that emerged from the region, notably semisubmersible designs for larger and larger drillships, cranes, and barges.

The sheer bulk of both concrete and steel platforms made them unsuitable for use in water depths beyond 1,000 to 1,500 feet. Any structure placed in the ocean "resonates" or sways in response to the rhythmic impact of waves, and as steel templates become taller, proportionately more steel is needed to ensure that they remain stiff enough to avoid swaying at the same rate as the waves. Exxon Production Research and Exxon Research and Engineering looked for long-term solutions to this problem, which became pressing as water depths reached 1,300 feet or so. By the late 1970s and early 1980s, plans went forward in the North Sea for the installation of a more "compliant" structure, a tension-leg structure consisting of a semisubmersible platform tethered to the ocean floor with cables. The first and most publicized such structure, Conoco's Hutton platform, was installed in the British North Sea in 485 feet of water in 1984 at a cost of $1.3 billion, or $11,800 cost per barrel a day of initial production. That depth could have been reached by a traditional steel-jacket platform, but Conoco's management, knowing that platforms for deeper water soon would be needed, decided that the Hutton field was deep enough to test the promising concept of a tension-leg platform.[93]

THE LENA GUYED TOWER

With the rest of the offshore industry, Exxon closely followed the progress of tension-leg structures, a much-heralded innovation. Exxon's interest was particularly strong because it was moving ahead at the time with its own much-acclaimed compliant-tower design, a guyed tower for the Lena field in the Gulf of Mexico off the coast of Louisiana. Exxon engineers had been working on possible platforms for water depths between 1,000 and 2,000 feet since the early 1970s. They had spent considerable time and effort testing and then constructing a platform design that featured a long, narrow, relatively light steel template that, unlike traditional platforms, did not widen at its base. Unlike the tension-leg platform, the guyed tower was attached directly to the ocean floor with an innovative piling system that allowed it to remain flexible; long steel cables, stretching from underwater off the legs of the platform out to the seafloor, provided additional stability. One observer noted that, from underwater, the guyed tower resembled "a giant maypole." This new design had few precedents, and it required creative thinking and innovative technology

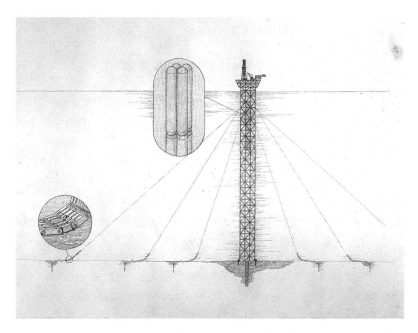

A schematic of the guyed tower in the Gulf of Mexico, 1980.
ExxonMobil Historical Collection, di_06251.

to move from the drawing board to a site in 1,000 feet of water some sixty-five miles southeast of Grand Isle, Louisiana, in the Gulf of Mexico.

The company's research groups—Exxon Production Research Company and Exxon Research and Engineering—worked together on what one longtime offshore engineer from Brown & Root called "a once-in-a lifetime or career project."[94] From the start, the guyed tower was viewed as both a long-term research project designed to generate new technology for use in deeper water and a practical effort to build a platform for the cost-effective development of a relatively small oil field. In its initial planning for the Lena field in 1979, Exxon USA had estimated that a conventional platform and the guyed tower design would cost roughly the same and decided to go with the more predictable conventional design. After discussion with then-president Howard Kauffmann "and others in New York," however, Exxon USA "shifted to the guyed wire concept."[95] Rising costs after design work had begun on the guyed tower later forced a reevaluation in 1981, but the company decided to continue its experiment with the new design. As with any new approach, there was an element of learning by doing. Not surprisingly, costs mounted as the company learned more about the part of the design that had never before been tried: the guyed wires and their installation.

Lena generated much excitement in the offshore fraternity. To the eye of the engineer, it was a beautiful structure, elegant in appearance and pathbreaking in technical innovations. As those working on it loved to remind any who would listen, at 1,300 feet in total length, it was then the tallest single-piece marine structure ever built—fifty feet taller than the Empire State Building. This was an epoch-defining statistic for an offshore industry that traditionally sought to convey the mammoth size of its platforms by setting a scale drawing down among the familiar skylines of major cities. Its size alone stretched to the breaking point all received wisdom about fabrication and installation. The list of major innovations and breakthroughs in scale required to build and install the structure included the first dynamically positioned derrick barge, which was used to help set the guyed wires; new designs for compliant underwater pilings; the components needed for the guyed wires; new designs for tower buoyancy and dynamic responses; and innovative methods for fabricating and launching the giant structure. Lena moved the industry forward in the development of deepwater technology needed to go beyond the limits of standard steel-jacket platforms to new and more flexible approaches needed for deeper water.

After twelve years of research and development, the actual launch and installation of Lena in 1983 was a dramatic and nerve-racking event. The tower and the equipment needed for its installation floated out into the ocean, a check worth hundreds of millions waiting to be cashed— or canceled. The mammoth barge built to transport Lena had support beams extending 500 feet out over one end and 300 feet over the other. Space-age, remote-controlled clamps secured Lena to the barge during the tow-out. To relieve the stress that would have been placed on such a long, single-piece structure during a "launch" off the front of a barge, which was the traditional method of launching steel structures, a side launch was used for the first time for a major platform. In essence, this required creating a system that allowed Lena to slide over the side of the barge into the ocean, where it could then be maneuvered into place over the site, tipped upright, lowered, and fastened to the seafloor with piles. Tether lines composed of cables five inches in diameter and 1,800 feet long extended out to 200-ton weights arrayed in a circle on the ocean floor around the platform—part of a complex technical system designed to keep Lena in place while allowing it to sway when needed.

The moment of truth was the side launch. Dean Guttormson, who had worked for Exxon in the Gulf of Mexico for years, vividly remembers it:

> It was a remarkable day in that the Gulf of Mexico was flat . . . just like a tabletop. . . . There were all manner of pieces of equipment out there—tugboats and launch barges and headquarters barges and helicopters. . . . At the appointed hour at a signal to be given, they were going to press the button, blow those explosive bolts, and Lena would slide off and float that way and then they would upend it and tow it to the site. . . . If it came off in any way sort of cockeyed, because it was so long and so slender, it could flex and it could have been trashed.

The possibility of disastrous failure put an edge on the festivities:

> [After the signal to launch] everybody's mentally [started to count]: one, two, three, four, five, six, seven, eight, nine, ten, eleven, twelve, thirteen—and wondering what had happened. It turned out it was nothing serious, but there was some electrical issue with the explosive bolt business, which they got resolved quickly. There was some scurrying around . . . but pretty soon, boom. Off it went. . . . And the rest is history, our first foray into a thousand feet of water.

To those who had helped the company move steadily over decades into deeper waters, this was a magical moment—the realization of the once-distant goal of oil production in 1,000 feet of water. The technical advances made in the Lena project filled the pages of the industry's annual Offshore Technology Conference proceedings in Houston, and discussion of the platform consumed one full-day session at its meeting in 1984, when Lena earned industry-wide recognition with the Distinguished Achievement Award of the Offshore Technology Conference, an award given to one company each year and sponsored by eleven major professional engineering societies.[96] Guttormson found it a time to reflect on the evolution of the "absolutely incredible technology" that had propelled the offshore industry into deeper waters.[97]

Guyed tower technology took the company past the thousand-foot mark, but only once. A victim of technological leaps in other directions, Lena's design was never again used. Exxon Production Research concluded that guyed towers were "less cost effective" than existing alternatives, a fact supported by Ellers's conclusion that its final cost of $800 million gave it a cost per barrel a day of production of $32,000. EPR argued that the guy wires were equivalent to "training wheels" that had to be removed to allow compliant structures to reach greater depths. The tension-leg platform had removed those training wheels, and ongoing advances in the size and strength of the semisubmersible platform as well as the cables used by tension-leg platforms foretold a promising future for this innovative design.

SUBSEA PRODUCTION

But even as work went forward on the tension-leg platform and other deepwater-platform designs, Exxon helped develop a key technology that took the entire discussion to new depths: subsea production systems. Moving various production functions from the deck of the platform to the ocean floor could change the game for offshore operations in very deep water. From the 1950s forward, the offshore industry had, in isolated cases, made use of submerged production facilities to produce oil from small and isolated fields. In the 1970s and 1980s, Exxon helped make this approach much more practical by taking the lead in the development of larger and more sophisticated submerged production systems. Such systems might substantially reduce the costs associated with building the massive, billion-dollar platforms being used in such areas as the North Sea. They might also facilitate the economic development of smaller or more isolated fields, as well as the development of distant portions of existing large fields. In combination with the use of floating production facilities, directional drilling, and other evolving technologies, submerged production systems seemed a good bet to help move the industry into still deeper waters.[98]

For this promise to become a commercial reality, however, an array of technical issues had to be resolved. Recognizing both the potential and the challenge of underwater production, Exxon and Shell agreed in 1974 to create the Joint Underwater Development Team to examine a range of options for subsea production facilities. Exxon and Shell brought a formidable collection of offshore experience, talent, and resources to the task. Both companies were pioneers in underwater processes, Shell in the Far East and Exxon in the Gulf of Mexico. From 1974 until the installation of the partnership's first major subsea project in the North Sea, the project team grew to more than one hundred strong, with experts from both companies drawn from around the world. This team moved steadily from the evaluation of different approaches to the application of the best of those to the development of the Central Cormorant area in the North Sea in 1982.[99]

Some of the Exxon members of the Joint Underwater Development Team had worked previously on an ambitious Exxon study of its submerged production system (SPS) in the Gulf of Mexico. In 1968, after it leased tracts off Southern California in waters up to 1,800 feet deep, the company began to examine options for producing oil at such depths and beyond without large platforms. Initial evaluations of subsea production began in a flooded pit near Ventura, California, before moving to the Gulf of Mexico in 1974. For the next five years, Exxon tested its initial SPS design using a manifold that controlled three wells drilled through its base, with oil delivered through pipelines to a nearby platform.

The company stood at the center of an impressive network of expertise. It drew talent and resources for this project from Exxon USA, Exxon Production Research, and other parts of the company. It benefited also from the cooperation of equipment manufacturers that would be building the first generation of subsea machinery. Tests covered the major systems needed to produce oil on the seafloor, including robotic devices controlled from the surface to help install and maintain subsea equipment.[100] The SPS was to be made as dependable and durable as possible while minimizing the use of divers. Ultimately, the system needed to be adaptable to even greater depths.

As with much of the high-tech equipment developed in the offshore industry, the SPS would do its work out of sight—largely unseen by and unknown to the general public. The basic design consisted of a template that contained and protected all the equipment needed to control production in an oil field, including compartments for wellheads, valves for regulating flow, pipeline connections, and the risers in which oil and gas would travel from the SPS to the surface. The manifolds that housed much of this equipment on the ocean floor grew into giant, sophisticated pieces of equipment. The SPS included numerous technically demanding subsystems. Each required the work of teams of specialists to develop, and Exxon and its collaborators regularly reported on the progress of its tests to professional organizations such as the Society of Petroleum Engineers and at the annual Offshore Technology Conference.

In 1976, the project team delivered to the conference a series of papers, coauthored by companies like Global Marine and General Electric, on a variety of technological "subsystems" being developed as parts of the SPS, including the robotic-maintenance system, the deepwater pipeline-connection system, and its marine production risers. On these and other aspects of the SPS, clusters of innovations were needed to move the subsea production equipment toward commercial application. The industry as a whole acknowledged the achievements of the network of experts Exxon had assembled for the SPS tests with the conference's Distinguished Achievement Award for 1980.[101]

Tests of full-scale equipment out in the rough waters of the North Sea were, of course, more demanding than tests in a controlled environment. The installation and operation of the underwater manifold center (UMC), an advanced version of Exxon's SPS, in the Central Cormorant area in 1982 marked a significant evolution of subsea equipment. Reports from Esso Europe to Exxon Corporation in 1981 summarized the thinking of the Exxon-Shell joint venture in choosing to develop this area with a subsea system instead of a fixed platform. Although a platform could be expected to recover a slightly higher percentage of the oil in the field, the subsea system would cost much less than even a small satellite platform. In addition, the platform would take longer to fabricate and install, and it would be taxed at a higher rate under prevailing British tax law. Much like the guyed tower at Lena, the proposed subsea system at Central Cormorant was an important element of an ongoing process of technological change. The Exxon-Shell partnership had made a significant, long-term commitment to subsea production as an important tool for the development of future projects in deeper waters.

The installation of the UMC at Central Cormorant went smoothly. A standard barge, tugboats, and a derrick barge transported and installed the structure, which stood about four stories high, measured about fifty yards long, and weighed far less than a platform. Designed for a field with an estimated 100 million barrels of recoverable oil—a size that made it a marginal candidate for development with a fixed platform—the manifold could operate satellite wells away from the template in addition to the wells drilled through the template. The manifold at Central Cormorant had been designed for 500 feet of water, but it could be modified for up to 2,000 feet. This was a project with an eye to the future.[102]

The development of the subsea production system illustrated the "technological loops" that took innovations in one offshore region, adapted them to others, and then returned them with improvements to the original region. From Central Cormorant, the ever-improving UMC system gradually made its way around the world. In the decade after its initial installation in 1982, for example, Exxon partnered with the Norwegian company Saga to develop the massive Snorre field in the Norwegian North Sea using both an advanced tension-leg platform and the UMC. This approach combined the stability and flexibility of the tethered, semisubmersible platform with the cost-saving advantages of the subsea system.[103] In later years, subsea systems encouraged the growth of complementary technologies such as sophisticated mooring devices and floating production, storage, and offloading systems. Indeed, the subsea production system was a central piece of the technological puzzle that redefined "deep water" after the 1980s, allowing production from depths that sound more like something out of science fiction than the latest chapter in an industry's ongoing quest for oil.

Other choices shaped by the North Sea also moved around the world in the years after the boom. In the 1990s, relying "heavily on experience in the North Sea," Exxon took advantage of "an otherwise idle casting basin built originally to make concrete sections for the now-completed Sydney Harbor Tunnel" to fabricate two concrete platforms, West Tuna and Bream B, which it installed in 200 feet of water in the Bass Strait of Australia.[104] Later, Mobil Oil applied its North Sea experience to the installation of a concrete-based platform at the Hibernia field in the icy waters off Newfoundland. Exxon also continued to develop advanced versions of fixed steel-jacket platforms in its work off California near the Hondo platform. In the 1980s and 1990s, the company installed two new platforms, Harmony and Heritage, both in more than 1,000 feet of water. Each was built in one piece in Korea and shipped across the Pacific Ocean on a newly constructed giant ocean barge for installation as a single unit. The platforms marked departures in fabrication and installation technology while also taking advantage of the growing globalization of the entire offshore industry. Bringing together its platform and subsea-systems research, Exxon connected the new platforms to onshore treatment and storage facilities at Las Flores Canyon with some of the first robotically installed, large-diameter pipelines. Those projects and many others to develop offshore fields around the world made use of technology developed in the North Sea before the oil-price bust, and many of the innovations passed through the research labs of Exxon on their way into general use.[105]

The tools available for the offshore industry certainly did not come only from Exxon or the company's partnership with Shell. Thousands of people in hundreds of companies contributed to the clusters of innovation required to move the industry farther offshore. As these clusters evolved, the trading of notes on new innovations became more and more global. Although national governments remained in control of leasing and taxes and terms of participation, neither technology nor the management of offshore operations was constrained by national boundaries. Engineers from around the world studied similarities and differences of conditions in different fields and the technical processes most appropriate for developing new fields. Technical groups such as Shell-Exxon's Joint Underwater Development Team brought together a fraternity of experts from the global operations of major oil companies, major manufacturers of offshore equipment, and offshore service companies. The growing global nexus of offshore technology could be a source of strength for industry leaders such as Exxon, which provided a gateway into the most advanced technical systems for those who needed access to that knowledge and experience.

As early as the 1980s, Exxon at times assembled management teams from other projects around the world to work on demanding offshore projects. The resulting teams could bring to bear diverse skills in installing complex and evolving technical systems while containing the kinds of cost overruns that had plagued North Sea development. More efficient management of giant projects improved financial results, and the growing cost of large projects encouraged Exxon to take greater advantage of its collective experience around the world in project management. The seeds of this change were planted in the years between 1973 and 1986, but the harvest came afterward, in the years of flat and relatively low oil prices.

———————————

A survey of the company's top ten fields in 1985 (measured by Exxon's interest in total daily output) puts in perspective the results of its quest for non-OPEC oil in the years after 1973. Prudhoe Bay, the company's top producer, is the only U.S. field on the list. Hondo, the largest producer for Exxon in the lower forty-eight states, is not on the list, although production later increased sharply with the addition of two more platforms. Groningen is number two, and the top two fields account for more than half the production on the list. All the company's hard work in the North Sea after 1970 pushed five new fields into the top ten spots, but just two of these, Brent and nearby Cormorant, supplied the bulk of production from the region. Because of its small share in the giant Statfjord field, Exxon's production from the Norwegian sector remained quite low in 1985 but increased substantially thereafter. Also showing up on the list were the early fruits of the company's operations in Australia's Bass Strait. Three fields there had a collective production approaching 150,000 barrels of oil equivalent in 1985, and this figure grew in the next decade. This list testifies to impressive advances by Exxon in several regions where it had little production before 1973, notably Alaska, the North Sea, and Australia. In these frontier areas, new Arctic and offshore technologies cleared the way for the discovery and development of oil fields that lay beyond the industry's reach in the early 1970s. One other fact of life shown on the list is the long lag time from discovery to production.

The company had devoted much of its technical and financial resources from 1973 to 1985 to the search for major new sources of non-OPEC oil.

Yet its annual reports paint a discouraging portrait in oil. In 1985, the company produced only 1.8 million barrels a day, which was about 25 percent of its production in 1973. Despite significant progress in offshore technology, and a variety of discoveries, it had replaced only a small portion of the oil lost through the nationalizations of the early 1970s. In light of the company's limited success in replacing the enormous losses of OPEC oil, one increasingly attractive alternative seemed to be to look outside oil for new sources of energy and new opportunities for investments.

CHAPTER FOUR

OUT OF OIL

DIVERSIFICATION AND DIVESTMENT IN AN ERA OF OIL PRICE SWINGS

L ooking back from the perspective of more than thirty years, Cliff Garvin identified a key assumption of the years from 1973 to 1982, when oil prices rose by a factor of ten: "We went through about a ten-year period there where we seemed to be working under the conviction that there would not be enough opportunities in the oil and gas business for the amount of cash flow that we were going to generate, and therefore we'd be remiss in our responsibilities as management not to look at other things."[1] Thinking that the oil industry might well be dying a slow death, Exxon and most major oil companies moved out of oil in search of opportunities for long-term growth. Exxon spent considerable capital, management effort, and research dollars on diversification into industries completely outside energy, as well as into energy industries other than oil and gas. But when oil prices sharply declined and economic conditions deteriorated in the 1980s, Exxon divested itself of most of its recently acquired businesses and refocused its attentions on its core businesses: oil, natural gas, and chemicals. Exxon had not neglected oil and gas during the era of diversification, but it emerged at the end with a sharper focus on its core businesses and a renewed sense that oil and gas would remain its priority well into the future.[2]

The rise and fall of diversification at Exxon raised questions about the capacity of the company to plan effectively when it could not predict oil prices in the near or long term. After a tumultuous decade marked by the enthusiastic announcement of diversification, followed at times by embarrassing announcements of divestments in the mid-1980s, fundamental questions arose from Exxon's ventures outside of oil. What were the company's core competencies and how could they be most effectively put to use? Could its capital, people, and technology be adapted to build new strengths outside energy or to become competitive in developing "alternative energies"? In short, was Exxon to remain an oil and gas company, or did it have the capacity and the incentive to evolve into an energy company or even a conglomerate with a variety of enterprises in and out of energy? The company had to answer those questions in the mid-1980s. In so doing, Exxon laid the foundation for its strategy for decades into the future.

CHEMICALS: THE LONG ROAD TO SUCCESS

Underneath all the stops and starts at Exxon as it moved into and out of numerous businesses in the 1970s remained one constant: the growth of chemicals into an important source of strength for the company. Because chemicals had been a byproduct of the company's refining operations since the World War I era, they were often overlooked in the debates about diversification. Looking back at this era, one longtime executive in chemicals observed, "One diversification worked out brilliantly . . . the chemical business." Lee Raymond later referred to many of the efforts to diversify in the 1970s as "excursions," but the move into chemicals was a journey down a long road to success.[3]

Refiners recognized the ties between chemicals and the oil industry in the early twentieth century. They came to realize that the "waste gases" left over from refining processes could be converted into valuable products. Beginning in 1920 with the production of isopropyl alcohol, previously flared gases increasingly became the raw materials, or "feedstocks," for making chemical products. The company's growing research capabilities in the years before World War II focused on the development of new cracking technologies to increase the yield of gasoline, but the company

also built a greater understanding of hydrocarbon chemistry and manufacturing. Under the demands of World War II, refiners made advances in
using petrochemicals as the raw materials for synthetic rubber and high-
octane aviation fuel. Butyl rubber and gasoline additives became more
important products after the war. Wartime manufacturing advances also
proved valuable; hydrogenation, for example, allowed the company to
produce more and better raw materials for chemicals from oil and gas. By
the end of the war, it was clear to many that chemicals held great promise
for the company. From Rockefeller forward, Jersey Standard had refused
to diversify out of oil unless there was "some special business relation
between its oil business and the non-oil business in question."[4] In the case
of chemicals, that special business relation had been firmly established
during and after World War II.

Jersey and the other oil companies faced stiff competition in chemicals
from large, profitable, technologically advanced chemical companies led
in the United States by DuPont, Dow, and Union Carbide, and in Europe
by companies such as BASF. Within Jersey, chemicals faced an uphill
battle to gain acceptance as an important part of a company that was
experiencing rapid global growth in its oil business. George Rizzo, whose
career spanned much of the postwar era, observed that the company often
seemed to treat chemicals as "a hobby."[5] The creation of the new Enjay
Chemical Company in 1947 addressed the problems of marketing chemical products, but the crucial manufacturing choices remained in the hands
of petroleum refiners. Until the early 1960s, those in charge of refineries around the world continued to add value to their overall operations
by expanding further into chemical production. Although the company
accumulated an assortment of chemical-manufacturing facilities, it did
not have a coherent strategy or organization to hold them together.[6]

This finally changed in 1963 with the formal separation of the company's chemical and petroleum operations: Humble Oil & Refining retained
management of chemicals within the United States, and the newly created
Esso Chemical Company took over management of chemicals outside the
country. In 1965, a further consolidation formed a worldwide chemical
company with four regional offices and a functional organization. Cliff
Garvin took on the difficult job of bringing order to existing chemical
operations within the new organizational structure. Many agreed with

Gene McBrayer, who would later become the president of Exxon Chemical Company, that the separation of chemicals from refining was "the key to the long-term success of chemicals."[7] At the corporate level, this gave chemicals greater standing, with the choice of Garvin as president presenting a clear symbol that this was an initiative to be taken seriously, although Lee Raymond would later remark that "in the chemical company there was always . . . a question about how much support they really had in the corporation. . . . [Part] of that was related to . . . the perception that not many people in the corporation really understood the chemical business."[8] By the early 1970s, Exxon Chemical had its own research arm, separate from Exxon Research and Engineering, the downstream research center. It had authority over some of its own hiring and its own strategy—subject, of course, to approval and financing from corporate headquarters.

At the plant level, the separation of chemicals removed final decision-making authority on chemicals from the refinery plant manager. The major refining and chemical complexes, such as those at Baton Rouge, Louisiana, and Baytown, Texas, named a chemical plant manager (in addition to the traditional refinery manager) to oversee the separation of facilities and people and then to manage operations. The division of equipment and units proved relatively easy, given the specialized technology used in refining and chemicals. In the division of personnel, personal choice was considered when possible, with an informal arbitration process set up to sort out disputes. The division of facilities was difficult, since the chemical plants had grown up within the refineries. The chemical company began to appoint separate staff managers as well as an overall head of chemical operations.[9]

The process of separating chemicals from refining at the plant level took three to six months. One vital decision, however, took longer. With chemicals standing on its own, some agreement had to be reached about the development of a fair and legal price for the feedstock that the refineries would provide to the chemical plants. The debates over the proper "transfer price" went on and on, since "a cent a gallon either way made a big difference in somebody's net profit." The negotiations became a "matter of grinding it down . . . a lot of lost time [was] spent on transfer pricing."[10] Although everyone involved understood the need for a durable agreement that could be adapted to later changes in technology, many of them no doubt shared Lee Raymond's impatience with a process that "chewed up hundreds of man-hours."[11]

The chemical company's strong ties to the refineries remained a source of strength after the separation process had been completed. Personal ties between those who had worked together in the refineries remained important for decades. Top managers had come up through the Exxon system and retained connections throughout the company hierarchy. Operational ties remained strong, since chemical employees continued to interact with their friends and former coworkers in the refineries, and Exxon's researchers became increasingly adept at creating processes that captured additional value from the streams of hydrocarbons that moved through the plants. The proximity of refining and chemicals in its large complexes gave Exxon a competitive advantage over "disassociated" chemical companies, which had to purchase feedstocks from other refineries. This advantage was particularly pronounced in the production of the basic commodity chemicals that were the building blocks of specialty chemical products. Exxon established an enduring strength in such commodity chemicals—and in selected specialty chemical markets. As a bonus, chemical profits were, in Gene McBrayer's words, "to an extent, countercyclical" to petroleum profits, giving Exxon a "smoother curve" of profitability over long periods. In fact, the continuing ties between chemicals and oil remained so close as to raise questions about the wisdom of separating the two businesses in the first place.[12]

But several fundamental differences between the two industries argued strongly in favor of separation. Ed Holmer, who ran Exxon Chemical in the 1970s, saw chemicals as "a different industry, different markets, different technology," requiring "different managers to run it."[13] Technological advances produced a steady stream of new products or new uses for old chemicals. Highly competitive markets also helped account for a recurring marketing problem in chemicals: successful new processes and products quickly attracted competition. One longtime chemical executive summed it up this way: "When times were great, people built new plants."[14] Overcapacity resulted. The pattern of rapid growth followed by hard times as products flooded existing markets has plagued the industry for most of its history. This was not the same as the overcapacity in oil caused by OPEC's inability to create an effective cartel, but rather the overcapacity of highly competitive markets operating in a cyclical business environment. All in all, as a separate company, Exxon Chemical could address distinctive characteristics of its industry while still benefiting from its close ties to Exxon's petroleum operations.

In the 1970s, largely under the leadership of Holmer, Exxon Chemical took advantage of its independence to create a bigger place for itself within the chemical industry and thus within Exxon. Its ultimate goal of making an impact on the corporation's bottom line was hard to achieve in a giant, successful concern such as Exxon. Doing so would require worldwide sales much larger than the $1 billion in revenues it generated in 1970. Exxon Chemical expressed a twofold goal for the 1970s: to contribute more to Exxon's profits through selective expansion, and to achieve a return on investment competitive with those of the world's largest chemical companies. The emphasis was return on capital invested, not on growth alone.

To produce better financial results, chemicals had to bring greater coherence to its varied investments in chemicals around the world. To do so required selective divestments. These included selling 80 percent of its underperforming Latin American investments and such businesses as a Canadian flooring company. At the same time, a simultaneous wave of new investments strengthened the best of the company's facilities, and further investments by the late 1970s were used to build modern new facilities around the world. Those investments included projects to produce synthetic twine and woven polypropylene fabrics, but the focus was on basic chemicals that served as building blocks for many intermediate products then produced by chemical companies. In the 1970s, olefins and aromatics remained the primary basic chemicals manufactured and sold by Exxon. The company later expanded more aggressively into the production of polymers and intermediate chemicals, and it correspondingly increased its own use of those chemicals.

Even so, moving beyond basic commodity chemicals and achieving leadership in selected "specialty chemicals" became an important strategic goal of Exxon Chemical. Specialty chemicals promised higher returns but were not large enough to carry the company forward alone. The growing confidence of top managers at Exxon in the future of chemicals was evident in the levels of investment approved for two large projects in the

1970s and early 1980s—a $500 million olefin plant in Baytown funded in 1977, and a $1.1 billion joint venture to build a linear low-density polyethylene plant in Al-Jubail, Saudi Arabia.

Impressive results eventually flowed from those and similar investments. In the banner year of 1979, Exxon Chemical earned a record $456 million, roughly 10 percent of the corporation's returns from energy-related operations in a very good year for oil. After a relatively strong year in 1980, chemicals endured a sharp decline in earnings in 1982 in what it called "very poor" conditions "unprecedented in the history of this traditional growth industry."[15] But earnings then climbed for most of the rest of the 1980s, surpassing $1 billion in 1988. The company had surely met its goal of returning more money to the corporation. In its internal comparisons, its return on investment mirrored that of the largest companies in the chemical industry. In the opinion of Gene McBrayer, who succeeded Holmer as the head of Exxon Chemical and served in that capacity from 1984 until 1990, those financial results ensured the final acceptance of Exxon Chemical "as a full-fledged, important part of Exxon. . . . Ed felt that we had to be profitable if we were going to survive with Exxon, and he was right. Sure, in time, Lee [Raymond] became a believer in chemicals, but I think the predicate for that was our first making money."[16]

For Exxon, a successful foray into diversification was one that made significant profits, but its experience with chemicals suggests insights useful for understanding what it takes for diversification to work. Close technical and operational ties to the oil industry were central to the success of Exxon Chemical. In this sense, Exxon's commitment to chemicals was an extension of its existing businesses as much as the creation of a new venture. It improved the company's overall business by adding value to the end products from oil and gas. Another critical factor on the long road to success for chemicals was patience bred of the confidence within Exxon that expertise developed in oil could be adapted to the needs of chemicals. As a result, Exxon's top management decided to stay the course by investing for long-term results across the cycles of overcapacity that plagued the industry.

The growth of Exxon Chemical illustrated the importance of a steady approach to diversification, one that did not begin with unrealistic promises or expectations of quick profits. Chemicals certainly did not

Eugene McBrayer, president of Exxon Chemical Company, 1980.
ExxonMobil Historical Collection, di_06147.

overpromise in its first fifty years of production in the company's refineries. In fact, the business overperformed once its management had gained experience and been given the independence to chart its own course. The most significant lesson for Exxon from its diversification into chemicals was straightforward: the search for profitable ventures should patiently build on the existing operations and expertise of the company. As will be discussed in later chapters, Exxon's chemical business repaid this patience by adding substantial strengths to the company.

IN AND OUT: DIVERSIFICATION AND DIVESTMENT THROUGH 1986

In the 1970s, Exxon neglected this lesson and searched for new opportunities outside its core expertise in oil, gas, and chemicals. This search took two paths. Jersey (later Exxon) Enterprises was created in the 1960s to identify potential targets for diversification for the corporation as a whole. Meanwhile, Exxon's regional companies pursued opportunities that arose during the operation of their businesses. In a few cases, Exxon moved completely outside its traditional core competencies, entering businesses as varied as office equipment, real estate development, and minerals production. The company also diversified into a variety of energy-related businesses, including the production and enrichment of uranium, solar energy, and electric motors. Even closer to home, Exxon applied its expertise in fossil fuels to the development of reserves of coal, oil shale, and oil sands. Those fossil fuels became the raw materials used by the company in an attempt to diversify into another energy-related area, the production of synthetic fuels, or synfuels.[17]

Almost all the major oil companies in the United States pursued similar strategies of diversification in the 1970s. Synfuels were popular investments, as were coal and other mining industries. Some large oil companies invested heavily in nonrenewable energy sources. Others made giant leaps outside oil. Mobil's purchase of Montgomery Ward in 1976, and Gulf's announced plans to acquire Ringling Bros. and Barnum & Bailey Circus in 1974, ranked among the most publicized of such "conglomerate" mergers.[18] Tenneco, originally a long-distance natural gas pipeline company, provided an extreme example of a major oil or gas firm acquiring a collection of companies active in numerous different industries. For a time, Tenneco's loosely coordinated bundle of unrelated businesses offered a much-discussed "model" of conglomeration, in which the corporate office became in essence the manager of an investment portfolio containing largely unrelated businesses.[19] Exxon never embraced that approach to conglomeration, but it did use its financial and research strengths to venture far outside petroleum.

DIVERSIFICATION INTO NONENERGY BUSINESSES

The company's longest steps away from its core businesses came under the direction of Jersey Enterprises, a division created in 1963 to explore nontraditional investment opportunities. It was given capital for new ventures and had access to Jersey Standard's far-reaching research capabilities. It could create new initiatives through venture capital, establish in-house business projects, support projects generated by the research and engineering company, or seek acquisitions. Its goal was to identify a limited number of investments with the potential to grow into major new businesses compatible with the company's projected future as a high-tech energy-based company.[20] Any such ventures would be expected to grow large enough to make a substantial contribution to the bottom line of Jersey Standard.[21]

By 1969, Jersey Enterprises had developed a "charter" to guide its activities. Its expanded business-development staff sought to add two to three new in-house developmental projects and three to four new venture-capital projects each year. Its budget of $8 million to $10 million a year included venture capital and funds approved to support internal research programs. In 1973, Jersey Enterprises and its affiliate, Jersey Nuclear Company, changed their names to Exxon Enterprises and Exxon Nuclear, respectively. Exxon Enterprises continued to envision a phased developmental cycle consisting of five-year intervals: it would explore numerous options in the first five years, focus more sharply on potential winners in the next five, and then push forward in one or two "areas of substantial future potential" in the early 1980s.[22]

Exxon Enterprises initially concentrated on the general areas of energy conversion and storage, information systems, and new-materials technology. These categories provided general guidelines for the search for new businesses, but the search ranged far and wide. During the 1970s, Exxon Enterprises examined energy-related opportunities in nuclear power, solar cells, higher-efficiency batteries, and service station equipment. It became involved with information-systems projects that applied emerging computer technology to office equipment, including electronic word processors, microcomputers, fax machines, and PBX (private telephone switchboard) services. It also tested the application of new materials to new products, notably the use of carbon fiber technology in such areas as golf club design, and looked broadly at the areas of food processing and health care. In short, it monitored the progress of clusters of far-reaching initiatives in an array of businesses.[23] Though several of the industries chosen by Exxon proved robust, most of Exxon's "excursions" in these areas ultimately failed.

OFFICE EQUIPMENT

Exxon Enterprises led a major foray into office equipment in the 1970s. Other than Exxon's use of office equipment in its global operations, there were no obvious similarities between that sector and energy. The company nonetheless spent almost a decade trying to build a presence in an industry undergoing rapid, far-reaching changes driven by advanced technology with which Exxon had limited experience. In this case, the company diversified in search of first-mover advantages in an emerging market for a new generation of business systems. The ongoing application of computing power to office equipment would eventually transform modern offices, in the process creating lucrative new markets. In pursuit of those markets, Exxon entered an unfamiliar arena inhabited by well-established competitors.

The entry of Exxon Enterprises into office systems began in earnest in 1975 with a venture-capital project aimed at creating an electric typewriter with memory. Development of this pathbreaking product went forward outside the company, and production began under the brand name QXY in 1977. In addition, Exxon Enterprises fostered the development of an early facsimile machine, which hit the market as QWIP; brought to market an innovative text-editing machine called VYDEX; and helped develop an early microcomputer chip called Zilog. These products held great potential, and they found early markets. Exxon Enterprises grouped them together in a category it called "office systems" and spent considerable effort improving management, lowering production costs, and marketing.[24] All the products embodied innovative applications of emerging computing technology, and all seemed on the cutting edge of a revolution in office equipment. So serious was Exxon about the growth of office systems that, according to Cliff Garvin, the company "came within an ace" of buying a major competitor of IBM.[25]

But there was soon trouble at the office. As Exxon Enterprises's investments in office systems increased in the late 1970s, growth stalled, and then the group began missing income projections, a bright red flag in Exxon's approach to financial controls. Within office systems, this was as much a comment on corporate culture as on management performance. The skills needed to manage a fast-growing and fast-changing collection of products in a highly competitive retail marketplace simply were not available in Exxon's core businesses. The attitudes developed in a mature oil business characterized by steady, systematic management, strict financial controls, and layers of bureaucratic oversight did not transfer well into the business environment in which new office products competed. Exxon hired a number of managers who had grown up in the office-systems business, but the company's deeply embedded tradition of nurturing its own encouraged it to look for homegrown managers well versed in the Exxon approach to business.

The big question underlying this critical phase in the development of the office-systems businesses was simple: could Exxon's products survive the impact of rapidly evolving technical innovations by competitors and prosper in the long run? With new applications of computer technology around every corner, one generation's electric typewriter with memory could go quickly from being the hottest new product in the office to ending up as a pile of outmoded machines stacked in a storage closet. Did Exxon have the resources, skills, and will to keep up with the pace of change or, more fundamentally, the depth of change brought about by the rapid development of computer capacity and flexibility?

According to Bob Winslow, the president of Exxon Enterprises, the individual products "had tremendous success initially and failed quickly." In effect, they rode the first wave of computer applications for office equipment to success before being crushed by the tidal wave of improvements that quickly followed. Exxon's electronic typewriter could not compete with the new digital word processors that were soon introduced. The company's fax business continued to develop analog technologies while competitors vaulted ahead using digital processes. Zilog's heralded eight-bit microprocessor did not remain the industry standard. As Exxon struggled to keep abreast of the waves of innovations undermining the continued profitability of its key office products, a tsunami hit the fledgling office-systems industry. Bob Winslow's simple statement of the source of this massive sea change serves as a useful epitaph for the death of Exxon's office systems business: "IBM announced the personal computer."[26]

Exxon could not succeed in office systems in the long term unless it made a commitment to fundamental research and development that could compete with IBM—and with the Apples of the future. In this sense, Exxon was out of its league. It had shown good instincts in targeting the extraordinary growth potential of office equipment and had early identified quite promising new products such as the fax machine and computer-assisted typewriters. But lacking the expertise to keep pace with the ongoing digital revolution and unprepared to meet the stiff competition in such a fast-changing area, it lowered the flag and exited the field. Its excursion into this new business exacted a high cost in capital invested and employees hired and fired, and the lessons learned about the company's limitations impressed themselves on many of Exxon's future senior managers.

REAL ESTATE DEVELOPMENT

Exxon enjoyed better results in several cases of diversification undertaken not by Exxon Enterprises but by regional affiliates as they went about their primary business. Some of them found opportunities in real estate development and minerals that remained promising parts of Exxon's operations for several decades. A brief look at these enterprises, which were spawned by and at least indirectly related to Exxon's core businesses, illustrates how new business opportunities could emerge, grow, and then be sold.

The Friendswood Development Company was chartered in 1962 as a joint venture between Humble Oil & Refining and the Del Webb Corporation. Its original project was the development of Clear Lake City, a planned community on land owned by Humble adjacent to land it had donated to Rice University in Houston with the agreement that Rice would then donate the land to the U.S. government as the site for the manned-spacecraft center (later renamed the Johnson Space Center).

There was a booming market for real estate development in and around Houston, which was in the midst of a prolonged surge of growth driven by its expanding oil industry and marked by suburban development. The area south of the city near the new manned-spacecraft center seemed particularly promising. Someone would make money developing this property as the space center grew, and Humble decided to try its hand at real estate development in conjunction with an experienced partner. As Friendswood Development gained experience, it moved away from its partnership with Del Webb and built master-planned communities and such commercial properties as shopping centers. It became one of the leading developers in the fast-growing Houston area.[27] In the mid-1970s, Exxon's Investment Advisory Committee lauded Friendswood Development's success in and around Houston, noting that the company "is generating all of its operating and investment cash requirements while making cash distributions to Exxon USA and owns assets which, if developed, would generate substantial future profits."[28]

In the early 1980s, Friendswood Development began to target opportunities outside Houston, choosing the Washington, D.C., area as its initial target for expansion. Ultimately, however, its returns in the volatile real estate industry lagged those of established parts of Exxon's oil business, and its residential-development business was spun off in 1995 to independent investors. This was a trajectory that almost all the enterprises originally based within Exxon Enterprises would have envied.

MINERALS

The company had decidedly mixed results in its involvement in minerals, which were the largest long-term commitments it made outside energy in the era of diversification. Most major American oil companies also moved into minerals in the 1970s as they searched for investments in which they could use their existing expertise to generate profits to supplement what appeared to be declining opportunities in oil and natural gas. Mobil, Gulf Oil, Amoco, ARCO, and Chevron all acquired or developed coal- and uranium-mining businesses, while Amoco, Chevron, and ARCO also moved into copper.[29] Like them, Exxon came to minerals through its earlier involvement in coal. Unlike coal, other minerals did not benefit from the "fossil fuel expertise" of oil companies, but they could, at least in

FIGURE 4.1. Major mineral holdings by Exxon, 1981

MINE	LOCATION	METALS	YEAR OF FIRST PRODUCTION
Mt. Hope	Nevada	molybdenum	1986
Golden Grove	Australia	copper, zinc	1987
Los Bronces (expansion)	Chile	copper	1987
Crandon	Wisconsin	copper, zinc	—
El Solado (expansion)	Chile	copper	1991

Source: *W. M. McCardell to M. E. J. McLaughlin, memorandum, October 1, 1981, Exxon Minerals, Exxon Management Committee. Exxon Corporate Archives, Irving.* Note: *In this era, Exxon also owned substantial U.S. coal reserves and had begun work on its giant El Cerrejón coal project in Colombia.*

theory, draw on the global reach of the oil companies' geologists. In the case of Exxon, large mining projects also offered the chance to take advantage of what the company considered a core competency: the planning, financing, and management of giant projects. It was a stretch to identify synergies between oil production and mining, but the steps from oil to coal to other minerals made the progression seem almost logical.

Exxon USA entered minerals production in the 1960s, buying coal mines in Illinois and uranium mines elsewhere. It expanded in the late 1970s with the addition of a large zinc and copper resource at Crandon, Wisconsin; large new surface-mining operations for coal in Wyoming; and a molybdenum mine in Nevada.[30] Expansion in the United States set the stage for international mining operations in the late 1970s as the company searched the world for promising large-scale investments. As shown in figure 4.1, Exxon identified good prospects for copper in Chile and zinc and copper in Australia. From 1977 through 1982, those in charge of the expansion of minerals developed an overarching strategy and a new organizational structure within which to move forward.

Developments in this era shaped Exxon's investments in coal and other minerals for the next twenty-five years. The symbol of this new commitment became Chilean copper. In early 1978, Exxon identified two existing copper-producing properties as potential investments. The first was the Los Bronces mine, about forty miles northeast of Santiago in the Andes at almost 12,000 feet of elevation. The second, the El Soldado mine, was eighty miles north of Santiago. Although smaller than the copper deposits at Los Bronces, those at El Soldado contained a higher grade of ore. A yearlong analysis of the two properties, which made the potential investment sound almost too good to be true, produced a proposal to buy and expand both of them. Indeed, the report estimated that an investment of approximately $1.6 billion could expand the two mines to a capacity of more than 100,000 metric tons a day, allowing the two open-pit mines to produce 340,000 tons of copper annually. If those numbers did not get the attention of the members of Exxon's management committee, surely their eyes focused on the projection that the $1.6 billion investment could be expected to "yield an ultimate net cash flow of $9.8 billion" and a higher-than-usual return on investment.[31]

Exxon's purchase of the properties accelerated the pace of change in its minerals business. By September 1980, Exxon Minerals Company, created through the consolidation of the company's previously separate domestic and international mineral companies, managed Exxon's noncoal mineral holdings worldwide—with the exception of Imperial's holdings in Canada. As it set to work defining a long-term strategy for its varied holdings, Exxon Minerals focused on the Chilean copper mines, the zinc deposit near Crandon, and several uranium projects. In early 1980, the company discussed the potential of twenty-two base-metal projects and seventeen uranium-mining projects scheduled for development by the year 2000 at a projected cost of $15 billion. This number made a clear statement that Exxon intended to establish a mineral business large enough to make a difference in its bottom line.[32]

The next year produced a more formal statement of strategy. It began with a decidedly optimistic statement of intent "to earn at least $750 million per year by 1990 with returns comparable to those achieved in the petroleum business." In pursuit of that goal, Exxon Minerals would undertake a program of global exploration shaped by many of the same considerations that governed oil exploration. The starting point would be to identify geologically attractive prospects in nations with acceptable political risks. The company preferred wholly owned ventures, but it would consider joint ventures "if adequate Exxon Minerals Company control is assured." Prospects, which would emphasize copper, zinc, lead, uranium, and gold, would need to be large in order to justify the involvement of Exxon. Within those guidelines, the company would seek to develop large ore deposits with a well-organized team "meeting the highest standards of operating and technical excellence."[33]

A year later, in 1982, the key goal of $750 million in earnings had been delayed from 1990 to 1995. The new focus was on the development of the five "world-class mines now in hand." These included the Los Bronces and El Soldado copper mines in Chile; zinc and copper mines at Crandon and Golden Grove, Australia; and the Mount Hope molybdenum mine in Nevada. The economics of those projects looked good enough to move Exxon Minerals on the pathway to profitability. Willing and able to spend money on the development of large-scale mines with the potential for outstanding profits in the long term, Exxon Minerals seemed poised in 1982 to become an important new source of profitable diversification for the corporation as a whole.[34]

Unfortunately, that was not to be. The first fundamental adjustment came with the abandonment of uranium mining in 1984 in response to the falling demand for uranium in the aftermath of the accident at the nuclear power plant at Three Mile Island, Pennsylvania, in 1979. Both copper and zinc followed a similar pattern. Substantial investments steadily increased production, systematic management efforts generated significant cost savings, and state-of-the art technology improved quality, but substantial profits did not follow. As in the oil industry, Exxon found itself competing against established companies and held hostage by highly volatile global markets for commodities. Soft prices plagued basic metals almost continually in the 1980s and 1990s; it was a rare year when high prices for copper and zinc brought profits to Exxon Minerals. The situation made a mockery of the earlier projections of annual earnings goals and of returns equal to those in the oil industry. In fact, despite a successful three-year program to triple the capacity of the Chilean mines from 1989 through 1992, annual earnings of Exxon Minerals in 1994–1998 averaged less than $50 million on average capital employed

Los Bronces copper mine, Doñihue, Cachapoal, Chile, 1990.
ExxonMobil Historical Collection, di_06231.

of about $1 billion. Such results led to Exxon's gradual divestment of all minerals, climaxed by the sale of its Australian coal and mineral properties in 2000 and of its Chilean copper mines in 2002. When judged on its own terms, the effort to create a profitable international mineral company capable of complementing Exxon's oil, natural gas, and chemical businesses had failed badly.[35]

Several patterns emerge from the company's ventures outside energy. The first is obvious. Although Exxon never had trouble finding promising prospects, establishing a profitable, large-scale business in an unfamiliar industry was harder than it looked. Exxon's core competencies, developed in oil and natural gas, were not easily transferrable to other endeavors. This reflected a general pattern in most of Exxon's ventures outside energy. For more than a century, it largely had followed John D. Rockefeller's example of sticking to its knitting as a vertically integrated petroleum company. A time of energy crises in a world highly dependent on oil and natural gas for energy was a strange time to decide to become an office equipment company or a copper company. Exxon's expertise was much more likely to produce profits in energy, especially in fossil fuels.

DIVERSIFICATION INTO ALTERNATIVE ENERGY

Throughout the 1960s and 1970s, Exxon seemed to identify good prospects for expansion in energy sources other than oil and gas. Indeed, Cliff Garvin argued in 1977 that "Exxon is in the energy business, as it is most broadly defined, rather than just the oil business."[36] The company was quite familiar with energy markets for transportation, home heating, industrial fuel, and the generation of electricity. It had technical and financial resources far greater than those of the leading companies in such alternatives to oil as coal and in renewable energy sources such as solar and wind power. Although the company entered the competitive arena for alternative fuels with great confidence, it would again have little long-term success in creating large, profitable ventures in energy other than oil and natural gas.

NUCLEAR FUEL

Exxon Enterprises took an important role in guiding the company into investments in energy sources other than oil and gas. It was the parent of Exxon Nuclear, which had been organized in 1969 to find new supplies of uranium from which to fabricate fuel for nuclear power plants. Exxon Nuclear appeared to be a good choice for diversification. The mining of uranium, at least indirectly, overlapped with the company's expanding involvement in minerals, including coal. Although the fabrication of nuclear fuel had few similarities with oil refining, it did require the sort of large-scale manufacturing operation that Exxon prided itself on building and operating efficiently.[37] This energy-related endeavor seemed to be an excellent fit for a major oil company.

Exxon had every reason to believe that the nuclear power industry would grow rapidly. In his report to the corporate management committee in 1974, the president of Exxon Enterprises laid out a strong general argument for such future growth: "Nuclear power is now accepted by the electric utilities throughout the industrialized Western World as the economic and preferred choice by central station electrical generating plants." Nuclear power had the added competitive attraction of being "an essential response to the growth problems of the environment and to the tightening supply of fossil fuel." In short, "Nuclear markets are thus assured as relatively predictable throughout the century."[38] Such in-house projections reflected the prevailing views of governments and utility companies around the world. In the United States, all three presidents in the 1970s made the expansion of nuclear power an important part of their alternative-energy programs.

Exxon Nuclear progressed steadily toward profitability in the early 1970s. It succeeded in finding new deposits of uranium and built a large uranium fuel-fabrication plant at Belleville, Washington. Consistent with the company's general strategy of vertical integration, Exxon Nuclear explored options for "optimizing opportunities within the total nuclear fuel product line, which means the development of an integrated fuel cycle."[39] The company hoped to take the last step in that cycle by moving into the enrichment of uranium, which it saw as an excellent business opportunity for a company with ample capital and technological expertise. In 1975, Exxon Nuclear announced that it had responded to an invitation from the U.S. government to submit a proposal "to design, build, and operate a uranium enrichment plant." Its proposal was one of several solicited from private companies by the Energy Research and Development Administration as a basis for contract negotiations pending the passage of legislation to allow private companies to become involved in uranium enrichment. President Ford initially supported this change. In a special message to Congress in February 1976, he urged the passage of legislation to allow for a competitive nuclear fuel industry. After Ford abruptly reversed course, however, Cliff Garvin met with him and was told, "This is reserved for the government." The enabling legislation did not pass Congress as antinuclear protests grew in early 1976 and presidential candidate Jimmy Carter expressed concerns about nuclear safety and the proliferation of nuclear weapons.[40]

Despite its inability to integrate into the backend of the fuel cycle, Exxon's uranium-mining and fuel-fabrication businesses continued to grow. As its orders increased within the United States, it also entered what appeared to be a promising market for nuclear fuel in Europe, where it made headway against strong competition from such heavyweights in the nuclear power industry as Westinghouse, General Electric, and Kraftwerk Union AG, a West German subsidiary of giant Siemens AG, which had a worldwide presence in the building of nuclear power plants and fossil-fuel plants. Exxon built on its management strengths and its strong capital base to expand in an industry characterized by extremely high capital costs and complex technology.

As Exxon Nuclear sought to turn the corner toward profitability in the late 1970s, however, the tone of its annual reports to the Exxon Management Committee changed sharply. In place of its earlier optimistic assessments of the future of the nuclear industry, its 1978 report sounded an alarming note: "The key words to describe the U.S. nuclear industry environment in 1978 are indecision and delay." After noting that sixty-seven existing nuclear plants in the United States produced 12 percent of the nation's electricity, the report voiced concern that "no new nuclear-plant orders have been placed thus far in 1978." From Exxon's perspective, the reasons for this were straightforward: "The problem is not one of comparative electricity-generating economics; most utility studies continue to show significant economic advantages for nuclear over coal-fired stations. Rather, the problem is one of uncertainty caused by U.S. Government indecision and delay concerning nuclear power policy."[41] Exxon Nuclear's 1979 report argued that projections of the nuclear industry's growth continued to be slowed by "government vacillation and inaction" and by "reduced forecasts of electrical demand growth." But, importantly, "further uncertainties have been added by the accident at Three Mile Island on March 28, 1979, and its effect on the risks perceived by utilities and financial institutions in ordering new nuclear plants." The company's financial results also had been hurt by delays in the licensing and start-up of its fuel-fabrication plant in Lingen, West Germany, and from the higher-than-anticipated unit costs in Lingen and in Richland, Washington, where some "70 percent of the work on European fuel is actually performed." In light of these delays and cost increases, Exxon Nuclear announced sharp reductions in its projected investments until "the direction" of the nuclear industry became clearer.[42]

Despite its strict financial controls and its systematic monitoring of financial performance, the company's planning process could not encompass the fundamental economic, political, and environmental uncertainties that plagued the nuclear industry after the accident at Three Mile Island in 1979. That same year, Exxon appointed a well-regarded executive named Lee Raymond to lead Exxon Nuclear, and his experiences at the

company provided a central business lesson that stayed with him throughout his career. In 1981, he moved on to become the senior vice president of
Exxon Enterprises, Exxon Nuclear's owner, where for two years he grap-
pled with the difficult problems raised by the company's nuclear business.

As time passed, Exxon grew increasingly disenchanted with the U.S.
government, whose strong support of nuclear power had encouraged the
company's initial investment in uranium. By the 1980s, however, governmental support had begun to waver, and environmental and safety policies increasingly delayed the construction of new nuclear plants. From
the perspective of Exxon's planners, the intersection of governmental
energy and environmental policies proved dangerous, with yield signs at
every corner and a malfunctioning yellow light in the center.[43] A company
investing millions of dollars in search of future returns from a booming
nuclear power industry could ill afford to mark time as the economics of
nuclear power worsened and the regulatory climate tightened.

False expectations about the growth of nuclear power plagued Exxon
Nuclear. From the 1960s through the early 1980s, its planners accepted
the prevailing projections of nuclear power's steady expansion as a vital
supplement to oil and gas and a central fuel source for the generation
of electricity. The company's planners consistently overestimated the
demand for nuclear power while underestimating the very real, though
unquantifiable, effects of political and environmental risks. They also
underestimated the impact of the double-digit inflation that followed the
oil-price spike of 1978–1979. As it turned out, their rosy view of the economics of nuclear construction led them to conclude as late as 1981 that
nuclear power remained economically viable. Their error was revealed by
the subsequent decline of new nuclear construction in the United States
and much of the rest of the world.[44] Giving up a long-standing investment
in nuclear fuel was difficult to do. The company's management had made
an enthusiastic commitment to it, as had governments around the world,
and the company only reluctantly abandoned a technology that once had
held such promise.

In the early 1980s, however, Exxon began to reevaluate its long-term
commitment to nuclear fuel. A combination of negative developments—
including the accident at Three Mile Island, the failure to privatize uranium enrichment, the lack of new U.S. nuclear-plant construction, and

some extremely unfavorable long-term uranium-supply contracts the nuclear company had negotiated—convinced Exxon that it had made the wrong bet on becoming a part of the nuclear-fuel cycle.[45] Even though Exxon Nuclear had finally eased into the plus column on "net-cash generation" in the early 1980s, the management of Exxon Enterprises had set a new course. Exxon's nuclear-fuel business had grown into the third-largest nuclear-fuel supplier in the United States, but its fate remained tied to that of the nuclear-power industry as a whole.[46] Lacking the capacity to reverse the stagnation of the U.S. nuclear industry, Exxon sold its nuclear fuel business to Kraftwerk Union in 1986.

SOLAR POWER

The company's entry into the solar-cell business began in 1969 with projects conducted by the research and engineering organization. Exxon Enterprises sought commercial applications for this research. In 1973, Exxon's Solar Power Corporation opened a facility for the manufacture of solar flat panels at Woburn, Massachusetts, near Boston, joining ARCO and Amoco as manufacturers of solar panels. The company gradually found a growing market for the relatively low-tech panels for use in remote and unattended locations such as railroad crossings and unmanned radio relays. In 1975, the company had sales in thirty-five countries, and in that year became a wholly owned subsidiary of Exxon Enterprises. Through a separate company, Daystar, Exxon Enterprises also began to develop more sophisticated solar panels for use in heating water and for space heating.[47] Within Exxon, solar power was a popular topic, with frequent articles about solar power in general and Exxon's solar-cell business appearing in such in-house publications as the *Lamp* and *Exxon USA*. Renewable energy seemed on the rise as a logical response to shortages in domestic oil and natural gas. A leading position in a small market, however, was not financially attractive to Exxon. The industry was growing, but its overall size remained small, and the costs of solar energy remained high. Solar power might eventually become price competitive and have an important long-term role as a major renewable energy source, but Exxon's core competencies in oil and natural gas had little direct application to solar power's operation or development.

Although Exxon's share of the global market for solar panels reached

5 percent in the late 1970s, Exxon Enterprises grew increasingly skeptical of the long-term prospects for the business—and weary of the short-term losses that piled up year after year. In its report to the Exxon Management Committee in 1979, Exxon Enterprises reported that it had shut down the Woburn manufacturing facility. The next year, it reported a decision to focus its research efforts on the development of "higher technology collector systems."[48] Then in 1981, Exxon announced the sale of Daystar. Three years later, *Energy Daily* reported the end of Exxon's fifteen-year commitment to solar cells under the headline "Exxon Flees Photovoltaics." Quoting Exxon sources, the article reported that Exxon Enterprises, after suffering about $30 million in losses on solar energy over its fifteen years in the business, had decided to exit the industry because the "economics are not very encouraging."[49] The solar business was small, and profits would come only far in the future, if at all.

Exxon came to realize that the petroleum and solar parts of the "energy industry" used fundamentally different technologies and required quite different types of management expertise. Exxon's mature businesses in oil, natural gas, and petrochemicals were capital intensive and well entrenched in global markets, while its solar enterprises were start-up companies in an industry that had not yet demonstrated competitiveness in the market for electricity. Although elected officials often discussed solar-energy technology, along with other renewable energy sources, as an essential part of the energy future, it was still in its infancy. Decades might be required for it to grow to a scale that would make a difference in Exxon's bottom line. Given Exxon's large size, its possible role in a fully developed solar industry was unclear, but the company had little financial incentive to move forward. It could not justify heavy investments of capital, management resources, and research and development in a relatively small industry with an unpredictable future.

RELIANCE ELECTRIC AND ELECTRIC MOTORS

Exxon's most controversial move into a nonpetroleum energy-related business came in 1979 with its acquisition, for more than $1.2 billion, of the Cleveland-based Reliance Electric Company, a medium-sized firm specializing in the development, manufacture, sale, and service of a broad line of industrial equipment. The acquisition of a company with more than 31,000 employees had its roots in research sponsored by Exxon Enterprises on a process called "alternating current synthesis" (ACS). Some within the company came to believe that this technology might hasten a breakthrough that could greatly increase the efficiency of electric motors.[50] Given the rising cost of electricity and the widespread use of electric motors by industry, including the oil industry, Exxon stood poised to reap substantial profits as soon as the new technology conquered the marketplace.

The decision to acquire Reliance Electric as a way to hasten the application of ACS technology came after an extensive examination of possible merger partners. Reliance was the most attractive of the companies Exxon Enterprises had studied. In the wake of the second oil-price shock, Exxon was not in a mood to go slow. It grabbed the attention of Reliance Electric with a much-publicized tender offer that was almost triple Reliance's book value. Even adjusted for "goodwill" and inventory changes, this offer proclaimed that Exxon considered Reliance Electric a valuable part of its push into the application of ACS technology in industrial markets.[51] In addition, the development of more-efficient electric motors could contribute to Exxon's growing commitment to fuel efficiency in its own operations and perhaps provide sales opportunities throughout the oil and gas industry.

There were doubters. One was the Federal Trade Commission, which slapped a stand-separate order on the merger partners as it studied the competitive implications of the deal for almost two years. Other skeptics included industry insiders. Looking back more than a quarter of a century after the acquisition, Cliff Garvin recalled a conversation with a golfing partner from General Electric who voiced doubts about the practical application of ACS and similar technologies. If, however, ACS did turn out to be a game-changing innovation, then Exxon's decision to acquire Reliance Electric would be an excellent investment.

Any dreams of success quickly disappeared, however, leaving the company shaken and embarrassed. In announcing the acquisition of Reliance Electric in its 1979 *Annual Report*, Exxon proclaimed that the "principal purpose ... was to obtain the means for rapid development and marketing of a new energy-saving technology called alternating current synthesis."[52] But only a year later the company sheepishly admitted that "Reliance has concluded that the original concepts underlying Exxon's alternating current synthesis will not produce a commercially viable product."[53] A wave of bad publicity understandably followed that announcement, dealing a harsh blow to a company with pride in its technical expertise. The title of a feature article on the Reliance Electric fiasco in *Fortune* magazine made the central point all too clear: "Exxon's $600 Million Mistake."[54] *BusinessWeek* asked a related question in the title of another article: "What's Wrong at Exxon Enterprises?"[55]

Without the promise of applications for ACS technology, Reliance Electric held little attraction for Exxon. Its far-flung holdings in a variety of industrial-equipment plants and its large workforce simply did not fit well with Exxon's existing operations. For several years after 1980, Exxon's management spent considerable time and energy trying to reshape Reliance into a profitable concern, or at least one that could be sold. Finally, in 1986, Exxon sold a company consisting of the original Reliance Electric facilities and properties from several other somewhat-related affiliates. The bad publicity surrounding the strange case of the purchase and divestment of Reliance Electric illustrated that the costs of diversification could reach beyond money and management time all the way to the reputation of the company.[56]

COAL: THE SOLID FOSSIL FUEL

Exxon had anticipated the need to move into other energy sources by acquiring coal reserves in the United States beginning in the mid-1960s. It later acquired deposits in Australia before investing in the massive Cerrejón coal project in northern Colombia in 1978. By 1979, it owned the fourth-largest coal reserves in the United States; by 1983, it ranked as the nation's fifth-largest coal producer.[57] Numerous other major oil companies moved aggressively into the coal industry in this era, raising fears that Big Oil would limit production of this competing fuel, as well as hopes that the same companies would help build a more modern and efficient coal industry.

Exxon's core businesses had clear and direct ties to coal. As a fossil fuel, coal shares the same basic geology and chemistry as oil and natural gas. A well-established, relatively inexpensive fuel, domestic coal could provide an important alternative to imported oil, especially as a fuel for electric-power plants, a market in which it competes with natural gas and nuclear power. And coal had the potential to be an important source of synthetic fuel. A final attraction of coal was the industry's competitive environment. Big oil companies such as Exxon seemed well prepared to gain market share in the "sick" coal industry, which had long been plagued by its regional organization, labor and environmental problems, and high transportation costs.

In an era when presidents Nixon, Ford, and Carter all put forward coal as a central component in the drive for energy independence, it seemed to be an attractive investment as an industrial fuel source. Throughout the 1970s, U.S. government policies encouraged the growth of the domestic coal industry. The most obvious of these was the Powerplant and Industrial Fuel Use Act of 1978, which prohibited the use of natural gas as fuel in new electric-power plants or in new industrial plants. This made coal and nuclear power the fuels of choice for a new generation of plants, and the growing economic and environmental problems of nuclear power in the late 1970s gave added encouragement to the growth of coal. The cards seemed to be stacked in favor of the rapid growth of coal production amid soaring oil prices after 1978, and Exxon was well positioned to place a profitable bet on coal.[58]

Against this backdrop, representatives of Exxon's operating companies from around the world met in February 1977 to discuss the long-term prospects for the expansion of the company's coal production. Their opening statement captured the tone of the times: "In view of the long-term energy picture and the increasingly prominent role that coal must play in satisfying growing energy demand, Exxon should make a maximum commitment to coal resource acquisition." The group went on to recommend "aggressive and innovative approaches" to acquire reserves in "Australia, Canada, the United States (including the Southern Rockies), and other areas as appropriate." This would mean "comprehensive exploration and resource acquisition assessments" in the "relatively unexplored areas of Central and South America, Africa, and the Far East."[59]

At the time of this meeting, Exxon USA already had a substantial underground coal mine in Illinois, which produced long-term supplies for Chicago-area utilities. Its giant new surface mine near Gillette, Wyoming, contained very-low-sulfur coal that held great promise in a marketplace falling under increasingly strict sulfur and emissions controls. As the Gillette mine moved toward completion, however, a lawsuit by the Sierra Club over its potential environmental impact produced an injunction by a district court that closed down work on the mine for a year until the U.S. Supreme Court overturned the injunction. This episode served as a clear reminder that environmental issues raised substantial barriers to coal's expansion.[60]

As Exxon's U.S. coal capacity expanded in the late 1970s, an interesting prospect for international growth came to the company's attention. In 1975, the government of Colombia invited seventeen international companies to submit proposals for the creation of a joint venture with Carbocol, the national coal company. The bid of Intercor, the Colombian operating company of Exxon, found favor with the government because of its offer of a high royalty rate and the reputation of Exxon in Colombia, where it had operated for more than a century. After a year of evaluation, Exxon concluded that the size, quality, and location of the Cerrejón coal deposits made them very attractive for development, primarily for export to Europe. Estimated to contain the world's fourth-largest coal deposits, Cerrejón lay in the sparsely populated La Guajira peninsula, a relatively short distance from the port of Puerto Bolivar near the mouth of Lake Maracaibo, Venezuela. Once a new transportation system linked the coal deposits to the port, European markets would be readily accessible.

This was a big project in every sense of the word. At an estimated cost of $3 billion to $4 billion, it made good use of Exxon's financial strength. Building a massive new coal-mining complex in a remote and mountainous region required the construction of basic infrastructure, including the mines, housing, and even a hundred-mile-long road to the sea. Such challenges called forth Exxon's great confidence in its ability to manage large, complex projects. Exxon faced other challenges, ranging from the politics of a successful joint venture with Colombia's national coal company to the social impact of the construction and operation of a huge industrial complex in a region with little previous development.[61] The biggest challenge of all was the development of a facility capable of competing over the long term in the demanding global market for coal.

Exxon moved quickly to build an efficient coal mine in the mountains of Colombia, spending several billion dollars as its share of the investment

Cerrejón coal mine loading port under construction, Guajira, Colombia.
ExxonMobil Historical Collection, di_06103.

needed by the joint venture to bring the mine online. By 1981, the company had negotiated long-term contracts for coal in Europe, and construction of the road to the sea and other vital infrastructure was underway. Initial production from Cerrejón came in 1984, and expansion of its capacity moved briskly toward its projected fifteen million metric tons per year. By 1988, the facility had become the world's largest coal mine for export, yet troubling signs of future financial difficulties had begun to appear.

Throughout the 1980s and 1990s, despite the sustained expansion of Exxon's coal capacity around the world, its coal operations regularly reported losses or, at best, scant earnings. Again, the villain was the declining price of commodities: the demand for coal was affected by the same collapse in demand and price that plagued oil in the years after the mid-1980s. After an unusually good year in 1991, regular losses resumed. As with copper, steady expansion combined with great attention to lowering costs was not enough to break this pattern. Exxon never solved the puzzle of how to earn adequate returns on its large investment in Colombian coal, and it finally decided that it could no longer justify further investment in the venture. After looking at long-term trends, the company's management decided in 2002 to sell its interest back to the Colombian government.[62] A determined effort of more than twenty years had failed to develop a large-scale coal operation capable of making a significant contribution to Exxon's bottom line.

The company also sold its large copper mines in Chile in 2002, ending its efforts to build a substantial global presence in minerals, one that would provide returns rivaling those of its petroleum operations. All things considered, Cerrejón and the company's big U.S. coal mines were probably the company's most disappointing experiences with diversification. Coal was, after all, a fossil fuel; the Wyoming surface mines were very efficient; and the Cerrejón project was a world-scale joint venture in a good location with a sympathetic government company, a combination that had proved successful in oil.

Its experiences in uranium, solar power, electric motors, and coal illustrated the difficulties facing Exxon as it tried to transform itself into a diversified energy company. The company's experiences suggested that there was no such thing as a unified energy industry. What the phrase so neatly implied could not be easily encompassed by technological and managerial systems. The core competencies of an oil, natural gas, and chemical company did not necessarily translate into successful operations in energy businesses as diverse as nuclear fuel, solar panels, or even coal. What scholars or public policy makers might lump together as the "energy industry" was in fact a complicated collection of separate industries with as many differences as similarities.

SYNTHETIC FUELS: IN SEARCH OF THE HOLY GRAIL

In the 1920s and the 1950s, synthetic-fuel bubbles developed in the United States in times of perceived shortages of domestic oil, only to burst after the discovery of new reserves drove down oil prices and removed fears of scarcity.[63] In 1925, the president of Jersey Standard, Walter Teagle, gave his opinion about the future of synthetic fuels to the head of the Federal Oil Conservation Board, the federal agency then studying the oil industry's views: "Any of the major products of petroleum will be displaced by substitutes as their cost advances to a level which will give substitutes a price advantage."[64] In the 1970s, as in the 1920s, price was the key to the growth of alternative fuels. High oil prices might foster the growth of synfuels, but only if they lasted long enough to allow major investments to create economies of scale and mature, tested technology. Synfuels had to overcome several inherent cost disadvantages before they could compete with conventional oil. Mining and retorting processes added costs, and development costs for synfuel technologies would remain high until they had moved through the cycle from research to pilot plants to commercial-scale manufacturing. In addition, it was clear that the new fuel would extract a high environmental cost because of its substantial air emissions and its large demand for fresh water. The combination of those factors meant that synfuels would compete with conventional oil only if the price of synfuels fell, perhaps because of new technologies and economies of scale, and if conventional oil's price remained permanently high—at least at the level reached in the early 1980s.

By the 1970s, Exxon and its industry had chased the elusive promise of synfuels for more than half a century. A variety of technologies had been used to separate liquid and gaseous hydrocarbons from a variety of fossil fuels, including coal, oil sands, oil shale, and heavy oil. Once separated, these hydrocarbons could be transported and refined with variations of processes used with conventional oil and natural gas. Synfuels could supply many markets served by oil and gas, and they could use much of the extensive infrastructure built by the oil industry. The established research agendas of oil companies and their associated chemical companies could be adapted and applied to synfuel development. All in all, synthetic fuels seemed to fit as least as well with the core competencies of the oil industry as did chemicals.

The most inviting targets for the production of synfuels were the vast deposits of oil shale in the American West and the large deposits of oil sands in Alberta, Canada. In combination with expensive processes for turning coal into either a liquid or a gas, these unconventional fossil fuels returned to the spotlight in the 1970s; major investments were made in processes designed to transform them into an important new type of conventional fossil fuel by 2000. Exxon joined many other oil companies and the U.S. and Canadian governments in trying to develop new synfuel processes. All three U.S. presidents in the 1970s promoted synfuels as an important part of the push to develop domestic energy sources, and public policies supported synfuels with research dollars and a variety of subsidies.

Exxon invested substantial amounts of money and time in efforts to bring synfuels to the market. In the decade after 1973, the company pursued ambitious research into technology to liquefy and gasify coal. One promising technology for coal liquefaction was the Exxon donor solvent (EDS) process, which drew on the Fischer-Tropsch process; the latter had been invented in the 1920s and used by Germany to produce synthetic fuels during World War II. The EDS process used a catalyst to speed the chemical reaction between pulverized coal and steam in order to produce a synthetic fuel in the absence of oxygen.[65] The project was the latest in a long line of technological innovations that Exxon and other oil companies had used to find alternatives to oil and natural gas.

Work on the proprietary process began in the company's research and engineering laboratories in 1971 and moved forward within a network of interested oil companies, with support from the Department of Energy after 1977. Exxon built an EDS pilot plant at its Baytown refinery, which went online in April 1980, processing 250 tons a day of various grades of coal and lignite.[66] Of the estimated $280 million budget, the Energy Department provided roughly half, Exxon Coal about 23 percent, and five other industry participants the balance.[67] All participants agreed to share any royalties from licensing the technology upon termination of the project.[68] By August 1982, the Baytown plant had logged about 10,600 hours of operation and handled more than 80,000 tons of coal and lignite. Tests convinced the project director of the technical feasibility of the EDS process, which, he concluded, was ready to be used in a commercial plant handling 20,000 to 30,000 tons a day.[69]

Exxon did not, however, construct a large-scale commercial plant.[70] Here, as with all of the synfuel projects Exxon undertook during this era, the fundamental problems were primarily economic, not technical. In September 1983, a *Journal of Commerce* article entitled "Exxon Coal Process Held Too Costly" reported that Exxon researchers estimated that the construction of a commercial-scale liquefaction plant using the EDS process would cost an estimated $7.4 billion.[71] At the time, that represented almost two years of earnings for Exxon. The sum would buy Exxon a plant using technology as yet untried on a commercial scale and capable of producing only 75,000 barrels a day of hydrocarbon liquids if it proved viable. The price was far too high and the risks were too great to justify moving forward.[72]

In those same years, Exxon conducted significant research on gasification of East Texas lignite, a low-grade and less expensive form of coal. Exxon borrowed the basic principles for its coal-gasification technology from the Lurgi-Ruhrgas process, which had been developed in Germany in the 1940s. By combining coal under pressure with steam and oxygen, the process produced an "intermediate Btu gas" that had the potential to compete with natural gas as an industrial fuel and perhaps even to become a feedstock for petrochemical production. As its research progressed, Exxon became increasingly enthusiastic about the gasification of lignite. For a brief time in the early 1980s, the company spoke of the possibility of a $4 billion project to begin operation in 1987 using 40,000 tons of lignite a day to produce synthetic fuel with an energy content equivalent of 65,000 barrels of liquid fuel.[73] As with its coal-liquefaction project, however, Exxon dropped this idea as construction costs skyrocketed and the price of oil began to soften. Although research continued, commercialization once again could not be justified by the project's high price per unit of output.

Both oil shale and oil sands held potential reserves large enough to alter fundamentally the position of North America in the world oil industry. At a time when Saudi Arabia's proved oil reserves totaled approximately 200 billion barrels, experts within Exxon projected that 550 billion barrels of liquid fuel "could potentially be produced from [oil shale] reserves in the western U.S." They also concluded that "Alberta oil sands alone contain about 150 billion barrels of recoverable oil."[74] Both types of synfuel seemed likely to become economically competitive with traditional oil if oil prices remained high in the 1970s, and both became more attractive to investors after oil prices rose to new heights in the early 1980s.

Synfuel enthusiasm at times helped experts look past the great difficulties in realizing this potential. To produce synthetic oil from shale or sand, expensive and technically challenging mining and refining processes separated the liquid oil from the solid mass that held it. The most promising reserves of oil sands and oil shale were located in relatively remote regions, so significant investments in infrastructure and in recruiting, training, and housing workers would be needed. Because the technical processes for producing synthetic fuels had not been demonstrated on a commercial scale, much remained to be done to perfect large-scale production facilities. Hovering above the technical issues raised by the commercial production of oil shale or oil sands was the ever-present question of the ultimate cost per barrel of synfuels. Waiting in the wings if the processes proved capable of commercialization were serious environmental issues, including the impact of their production on air quality and water supplies, especially in regions already plagued by a scarcity of water.

But differences between oil shale and oil sands (also known as tar sands) permitted economic production of the latter. The Athabasca oil sands in Alberta, Canada, had attracted public attention as early as the 1830s. Located in a remote section of northern Alberta, the sludge-like mixture of oil and sand near Fort McMurray fascinated the earliest oilmen, who could only imagine the magnitude of the vast deposits of hydrocarbons trapped in the sand. For almost a century, however, the deposits went undeveloped, awaiting a combination of higher prices for oil and the development of an effective process for separating the hydrocarbons from the sand. Efforts to build pilot plants capable of creating synthetic oil from the bitumen contained in the oil sands began in earnest in the 1950s, but the pace of research and development accelerated markedly in 1973 with the creation of Syncrude Canada Ltd., a consortium of private companies and the governments of Canada and the provinces of Alberta and Ontario. Imperial Oil, Exxon's majority-owned Canadian affiliate, was an original member, and it became the largest individual partner after the reorganization of the consortium in 1975.[75]

By 1978, production of synfuels had begun, using gigantic draglines to surface-mine the oil-impregnated sands and then transport them to a nearby retort. There, water heated to about 1,000 degrees Fahrenheit converted the bitumen to solid coke, gas, naphtha, and distillate. After sulfur removal, the gas was used to heat the naphtha and the distillate to form synthetic crude oil, which could then be transported via pipeline to oil refineries for further refining. This technology produced high-quality syncrude. But it required large amounts of water even as it produced tailings from spent sands, air pollution, and land in need of reclamation. Such environmental damage was the much debated cost of oil sands

*Strip mining bucket at Syncrude plant, 1978. ExxonMobil
Historical Collection, di_06245.*

development, which promised to boost the economy of Alberta while
providing a significant addition to energy supplies.[76]

As the Syncrude consortium moved toward production, Imperial pursued its own heavy-oil project near Cold Lake, Alberta, south of Fort
McMurray. Because the thick layers of oil were not near the surface at
·Cold Lake, as the oil sands were at Fort McMurray, surface mining could
not be used. Instead, Imperial developed an innovative steam-injection
process to recover bitumen from some 1,500 feet underground. The injection of steam under intense pressure from multiple wells into the heavy
oil at Cold Lake thinned the thick bitumen, causing it to begin to flow.
Then, with the steam shut off, the injection wells could be used to pump
the bitumen to the surface, where it could be sent to refineries to be processed into crude oil or sold in unrefined form for such uses as producing
asphalt for roads.[77]

Syncrude enthusiasts held great hopes for Imperial's Cold Lake project
in the boom years for synthetic fuel in the decade after 1973. Indeed, the
company announced plans in 1978 to acquire permits for a giant commercial facility costing about $4 billion and capable of producing 140,000

barrels of oil equivalent per day at Cold Lake by 1986. Only three years later, however, the optimism underlying that announcement had dissolved, and the company considered abandoning Cold Lake. In 1983, it chose instead to continue the project, but more slowly than originally envisioned, with a phased development designed to match output more closely to market demand. The Canadian government encouraged this approach by reducing its royalties and lowering its taxes until Imperial had recouped its investment costs.[78]

The federal and provincial governments in Canada assisted Imperial in staying the course at Cold Lake because they viewed themselves as partners in the development of synthetic fuels from oil sands. The companies and governments involved in the Canadian oil sands all acknowledged the importance of the synfuel industry for the reduction of oil imports, the growth of Alberta's oil industry, and the overall health of the Canadian economy. The participation of Canadian governments in the Syncrude consortium helped it move quickly toward production in the mid-1970s, and that fast start helped create a young industry strong enough to survive the price downturn of the mid-1980s. Government assistance in the form of lower taxes at Cold Lake helped that project remain in operation at a reduced scale until better economic conditions for the development of synfuels returned. Thus encouraged by strong governmental support, and aided by a less expensive technology, oil sands development in Canada forged ahead of oil shale development in the United States.

Exxon had identified both oil sands and oil shale as potential supplements to traditional oil as early as the 1960s, and company planners monitored developments in both industries. In April 1975, the Exxon Management Committee voiced no objection to Imperial's investing almost half a billion dollars in order to take a leading role in Syncrude Canada's project to manufacture "high-quality synthetic crude oil" from the Athabasca oil sands. That same month, a study by Exxon USA suggested that commercial-scale oil shale projects enjoyed a "considerably lower cost" than those involving the oil sands, namely, $12,800 rather than $18,700 for the investment cost to produce a barrel of synfuel. Despite Exxon USA's views, Exxon's corporate management remained skeptical of oil shale. In 1975, the outgoing CEO, Ken Jamieson, concluded that "shale is a very high cost energy source, and it produces a great amount of solid waste. . . . Oil from shale is still a long way down the road."[79]

Only four years later, his replacement, Cliff Garvin, wrote of the "need for synfuels," arguing that they were critical domestic alternatives to high-priced oil imported from dangerous regions. The next year, Exxon USA bought a majority share of the Colony project, a large oil shale project being developed near Parachute, Colorado, thus quickly emerging as one of the nation's most prominent supporters of oil shale development. Echoing remarks previously made by Garvin, Randall Meyer, the president of Exxon USA (which managed the project), wrote in 1981 of the great potential for oil shale and other synfuels. Based on what turned out to be far too optimistic internal projections, he asserted that the United States could build "a 15 million-barrels-per-day-oil-equivalent synthetic fuels industry over the next thirty years." Such an industry "would employ directly 870,000 people" and cost "$850 billion in today's dollars." For perspective, Meyer noted that this total "is about 1 percent of gross national product at the peak of development," or roughly the "percentage of GNP invested by the petroleum industry today in conventional oil and gas exploration and development." Such an investment would create a diverse synfuel industry led by oil shale but also including oil sands and coal liquefaction and gasification.[80]

Exxon's *World Energy Outlook* (an annual publication) for 1980 published a rosy analysis of the promise of synfuels. In articles, speeches, and company reports, Exxon spokespersons laid out the prospect for an energy future dominated by synfuels. They neither minimized the economic and environmental challenges facing those who would create such a future, nor directly advocated the sort of massive investment in synfuels needed to achieve fifteen million barrels a day of production. But by discussing a far more ambitious future scenario for synfuels than generally put forward elsewhere in industry or by the government, Exxon made itself into a prominent symbol of synfuel enthusiasm.[81]

The Colony project, begun in the 1950s, had endured several stops and starts before Exxon entered the picture. The technology used had been under development since 1955. In 1964, TOSCO (The Oil Shale Company) had created the Colony project with Sohio and Cleveland-Cliffs to build and operate a demonstration plant west of Rifle, a small town in western Colorado. After the suspension of those operations in 1967, a second retorting demonstration at Colony took place from 1970 to 1972. TOSCO's partners changed over time. ARCO took a 60 percent ownership interest and then decided to withdraw from the project and focus its resources on the development of its oil and gas on the North Slope of Alaska. By this time, with the help of a government-guaranteed loan, TOSCO had developed a technical process that could compete for leadership in what appeared to be an oil shale industry on the verge of rapid growth. Enthusiastic about the prospects of the Colony project, Exxon bought ARCO's 60 percent share for $300 million, with a promise to pay another $100 million if a successful commercial plant was in operation by the late 1980s. Other oil companies were at the time developing their own technologies to develop oil shale in several sections of the country.[82]

Synfuel enthusiasm was in the air, bolstered by the doubling of oil prices after the Iranian hostage crisis. Against this backdrop, Congress passed, and President Carter signed, the Energy Security Act of 1980, which created a new federal agency, the Synthetic Fuels Corporation, and provided billions of dollars in governmental funding to foster the growth of a synfuel industry. The act put forward aggressive goals for synfuel development, calling for 500,000 barrels of oil equivalent a day by 1987 and 2 million barrels per day by 1992. The race was on.[83]

By 1980, economic conditions had changed so dramatically that Garvin noted that "the least expensive synthetic fuels—shale oil and intermediate BTU gas from coal—have become competitive with imported crude oil." For synfuels to be economic in the long term, however, their price would have to remain competitive with oil for the decades needed to construct the plants and operate them at a profit. In the chaotic conditions brought by the second oil-price shock, this seemed possible and even likely to many in the petroleum industry. As oil prices shot through the roof and numerous synfuel processes seemed to be moving toward commercialization, the trend lines for the prices of the two fuels seemed likely to cross. Indeed, it was not far-fetched to think that economies of scale from increasingly large synfuel projects, set against increases in oil prices because of growing scarcity, might drive the future price of some synfuels below that of oil.

Garvin predicted that by the year 2000, synfuels could account for "nine million barrels a day," as much as 4 percent of total world energy supplies, if they were "developed aggressively."[84]

At this point in Exxon's history, its synfuel enthusiasm even overrode the company's traditional commitment to strict financial controls. Exxon USA reached its decision on the Colony project outside of what it called the company's "traditional approach of progressing the project through a series of checkpoints, making a limited commitment at each stage." Instead, it took "a second approach . . . to make a strong initial, public commitment to a shale oil project—which would be subject to relatively few conditions." Those in charge of the project felt that "making a strong public commitment will be required to achieve the proposed resources exchange [in which Exxon traded lands with the state of Colorado] and to obtain the necessary environmental permits on a timely basis." While noting that there were risks associated with a new industry, they argued that "the potential economic variability is not likely to drop the ROI [return on investment] to an unacceptable level."[85]

In retrospect, it is clear that an era of irrational exuberance for synfuels had begun at Exxon, in the oil industry as a whole, and in Washington, D.C. Oil executives and government officials confronted unprecedented conditions of runaway oil prices and shortages, which seemed to demand decisive action. As the world economy groaned under the impact of the rising cost of energy, pessimism grew about the long-term supply of oil. Fears arose that supply, particularly from domestic sources, could not keep pace with demand even if oil prices continued to rise to $100 a barrel, as projected by many experts. More than corporate profitability was at risk. The nation's national security and economic well-being seemed to hang in the balance. Those fears ultimately proved overblown as high oil prices and a global recession dampened the demand for oil products, but not before many energy-related institutions had made decisions, which they would come to regret, based on shaky assumptions about the future of oil shared by almost everyone in the oil industry.

Risks were all around, but the synfuels bubble and the high price of oil blocked them from view. In June 1981, the *Oil and Gas Journal* presented an overview of the major oil shale projects around the nation and proclaimed that the industry "was heading for commercial operations—the earliest possibly in two years." In November 1981, the *New York Times* picked up the same theme in a long article under the headline "Shale Oil Is Coming of Age." The next day, *U.S. News & World Report* published "As the Synfuels Industry Picks up Steam," an article which discussed the synfuels-led boom in the western United States. All those articles highlighted the Colony project as an important part of a boom in the making. The *U.S. News & World Report* article reported: "The federal government has earmarked 17.5 billion dollars to underwrite ventures by 1985, with the option of spending another 68 billion if needed. Energy companies are prepared to spend billions more."[86]

Exxon earlier had accepted government subsidies for synfuel pilot projects, but it decided early on not to accept them for commercial-scale plants such as the one being built by the Colony project, even though its partner, TOSCO, had long made use of them. The lack of subsidies would reinforce the financial discipline Exxon needed to ensure that the project would be competitive upon its completion. Against this backdrop, work went forward in and around Parachute, Colorado, preparing the way for construction of the manufacturing complex. Exxon and TOSCO spent an estimated $400 million on this phase of work on engineering, design, and field-construction development. A broad section of western Colorado bustled with activity, as numerous synfuel projects took shape in oil-shale-rich hills framed by the Colorado River and Interstate 70.

The project's proposed commercial plant at Colony was designed to use about 60,000 tons of oil shale per day to produce approximately 48,000 barrels a day of liquid fuel. The technology developed by TOSCO had already proved successful at a pilot plant. With a projected completion date of 1985 at a cost estimated at $1.7 billion in June 1981, the plant had the inside track on becoming the first commercial-scale oil shale facility in the United States.[87]

The oil shale would be mined using conventional surface mining, crushed to reduce the size of the ore, heated, then mixed in a large rotating drum with heated ceramic balls to vaporize kerogen (a usually insoluble mixture of organic solids) in the shale. The process would produce a variety of hydrocarbon products. Light gases would be used as fuel at the site; further treatment would purify the remaining light and heavy oils by removing hydrogen, nitrogen, and sulfur. The final product was

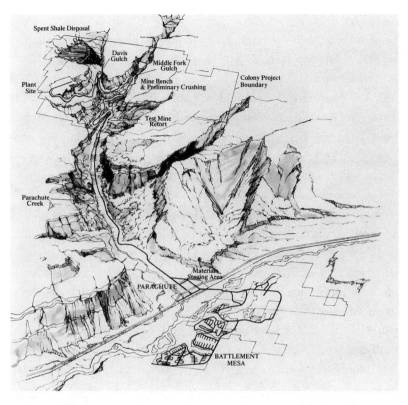

Colony Shale Oil Project and Battlement Mesa Community, ca. 1981.
ExxonMobil Historical Collection, di_08136.

high-quality synthetic oil that could be shipped by pipeline to conventional oil refineries to be made into gasoline, jet fuel, or diesel fuel.[88]

As the Colony project moved forward, Exxon began a series of detailed studies that revealed a disturbing trend. Costs on all aspects of the Colony project were rising dramatically. Early in 1980, TOSCO had estimated a $1.4 billion cost for the completion of the project. By early 1981, TOSCO projected a final cost of $3.2 billion when it applied for guaranteed loans from the Department of Energy. The next year, it revised this figure upward to $3.7 billion. Exxon's internal studies in 1982 startled the company's management by projecting a final cost of $6 billion to $8 billion for a plant capable of producing less than 50,000 barrels a day of synthetic oil. For perspective, this projected cost was roughly the cost of the recently completed Trans-Alaska Pipeline System, which could deliver as much as 2 million barrels of oil per day, about forty times the projected daily capacity of the Colony project.[89]

Exxon soon fell out with its partner over costs. Spokesmen for TOSCO continued to voice public optimism about the project, while Exxon increasingly expressed private doubts. Changing oil prices cut two ways. The sharp increase in oil prices after the Iranian Revolution dampened global oil demand while also fueling high inflation, which raised construction and material costs. Then, the softening of oil prices from 1982 onward raised doubts about the price competitiveness of synfuels from oil shale. In early 1982, TOSCO optimistically projected that, at completion, the Colony facility would produce oil from shale that could be sold for $30 a barrel.[90] Although OPEC's base price remained $34 a barrel at the time, discounting already had begun to put the price of some grades of OPEC oil below $30. Exxon's planners, along with many others in the oil industry, began to sense that prices would come down as lower world demand and growing production from non-OPEC nations created a surplus of oil. They were right. From 1982 through 1985, oil prices slid downward before plummeting to less than $10 per barrel in 1985 and 1986 as Saudi Arabia reasserted its control within OPEC by greatly increasing production.

After considering the increasing costs of the project and the possibility of sharply lower oil prices in the near future, Exxon's executives could no longer justify their investment in oil shale. On a quiet Sunday afternoon on May 2, 1982, Exxon announced the suspension of funding for the Colony project. The president of Exxon USA gave this explanation of the decision: "While construction has been progressing satisfactorily . . . Exxon believes the final cost would be more than twice as much as we thought it would be when we entered the project. . . . In our judgment, the investment economics no longer support our continuing to fund the present project."[91] Two weeks later, Cliff Garvin expanded on this topic at the annual shareholders' meeting: "Because OPEC nations have so much oil and such flexibility to increase or decrease output, they will continue to have a major impact on world oil markets." Exxon and other oil companies thus faced the problem of "how to plan for the long run in the face of such uncertainties." He acknowledged that the company "knew that it [Colony] was a risky venture and that we would have to find our way among many uncertainties." But with changing economic conditions, "even when giving the project all the credits we could for its newness and eventual desirability, the economics were no longer attractive."[92]

TOSCO spokesmen forcefully disputed Exxon's figures, publicly calling its partner's decision "a grave setback to the national program to launch a commercially viable synthetic fuels industry."[93] Public reaction also was intense, with the general sentiment captured in the headline and subhead of a *New York Times* article on the announcement: "Exxon Abandons Shale Oil Project; Entire Synthetic Fuel Industry Seriously Eroded by Action." *Newsweek* magazine called the decision "the 'Death' of Synfuels," and *Time* said simply "Setback for Synfuels."[94] Those reports acknowledged that other companies, notably Union Oil, remained committed to oil shale development. But Exxon, the largest oil company, and the Colony project, one of the largest ongoing efforts to build a commercial oil shale facility, had great symbolic importance.

The head of the Synthetic Fuels Corporation, Victor Schroeder, made determined appeals to Exxon to reconsider its decision. In a face-to-face meeting with Garvin in June 1982 and a later exchange of letters, Schroeder stressed that "our nation's energy security requires that it have commercial-scale facilities to prove and improve synthetic fuels capabilities, and to provide a base for rapid expansion in response to an oil supply crisis." He reminded Garvin that the Energy Security Act of 1980 provided the SFC with funds to "reduce the risk and improve the return to make well-conceived synthetic fuels projects attractive to private companies." Schroeder pleaded with Garvin to "explore the possible ways that the Colony project or any feasible synthetic fuels process can be considered for the production experience and the insurance."[95]

Garvin's direct response to Schroeder left no doubt that Exxon's decision on the Colony project would not be reversed unless economic conditions changed. Garvin explained that Exxon had not abandoned the idea of synfuel production in the future, but that for the present, "the anticipated investment costs had risen to the point where . . . the project would simply not produce an adequate return on our very large investment." He also reiterated that the sort of financial assistance available through the Synthetic Fuels Corporation would not alter Exxon's thinking: "It is simply that with costs as we see them today, such projects will not produce satisfactory returns. The only obvious correction for this would be a direct subsidy, a step which I would not be willing to recommend for a commercial-size plant." After affirming his belief that "a commercial, fully private industry will emerge at some point," Garvin concluded that this was where conditions "are likely to stay until a significant breakthrough is made in investment costs, or unless this country, for security reasons, wishes to put government in a different role."[96]

Several months after Exxon announced the suspension of its Colony project, Rawleigh Warner Jr., the CEO of Mobil, wrote to Garvin suggesting that "all of us give serious thought to a cooperative industry effort (with appropriate government participation) to spread the risks and finance a major shale oil project now, so that all of us can be ready for full-scale exploitation at the time we can forecast the economics that make individual ventures feasible." Garvin's response was straightforward: "We [Exxon] see nothing in the nation's energy future that changes our conviction that shale oil development will ultimately be a necessary part of our energy supply. At the same time, however, given the current economic climate, the tremendous capital commitments that such development will require are not being made by the private sector. Also, we doubt that many, if any, in industry would be supportive of a major government-financed program."[97]

With that, Exxon backed away from an investment that only two years before had been announced with great fanfare. All in all, Exxon's brief venture into oil shale produced perhaps a billion-dollar loss. Additional costs to the company included a substantial investment of managerial resources and a public relations black eye from jumping in and out of such a highly publicized investment. Exxon USA's strong support of this project would later be used as an argument in support of greater control over its activities by Exxon Corporation.

Although numerous other companies remained in oil shale development immediately after Exxon's withdrawal from Colony in 1982, the oil shale industry effectively ceased to exist in the United States within three years. Already in late 1983, Exxon officials noted the "marked reduction of industry and government interest and support for synfuels over the past two years, primarily brought by declining oil prices." At that time, the company conducted studies that "support shale as the preferred initial synfuel option for commercialization after Canadian oil sands," but the timing of future synfuel development remained in doubt.[98] Although the company retained a commitment to conduct research into a range of possible synfuels, the bubble had clearly burst, both within Exxon and within the oil industry as a whole.

Once cheap oil returned and the interest of private companies in synfuels waned, government-subsidy programs in the United States faded away. Officials in the Reagan administration had little interest in expanding the mission of the Synthetic Fuels Corporation to include a government-led oil shale program and little enthusiasm for retaining subsidies for private companies. The oil sands in Canada continued to produce synfuel during the next two decades of relatively low oil prices and then enjoyed a boom with the return of high oil prices after 2004. Until that time, little development of synthetic fuels went forward in the United States. In this sense, Exxon's investments in synfuels in the oil price boom of the decade after 1973 shared the fate of almost all its forays into energy sources other than oil and natural gas: what looked like promising investments in a high-oil-price era looked decidedly less promising after oil prices plummeted.

Oil prices were not, of course, the only determinant of the success or failure of Exxon's ventures into synfuels. The timing of entry obviously played a role, as the company entered oil shale just ahead of the collapse of the industry. Stronger, long-term federal support might have helped, although Exxon's reluctance to accept government subsidies for commercial plants probably would have caused it to decline such aid. Extreme oil-price swings revealed a harsh reality forgotten during the race for alternative energies in the 1970s: there was no economic alternative to inexpensive oil. Blinded by the bright light of high oil prices, the company made a series of mistakes in the process of diversification. But as prices softened and then collapsed in the mid-1980s, it stopped digging itself into a hole and reversed course.

———————————

The mothballing of the Colony project marked the end of Exxon's enthusiasm for both synfuels and diversification. Exxon's divestment by 1986 of most of the businesses it had acquired outside oil and natural gas was a strong statement of its resolve to refocus on its core businesses. The company had labored mightily to find new businesses capable of offsetting the projected decline of oil and natural gas supplies, but it had come up empty. Its overall returns from the time and money spent on diversification were disappointing, with losses of several billion dollars from failed investments and operating costs for unprofitable businesses. A greater cost for the company was the time and energy spent by top executives in planning diversification and then attempting to build the new companies, along with substantial investments of time and money by the company's research centers in work on technical processes for businesses that ultimately did not remain in the company. Yet Exxon's excursions into other industries did not permanently harm its core businesses. In the decade after 1973, the company spent several billion dollars on diversification at a time when its annual profits stayed in the range of $3 billion to $5 billion. Oil, gas, and chemicals continued to absorb the great majority of the company's capital, its technical expertise, and its managerial resources.

Among the few significant returns for Exxon from its investment in diversification were several key lessons learned. The most obvious was the need to improve corporate planning. On the fundamental issue of projecting the price of oil, company planners were wanderers in the wilderness of OPEC-led oil pricing, where no signposts pointed the way back to the comfortably predictable oil prices that had prevailed from World War II to 1973. The height of the planners' folly within Exxon—as throughout the oil industry—came just after the second price shock. The company's extremely high projections of both the price of oil and the future growth of synfuels in its *World Energy Outlook* of 1980 illustrated the groupthink that plagued the oil industry—and government officials and academic experts—in those years.[99] Indeed, underlying many of the bad decisions by corporate executives and government policy makers alike were sharp and unpredictable swings in oil prices. After the oil-price bust, Exxon cut through the uncertainties of projecting oil prices by using very low oil-price projections for planning. In practice, its approach was to guess low, invest in projects that met the company's investment criteria at that level, and count anything higher as a bonus.

Other lessons involved the process of selecting new ventures. Exxon identified new opportunities outside oil through the systematic approach of Exxon Enterprises and the happenstance approach within regional companies. Happenstance worked better. Opportunities ranging from chemicals to the electric power industry in Hong Kong (discussed in chapter 8) proved profitable in part because they had concrete ties to the company's daily operations. On the other hand, as Exxon Enterprises sought lucrative businesses outside petroleum, such ventures almost certainly were already in the sights of other major companies. Office equipment invited competition with IBM on its home court. Had it succeeded, Exxon's purchase of Reliance Electric could have placed the company in competition with GE. When a golfing partner from GE told Garvin that his company had "the same technology sitting on our shelf," Garvin thought that "if those guys get involved, our head start won't make much difference."[100]

In several cases, much-exaggerated projections of long-term profitability produced unrealistically high expectations. The projections poisoned the well when reality set in. No doubt that pattern encouraged Exxon to sour on poorly performing businesses and sell them quickly, making investors wonder about the judgment of the company's top management. The regular overselling of new ventures caused some managers within Exxon to begin to question the entire concept of diversification. The president of Exxon Enterprises, Bob Winslow, looked around in 1979 and saw the declining performance of office systems, the cutback in investment by Exxon Nuclear, and the impending death of the solar business; he responded by calling for various improvements in the management system.[101] After three more years of flowing red ink and projections of profitability being pushed into the future, Winslow had more fundamental concerns. The capital costs and the opportunity costs of Exxon Enterprises's efforts to develop new businesses led him to state the obvious: "An issue for the future would appear to be Exxon's needs for and interest in 'diversification.'"[102] Even a leading company such as Exxon could not easily build profitable enterprises in businesses outside its traditional strengths.

Exxon's enduring lesson from the era of diversification was simple, but powerful: when searching for promising opportunities, do not underestimate the vitality and flexibility of the oil and natural gas industries. The fundamental—and fundamentally flawed—assumption underlying diversification was that the company's core businesses would cease to grow and to produce long-term profits. By the mid-1980s, that assumption had to be reevaluated. The company's core industries could be expanded as new technologies became capable of finding and producing oil and natural gas in new frontier areas, such as deep water offshore. Such technologies would be costly, but even with the end of easy oil, oil and gas offered far greater opportunities for growth than had been apparent in the chaos after the first and second oil-price shocks of the 1970s. Those dependable, flexible, and historically inexpensive fuels would continue to supply a majority of the world's energy well into the future, and oil companies would continue to find ways to expand both the supply and the definition of "conventional" oil and natural gas. Exxon's core industries could be expanded if the company focused its considerable strengths more sharply on oil and gas, not on electric typewriters or copper or even coal. To do so, however, would require the reorganization and revitalization of core strengths developed by more than a century of leadership in the global oil and gas industries.

CHAPTER FIVE

REVIVAL

ORGANIZATIONAL INNOVATIONS
AFTER THE OIL BUST OF 1986

F rom December 1985 through the summer of 1986, all hell broke loose in the global oil industry as the oil bust of 1986 dropped oil prices from about $25 a barrel to less than $10 a barrel in a blink of the eye. After oil prices had begun to slide downward from a high of about $35 a barrel in 1983, "experts" projected that they would "settle in" at about $25 before rebounding. Instead, in the months after December 1985, prices plunged day after day before finally bottoming out briefly at about $8. Few then active in the oil industry had seen anything quite like that free fall in prices, since the last such plunge had come during the Great Depression. In centers of oil-related activity such as Houston, New Orleans, and Midland, Texas, the Great Oil Depression caused the widespread loss of jobs and money; almost no individual or company in the petroleum industry escaped unscathed. Even conservative oil companies and banks that had planned ahead in anticipation of lower prices suffered badly. It would be a long time before prices returned to the mid-$30 range, which had so recently seemed to herald an era of continually rising oil prices. A desperate tone prevailed as confused industry leaders surveyed the wreckage and wondered what the future of oil might hold.[1]

Before the bust, the conservatively run Exxon had prepared for a

Clifton Garvin, chairman and CEO (left) and Lawrence Rawl, president, Exxon Corporation, 1986. ExxonMobil Historical Collection, di_06155.

downturn, but not for disaster. As oil-price increases stalled and then softened in the early 1980s, Cliff Garvin responded by selling off unprofitable businesses, deferring large investments, and cutting costs. In his last year as CEO, before his mandatory retirement in 1986, Garvin ceded some of his authority to the incoming CEO, Lawrence Rawl, who would be responsible for guiding the recovery at Exxon. Rawl later called Garvin's actions between 1982 and 1986 as "deliberate steps," but as Garvin walked off into retirement, it was clear that the devastation wrought by the oil-price collapse of 1986 demanded stronger responses.[2]

With the close cooperation of his president, Lee Raymond, Rawl responded with a vengeance to the crisis at hand. He pressed forward in refocusing on Exxon's core businesses, oil, gas, and chemicals, which were the key to reviving the company's fortunes. Over the years from 1986 to the Mobil merger, in 1999, this effort steadily grew into a broader endeavor: refocusing on the company's core operating values to renew the company, returning it to its position as the low-cost competitor in its industry. A renewed emphasis on financial discipline and cost management moved the company toward a new generation of economies of scale. Technical leadership remained an important component of the ongoing effort to increase the efficiency and lower the costs of operations. Organizational innovations helped define a company-wide, global approach to strategy and the allocation of capital. As in the days of John D. Rockefeller, a small group of top managers would make key strategic choices; others in the company would manage the day-to-day business within a clear organizational framework. At the heart of the transformation of Exxon in this era was an old vision of the company made new: it would strive to set the industry standard for efficient and profitable operations.

A MANDATE FOR ACTION

The collapse of the petroleum industry slashed revenues and profits throughout the petroleum industry. Exxon's revenues dropped from $92.9 billion in 1985 to $76.6 billion in 1986, a fall of nearly 18 percent. Its earnings remained strong in 1986, but then dropped significantly, and failed to return to 1986 levels until 1991. What had looked like bad times in 1985 looked like the good old days by the end of 1986. The company's annual report for 1985, published in early March 1986, directly addressed deteriorating market conditions. In their "Letter to Shareholders," outgoing chairman Garvin and incoming chairman Rawl conveyed a sense of urgency about the far-reaching impact of the "most drastic drop" in spot-crude oil prices "in the modern history of the oil industry." In response, the company would have to "rethink [its] entire strategy": "Exploration ventures, capital investments, the lines of business we are in—all must be reexamined to make sure they continue to make sense in a radically new environment."[3] Richard Kruizenga, the vice president of corporate planning at the time, noted, "It was Garvin who blew the whistle and saw this changed environment . . . and said, 'We've got to rein ourselves in; we're going overboard.'"[4]

In the first quarter of 1986, Rawl and Raymond met with Garvin to outline the changes they thought Exxon needed to make in order to become more responsive to market conditions. According to Raymond, Garvin agreed with their proposals. They then suggested that he might want to wait until after his retirement at the end of 1986 before the wrenching series of changes were made. Raymond later recalled Garvin's response: "No, no. Don't wait for me. Don't ever wait for me. Let's get going, and whatever you want me to do [to make the process work], I'll do."[5] The three worked together until Garvin's retirement, but in the full-blown crisis after 1986, Rawl as CEO took the lead in reviving the company with the help of Raymond and many other strong Exxon executives.[6]

Rawl was an unusual choice for the chairmanship. He was born in Ridgewood, New Jersey, one of six children. His father worked for the Railway Express Agency. In 1945, when he was only seventeen, he enlisted in the U.S. Marine Corps, where he ultimately earned the rank of sergeant. After his discharge, he took a job in the oil fields in Oklahoma and then entered the University of Oklahoma on the GI Bill and graduated with a degree in petroleum engineering. He turned down a job offer from Standard Oil Company (New Jersey) because, in his words, "I knew I didn't want to work for the world's biggest oil company. You couldn't get ahead."[7] Instead, he took a job at Humble Oil & Refining, only to discover later that Jersey Standard owned a majority share in the company.

Humble first assigned Rawl to supervise an exploration crew in South Texas. Some of his early experiences suggested how his personality might affect his work within the company. Once, after the young Rawl told one of his long-experienced drillers how a well should be drilled, the man dryly informed him that he had been in the oil fields for a while. Rawl retorted: "If you want to be here a couple more weeks, do what I tell you." After learning of the incident, Rawl's supervisor told him that he understood he had been giving orders to people. Rawl's reply: "So what? Who's in charge out there, me or the driller?" The supervisor replied, "I am," and told Rawl to back off.[8] The episode captured Rawl's self-confidence and his demanding nature, and it also illustrated his abrasive side, his impatience with poor performance, and his characteristic bluntness.

Rawl spent a number of years in drilling jobs in South Texas, moving more than a dozen times. He and his wife, Betty, began to have children, one of whom he helped deliver when they could not get to a hospital in time. In 1960, he was assigned to Jersey Standard's New York headquarters to assess overseas exploration prospects. He did well and was soon sent back to Texas, where he gained experience in planning and production. His outstanding performance led to a job as the executive assistant

Lawrence Rawl, chairman and CEO of Exxon Corporation, 1986.
ExxonMobil Historical Collection, di_06151.

to Exxon's chairman, Mike Haider, in New York City. He then returned to Humble in Houston, and within nine years rose to be the executive vice president of the newly named Exxon USA.

Having spent his career to date in the United States, Rawl became the executive vice president of Esso Europe, the regional headquarters for Exxon's European affiliates. There, the rough-edged Rawl presided over a rather cosmopolitan group, which came to tolerate and even appreciate his direct manner. In 1980, Rawl returned to New York as senior vice president and director of Exxon Corporation. He was fortunate in that Howard Kauffmann, the company's president, was just two years younger than Garvin and therefore unlikely to succeed him as chairman when he reached mandatory retirement age in 1986. When Kauffmann's retirement was announced at the annual meeting in May 1985, Rawl was named president, thereby becoming the leading candidate to replace Garvin.[9] The next year, he was named as Garvin's replacement, becoming the chairman and CEO of Exxon at age fifty-seven.

Rawl's personality left a lasting impression on all who worked with him. He was obstinate and argumentative. He gave scant attention to the traditional polite tone of the company and relished challenging existing approaches to the oil business. He respected those with the self-confidence to argue with him, as long as they made useful comments and did not argue too long. This did not happen often, since he had the ability to get to the heart of an issue. He had little patience with people he considered poorly qualified, and "could be damn brutal internally."[10] An article in *Fortune* reported that "outside directors and former top managers in the company heap compliments upon the man."[11] One executive recalled "that as a human being, [Rawl was] probably one of the nicest people I've met in the company, although at times he could be quite severe with those . . . that didn't share his [business] point of view."[12] In short, Rawl was a man of many contradictions: a self-styled cowboy from New Jersey and a marine sergeant serving as the general of Exxon. In the context of the crisis he inherited, his decisiveness was a strength. To fill weaknesses such as his lack of experience with finance, he could turn to others in a company rich with executive talent.

As president under Rawl, Lee Raymond complemented his CEO in both experience and style. Both men grew up without privilege and made their own way in life. At Exxon, both found an organization that rewarded merit, and both worked hard to move to the top. Raymond was born in Watertown, South Dakota, in August 1938. His father had quit school at thirteen years old to support his sick mother, since his own father was no longer at home. He became a railroad engineer and worked for the same company for fifty-five years. A strong proponent of education, he once told Raymond and his brother, "You have to get an education and get out of here. There's not enough opportunity."[13] Raymond attended public schools and played sports and hunted and fished for fun. He excelled in math and science, and he was a skilled debater.

After high school, Raymond attended the University of Wisconsin in Madison, majoring in chemical engineering. He then earned a Ph.D. in chemical engineering in 1963 from the University of Minnesota. Along the way, he met and married his wife, Charlene, and the family expanded dramatically with the birth of triplet sons. Raymond began work at an affiliate of Exxon as a production research engineer in Tulsa, Oklahoma. His subsequent career path within Exxon indicates that the company's management-development program quickly identified him as a young person with extraordinary promise, and he received a series of increasingly demanding assignments that propelled him upward at an uncommonly rapid pace. In 1977, he took charge of the company's large refinery in Aruba, which at the time was losing $10 million a month while refining Venezuelan crude. By cutting costs and convincing the Venezuelans to provide less expensive, extra-heavy crude oil, he helped turn Aruba's losses into profits. This turnaround helped establish his reputation within the company as a hard-charging problem solver. He next became head of Exxon Nuclear, where he renegotiated unfavorable contracts for uranium ore. Then, in 1981, he was moved to the top position in Exxon Enterprises, where he prepared the way for the divestment of poorly performing companies in a variety of nonenergy businesses. Those experiences convinced Raymond that Exxon's basic strengths in oil did not necessarily translate into success in other, unrelated businesses, a conclusion he retained throughout his career.[14]

Following his tenure with Exxon Enterprises, Raymond moved to the top job in Esso Inter-America, the regional company that managed the company's holdings in South America and the Caribbean. Here he became reacquainted with the conventional petroleum business, particularly the marketing function that dominated Exxon's activities in the region. In that position, he again demonstrated to his superiors a willingness to make hard decisions and an ability to negotiate agreements favorable to the company.

Successful in his role as a "fixer" of poorly performing businesses; conversant in oil production, oil refining, and marketing; and experienced in both the United States and abroad, Raymond became a senior vice president of the corporation in 1984. He remained in that position until his elevation to president in 1987. He had been groomed for leadership throughout his career at Exxon, and now his training and experience in meeting challenging situations would be tested at the highest level in the midst of one of the most severe crises Exxon had faced in the post–World War II era.

Rawl and Raymond had worked together at times during their many moves throughout Exxon's far-flung operations. Indeed, the company's management-development system often brought together promising young employees who were later reunited at higher levels within the company. Working closely together at corporate headquarters in New York in the years just before the oil bust in 1986, they often discussed where the company should be going and what needed to be done. They saw many of the same problems and solutions, and they agreed on the need for basic changes within Exxon. When their time at the top came, they led the transformation of the company.

The approach to management of first Rawl and then Raymond marked a generational change in outlook at the top. They shared with many in Exxon the view that the market crisis had placed upon them the responsibility to set things straight. Raymond recalled the attitude of the new top management: it was time "to get this place going again." He continued: "I won't say the company had been floundering, but the company had kind of been treading water and people were [thinking] what are we going to try and do and [what] aren't we going to try and do. . . . [There] was the [Exxon] Enterprise debacle that nobody liked and research was all screwed up. . . . Esso Europe hated Exxon USA and Chemical wouldn't talk to anybody. . . . And you just had this [feeling] of like, 'Who the hell's in charge?'"[15] The rapid deterioration of market conditions reinforced such attitudes, and Rawl, with considerable confidence in his own ability, set about shaking Exxon out of its confusion.

"WHO THE HELL'S IN CHARGE?": ORGANIZATIONAL TENSIONS

Reorganizing the company to eliminate structural barriers to efficiency was a pressing need. In the forty years after World War II, the company's steady international expansion in an era of difficult travel and slow communications spawned powerful national affiliates around the world. One of Raymond's contemporaries, Morris Foster, recalled his time as head of Esso Malaysia: "I mean, I was the king. I did my own thing, and I didn't let anybody bother me. . . . I was . . . thirteen hours out of cycle with them [his superiors in the United States], so I could do anything I wanted to."[16] In North America, Exxon USA had long held a special status as the largest producer and refiner in the Exxon system, and Imperial Oil had similar independence because of a 30 percent minority interest that Exxon was hesitant to challenge—at least for as long as the company remained successful. Efforts to assert more systematic oversight and control over the national companies led to the creation of an additional layer of bureaucracy in the 1960s—regional companies that managed a number of nations in broad geographic areas. Adding to the organizational confusion and overlap built into this management system were the businesses acquired through diversification in the 1970s.

By then, Exxon had become a sluggish giant, slow to make even important decisions and prone to stifle creativity under layers of oversight. In August 1980, when Exxon was optimistic and flush with cash from high oil prices, the *New York Times* published a mostly positive appraisal of its management system. The reporter enjoyed rare access to a meeting of the corporate management committee, which he identified as the men "who really rule Exxon." The eight-person committee met approximately three times a week to evaluate proposals brought to New York by representatives of the regional affiliates. The article likened the presidents of the regional companies to "provincial governors" with "substantial autonomy, but within a top-to-bottom network of checks and balances." It noted that Exxon USA enjoyed a status as "first among equals" in the pecking order of the regional companies. Tensions arose between the regional representatives and corporate headquarters in New York City, where a large, powerful staff compiled volumes of data to support the deliberations of the corporate management committee and the corporate investment advisory committee. Projects put forward by national companies faced a long journey to final approval; they were examined closely at the national level and at regional headquarters before being presented to the corporate management committee. As they neared the finish line in New York, however, proposals requesting more than $25 million also faced a detailed financial analysis by the corporate investment advisory committee. Only after clearing that daunting series of hurdles would a request reach the management committee. The multilayered and drawn-out deliberations ensured that by the time a proposal had moved up to the top of the hierarchy, there would be "no surprises," which the reporter labeled "a favorite phrase around Exxon." The article concluded that Exxon Corporation was in fact less like a corporation than a "fabulously wealthy investment club with a limited portfolio."[17]

Rene Dahan, who participated in deliberations in the same conference room before the same set of corporate committees early in a career that led him to the top level of Exxon's management, had quite a different memory of the corporate management committee. He recalled the headquarters building as "51 stories of people" who busily collected and analyzed detailed data on every aspect of the company's operations. He noted that "the corporation was very rich in committees," which were "very political, very slow, and not particularly dynamic." Indeed, Dahan recalled that he and his colleagues referred to the deliberations of the committee system at Exxon as "trying to . . . push things with a wet noodle." More telling to Dahan was the tone of the company in these years: "Exxon had a long, long tradition of being very much focused on efficiency, and yet, if you asked me, from the days I joined the company in the early sixties, in the first twenty years of that, I saw little to . . . reinforce that kind of dedication to efficiency . . . to what I would call execution [of] the work we do every day and the quality of that work, both in money and in performance."[18] From his point of view, the core operating values that had given the company its reputation and it success had been submerged under layers of bureaucracy.

Rawl had similar reactions to his own early experiences within the inherited decision-making system. To him, the structure and process were sclerotic and unnecessarily costly. He did not have fond memories of working with the headquarters staff in New York City: "We just had a lot of people working for other people who were going to meetings of committees. . . . You came in, sat around, and generated numbers for some guy on the 51st floor, wondering why he needed them."[19] Under that system, after lengthy discussions of proposals developed in detailed deliberations within the regional companies, the corporate management committee generally stated its approval by "expressing no objections." According to Raymond, Rawl believed that top decision makers ought to participate more directly in defining the agenda for debate, shaping key choices, and making final decisions in their areas of responsibility. He wanted the corporate executives in New York to exercise authority and responsibility as opposed to sitting on the sidelines and sniping. He wanted them to take the attitude that "we were all in this together." Raymond recalled Rawl commenting, "We have too many checkers checking the checkers. You're not allowed to sit on the sidelines. . . . We don't have time for that." [20]

With that attitude and inclination, Rawl was eager to change Exxon's structure and procedures. As president in 1985 and 1986, he concluded that the company's regional structure had outlived its usefulness, particularly since advances in technology allowed operating companies to communicate faster and more directly with corporate headquarters. Intermediate-level staffs at regional levels no longer appeared useful. Rawl knew from experience that the company needed to be nimbler and more flexible in responding to competitive pressures. He colorfully described his goal as "making the elephant dance" or, alternatively, as making the global giant Exxon operate like an independent oil company.

Doing so required fundamental changes in the overall organization of the company. Such changes are never easy in large organizations, particularly those with long histories of success and traditions of lifetime employment. In the late nineteenth century, John D. Rockefeller had pushed through organizational innovations that created the first vertically integrated oil company. A century later, Rawl pushed for another set of organizational innovations designed to improve Exxon's operations by increasing the capacity of top managers to take an overall, corporate view of the company's global operations and a more active role in managing.

CHEMICAL STEPS OUT FRONT

Others within the company had not waited to address some of the same fundamental problems that plagued the company's oil and natural gas businesses. Ed Holmer, the president of Exxon Chemical Company, came to believe in the early 1980s that the matrix organization the company had used for years was too cumbersome and costly. In that structure, a person running the plastics business in Europe, for example, would report to both a regional vice president in Europe and a plastics vice president at the company headquarters in Darien, Connecticut. This dual reporting structure had been useful in the years following the split of chemicals from the petroleum company in the 1960s, as it ensured that the chemical company's business plans were carefully vetted from the perspective of both the region and the product line. By the early 1980s, however, Holmer concluded that such redundancies had become counterproductive.

By 1985, the chemical company's senior executives believed that they had developed a large number of managers with experience in chemical production and marketing as well as broad exposure to the business of their sister petroleum company. Moreover, Exxon Chemical had put together what it considered an outstanding management-development program. The company had been an early practitioner of moving executives across product lines, countries, and operations, and it had developed a cadre of internationally experienced executives.[21] In short, the matrix structure seemed to offer few continuing benefits for the maturing company, but merely raised costs and slowed decision making.

Accordingly, in the fall of 1985, Holmer appointed a task force to assess the company's organization and recommend changes. Exxon Chemical executive vice president Gene McBrayer headed the seven-member task force, which toured the company's facilities around the world, interviewed almost 200 people in a wide variety of positions in the company, reached out to consultants, and debated alternatives before making recommendations to Holmer.[22] In assessing the existing matrix structure, McBrayer noted that a large majority of employees interviewed "felt that they were over-managed and underutilized." And this had impeded efficiency: "There was a general feeling that for many matters we had kept decision making far too high in the organization. . . . We needed to be a much more market-driven, outward-focusing company."[23] In March 1986, Holmer retired and McBrayer took over as president of Exxon Chemical. McBrayer quickly implemented the study's recommendations in three areas: employee reductions, simplification of product lines, and cost controls. Acting on the study's conclusion that one-third of managers at the vice presidential level and above were unneeded, the company offered

1,000 employees early retirement or separation packages. The company trimmed its employees to 16,600, a cut of 6 percent.

Exxon Chemical had previously operated with ten product-line groups and with regional organizations that included the United States, Latin America, Asia, Europe, Middle East, and Canada, each with its own management. The redesigned company had only three major product groups; each included related products, and each interacted with nationally based companies. These groups were the following:

BASIC CHEMICALS: olefins, aromatics, normal paraffins, methyl tertiary butyl ether (MTBE), and fertilizers;

POLYMERS: polyethylene, polypropylene, butyl polymers, ethylene-propylene rubber, and polyisobutalene, as well as related adhesives, film, fabrics, and twine; and

PERFORMANCE PRODUCTS: engine-oil additives, chemicals used in petroleum production, refinery chemicals, solvents, plasticizers, intermediate plastics, some acids, and two separately organized affiliated companies, Callaway Chemical and Tomah Products.

The company also simplified its geographic structure by creating three regional headquarters in Houston, Toronto, and Brussels. A primary duty of the headquarter groups was to maintain contact with major customers as well as governments and industry associations.

Both Holmer and McBrayer sought ways to make the reorganized company more competitive in a dynamic industry. After benchmarking the leading chemical companies in order to better understand competitive conditions, they concluded that Exxon Chemical had to find ways to reduce its costs year after year. McBrayer determined that cost reductions from "de-bottlenecks, cost efficiencies, [and] energy-efficiency projects... required lowering of real costs": "We just went back to the drawing board and said, 'That's not good enough. We've got to do better.'"[24] McBrayer added that the company's investment strategy had to change as well: "We knew our cost structure. We had learned to start managing the cycles so that we could take advantage of bust periods to put in capacity for the next boom, as opposed to waiting until the boom comes and investing such that it would be coming onstream when the next bust came."[25]

The restructured Exxon Chemical quickly enjoyed improved financial success. Worldwide earnings in 1985 were $249 million, split evenly between the United States and international areas. In 1986, the first year with the new structure, earnings rose to $470 million, though a reduction in the cost of raw materials was undoubtedly a factor. In 1987, global earnings were even higher, $750 million, and then, in 1988 and 1989, they broke the billion-dollar level with profits of $1,306 million and $1,082 million.[26] The quadrupling of profits between 1985 and 1989 seemed to vindicate the new structure, but profits did not remain at those levels, falling back to $522 million in 1990.

The importance of the 1986 reorganization of Exxon Chemical went beyond the resulting increase in profitability. The redesigned chemical company became a symbol to many within Exxon of the benefits of global organization around product lines, as opposed to a regional organization. The geographic groups that remained within Exxon Chemical were more for the convenience of interacting with governments than for dealing with commercial customers. At the time, the company's globalized organization was an unusual departure from the popular matrix structure. As Exxon Chemical gained experience with the new structure, the management of both the chemical company and the corporation as a whole became more familiar with its advantages, including generally lower costs. In addition, proponents of a more global organization for the corporation as a whole now had a case study that supported their position.

ECI: A BEACHHEAD FOR ORGANIZATIONAL CHANGE IN OIL

In oil, Rawl began reorganization with a bold, controversial decision to abolish the major international regional organizations and replace them with Exxon Company, International (ECI). Headquartered in Florham Park, New Jersey, near Exxon Research and Engineering's headquarters, the new organization absorbed all the existing regional companies except Exxon USA and Imperial. This meant that Esso Europe, Esso Eastern, Esso Middle East, Esso Africa, Esso Inter-America, Esso Exploration, and Exxon International Company disappeared as independent operating companies.[27] Exxon Chemical and the research companies—which provided services for all the divisions of the corporation—also remained outside ECI.

To head the new company, Rawl and Raymond favored Richard G. Reid, at that time the president of Esso Europe. Reid had been Rawl's boss when the new CEO was executive vice president of Esso Europe. Raymond had dealt at length with Esso Europe and considered Reid to be an extremely organized manager. Both men knew that Reid agreed with them on the need for fundamental structural changes.[28] Reid was slated for retirement in 1987, and his probable successor at ECI would be Sidney J. Reso. After Garvin went along with his subordinates' recommendation, the naming of other key executives for ECI soon followed, and the new entity began operation in 1986.[29]

ECI had a conventional management structure, with functional divisions supported by standard staff departments. Under the president were two executive vice presidents, one responsible for the upstream and one for the downstream. Three vice presidents had responsibilities for exploration, production, and natural gas. The company included a marine-transportation group that had responsibility for the shipment of crude oil and products. The downstream part of the business included refining and marketing. Support functions encompassed standard groups: finance, public affairs, planning, computer systems, legal, medical, and human resources. One special regional group at ECI headquarters focused on the Middle East. ECI also set up a special office in Belgium to follow developments in Europe. Otherwise, the managers reported directly to the headquarters department appropriate for the problem at hand. The head of each national company was given a primary contact at headquarters.[30]

The creation of ECI altered historical balances within Exxon. Long used to a dominant position, Exxon USA was now overshadowed by the larger ECI, which held the bulk of the company's production, sales, and profits (see figure 5.1). In all but two of the categories included on the chart (natural gas reserves and chemical's return on capital employed), the relative share of the United States was below that of the rest of the world, sometimes by a large margin. What took place in ECI had a larger impact on corporate fortunes than what transpired in Exxon USA or Imperial Oil. Growing reliance on foreign crude and the relative decline of North American production after the early 1970s had been moving Exxon steadily in this direction, and the creation of ECI meant that a new day had arrived. But organizational tensions between the old leader,

FIGURE 5.1. ECI within Exxon, 1987

CATEGORY	NON-U.S.	NON–NORTH AMER.	U.S.	CANADA
Employees	62		38	
Crude oil reserves		54	34	12
Natural gas reserves		48	43	9
Net undeveloped acreage		86	8	6
Petroleum product sales		63	26	11
Refining capacity		54	34	12
Net investments (petroleum & chemicals)	51		49	
Earnings from petroleum	68		32	
Return on capital employed				
Exploration & production	31		10	
Refining & marketing	6		1	
Chemical	17		22	

Source: *1987 Financial and Statistical Supplement to the Annual Report*
Note: *All figures are percentages.*

Exxon USA, and the remainder of the corporation continued to fester. As Lee Raymond had begun to realize in the 1970s: "The future of the company was outside the United States. It was not inside the United States, and that means we had a lot to clean up."[31]

The creation of ECI was a part of a general trend throughout Exxon of reducing costs by streamlining operations in such areas as refining, shipping, and retail marketing. Other divisions within Exxon also were cut back. Exxon USA reduced the number of its production districts and divisions, consolidated exploration activities within fewer districts, reduced the number of retail marketing regions, and reorganized the existing industrial and consumer business groups into fewer marketing areas. In addition, the company redesigned service organizations to handle larger portions of the operating groups and cut staff in headquarters departments. The Public Affairs Department, for example, moved its management staff into the Houston headquarters and eliminated the colocation of field managers with operating units.

REORGANIZING EXPLORATION

ECI's consolidation of exploration outside North America saved money and improved coordination throughout the corporation's international operations. It also paved the way for the global management structure put in place after the merger of Exxon and Mobil. But ECI held a broader appeal to Rawl and others. It was the key to finding more oil. As an old hand in the upstream, Rawl paid close attention to the company's exploration results. Although Raymond had less experience than Rawl in exploration and production, its importance had been impressed upon him as he climbed the corporate ladder. He remembered a conversation in the early 1970s with James Dean, then the head of Esso International. Overhearing Raymond grousing about his assignment to participate in a study of the company's Middle East concessions, Dean told him, "You can engrave this on the stone at the corner of the Exxon building on the Avenue of the Americas: 'Crude oil is the bedrock of the company.'"[32]

In their first letter to shareholders in the annual report for 1986, Rawl and Raymond emphasized this point: "Our organization is now better prepared to address the key problem facing our industry—finding new sources of oil and gas. For us, as for others, finding new supplies at reasonable cost has become an overriding objective." They acknowledged that changes had been made: "Our own program has been scaled down somewhat, though we still have one of the largest exploration budgets in the industry." The company had a "large resource base . . . that we can develop into proven reserves as these investment opportunities become commercially attractive."[33]

The *1986 Annual Report* affirmed the company's commitment to continue projects underway in Prudhoe Bay, LaBarge (Wyoming), offshore California, Europe, Canada, Australia, Malaysia, and Yemen.[34] It also revealed, however, cuts in capital spending for exploration and production. In fact, spending for exploration and production dropped nearly

40 percent in 1986, with much of the reduction concentrated in the United States.[35] Spending in those areas would not approach 1985 levels again until 1989.[36] Such cuts had an immediate impact on exploratory drilling. In 1985, the company drilled 433 net wells; in 1987, the figure declined to 184. The decline continued through 1990, when Exxon drilled only 139 net exploratory wells.[37] The company was in a difficult bind. It badly needed new reserves, but economic hardships required cuts in its exploration budget, and the low price of oil ruled out drilling in high-cost regions. Simply put, Exxon lacked promising prospects that could be developed economically at the low prevailing prices of oil.

As a result, its proved reserves declined. In 1980, Exxon had proved developed and undeveloped reserves of crude oil and other liquids of 7.64 billion barrels, and 45.44 trillion cubic feet of natural gas. In 1987, the petroleum number fell slightly, to 7.44 billion barrels, while natural gas reserves declined by a larger amount, to 38.76 trillion cubic feet, in part because of a reevaluation of Prudhoe Bay natural gas reserves. Accounting rules required the company to lower reserve estimates if there was no near-term prospect of producing the gas economically at existing prices, and the collapse of plans for the natural gas pipeline from Prudhoe Bay to existing gas markets forced the removal of North Slope gas from the figure for proved reserves.[38] The lower level of proved reserves would hold even in 1988.[39] Those reserves remained in the ground for future development when, or if, prices rose. But at lower prices, the revision of proved reserves downward presented a more realistic reflection of what the company could expect to produce in the near term.

Reserve replacement was a key measure used by stock market analysts to assess oil companies. In Raymond's view, "If you wanted to have a stock price that had a premium on it, you had to build a base of why you should get the premium. And one of the clear things that would let you do that would be a continuous reserves replacement."[40] Raymond's perspective on the importance of replacing reserves was underlined in a rambling article in *Fortune* in 1990. After lamenting the company's recent accidents (including the *Exxon Valdez* spill), describing poor company morale, and commenting unfavorably on the company's senior management, the authors wrote: "For all its strong financial performance in the 1980s, in the basics of oil and gas Exxon had lost its once fine edge. Measured by

Lee Raymond, upon becoming a member of the board of directors of Exxon Corporation, 1984. ExxonMobil Historical Collection, di_06242.

such critical gauges as the amount of production it has replaced with new reserves and how much it paid for them, the company usually scored lower in the past decade than Mobil or Royal Dutch/Shell."[41] Though they disagreed with the negative tone of the article, Exxon's top two executives shared concerns over the company's exploration record. They came at the problem, however, from slightly different perspectives. They believed that the exploration division had to greatly improve the management of its drilling program and find better ways to report its results.

To improve exploration, Rawl turned to organizational innovations. He wanted to find reserves that would be more profitable to produce, which meant focusing on the search for larger reservoirs. He wanted also to rationalize the company's method for ranking prospects. Before the 1986 reorganization, the company's exploration efforts had been fragmented by region. Each regional or corporate division prepared a plan for future exploration and presented it for approval to the Exploration Department in New York. The corporate management committee then approved funding for exploration drilling and assessment, with a heavy bias on prior funding in the allocation of funds to each region. The corporation, in effect, rank-ordered prospects in each region, but did not systematically compare prospects across the regional companies. This meant that Exxon USA might be drilling prospects in the United States—a relatively mature exploration area—that were far less promising than projects in less explored areas of the world. Rawl knew that this was an inefficient way to develop the company's reserves, and he looked for ways to force changes. Raymond recalled, "Somehow we had to get a worldwide system where there was a worldwide seriatim [list in priority order] independent of the fact that Australia used to be big or the United States is the United States." According to Raymond, Rawl felt strongly that "we weren't using all of our experience and expertise to try and help us figure out where to go."[42] Exxon needed an exploration process that, in a global perspective, combined the best possible geological data with previous experience.[43]

The first step was to find the right person to lead the effort. That man was Jon Thompson. He was born in May 1936 in Jacksonville, Florida, where he grew up and attended high school, playing sports and pursuing a strong interest in music.[44] At the University of Florida in Gainesville, he originally studied engineering, but switched to geology, which he considered ideal: "Geology is not a pure science like physics or chemistry or biology. It is not a prescribed science like engineering. . . . And it is like putting puzzles together and taking them apart and putting them together, so there are an infinite variety of potential solutions. You need data and you need intuition and you need a strong science background."[45] Thompson majored in geology and minored in chemistry, then went on to earn a master's degree in geology in 1962.

He then accepted a job at Humble, which he deferred while serving a

Jon L. Thompson, president, ExxonMobil Exploration Company, 1999.
ExxonMobil Historical Collection, di_06128.

two-year stint in the army. He rejoined the company as a paleontologist. At the time, geophysicists made common cause with paleontologists in order to determine the shape and pattern of potential petroleum reservoirs. Thompson gained experience in assessing sediments in the Gulf of Mexico during a period of extraordinary technical advances in geological understanding. He soon became a production geologist on an offshore drilling rig, where he worked with Harry Longwell; both subsequently became senior executives in Exxon's upstream operations. Thompson helped discover oil offshore California, worked in the Alaskan oil fields, moved to Denver to work the hard-rock geology of the Rocky Mountains, and then returned to Alaska. His rich experience also included a position as exploration operations manager for Esso Europe in London, where he gained familiarity with fields in the North Sea and Continental Europe. In that job, he dealt extensively with Shell Oil, Esso's partner in many European exploration and production ventures. He also worked in the Ivory Coast, gaining his first exposure to the geology of Africa.

Then it was back to the United States to focus on the Gulf of Mexico. At a meeting to discuss a lease sale, he formed early impressions of Larry Rawl: "Rawl was . . . a Renaissance man in wolf's clothing. . . . He'd grown up in Exxon USA. He'd seen the functional problems. . . . I was very taken by him and his breadth of understanding of the business. . . . But you'd go [to New York] and it appeared to be very structured, very structured—except for Rawl, who's not structured at all. . . . But he had a tremendous feeling for the business."[46] Thompson must have made a good impression on Rawl, who summoned him to New York in early 1985 to offer him a new job.

Thompson understood that top management was unhappy with the various company fiefdoms and with the meager exploration results: "How can we spend all this money and not have much to show for it? How can we . . . break this prison that we've built for ourselves, organizationally? So what they asked me to do at that meeting was [to] set up the Exploration Technical Assessment Group, which [would] report to the corporation."[47] Rawl told Thompson to pick the people he wanted in a new Exploration Technical Assessment Group (ETAG), which would conduct independent analyses of every exploration proposal from every region. Rawl promised Thompson access to any data he wanted, and guaranteed him full support: "If anybody, anywhere along the line, refuses or gives you a hard time, you let [me] know and [I'll] take care of it. . . . We're going to tell all these regions what we've done and what we want done and that we want you to go do it. Because something's broke and we've got to get it fixed."[48]

With this ambitious charge, Thompson assembled about a dozen people experienced in exploration and set up offices in North Houston. The group's members spent the better part of 1985 collecting information from throughout the corporation and using it to put together a worldwide evaluation of prospects. Their work confirmed the value of ranking prospects around the world. When the 1986 oil crisis hit, ETAG already had marshaled a great deal of information and had begun to form preliminary conclusions about the company's worldwide priorities in exploration.

The formation of ECI in 1986 created a new organization ready to act on the data developed by the Exploration Technical Assessment Group. Thompson became ECI's vice president of exploration, reporting to its executive vice president, Sidney Reso. Thompson's department had two groups. The first, based at ECI headquarters in New Jersey, directed the exploration efforts of existing affiliates; the second, New Ventures (based in Houston), contained the residue of Esso Exploration and operated in areas without established affiliates. The creation of ECI greatly simplified Exxon's exploration structure. But in 1986, it did not include two of the largest regions: Canada, where Imperial Oil managed exploration, and the United States, where Exxon USA still retained an exploration group.

ECI's exploration group quickly went to work, using all the information it could find within the corporation. According to Thompson, "We set out a map of the world, and I wanted them to create regional studies which zippered together so that when we finished we had a worldwide understanding of all the [geologic] basins in the world."[49] ETAG took an independent look at those results while also providing an independent assessment of the plans of Exxon USA and Imperial. With the study completed and its new structure in place in 1987, the exploration organization began the demanding task of evaluating Exxon's worldwide prospects.

The leaders of ECI's exploration group met key government officials from around the world, brought affiliate exploration groups into the new structure, and established the Ventures entity. Within a few months, the new organization had completed several regional studies, and Thompson traveled to New York to review the first of these with the Exxon Corporation board of directors. This was a "regional" look at eastern South America and western Africa. The presentation, which combined discussion of the two regions, reflected conditions eons in the past, before the continents had separated. The study raised the tantalizing prospect that oil resources could be found in the deep water bordering the two continents.

Oil had been produced from onshore and shallow offshore deposits in both regions. The deepwater prospects were new, however, and had never been fully assessed. Indeed, at the time, the technology needed to produce oil economically (given the low oil prices then prevailing) from waters at those depths had not yet been demonstrated.

For technical assistance, ECI and the other exploration groups looked to Exxon Production Research Company in Houston, which was then headed by Fred Perkins. As Exxon's primary upstream research organization, the research company was responsible for developing new exploration technology. In Thompson's view: "[Perkins] had an anti-silo mentality and he saw through these things; [he was] very intelligent, and he would tell Rawl how it was. Perkins and Rawl went way back, and Rawl respected Perkins's judgments probably as much as any other person."[50]

Thompson would need all the help he could get in convincing Rawl and the Exxon Corporation board to seek offshore reserves in depths greater than 1,000 feet. Deepwater exploration was not widely championed within the company. In 1985, Exxon USA had passed on bidding for any prospects in the first round of leasing of deepwater tracts in the Gulf of Mexico. Shell, in contrast, believed that it could economically develop fields at that depth as long as they contained large reserves.[51] It had aggressively sought deepwater leases; in a 1985 deepwater sale, Shell obtained leases in water depths as great as 6,000 feet. According to Thompson, the management of Exxon at the time felt that "these [people at Shell] are fools for paying this kind of money for these things way in deep water."[52] Thompson believed that Shell was right, but he had a high hurdle to clear in the person of Larry Rawl: "Rawl was not a big advocate of the deep water. . . . He thought the technical challenges were going to be so immense and it was going to cost so much and here we're . . . looking at twelve-dollar oil. . . . He said: 'There's no way we're going to do that.' So I think Rawl kind of made a little bit of an error in [not] seeing through to the potential."[53]

Thompson saw great potential for deepwater exploration, and he was a good salesman. In a presentation to the board of directors of Exxon Corporation in 1987, he compared the trajectory of the development of the North Sea with the deepwater basins, concluding that "we need to be there."[54] Whatever his private misgivings, Rawl took no exception to Thompson's conclusion, and the board agreed. Thompson had a green light to move ahead to seek deepwater reserves. Exxon USA's exploration efforts supported Thompson's enthusiasm. In 1986, Exxon USA found gas in 3,000 feet of water, and oil in 2,500 feet of water, near the Lena guyed tower in the Gulf of Mexico. Then, in 1987, it made a discovery in 1,700 feet of water in the Gulf. Although these discoveries were in waters far shallower than the deep water Thompson coveted off Africa, such results in the Gulf of Mexico encouraged Rawl to endorse the acquisition of leases in deeper waters.[55]

As Exxon USA made these acquisitions, Thompson continued the work of ECI's Exploration Department by rationalizing and prioritizing its exploration program. He also moved forward on new deepwater prospects off Africa. Meanwhile, he worked closely with Exxon Production Research to improve deepwater exploration and production technology. Thompson remembered 1986 and 1987 as a very demanding time: "Here we're going to try to handle the whole world out of Florham Park, New Jersey . . . and [it] liked to kill us all. . . . We'd go from one meeting with one affiliate to another, then a meeting with Shell. . . . And we still had ETAG going on."[56]

By the early 1990s, both reorganization in general and exploration in particular had begun to prove their value in improving exploration results. Yet the consolidation of global exploration into ECI remained incomplete. Imperial and Exxon USA retained separate exploration groups, although their share of the corporation's total exploration activities and success continued to shrink. From 1987 to 1991, the average reserve replacement ratio had been 91 percent in the United States but 123 percent elsewhere.[57] Despite those results, senior management at both Exxon USA and Imperial resisted folding their independent exploration groups into ECI.

Exxon USA—the old Humble Oil of industry lore—had played a central role in the history of Exxon in the "glory days" when the United States dominated world production and Humble dominated U.S. production. Humble executives often had risen through the organization to head Exxon. Wallace Pratt, one of the most famous geologists in oil history, and several generations of successful finders and producers of oil had come up through Humble. Many of the leading executives in Exxon in the 1980s and 1990s had served apprenticeships in Houston and in the oil fields and refineries of Texas. Beginning in the 1960s with the movement of chemicals out of Humble and into Esso Chemical, Exxon had also pulled coal and other minerals out of Exxon USA and placed them in international affiliates, but exploration for oil and natural gas was another matter entirely. If Exxon USA lost control of exploration, its importance within Exxon would be greatly diminished.[58]

Rawl believed, however, that the growing importance of international production called for a coordinated global approach to exploration, and he decided to force the issue. The showdown over the fate of exploration at Exxon USA finally came in late 1991 at a meeting of senior executives at the Tomas Ranch in South Texas. The location was heavy with symbolism; Humble Oil had used the Tomas Ranch for executive retreats during its heyday within Jersey (Standard), the 1930s through the 1960s. Rawl solicited the views of those present about the best organization for exploration. According to Raymond, a spirited debate ensued, with William Stevens, the head of Exxon USA since 1987, and Sid Reso, the president of ECI, arguing against the change.[59] According to Raymond, "The first night we're down there and bitching and moaning and complaining." The group went out quail hunting the next morning, and then in the afternoon, Rawl said, "Okay, we heard all that and here's what we're going to do."[60] Rawl arrived at this momentous decision in a process much different from the "no surprises" approach of the old management system at Exxon. He told the group that the company was moving to a global exploration company, separate from all other divisions, with responsibility for worldwide exploration. It would include the exploration activities of Exxon USA and Imperial, as well as the Exploration Department of the Ventures Group in ECI. The new Exxon Exploration Company would join Exxon Chemical and the two research groups as truly global organizations. Jon Thompson would head it.

Thompson hit the ground running. The new company officially opened for business at the beginning of 1992, with its headquarters in Houston. Its creation marked the most important step yet taken in the transformation of Exxon from a corporation composed of national affiliates grouped into regional companies into one with its function organized globally.

The two primary dissenters to the creation of a global exploration company—Bill Stevens of Exxon and Sid Reso of ECI—had abbreviated careers within Exxon, but for very different reasons. At the time of the 1991 meeting on exploration, Stevens had the misfortune of being in charge of a division with declining profits and of having presided over the *Exxon Valdez* accident and other recent operational failures (described in chapter 6). He left the company in early 1992 at only fifty-seven, joining the independent oil company Mitchell Energy & Development as president and chief operating officer.

Sidney J. Reso was fifty-six in 1991, and had led ECI for the four years following the retirement of Richard G. Reid. Reso's tenure at ECI had been a successful one, and planning was underway for his next high-level assignment at the corporation. Those plans ended abruptly with his murder in a failed kidnapping attempt in the spring of 1992. Reso was abducted from his car at the end of the driveway at his home in Florham Park, New Jersey, near ECI headquarters. The FBI led the prolonged negotiations for his release, which eventually produced an agreement for the delivery of an $18.5 million ransom.[61] Six weeks after Reso's disappearance, authorities arrested a former security guard at the ECI facility and his wife as they tried to pick up the ransom. Interrogations revealed that Reso had been shot in the original abduction and had died soon afterward in gruesome circumstances, although his abductors buried his body and continued to negotiate for a ransom.[62] The would-be kidnappers went to prison for their crime, with the ringleader receiving a life sentence. Reso's murder was a painful ordeal for his friends and coworkers within Exxon and for the company as a whole. One lasting legacy of was the strengthening of executive-security measures.[63]

Reso's untimely death added to the challenge of executive succession presented by the departure of William Stevens. Substitutes were soon in place for both men. Reso had been slated to move into the corporation as senior vice president the next year, but with Reso's death, Mel Harrison was brought to Dallas instead.[64] Harrison, another seasoned executive with broad experience in exploration and production, assumed direction of the corporation's upstream portfolio. Meanwhile, Rene Dahan replaced Reso at ECI. Dahan later moved to corporate headquarters, where he became one of the planning architects of the Exxon-Mobil merger. In Exxon USA, Stevens's position was filled by Harry Longwell, an experienced upstream executive who devoted considerable effort to improving the operational performance of that company.

Harry J. Longwell, senior vice president and member of the board of directors, Exxon Corporation, 2004. ExxonMobil Historical Collection, di_06119.

Longwell understood Exxon USA and he understood global production. His career at Exxon split roughly in half, the first twenty years spent in the United States and the second twenty in international assignments and corporate-level jobs in Irving. After graduating with a petroleum engineering degree from Louisiana State University, he went to work for Humble Oil in 1963. He served his apprenticeship in production engineering at Exxon USA offshore Louisiana, at the King Ranch, offshore Santa Barbara, and in Alaska, where he worked on many phases of the planning and building of the Trans-Alaska Pipeline. His first international experience came in Esso Europe in joint ventures with Shell in the North Sea. He then passed through corporate headquarters in New York, serving for a time as an executive assistant to Cliff Garvin, before moving to ECI in 1987 as an executive vice president.

He thus brought a breadth of experience to the presidency of Exxon USA, and he took as his mandate the revitalization of a proud company that had made a series of costly mistakes in the 1980s. Longwell knew that those in charge of Exxon USA were not simply "defending a kingdom" but also following long-accepted practices that had granted them extraordinary autonomy because of Humble/Exxon USA's past success and its historical importance within Exxon.[65] He sought to change long-standing patterns in order to align the goals and procedures of Exxon USA with those of Exxon Corporation. After beginning the process of organizational change during a three-year stay in Houston, he joined corporate headquarters in Irving as a senior vice president and corporate director. He retired as a senior vice president of ExxonMobil in 2004, leaving his impact on many important projects and many people who worked with him.[66]

Executives the caliber of Harry Longwell and Rene Dahan did not emerge by accident. They were the product of Exxon's emphasis on executive development. A painstaking and continual evaluation process, as well as the management training and regular job rotation of executives, built a corps of able, well-trained, and loyal managers. Longwell called them "generational managers" who came up the ranks together and emerged well prepared and with confidence in one another.[67] The resulting depth of talent illustrated the strength of one important part of the traditional system of management at Exxon, the systematic and continual approach to hiring, evaluating, and training its executives.

EARLY RESULTS IN EXPLORATION

It is impossible to say with any precision how the global organization of exploration affected the addition of new reserves in subsequent years. In an era when political turmoil shaped oil exploration almost as much as geology in much of the world, trends in Exxon's oil and natural gas

discoveries from 1986 through the Mobil merger in 1999 provide no conclusive answer to the question of the impact of reorganization. Case studies (discussed in chapter 7) illustrate several obvious successes in Angola,
Russia's Sakhalin Island, and the deep water in the Gulf of Mexico. As
measured by the traditional definition of net proved reserves (developed
and undeveloped), Exxon more or less held its own in the years just after
the creation of Exxon Exploration, with a high of about 7.5 billion barrels
of oil in the late 1980s, and lows of around 6.6 billion in the early 1990s.
Proved reserves of natural gas dipped from a high of about 47 trillion
cubic feet in 1984 to a low of about 39 trillion cubic feet before leveling
off at approximately 42 trillion cubic feet in the 1990s. For the ten-year
period 1989–1998, Exxon's average reserve replacement for oil was 95 percent; for natural gas, 122 percent; and for the two combined, 110 percent.
Such figures were achieved with expenditures ranging from a high of $2.7
billion in 1984 to lows of almost $1 billion in the early 1990s. Return on
investment on expenditures for exploration ranged from a solid 15 percent
in the early 1990s to an impressive 23 percent in 1997.[68] Those returns
reflect the effect of greatly improved technology in driving down the cost
per barrel of new discoveries. They also suggest the early impact of Exxon
Exploration in identifying good prospects. Taken as a whole, the figures
suggest a giant company struggling—along with the rest of its industry—
to find new sources of oil and natural gas in a low-oil-price environment.

Exxon understandably interpreted the figures optimistically. In its
annual reports, the company made the case that traditional measures of
success in exploration had been rendered less useful by changes in technology. In this view, the old definition of "proved reserves" did not give
an accurate measure of a company's success. Historically, "proved" meant
proved by the bit; that is, drilling had produced a reliable estimate of
the amount of oil or gas that might be recovered from a field at existing
prices and technology.[69] Yet astonishing advances in three-dimensional
seismic surveys had increased the capacity of companies to "see" beneath
the earth's surface. In addition, new technology for finding reserves in
ever-harsher environments and for enhancing production from new and
old fields had changed the underlying realities of reserve accounting. In
traditional reserve accounting, the negative term "unproven" was used

to classify identified reserves that had not been thoroughly investigated. Exxon had large volumes of unproven reserves of oil and natural gas that the company considered almost certain to be produced at some future time. In 1990, the company began reporting such oil and gas resources it held as "static" reserves—that is, reserves "which had been discovered but which needed further field delineation, market development, new technology or some combination of lower development costs or higher prices before they could be produced." The company showed static reserves almost as large as its proved reserves, painting a rosier portrait of its future for investors.[70] The company ultimately lost the debate; "static reserves" did not become a category widely accepted by others. But the issue raised was real and important, particularly for a company that was a leader in technology and took a long-term view of its business.

A second, more prominent consequence of Exxon's performance in exploration and production in those years was the much-publicized fact that Royal Dutch Shell had grown larger than Exxon by several standard measures. By the mid-1980s, it was producing more petroleum and selling more petroleum products than Exxon.[71] Periodic internal reports reminded the corporate management committee of the performance gaps between Exxon and its closest competitor. Raymond recalled that this seemed to bother many in the upstream.[72] But he and Rawl reacted differently. It rankled both that Exxon had been surpassed, but they believed strongly that profits, not production or sales, were the best measure of success. Rawl and Raymond emphatically placed profitability at the center of corporate strategy. Raymond was not impressed by higher sales that were unaccompanied by profits: "The fact that Shell wasn't making any money when they were [increasing volume] . . . was lost on a lot of people. . . . There's nothing sacred about volume. Volume for volume's sake isn't particularly useful. . . . [We wanted to] make sure that the assets we have were really assets that are going to add value to the company. . . . If you focus on return over the long haul, you will prevail."[73] Financial efficiency, operating efficiency, and return on investment would guide Exxon's efforts, and long-term profitability would be the key measure of success. In light of Exxon's extraordinary financial results in subsequent years, it is clear that it succeeded on its own terms.

INNOVATIONS IN FINANCE

Strict financial controls had been a core value of Exxon since the days of Rockefeller, and several important innovations by Jack Bennett, the de facto treasurer of Exxon for much of the 1980s, contributed to the more efficient use of capital in those years. Bennett's most inventive and productive period began in 1982, when he introduced a series of financial reforms that included the systematic repurchase of large quantities of shares—a policy that Exxon continued and then expanded in the 1990s.

Bennett had an unusual career at Exxon. Born in Macon, Georgia, in 1924, he earned an undergraduate degree from Yale and a doctorate in finance at Harvard at a time when Ivy League degrees were uncommon at Exxon. After service in the navy, he took a job in Washington, D.C., on an Eisenhower-sponsored commission to study foreign economic policy. Noticed in that job by an Exxon director, he accepted an offer to join the company in 1955 at the age of thirty-one. His subsequent whirlwind career, marked by a series of moves to a variety of increasingly important jobs, very much fit the Exxon pattern for those who demonstrated great potential. He worked in finance in New York and London, then as an assistant treasurer, assistant to Jersey Standard's chairman, and head of corporate planning. Switching gears, he moved to Houston to lead Exxon USA's Supply Department, which was in charge of trading crude oil and petroleum products. In informing Bennett of this move, Exxon's chairman told him that there was "not a single job in that department for which you are qualified by experience or knowledge . . . so we're going to make you the head of it."[74] After three years in that job, he returned to New York to lead the company's international trading group.

Bennett then made an unusual move for an Exxon executive on the way up: he left the company and returned to Washington as deputy undersecretary of the treasury. In four years in Washington, he rose to the job of undersecretary of the treasury for monetary affairs, serving under George Shultz and William Simon. Exxon wanted him back, and in the summer of 1975 he returned as a senior vice president and director. Whatever the job title, he was the company's de facto chief financial officer, embarking on a second, fourteen-year career at Exxon in which he established himself as one of the most creative financial executives

Jack F. Bennett, senior vice president and a member of the board of directors, Exxon Corporation, 1975. ExxonMobil Historical Collection, di_06157.

in American business, while netting the company hundreds of millions of dollars.

Bennett mentored a generation of exceptionally capable financial executives. These included his assistant treasurer, W. Allen Harrison, as well as future treasurers Edward A. Robinson, Ulysses LeGrange (later involved in helping manage the *Exxon Valdez* oil spill), and Frank B. Risch. Far from aloof, Bennett was unusually approachable and clearly valued ideas. Risch lived near Bennett in Connecticut, and though Risch was junior to Bennett, the younger man had warm memories of their collaboration: He "would come over to my house. He would call me up and say, 'I have got a new idea . . . [and] I have kind of written it out. I would like to bring you my notes and ask you to read them . . . and maybe you can tell me what you think.'"[75]

Bennett's most visible initiative was the systematic repurchase of Exxon's shares. This buyback program began in an era of great uncertainty in the oil industry, in the years just before the oil bust of 1986, when many companies sought greater security and additional oil reserves by acquiring other oil companies. The merger wave peaked in 1984, when Chevron paid $13.4 billion for the troubled Gulf Oil Corporation, Mobil paid $5.7 billion for the large independent Superior Oil Company after a hard-fought hostile takeover, and Texaco paid $10.1 billion and endured an expensive legal battle to acquire Getty Oil. Such major mergers generally required the acquiring companies to take on considerable debt, and the long-term performance of the merged companies was unpredictable, given conditions in the industry.[76] Cliff Garvin acknowledged as much to shareholders in March 1985: "From time to time we have looked at the possibility of acquiring entire companies rather than just individual properties, but we have not found opportunities that in our judgment were in the best interests of our shareholders."[77] The company did, however, identify an attractive and profitable target of opportunity: Exxon itself. With substantial funds and limited investment opportunities, in July 1983 it took the lead in the industry in buying back its own stock. This proved to be an important long-term financial strategy. Only eighteen months after it had begun these buybacks, Exxon had purchased about 10 percent of its outstanding shares.[78]

Thereafter, the company regularly repurchased large blocks of its own stock, absorbing them into the company's treasury and accumulating billions of dollars worth of shares. The buybacks bolstered stock value by reducing the number of outstanding shares and by reassuring those who owned shares that they would have a ready buyer for their stock, even in volatile markets. Repurchasing had the additional advantage of preserving the number of authorized shares, which allowed Exxon to reissue those shares if changing economic conditions warranted. According to Bennett, Exxon was not "the first U.S. corporation to buy back its shares for the [corporate] treasury," but it was "the first large oil company to carry out a large and continuing purchase."[79] Detractors argued that the money used for buybacks would be better spent on tangible investments, such as the search for new energy sources, or returned to shareholders in the form of higher dividends.[80] Bennett disagreed with the assumption that funds spent on stock repurchases were needed elsewhere: "We wouldn't want to pay out the money that way if at the time we had an investment waiting that required that money. So that it would have been silly to pay it out and bring it back after tax. But if we didn't have enough current opportunities to use that money, better to give it to shareholders [via share repurchases]."[81] In addition, the repurchases offered tax benefits for some large shareholders. Had those shareholders received the funds in the form of larger dividends, the income tax rate would have been higher than the rate paid on capital gains when they sold the shares.

In a 1988 speech to the Exxon Research Club, Bennett detailed the major concerns that had been raised about share repurchases, in particular the idea that "those purchases are evidence of liquidation of the company and a sign that management has lost confidence in the future of the business." He was having none of that. The company was growing, not shrinking, and he assured the audience that management definitely had not lost confidence in the business.[82] Bennett voiced Exxon's motivation clearly: "We serve the shareholders. We held up the market price. And we made a good investment because, as it turned out, those shares that we bought had been sufficiently underpriced in the market, that it was a very good investment for the company to buy those shares."[83]

Bennett understood that share buybacks could be abused if used to boost stock prices and prop up underperforming managers and their stock options. Believing that the market, not Exxon, was underperforming, however, he viewed the repurchase of shares as similar to buying a tangible asset: "So in a sense, we were investing in real assets. One [option] was going out and buying the assets, the other was buying the shares that owned the assets."[84]

Many other companies were convinced, and they followed suit in buying back their own shares. In April 1985, *Fortune* magazine compared the performance of companies using buybacks to those that did not. Its finding was unequivocal: "The outcome is spectacularly decisive. The

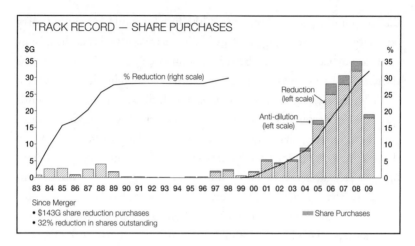

FIGURE 5.2: Source: *Exxon Mobil Corporation*

shareholders in the buyback companies earned superb returns, far exceeding those accruing to investors as a whole. . . . The buyback companies showed a median total return . . . of 22.6%. The equivalent return for the S&P 500 was only 14.1%."[85] Such statistics help explain Exxon's growing use of share buybacks (see figure 5.2).

The early round of purchases from 1983–1989, which seemed large at the time, dipped following the *Exxon Valdez* accident in 1989, flattened out in the 1990s, and then rapidly accelerated after the 1999 merger with Mobil, which was facilitated by Exxon's access to the ready capital represented by its retained shares. The company also used some of the purchased shares to avoid dilution of share prices from the payment of executive bonuses. In the decade from 1999 to 2009, ExxonMobil spent $143 billion dollars buying back shares, reducing its shares outstanding by nearly one-third and significantly boosting the underlying per-share assets. Share repurchases provided a hedge against fundamental uncertainties in an industry subject to wild price swings.

Other financial innovations by Bennett took advantage of Exxon's size and financial strength. One of these was "shelf registration," a creative new way to issue debt made possible by a new SEC regulation (Rule 415) governing the information disclosures required for new debt or equity issues. Before the rule was in place, a company wishing to issue debt had to provide a new registration statement defining the full terms of the bond issue. The preparation of the registration statement was time-consuming and costly, and it also provided a clear signal to knowledgeable financial analysts that the issue was imminent. With shelf registration, on the other hand, a company prepared a more generic registration statement, held it until conditions for a debt issue appeared favorable, and issued it rapidly, with a minimum of additional effort or prior public knowledge. Shelf registration saved money while providing flexibility that a company could use for tactical financial benefit.

Exxon used those advantages and even took them a step further by issuing the debt itself rather than hiring an investment bank. This allowed the company to avoid paying the considerable bank fees typically charged as a risk premium for ensuring a debt issue was sold. Bennett and his assistants were "enamored" with the idea that given its "tremendous financial strength, size, widespread shareholding, [and] tremendous creditworthiness," Exxon did not need "the investment banking community in the same way that much smaller companies would need those kind of services."[86] Bennett questioned the idea that the company gained anything by paying investment bankers to assume the risks associated with the bond sales: "We don't need to pay people to take risk from us. . . . We know how to manage risk, and we don't need . . . risk insurance."[87] When the company began to sell debt issues internationally without an intermediary, it introduced a second unorthodox financial feature.

Shelf registration and international self-selling did not endear Bennett or Exxon to investment bankers. Bennett recalled a conversation with a former head of the investment banking firm Morgan Stanley, who told him, "You know, when I was a young man working for Morgan Stanley, I heard the name 'Bennett,' but I never realized you had a first name that could be used in polite society."[88] However he may have been viewed by investment bankers, Bennett's initiatives saved money for Exxon.

The benefits obtained from the new ways of selling debt directly influenced Exxon's later views on its need for third-party insurance coverage. Rather than paying premiums to intermediary insurance companies for risk coverage, the company eventually began to self-insure. It had sufficient financial resources to pay for any realistic calamity. And by paying careful attention to the integrity of its operations, Exxon would not often need to devote significant monies to cover calamities. This strategy was called into question by the *Exxon Valdez* disaster, but in that case Exxon already had the maximum coverage available through industry-wide shipping-insurance arrangements. In other circumstances, third-party insurance was required by law. But unless constrained by factors such as legal rules or industry-wide insurance schemes, the company began to self-insure more and more of its activities.[89]

Bennett retired in 1989, but his impact on Exxon's financial arrangements continued. His creative financial initiatives underscored the company's emphasis on shareholder value, as well as its willingness to ignore Wall Street traditions and take innovative approaches to managing its own finances. Financial discipline was a core value of Exxon, and Bennett's efforts expanded its traditional definition by demonstrating new ways the company could take advantage of its size and long-term financial strength. His work attracted a new generation of financial experts who remained with the company for decades.

THE ORGANIZATION AND FOCUS OF RESEARCH

A commitment to leadership in technology was a core value at Exxon. In the demanding years after the oil bust, Exxon's efforts to improve its financial performance led it to take a hard look at the organization of its research efforts. Technical leadership had been a hallmark of the company's success and an internal symbol of its commitment to excellence for more than a century. During his years as president, Raymond was the primary contact for research on the corporate management committee. He found the company's research efforts to be poorly structured and unfocused. With his academic training and business background in research, Raymond strongly supported research within the company, but he believed that it should be of greater practical benefit. He was particularly concerned about the direction taken by Exxon Research and Engineering, the company's primary research organization for downstream operations.[90] In 1977, Cliff Garvin had hired Edward E. David Jr., to run Exxon Research. David, with training in electrical engineering at MIT, had served as the executive director of research at the prestigious Bell Laboratories and had been a science advisor to President Nixon. His consulting group advised companies, universities, and governmental agencies on technology matters.[91] Not surprisingly, given his background, David increased the emphasis on basic research at Exxon.

Raymond wanted Exxon Research to focus more sharply on applied research—on projects with more direct application to the company's ongoing business. He was also unhappy about the lack of cooperation among the various research institutions: "Everybody in the organization was carping about it. . . . When ER&E was criticized, they'd just run to New York and get a bunch of money. . . . Chemicals had their own big research organization. Exxon USA had their own big engineering organization. . . . I mean, it was a shambles."[92] One member of the research group at the time, Frank B. Sprow, who later became vice president for Safety, Health and Environment, recalled that David appeared to believe that "hiring some outstanding researchers and giving them a tremendous amount of freedom uncoupled to the business world would, through some process, generate opportunities which the company could take advantage of, particularly in diversification-type activities." He noted that David and his head of the Corporate Research unit, Peter Lucchesi, "had hired a number of truly world-class people but kept them largely in the dark about the company's business, feeling that it would probably limit their creativity."[93]

Sprow felt that the move toward basic research had gone too far. At one point, he asked his group in Corporate Research whether anyone could tell him the difference between the upstream and the downstream. No one could. "Here you had world-class catalyst experts, surface-science people, people skilled in spectroscopy, molecular physics, materials science," yet when asked whether anyone knew what a catalytic cracker unit was, no one knew. According to Sprow, the situation became bleak: "The wheels largely came off the wagon. . . . I think [that] if there had been a vote of the senior [business] people at the time, 'Keep [Corporate Research] or sink it,' the answer would have been to sink it." Sprow recalled that "Lee Raymond, who was clearly very dissatisfied with the way things were going at the time, still thought [Research] was worth saving."[94] In fact, Raymond supported a substantial—though reduced—amount of corporate research, but he wanted researchers to attract support from business groups and enter into partnerships with them.

Raymond also insisted that the company institute a "system of per-formance" that would more sharply focus the goals of research: "We're not going to be the next Bell Labs. We're going to quit building all these damn buildings for [the researchers], and they are going to have to start producing something that makes sense."[95] This approach was inconsistent with the orientation of Ed David, and he departed in October 1985 to pursue other research and business interests; Peter Lucchesi followed in February 1986. The departure of those executives presented an opportu-nity to reorient Exxon's research efforts under the management of David R. Clair, who took over as president of Exxon Research in October 1986, and Robert Epperly, who replaced Lucchesi. Also in 1986, Fred Perkins replaced L. W. Welch Jr. as head of Exxon Production Research Company, the company's primary upstream research center.

In both research companies, the primary mandate for the new pres-idents and their management teams was to align research more closely with business objectives and needs, yet still preserve some measure of sup-port for speculative research linked with potentially broad, high-value applications. The immediate task facing the new management teams, unfortunately, was not to realign research but reduce their workforces. Neither Clair nor Welch (before his 1986 retirement) wanted to make the cutbacks as rapidly as did corporate management. Clair favored a mea-sured reduction over two years. Rawl and Raymond, who were looking months, not years, ahead, rejected that approach out of hand, ordering immediate cuts.

As soon as Epperly was named the next general manager of Corporate Research, and even before the cutbacks, he was asked to reassess the direc-tion Corporate Research had been taking.[96] In early 1986, he completed a series of studies with the goal of reducing the level of Corporate Research activity by 20–50 percent while refocusing on Exxon's core businesses and improving technology transfer to the operating organizations. Such was the disillusionment with Corporate Research that Exxon Research reduced it by about half, a greater reduction than the overall corporate-wide decline. At that point, in March 1986, Sprow became Epperly's boss as director of Corporate Research, and Sprow delivered the bad news that the unit's research activity would be downsized and its mission modi-fied. The resulting cutbacks took place during 1986, and they damaged the company's reputation in the academic community. Sprow felt that it became "tough for a few years after that to maintain [the previous] level of college contacts."[97] Nevertheless, in the consultations within the company that followed, the business units began to realize that Exxon Research was committed to becoming a more useful partner. This did not mean that Corporate Research would focus exclusively on applied research to extend existing technology, since both Exxon Research and Exxon Production Research continued to conduct basic scientific research on key issues, looking for step-out innovations.[98]

Exxon's overall expenditures for research and development fell substantially during the cutbacks of the mid-1980s. Despite such cuts, technical leadership remained a core value at Exxon. This was communicated to shareholders in the 1988 annual report, which for the first time devoted two full pages to a discussion of the company's research, with sketches of innovative research in areas including deepwater production systems, three-dimensional seismic mapping, pollution control, and energy efficiency from the cogeneration of power and steam at company refineries and chemical plants.[99] Although of necessity incomplete, the list illustrated the richness and diversity of the company's research into the many technical systems and processes required to produce products from oil, natural gas, and chemicals.

One key organizational tool devised to improve applied research was the Corporate Research Advisory Committee (CRAC).[100] The committee consisted of the top technology managers from each of the main business functions—the upstream, the downstream, and chemicals—as well as a representative from Exxon Corporation. The committee reviewed and endorsed the Corporate Research plan, with an emphasis on sponsoring research to identify and pursue leading-edge technologies that could eventually be applied to practical business needs. In the jargon of the day, the investigations were to pursue "relevant science" that would ultimately lead to "connected science." Experience with this process led to further modifications of Corporate Research during the tenure of Terry Koonce as head of Exxon Research from 1990 to 1993, and under his successor, Clarence Eidt. The advisory committee was discontinued in the mid-1990s as the business units became more firmly integrated into the designation of research needs and as Corporate Research became more responsive to business suggestions. The 1999 merger with Mobil brought additional research resources and technology expertise. But the initiatives undertaken in the late 1980s and through the early 1990s—a systematic approach to applied research that would be integrated with the needs of the company's operating businesses—remained the central method used by Exxon and then ExxonMobil to extract maximum value from its research and development expenditures.

IRVING, TEXAS: SYMBOL OF A NEW AGE?

In the 1980s, Exxon gradually reduced its presence in New York City; it then left altogether in the 1990s. In ways not readily apparent on the surface, the move of Exxon's corporate headquarters from Manhattan to Irving, Texas, provided an appropriate symbol for the broad changes that had occurred in the company after 1986.

Larry Rawl had never been comfortable in New York City, even though he was originally from nearby New Jersey. To him, Manhattan meant expensive housing, high taxes, long commutes, location premiums to enable employees to meet the high costs of living, high crime rates, and harsh winters.[101] In 1985, the company sold its headquarters building, taking advantage of a real estate boom that was driving the price of office space in New York City sky-high.[102] In late 1985, Mitsui Real Estate Development purchased the Exxon Headquarters at 1251 Avenue of the Americas for $610 million.[103] The sale came at an opportune time for Exxon, since the 1986 cutbacks and creation of offices for Exxon Company, International, in New Jersey sharply reduced the number of employees in the New York headquarters. The sale to Mitsui was also well timed, since other firms had begun to leave New York City, and real estate prices stagnated before falling in the early 1990s.[104]

Exxon's time was running out in a city where it had had its headquarters since 1883.[105] As the nation's media capital, New York had always shone a spotlight on the major companies headquartered there. The political environment in New York became especially unpleasant for Exxon after the *Exxon Valdez* accident in 1989, when the *New York Times* and other local media regularly attacked the company. But the move out of Manhattan ultimately was not a political statement. Deliberations moved

Exxon Corporation headquarters building located at 1251 Avenue of the Americas, New York, New York, ca. 1972. ExxonMobil Historical Collection, di_03933.

slowly, since both Rawl and Raymond assumed that Cliff Garvin would not agree to a move from New York while he was chairman. But in late 1987, after Garvin retired, discussions of a move reemerged. According to Raymond, Rawl's concise guidelines for the choice of a new location were characteristically blunt: "We're not going to be where it snows . . . and we're not going to be where we get screwed on taxes."[106]

With those guidelines in mind, Raymond and Jack Clarke began to assess new locations. Florida, North Carolina, Arizona, Georgia, and Texas met the criteria, and Exxon USA's Friendswood Development Company secretly investigated specific locations. The company settled on Texas in 1988, and reviewed sites in Houston, Austin, and Dallas. Houston, the self-proclaimed "energy capital of the world" and home to substantial Exxon operations, seemed the logical choice. Rawl, however, opposed its selection, in part because of his memories from his early career when he worked in Houston and higher-ups from Exxon USA's head-quarters in the same city could easily come by and look over his shoul-der. Dallas and Austin offered more separation of top management from operational management, allowing both groups to focus more clearly on their jobs. Exxon ultimately chose Irving, a small, business-oriented com-munity halfway between Dallas and Fort Worth.

The company then quietly purchased land and solicited designs from a small number of architects, who were told to prepare a design that was timeless, not ostentatious, and adequate for only a limited headquarters staff. Rawl deferred to Raymond's judgment of the designs, since it was clear that he would soon inhabit the building. The St. Louis–based firm Hellmuth, Obata, and Kassabaum had the winning design, which evoked Frank Lloyd Wright's prairie style. This appealed to Raymond, whose boy-hood home was not far west from Wright's studio in Taliesin, Wisconsin. The firm had earlier designed Houston's pathbreaking Galleria shopping mall, the National Air and Space Museum in Washington, D.C., and BP's headquarters in Cleveland. With the land acquired and the design picked, Exxon announced the move in October 1989.

The company's headquarters began the move to Irving in 1990, occu-pying rented space until the completion of its new building in 1996. The move to Irving was a move to a well-established center of the world oil industry: Texas, a probusiness and pro-oil state. The new building had tight security and was located in an isolated area. Irving had easy access to a major international airport, meeting a primary need of a global corporation. The region had little snow, and the state had low taxes. Excellent and relatively inexpensive housing surrounded the new site. The company's departure was not surprising; only 300 Exxon employees remained in Manhattan. City government there put a brave face on the loss, which followed earlier departures by J. C. Penney & Company (which moved to Plano, not far from Irving), Mobil Corporation, and Texaco. As the company severed its century-old tie to New York City and departed for Texas, there was a sense that a new era had begun.

In fact, that era had been underway since at least early 1986. The move to Irving was a clean break for a company shaped by a quarter century of steady and relatively easy growth after World War II and then by a hectic period of boom and bust in oil prices. Along the way, Exxon had become a giant, bureaucratic organization inhabiting a Manhattan skyscraper stacked with analysts and committees and number crunchers to serve and oversee two other levels of decision making at the national and regional levels. After cutting layers of this bureaucracy, the company traded the skyscraper for a much smaller building; its size limited the number of people who could work at corporate headquarters. The building's design and its tranquil grounds created a relaxed setting that encouraged top-level managers to collaborate in fulfilling their primary mission: the definition of long-term corporate strategy. This was especially important in the restructured and refocused Exxon that emerged from the turmoil of the 1980s. A sustained focus on the execution of corporate strategy and excellence in day-to-day operations required strong, clear direction from the top.

CHAPTER SIX

EXXON VALDEZ

RESPONDING TO ENVIRONMENTAL DISASTERS

At 9:12 p.m. on March 23, 1989, the supertanker *Exxon Valdez* left the port of Valdez, Alaska, bound for California with a cargo of 1.25 million barrels of North Slope crude oil. After clearing the harbor into Prince William Sound, the captain, Joseph Hazelwood, heard reports of floating ice in the normal outbound lane. He requested permission to move temporarily to the more eastern, inbound shipping-traffic lane to avoid the ice hazards. The local coast guard agreed to the diversion, a standard practice in such conditions—in fact, a course taken by the previous outbound tanker. Once past the ice, the tanker would need to move back into the proper lane to avoid the danger of grounding on an underwater reef near Bligh Island. Captain Hazelwood gave orders for this routine maneuver to his third mate, who was to ensure that the helmsman made the course correction at the appropriate time. Then Hazelwood left the bridge to go to his cabin. The vessel moved on through the night, passing the point where the course correction should have been made. As it approached Bligh Reef, an emergency maneuver came too late. At a little after midnight on March 24, hard metal met harder rock, and the tanker grounded on the reef. The first of nearly 260,000 barrels of crude oil began to flow from a long gash in the tanker's hull.

The tragedy in Prince William Sound, which created the largest oil spill up to that time in American history, captured the attention of people around the world. The spill caused extensive damage to the shorelines and waters off southern Alaska, threatening both the livelihoods and the way of life of many in the region. Those directly affected were outraged at the extent of the damage, the carelessness of Exxon before the accident, and its ineffectiveness in the initial stages of the cleanup. A firestorm of criticism around the nation and the world continued for years, causing enduring damage to the company's public image and leading to the passage of strong new regulations on oil tankers. The name on the tanker identified both the company involved and the location, and "*Exxon Valdez*" or "*Valdez*" or just "Exxon" became synonymous with environmental disaster.

It was a public relations disaster, but much more. Exxon's performance after that accident and several following ones called into question its basic competence. Rene Dahan, an executive who lived through the trauma of the *Exxon Valdez* oil spill, captured the sentiment of many in the company when he recalled "the pain we experienced, the deep, deep pain, and in a way the shame as a very proud organization."[1] The company could not go back and alter the series of events that led to the spill, but it could and did develop a more effective system to improve its everyday operations, making the company far less likely to have accidents in the future. Indeed, the worst disaster in Exxon's history marked a turning point in its systematic management of matters related to safety, health, and the environment.

THE ACCIDENT AND THE EARLY CLEANUP

As news of the accident spread, observers from around the world wondered how it could have happened. The early reports focused on the role of Captain Hazelwood. He had made a critical error by leaving the bridge. Company policy required two officers on the bridge during especially important maneuvers, yet only the third mate, Gregory Cousins, was present to supervise the helmsman. Moreover, Hazelwood was the only person onboard licensed to navigate that part of Prince William Sound. After turning away from the iceberg and temporarily entering the inbound channel, he had placed the tanker on automatic pilot, and the subsequent failure to release the autopilot meant that the course corrections he later ordered could not be made in time. Hazelwood also took controversial actions after the grounding: he ordered the ship put into reverse in order to try to extricate it from Bligh Reef, a step that could have caused the ship to founder and spill much more oil. The captain waited more than twenty minutes to notify the U.S. Coast Guard of the grounding and spill. The coast guard responded to his notification, boarded the stricken *Valdez*, and gave Hazelwood a blood test for alcohol, the results of which were later contested in court. Speculation about alcohol impairment increased after trial testimony indicated that he had been drinking before boarding the *Valdez* and that he had a history of alcohol abuse and rehabilitation efforts, all known to responsible company managers.[2] Much of the public, following the lead of late-night comedy-show hosts, came to a simple, straightforward interpretation of these events: a drunken sailor at Exxon had wrecked a supertanker in one of the most beautiful areas in the world. Such an oversimplification was unfair. No explanation of the events on the bridge that night, however, could be interpreted in a good light for Exxon. Human errors impossible to justify in a well-run company turned a routine voyage out of Valdez into a catastrophe.

The courts later spent almost two decades reaching final decisions about the damages the spill caused. But the pressing task in the hours just after midnight on March 24 was to save the badly damaged ship. Later inspections revealed that 500 feet of its hull had been peeled back, rupturing eight of eleven cargo tanks as well as three saltwater ballast tanks.[3] Despite the enormous damage, 80 percent of the ship's cargo, or approximately one million barrels of oil, remained onboard. Although the tanker remained afloat, it was in danger of sinking.

The grounding was reported to Exxon Shipping and its president, Frank Iarossi, who notified his immediate superiors at Exxon USA in Houston. They informed corporate management in New York City of the situation in Valdez. Under Exxon's procedures at the time, handling the accident and oil spill were the responsibility of Exxon USA and its affiliate, Exxon Shipping. Iarossi and his assistants flew to Alaska early on the morning of March 25, followed by experts in ship stabilization and handling. While Iarossi worked with the shipping experts to save the ship, he also worked with state and federal officials to determine how best to recapture the spilled oil.

The crippled Exxon Valdez *being lightered, 1989.*
ExxonMobil Historical Collection, di_06237.

The group assigned to board the ship and begin removing oil faced a dangerous situation in an isolated area subject to harsh weather conditions. Bob Nicholas, the general counsel to Exxon Shipping at the time of the spill, described his journey out to the grounded vessel: "The water was very calm out there at the time. There were floating pieces of ice all over the place. . . . The person piloting the small boat that we were on turned on a spotlight to pick our way through the ice pieces. And we were about halfway there when the light burned out. And I could remember thinking . . . we are going to have to go back through this in the dark."[4] On the *Exxon Valdez*, he found noxious fumes, a vessel hard aground with serious damage, and the ever-present danger of fire or explosion from the volatile hydrocarbons.

Over the next several days, the rescue crew sealed the deck, pumped air into the damaged tanks, and floated the ship on what was in effect a bubble of air. One shipping expert from outside of Exxon commented that "to lose a third of the bottom and keep the ship from capsizing was an incredible feat of seamanship."[5] Exxon's salvage manager on the scene recounted the situation: "We had an unstable vessel. . . . She would have gone down eventually if she had come off the rocks that night. She still had more than 42 million gallons [or one million barrels] aboard . . . and we wanted very much to spill no more."[6] The tanker *Exxon Baton Rouge*, en route in ballast to Valdez, rafted alongside the stricken tanker and began offloading the oil that remained aboard. The success of those operations significantly reduced the potential impact of the accident. Had they not gone well, the *Valdez* oil spill could have been much larger, and the gradual release of oil from a sunken ship might have continued for years. Fortunately, the seas remained calm in the days immediately after the grounding, and the ship was eventually refloated on April 5 and moved nearby for temporary repairs.

The oil discharged from the tanker had spread broadly around it, but calm seas presented the opportunity to contain the spill. Nicholas described the scene from the air as he flew into Anchorage the day after the spill: "There was a small vessel that looked like it was attempting to string some boom and here is this massive slick which I guess extended out several miles from the vessel. So, they would have had to have a thousand times more boom—this is my guess."[7] For three days after the grounding, calm conditions provided the chance to contain the spill by recapturing some it with skimmers and burning or dispersing the oil on the surface. But confusion reigned. Delays resulted from a lack of adequate equipment. There was divided authority among Exxon, the Alyeska Pipeline Service Company (the consortium that operated the Trans-Alaska Pipeline and its terminus at the port of Valdez), and the state and federal governments. The lack of experience with large spills in icy waters presented problems. The slow start shaped public perceptions of the response to the spill. For much of the public, whatever Exxon did in the days after the spill began to spread was too little and too late.

Under contingency plans for possible spills, last approved in 1987, Alyeska, under the leadership of British Petroleum, had initial responsibility for the cleanup. It quickly became apparent, however, that Alyeska lacked the resources, trained personnel, or experience to handle the disaster. It also lacked quick access to the equipment needed to collect or corral the oil. Indeed, its only major containment barge in Valdez was in dry dock for repairs, and equipment on hand could contain, at most, 2,000 barrels of oil—less than one-hundredth of the oil spilled in Prince William Sound.[8] By the end of the first day, about thirty local boats had deployed some two miles of boom.[9] Recognizing the need for a much more aggressive response to the spill, on the second day Exxon sought to obtain more booms and additional boats locally. The company also ordered other equipment from the lower forty-eight states and from several international oil-spill cooperatives, but days would pass before this equipment would arrive. Exxon conducted an early test of burning the oil on the water's surface, but the results were disappointing and also raised concerns from the State of Alaska about the amount of airborne pollution a larger burn might produce.

Exxon and the State of Alaska also disagreed about the use of chemical dispersants to break up the oil and cause it to spread throughout the water, reducing its concentration and its effects on surface wildlife, including birds and otters. Alaska had preapproved the use of these dispersants for parts of Prince William Sound. Their use in other designated areas, however, required additional permission from the Alaska Department of Environmental Conservation (ADEC). The agency hesitated to do so until convinced that dispersants would not harm fish and other wildlife, and ADEC's approval for widespread use was not given until the evening of March 26, three days after the spill.[10] Exxon cited this delay as part of its public and legal explanation of how state officials prevented it from taking quick steps to clean up more of the spill. Others disagreed, arguing that the supply of dispersants on hand was inadequate for the size of the spill and that calm conditions would have limited the effectiveness of the dispersants, which worked best in choppy conditions.[11]

The delays caused by the lack of equipment and the debates over the best method to treat the spill proved costly. Efforts to apportion blame for such delays became a staple of published reports about the response to the accident and later reappeared in trials over liability for damages. Alyeska, Exxon, ADEC, other Alaskan agencies, and the U.S. Coast Guard all debated the best way to address the cleanup. Legal responsibilities were confused, and little effective action occurred in the crucial days before a storm dramatically broke the prevailing calm with seventy-mile-an-hour winds that blew away the few booms that had been deployed. Stormy conditions soon roiled oil floating on and near the surface into tar balls and hard-to-collect mousse. During the next four days, high winds and rough seas pushed oil up to ninety miles from the site of the grounding.

Over the following weeks and months, what had been a very severe

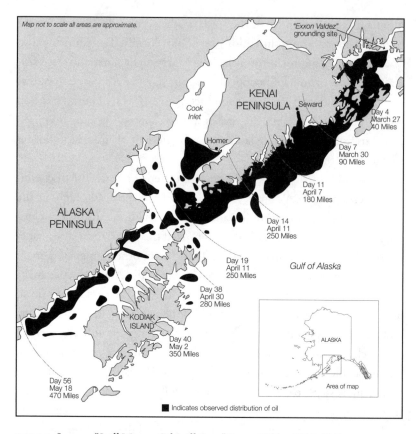

Map not to scale all areas are approximate.

"Exxon Valdez" grounding site

KENAI PENINSULA

Cook Inlet

Seward

Day 4 March 27 40 Miles

Homer

Day 7 March 30 90 Miles

Day 11 April 7 180 Miles

ALASKA PENINSULA

Day 14 April 11 250 Miles

Day 19 April 11 250 Miles

Gulf of Alaska

Day 38 April 30 280 Miles

KODIAK ISLAND

Day 40 May 2 350 Miles

ALASKA

Day 56 May 18 470 Miles

Area of map

■ Indicates observed distribution of oil

MAP 6.1: Source: *"Spill Maps—Oil Spill Facts,"* Exxon Valdez *Oil Spill Trustee Council, Anchorage, Alaska.*

but localized spill became a massive regional problem. Oil from the spill ultimately spread 470 miles south of Bligh Reef, contaminating shores throughout much of Prince William Sound and out into the western Gulf of Alaska (see map 6.1).[12] Higher-than-usual tides coated shorelines with oil above the normal zone of wave action, complicating future oil removal by natural means. In all, the spill affected some 1,300 miles of shoreline, roughly the distance from New York City to Jacksonville, Florida, or from Seattle to Los Angeles.[13]

But the spill was not in Los Angeles or New York City. It was in Alaska, which had long represented America's last natural frontier. The original battle over the Trans-Alaska Pipeline, which included the oil terminal at

Valdez, had been long and hard fought, with environmentalists squaring off against the Alyeska partners on the issues raised by the development of Prudhoe Bay's oil. As discussed in chapter 2, the struggle delayed the construction of the pipeline for more than four years and focused the nation's attention on two competing interests central to the nation's future: the supply of more domestic oil versus the protection of the natural environment. When the oil spill refocused attention on the pipeline and extensive damage to a large section of the Alaskan coast, critics of Big Oil reacted with anger tinged with a sense of betrayal. The system had been approved with assurances that all possible steps would be taken to prevent such a spill.[14] The sheer physical beauty of Prince William Sound intensified the reaction to the oil spill. A city manager of the town of Cordova had this to say: "I referred to Prince William Sound as one of the two most beautiful places on earth. I leave it to each of you individually to decide what the other one is."[15] Many of those who lived in the region fished for a living, depending on the richness of the estuary to provide them the opportunity to live in such a special place.

An enduring symbol of the devastation was the wildlife that suffered and died from exposure to oiled beaches and water. Regular media reports with gruesome photographs of oil-covered birds and otters being pulled from the water burned into the public mind scenes of devastation. The *Exxon Valdez* Oil Spill Trustee Council later estimated that the spill killed 170,000–300,000 common murres, 1,000 harlequin ducks, 8,000–12,000 marbled murrelets, 300 harbor seals, 13 killer whales, 3,500–5,500 sea otters, and more than 200 bald eagles.[16] A widespread concern in Alaska was the potential impact of oil pollution on commercial fisheries, especially the salmon farms that dotted several of the inlets of the sound. As the spill spread, fishermen, as well as Exxon's crews, placed booms around the fisheries to protect them from the oil, but fears of potential contamination nonetheless reduced consumer demand for Alaska salmon. The spill threatened other fisheries, prompting the state to cancel some of the open periods for fishing in the sound. Later, during the trial over the spill's damages, the loss of income from those and other fisheries became a central issue. Exxon's reassurances that it was doing the best it could to protect fisheries, and even the company's policy of quick payments of compensatory damages to fishermen harmed by the giant spill did little to dampen the outrage of those who saw their livelihoods and their way of life threatened. These were among the angriest of all Alaskans, and they led the way in organizing both legal and political challenges to Exxon.[17]

In the immediate aftermath of the oil spill, a series of newspaper reports, congressional hearings, and speeches by governmental officials criticized the failure of Alyeska and Exxon to fulfill the promises made in their contingency plans. Early in the permitting process for the Trans-Alaska Pipeline in the 1970s, Alyeska had put forward a variety of promises that safeguards would make major spills highly unlikely. In plans from the early 1980s and then in a voluminous plan in 1987, Alyeska assured government officials that it had adequate containment equipment, sufficiently trained spill-response workers, and a realistic plan to contain and treat potential oil spills in Prince William Sound. Just after the *Valdez* spill, a *Wall Street Journal* article entitled "Broken Promises" detailed the cutbacks and the attitudes that undermined those plans. The *Houston Post* and *Newsweek* published similar exposés that portrayed a steady retreat from preparedness by Alyeska—and the State of Alaska. Some of this could be blamed on budget cuts by the company and by regulatory agencies after the oil price bust of the mid-1980s. Such cuts helped explain why Alyeska had eliminated its twelve-person emergency response team in the 1980s and why ADEC had reduced its workweek to four days in the same period. Other problems arose because of Alyeska's attitude toward regulators, an attitude that one official labeled "utter contempt." One Alaska state inspector's memorandum to his superior about a preparedness drill he witnessed in 1984 reported that Alyeska's spill-response capability had "regressed to a dangerous level." Another inspector recalled that "drills were a farce, a comic opera."[18]

Some problems reflected the general difficulties of contingency planning for an extremely unlikely, but potentially devastating, accident. Almost 9,000 oil tankers had made the trip from Valdez with no major accidents during the twelve years between the opening of the pipeline in 1977 and the *Valdez* spill. That record, along with safeguards in the original construction and planning of the pipeline, safe operating procedures, and government regulations, combined to convince company and government officials that a major spill was highly unlikely. The 1987 contingency plan did, however, include plans for responses to a spill of

8.4 million gallons of oil thirty miles out in the sound from Valdez, a scenario similar to what occurred in the actual *Exxon Valdez* spill. In a wildly optimistic projection, Alyeska estimated that only 5 percent of such a spill would not be recovered or dispersed. In testimony before Congress after the spill, the president of Exxon USA more realistically interpreted the 1987 plan when he noted that "the approved plan recognized that a spill of that magnitude [200,000 barrels] could not be fully contained, large volumes of oil would reach the shore, and a significant cleanup effort would be required."[19] A projection in congressional hearings that a spill as large as 200,000 barrels might be expected to happen only once in 241 years brought a memorable and telling reply from Jack Lamp, a member of the Cordova District Fishermen United: "There's a saying 'only one in 100 Alaska brown bears will bite.' Trouble is, they don't come in numerical order."[20] Even though the worst-case scenario was statistically unlikely, its vast impact could not be safely ignored. Complacency was a dangerous frame of mind given the extremely damaging consequences of a serious accident on the 9,001st tanker trip.

After the spill, most major media raked Alyeska and Exxon over the coals for their poor responses. The *New York Times* reported that "Exxon seemed to respond to the oil spill off the Alaskan coast in slow motion."[21] *Newsweek* said that Exxon and the oil industry were not prepared to handle a major spill. In another article, it called the initial response to the spill "confusion bordering on chaos," and blamed "complacency borne of the belief that no spill could be this bad."[22] Government officials came down even harder on the oil companies. The U.S. secretary of transportation concluded that "no one was ready" and that the 1987 contingency plan should not have been approved. The head of ADEC derided Alyeska's claims that the promises of adequate equipment put forward in the plan were merely "guidelines," not requirements. Senator John Chafee (R-Rhode Island) captured the overall tone of the criticism when he concluded that "the cleanup crews initially responding to this spill acted more like Keystone Kops than the well-trained oil spill response teams described in the industry's contingency plan."[23]

A thorough investigation by an intergovernmental committee headed by the secretary of transportation and the administrator of the Environmental Protection Agency put forward similar complaints about the initial response to the spill. It noted the lack of sufficient equipment on site, the absence of an adequately trained response force, the long delay in bringing people and equipment to the scene, the confusion caused by the existence of three competing contingency plans, and the lack of preparedness for dealing with a major spill. Exxon and its partners in Alaska had designed and built a technologically advanced system to develop giant reserves of oil on the North Slope of Alaska; transport it 800 miles to Valdez via a large-diameter pipeline over mountain ranges, major rivers, and earthquake zones; and then ship it in modern tankers capable of hauling more than a million barrels of oil to markets. They had not, however, put in place a technically advanced system to contain a major spill at sea should one occur. The technological and managerial innovations needed to produce oil in a harsh and remote environment had not been matched by equivalent advances in technology to protect the marine environment. The report found plenty of blame to go around: "Government and industry plans, individually and collectively, proved to be wholly insufficient to control an oil spill of the magnitude of the *Exxon Valdez* incident."[24]

Most critics focused on Exxon, and CEO Larry Rawl came in for special criticism. For the first week of the spill, he remained out of the spotlight and out of the public's vision. By the time the top official of the Exxon Corporation became more visible in the cleanup, the court of public opinion had found him guilty of failing to take decisive steps in the initial response to the spill. Many felt he had shown disdain for the public by delegating responsibilities for the spill to others in the corporation. Even experienced executives within the company felt that Rawl had made the wrong choice, making a bad situation worse. In particular, he had failed to step out in front of the disaster by making a trip to Alaska to survey the damage and giving a public expression of regret and a loud and clear commitment to remedy the situation. His approach to crisis management clashed sharply with the realities of politics and public opinion in an outraged democracy. In short, the company's initial handling of the *Exxon Valdez* oil spill became the basis for case studies of what not to do in response to a major corporate disaster.[25]

Rawl's actions immediately after the spill were in keeping with Exxon's approach to management. Orders flowed through a well-established hierarchy to be carried out by those nearest the problem. Lee Raymond recalled that Rawl's initial reaction was that the cleanup was the shipping company's job. Rawl's personality and his management style worked against his successful participation in public relations. He was known for taking a low-profile stance in public. He felt unfairly maligned by public criticism, and he had no intention of flying to Alaska for a day, putting on a slicker suit, and taking to the beaches at Prince William Sound for a photo opportunity. According to Raymond, Rawl commented, "What the hell would I have done?"[26] One answer to that question came from an Alaskan named Art Davidson, the author of one of the first books about the spill, *In the Wake of the "Exxon Valdez"*: "Rawl's presence on the beaches of Alaska could have helped show that Exxon gave a damn—if Exxon *did* give a damn."[27] Many in the general public wanted more visible action from the man in charge of Exxon. Rawl's failure to respond in a highly public way fed perceptions that Exxon was indifferent to the impact of the oil spill, leaving an enduring impression that the company lacked a full commitment to rectifying the damage done.

Rawl had a well-earned reputation for a combative approach to management.[28] That approach had been effective in his efforts to streamline the company in the mid-1980s, but it did not serve him well when he moved into the public spotlight. At the first shareholders' meeting after the spill, in May 1989, good news about rising earnings and promising new exploration and production was overshadowed by protestors outside the meeting auditorium, angrily shouting their dismay over the company's response to the oil spill. When such sentiment reached the floor of the meeting in the form of a shareholder resolution calling for Rawl to step down, he responded, "I won't. It would be counterproductive." He then reminded those who presented the resolution of another method of removing him: "There are ways of getting me out. Vote your shares." Both sides knew, of course, that Rawl held proxies for a majority of the votes. Later, faced with a proposal from the floor to establish a billion-dollar trust fund to cover future restoration, Rawl voiced his frustration: "It's not like we're deadbeats. We'll stay as long as it takes and pay what it takes."[29]

Exxon spokesmen had a difficult time finding an effective voice with which to communicate with the broader public. Sometimes their comments were incomplete.[30] Sometimes they were delivered in "engineer-speak" and confused or angered the public. And sometimes they were reported in a way guaranteed to draw an unfavorable response. In a *News-week* article, one company official hard at work in Alaska observed, for example, that "the public's reaction is totally irrational." A spokesman for the company reminded reporters soon after the spill of the common occurrence of oil seeps in nature. One national news story reported comments by Otto Harrison, who managed Exxon's cleanup efforts, under the misleading headline "Exxon Exec Says Valdez Spill Was Good for Alaska." Even carefully framed comments from Lee Raymond sounded off-key. The *New York Times* quoted him on the company's reactions to the spill: "We are chagrined, we're disappointed, we're even devastated to a degree."[31] If there was anything the company could have said to soothe public anger or increase public understanding of its efforts to clean up the spill, it had trouble finding the words or the tone with which to do so.

Efforts to adjust the public relations message and its tone began soon after the spill with a public apology from Rawl in a series of newspaper advertisements. He returned to this message in congressional testimony in April 1989: "I want to repeat what I've said in print and on television a number of times; how sincerely and profoundly sorry I am that this accident happened. I speak not only for myself, but also for the thousands of Exxon employees who, because of their loyalty and commitment to Exxon, share my distress."[32] In June 1989, Rawl even confided to an interviewer from the *Wall Street Journal* that he had wanted to go to Valdez immediately after the spill, but had been dissuaded from going since he would only have gotten in the way of "people who were already up to their necks in alligators." He recalled thinking that "even if it [the trip] had been cosmetic, it would have been productive. . . . Frankly, I was a little naïve." He said that he woke up "in the middle of the night" questioning his decision to stay home.[33]

After absorbing a year of constant criticism and second-guessing by the media, Rawl responded aggressively to a scathing attack on him and his company in *BusinessWeek* in March 1990. The article quoted an unnamed former Exxon executive as follows: "Larry [Rawl] simply saw it [the *Valdez* spill] as an engineering problem. He didn't realize it was also a leadership and a vision problem."[34] The article called into question Rawl's overall strategy for Exxon, suggesting that his cutbacks from 1986 onward had "created an accident-prone system," particularly in areas responsible for environmental issues. An accompanying editorial, entitled "Exxon Should Live Up to Its World Stature," criticized the company's "lead-footed response to the accident." It portrayed Rawl as an incompetent leader whose strategy was "unworthy of Exxon's stature and history."[35] It even included a quote suggesting that "outside directors should appoint a new chairman committed to making Exxon the proud giant it once was."[36]

In a quotation included in the article, Rawl defended himself by arguing that Exxon would have received "the same amount of hell" over the *Valdez* spill even if he had done a better job of "cosmetic PR."[37] After the article's publication, he responded more forcefully in a carefully crafted letter to the editor of *BusinessWeek*. In a sense, he wrote for all of the employees within Exxon who were, in the words of Harry Longwell, "still catching unbelievable grief from people on the outside"; Longwell added, "I can see how that could sour your attitude a little bit."[38] Rawl defended the company's record and the health of Exxon with a detailed rebuttal of many of the points made in the article. He argued, "Your magazine has rendered a severe judgment about the direction Exxon is taking. We feel that judgment is flawed by the dubious quality of your information and your simplistic analysis."[39] In conclusion, he stated his confidence that Exxon would enjoy continued success in the future by following the strategy that had served the company well for more than a century.

Morale had suffered as Exxon had endured almost continual attacks on its performance in Alaska, and Rawl's letter, which was distributed to employees throughout the world, rallied the troops with a reminder that they worked for one of the "world's premier petroleum and chemical oil companies."[40] A more thorough presentation on this broad point also was presented by executives in meetings with their employees throughout Exxon. In the fall of 1989, Rawl thanked employees for their efforts in the cleanup, taking the tone of Exxon's tradition of quiet public relations: "Their efforts—and results—demonstrate again that Exxon cares a great deal about the environment and that we continue to stand ready to prove it with deeds, not just words."[41] Near the one-year anniversary of the spill, he made his fullest statement of the traditional Exxon approach to public relations in a letter to shareholders: "The depth of our regret for the accident has been expressed by the determination we showed in taking responsibility for the cleanup immediately after the accident and the lengths to which we have gone since then."[42]

TAKING RESPONSIBILITY FOR THE CLEANUP

The cleanup would be a long and demanding process. The first order of business was to clarify lines of authority and responsibility. Having taken charge of the cleanup from a hapless Alyeska, Exxon joined state and federal officials to coordinate an approach for marshalling needed personnel and equipment. That effort included steps to clarify the responsibilities of all parties involved in the spill response. The governor of Alaska, Steve Cowper, surveyed the scene of the spill on March 24 and promptly requested federal involvement and oversight. ADEC also had the responsibility to respond to oil spills in Alaskan waters, and it established a modest cleanup capability that continued for some time, largely independent of the efforts coordinated by Exxon and the U.S. Coast Guard's on-scene commander.[43]

The U.S. secretary of transportation, Samuel K. Skinner, in office only since early February, placed the coast guard in charge of the response. Admiral Paul A. Yost Jr., commandant of the coast guard, assigned Vice Admiral Clyde E. Robbins the specific responsibility for overseeing the cleanup in Prince William Sound. Lee Raymond later referred to both Yost and Robbins as "first-rate," and the navy and the coast guard proved effective in obtaining federal assistance for the cleanup.[44] Under the National Contingency Plan, in effect as of 1989, the U.S. Coast Guard's captain of the port where a spill occurred had the authority to manage the government's response, acting as an agent of the president. As the "federal on scene coordinator," that official could choose to direct the cleanup using federal funds and resources or monitor the cleanup carried out by the party responsible for the spill. Yet Vice Admiral Robbins gave an honest answer when asked about his role as coordinator: "As far as my actual authority over the cleanup, I have none, unless I take over the spill. My only hope is to get Exxon to do what I want to get done through jawboning and coercion."[45] Given the magnitude of the *Exxon Valdez* spill, Robbins made the practical choice to monitor and assist Exxon's efforts, since the company could bring to this work far greater resources and

Melvin Harrison, executive vice president, Exxon Company USA, 1989.
ExxonMobil Historical Collection, di_06102.

oil-related expertise than the coast guard. In effect, the coast guard had official oversight authority, and Exxon had the practical responsibility to manage the cleanup.

Before Exxon could work effectively with government agencies, it needed to define more clearly the lines of authority over the spill within the company. Rawl, Raymond, and William "Bill" Stevens, the president of Exxon USA, held an all-night meeting a week after the spill to decide how the company would approach the monumental problems resulting from the disaster. In early April 1989, Raymond informed Stevens that he would like to attend a meeting that had been scheduled with Stevens, Skinner, and Yost a few days later. It was clear from those meetings that Exxon Shipping was simply too small to manage an effective cleanup. A much larger effort, drawing on resources across the corporation, was needed, as was a leader with strength and experience. Mel Harrison had both. He had the strength of a poor boy made good. Born during the Great Depression in a small town in East Texas, he earned a petroleum engineering degree at Texas A&M University, supplementing a partial scholarship by working in the oil fields during the summers. He went to work at Humble Oil in 1952 and gained experience throughout Texas and California. As the head of Exxon's affiliate in Libya, he was one of the last ones out in the early 1980s as Qaddafi's supporters took charge of the company's LNG plant. After a stint in corporate planning, he became an executive vice president of Exxon USA. Harrison gradually "assumed responsibility of Exxon USA [in Alaska] instead of Bill Stevens," who "continued to manage the rest of [its] operation." Harrison recalled that "Larry Rawl was very involved at the start, and then he delegated that to Lee Raymond at the corporate level."[46] By the time the cleanup began to pick up steam, the top Exxon executives overseeing the effort had become Lee Raymond, Mel Harrison, and Jack Clarke, who from the earliest days served as the "point person" for legal questions.

To manage the cleanup on the ground in Alaska, Exxon's leaders chose a man known to them all—Otto V. Harrison. The son of an oil-field roughneck, Harrison was born in a tent next to a drilling rig. He grew up in the small town of Algoa, Texas, in Galveston County, working on dairy and pig farms and in the rice fields. After working his way through the University of Texas and graduating with a degree in petroleum engineering, he went to work for Humble Oil & Refining. He gained experience on various production projects and eventually worked with Rawl in planning at Exxon USA. He also spent a year on loan to the Environmental Protection Agency in Washington, D.C. At the time of the *Valdez* accident, he was in Australia helping bring new oil-production projects onstream.

A telephone call from Exxon headquarters abruptly changed Harrison's life. He was told that he had been chosen to head Exxon's Alaska oil-spill task force, and that he should catch the first plane out for Alaska and take responsibility for leading the cleanup. Soon thereafter, Rawl told him, "I want you to clean this up. I'm going to give you all the authority that I've got—you've got it all. And if anybody gets in your way, you just tell me." Harrison noted that "most people have an authority that'll get you to a million or a hundred million.... Mine was unlimited. Of course, I spent $2.5 billion.... But that was just Larry.... You got the job, now go do it, don't let anything get in the way of it, and move on along."[47]

Otto Harrison was an inspired choice. He managed the acquisition of needed equipment and the actual cleanup of the shoreline while also handling the press and meeting with governmental officials. Workers drawn from Exxon's global operations traveled to Alaska to help with the effort. Some handled early damage claims. Others scrambled to find the array of equipment needed. Still others developed plans for hiring local contractors and citizens to help. Researchers set about finding ways to capture oil from the sea and to clean it from beaches and rocky shores.

Harrison made an embarrassing misstep as he began to marshal the resources needed to get started. In his first days in Alaska, he had a trained crew of workers, but the vessels needed to put them to work were not yet ready. He did not "need anyone winding up in a bar or fistfight." To keep these workers out of trouble, he sent them to wash contaminated rocks manually, wiping the oil off one rock at a time. A photographer in search of an action shot saw the crew at work and snapped their photograph, cleaning rocks with towels on a heavily soiled beach in a plainly futile exercise. Harrison realized that "from a public relations perspective, that was a dumb, dumb decision," since the often-reprinted photo conveyed to the public the impression that Exxon had no idea how to clean up the spill.[48]

While other spills around the world had been larger, the scope of the *Valdez* spill, its remoteness, and the fragility of Prince William Sound were all outside the experience of the oil industry.[49] To help in the cleanup, members of Harrison's team sought local allies. At all public meetings, they made it a point to apologize and take responsibility for the spill. Tom Cirigliano, a Public Affairs Department manager in Alaska, recalled that at "a typical Exxon presentation . . . we got up, told the facts, no spin, no gloss over, simply facts. . . . Our company culture embodies the belief that if you do the best job you can, people will understand."[50] Of course, many in the region remained highly skeptical of Exxon, and tensions were high as the cleanup moved forward. Local fishermen and others often disrupted company press conferences, and unfriendly state officials released information contradicting Exxon's reports about the progress of the cleanup, at times considering them to be all spin and no facts. It was not a time and place to reason together. Every fact was disputed; every motive was questioned.[51]

One area of special concern was the payment of damages to those harmed by the spill. According to Mel Harrison, the company had a claims office up and paying claims "within weeks." He recalled that Exxon chose not to take the "typical" approach in which those who received payments to settle their claim had to sign an agreement forgoing future payments. Instead, Exxon "left that open-ended so that they could come back and claim additional damages or funds"; the company was "paying money without an agreement on the final settlement of damages with individuals and organizations—villages, cities, fish plants, processing plants, fishermen and so forth."[52] The company sought to get quick relief to those harmed by the spill. In the months after the spill, by its own count, Exxon distributed approximately $300 million through that process to more than 11,000 Alaskans. In addition, the company hired fishermen and other people who had already been compensated for economic damages to work on the cleanup.[53]

The company used an array of equipment and techniques to capture oil, restore the shoreline, and mitigate the damage.[54] Unfortunately, existing cleanup technology was rudimentary and largely untested on a large spill in Arctic conditions. The potential long-term harm from approaches such as the steam cleaning of beaches and rocks had not been thoroughly studied, nor had the possible long-term health implications for those engaged in the cleanup. Inevitably, the definition of "cleaned beach" was much disputed, particularly regarding oil that remained beneath the surface of beaches and rocks. Almost everyone understood that over long periods of time, natural forces such as weather and tides would gradually work to improve the condition of the shoreline and restore the health of wildlife populations. The practical and political imperative, however, was to remove oil as quickly and effectively as possible.

Under coast guard supervision, Exxon provided the funding and the general direction for the massive effort. One company executive later recalled: "It was like war. I mean, the esprit de corps was so high—all the people working up there were just as dedicated as they could be, and they would work sixteen hours a day and go get four or five hours sleep and be up and at it again."[55] The war required an army of workers, a fleet of cleanup vessels, and logistical support for all of them. Exxon contacted five oil-spill-response organizations—three in Alaska, one in California, and one in England—for help. Much of the equipment and supplies needed by those groups had to be shipped into the region, and such shipments steadily increased over the summer. Local vessels fought the spill, both under Exxon's direction and in independent actions by their owners, and the "mosquito fleet" of local boats played an important role in the cleanup. At its peak in August, the cleanup employed almost 1,500 boats of assorted types. The U.S. Navy supplied—with company reimbursement—amphibious-support ships to provide berths for workers; others lived on modified barges. Landing craft hauled people and equipment around the broad area affected by the spill and served as platforms for shoreline-treating equipment. Other purpose-built barges provided logistic support and handled special treating equipment.

People to work on cleanup crews also were in short supply. Early discussions between Exxon and the coast guard regarding the size of the crew needed convinced the company to ramp up its plans for staffing.[56] Exxon sent hundreds of employees to Alaska to help with the cleanup. The company turned to contractors to find additional workers to do an array of jobs. VECO, the company's primary cleanup contractor, recruited, trained, and deployed workers. The number of cleanup workers grew quickly through May, and then increased at a more moderate pace. Employment peaked in late July, when more than 11,000 people were on the cleanup rolls. Most were Alaskans. Many were assigned to work in six task forces, each with an average of 500–700 people and using about 100 boats of all types. Half the people in each task force directly treated the shoreline. The other half provided the logistical support to meet the needs of the six task forces, which each day required about 30 tons of food, 102,000 gallons of fuel, 66,000 gallons of water, and 18 tons of other materials.

Scott Nauman, an Exxon employee then in his early thirties, worked two levels beneath Otto Harrison as an "operations coordinator" managing several of the task forces. His memories of his time in Alaska provide a close-up view of the operation. When Nauman walked off the plane for the first time at the small airport in Valdez, a man with a clipboard greeted him, asked him to sign a document, and then informed him that he now had approval authority for individual invoices up to $1 million. Noting that his previous limit as an operations coordinator had been $25,000, he "knew at that point that this was going to be a completely different experience."[57]

As he plunged into the work of managing his task forces, he quickly realized the vast scale of the cleanup. After working his way through the paperwork for a stack of invoices one evening, he was startled to realize that he had just approved expenditures of $17 million. His job was "basically to ensure that our operations were moving forward, that they were being done in a safe fashion, and really making sure that we were making the progress that we needed to make in the cleanup." Working for him were "thousands of people that were actively involved in the cleanup. . . . Each task force had fifteen to twenty [Exxon people] and they worked in shifts, two weeks on, and two weeks off." Most of these Exxon employees were volunteers from all parts of the company. Some took to the demanding, stress-filled conditions in Alaska and stayed; others did not adapt well and returned to their regular jobs. Part of Nauman's job was giving brief tours of the cleanup to visitors, including "senior executives from our company, politicians, news people, senior executives from other energy companies." The "spectators" "always said the same thing . . . they all said they had no idea how big the cleanup effort was . . . how many people, how many ships, how much area, how much logistics required. . . . It struck me that every person who came up there to get a look, they were just about overwhelmed by the scope of it."[58]

The task forces tried various means to clean the beaches. They used deflection and containment booms to control the flow of the oil and to protect sensitive areas. Every sort of skimmer available was put to use in the cleanup. Dredges scooped oil out of shallow-water bottoms. Skimmers loaded on special barges transferred oil to disposal sites. To collect oil fouling the shoreline, the company developed and deployed a series of purpose-built barges with specialized equipment. These included "cold-minis"—landing craft fitted with pressure washers and cold-water pumps

A shallow-draft barge cleaning up oil from the Exxon Valdez *on the beach in Prince William Sounds, Alaska, 1989. ExxonMobil Historical Collection, di_06227.*

for washing oil off the beaches; "hot-minis"—landing craft able to heat water for the same task; and for use in very rugged areas, "maxi-barges," which had handheld hoses on the shoreline and larger hoses suspended from man-lift buckets that could be suspended over beach areas. The number of such specialized cleaning mini-barges rose from fewer than ten in April to about seventy of all types by the end of June to a late-August peak of almost ninety barges.

In the summer of 1989, Exxon applied nutrients to about seventy miles of shoreline to accelerate the natural biodegradation of the oil.[59] Not all techniques worked as well as desired, and the learning curve was steep, and at times costly. Some of the approaches had unintended consequences. For example, hot-water washing of oiled beaches to remove oil also could kill beneficial bacteria that might help degrade the oil naturally. Despite such problems, extensive efforts by Exxon and others had removed much of the most visible oil from the shoreline by the end of the summer of 1989.

With the approach of winter weather in September, bay operations became hazardous, forcing the reduction of cleanup work. By October, the 2,000 remaining workers were rapidly demobilized. The company assumed correctly that rough winter weather would improve the condition of many oiled beaches. When the company resumed cleanup operations in 1990, the improvement was obvious, and cleanup crews used different techniques to treat the remaining oil in some areas.[60] Workers used hand tools to remove small patches of oil. In other locations, workers tilled beaches to expose subsurface oil to wave action and bioremediation. Only about 1,000 people took part in the cleanup in 1990. The number dropped to half that in 1991 and to fewer than 100 in 1992. In that year, the U.S. Coast Guard—advised by the National Oceanographic and Atmospheric Agency—decided that further cleaning would not provide a net benefit and declared the cleanup complete; the State of Alaska reluctantly agreed. Exxon reported that it had spent more than $2 billion dollars to ameliorate the impact of the spill.[61]

There was, of course, much controversy over the success of the cleanup. The surface of the shoreline had been cleaned to the extent that human effort could quickly clean it. But the restoration of the sound and its shoreline would be a long-term process. In an issue published soon after the spill, *National Geographic* published an excellent article that surveyed the devastation and asked, "Can the Wilderness Heal?" On the tenth anniversary of the spill, an article in the magazine answered: "yes, with scarring."[62] Environmentalists and Exxon consistently disagreed about the extent and the seriousness of the scarring. The company wrote of "the remarkable recovery" as early as 1993, concluding that "a new body of scientific work confirms that the environment of Alaska's Prince William Sound is essentially recovered." On the tenth anniversary, Frank Sprow, then the company's vice president for Safety, Health and Environment recalled his own ten-year involvement with the cleanup by noting evidence of the sound's "truly impressive" recovery. He mentioned the return of most wildlife and the health of the salmon population. The article in the company magazine that includes Sprow's interview reported: "Scientists representing Exxon, government agencies and independent institutions have investigated the impact of the spill on wildlife and the environment. They've developed a broad consensus: The region has essentially been restored thanks to nature's resiliency and the massive cleanup."[63]

The tone of the company's reports offended many critics. As in most aspects of the spill and its cleanup, the views of Exxon on the overall success of the effort differed sharply from those of many fishermen in the region and environmental groups. Each upbeat Exxon report on the progress of the cleanup was met by skepticism. Decades after the disaster, complaints about the persistence of oil in Prince William Sound continued. On the twentieth anniversary of the spill, the *Exxon Valdez* Oil Spill Trustee Council—which had been created to oversee restoration of the regional ecosystem using funds from a $900 million settlement— reported that some spots remained toxic and that the remaining oil might "take decades and possibly centuries to disappear entirely."[64] The question "How clean is clean?" has been debated since the summer of 1989, often with what one newspaper called "dueling findings of scientific studies."[65] The long court battle over punitive damages no doubt heightened those duels, but at their heart were different views of what is possible and what is necessary to restore the regional ecosystem.

The company struggled to regain credibility with the general public, politicians, and the media. It found almost no support among environmental groups. One longtime leader within Exxon's philanthropic foundation noted the company's sense of betrayal: "Prior to the Valdez accident, Exxon had a good relationship with a number of the sort of signature environmental organizations. It had funded projects with many of them. With the accident, these environmental organizations turned on the company."[66] More distressing within Exxon was the reporting of the major business publications, which remained highly critical of the company for several years after the oil spill. A company long satisfied to keep a low public profile was frustrated by its new image as the poster boy for irresponsible corporate behavior.

Two episodes illustrated the difficult task facing Exxon as it sought to defend its actions and its credibility in the days before and after the spill. The first is a story told by Otto Harrison about the first time he escorted Exxon's board of directors on a flying tour of the damage to Prince William Sound. The plane flew over one arm of water that had not been contaminated by oil, but was filled with black lichen. Harrison recalled that when he explained this to the board members, "They flat out did not believe me. . . . So we went back and we took some boats and brought them back up in there and showed them what that was. So [you can] see what the public perception was we were fighting. . . . But I mean to tell

you, they were ready to throw me out of the airplane the first time I was
. . . telling them what we were looking at."[67] The second episode came
almost a decade later, during the merger of Exxon and Mobil. The board
of Mobil did not vote unanimously to approve the merger, because one of
its members was a strong conservationist who, according to Mobil's chairman, Lou Noto, "could never forgive Exxon for *Valdez*."[68]

PUBLIC POLICY RESPONSES TO THE SPILL

The *Exxon Valdez* accident was the catalyst for a major piece of U.S. legislation: the Oil Pollution Act of 1990 (OPA 90). Shocked by the severity
of the spill, Congress took up legislation to improve the nation's ability
to prevent and respond to oil spills. Despite a number of controversial
elements in the legislation, it passed with overwhelming congressional
support in August 1990. The new law marked a return to the "command
and control" approach to environmental legislation that had prevailed in
the 1960s and 1970s. It enhanced the ability of the federal government
to prevent oil spills and to respond more rapidly when they occurred.
The law required the government to take direct control of a major spill.
It established a $1 billion Oil Spill Liability Trust Fund funded by a five-
cent-a-barrel tax on imported oil to help pay for spill damages when a
responsible party could not be determined. It also raised the liability for
damages on those responsible for oil spills up to $75 million. Other provi-
sions required more thorough contingency planning for spills.[69]

The oil industry responded to the mandates by funding coordinated
response teams of unprecedented size and resources. Exxon joined other
companies in creating two nonprofit organizations: the Marine Preservation Association, to fund an industry-wide response effort, and the
Marine Spill Response Corporation, to purchase equipment, hire staff,
and train responders. This fostered the transition of the oil-spill-response
business from a cottage industry to a profession with a much greater ability to respond to spills. The response corporation was at the high end
of the business, with dues-paying members from major oil companies,
oil terminals, public utility companies, and shipowners. With its equipment, personnel in place, and ongoing training, it could respond much
more rapidly and efficiently to major spills than was previously possible.[70]

To reduce the severity of future oil spills, OPA 90 required tankers in U.S. waters to have double hulls by 2015. During the debate over the bill, Exxon opposed this provision, arguing that double-hull tankers might lose their stability after a major accident, potentially resulting in larger oil spills instead of smaller ones. Exxon's arguments on the matter had little impact.[71] In the heated political climate of the time, the company had lost its place at the bargaining table in the debate that produced OPA 90.

After the United States acted unilaterally on double hulls, the International Maritime Organization soon followed. It duly established double-hull standards in the 1992 International Convention for the Prevention of Pollution from Ships (known as MARPOL, short for "marine pollution"). This convention required tankers delivered after July 1996 to have double hulls, and ships constructed before that date would need double hulls once they reached twenty-five to thirty years of age—effectively banning such ships from oil carriage at that point, since the expense of retrofitting a double hull is prohibitive. The European Union, faced with those developments, passed regulations to accelerate the phasing out of single-hull oil vessels trading with its members.

One final provision of OPA 90 banned any vessel that had caused a spill of more than one million gallons after March 22, 1989, from operating in Prince William Sound. The company challenged this provision in court as a bill of attainder aimed at Exxon and the *Exxon Valdez* alone, but the Ninth Circuit Court of Appeals rejected this argument in 2002.[72] The company completed repairs on the *Exxon Valdez* in June 1990, renamed it the *SeaRiver Mediterranean*, and eventually sold it in 2002. In 2012 it was sold for scrap.

All tankers that remained in the business of transporting oil from Valdez faced tighter supervision as a result of new public and private regulations governing shipping in Prince William Sound. The oil companies and various state and federal agencies worked together to develop new rules and safeguards to prevent major accidents and to be prepared to respond if one occurred. Each outbound tanker had to be escorted by a vessel to scout for ice or other threats and followed by a tugboat to help any tanker that lost power. Spill-containment equipment on the escort boats made them potential first responders in the event of an accident. Alyeska added to its stock of response equipment, including both skimmers and chemical dispersants. The company also began to check departing crews for alcohol impairment. The coast guard upgraded its tanker-tracking system and began monitoring loaded tankers via satellite throughout their trip out of the sound. New rules assigned specially trained marine pilots with experience in the sound to accompany tankers farther south than had previously been done and also required outbound tankers to travel slower and sail under stricter weather rules.[73] Similar changes made oil-spill planning much more rigorous. New contingency plans mandated the inclusion of plans for spills up to 12.6 million gallons, and required annual drills. Responders placed skimmers capable of recovering 300,000 barrels of oil within seventy-two hours (ten times the capacity of skimmers available at Valdez in 1989) around the sound, as well as seven barges for taking on the recovered oil. Much larger supplies of dispersants and booms were also stockpiled.

In short, the response to the *Exxon Valdez* spill made the port of Valdez safer and much better equipped to respond to spills. These logical and obviously positive changes pose an important question: why was a major catastrophe required to put them in place? The new safety system illustrated that the self-interest of numerous public and private concerns, including Exxon, was bound up in ensuring the safest possible shipment of this crude. But those involved had not recognized the need for new procedures and equipment until a disaster shattered the assumption that such spills would not, almost could not, occur. More than a decade of tanker operations at Valdez before 1989 without a major accident had reinforced that assumption, feeding a sense of complacency that made contingency planning for a giant spill more a routine bureaucratic task than preparation for a real-life event with far-reaching effects on a region, a company, and an industry.

MORE WARNING FLAGS

More bad news rocked the company as it struggled with the aftermath of the *Exxon Valdez* spill. In the nine months after the spill, two other major accidents raised public concern about Exxon's operational performance. The accidents embarrassed the company, convincing it to redouble its efforts to improve safety throughout its operations. Coming soon after

Robert E. Wilhelm, senior vice president and member of the board of directors, 1999. ExxonMobil Historical Collection, di_06116.

the *Valdez* spill, they forced the company to acknowledge that it had serious safety problems and to act to remedy them.

The first of the post-*Valdez* accidents was a modern recurrence of one of the oil industry's worst nightmares—a major refinery explosion with fatalities. On Christmas Eve 1989, a thunderous explosion shook the company's refinery in Baton Rouge, Louisiana, setting three large heating-oil storage tanks on fire and killing two workers. In the fifteen hours it took to extinguish the fire, almost 4.5 million gallons of heating oil and lubricating oil had burned.[74] Robert Wilhelm, an Exxon executive with considerable downstream experience, went to Baton Rouge to inspect the refinery after the explosion. In earlier inspections, he had been struck "that the incidence of improperly installed material was higher in Exxon USA than it was in some of the foreign operations." At Baton Rouge, he found "that the emergency shutoff procedures in that part of the refinery [where the explosion occurred] were different than in any other refiner- ies and different than in other parts of . . . the same refinery." When he asked why the same procedures used in other facilities were not followed, the reply was, "Well, that's the way we do it in Baton Rouge."[75] A major accident, particularly one involving fatalities, raised a disturbing question: why had a plant been allowed to follow practices that did not come up to the standards of the best practices within the company?

A week later, on New Year's Day 1990, a heating-oil pipe that connected Exxon's Bayway refinery in Linden, New Jersey, with its products terminal in Bayonne, New Jersey, ruptured, leaking petroleum into Arthur Kill, a narrow waterway that separates New Jersey and Staten Island. Investiga- tions after the accident revealed several disturbing operational failures. A leak-detection device that was supposed to sound an alarm and shut off the flow of oil when a leak was detected had never properly functioned. Instead of fixing it, company employees simply turned it off and then reset it. On the night of the leak, the alarm went off at 10:30 p.m., only to be turned off and the valves reopened. Not until the alarm went off again four and a half hours later did workers discover the spill. They com- pounded their mistake by not reporting the spill to the coast guard for twelve hours. To make matters even worse, the company's initial public estimate of the size of the spill was 5,000 gallons. That estimate proved to be off by a factor of more than one hundred; regulators later placed the size of the spill at 567,000 gallons.[76]

As with the *Exxon Valdez* disaster, Exxon had suffered multiple fail- ures in its operating procedures. As the truth about the New Jersey spill trickled out over a week of increasingly hostile media reports, public con- cern and anger grew. The treatment of the leak-detection device seemed beyond indifference, and the delay in informing the coast guard seemed almost criminal. The confusion over the size of the spill seemed either devious or incompetent. All aspects of the accident were difficult to imag- ine occurring in a well-managed company.

Such behavior drew intense criticism of the company's operational performance, a sentiment greatly amplified by the fact that the spill took place in the shadow of New York City, the nation's media center. Adding to the public outrage was the fact that Arthur Kill was a breeding ground for herons and egrets. Several hundred gulls and Canadian geese died in the incident, and experts voiced fears about the spill's danger to other migratory birds as they returned to their nesting sites in the spring. As at Valdez, photos and news reports featuring birds soaked in oil were power-ful reminders of the impact of the company's negligence.[77]

The *New York Times* reported that after the spill, Exxon "faced weeks of relentless criticism." Some of it came from the *Times* itself, which intro-duced one story with the headline "Corporate Error—and Arrogance." The governor of New Jersey, Jim Florio, echoed that criticism: "What made the spill all the more galling was the apparent incompetence, and, yes, arrogance, that caused the problem." Officials from the EPA, focusing on the problem with the leak-detection alarm, complained that Exxon's response to their questions had been "disingenuous at best." The com-pany's previous explanations of its failure to replace the faulty alarm were not reassuring. One Exxon spokesman admitted that the pipeline was "simply not a priority item." Another reportedly said that the company "preferred to have an alarm system that erred too often on the safe side to one that never erred." An editorial in *Time* magazine noted Exxon's "attitude problem" and argued that the company was "earning a reputa-tion as a careless and callous despoiler of the environment." As at Valdez, several government agencies shared Exxon's misery. Both the coast guard and the company acknowledged that they "did not have enough spill con-tainment equipment at hand" and had to bring it in from as far away as Alabama and Georgia. The federal agency involved—the Office of Pipe-line Safety, within the Department of Transportation—admitted that it lacked jurisdiction over the oil spill and that it did not know "the number and location of all pipelines that pass under New York Harbor."[78]

Local and state governments were not in a forgiving mood. Criminal and civil claims were soon brought against Exxon by the State of New York, the State of New Jersey, the federal government, and the City of Elizabeth, New Jersey. Fifteen months later, Exxon resolved the charges by agreeing to an omnibus settlement. On March 20, 1991, the com-pany pleaded guilty, under the Clean Water Act, to a criminal charge of negligence in the training of personnel. Exxon agreed to pay a total of $5 million to the two states and the federal government as part of the criminal penalty, and an additional $10 million to settle civil litigation with the local and state governments. Coincidentally, the settlement came just a week after Exxon had entered a guilty plea on four federal criminal counts that arose from the *Valdez* spill, agreeing to pay $100 million.[79]

Looking back at these accidents after the passage of almost twenty years, Rene Dahan placed the period from 1989 through 1990 in perspective: "I think the *Valdez* was a wake-up call that has been very painful to many of us. . . . You know, we had a large number of very serious incidents that if you combined them with the *Valdez*, left you no escape out of concluding that there was something fundamentally broken."[80] How could these problems be fixed?

The search for answers quickly led to the subsidiary directly responsible for all three major accidents, Exxon USA. The company enjoyed considerable autonomy within the corporation because of its historical leadership in production and refining and its primary role in representing the corporation before U.S. regulatory authorities. But as its production declined, so did its special status. Even before the accidents in 1989 and 1990, Exxon USA had lost favor with corporate officials as a result of its failed attempts at diversification in the 1970s.

As top management at Exxon Corporation sought to foster a global, corporate perspective within the regional companies that had long dominated the company's overall agenda, the three major accidents in rapid succession on Exxon USA's watch came under intense scrutiny from above. Raymond recalled a budget meeting in the fall of 1990: "Exxon USA came up [to New York] and said that their safety record for the year had been below the industry average and their objective was to get above the industry average. And I said, 'That is ridiculous. You can have only one objective and that is to be the best.' And Larry [Rawl] didn't say anything for a couple of minutes and then he said, 'This meeting is over . . . Until you guys get your heads screwed on right, I don't want to hear from you,' and he got up and left."[81] Safety was becoming a top corporate priority, and any regional company—no matter how prominent and self-contained in the past—would be held accountable for it. The final break came in 1991, when Harry Longwell replaced Bill Stevens as head of Exxon USA.

Longwell's task was to fix whatever had gone wrong in the company, and he plunged into an in-depth review of its operations, with an eye to improving both operations and profitability. But the problems in Exxon went beyond the short-term effects of Exxon USA's recent accidents or even its long-term decline in oil production. Rawl and Raymond concluded that the corporation as whole had to take a far more disciplined approach in all its operations. It had to improve its record on the environment and on operational safety. The reforms that resulted marked a turning point in the company's commitment to safety, health, and the environment. Its thorough and systematic approach created a common system for improving safety around the world, helping move Exxon still another step toward truly global operations.

OIMS: RISING FROM DISASTER

On January 1, 1990, the day of the Arthur Kill oil spill, Edwin J. Hess was appointed to the newly created position of corporate vice president for environment and safety. To emphasize the seriousness of the initiative, Hess was named Lee Raymond's executive assistant as well, giving him direct access to the corporation's president. This was more than a symbolic move, since Hess quickly took on important new responsibilities that had a significant impact on the company. His mandate was simple yet critically important for the company: fix the embarrassing and costly problems that had created the crises.

Hess had grown up in New Jersey, earned a degree in mechanical engineering from the Stevens Institute of Technology in Hoboken, New Jersey, and then an MBA from the Harvard Business School. During the summer between his two years at Harvard, he worked at the Bayway refinery, and he took a permanent job there in 1957. His career took him through Exxon USA, where he served as an executive assistant to Mike Wright before moving into marketing under Randall Meyer. He then rotated from Houston through the New York headquarters for assignments in public affairs and marketing; back to Exxon USA, where he was eventually named to that company's management committee; and then to ECI as senior vice president for downstream operations. Hess was well prepared to head the corporation's new Safety, Health and Environment

*Edwin J. Hess, vice president, Safety, Health and Environment,
Exxon Corporation, 1990. ExxonMobil Historical Collection, di_06161.*

Department. He was an experienced manager known for his command of
detail, and he enjoyed the confidence of the corporate leadership.

Hess decided that fundamental change was called for: "If we were
really going to do something meaningful about environment and safety
throughout the organization, it was going to involve a modification to the
culture, the ingrown culture of the company."[82] He first created a small
department with four leaders and a staff of experts who could guide the
operating companies. They set about creating a process for improving
performance throughout the corporation. Hess's group did not have to
start from scratch. It could borrow from a successful system developed
in Exxon Chemical that had drawn from the industry-wide "responsible
care" movement to build a process for continual improvement in environmental quality and safety.

During this period, some external groups were looking at new
approaches for forcing corporations to improve their performance on

issues relating to safety, health, and the environment.[83] Exxon accepted the need for those kinds of reforms, but instead of working within a broader organization, it decided to create its own initiative. It defined its own principles, implemented them systematically throughout its global operations, and used them to pursue industry-leading standards of operational excellence.

At the heart of the process of change was continuous improvement in the management of safety. This involved the steady improvement of best practices and the adoption of those practices throughout the global organization. Whatever was adopted would need to incorporate long-standing corporate policies on safety, toxic substances, and the environment. Hess had to establish a useful set of principles and strong operational guidelines that could be adopted worldwide, with allowances for legitimate local variations. Exxon's approach became known as the Operations Integrity Management System, or OIMS.

A starting point for Hess was "an inventory of where we stand." One interesting place to start was the company's marine operations around Arthur Kill. In early 1990, Exxon shut down the facilities for three months as it studied what had gone wrong before the New Year's Day oil spill and what could be done to improve operational performance. Before the spill, Exxon had met applicable laws and operated according to commercial standards of safety, which were not as high as the new standards Exxon sought to adopt. The company upgraded its facility by adopting more rigorous inspection systems, including inspections of tankers owned by others that docked at its terminals in Linden or Bayonne. New safety procedures required up to four tugboats to accompany vessels, with another equipped to contain spills standing by. One company spokesman assured reporters that Exxon was "trying harder now." "It's important," he said, "that we do our job right and that we continue to look for ways to do it better." One environmentalist responded with a combination of both support and skepticism: "Yes, they have undertaken a number of measures that go beyond what they've done before . . . but that does not guarantee that they'll continue to implement these measures once the spotlight has been removed from Exxon and Arthur Kill."[84] For the company to meet that challenge, OIMS had to define new operating principles, embody them in procedures and attitudes that fostered continual improvement in operations, and communicate the change to the public.

Work on OIMS began in 1990 with the formation of a steering committee made up of managers of at least senior vice president rank from the company's operating organizations, including Exxon Chemical and Imperial Oil. The committee began with a set of expectations developed by Hess, Raymond, and Rawl. As summarized by Hess, its charge was to "find a way to get the organizational culture to put proper emphasis and priority on environmental and safety issues and get it integrated into the whole operating philosophy."[85] While recognizing that the company encompassed a wide range of practices in its regional operations, Raymond was clear that OIMS would be a single program adopted by the entire organization: "We're not going to have one system for one and one system for another. . . . We're just not going to do that anymore. We've tried that for years. That was a disaster."[86] The committee came back in 1991 with a set of eleven elements that comprised OIMS (figure 6.1). Each element formed a "management expectation" of how affiliates would operate.

Improvement in operations required more than a list of priorities. It took a well-organized, systematic approach to the enforcement of those principles. Success or failure depended on Exxon's own seriousness of purpose. Self-regulation by business has a long and largely unsuccessful history in the United States.[87] A general list of "elements" or "management expectations" could easily become a bureaucratic exercise in deflecting outside scrutiny. Successful self-regulation required a clear statement of policy, the forceful communication of a strong company commitment, and reliable measures of improvement. Also required over the long-term was an enforcement mechanism and a demonstrated commitment to "hang scalps" if necessary to alter attitudes and behavior. The eleven OIMS elements presented a straightforward statement of general principles. In the shadow of the disasters of the previous years, Exxon employees understood that something was broken and that top management was strongly determined to fix it. Referring to the punitive damages levied against the corporation after the *Exxon Valdez* spill, Hess also noted that there is "nothing like a $5 billion jury award to get your attention."[88]

Implementation of the OIMS system left little doubt that employees would be held accountable. OIMS required annual internal audits by each

FIGURE 6.1. Elements of the Operations Integrity Management System

---

1. *Management leadership, commitment, and accountability*
   Employees are held accountable for safety, security, health, and environmental performance.

2. *Risk assessment and management*
   Systematic reviews to evaluate risks to help prevent incidents.

3. *Facilities design and construction*
   All construction projects, from small improvements to major expansions, are evaluated early in their design for safety, security, health, and environmental impact.

4. *Information and documentation*
   Information that is accurate, complete, and accessible is essential to safe and reliable operations.

5. *Personnel and training*
   Meeting high standards of performance requires that employees are well trained.

6. *Operations and maintenance*
   Operations and maintenance procedures are frequently assessed and modified to improve safety and environmental performance.

7. *Management of change*
   Changes must be evaluated for safety, security, and environmental impact.

8. *Third-party services*
   Safe, secure, and environmentally responsible operations are required.

9. *Incident investigation and analysis*
   Incidents and near misses are investigated.

10. *Community awareness and emergency preparedness*
    Thoughtful planning leads to appropriate community involvement.
    Careful preparation can significantly reduce the impact of an incident.

11. *Operations integrity assessment and improvement*
    A process that measures performance relative to expectations is essential to improve operations integrity.

Source: *ExxonMobil Safety, Health and Environment Progress Report 2000*

operating unit and additional "outside" audits every three years to be conducted by company employees who were not a part of the operating unit.
This ensured that new sets of eyes regularly evaluated procedures and suggested improvements drawn from best practices used by the company and
by benchmarked competitors such as DuPont, long considered the leader
in safety in the chemical industry. Managers of all major operating units
had to make an annual report to the corporate management committee
on their progress in improving performance and their plans for continual
improvement. Any doubts that measures of performance would be taken
seriously were removed by the deliberations of the company's in-depth,
multilayered employee-evaluation system. Under OIMS, safety and environment became more important in promotion and advancement. The
message was forcefully communicated: "The corporation is not going to
accept you as a top-level manager if you cannot run a safe operation."[89]

To quantify goals and the criteria for meeting them, OIMS used measures such as "lost time due to job-related injury or illness." Those measures could be used to compare Exxon's current performance with its past
performance, and with the performance of other companies. In pursuit
of a record of continual improvement, each unit kept track of trends in
safety, health, and the environment, posting results for all employees to
see. Exxon celebrated things such as long periods of operation without
time lost from injuries. Exhortations to improve could motivate employees to a degree, at least if top management did the exhorting. But over
the long run, there was no substitute for regular and visible rewards and
punishments. The audits had to be real. The results had to have a clear
impact on resources and personal advancement. The inclusion of contractors in the calculations was a significant departure from past practices in
the company and the industry, and it heralded a new era in worker safety
in an industry with growing numbers of contractors.

The working environment fostered by OIMS differed markedly from
that found during previous eras of the petroleum industry. As Hess sought
to convince employees to get with the new program, he had to overcome
traditional attitudes from operators who "took pride in . . . dealing with
emergencies in an innovative way and keeping everything going, and not
having to shut it down for economic purposes." OIMS, on the other hand,
sought to systematize and rationalize responses to unplanned events:

"People need to know where the priorities are, and how to better draw the balance between taking a risk that is calculated and is a good risk to take, and doing something that goes over the line." As he went about selling OIMS within the company, Hess talked about an incident in the field early in his career at Exxon. Something was wrong at a drill site, and he watched as one worker climbed up a stack with a big wrench and started "tightening the damn thing." Hess thought, "If that thing had ever blown with him on there, he would have been the first astronaut in space, because the pressures were terrific." Other people "were saying what a great job this guy did . . . but it was a risk that this fellow took," which could have led to a fatality; "there should have been established procedures for a situation like that."[90] OIMS embodied such procedures in a global system, and it gradually succeeded in making safety a top priority at Exxon. In the post-*Valdez* era, the company's employees and its corporate culture gradually accepted the truth that an unsafe workplace was a poorly managed one.

Skepticism of OIMS within Exxon diminished as the company's operational results began to improve. In the five years from 1990 to 1995, the company's "significant incident" rate—defined as any accident costing more than $25,000—declined by more than 50 percent. Time lost because of accidents fell well below the levels experienced by other energy companies and U.S. manufacturing as a whole. Contractor safety also improved. Emissions from U.S. facilities required to be reported under the Superfund Amendments and Reauthorization Act of 1987 declined by 50 percent. Oil spills from Exxon-operated vessels declined by 80 percent. The chemical company reduced its hazardous wastes by 75 percent. Air-quality exceedances declined significantly, flaring was reduced, and energy efficiency at Exxon's facilities improved by 35 percent, which helped reduce greenhouse-gas emissions.[91] Such figures could not be easily ignored. Something good was happening within the company.

These systematic approaches improved the reliability of data collection and the comparability of information. They made it easier to accomplish process-oriented activities with lower-skilled employees, a particularly useful capability as Exxon expanded its operations in developing countries. They provided better information to senior managers, thus allowing them to focus more of their attention on broader business issues. This was clearly a factor in allowing an increasingly smaller group of very senior executives—the number on Exxon's management committee was eventually reduced to two or three—to oversee an extremely complex global business.

OIMS and its successor programs rested on three common principles. The first was the key lesson of the *Exxon Valdez* oil spill. Even if disasters are highly unlikely, serious efforts to prevent them are justified by the high costs in money, time, and public image that they incur. As vice president for environment and safety for Exxon in the 1990s, Frank Sprow preached this new gospel from every available pulpit. He repeated the old saying "An ounce of prevention is worth a pound of cure" and backed it up with the argument that "a company has to earn its good standing every day. . . . Exxon does it by running its operations as safely as possible and by doing what we say we'll do." This included real and effective plans for responding when disasters struck: "OIMS also ensures that the company can and does take a disciplined approach to emergency planning."[92] The second principle was that an effective program had to be global. Differences in procedures around the world added to confusion and uncertainty, and a common, systematically enforced program built a sense of unity and encouraged the worldwide sharing of best practices. The final principle was fundamental to Exxon's success in the years after the *Exxon Valdez* oil spill: operational excellence was not simply an objective, it was a central part of the company's strategy for building competitive advantage.

LEGAL WARS

A long, complicated series of criminal and civil lawsuits arose from the *Valdez* oil spill. The primary civil lawsuit, involving a jury award of $5 billion in punitive damages, was not resolved until a Supreme Court ruling in June 2008, more than nineteen years after the accident. In those prolonged legal battles, Exxon pursued a strategy that reflected its traditional corporate culture. This was not a company that used its deep pockets to settle lawsuits and make them go away. Instead, when it felt that it was in the right, it mobilized its substantial legal resources and fought to the end. The company strongly believed that it had fulfilled its responsibilities to clean up the spill and to compensate people promptly for their economic losses. Exxon's leaders found the judgment for $5 billion in punitive damages unfair and excessive, and the company fought through every legal channel available to overturn the decision. Principle as well as money motivated the company to pursue the matter to the end despite the legal costs and the public relations costs of continuing to appeal.

That said, it is important to note that those opposing Exxon pursued a different set of principles and had profoundly different perspectives on events. Their point of view was presented forcefully in *Not One Drop: Betrayal and Courage in the Wake of the Exxon Valdez Oil Spill*, a book on the spill and its aftermath written by Riki Ott, an Alaskan fisherman trained in marine toxicology, a claimant in the Alaska spill, and a frequent Exxon critic. Ott portrayed Exxon as motivated "by a single goal: to maximize profits regardless of the environmental and social costs." Exxon's conception of damages as purely financial losses, she argued, was incomplete: "The oilmen couldn't even begin to comprehend what we have lost. Motels and our fishing business! What about our lifestyle? The Natives' subsistence foods? Our beautiful Sound?"[93] The passion of those seeking punitive damages flowed from both the desire for financial rewards beyond simple compensation for actual losses and the yearning to punish a big oil company for causing serious damage to a way of life.

The trials began with Captain Hazelwood, who faced four charges for his role in the spill, including felonies, and his criminal case went to trial in January 1990. The jury heard considerable testimony about his drinking, but it also was told of delays in the testing of his blood-alcohol content. On March 23, it acquitted Hazelwood of all felony charges and convicted him only on the misdemeanor offense of negligent discharge of oil. Leaving the bridge met the legal definition of negligence, according to the jury, but not of reckless behavior.[94] In a case in 1991, the coast guard cleared Hazelwood of charges that he was impaired while in command of the *Valdez*, but it temporarily suspended his license for leaving the bridge at a critical moment. Hazelwood ultimately completed 1,000 hours of community service spent picking up trash along Alaskan highways, and in May 2002 paid a fine of $50,000. He also paid a high personal price by being labeled forever in the public mind as the man responsible for the massive spill.

Other suits went forward in a variety of venues and jurisdictions. The federal government and the State of Alaska brought criminal charges

*Jack G. Clarke, senior vice president and member of the board of
directors, 1975. ExxonMobil Historical Collection, di_06162.*

against Exxon. Most civil lawsuits filed on behalf of individuals were
combined in a single cause of action and argued in federal courts under
U.S. admiralty law. Native Americans pursued a separate legal challenge
against Exxon, and the company sued insurance companies that disputed
claims for damages.

Within Exxon, both Rawl and Raymond followed the cases closely,
though Raymond was more deeply involved. They were advised on the
company's legal strategy by Jack Clarke, an eminent and highly respected
figure within Exxon. He had been the corporation's general counsel in
the early 1970s, when he served as a central figure in negotiations with

OPEC nations on equity-oil matters. After 1975, he became a senior vice president and director, positions he held until he retired in August 1992. After his retirement, Exxon retained Clarke for his valued advice and his deep familiarity with the *Valdez* case.

During the period before the major civil trial, Exxon's management settled the criminal charges brought against it by the federal government and the State of Alaska. The state filed suit against Exxon and the owners of the Trans-Alaska Pipeline on August 15, 1989, seeking damages for environmental, economic, and social harm. In late October, Exxon responded with a countersuit, arguing that the state's delay in approving the use of dispersants had handicapped the cleanup efforts, making damage from the spill much worse. Meanwhile, the federal government convened a grand jury in Anchorage and presented charges against Exxon. In late February 1990, the grand jury returned a five-count indictment, including two felonies, against the company. In the announcement of the charges, U.S. Attorney General Richard Thornburgh indicated that Exxon could face fines of at least $600 million if convicted.[95]

Before the federal trial, discussions took place about a possible settlement of the federal and state charges. When Walter Hickel, a former secretary of the interior in the Nixon administration, took office as the governor of Alaska in 1990, he accelerated the talks. According to Lee Raymond, he, Rawl, and Clarke traveled to Juneau to meet with Hickel, who was joined by the attorney general of Alaska, Charlie Cole, and Secretary of Transportation Samuel Skinner. Hickel opened the meeting by saying, "Look, I think we need to try to get this behind us. We need to try and settle this thing." He then suggested a settlement figure of $1 billion, which Rawl agreed to consider.[96] A subsequent meeting at the Department of Commerce in Washington brought Exxon together with representatives of the interested federal agencies. Secretary of Commerce Robert Mosbacher, an oilman, recused himself, but Secretary Skinner was present, along with representatives from other executive-branch departments. Hickel also attended. After the meeting ended inconclusively, Raymond returned to New York, where Skinner called to suggest that the government and Exxon try to cut a deal. They then came up with a rough formula that both judged acceptable as the basis for further discussions.[97]

Raymond returned to Washington, and in a long, contentious meeting with federal officials, he helped hammer out a more detailed framework for an agreement. Exxon initially rejected the EPA's demand that the agreement could be reopened if damages proved greater than expected. Eventually, the corporation agreed to a provision to add an additional $100 million if later evidence indicated greater and longer-lasting harm. Other aspects of the agreement took longer to negotiate. Central to Exxon's acceptance was the stipulation that the coast guard would determine when the cleanup was complete, with any expenditure after that point becoming the responsibility of the State of Alaska.

Hickel announced that a settlement had been reached on March 13, 1991: "Yes, we signed it and, yes, this is a very, very good thing for the people of the State of Alaska."[98] A thirty-day period for public comment and a further fifteen-day period during which any party could withdraw its support followed. After reviewing many unfavorable public comments, U.S. district court judge H. Russel Holland rejected the settlement. He may have been influenced by a March press conference in Irving, Texas, at which Rawl remarked that the settlement "looks pretty good," but then committed a serious public relations blunder by noting: "It will not have a significant effect on our earnings," adding for good measure, "The customer always pays everything."[99] Then, on May 2, the Democratic-controlled Alaska House voted down the agreement. On May 3, both Hickel and Exxon pulled out of the deal, which looked dead.

It was not. After a cooling-off period, the parties renewed discussions in mid-September, when the Department of Justice invited all participants to Washington. The new arrangement being negotiated increased payments to Alaska. This time around, Rawl struck a very different tone. Appearing before Judge Holland, he apologized: "We regretted the spill very much. . . . We have done all we could possibly do at this point to get this cleaned up and to take care of all people who came forward with claims."[100] A new proposal acceptable to all parties was drafted and announced on September 30. Exxon agreed to pay a criminal penalty of $125 million, $25 million more than in the proposal rejected by Judge Holland. Included was a payment of $100 million in restitution to help restore Prince William Sound, twice the amount for that purpose in the earlier agreement. Exxon would also pay, over a ten-year period, an additional

$900 million in civil penalties.[101] The federal and state governments had enhanced the chances for the approval of the arrangement by agreeing the week before to share their legal and scientific data with private Alaskan plaintiffs in exchange for their agreement to drop lawsuits against both the state and federal governments.[102]

The Department of Justice delivered the new agreement to Judge Holland on September 26. He approved it on October 8, in the process calling Exxon "a good corporate citizen" that was "sensitive to its environmental obligations."[103] Rawl appeared before Holland at the October 8 hearing to plead guilty to the charges that had been a part of the previous settlement. He was contrite and apologetic. This time, Hickel did not have to present the agreement to the legislature, but a House Democrat praised it as a "much nicer deal."[104] In mid-November, Exxon paid a criminal fine of $125 million. The next month, it paid the first installment on the $900 million civil settlement.

Numerous other suits remained. One group of cases included those brought against Alyeska Pipeline Service Company for its negligence in the spill. The company settled a suit filed against it in 1992 by the federal and state governments for damages to natural resources and for loss of tax revenues of $31.3 million. Numerous Alaska Natives, commercial fishermen, businesses, and others brought a civil action against Alyeska, which settled for $98 million in July 1993. That settlement, from which many law firms realized fees, helped fund the major civil litigation against Exxon that began in 1994.[105] A second group of cases involved damages to some municipalities, a few dozen commercial fishermen, and Alaskan Native corporations. In late December 1993, Judge Holland removed those plaintiffs from the consolidated lawsuit and sent them to state court, which ultimately disallowed their claims. A third group of cases involved Exxon and its insurers, which included Lloyd's of London. Exxon had tried unsuccessfully for more than four years to obtain insurance reimbursement in excess of $1 billion of its losses and costs. After winning a jury verdict in Houston in June 1996, Exxon and the insurers entered into negotiations that produced a settlement of $480 million.[106] Coupled with an earlier payment of $300 million, Exxon finally recovered $780 million of its costs from its insurers.[107]

As those cases moved forward, the main civil action was also tried and appealed. The federal civil case was filed as *Grant Baker et al. vs. Exxon Corporation*, with Judge Holland presiding. Holland consolidated the plaintiffs into one class and divided the trial into three parts. Phase one would determine if Exxon and Hazelwood had acted recklessly in causing the grounding. If the jury found them guilty, the second phase would determine the actual spill damages. Phase three would then assess whether Exxon should have punitive damages levied against it, and if so, in what amount.

During phase one, which began in May 1994, attorneys for Exxon conceded that errors made by a variety of parties—Exxon, Hazelwood, the crew of the *Valdez*, the U.S. Coast Guard, and others—had resulted in the grounding of the tanker. But the company asserted that the errors did not rise to the legal definition of recklessness. The plaintiffs disagreed. They presented evidence of Exxon's prior knowledge of Hazelwood's drinking problem, the company's ineffective steps to address that problem, drinking by Hazelwood before sailing, and an overtired crew. Hazelwood's trial focused on the evidence of his drinking, but his defense pursued the problems that had occurred in the chain of possession of his blood sample, and pointed to the testimony of a number of people who had seen him after his drinking in Valdez but had noticed no impairment. The jury found Hazelwood guilty of negligence and recklessness, and Exxon guilty of recklessness.

In the next phase of the trial, which began June 20, the jury assessed compensatory damages. After largely technical presentations of evidence regarding damages that plaintiffs had suffered from the spill, the jury placed compensatory damages at $287 million, much less than the nearly $900 million the plaintiffs had requested to cover losses in fishery income. Both parties agreed that Exxon could deduct $130 million in payments made immediately after the spill. Hence, the net effect of the award was to provide fishermen with an additional $157 million. That amount was reduced further, to $76 million, in September 1995, when Holland offset the award with additional payments received by the plaintiffs from the Trans-Alaska Pipeline Liability Fund and from the settlement with Alyeska.[108]

The main event, the assessment of punitive damages, began on August 22. The plaintiffs asked for only $1 from Hazelwood, but suggested that the jurors, in considering the amount to be awarded from Exxon, should take into account the corporation's worldwide net income.[109] In reply, Exxon's lawyers focused on how much had already been paid to those injured and how much had been spent by Exxon to clean up the spill. The jury lacked clear guidelines for determining damages for an accident the size of the *Exxon Valdez* oil spill, and it had considerable difficulty framing its discussion. After jurors proposed punitive damages ranging from zero to $15 billion, compromise seemed impossible. The jury reported an impasse on day five, but the judge instructed the jurors to continue to debate the matter. On the thirteenth day of deliberations, the jury reached its verdict: Hazelwood would pay $50,000; Exxon would pay $5 billion.[110] The plaintiffs celebrated; Exxon prepared its appeal.

Judge Holland then learned of a previously secret agreement Exxon had made with seven Seattle fish-processing companies in 1991.[111] Exxon had paid the "Seattle Seven" $63.75 million in exchange for their agreement to pay Exxon their share of any future punitive damages, should they be awarded. The share of the $5 billion judgment due the fish processors was about $750 million, all of which would, by the terms of the agreement, be repaid to Exxon. Holland was livid, and ruled in June 1996 that "the court will not countenance Exxon's astonishing ruse and allow it to manipulate the jury and negate its verdict."[112] Exxon appealed Holland's ruling negating its agreement with the Seattle Seven, and the Ninth Circuit Court of Appeals both reversed his decision and noted that to have revealed the arrangement would have been improper. After that dustup, the judge required Exxon to post a bond for the full amount of the award.

In June 1997, Exxon appealed the punitive-damages verdict to the Ninth Circuit, beginning an appeals process that would last more than eleven years. The company argued that the judgment was excessive under maritime law, which generally did not allow punitive damages. At the time, however, few precedents existed on the issue. Judge Holland appeared to believe that the jury's decision should be respected, and he consistently resisted reducing the award when it was returned to him on appeal for reconsideration. Exxon, of course, wanted the jury reward reduced, a view that gained legal support as a series of cases on the size of punitive damages made their way to the Supreme Court while the company's appeal moved forward.

Supreme Court decisions favorable to the company's case, growing concern over lawsuit abuse, and new research all contributed to a gradual modification in the treatment of punitive damages. Exxon anticipated the impact that evolution might have on the *Valdez* case. Lee Raymond recalled, "We made a decision very early on [that] time is on our side. To the extent we can draw it out, the legal system was gradually going to close down on punitive damages."[113]

The Ninth Circuit took nearly four and a half years to rule on Exxon's initial appeal. In November 2001, it remanded the $5 billion award determination to the district court for reconsideration as being excessive. Thirteen months later, in December 2002, Judge Holland reduced the award by $1 billion. Ten weeks later, ExxonMobil appealed the judge's ruling to the Ninth Circuit. The appellate court vacated Holland's decision in mid-August 2003 on the grounds that it seemed inconsistent with recent Supreme Court decisions and once again sent it back to him for reconsideration. In January 2004, Holland's irritation showed when he raised the award to $4.5 billion. ExxonMobil promptly appealed that surprising result, arguing to the Ninth Circuit that it should make a decision itself rather than remand again to what was obviously a recalcitrant lower court. In December 2006, almost two years later, a three-judge panel of the Ninth Circuit reduced the award to $2.5 billion. Two months later, ExxonMobil again asked the panel to reconsider. When it refused to do so, the company appealed the Ninth Circuit decision to the U.S. Supreme Court, which accepted the case on October 29 under its authority to hear cases governed by maritime law.

The case went before the Supreme Court on February 28, 2008. ExxonMobil suffered a blow when the conservative justice Samuel Alito recused himself from hearing the appeal, presumably because he owned ExxonMobil stock.[114] His recusal left the court with eight justices, which meant that a decision favorable to the company would have to carry by at least 5–3, since a tie vote meant the lower-court decision would stand. The company based its appeal on three key questions. First, was the owner of a ship liable for punitive damages if the owner had not condoned the actions of the captain? On that question, the court split 4–4, meaning that the circuit and district court rulings on Exxon's liability stood. Had ExxonMobil's arguments won on that issue, the trial court's decision would have been overturned, punitive damages would have been disallowed entirely, and the case would have been returned for trial in the Alaska district court under different instructions. The second question involved jurisdiction. ExxonMobil argued that the Clean Water Act established penalties for oil spills, thus prohibiting the courts from allowing private parties to sue for such damage. The court dismissed that argument 8–0. The final question was whether maritime law limited the size of punitive damages. The Supreme Court is the final arbiter of maritime law, so on this matter it had the authority to determine such damages. In line with precedent, it limited punitive damages to the amount of compensatory damages. In the *Valdez* case, that formulation dramatically reduced the existing $2.5 billion award to $507 million, with interest to be calculated from an earlier date and added to that figure.[115]

The case was finally over, thirteen years after litigation began and nineteen years after the accident. Despite the favorable Supreme Court decision, the damage to Exxon and ExxonMobil from the *Valdez* grounding was significant. The cleanup had cost billions. Fines and voluntary payments had been high. Legal costs had been high, and even the final civil judgment was costly. And public relations costs were high, since the trial and ongoing appeals periodically reminded the public that the company had caused an environmental calamity.

More than twenty years after the *Exxon Valdez* spill in Prince William Sound, Exxon's public image still carries a stain from the disaster. The discussion of every major oil spill still calls forth media comparisons to it, prodding the public's memory with sound bites and photographs of oil-soaked wildlife. It was large. It despoiled a place of stunning physical beauty. It killed wildlife and damaged the fisheries upon which the livelihoods of many fishermen depended. And above all, it was caused by Exxon, the largest and most profitable of the oil companies. Few events in the recent history of the energy industry or the U.S. environmental movement have retained such a grip on the public mind.

For twenty years after its occurrence, the spill remained the benchmark against which all other oil spills were compared. Then, in the spring of 2010, BP's Macondo blowout in the Gulf of Mexico placed the *Exxon*

Valdez accident in a new historical context. There were obvious differences between the two spills. The *Valdez* spill, which resulted from a tanker accident in a fragile environment off the coast of Alaska, totaled about 260,000 barrels of oil. The Macondo spill, which resulted from a blowout during the drilling of a deepwater well, dumped an estimated five million barrels of oil off the coast of a fragile wetlands environment. But numerous questions quickly emerged in the Gulf of Mexico that previously had been difficult to answer in Prince William Sound. Who was in charge of the emergency response? How should the various local, state, and federal governmental agencies cooperate with the companies involved? How effective were dispersants? How effective was the technology of spill control? How much equipment was needed to respond to such a spill, and where should it have been stored? What role did complacency play and how could it be prevented in the future? Almost none of those questions had been fully answered in the twenty years after the *Exxon Valdez* spill. Neither the oil industry nor government regulators seemed significantly better prepared for a major oil spill in 2010 than they had been in 1989.[116]

Those who read the fine print of the reports on the Macondo spill, however, found one strong lesson from the *Exxon Valdez* disaster. After a string of accidents that began with the *Valdez*, Exxon had taken to heart its responsibility to work harder and more systematically to prevent future accidents. It had taken self-regulation seriously, and the OIMS approach had taken hold in the company over time. William Reilly, cochair of the president's National Commission on the BP Deepwater Horizon Oil Spill and Offshore Drilling, cited ExxonMobil's leadership in this area by calling its safety culture and systems the "gold standard" to which all companies should aspire.[117]

OIMS took hold at Exxon in part because it reflected the core operating values that had guided the company's internal operations since the days of Rockefeller. Early on the company had built competitive advantage by paying systematic attention to the details of its daily refining operations. In essence, OIMS extended Rockefeller's approach to areas that had not been at the top of any company's list of priorities in his era: safety, health, and the environment. It was both good citizenship and good business to minimize the likelihood of future accidents. The spill's damage to the company's public image was severe, much as Rockefeller's battle over antitrust had been. Public outrage over the tone as well as the behavior of the company was similar in both episodes.

In the long term, OIMS was the key to the company's efforts to repair the damage to its public image caused by the *Exxon Valdez* spill. This was best done not with advertising campaigns, but by operating efficiently over a long period without causing any major disasters. The *Exxon Valdez* oil spill and the two serious accidents that followed were, first and foremost, failures of the company's long tradition of engineering and operational excellence. OIMS addressed the root causes of those failures. It remains today a reminder to business and government that serious, systematic, and continual concern for operational excellence is the central element in reducing accidents and enhancing worker safety. From his point of view as an operations coordinator on the ground in Prince William Sound, Scott Nauman had an up close and personal view of cleanup. He earned the last word on the topic: "The obvious lesson is you need to keep something like this from happening in the first place, because to remedy it after the event is a horrendous undertaking, and that is the heart of a lot of the OIMS activities that we do today and the drills we do today."[118]

CHAPTER SEVEN

NEW FRONTIERS

BEYOND TRADITIONAL POLITICAL RISKS

I n 1989, the same year the *Exxon Valdez* ran aground, the Berlin Wall fell. The collapse of communism in the Soviet Union and the Eastern Bloc then followed with stunning swiftness, introducing a new era in globalization. As Cold War divisions ended, the international oil companies entered large sections of the world previously closed to the West. In the 1990s, Exxon developed a presence in Russia, Azerbaijan, and Kazakhstan. The company went searching for oil and profits, but it also shared a vision of the future in which the former communist nations would be integrated into the global economy.[1] At roughly the same time, Exxon reentered Venezuela during a time of growing political tension there, and it pursued large projects in the African nations of Chad and Angola, where history and poverty caused difficult political and social problems.

In the new world after the fall of Soviet communism and the end of the Cold War, Exxon encountered almost unmanageable uncertainties that went far beyond traditional definitions of "political risks." Yet the potential reserves seemed too great to ignore, and the company forged ahead in regions where the prospects for high rewards were matched by the possibility of substantial losses. Political forces driven by resource nationalism challenged Exxon and then ExxonMobil around the world at every turn.

The associated risks reflected the reality of producer power and the growing global demand for oil; they tended to rise with the price of crude as producing countries flush with oil revenues explored options for developing their reserves.

This political frontier presented challenges as difficult in their own way as the technical and managerial challenges in the North Slope of Alaska or the North Sea. The company needed new supplies of oil and gas, however, and with limited access to Middle Eastern reserves, it had little choice except to pursue those in promising regions, despite political turmoil. In nations with quite different political systems, histories, and cultures, Exxon had to build a durable accommodation with each government based on mutual self-interest. The four case studies in this chapter—Russia, Venezuela, Chad, and Angola—illustrate the company's responses to the diverse political demands it encountered in its quest for oil and gas reserves around the world.

In its long history, Exxon had learned—often through painful failures—the long-term benefits of expanding the boundaries of good corporate citizenship. In the years after 1973, it made a broader commitment to training local workers and purchasing goods and services in local markets. It also expanded its philanthropic efforts to address poverty, education, health care, and economic opportunity. Those efforts did not contradict its often-repeated pledge to stockholders that "maximizing shareholder value is the guiding principle for all we do in managing and operating the company."[2] Instead, in an industry marked by multibillion-dollar projects built and operated over decades, long-term profitability required strong and durable partnerships with both the governments and the citizens of producing nations.

RUSSIA: A MAJOR PRODUCER IN TRANSITION FROM COMMUNISM TO SOMETHING ELSE

The fall of communism in the Soviet Union and the Eastern Bloc altered the landscape of the global petroleum industry. In the early 1990s, the Union of Soviet Socialist Republics rapidly split into numerous independent nations referred to collectively as the Commonwealth of Independent States. Almost all those nations made fundamental changes to their economic and political systems. Each took a different path, but all faced transitional eras of confusion and uncertainty. Several of the new nations were major oil and gas producers or held promising petroleum reserves, and the disposition of those resources became an important part of their transformation from communism to something else.

In Russia, the core of the Soviet Union, the end of communism brought an era of chaotic change marked by economic stagnation and political flux. Throughout most of the 1990s, Russian leaders followed the "Big Bang" approach recommended by international lending institutions and other Western advisors. The Big Bang sought to move a nation with a seventy-year history of communism as quickly as possible toward democracy and capitalism. Boris Yeltsin's government (1992–1999) opened the Russian economy to foreign direct investment, made fiscal reforms, privatized large sections of the economy, and moved toward private property. It also accepted loans from the International Monetary Fund and the World Bank to assist in the transition from communism. In the political sphere, reforms encouraged greater freedom of expression and citizen participation in political activities. These sweeping changes in the political economy were far from orderly in the 1990s.[3]

For the international oil companies, the new era seemed to promise expanded access to oil riches. Under communism, the Soviet Union had found the world's largest natural gas reserves and had developed substantial oil and gas production. The nation produced a staggering 12 million barrels of oil a day in the 1980s. The chance to enter the former Soviet Union was a dream come true for the international oil companies. One of the largest oil- and gas-producing regions in the world suddenly opened its doors to Western companies that had been excluded for most of the twentieth century. The region needed infusions of capital and new technology. Exxon and its competitors needed large new reserves, particularly from producing regions not affiliated with OPEC. In Russia and the other USSR successor states, geological risks in some regions were quite low, but political uncertainties were dauntingly high.[4]

No one could predict with confidence the pace or direction of political change in the region. For an undetermined period, there would be no generally accepted rules of the game. In Russia, this meant no effective petroleum law, no laws to protect property rights, and nothing equivalent to contract law. A government accustomed to exercising centralized authority over the Soviet economy had lost control of vast areas of the former Soviet Union. As central planning collapsed, the lack of clear lines of political or administrative authority left a void in decision making, and at times corrupt officials filled this void. Exxon and other companies had no way of understanding which official or agency had the power to make binding decisions as fundamental as the granting of the rights to develop an oil field. The tax system was in flux. The banking system was in transition from a Soviet model of state control to a hybrid system in which financial entrepreneurs took risks backed by government funding in emerging Russian markets such as oil and natural gas.[5]

Beyond such practical problems was the vast gulf between the centrally planned Soviet economy and the market-based system of democratic capitalism. Cultural differences were readily apparent to Terry Koonce, one of Exxon's early executives in Russia, not least regarding the basics of corporate finance: "The Russians had to be taught that capital . . . had a cost. . . . Capital had always been handed to them by the government."[6] The communist planning system had focused on meeting quotas assigned by the state, not on making efficient use of resources to create profit. The great Cold War rival of the Soviet Union had, after all, been the United States, the symbol of modern capitalism. Students under communism had learned that profits were the ill-gotten gains that capitalists wrung from their workers.

The mentality of the quota system and the five-year plans that were central to communist economics did not translate well into the workings of capitalism. Koonce recounted one example of the stark differences: "They had a five-year plan that they were going to drill twenty wells on a prospect; they would drill twenty wells no matter what, and, in fact, be very proud of it." When asked what happened to the first few wells, the Russians replied, "Well, they were dry." In fact, all twenty wells came up dry. So why did they persist? "Their job was to drill twenty wells. They drilled dry holes . . . and just kept on drilling. They did not analyze or back off or wonder why those were dry and should they move somewhere else?"[7] The Russians were not yet fluent in the language of international business, particularly the language of financial analysis, which was so important in Exxon. Mutual understanding was thus in short supply as

K. Terry Koonce, vice president, ExxonMobil Production Company, 1999.
ExxonMobil Historical Collection, di_06117.

foreign companies poured into Russia in the 1990s. Had the tables been turned, Americans would have had an equally difficult time accepting instructions in Russian from Siberian petroleum engineers on how to use central planning to develop oil fields in the United States.

Jersey Standard (Exxon) had been a frequent observer of the Soviet Union since the early years of Bolshevism, when it spent seven years (1920–1927) in futile pursuit of an opportunity to enter the country as a part of a consortium in the Caspian region, the major producing area of the Soviet Union at that time. A report in 1920 by one of the company's top executives concluded that "the Russian oil regions were not only a production engineer's dream but also a wildcatter's paradise."[8] Fifty years later, in the 1970s, Exxon got another brief glimpse inside the Soviet Union during a trip there by several top Exxon executives. Tom Barrow, a geologist who rose to the top layer of management at Exxon, later recalled his impressions of the tour. He traveled all the way to the USSR's eastern edge, Sakhalin Island, where oil fields had been discovered but only partially developed. He judged the Russian engineers he encountered as "ten to fifteen years behind us." They had the technical capacity to find giant reserves in their resource-rich nation, but lacked any incentive to develop the new generation of technology that came pouring forth from the Western oil companies in the late twentieth century.[9]

In the early 1990s, at the end of the Soviet era, the "petroleum engineer's dream" and "wildcatter's paradise" proved irresistible. Exxon and other companies that wanted to remain leaders in the industry felt that they had to take their chances in Russia, which in 1992 had an estimated 170 billion barrels of proved oil reserves, almost six times those of the United States. Estimates of Russia's recoverable natural gas reserves in 1991 were the largest in the world at an estimated 1,900 trillion cubic feet, more than ten times those of the United States.[10] Even though oil production had fallen to about 6 million barrels a day in Russia in 1992, that figure could be expected to rebound dramatically when the nation's economy recovered.

In 1992, Exxon opened its first office in Moscow, the home of the newly created Exxon Ventures (CIS). For the first year, Nicolas Govoroff, a Frenchman who spoke Russian, managed a small group of Exxon employees whose primary function was to keep "an ear to the ground about what was happening." In 1993, the company expanded the office, making Exxon Ventures (CIS) an operating affiliate responsible for exploration and production throughout the former Soviet Union. The president was K. Terry Koonce. He had joined Exxon in 1963 with a Ph.D. in chemical engineering from Rice University, and worked in research before taking a series of positions in production in Alaska, California, and Canada. After next serving as the president of Exxon Research and Engineering, he remained the head of Exxon Ventures until its reorganization after the Mobil merger.[11]

Koonce began by ramping up staffing, expanding the workforce from a handful of people to a staff of several hundred. Exxon Ventures quickly established additional offices on Sakhalin Island; in Almaty, Kazakhstan; and in Baku, Azerbaijan. Much of the support staff worked in Houston, as did Koonce, who commuted to work by making fifteen to twenty flights to the region each year. If Koonce had any doubts about the importance of the region to Exxon, he had only to look over the roster of those assigned to work with him: "Man, they gave me the best people in the company. The top explorer [Tim Cejka] now [in 2007] was my exploration vice president and the [current] chairman of the company [Rex Tillerson] was my production vice president. We had a heck of a team."[12] Sorting through the many potential prospects in the region, the team ultimately focused on five general regions: Sakhalin Island, western Siberia (under a cooperative agreement with Mobil), the Timan-Pechora Basin, and the Caspian region in both Azerbaijan and Kazakhstan. All had known reserves and outstanding prospects, and Exxon was one of many companies competing for the right to develop them.

On his first day in Moscow, Koonce saw firsthand an extreme version of the "Big Bang" in Russia. He arrived on the day when President Boris Yeltsin dissolved the Duma (legislature) and the shelling of governmental offices in Moscow began: "It was a little bit on the chaotic side, you know. . . . You kind of wondered what you had stepped into."[13] After difficulties arose in accessing interior oil prospects, Exxon pursued a "peripheral strategy" that stressed oil developments near ports, where oil could be shipped by tankers to global markets. Sakhalin Island quickly emerged as a primary target for Exxon, and it pursued the promising prospect patiently and systematically throughout the 1990s.

Sakhalin Island lies off the far eastern coast of Russia, north of Japan. The island's northernmost portion is about 800 miles south of the Arctic Circle in the Sea of Okhotsk, so the climate can be brutal in the winter, with frigid winds coming off the vast Siberian interior and an ice pack three to five feet thick. Offshore, the fall can bring hurricane-force winds. Such conditions limit activity offshore to about five months out of the year. Oil seeps had been observed there as early as the 1880s, and the region had produced oil since the 1920s. In the early 1970s, the Russian concern Sakhalinmorneftegas, a well-established oil company that had operated in the region for more than seventy years, began exploring for additional oil and gas. Strapped for cash, the Soviet Union in 1975 signed an agreement with the government of Japan to help finance exploration in the high-cost area. Several Japanese companies joined Sakhalinmorneftegas to create the Sakhalin Island Oil & Gas Development Company consortium, which discovered two fields in the late 1970s. A decade later, in 1989, it found the Arkutun-Dagi field. After the breakup of the Soviet Union, the new Russian government held a tender (the closest equivalent to leasing in that era in Russia) for acreage off Sakhalin, which attracted several international bidders, including Exxon and Shell.[14]

In search of a major partner with experience in developing large, difficult projects, the consortium brought Exxon into its discussions of Sakhalin Island with the Russian authorities. Harry Longwell recalled that the Japanese group "was really a consortium of the oil and gas industry in Japan and the industrials that . . . were working as a group with the Russians." Included were the Japanese National Oil Company, JAPEX (its exploration company), and Mitsubishi. Sakhalinmorneftegas remained part of the group. Koonce described the inclusion of the Russian company as "part of the deal" brought by the Japanese when they approached Exxon. This Russian partner provided an excellent point of contact with local and federal government officials and expert knowledge of the people and the conditions on Sakhalin Island. Its inclusion became increasingly valuable as Russian nationalism reasserted itself after 2000.[15]

The Japanese talks with the Russian government focused on the rights to negotiate a production-sharing agreement (PSA) for Sakhalin-I, as the project came to be known. Early on, Exxon remained primarily an observer. Koonce recalled the confusion over who had authority to make a deal for the Russian state: "We negotiated with a deputy minister of energy. . . . He asserted that he was authorized to do it, and it turned out that he was."[16] Negotiations proved difficult because of frequent changes in ministers during that era of upheaval. The local governor of Sakhalin Island, Igor Farkhutdinov, also took an important part in the negotiations.[17] Exxon gradually took a stronger role in the talks, which finally produced the company's first concrete success in Russia, announcing in

1993 that "Exxon and its partners had obtained [exclusive] rights to negotiate a production-sharing agreement [PSA] for already discovered but
undeveloped fields offshore Russia's Sakhalin Island and to explore two
other large offshore blocks in that area."[18]

Two years of negotiations followed over the terms of the PSA, a type
of agreement insisted on by Exxon because it was particularly useful in
a nation without a formal petroleum law. PSAs provide great flexibility,
since they can include a variety of stipulations about everything from
basic financial terms to the training of local workers. These agreements
allow the companies to cover all their development costs before beginning
to share the oil from the project with the government. This was no small
matter for Exxon's Sakhalin-I project or for Shell's Sakhalin-II project,
which covered a large reserve in a different area of the island. The costs of
the two projects ultimately totaled about $35 billion. Under the terms of
the PSAs signed by Exxon and Shell in the mid-1990s, once those costs
had been covered, the government would begin to receive its share of the
oil, a proportion that would increase over time. The favorable terms for the
companies reflected the realities of a time when the nation badly needed
capital and expertise to rebuild its vital oil and natural gas industries.[19]

Once the terms of the PSA had been reached, in April 1995, Exxon
addressed its vulnerability to future political and legal challenges. First,
the consortium, now led by Exxon, had the agreement formally signed
by the Russian government in Moscow in June 1995. Koonce recalled
some of the legal hurdles the company faced: "[While we were] definitely
happy with it [the PSA], the lack of a fully functioning legal system posed
problems. There was no production-sharing law for the longest time as we
were negotiating . . . Even after it had been signed, we had a provision in
it that it would not be effective until there was a production-sharing law
that covered it."[20] Exxon CEO Lee Raymond made the trip to Moscow to
emphasize to President Yeltsin that "if you're serious about having it [the
Sakhalin-I project], you're going to have to have the PSA law." After long
and complicated political bargaining, the Duma finally passed a PSA bill,
which was signed into law in January 1996, but even that law contained
ambiguities and did not provide Exxon with the legal protection it felt it
needed to move forward on Sakhalin-I. Koonce reiterated the company's
stand to the Russian energy minister: "We are not going forward until

we know absolutely that the law covers our project."[21] After more debate, Exxon received the legal protection it needed. According to Koonce: "We actually got resolutions out of the Duma that said our project [along with two others] was covered. It was grandfathered. That no matter what else happened, these three projects are covered by the law. And it was on that basis that we then actually went forward."[22]

The long debates about the PSA law illustrated the confusion that reigned in Moscow about oil policy in the 1990s. Events in the oil and gas industry mirrored those in many other large Russian industries. One key reform was the reorganization of the highly centralized petroleum industry, a structure inherited from the communist era. Another was the substitution of market-based incentives for the quota-driven system of central planning. Foreign companies at times became frustrated at the slow pace of change. But it was unrealistic to expect new laws, new industry structures, and new competitive attitudes to emerge quickly in a longtime communist system undergoing fundamental political, economic, and social changes.[23]

Privatization in the Russian oil industry in the 1990s went forward with little governmental guidance in a process that had long-term implications for Exxon and the other foreign oil companies in Russia. In the four years immediately after the 1991 breakup of the Soviet Union, the communist-designed oil industry was gradually split into pieces; managers from the previous regime took a leading role in creating and spinning off these alliances. Then, in 1994 and 1995, Boris Yeltsin, who was struggling toward a presidential election in 1996, cast his lot with a group of bankers who had access to capital and the ambition to become the new entrepreneurs who would remake the Russian economy. In an arrangement that came to be called "loans for shares," they offered short-term loans to sustain operations at some of the large companies at the heart of the Russian economy, including major companies in the petroleum industry. When the loans were not repaid on time, the bankers were paid in greatly undervalued stock, allowing them to take control of major companies at bargain-basement prices.[24]

By 1998, an array of Russian companies had emerged within the evolving market structure in Russian oil and natural gas. These included the government-owned natural gas giant, Gazprom; Mikhail Khodorkovsky's high-flying Yukos, which seemed destined to become one of the largest petroleum companies in the world; and Lukoil, the privately owned, government-supported prototype for a Russian international oil company. Because of their size and their potential role in global oil markets, the companies drew great attention from the international press and investors. Although most of the ambitious projects put forward by foreign oil companies in the early 1990s made little progress, the companies sought joint ventures with Russian companies while at times buying their stock. The possibility of mergers with, or acquisitions of, the Russian companies remained a part of the long-term calculations of the largest international oil companies.[25]

Conditions in the Russian economy as a whole and in the oil industry in particular took a dramatic turn after a severe financial crisis in 1998. Before then, the Russian government had borrowed much-needed funds from the International Monetary Fund and the World Bank. The loans came with strict conditions that dictated adherence by the borrower to a collection of policies collectively labeled "the Washington Consensus," which included the opening of the economy to outside investment and a range of domestic and trade policies that imposed monetary and fiscal reforms designed to create a healthier economy.[26] Faced with a deteriorating economy, Russian officials took charge of their own economy. They ended the nation's dependence on loans from the IMF and the World Bank and sought different paths out of the economic stagnation of the 1990s. This process began in 1998 and gained momentum after Vladimir Putin assumed the presidency in December 1999. Bolstered a few years later by rising oil prices, his increasingly nationalist economic and foreign policies altered the political situation in Russia, including the treatment of foreign oil companies.[27]

Looking back at the period of political turmoil during his years at Exxon Ventures (1993–1999), Terry Koonce perceived no real plan by the Russian government for the petroleum industry: "I do not think at any point—in those six years anyway—they had some plan in a back room that . . . here is what we really want to get out of Sakhalin-I and here is what we want to get out of Sakhalin-II, etc. . . . . They have been political footballs." Given the great uncertainties of the era, Exxon took a low profile politically. In Koonce's words, the company "just kept on churning."[28]

That stance was essential from 1998 through the early 2000s, when Russia went through far-reaching political changes while Exxon planned and executed its merger with Mobil. Koonce took on added duties as part of the merger transition team, leaving executive Rex Tillerson (a production engineer by training) and Tim Cejka (a geoscientist) with greater responsibilities at Sakhalin Island. In Tillerson's words, "The project . . . was just stuck." In 1999, Tillerson had his first meeting with the emerging Russian leader Vladimir Putin, who stopped at Sakhalin Island en route to Japan on the first overseas trip during his transition from prime minister to president.[29] According to Tillerson, keeping the project alive in the turmoil during and after the 1998 financial crisis and then getting it moving again as Putin asserted control required "an enormous amount of persistence and patience."[30] Exxon exercised caution amid the considerable uncertainty surrounding its future in the Sakhalin Islands.

In the years after the passage of the PSA law for Sakhalin-I in 1996, Exxon appraised the fields involved in the first phase of the project while waiting for the Russian economy to stabilize and the government to approve its development plans. The consortium made plans to produce oil and gas from the complex rock formations off Sakhalin Island while working to reach an agreement with the Russian government on how best to market the natural gas from Sakhalin-I. The company acknowledged in 1998 that "progress in Russia has been hindered by political and economic problems," and that it had taken "a step-by-step approach to develop the high-potential resources of Sakhalin Island."[31] In addition to political risks, Exxon's deliberate approach reflected the high technical and financial risks of a project with an estimated price tag of $12 billion. While waiting out governmental delays in the issuing of permits to begin construction on Sakhalin-I in the late 1990s, the company conducted a $200 million to $300 million appraisal program, complete with extensive new three-dimensional seismic mapping and the drilling of numerous wells. It also completed an encouraging appraisal well at the project's Chayvo field. Then, in 2001 came the news that the Russian government had finally approved the "declaration of commerciality" needed so the company could begin work on the project.[32]

The consortium went to work in 2001 to build the first phase of Sakhalin-I, which had estimated recoverable oil reserves of about 1.5 billion

Sakhalin extended-reach drilling schematic. Exxon Mobil Corporation.

barrels, gas reserves of 1.5 trillion cubic feet, and a peak capacity of 250,000 barrels a day (75,000 b/d to Exxon for its 30 percent share). By this time, the consortium's membership had changed. Exxon remained the operator, under the name Exxon Neftegas Limited, and Sakhalin Island Oil & Gas retained a 30 percent interest. But the Russian partners invited India's ONGC Videsh Limited to join with a 20 percent interest. In addition, the Russian participation shifted to Sakhalinmorneftegas-Shelf, a subsidiary of Rosneft-Sakhalinmorneftegas (the original Russian partner), with an 11.5 percent interest, and RN-Astra (a new Russian partner) holding the remaining 8.5 percent. The facilities and equipment needed included an onshore processing plant, a giant onshore drilling rig, and a massive offshore concrete production platform. The project also required the construction of a twenty-four-inch-diameter, 136-mile-long pipeline under the Tatar Strait west of Sakhalin Island and on to an oil export terminal on the Russian mainland, where the original plan called for the loading of tankers at an offshore single-point mooring tower for shipment primarily to Asian markets. Negotiations continued with potential buyers in Japan for the project's natural gas.[33] For basic facilities on Sakhalin Island, ExxonMobil used modular construction, as it had done on Alaska's North Slope. Prefabricated facilities reduced the need for construction in the harsh island climate, helping the company meet a tight production schedule.

The choice of technology also hastened first production. After considering the design and construction of a new concrete platform to drill wells in the extreme ice and wind of the Chayvo field off Sakhalin, the company decided instead to tow a concrete island drilling system originally developed and used in the Beaufort Sea off Alaska, a distance of 3,000 miles. The platform underwent significant modifications to strengthen it against ice floes before being installed. Even more important was the one-of-a-kind onshore drilling rig (named Yastreb, Russian for "hawk") that had been specially built for the project. Called "the world's most powerful land drilling rig," it stood twenty-two stories tall and had the power to complete the ambitious plans for horizontal, "long-reach" drilling that was central to Sakhalin-I's development.

When Harry Longwell had first examined data on the Chayvo field in the early 1990s, he had found the economics "very, very marginal" because of its "thin reservoirs."[34] The Yastreb drilling rig altered that assessment, since it could sit onshore and drill a record-setting seven miles out under the ocean. It reached the offshore reservoirs 50 percent faster than available offshore drilling rigs, at a cost savings estimated at $200 million. The ability to drill such long distances horizontally and to hit faraway targets with extraordinary precision had been developed from "downhole" research done at ExxonMobil and other oil companies. The research created new ways for drillers to understand and control what was going on at the end of the pipe far under the surface.[35] Such innovations were revolutionizing many aspects of fast drilling and long-reach drilling, giving oil companies new tools for developing complex fields. Exxon's global-exploration function had helped identify new prospects around the world, and its global-development function brought an expanded set of tools, and growing experience in applying them, to the task of quickly and efficiently constructing new projects. The "early production system" used on the project allowed the first oil and gas sales to occur in 2005, and peak production was reached in early 2007.[36]

As required by its PSA and reinforced by its own commitment to build partnerships in producing regions, ExxonMobil trained local workers and made use of regional businesses and contractors when possible. Company training sessions on the English language and on technical topics helped prepare local workers for employment. The company also partnered with a technical college on Sakhalin Island to design and fund a training program for professional welders. The PSAs for the project required the consortium to donate $100 million over five years to the Sakhalin Development Fund, which was to be used to improve the island's infrastructure. Those funds encouraged local hiring and training and the growth of local construction and supply businesses.

ExxonMobil found and developed regional contractors capable of supplying services and supplies required for the Sakhalin-I project. The company publicized opportunities for bidding on oil-related work. It heavily recruited Russians to become employees in the operations group when the project began production.[37] It sought the aid of its Russian joint-venture partners in helping manage the project. In short, Exxon took concrete steps to create jobs and economic growth; it trained local citizens for participation in the project; it went beyond its legal obligations on matters such as local content; and it followed global standards on issues involving the environment, health, and safety. Russian officials took note. A member of the consortium who was also an executive of the Russian national oil company Rosneft voiced his pleasure at being a part of the Sakhalin-I project: "I am quite proud and pleased that two-thirds of the Sakhalin-I project's contract spending [more than $3.2 billion] is going to pay for the services of Russian contractors and suppliers."[38]

As the company moved forward with Sakhalin-I, however, political forces beyond its control brought a new order to the Russian political economy. In the early 2000s, a Russian petroleum policy finally emerged, and it greatly altered the prospects for foreign oil companies. The new policy was an important part of President Putin's reassertion of the power of the central government. Petroleum and natural gas played starring roles in his efforts to rebuild the Russian economy. Their availability in Russia at below-market prices subsidized the development of the domestic economy. Oil and gas exports generated much-needed hard currency.

Putin came to office at a most opportune time. Russia had revalued the ruble in response to the 1998 economic crisis, and doing so proved to be a strong stimulus for the domestic oil and gas sectors. Then, after Putin took office, the global price of oil began to climb steadily, giving Russia a welcome economic boost. With the cushion provided by expanding oil and gas revenues, Putin strengthened the economic and political power of Gazprom, the national company that controlled most of the nation's giant natural gas reserves and the export of gas from Russia. More broadly, his government assumed greater control over the general direction of oil and natural gas policy, by, for example, reducing the role of foreign oil companies, moving toward stricter controls over their operations, and limiting their ownership of Russian reserves and companies.[39]

In early 2003, BP purchased a 50 percent share in a major Russian oil company, TNK. Both ExxonMobil and ChevronTexaco began discussions with Khodorkovsky, who owned 44 percent of Yukos, about the possibility of obtaining a stake in that company. After Khodorkovsky suggested to Lee Raymond and Rex Tillerson that such a purchase would be supported by the Putin government, they arranged to meet Putin in September 2003 to discuss the matter. How large could the share be? In *The Quest*, Daniel Yergin reports that Khodorovsky was "in talks with both Chevron and ExxonMobil about selling controlling interest in Yukos." This was a logical purchase for Exxon, since it would reinforce the company's world leadership while firmly establishing it in an important producing region. Putin, however, was growing increasingly concerned about foreign companies acquiring large ownership positions.[40] Soon after meeting with both ExxonMobil and Chevron concerning the possible sale of Yukos, Khodorkovsky was arrested on charges of tax evasion. After a trial, he was convicted in October 2005 and sent to prison in Siberia. Yukos was auctioned off by the government and sold at a deep discount to Russian companies acceptable to the Kremlin.[41]

Soon, the second major oil and gas project on Sakhalin Island, Shell's Sakhalin-II project, came under governmental scrutiny. The project had been developed under a PSA signed in 1994. Its lack of a Russian partner made Sakhalin-II vulnerable in an era of resource nationalism. Shell sought to address this problem by adding Gazprom to its consortium through a trade of properties and interests. There matters stood until the summer of 2005, when Shell made a stunning announcement. The costs of developing Sakhalin-II would be $20 billion, double the original estimate. Under the terms of the PSA, Gazprom and the Russian government would not begin to receive payments from the project until those costs had been covered. The government found that unacceptable, and it turned up the political heat on Shell to renegotiate the PSA. Environmental violations previously overlooked suddenly became the focus of new demands by the government for billions of dollars in fines. Shell resisted what it considered a perversion of the rule of law. Its resistance waned, however, as it became clear that its multibillion-dollar investment in the project was at risk—as were other plans it had made for Russian projects. In December, the ordeal ended with Shell's agreement to sell 50 percent plus one share of Sakhalin-II to Gazprom at a bargain price. Shell retained 27.5 percent, but lost effective control of the project.[42]

ExxonMobil too faced challenges from the Russian government. In October 2005, the company received word that the government had decided to delay the first shipment of crude oil from Sakhalin-I until health and safety inspections were completed. ExxonMobil, with the help of its Russian partners, its record of efficient completion of the technically difficult project, and its giant investment in Sakhalin-I, managed to come through the episode with its project largely intact. But it paid a price. The natural gas from the project would go into the pipeline system of Gazprom, and that company, not ExxonMobil, would decide its destination for sale. ExxonMobil also lost the right to develop Sakhalin-III, with estimated recoverable reserves of five billion barrels of oil. The government ultimately awarded that project to Gazprom and to the government-owned Rosneft.[43]

The oil and gas industries were too important to the Russian economy, its national security, and its self-image as a superpower for the government to allow majority ownership of them by foreign petroleum interests. Evaluating the company's position in Russia, Terry Koonce said in 2007, "I think ExxonMobil is doing about as well as you could hope . . . given all of the political problems."[44] The problems went far beyond the traditional conception of political risks, involving as they did the historic transformation of the political economy of one of the most powerful nations in the world. As Exxon and its competitors had learned in dealing with the OPEC nations in the 1970s, there was little that could be done to "manage" political risks when a sovereign nation asserted greater control of its oil and natural gas.

Despite the political turmoil in Russia in the 1990s, Exxon and its competitors had placed their bets on the nation's extraordinary reserves of oil and gas. Most of the companies lost both time and money in Russia. Exxon did better. It developed a large, innovative project on Sakhalin Island that returned a profit, employed many Russians, paid taxes, produced much-needed supplies of crude, and gave the company the opportunity to expand its technical capabilities in near-arctic conditions and in horizontal drilling. In the new Russia, the company moved far up the learning curve in coping with political uncertainties.[45]

KAZAKHSTAN AND AZERBAIJAN

Exxon found quite different political circumstances in Azerbaijan and Kazakhstan, two oil-rich nations in the region surrounding the Caspian Sea. These former Soviet republics used their oil to protect their newly won national independence. In Azerbaijan, one of the oldest oil-producing regions in the world, President Heydar Aliyev used a very promising oil field in the Azeri waters of the Caspian to attract international oil companies to his new nation. The result was the signing in September 1994 in Baku of what Aliyev called the "contract of the century," which set the terms for the development of several fields in the Caspian Sea with a potential maximum production estimated to be as high as 700,000 barrels a day. Exxon was not an original signatory of the deal, which included Amoco, BP, Lukoil (Russia), Pennzoil, Unocal, Statoil, the Turkish State Oil Company, SOCAR (Azerbaijan's national oil company), and several oil-service companies. But Exxon quickly bought a 5 percent stake in the project, which it raised to 8 percent in 1996. Geopolitical considerations in Azerbaijan, unlike those in Russia, benefited the company. President Aliyev was eager to bring into the deal as many oil companies from as many nations as possible, hoping that their home governments might help his nation resist any effort by Russia to assert control over its much smaller neighbor's oil. The investment paid quick dividends for Exxon when it produced oil in 1997, marking the company's initial production in the former Soviet Union.[46]

Kazakhstan, a large nation across the Caspian from Azerbaijan, presented a trickier political situation. After the breakup of the Soviet Union,

Nursultan Nazarbayev rose to the presidency. In the early 1990s, a joint venture including Chevron and Mobil won the right to develop the giant Tengiz field on the Caspian's eastern shore. With an estimated seven billion barrels of recoverable oil, the field might produce as much as 700,000 barrels a day when fully developed. The road to production would be far from easy, however, since the oil was under unusually high pressure and contained high levels of dangerous hydrogen sulfide. In the early 2000s, the even larger Kashagan field was discovered. Exxon had a small presence in Kazakhstan, but was not involved in those large projects before its merger with Mobil; thereafter, ExxonMobil had a 25 percent share in Tengiz and a 17 percent share in Kashagan in 2001.

Flush with enthusiasm for its future in Kazakhstan, the company announced in 2002 that "several phases of exploration will be required to fully develop this world-class discovery [the Kashagan field]—the largest gross resource that ExxonMobil has participated in developing in more than thirty years."[47] In 2006, ExxonMobil took a highly publicized hit to its reputation when a former Mobil executive was convicted for his failure to report income on several million dollars that prosecutors described as kickbacks from a Mobil payment to Kazakh officials. The payments appear to have been part of a much-larger scheme of oil-related payoffs in Kazakhstan. In 2007, the government shut down work on the Kashagan field amid growing demands on the foreign oil companies from a government touched with the fever of resource nationalism. By 2010, the estimate of the first production from the field had been pushed back from 2005 to 2012, and estimates of its final cost had risen to as high as $100 billion.[48]

Terry Koonce recalled his time in the former Soviet Union philosophically, commenting that it was "kind of profound . . . to live a part of history."[49] One part of that history must have been profoundly frustrating as Exxon's leaders in the region watched big projects drift away on the winds of political change as nations struggled to make the transition from communism to some still-undetermined future.

VENEZUELA AND RESOURCE NATIONALISM: ROUND TWO

Twenty years after Venezuela under President Carlos Andrés Pérez nationalized Exxon and other foreign oil companies in 1976, Exxon reentered this major oil-producing nation.[50] Why would a company return to a nation in which oil production had been nationalized? The easy answer was that both Venezuelan politics and the nation's massive reserves seemed to have changed for the better. Ironically, the leader of the political change that produced a new "opening" to foreign oil companies in the 1990s was Pérez, who was again elected president in 1988. As in the 1970s, Pérez represented the reformist wing of Venezuelan politics, and he responded to bad economic conditions in the 1980s by seeking ways to jump-start a stagnant economy. Since petroleum remained the dominant engine of growth, policies to encourage the expansion of production offered one path to revitalization.[51] In Venezuela, as throughout much of the world during the wave of globalization of the 1990s, foreign direct investment by international oil companies seemed to be one logical way of spurring such growth.

The companies had made headway in the development of technologies that might finally unlock the great potential riches of the heavy-oil deposits in the Orinoco region of Venezuela. By the early 1990s, estimates of the nation's recoverable conventional oil reserves were a highly respectable 90 billion barrels, but its heavy-oil belt held as much as 250 billion additional barrels of recoverable reserves—if ways could be found to develop those resources at prices competitive with conventional oil. Exxon's previous experience with Canadian oil sands and the heavy-oil deposits at Cold Lake, also in Canada, along with its research on synfuels, made it a logical company to develop the technology needed to transform the long-touted promise of heavy oil into a bonanza for Venezuela.[52] In an effort to find out, the Pérez government offered attractive terms to Exxon and other international oil companies to return to Venezuela. Given its past experience there and its commitment to financial discipline, Exxon moved deliberately. The country's political affairs were hardly stable. Soon after his election, Pérez had faced an attempted military coup led in part by then-Colonel Hugo Chávez. Although the bloody coup failed, it put Pérez on notice that he and the nation's democratic institutions were in danger. As Exxon studied conditions in Venezuela, it had to look ahead into Venezuela's uncertain political future and try to predict the direction of political change. In addition, the economics behind the recent overtures to foreign oil companies gave the company pause. In an era of low oil prices, the government needed foreign capital and technology to develop its oil reserves. Would this remain true over the long period needed to develop the heavy oil? In short, did long-term political and economic trends merit large investments in a nation whose modern history had been shaped by recurring periods of political challenges to international oil companies?

Although Exxon took a small stake in a traditional oil project in Venezuela early in the era of reopening, it took a "go slow" approach to the heavy-oil sector in the first round of contracts for large new projects. Many of its competitors did otherwise. Conoco, Mobil, Total, Statoil, ARCO, Texaco, and Phillips joined PDVSA in signing thirty-five-year contracts with very low royalties and tax rates. Those projects were planned to produce the region's very thick heavy oil and then upgrade it to a lighter syncrude through refining. Some of the refining would take place in plants owned by the foreign companies on the Gulf Coast in Texas and Louisiana. Mobil's Cerro Negro project (which came into ExxonMobil through the merger in 1999) involved potential production of 120,000 barrels a day by 2001, with most of the upgrading to be done at a refinery in Chalmette, Louisiana, jointly owned by Mobil and PDVSA. Mobil, the operator, had a 41.7 percent share in the project.[53] The low tax and royalty rates on the heavy-oil projects made them attractive despite the prevailing low prices for oil.

Exxon was not a partner in any of the four first-round projects, but it continued negotiations for Hamaca Este, a project designed to produce about 170,000 barrels a day of syncrude by upgrading heavy oil from Venezuela in the company's Baytown or Baton Rouge refinery. Exxon continued planning as well for a $3 billion petrochemical complex in Venezuela with Pequiven, the state-owned petrochemical company. Finally, it took part in the latest proposal for the Cristobal Colon LNG project that had emerged in the 1970s and then reemerged in the early 1990s.

After Chávez won the presidential election in 1998, he began to consolidate his political power in ways that did not bode well for foreign oil companies. His Venezuelan-style socialism featured a variety of programs to improve the education, health, and welfare of the poorest segments of the society—paid for largely by increased payments by foreign oil companies. He backed those programs with aggressive rhetoric against U.S. foreign policy. Early in his term, he denounced as illegal the 1990s contracts with the international oil companies, putting the companies on notice that they could remain in Venezuela only on his terms.[54]

A turning point in his presidency came when Chávez won a dramatic showdown with PDVSA, the national oil company of Venezuela. After the nationalization of foreign oil companies in 1976, PDVSA had evolved into what a *New York Times* article once characterized as "perhaps the best-run national oil company ever."[55] "Best run" from a U.S. perspective suggested that it had become more like a privately owned international oil company, gaining respect for its professional operations and its focus on oil and natural gas, not on social welfare programs. PDVSA's management assumed that its ample tax payments, its role as the largest employer in Venezuela, and its provision of gasoline within the country at subsidized prices were sufficient contributions to the nation. When Chávez sought to tie PDVSA's goals more closely to his own, the company's leaders resisted. Tensions came to a head in December 2002, when about half of the company's workers staged a national strike that shut down the company's operations for more than two months. Chávez took a hard line, firing some 18,000 strikers, including many of the company's professionals and managers, and replacing them with people loyal to him. When he took office, he found PDVSA to be operated much like a multinational oil company; now he had the leverage to harness its goals and its operations to his social reforms. Almost overnight, he transformed PDVSA from an efficient oil company run by engineers into an organization shaped by Chávez loyalists into a source of revenue for his reforms.[56]

The way was now clear for direct challenges to the foreign oil companies. Higher government revenues from steadily rising oil prices encouraged Chávez's resource nationalism. The speeches of the president and his oil ministers heated up, with references to the deals cut with the foreign oil companies in the mid-1990s as "criminal" and "treasonous giveaways."[57] The government backed its rhetoric by announcing that contracts for conventional oil projects written in the 1990s would be revised. ExxonMobil was reportedly "alone in resisting contract changes for 32 privately run oil fields that [would] be dominated by PDVSA under new joint ventures."[58] The company responded to Chávez's decree by selling its holdings in its project instead of agreeing to alter its contracts.

The Chávez regime then moved on to heavy oil. In 2004, the government unilaterally raised the royalty rate on the Orinoco projects. In 2006, Chávez demanded changes in the original thirty-five-year contracts to significantly increase taxes and royalties while giving PDVSA majority control of each project. All the companies involved faced a difficult choice: accept those changes or leave Venezuela. Collectively, "a half dozen international companies" (including Exxon) had already invested "upwards of $20 billion" in partnerships with PDVSA in the heavy-oil fields and in refineries needed to upgrade the approximately 600,000 barrels a day of syncrudes flowing from the projects.[59] Most of that investment, including advanced technology being used to produce the heavy oil, could not be moved out of Venezuela.

ExxonMobil had backed away from a threat of international arbitration after the earlier round of royalty increases, but it held its ground in 2006. With oil prices rising steadily, the Venezuelan government also stood firm. After ExxonMobil indicated that it could not make an adequate return under the proposed new taxes, the Venezuelan oil minister responded with disdain. If the company preferred to leave rather than to adjust, he said, "We don't want them to be here then. . . . [If] we need them, we'll call them."[60] The minister reminded Exxon that plenty of other oil companies around the world, particularly national oil companies, had expressed interest in entering the heavy-oil developments in Venezuela.

After almost a year of this war of words, Exxon announced its decision to leave Venezuela. Conoco was the only other foreign company in the heavy-oil projects that made the same choice. Before Exxon's departure, Chávez had proclaimed, "The Orinoco belt is still a living symbol of what was an important part of the oil opening. We must eliminate this symbol." While accomplishing that goal, Chávez had punctuated his political victory by refusing to back down to ExxonMobil, the largest foreign oil company, and one based in the United States, the nation he most loved to challenge.[61]

Exxon paid a price for its decision to resist Chávez. It sold one traditional oil field in Venezuela, lost its stake in the Cerro Negro heavy-oil project, and was eliminated from further consideration for a $3 billion petrochemical project and an even larger LNG project. Yet its highly publicized confrontation with Chávez yielded some long-term benefit by announcing once again that the company believed strongly in the sanctity of contracts and was willing to stand up for its principles. And the company had grown skeptical about the long-term prospects for all the projects in Venezuela in light of the increasingly hostile political environment there and the volatility of oil and gas prices. Reentry into Venezuela had looked interesting in the mid-1990s. Events in Venezuela after the election of Chávez in 1998, however, showed how quickly political risks could mount, particularly in times of rising oil prices.

WEST AFRICA: FIGHTING THE OIL CURSE

Exxon had substantial oil and natural gas production in Libya until its expropriation in the late 1970s. It did not move aggressively back into Africa until the 1980s, when it became active in Chad, Cameroon, and Angola in the Gulf of Guinea region of West Africa (see map 7.1). There, the company developed oil projects in impoverished countries where the lingering impacts of colonialism, civil conflict, limited educational opportunities for the population, and deadly diseases were all added to the normal political risks associated with finding and developing petroleum resources.

When it entered Africa, Exxon also became part of an ongoing debate about the impacts of oil-led development there. One prevailing argument focused on what came to be known as the "oil curse," which held that oil-led development often harmed rather than helped poor nations. In that view, oil production encouraged political corruption, a lack of transparency, unhealthy domination of the economy by the oil sector, and exploitative behavior by the major oil companies. Too often, went the argument, oil production enriched foreign companies and governing elites while contributing little to society as a whole.[62] This had been the basic argument of Venezuelan reformers as early as the 1920s, and it applied most convincingly in nations whose poorly developed political systems were tightly held by small groups that were not representative of the people as a whole. Foreign oil companies faced a difficult decision when entering such nations, since they could gain access to oil reserves only by making agreements with the existing government. Oil revenues then flowed to those who controlled that government, reinforcing their power and opening the way for heightened corruption. Almost inevitably, when citizens and the nation as a whole received little benefit from oil-led development, they voiced their anger at the foreign companies.

Such criticism certainly was nothing new for a global company such as Exxon. But parts of Africa in the 1980s and 1990s presented the dual challenges of extreme poverty and corruption amid oil riches. The company knew that it would face scrutiny when it entered less developed African nations with economies highly dependent on oil. If the established governments, to which it paid taxes, were repressive or unrepresentative or corrupt, sooner or later the company would be blamed for the societal problems that resulted. If the society as a whole saw few direct benefits from oil production, then public sentiment could turn against both the government and the foreign oil companies. Exxon had experienced this in Venezuela, Iran, Libya, and other nations.

In Africa, the oil curse was most often discussed in relation to Nigeria, one of the largest and most populous African nations, and one of the richest in oil and gas reserves. For much of its postcolonial history (since 1960), Nigeria has been a troubled nation, plagued by civil war, violence, political corruption, and widespread poverty. In the 1980s, Exxon had decided against entry into Nigeria after being solicited for a bribe in preliminary negotiations.[63] It had watched as other international oil companies faced mounting criticism for not improving conditions in Nigeria. As Exxon entered West Africa, it sought ways to avoid the worst problems often associated with the oil curse.

CHAD AND CAMEROON: AN EXPERIMENT IN OIL-LED DEVELOPMENT AND RISK MITIGATION

The company faced a difficult situation in Chad, a very poor, landlocked country in north-central Africa. The unelected government struggled to establish legitimacy with its citizens and to build its own capacity to govern a large, sparsely populated, agricultural nation. In the early 1990s, Chad was one of the poorest countries in the world, with some 80 percent of the population living on less than $1 a day. With around eight million people living in an area of about 500,000 square miles, Chad remained a nation of small agricultural villages without basic infrastructure. The country had never had a major railroad, and it had less than 200 miles of

Construction of a new road in Chad, 2002. Exxon Mobil Corporation.

paved roads, scant telephone service, and irregular electric supplies in limited regions.[64] Those conditions existed before oil development, reflecting
the long-term impact of French colonial rule and the prolonged violence
that accompanied the battle for political power following the withdrawal
of the French in 1960. They posed stiff challenges to Exxon as it sought to
develop new reserves in Chad.

Political upheaval racked the nation for more than thirty years after
independence as rival factions vied for control. A military junta briefly
asserted power from 1975 to 1978, but armed conflict among determined
groups with outside backing marked the next two decades. The effort by
one faction to unite Chad with Libya escalated the violence by igniting
cross-border fighting with that country. The French intervened to help
Chadian forces repel the Libyans and their allies. Those conflicts claimed
as many as 20,000 lives. General Idriss Déby, a French-trained army officer who seized power in a coup in 1990, imposed a measure of national
authority on the nation.

Throughout that era of incessant fighting, Exxon retained an interest
in several oil fields that had been discovered in Chad's Doba Basin before
the onset of civil war. After obtaining the original concession in 1969,

Conoco made several promising discoveries in the early 1970s. It spread its risks by creating a joint venture with Exxon, Royal Dutch Shell, and Chevron, but the escalation of the civil war in 1981 forced the consortium to suspend all exploration. The return of a tenuous peace in 1986 led to the reopening of negotiations with the government, and the consortium and the government reached an agreement in 1988 for a thirty-year concession to develop the oil fields in the Doba area and transport the oil to export markets via a pipeline through its neighbor to the southwest, Cameroon, which had 250 miles of coastline on the Gulf of Guinea and several major ports.[65]

Almost as soon as the agreement was in place, however, the original consortium began to unravel. With an eye on the political risks and social upheaval in Chad, Conoco sold its share of the fields to Exxon, which became the operator, with a 37.5 percent interest, the same as Shell's existing ownership share. Then, in the early 1990s, Chevron also lost confidence in the project and offered to sell its share to the French company Elf. At that point, Exxon and Shell acquired Chevron's holdings by exercising rights of first refusal included in the existing agreement. Elf responded by lobbying the French government to intervene on its behalf with President Déby, who had enjoyed the military support of France during his rise to power. At Déby's request, Exxon and Shell reluctantly agreed to offer Elf a 20 percent ownership in the joint venture, with Elf paying Chevron $30 million for the share.[66]

In 1994, Exxon selected Dean Guttormson and André Madec to manage the extremely complex project. Guttormson was a production specialist who had spent much of his career in Exxon Company USA. A graduate of the University of Minnesota and Princeton, he had worked on projects in Australia, Canada, the King Ranch in South Texas, and Tyler in East Texas, as well as on offshore projects from New Orleans. Madec's career had been largely in international operations. After joining the company in 1972 in France, he moved to the United States in 1986 and worked on various upstream projects. He played a central role in the Chad assignment for eight years before moving to a job in Exxon Corporation Public Affairs in 2002. The politically astute and French-speaking Madec became the primary contact for Exxon with the governments of Chad and Cameroon on many key issues.

The two executives sought ways to manage the intricate political and economic risks associated with the project. Madec later recalled, "The corporation was concerned with the political risks that we were taking . . . and the fact that the economics of the project were shaky." The company was willing to take the technical and economic risks, but was "much concerned about the political risk."[67] That concern was certainly justified. According to a Harvard Business School case on the pipeline project, "by any measure, Chad [in the 1990s] was one of the riskiest places on Earth to invest."[68]

The company's search for ways to manage those risks led to an innovative arrangement with the World Bank.[69] The treasurer of Exxon Company, International had noticed that the World Bank had begun to provide some funding for select resource-extraction projects in developing countries. In light of the extreme poverty in Chad, he suggested that the company explore the possibility of the World Bank's involvement in oil development in Chad and Cameroon. He understood that although "the involvement of multinational institutions and other lenders adds complexity, their presence can enhance country commitment and mitigate political risks."[70] Funding from the bank would mean that any default by either Chad or Cameroon on its obligations would have broader repercussions for the country than a default on a purely private loan. The World Bank Group could provide concessionary funding directly through grants or loans to Chad and Cameroon, lowering the costs as well as the financial risks to the private companies.

In mid-1994, Exxon approached the bank, which saw the proposal as "a prime opportunity to help Chad increase its fiscal revenues and ensure that the new funds would be dedicated for the most part to poverty alleviation." It also hoped to "ensure that the Project would be carried out in an environmentally and socially sound manner," and to "catalyze private sector investment in a difficult environment by mitigating political risks identified by the private sponsors."[71] Chad and Cameroon supported the World Bank's involvement, without which the private companies were unlikely to move forward with the project.[72]

In late 1994, the bank formally agreed to work with the companies and the two governments. Conceding that neither Chad nor Cameroon had been paragons of good governance, the bank—now led by James D.

Wolfensohn—nevertheless decided that the desperately poor countries might benefit from a properly organized project with strict supervision of the use of oil revenues. The project was a departure for the World Bank in its scale and in the cooperation it called for with international oil companies. Taking seriously its mission to reduce world poverty, it chose to underwrite a controversial project that might make a difference in a very poor region.

In 1995, the bank, the consortium, and the two governments began four years of negotiations on the structure of the project and the obligations of all parties. In 1996, a treaty between Chad and Cameroon defined procedures for project construction, including environmental and social safeguards, as well as Cameroon's revenue share from petroleum transportation. The final World Bank–approved plan in 1999 included general plan for project management, for detailed environmental-impact assessments by the consortium, and for addressing the potential social impacts in the construction and operation of the project. It stipulated detailed conditions concerning the use of oil revenues for social betterment.[73] At the time, the total project was projected to cost about $3.7 billion, though the figure eventually grew to more than $4.8 billion. Of that sum, approximately $4.1 billion would be provided by the members of the consortium. Additional funding would come from private investors, the governments of Chad and Cameroon, the European Investment Bank, and the World Bank, either in the form of loans to the governments or the consortium, or as grants to the countries in the form of technical assistance. Only a little less than $50 million was an outright grant to Chad and Cameroon for technical assistance. The equity investment of the two African countries was about $120 million, a bit over 2.5 percent of the cost.[74]

The Revenue Management Plan included in the agreement went far beyond traditional financial agreements for loans from international lenders or contracts with private corporations. The tax rate on the consortium, 12.5 percent, was low even by African standards, and restrictions on the government's discretion over the resulting revenues were unprecedented. The agreement placed the first 10 percent of those taxes in a "Future Generations Fund" for use when oil production ended. It set aside 80 percent of the oil tax revenues for poverty-reduction programs in such areas as health, education, and public works. That left 5 percent for distribution to communities in the oil region and the remaining 5 percent for the government's general use. All oil revenues would be placed in an escrow account in London, to be made available for transfers to Chad only as long as the government remained in compliance with the agreement. Bank-appointed oversight committees would review and approve expenditures within Chad and monitor the environmental impacts of the project. The Petroleum Revenue Management Law, passed in 1999, made the agreement part of the nation's laws.[75]

The demands on the government of Chad included unprecedented outside control over government expenditures from oil revenues.[76] In retrospect, perhaps the demands were overly ambitious, covering too much of the total oil revenue without also creating suitable arrangements for developing worthy projects for funding. One human rights specialist called the bank's revenue-management program "a challenge to the sovereignty of undemocratic rulers." The agreement came under close scrutiny from other critics. Environmentalists decried the destruction that they expected from the construction of a major pipeline through the rain forests of Cameroon. Other groups cited the records of the governments of Chad and Cameroon on human rights, closed government, and corruption before voicing fears that the revenues from the pipeline project would only make things worse. Some called the World Bank's loans "corporate welfare" that used public funds to cushion private-sector risks. On a practical level, many voiced pessimism over whether the government would comply with the agreement once the pipeline had been constructed.[77]

Not all observers were so pessimistic. In May 2000, an article in *Le Monde* headlined "Chad-Cameroon Pipeline: A Chance for Africa," spoke of the project with guarded optimism. It argued that World Bank specialists on environmental and social impacts had played a central role in creating a well-designed project. It noted that the pipeline route had been significantly modified, the tropical forests only slightly affected, two new national parks created, and arrangements put in place to help guide 90 percent of the project's revenues into funds devoted to future needs and social development.[78] It recognized too the prevailing skepticism that the agreement would be respected. World Bank officials acknowledged both the controversy and the difficulties facing the project: "It is a bit of an experiment. . . . If we don't do it today, somebody will develop [the project] without the safeguards" contained in the agreement.[79]

As negotiations between the bank and the companies stretched on, the Chadian government grew increasingly impatient. In mid-1999, it told the consortium to get started on the project or lose its concession. In response, Lee Raymond and the chairman of Shell, Mark Moody-Stewart, met with Wolfensohn in October 1999. Both Raymond and Wolfensohn were ready to proceed, but Moody-Stewart was not. Soon afterward, both Shell and Elf formally withdrew. They did so in a climate of growing criticism of international oil companies in Nigeria and other African nations, spearheaded by well-organized nongovernmental organizations—as well as by rising costs for the project and the prevailing low price of oil. Coming near the end of what had been a long and complex negotiation, the sudden change in consortium membership threatened the project as a whole. Not wanting to go it alone, Exxon found new joint-venture partners.[80]

First, however, came the ordeal of informing the government of Chad of the departure of Shell and Elf. Guttormson recalled his trip to N'Djamena, the capital of Chad, to reveal the sudden turn of events to the government. He and Madec and representatives of Shell and Elf first met in the prime minister's office with the heads of various ministries, including the petroleum ministry. After the prime minister berated Shell and Elf for their lack of goodwill in waiting until the last moment to pull out, he informed those present that the next step was to talk with the president. According to Guttormson, the prime minister concluded the meeting by inviting the ministers and "you, Esso . . . to go up and talk to the head of state, but you, Shell and Elf, are unwelcome in this setting. . . . He made it quite clear they were unwelcome in very strong terms."[81]

Since the project was so important to the future of Chad, responsibility for it "was held tightly by the president," who had worked closely with the companies and with the government of Cameroon to push the project forward. In a tense meeting at the palace, President Déby expressed his disappointment, reminding those present that the government of Chad had, as Guttormson recalled the conversation, "facilitated progress in any way they could, had made concessions that some might argue . . . were beyond what should be expected of a sovereign government." At the conclusion of the meeting, the president asked all those present except Guttormson and Madec to leave. He asked the two executives, "Tell me, what we are going to do?" They responded that the company planned to find new joint-venture partners, and they made the president a critical promise: "If [new partners] come aboard, they come aboard for the deal that's now in place such that it does not represent a five-year delay in your project. This is important to us. It's important to you." The president responded favorably, applauding the pair for coming to him with a potential solution, not just a problem. He asked them to keep him informed of their progress with a weekly telephone call directly to him.[82]

Back in Houston, the company quickly put that plan into action. Within about four months, Chevron and Petronas (the Malaysian national oil company) had agreed to purchase an interest in the project. Guttormson and Madec then took "our new partners on the same trip we did before. [We] flew to Chad and had another meeting to introduce them. . . . The government, as well, had to agree to their arrival." In the meeting with President Déby, Exxon's general point was clear: "When Exxon says something, they do it." Guttormson moved almost immediately to Angola to work on deepwater projects there, where he found that the message of Exxon's experience in Chad had preceded him: "That legacy stayed with us, that if you guys say it . . . you'll by golly do it. . . . You'll be tough as a brick getting there, which also preceded us, of course. . . . But having reached a deal, we'll do it." Another part of Exxon's reputation that had made its way to Angola was its commitment to avoid bribery: "It doesn't take long for the street to realize that this company ain't going to play that game. They'll come at you, and they'll test you, but they quickly realize that that's just not the way you do business, which is the reason why you can never, ever . . . make a single exception, because as soon as you do that, you're dead."[83]

Despite the turmoil created by the reshuffling of the consortium members, the World Bank Group formally approved the agreement in June 2000. This solidified the resolve of the companies and provided a framework for additional loans from commercial lenders and other intergovernmental groups such as the European Bank for Reconstruction and Development. After years of discussions, this experiment by public and private institutions to produce oil in a way that might reduce poverty in a very poor region of Africa finally moved forward.[84]

With the agreement in place, construction of the large and expensive project began in late 2000. The first part involved the development of facilities to produce oil from the Doba Basin, where the consortium initially drilled more than 300 wells to tap reservoirs with estimated recoverable reserves of more than 900 million barrels and a projected peak production of about 250,000 barrels a day, which might be sustained for a portion of the twenty-five-year life of the fields. The heavy crude in the fields proved difficult to produce, but no more so than Exxon had encountered in other fields around the world. Part two was the construction of a system to transport the oil for export through a 655-mile-long buried pipeline from the fields to the Cameroon port of Kribi.[85]

The consortium recruited the majority of its workers in Chad and Cameroon and trained them to do the unskilled and skilled labor required to lay a pipeline. The company later estimated that it had employed more than 35,000 workers during the construction phase of the project, with a peak employment of about 13,000. In a nation lacking basic transportation infrastructure, the consortium also had to build approximately 375 miles of roads, bridges, and airstrips to supply the material needed along the right-of-way. Careful planning allowed construction to continue through the rainy season. Madec described how crews would "work all the low grounds during the dry season and then . . . during the rainy season work on the high ground."[86] All such demands were well within the experience of the major companies in the consortium, which completed the pipeline in three years—six months ahead of schedule.[87]

It was clear from the start of the project that social and political issues would be as difficult to deal with as technical issues. To better manage the social issues, the joint venture developed an innovative but time-consuming approach to educate the people of Chad and Cameroon about the project and to listen to their concerns. In 1994 and 1995, long before the final approval of the project, Exxon began holding meetings in local communities to consult with citizens about questions raised by the project. Spearheading those efforts was Ellen Brown, an American anthropologist who spoke many of the local languages and had worked in Chad for more than two decades for the U.S. Agency for International Development and for independent nongovernmental organizations. In Cameroon, a variety of people were used for similar consultations, most with experience working in the area.

The consultations often included basic facts about the oil industry, the companies involved, and the project itself. Also discussed were questions about how much land would be needed for the pipeline and how people would be compensated for use of the land. Agreements on compensation could be tricky to arrive at, since local politicians had in some cases created unrealistic expectations of riches from land sales.[88] More difficult to overcome was the fact that Chad had no tradition of land ownership. Instead, rights to use land in much of the nation simply had been passed down for generations.

The company worked hard to reach agreements involving either in-kind trades of land or straightforward payments of cash. The cash injected a stream of money into local economies with no established banking systems and limited use of currency. Along with wages paid to workers on the pipeline, the land payments gradually expanded opportunities for some villagers to buy equipment for farming or to open small businesses. Thousands of consultations took place in local communities over a fifteen-year period starting in 1993. The meetings led to more than twenty changes in pipeline routing; in Cameroon there were changes to protect the settlements and hunting grounds of the Bagyeli-Bakola pygmies and to avoid environmentally sensitive areas such as the Mbéré Rift Valley and the Deng Deng forest areas.[89] The final World Bank evaluation of the project praised the "innovative" and "participatory" approach taken by the consortium: "The consultative process not only gave stakeholders room to understand the Project better, it equally gave the sponsors opportunity to take stakeholders' concerns into account with regard to impacts, benefits, mitigation measures, and compensation. And it strengthened local civil society organizations that lacked capacity at the beginning of the Project."[90]

Optimism was in the air in October 2003 at the celebration of the first oil to flow through the pipeline. An article in the *Houston Chronicle* reported the opening of the pipeline under the headline "African Pipeline Born of Promise to Spread Wealth." It reported that "the World Bank broke precedent and put money into the high-risk . . . project to prove that its developmental experts could reverse history and ensure that the new oil money could work for all citizens and not just the elite." It quoted a World Bank official's statement that "if we didn't take some risks, we'd never get anywhere."[91]

This optimism proved short-lived. Tensions grew in 2004 and 2005 as the Déby government became increasingly impatient with the lack of projects being undertaken with oil-revenue funds, particularly in light of a spike in the price of oil that built the fund more quickly than had been anticipated. In addition, a growing stream of refugees fled to Chad from Darfur in neighboring Sudan to escape the violence in their region. Opponents from inside and outside Chad posed a threat to the survival of the government of the country, which had cut its spending on armed forces in half during negotiations over the revenue-management program. Strapped for cash to meet these unanticipated challenges, the Déby government unilaterally rewrote the existing petroleum law in December 2005 to alter its agreement with the World Bank. The revised law eliminated the Future Generations Fund and transferred its $36 million balance to the general budget. It also increased the amount of oil revenue targeted for nonpriority sectors not subject to oversight and added new sectors, including security, to the list of priorities.[92]

As early as 2000, the World Bank had looked the other way when the government purchased weapons with a portion of a special $25 million payment required of Chevron and Petronas when they entered the consortium. But those payments had not been included in the official agreement with Chad. In response to the changes in its basic agreement with Chad, the World Bank suspended payments. This placed Exxon and the consortium in a difficult position, since the bank's actions suspended payment of $124 million the companies owed to Chad. Vigorously protesting such "blackmail," the government threatened to shut down the oil fields if payments were not forthcoming. The companies had to take the threat seriously. In the forced negotiations that followed, it was clear that the balance of power between the parties to the agreement had shifted dramatically. The World Bank had held all the cards during the early discussions of the agreement. But now that the oil field and the pipeline had been completed, the government of Chad held the trump card. An agreement at least temporarily acceptable to all sides was reached in mid-2006.

The bank relented and released the funds while modifying the agreement to make it more to Chad's liking.[93]

That short-term resolution imploded in February 2008, when rebel forces crossed the border with Sudan and attacked N'Djamena. The Déby regime responded by declaring a state of emergency, which allowed the president to approve the nation's budget by decree. In effect, this removed the oversight of oil revenues from the committee created for that purpose in the 1999 law. This marked the beginning of the end of the World Bank's continued participation in the pipeline agreement. In 2008, higher oil revenues allowed the government of Chad to pay off most of its loans from the World Bank early, escaping the strict supervision of expenditures that had been at the heart of the agreement in 2000. The World Bank then withdrew from the Chad-Cameroon pipeline project, although the World Bank Group's International Finance Corporation remained in Chad through a $100 million investment in the consortium's project. The bank's final internal review rated the project "unsatisfactory," concluding that it had failed in its "fundamental development objective of reducing poverty and improving governance in Chad through the best possible use of oil revenues."[94]

The bank's withdrawal did not, of course, end the pipeline project. ExxonMobil, Chevron, and Petronas remained in Chad and Cameroon. With more than $4 billion invested in a permanent pipeline and production facilities that could not be moved, they had very strong incentives to find an accommodation with the government and continue to produce oil. Throughout the controversies, the basic contract between Chad and the consortium had remained intact, with both parties enjoying the benefits of higher oil prices under the original terms of the contract. Indeed, by 2008, five years after first production, oil shipments through the pipeline to a marine terminal off the coast of Cameroon had reached a total of more than 266 million barrels and had grown to about 130,000 barrels a day.[95]

The company had taken part in an experimental partnership with the World Bank to try to find new ways to avoid the oil curse. Although large portions of the experiment failed, the goals embodied in the agreement signed in 2000 remained important. Innovative ways still needed to be found to manage—in the broad interests of the nation as a whole—oil revenues in producing nations without well-established political and economic institutions. Oil companies still needed creative and more effective ways to mitigate political risks. The World Bank still needed inventive ways to address the problems of poverty in the poorest regions of Africa. Perhaps those facing similar issues in the future will look to the case study of the Chad-Cameroon pipeline project for positive and negative lessons on how to proceed.

ANGOLA: LESSONS APPLIED

Exxon's deepwater developments offshore Angola symbolized a new era of global exploration and production for the company. Initial identification of the extraordinary deepwater potential of Angola came in the geological surveys completed by the Exploration Technical Assessment Group in the late 1980s. In developing deepwater prospects, the company made use of its expanding technological expertise and its evolving global development organization. Just as important was its management of political risks. In both Angola and Chad, those risks had to be interpreted broadly to include concern for social issues such as improvements in education and health and the reduction of poverty. By applying lessons learned around the world, the company sought to create a durable partnership based on mutual self-interest in Angola, where the rapid rise in oil production had the potential to improve social conditions and to enhance Exxon's long-term profits.

In Angola, as in Chad, the government faced difficult economic challenges, including a lack of modern infrastructure and a limited supply of trained industrial and technical workers. Poverty, lack of health care, and minimal education also limited the prospects for sustained growth, as did governmental institutions weakened by centuries of colonial rule under Portugal and decades of civil war in the postcolonial era.

Yet despite such broad similarities, Angola enjoyed several distinct advantages over Chad. The first was fundamental to Exxon's plans. Even before the 1990s, Angola had a tradition of oil production, with laws governing production, job training, and local content inherited from an earlier era, along with a national oil company, Sonangol. Angola's small population and giant reserves placed it in an excellent position to spread the wealth from oil. Unlike Nigeria, with a population of more than 150 million, Angola could concentrate on using oil revenues to improve living conditions for a much smaller population of about 11 million. Its citizens shared a desire to end the violence from a civil war that had stretched over almost three decades, splintering political institutions and civil society. A final difference between Chad and Angola had significant long-term implications: Exxon's project in Chad was onshore and required a large temporary workforce to lay an underground pipeline. The projects in Angola were offshore and involved many fewer workers initially, but a greater number of technical and professional employees over the long term.

For more than a decade before the end of Portugal's colonial rule in 1975, a war for independence devastated Angola.[96] Fighting over control of the postcolonial government continued until a cease-fire was signed in 2002. The twenty-seven years of civil war killed an estimated 550,000 people and displaced millions more. The war destroyed most infrastructure, including basic health and sanitation facilities. By war's end, average life expectancy in Angola had been reduced to a little more than forty years, and adult literacy stood at only 42 percent. After 1975, mass migration from the countryside to the nation's major cities drastically altered the way of life in Angola. A nation previously capable of feeding itself now had to import vast amounts of food. A once-rural society found itself squeezed into cities ill-prepared to provide even the basic needs of their swelling populations. The mass of the population lacked access to clean water, basic sanitation, and health services.[97]

Cold War tensions added to the damage and confusion of the civil war era. The battle for control in Angola became one of the "proxy wars" fought between the superpowers. José Eduardo dos Santos, who had been trained as a petroleum engineer in the Soviet Union, led the communist-backed MPLA party. He took over the presidency in 1979 and thereafter held the official reins of government. Dos Santos enjoyed the support of the Soviet Union and the Eastern Bloc, and Cuban troops played a highly visible role in his coalition. Opposing him was the UNITA rebel faction led by Jonas Savimbi, who at different times during the long war had the support of the United States and China. Access to oil was one objective of those seeking to influence the outcome of the civil war, but

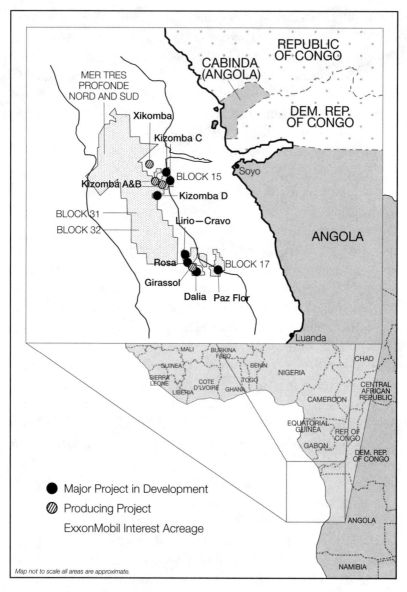

MAP 7.1: Source: *ExxonMobil,* 2005 Financial and Operating Review, *p. 48.*

much broader Cold War objectives were also in play. The extraordinarily complex international politics swirling around the combatants in Angola created strange bedfellows. At one point in the war, for example, Cuban troops protected the production facilities of U.S.-based Chevron against threatened attacks by rebel forces backed by the U.S. government.[98]

Oil had been discovered in Angola in the 1950s, and Gulf Oil (absorbed into Chevron in 1984) developed a substantial offshore oil field in shallow waters off the coast of the northern province of Cabinda in the 1960s. Both offshore and onshore activities in that region continued during parts of the civil war, which included armed conflict between separatists in oil-rich Cabinda and the troops of the Angolan government. Oil and diamonds provided exports in the 1980s and 1990s, but neither industry could expect to grow amid the violence and confusion of a civil war. Not until the end of the fighting after 2002 did the move into deeper waters offshore begin in earnest, marking a new era for the Angolan oil industry.

As noted in chapter 5, Exxon entered Angola in the 1990s after its newly created global exploration group concluded that the area off western Africa in the Gulf of Guinea held great potential. Exxon decided to make a big push in that general area. But where? After looking up and down the coast, Exxon focused on Angola, which had source rock with high potential for giant discoveries. Indeed, company experts estimated that as many as fifteen billion barrels of oil equivalent might be recoverable offshore there.[99] The deep water off Angola was little explored, and the time seemed right to enter the country boldly in search of major fields that would make a significant difference in Exxon's production.

The company sought to be one of the first to develop Angola's deepwater prospects. Initially, Exxon faced a tricky political problem: it would have to deal with President dos Santos at a time when the U.S. government still favored his opponent. Harry Longwell and Jon Thompson approached dos Santos with the argument that Exxon had the best technology and project-management skills with which to develop the massive fields that might lie in Angolan waters. Early on in the process, Longwell and Thompson hedged their bets by also meeting with his American-backed rival, Savimbi. At one memorable meeting of the United Nations in New York City, the two Exxon exploration specialists

Deep-draft caisson vessel under construction for the Block 15 concession off
the Angolan coast, 1998. ExxonMobil Historical Collection, di_06205.

met separately with both men to discuss the possibility of obtaining leases in Angola's deep water.[100]

The negotiations with dos Santos led to a joint venture, operated by Exxon with partners BP, ENI, and Statoil, in Angola's deep water. In 1994, the partners signed a production-sharing agreement for the project with Sonangol, Angola's national oil company. Four years later came the announcement of the discovery of four large oil fields. The next year, 1999, brought news of two more major discoveries; the year 2000, three more. Savimbi's death in battle in 2002 marked the effective end of the civil war, allowing the dos Santos government to focus on economic development, and Exxon and other international oil companies in the deep water off Angola played an important role in his efforts. Construction of facilities to produce oil from those fields quickly began, and work went forward rapidly. The first production from Block 15 came in 2003. By 2009, the fifteenth anniversary of the signing of the original production-sharing contract, the joint venture had identified in Block 15 recoverable reserves estimated at more than five billion barrels of oil equivalent.[101]

After the company had made headway in Angola, it put together an internal presentation on the keys to success in its entry into Angola. The filmed report stressed the need to "get in early," put a trusted person on the ground to collect data, learn the lay of the land, and establish the knowledge and relationships needed for success.[102] Strategists have long stressed the value of "first mover advantages," and Exxon recognized the great attraction of being first, when it is "never cheaper, never better." Exxon's Angola group also noted the need "to keep the aperture of knowledge open wide at the beginning" of a project, since broad information and a comparative perspective produce the best long-term choices. In western Africa, this meant keeping an open mind about the potential of several nations and about the various blocks put forward for competitive bidding. Exxon watched several of its key competitors focus so sharply on specific blocks that when those could not be obtained or they came up empty, the companies lost ground in one of the major oil-producing basins in the world.

Another key part of Exxon's approach in Angola was to "establish strong relations." This seems almost too obvious to include, but the broad discussion of effective relationships is instructive. Included were good working ties to superiors within Exxon's management, the various parts of the Angolan government, and the company's joint-venture partners. Although the best approach was easily stated, it could be difficult to follow in practice: keep your partners fully informed and justify your choices to them; use straight talk; and do what you say you will do. One obvious example of that approach in Angola was a presentation to the government early in the development process that illustrated how the country would benefit from streamlining the permit processes. Revenue would flow steadily and more quickly to the government if the company could move forward without delays.

Straight talk about mutual self-interest also proved important in another critical decision, the choice of the operating company for Block 15, which proved to be a giant producer. At one point, the block had been set aside by the Angolans for BP, but Exxon took advantage of its own reputation and bargaining leverage to become the operator, with a 40 percent ownership share. With the help of the American ambassador to Angola, Exxon successfully made the case that the award of Block 15 to an American company (Chevron was also in the running) might help convince the U.S. government to offer recognition to the dos Santos government.

Straight talk included direct information about how the company planned to build a long-term relationship that would benefit Angola, energy consumers around the world, and Exxon shareholders. To do so required Exxon to understand the aspirations of the nation. The best way to do this seemed obvious: "Learn by listening to their needs." Unfortunately, that had not been the common approach of international oil companies historically in their dealings with less developed producing nations, and Exxon had to take a new, more responsive stance in Angola.

The company had the finances, people, and technology to make a convincing argument. It had a wealth of experience, from Hondo off California to the North Sea to Lena in the Gulf of Mexico, that it could bring to bear in Angola's deep water. It also had strong incentives to perform well, since it considered Angola an important part of its future. As Exxon searched for new reserves large enough to have a significant impact on its own total reserves and production, few regions were more promising. The potential size of the reserves and their location under 3,000–5,000 feet of water made deepwater Angola an ideal fit for a company seeking to bolster its position as a leader in deep water throughout the world.

Exxon's performance in Angola was shaped by the deepwater technology it had helped develop around the world—and in the labs of Exxon Production Research Company (known as the ExxonMobil Upstream Research Company after the merger). Advanced three-dimensional seismic mapping identified the offshore fields. In developing them, Exxon took to new levels the technology it had helped pioneer in the use of floating production, storage, and offloading (FPSO) vessels, building vessels with a capacity of 2.2 million barrels. They were the largest such vessels yet used to produce, store, and transfer to tankers large quantities of oil. The company also relied on advanced subsea production systems that it had helped pioneer in other regions. At the Kizomba field, the subsea equipment separated oil from natural gas and water on the ocean floor and then reinjected the gas back into the field to maintain pressure in the oil-bearing reservoir. An essential part of the subsea system was an ambitious program of long-distance drilling that stretched out as far as four miles horizontally to tap oil deposits in thin reservoirs. The

*Kizomba A FPSO (floating production, storage, and offloading) vessel about
200 miles off the coast of Angola, 2004. Exxon Mobil Corporation.*

Angolan developments did not require Exxon to create completely new
technologies, but the company extended its technical capabilities every
step of the way.[103]

It also made innovative use of new approaches to development. Here,
the company could see practical benefits from the functionally organized structure it built after the merger with Mobil. Its global development function brought lessons learned from other large projects around
the world to Angola. Important to the government's finances was the
use of what Exxon called the "fast production system." First applied in
offshore projects in Nigeria, the system used converted tankers to begin
to recover oil for market as much as two years before the completion of
the permanent production facility. The system was particularly attractive to host governments because it sharply reduced the time required to
reach first production—and first oil revenues. The first head of Exxon-
Mobil's global development function, Morris Foster, proudly noted,
"It's this kind of innovation that has helped make ExxonMobil become
a partner of choice."[104]

To speed production from its leases while also cutting costs, the company took a hard look at the expense and time required to design and build the complex equipment required for deepwater production. In the past, each new field generally had required a specially designed production facility matched to its water depth and location. Deepwater development using subsea production systems and FPSO vessels, however, presented an opportunity to use generic designs suitable for general conditions. Off Angola, ExxonMobil aggressively reduced the time traditionally required to design, build, and test production platforms by adopting the principle "design one, build multiple." This Henry Ford–like approach produced not Model Ts but rather giant FPSO vessels that were at the center of operations for much deepwater production.

The obvious benefit was a much shorter turnaround time for placing the equipment on site. In addition, since repairs and operations of the vessels were more uniform around the world, those who worked on them or repaired them could use others' experience to help them master their jobs. Lisa Waters, who managed the design and construction of the first two FPSO vessels used in the Kizomba A field, observed in 2004, "The hull and the marine systems for the two vessels are identical. We transferred what we learned on Kizomba A. As a result, the construction of Kizomba B is well ahead of schedule. We're one of the few oil companies that has the global reach and technology strengths to be able to pursue this concept."[105] That global reach included the use of low-cost builders in major shipbuilding regions around the world for the specialized equipment needed in deep water.

Exxon's technical and managerial strength thus became primary tools in the management of political risks. The capacity to deliver oil production and thus oil revenues in record time cemented its relationship with the Angolan government. Early on, the company had judged dos Santos to be a person who could achieve political stability and lead the nation toward economic recovery. Negotiations with him and other officials had convinced Exxon that his government had very strong incentives to respect the sanctity of contracts, a basic principle that shaped the company's choices around the world.

Once the company entered Angola, it became clear that the nation had in place a legal and regulatory framework to encourage the development of its oil industry. It had a tradition of entering into production-sharing agreements that recognized the risks to the international companies of deepwater exploration, and its tax system was in line with those used by major producing nations around the world. Angolan law reserved ownership of all hydrocarbon resources for the nation. Its national oil company, Sonangol, had been created in 1976 and had become the sole concessionaire for the nation's oil and gas development in 1978. It functioned much like national oil companies created in the 1970s by other major producing nations. It worked with foreign companies through production-sharing agreements and joint ventures, with its share of expenses funded through oil-backed borrowing.[106]

As in Norway, the national oil company's work in joint ventures prepared it to evolve into an independent oil company capable of developing fields on its own. It also oversaw the operations of foreign oil companies, recommended areas to be opened for exploration, conducted bidding for leases, and managed the development of petroleum services.[107] An independent Ministry of Petroleum designated blocks for bidding, approved field-development plans, regulated production levels, and reviewed Sonangol's investment programs. All in all, the organization of the oil sector in Angola mirrored that of most of the OPEC nations, with responsibilities shared among top government officials, a ministry, and a national oil company. In fact, as its oil production increased, it became a member of OPEC in 2007.

After its prolonged civil war, Angola confronted developmental problems that had been common in many other OPEC nations decades earlier. Angola lacked the infrastructure and the trained workforce to benefit over the long term from oil-led development. The country had few of the support industries that had grown in other producing nations during decades of steady expansion of the oil sector. Angola did have laws dating back to 1982 that mandated the training of local workers and the participation of local businesses in oil-based purchasing and contracting; the enforcement of those laws became the focus of much effort by Sonangol. Laws requiring both the payment of a "training tax" and "local content" in oil-related manufacturing became a part of the basic leasing agreements.[108]

Such demands were hardly new for Exxon. During the last half of the twentieth century, the company had steadily increased its commitment to train local workers for technical and professional positions. Creole in

Venezuela and Aramco in Saudi Arabia had built early models for the technical training of nationals, and that experience was used time and again in places as diverse as Malaysia, Angola, Papua New Guinea, and Chad. Over time, training programs grew in scale and sophistication—at times under the impetus of new laws requiring their expansion. In Libya in the late 1970s, for example, the government required two-thirds of Exxon's workforce to be Libyans.[109]

In 2004, Esso Exploration Angola pointed proudly to the fact that 65 percent of its 580 employees were Angolans and that many more Angolans found work with "contractors and subcontractors in Angola who work to support our ongoing operations." The company put in place programs to provide technical training for current and future workers, and the number of workers then grew with the expansion of the company. In the long term, training for those workers helped prepare them to take more extensive control of the development of their own reserves. At another level, the globalization of the oil industry gave Exxon a strong incentive to train people fluent in the languages and familiar with the cultures of nations around the world for future technical, professional, and managerial positions within the company. In effect, the training programs helped produce a pool of future employees for both ExxonMobil and the national oil companies.[110]

The need for training in Angola went beyond the oil sector. The nation badly needed a new generation of professionals, businessmen, and civic-political leaders to rebuild the nation following decades of war. It needed entrepreneurs with the skills to develop local companies that could supply the requirements of the oil companies while also creating unrelated businesses. For its part, Exxon held local workshops for its workers; it also provided extended periods of training at international universities for Angolans who showed great promise. As required by law and encouraged by the company's experiences in other nations, it sought Angolan partners in development by purchasing from local companies. The management of long-term political risks thus demanded concern for the improvement of the social conditions that had the potential to dash the rising expectations of Angolans and lead to the return of civil strife.[111]

Harry Longwell summed up the situation as he saw it: "Angola's rich in human resources. It just suffers from 300 years of slavery and 150 years of colonial rule, and 30 years of civil war . . . So it's a country that has tremendous natural resources and human resources."[112] Given Exxon's relatively small workforce, it would be difficult for the company to fundamentally alter Angola's economy. The needs of the nation were large, including the reconstruction of health care infrastructure, schools, roads, and water supplies, along with the creation of basic services for the millions who had migrated to the cities. But Exxon sought to be a responsible citizen by contributing to the solutions to these problems. It did so because it was good business to help improve conditions in the country. History suggested that oil-led development managed in part by international oil companies would not continue unless in the long term, the government and citizens of Angola viewed it as being in their interest.

Exxon had long experience with philanthropic activities in more-developed nations. It extended those efforts to Angola through basic anti-poverty programs, usually in cooperation with government, local institutions, nongovernmental organizations, and global organizations such as the World Bank or the United Nations. After the Exxon-Mobil merger, the company streamlined and centralized its philanthropic activities, and one area that came in for special attention was its programs in western Africa, where the newly merged company had a large presence.[113]

Of special interest to the company were the improvement of the region's health care infrastructure and the prevention of disease, not only in Angola but also in Chad, Cameroon, and other at-risk countries. The most serious disease was malaria, which killed as many as one million Africans a year, with perhaps 90 percent of those deaths in sub-Saharan countries. According to Edward Ahnert, the head of the company's philanthropic foundation from 1990 to 2005, the African countries in which ExxonMobil operated "had some of the highest malaria rates in the world." As a result, the company "saw an opportunity to mount both an internal health policy around malaria prevention and a publically oriented philanthropic program to reduce the impact of malaria in those work areas."[114]

The initiative took many forms, including large, continuing contributions to global organizations such as Roll Back Malaria, created in 1998 by the World Health Organization, UNICEF, and the World Bank. The company both joined the partnership and organized its own efforts under the Africa Health Initiative in 2000. Though other tropical

Africa Health Initiative on bed nets. Exxon Mobil Corporation.

diseases were included, a central target of the initiative was malaria prevention, control, and treatment. An early $1 million grant was given to
the Harvard Malaria Initiative, and the company associated itself with
numerous other global programs and groups dedicated to eradicating
malaria and other African diseases. From 2000 to 2009, ExxonMobil
contributed more than $50 million to an array of antimalaria groups,
international and Angolan, and sponsored antimalaria conferences in
Angola and other nations.[115]

Among its other measures, the company supported campaigns to combat the spread of HIV/AIDS in Africa through assistance to local clinics.
ExxonMobil addressed the societal need for better educational facilities
through contributions to Angolan universities for building libraries and
other facilities. As in other parts of the world, company employees vol-
unteered their time and money to assist in efforts to improve health and
education in Angola. [116]

Of course, a corporation, no matter how large, could not solve such
problems alone. But ExxonMobil's philanthropic efforts helped local citizens while also providing symbols that the company cared about social
problems in Angola and elsewhere. The company's primary contribution

to the nation's long-term well-being was its production of oil, which generated funds for the government while also directly and indirectly providing jobs. ExxonMobil and the other international oil companies could point to a combined economic impact sufficient to improve economic and social conditions through revenues paid to government, training programs that over time would produce a growing number of professional and technical workers, and philanthropic programs that addressed the broad needs for improved health care and education.

In 2009, Angola produced almost two million barrels a day of crude oil, surpassing Nigeria to become Africa's largest producer in that year. By then, ExxonMobil had established a solid competitive presence in Angola and in Africa as a whole, with large developments in Chad, Nigeria, Equatorial Guinea, and other African nations brought into the merged company by Mobil. ExxonMobil was a prime beneficiary of Angola's growth in oil production. After acquiring rights to significant acreage in Angola in the early 1990s, the company had built substantial production at a pace seldom before seen in the global oil industry. The 1,600 square miles in deepwater acreage covered by Block 15 proved especially productive, providing the company with one of the most prolific properties in its long history. Its 40 percent ownership of that block yielded much-needed reserves (about 1.8 billion barrels of an estimated 4.5 billion barrels) and production (about 320,000 barrels a day of an estimated peak production of 800,000 barrels a day).[117]

Within Exxon before and after the merger with Mobil, Angola became a test case for the company's new global organization in exploration and development. It passed with flying colors. Equally important was the company's growing confidence in its capacity to manage political risks, broadly defined. Those included the long-term risk that poverty, corruption, and growing extremes of wealth might undermine the political stability of a developing nation attempting to build a stronger economy around the production of oil. In its first fifteen years in Angola, the company drew on its experiences from around the world to operate so as to make long-term profits while also trying to demonstrate that oil-led development in an aspiring nation could be a positive force, not a curse. ExxonMobil had made impressive progress toward this goal by 2005. Time will tell whether its efforts succeed in the long term, which is the only realistic time frame within which to expect a nation to overcome deeply rooted problems spawned by colonialism, civil war, and poverty.

A traditional saying in the petroleum industry is "Oil is where you find it." Thus, ExxonMobil's choices to enter politically volatile regions were decided in part in geologic time, millions of years before the fall of communism, or revolutionary socialism driven by resource nationalism, or the resource curse. An oil company as large as ExxonMobil needs big projects such as Prudhoe Bay—and Block 15 off Angola. Unfortunately, large oil fields are as likely to be found in politically demanding locations as they are in technically and physically demanding ones. Over its long history, ExxonMobil has gradually developed greater capabilities for addressing political risks, which have become even more difficult to manage since the coming of producer power.

The company managed political risks with a variety of tactics. True to its reputation as financially conservative, it moved cautiously in Russia, Chad, and Venezuela, waiting for as much political clarity to be achieved as possible before making large investments. A company the size of Exxon could afford to do so in part because it had the financial clout to buy in later if it was not a first mover. The company's image and capabilities gave it some leverage in negotiating good terms of entry, since nations usually understood that they would benefit from the involvement of a large, technically advanced leader in the oil industry. Leverage shifted sharply toward the country once a major investment had been made, however, since most oil-producing facilities could not be moved. This reality reinforced Exxon's impulse to negotiate for as long and as hard as necessary to dot the i's and cross the t's in its agreements. Unfortunately, as illustrated in two different eras by events in Venezuela, governments could and did unilaterally rewrite agreements, especially when resource nationalism shaped national politics and when high oil and natural gas prices raised oil revenues.

One other lesson emerges from the case studies of Russia, Venezuela, Chad, Cameroon, and Angola. In each case, geopolitics, as well as national politics, shaped the outcome of events. The end of the Cold War with the Soviet bloc did not eliminate international tensions. Instead, new issues pushed to the forefront of international politics, affecting the operations of international oil companies. President Putin's drive to reestablish the global influence of Russia reshaped both the nation's energy policy and the options of international oil companies. Hugo Chávez's pursuit of a Latin American socialist revolution financed in large part by Venezuelan oil and natural gas became the linchpin for an oil policy that forced Exxon to withdraw. In Chad, the government's decision to alter the terms of the deal with the World Bank resulted in part from an invasion by outsiders. Throughout Africa, the growing competition for oil among companies from many nations, including China, promised to raise geopolitical tensions in the future. The importance of oil in international relations ensured that Exxon's efforts to manage political risks would go forward amid geopolitical concerns.

In a presentation in the late 1980s to Exxon's board of directors on regional geologic studies conducted by the Exploration Technical Assessment Group, Jon Thompson noted the tremendous prospects in West Africa. He spoke of the large increases in oil and gas if the company could return to "the Russias and the Iraqs," and then concluded, "We now know where we want to be; we have a very good idea of the specifics of it—what we need to do, how much we'll find, what technologies will be necessary. . . . We have come to where we want to come. We're now at the mercy of the political world, the price world."[118] The demands of politics and oil price swings showed little mercy for Exxon in the two decades after Thompson's presentation, but the company nonetheless held its own in its struggle to develop reserves on a frontier that will remain critical to its long-term prosperity—the frontier of political risk.

CHAPTER EIGHT

UPGRADING DOWNSTREAM

OPERATIONAL EXCELLENCE IN REFINING AND CHEMICALS

The view of a refinery or a petrochemical plant from the highway is much the same around the world. Behind a high, sturdy chain-link fence sits a mass of silver towers and white storage tanks, with pipes reaching in every direction and steam floating up from the stacks. The sense of most of those who drive by is that nothing much changes over time. Yet inside the fences, some sort of construction is almost always going on, and change is continual and far-reaching. The pace of change at Exxon accelerated after 1973, when refining and other downstream operations faced major adjustments. As the company searched the world for new sources of crude, refiners within the company had the equally challenging task of adapting to fundamental changes in the market for petroleum products.

As the largest refiner in the world and one with a decidedly global presence, Exxon had to adjust its refining capacity in different regions to new patterns in demand. Its initial response in the 1970s was to reduce the wide gap between its total refining capacity and the much lower capacity required to meet the falling demand for refined products that was being driven by higher oil prices. In the two decades after 1973, the company reduced its overcapacity by shuttering or selling its least efficient plants, but it still faced the downward pressure on sales exerted by overcapacity throughout the industry. In the long term, however, the company faced a broader challenge more difficult than reducing idle refining capacity. It had to transform the cost structure, scale, and efficiency of its vast refining system while also adapting to ongoing regulatory demands for greener operations and cleaner-burning fuels.

From the mid-1980s onward, Exxon pursued a long-term strategy designed to return the company to its historical position as a low-cost producer and marketer of high-quality petroleum products. Doing so required fundamental changes in downstream operations. The consolidation of plants and the elimination of smaller refineries created economies of scale; a variety of new management systems focused on the systematic, relentless reduction of downstream costs; new technology allowed its refineries to make cleaner, better products from less expensive grades of crude oil; and organizational innovations steadily increased the sharing of best practices in Exxon's far-flung global system for transporting, refining, and marketing oil and petroleum products. Another important initiative was the closer coordination of the operations of large refining and chemical complexes in order to maximize the value added to feedstocks. The impact of those changes was particularly evident in Singapore and other Asia-Pacific nations, since a final part of downstream strategy was expansion into that fast-growing region.

CONFRONTING THE PRESSING PROBLEM OF OVERCAPACITY REGION BY REGION

In the decades after World War II, oil consumption boomed in North America, Europe, and Japan, encouraging the spectacular expansion of downstream operations. "Free world" demand for petroleum products jumped from about 10 million barrels a day in 1950 to almost 50 million barrels a day by 1973. This stunning 400 percent growth in less than a quarter of a century shaped patterns of investment and behavior within Exxon. Its refining business boomed, with much new growth in western Europe and Japan—two war-ravaged regions that rebuilt with dramatic increases in the use of oil. North American refining grew less rapidly, but it nonetheless contributed to the spectacular expansion of the company's worldwide refinery runs (the amount of crude oil processed) from 1.6 million barrels a day in 1950 to about 5.8 million barrels a day in 1973.[1] That growth required extensive investments in new refineries, service stations, and transportation facilities, everything from pipelines to tankers. The company prospered by building far-flung operations around shipments of high-quality, low-cost crude oil from Venezuela and the Middle East, and it entered the 1970s seemingly well positioned to continue to do so. All that changed in the turmoil of the 1970s, and Exxon faced a very difficult period of transition as sustained growth gave way to reduced demand.

As shown in figure 8.1, the company's worldwide refinery runs declined by about 1.3 million barrels a day (mb/d) from 1973 to 1979, then fell by another 1.4 mb/d by 1986. That reduction, almost 50 percent over thirteen years, allowed Exxon to establish a new refining equilibrium by the early 1990s, with about 3.6 mb/d of refinery runs from about 4.1 mb/d of capacity, for a utilization rate of around 88 percent, a far cry from the utilization rates of around 70 percent that prevailed in 1975–1986, and even better than the 85 percent utilization in 1973.

Idle capacity created a drag on the performance of the company's downstream operations for much of the era. As the company sought to recover from the devastation caused by nationalizations of its largest sources of crude, it needed a stronger financial performance from downstream operations.

The company-wide struggle to reduce idle capacity and increase profitability went forward region by region. As Exxon entered the 1970s, each major region had its own refining operations, and the approach to reducing idle capacity reflected the history and practices in particular regions. Although the pace and timing of downsizing differed by region, the overall results were the same. During a painful period of adjustment, the company sharply reduced idle capacity and began to expand and improve the operational performance of the plants that remained.

The problem of overcapacity was most severe in Europe, which accounted for about 40 percent of Exxon's global refining runs in 1970. (See figure 8.2 for the relative size over time of refinery runs in Europe, the United States, Canada, Latin American, and the Asia-Pacific area.) Although the company had had a strong marketing presence in Europe from the late nineteenth century onward, it had only about 70,000 barrels

FIGURE 8.1. Exxon Refineries Worldwide: Runs, Capacity, Utilization (millions of barrels per day)

YEAR	RUNS	CAPACITY	UTILIZATION
1973	5.7	6.7	85%
1974	5.2	6.7	78%
1975	4.3	6.7	64%
1976	4.4	6.1	72%
1977	4.3	6.3	68%
1978	4.4	6.2	71%
1979	4.4	6.0	73%
1980	4.2	5.8	73%
1981	3.9	5.6	70%
1982	3.5	5.4	65%
1983	3.3	4.7	70%
1984	3.2	4.6	70%
1985	2.9	4.3	67%
1986	3.0	4.1	73%
1987	3.0	3.9	77%
1988	3.0	4.0	75%
1989	3.3	4.1	80%
1990	3.5	4.2	85%
1991	3.6	4.1	87%
1992	3.6	4.2	87%
1993	3.6	4.1	88%
1994	3.7	4.1	88%

Source: *Exxon Financial and Operating Reviews, 1973–1994.*

FIGURE 8.2. Regional Distribution of Exxon Refinery Runs by Region, 1970–2005

	EUROPE	U.S.	CANADA	LATIN AMERICA	ASIA- PACIFIC
1970	40%	19%	8%	22%	6%
1975	36%	27%	9%	16%	9%
1980	38%	30%	11%	10%	11%
1985	34%	36%	12%	3%	14%
1990	40%	27%	14%	NA	12%
1995	39%	27%	12%	4%	19%
2000	28%	33%	8%	2%	26%
2005	29%	31%	8%	2%	26%

Source: *ExxonMobil Financial and Operating Reviews, 1970–2005.*

a day of refining capacity in ten small plants scattered throughout Europe before World War II. Seven of the ten were destroyed during the war, and the company faced serious strategic issues when it reentered the region. Its answers propelled a thirty-year record of sustained expansion of refining in Europe.

REGIONAL ADJUSTMENTS IN REFINING

The company's choice of a European strategy was logical in the context of the postwar era. It chose to rebuild most of its refineries and build a new generation of much larger plants in Europe in an effort to achieve "the maximum outlet for its crude."[2] That approach promised profits for both downstream and upstream operations, with a growing volume of relatively inexpensive Middle Eastern oil flowing to an expanding market for petroleum products. As Europe rebuilt from the war and embraced oil over coal for many uses, its demand for petroleum surged, and the company responded by increasing refining capacity. It built large plants at Fawley

(UK), Rotterdam (Netherlands), Port Jerome (France), Antwerp (Belgium), Cologne and Karlsruhe (West Germany), Augusta and Trecate (Italy), and other sites. Into the early 1970s, it continued to invest heavily in building and upgrading downstream operations in Europe, expanding refining capacity from about 800,000 b/d in 1960 to more than 2.7 million b/d in its twenty-one European refineries by 1973. Despite the weakening of demand after the onset of the energy crisis, Exxon's refining capacity in Europe did not peak until 1976 (at more than 2.8 mb/d) because new plants were under construction in the early 1970s based on estimates made before the oil-price shock of 1973–1974 for a growing demand for refined products.[3]

The drop in oil demand in the 1970s devastated Esso Europe's downstream operations. Indeed, refinery runs in Europe dropped from 81 percent of installed capacity in 1973 to 56 percent in 1975 and remained in the low 60 percent range into the 1980s. Despite plunging refinery runs, overall capacity proved hard to reduce; in 1980, Exxon's refining capacity in Europe remained at almost 2.5 mb/d, with 37 percent of capacity idle. Against that backdrop, a determined effort began to reduce capacity. The company announced the shutdown of its Cologne refinery in 1981 and then sold it the next year, launching a rapid-fire round of cutbacks. In 1982, it sold minority interests in one plant in Ireland and one in France, and also disposed of its interests in a Jamaican refinery. The next year it shut down two more European plants—Milford Haven in the UK and Bordeaux in France—then sold its Thessalonica refinery in Greece to the Greek government and shuttered a refinery in Montreal. A refinery in Denmark was sold to Statoil in 1986, and the sale of a large plant in Hamburg followed in 1987. From 1980 to 1990, sharp cuts in capacity, combined with a slight increase in runs, reduced the company's refining capacity in Europe by almost one-third while boosting the utilization of its refineries by more than 15 percent. In 1993, Exxon reported that the "significant restructuring and operating cost reductions initiated in the early 1980s resulted in a well-balanced European downstream network," which made Europe the company's "largest source of downstream income."[4]

In the United States and Canada, the problems downstream in those years were not as severe, and so the initial capacity reductions after 1973 were not as drastic. The United States was second to Europe in refining capacity within Exxon in 1973. It operated only five refineries in the United States: two large Gulf Coast plants at Baytown, Texas, and Baton Rouge, Louisiana; its oldest refinery, in Bayway, New Jersey; a smaller plant in Billings, Montana; and a newly completed refinery with an initial capacity of about 70,000 barrels a day in Benicia, California. The plants had grown in response to the postwar boom in oil demand, and for the most part they refined crude oil from the southwestern United States and Venezuela, which also shipped substantial quantities of refined products into Exxon's domestic markets from both Venezuela and Aruba, in the Netherlands Antilles. The five Exxon USA refineries combined entered the energy crisis with utilization rates of 97 percent in 1973. Although the rate decreased to the mid-80s in the late 1970s, it dipped below that only briefly amid the oil spike of 1979–1982, when gasoline demand in the United States fell sharply. One response was the reevaluation of the role played within Exxon by the Bayway, New Jersey, refinery; the company made substantial cuts in capacity there in 1982 before announcing the sale of the plant in 1992. Besides increasing the company's overall U.S. utilization rate, the sale of Bayway pushed demand toward the two large, technically advanced refineries on the Gulf Coast, allowing them to utilize more fully their recently upgraded capacities.[5]

Canada entered the 1970s with its downstream in good shape, in part because of basic adjustments made early in the decade. Imperial had expanded rapidly after World War II while also moving steadily westward to Alberta in both upstream and downstream operations. In 1976, the company opened a large, modern refinery at Strathcona, Alberta, and then closed four older refineries. In the 1970s and 1980s, Imperial regularly invested in upgrades and expansions at Strathcona while also upgrading older plants in Nova Scotia and Ontario. Its idle capacity remained roughly the same as that of Exxon USA's operations and less than that of the company's European plants.

A new wave of adjustments in Canada began in 1989 when Imperial acquired 78 percent of the operations of Texaco Canada for more than $4 billion. Included were promising upstream prospects along with several refineries and a large collection of service stations.[6] Canada's Bureau of Competition Policy began the process of downsizing those holdings when it required Imperial to sell Texaco's 20,000-barrel-a-day refinery in

Nova Scotia, some 638 service stations, and an oil terminal before approving the acquisition in early February 1990.[7] More cuts were in store. The purchase added to Imperial's debt burden, and Imperial's downstream business experienced a loss in 1990, the first in the company's history.[8] Robert Wilhelm, a senior vice president at Exxon with long experience downstream, visited Imperial and reported back ominously to New York: "We have a real mess on our hands." He noted that the company, not particularly cost-efficient to begin with, had "absorbed all this overhead and cost structure from Texaco." His verdict: "They should have fewer facilities, less assets and less people." What was required was "a lot of come-to-Jesus meetings, where Imperial was charged with getting their operations reconfigured to be competitive."[9]

Wilhelm was astonished that in the midst of its financial problems, Imperial had purchased land in Toronto for a new headquarters building, when in his view it should have cut costs by moving to Calgary. The problem, he concluded, was the attitude of Imperial's management: "At the time, they really thought of themselves as being the preeminent company in Canada. But you know, the preeminent company in Canada can't lose money."[10]

In 1992, a new CEO, Robert Peterson, took charge and began the process of downsizing and cost cutting. Under Peterson's leadership, Imperial closed 1,000 service stations, reduced its workforce by 1,700 employees, and reorganized by consolidating chemical, petroleum, and other operations. In 1992, it shut its refinery in Port Moody, British Columbia, and in 1994, it sold Cascade Fertilizers, which it had held for less than five years. Those cutbacks, though painful, allowed Imperial to repay the cost of the Texaco Canada acquisition and moved it back into the black.

Despite that impressive comeback, Imperial's purchase of Texaco Canada underscored the long-term tensions caused by the large minority interest; in Lee Raymond's recollection, "All we heard from Imperial for years was the [need to consider] the minority shareholder."[11] Similar problems arose, however, in Exxon's fully owned affiliates, which at times asserted considerable authority to shape their own destinies—even when their choices might be at odds with the long-term interests of the corporation as a whole.

From the mid-1980s onward, top management at Exxon Corporation gradually asserted more complete control of the company as a whole. The movement of Exxon Chemical to a global organization in 1986 required a cooperative agreement with Imperial that gave Exxon Chemical the final say over chemical operations in Canada, with regular reports to Imperial's board.[12] Under that arrangement, proposals for investments by Imperial on chemical issues went to Exxon Chemical, which then brought them before Exxon's corporate management committee. There, Lee Raymond and others committed to financial discipline had the power to say no. Such was the case when Imperial kept requesting the capital to build a "big chemical plant up in Edmonton." According to Raymond, "Every year they would come in . . . [and say we] want to build this plant. And we just said, 'No. We're just not going to do that.'"[13] Such organizational tensions were more directly addressed after the Mobil merger, when ExxonMobil took Mobil's holdings in Canada and organized a Canadian affiliate independent of Imperial. The break illustrated the difficulties that could hamper systematic efforts to increase efficiency by cutting facilities and costs, particularly when top management hesitated to impose its authority.

Top management had little choice in the key events that led to drastic reductions in the company's downstream business in Latin America. Venezuelan oil had played a central role in the growth of Exxon from the 1920s into the 1970s, with a large refinery on the island of Aruba and the Amuay plant on the Venezuelan mainland supplying as much as 20 percent of the company's global refining capacity by the early 1970s. In the postwar years, petroleum products from those plants flowed to the United States and Europe and around the world, and the company's loss of that capacity after the energy crisis resulted in both a giant drop in its refining capacity and basic adjustments to its patterns of marketing.

Exxon lost access to Amuay through nationalization on the last day of 1975. At the time, it was one of the largest refineries in the world.[14] The refinery's location had been chosen after World War II by the Venezuelan government, in part in response to its desire to have major facilities that processed Venezuela oil inside the country. When the government made that "request," it had much in mind the history of Exxon's second refinery that processed Venezuelan crude, its large plant on Aruba. Standard Oil of Indiana (later Amoco) had built the plant in 1929 because it was near

Venezuelan oil (less than seventeen miles offshore), but outside the reach of the Venezuelan government (Aruba was and is a Dutch possession). Standard of Indiana completed the refinery just before the onset of the Great Depression, and circumstances forced it to sell the plant along with its substantial holdings in Venezuela to Jersey Standard in 1932. In the postwar era, the plant prospered along with the Venezuelan oil industry, expanding steadily from 250,000 barrels a day to 500,000 barrels a day in the early 1970s.[15] As Exxon sought to retain access to Venezuelan oil despite the pending nationalization of its properties there in the 1970s, the Aruba plant remained an important consideration.

The plant remained profitable after nationalization primarily because of a highly advantageous arrangement for the purchase of Venezuelan crude, which had been negotiated by Lee Raymond, then the plant manager. Raymond understood that both Exxon and the Venezuelan government had strong incentives to keep oil flowing through the plant in the aftermath of nationalization. By the early 1980s, however, the Venezuelans wanted out of the contract to supply Aruba; they had developed the capacity to refine the heavy crude oil in their owned refineries.

The push was on within Exxon to reduce excess refining capacity in 1984 when Raymond, then the contact director at the corporate level for downstream operations, looked again at the fate of the Aruba refinery.[16] One of his first steps was to endorse the recommendation of Robert Wilhelm, at that time the head of Esso Inter-America in Coral Gables, Florida, to dispose of the refinery.[17] Wilhelm knew that if the refinery could not process advantageously priced Venezuelan heavy crude oil, it would be unprofitable to operate. After exploring other options, Wilhelm advised shutting down the refinery. Raymond agreed with Wilhelm's main point: when the favorable crude-oil supply arrangement with Venezuela "goes away, this refinery is right back to where it was before. . . . [The Aruba refinery is] not going to make it."[18]

Looking back on this and other decisions about reducing downstream operations during that era, Raymond expressed the belief that the company began to concentrate more on return than volume: "We had built way too much refining capacity to begin with, and [the reductions were] getting away from the notion that the company was driven by volume. . . . We started to say, volume isn't the name of the game. Ultimately what the shareholder's interested in is return. So if we're going to get the return up . . . you have to get the P&L [profit and loss] up by managing the costs and becoming more efficient . . . by getting rid of a bunch of assets that are never going to be able to help us."[19] Good asset management required hard-nosed realism; at times, historical patterns had to be altered, with losses cut so that resources could be shifted toward more promising investments.

Latin America had been a favored place for foreign investments by Exxon for much of the twentieth century. In the early 1970s, the company still had marketing operations in many Latin American nations and active exploration and production in several of them. But the loss of the linchpin of its investments in the region—its strong position in Venezuelan production and its two major refineries for that nation's oil—undermined its continued prosperity there. Low economic growth, national price controls in Argentina and elsewhere, the selling off of mineral ventures in Colombia and Chile, and competition from preferentially treated national companies all influenced Exxon's decision to limit future investments in Latin America.

In the 1980s, a clear alternative had emerged: the Asia-Pacific region. Exxon's presence in Australia, Japan, and Malaysia had been growing since the 1950s, and the company aggressively expanded its presence in the area from the 1980s onward—one of its defining strategic choices of the late twentieth century. Exxon in Asia is treated at length at the end of this chapter, but one statistic regarding refining capacity is instructive: from 1970 to 2005, Latin America's refining capacity as a percentage of the total capacity of Exxon and then ExxonMobil fell from 22 percent to 2 percent, driven by the loss of its Venezuelan and Aruban refineries. In the same years, Asia-Pacific refining rose from 6 percent of the company's total global refining capacity (almost all of which was in Japan) to 26 percent (which was spread through the region, but centered in Singapore). That growth made Exxon's refining capacity in the region roughly equal to its capacity in both Europe and the United States by 2005.

Growth in the Asia-Pacific region occurred as the company went about the work of shuttering or disposing of "high-cost running capacity" in other parts of the world. The resulting reductions fundamentally altered the location, size, and cost structure of Exxon's global system of refineries.

The number of Exxon refineries fell from fifty-five in 1975 to fewer than forty in the mid-1980s and to the low thirties by 1995. In the twenty years after 1973, the company slashed almost 40 percent of its refining capacity worldwide, dramatically reducing idle capacity. That restructuring was an important part of a broader movement toward a smaller total refining capacity handled by fewer and larger refineries—a configuration more suited to changing patterns of global supply and demand and the capture of economies of scale.[20]

INTERNATIONAL MARINE: THE RISE AND FALL OF EXXON'S TANKER FLEET

A somewhat similar process shaped fundamental changes in the company's tanker fleet in the late twentieth century. In the decades before the 1970s, the company had built new tankers to keep pace with its marine transportation needs in a market for oil that was later greatly altered by the dislocations and wild price swings of the post-energy-crisis world. The fleet transported increasingly large volumes of crude oil from fields in Venezuela and the Middle East to refineries near markets in North America, Canada, and Japan. The temporary closing of the Suez Canal in the late 1950s convinced many in the petroleum industry that extremely large "supertankers" could dramatically lower transportation costs even if they had to make longer voyages in order to avoid the canal. The industry built more and bigger tankers during the rapid expansion of the 1960s. Most large international oil companies owned their own fleets, but supplemented them with a growing number of vessels available on the charter market.[21] Higher oil prices reduced demand after the energy crisis, forcing a reevaluation of all downstream operations built in response to the sustained expansion after World War II. In marine transportation, as in refining, Exxon found itself with a large overcapacity in tankers, and considerable uncertainty about the future of the market for shipping crude.

By the earlier 1970s, Exxon had an impressive "navy" at its disposal, with more than 300 total vessels and a capacity of more than ten million deadweight tons (dwt). Anticipating that the need for large tankers would continue to grow in the 1970s, the company had numerous new tankers on order in 1973, and it continued to accept delivery of new tankers into the late 1980s. By the mid-1970s, it listed the "average capital employed" by its international marine company as slightly less than $2 billion. As shown in figure 8.3, the company's owned tanker capacity peaked at 17.3 million dwt in 1978; its total capacity, including chartered vessels, had peaked the year before at 25.4 million dwt. This was a significant business, but one with an unpredictable future. Much higher oil prices might substantially reduce global demand, drastically reducing the need for long-distance shipments. The discovery of new sources of crude nearer or farther from major centers of oil consumption also might disrupt old patterns of transportation. Finally, the frequently proposed development of new sources of domestic energy in major consuming regions might cut deeply into the tanker market, making it a relic of an age of growing imports.

Exxon allowed the tanker market to sort itself out before making decisions about the future of its own fleet. In 1976, the company chose to continue to reduce the number of vessels in its fleet while increasing the efficiency and size of its ships. This required purchasing the most modern large tankers and selling or scrapping older, smaller vessels. As suggested by figure 8.3, the company had a bias toward using tankers it owned, and it steadily reduced the company's use of chartered vessels, which fell from about half of the capacity used by the company in 1973 to less than 15 percent by 1986. From 1976 onward, the company sold or scrapped five to ten tankers each year, steadily reducing its total deadweight tonnage to approximately 8.7 million by 1986—or about half the capacity it had owned only eight years earlier. The growth in demand for oil in response to much lower prices after 1986 led to a brief reversal of the trend as Exxon brought previously idled tankers out of storage to transport the larger volumes of oil. In 1988, it reported that its international tanker fleet had been "fully utilized" for the first time in six years.[22]

The next year, the *Exxon Valdez* oil spill focused the attention of the world on the company's tanker fleet. That vessel was one of the largest and most modern in the fleet when it was delivered in 1986; after 1989, it became a symbol within the company of the environmental risks associated with the ownership of a major fleet of tankers. The oil spill placed an edge on discussions of tanker ownership by Exxon.

The harder edge in the debate had long been clear in the financial statistics so important to the management of Exxon. From 1973 through 1986,

FIGURE 8.3. Decline of Exxon's Owed Tanker Capacity, 1970-1990 (million dead weight tons)

	MDWT			MDWT
1970	8.1		1981	16.8
1971	9.5		1982	15.2
1972	10.3		1983	13.3
1973	11.6		1984	12.0
1974	13.5		1985	11.2
1975	15.2		1986	8.7
1976	15.0		1987	8.1
1977	16.4		1988	8.2
1978	17.3		1989	7.9
1979	16.6		1990	7.0
1980	16.7			

Source: *ExxonMobil Financial and Operating Reviews, 1970–1980 and 1973–2005*

the international marine function lost money in more years than it made money. Its average capital employed peaked at almost $2 billion and then plunged steadily down to $490 million in 1986. From 1975 through 1986, its highest return on capital was about 5 percent (in 1976), and it lost money in seven of the next ten years. Larger, more efficient tankers had not improved financial results in a depressed shipping market at a time of falling demand for oil.

Thus, in 1988, the company announced the "completion of a major fleet restructuring program" that had greatly reduced both the number of vessels owned by Exxon and their carrying capacity, improving "the economic utilization of the international marine fleet."[23] Then in 1990, after the *Exxon Valdez* accident, it announced the completion of the sale of its last four "ultra-large crude carriers," the largest category of tanker.[24] After that, no other announcements about the tanker fleet were made in

Esso Atlantic, *an ultra-large crude carrier (ULCC), offloading to another tanker in the Gulf of Mexico, March 1978. ExxonMobil Historical Collection, di_06235.*

the annual reports or the supplemental financial and operating statistics. The company had decided that it had better uses for its capital than the maintenance of a large fleet of generally unprofitable tankers, which carried a very high hidden cost in the event of an oil spill. It could more safely and cheaply charter the capacity it needed in a renters' market. Those decisions exemplified Exxon's efforts to manage assets to ensure their efficient overall use within the company, and to manage risks so as to avoid large-scale liabilities. Marine transportation was no longer considered a core function of Exxon; it was past time to cut the losses and move on to more pressing problems.

TOWARD A COMPREHENSIVE, EXPLICIT DOWNSTREAM STRATEGY

The core downstream function was refining. Reducing idle capacity and eliminating the smallest and least efficient plants were necessary steps in a long-term adjustment in the location, operating efficiency, and product mix of the company's refineries. Indeed, new management acknowledged in 1990 the importance of the "decisive rationalization of excess refining capacity" from 1980 to 1985, when, "acting ahead of our competitors, Exxon reduced high-cost running capacity by 1.5 million barrels per day, or 27 percent."[25] Going forward, Exxon would need further fundamental changes to continue to improve its competitiveness by forcing refining costs down.

One clear impetus behind the change in those years was the commitment of top management to take charge of the definition and implementation of strategy. The genesis of the change was the frustration of Rawl and Raymond, at the time of the 1986 cutbacks, over the lack of a process for assigning and assessing managerial responsibility. As explained by Raymond: "[The problem was] who's really responsible for this? Who wants X to happen? Who's really responsible for making X happen? And does the person know he's responsible? And . . . if he's responsible, then have we delegated a kind of authority the person needs to be able to get [things] done? . . . People need to know what it is that they are trying to do. So how do you communicate that?"[26] The company needed clearer lines of responsibility, with sufficient authority and power vested in top management to hold executives responsible for their success or failure in implementing strategic objectives.

The downsizing of the 1980s was accompanied by the upgrading of facilities. New refineries replaced older ones; larger tankers took the place of numerous smaller, less efficient ones. Such changes, however, moved forward in the absence of an explicit strategy for long-term improvements in refining. As late as 1989, the company's annual report still discussed downstream activities under a series of headings that would have been applicable throughout the decade. These included positioning the downstream for new growth, adding convenience stores, improving consumer convenience when paying at the pump, building more flexible refining facilities, and focusing on product specialty markets. In the 1990s, those objectives and strategies coalesced into a more comprehensive, explicit strategy for downstream operations.

By 1991, the company had defined the new business strategies. Rather than dictate goals and objectives, corporate leaders asked each business segment to submit a list of its own goals. If Rawl and Raymond felt the appropriate strategies had been identified, they endorsed the list. If not, they suggested modifications. They sought to go beyond the old "no objections" approach of the corporate management committee. They wanted to be strategists, not overseers. The duty of top management was to plan the way forward for the company and then to allocate resources to those in the organization who could make the plans come true. Corporate goals took priority over regional or business functional goals, thereby creating a sense of managerial and operational unity throughout the corporation.

Raymond expressed this as follows: "One of the overarching themes that we started in the late 1980s and continued is 'Hey, guys, we're all in this together. . . . We all succeed or we all fail.'" He also remembered, however, that Rawl usually added a pointed reminder: "If you guys out there come in here and tell us here's what we want to do and we say yes and it fails, we [all] fail . . . [but] if you guys out there do something and you don't tell us and it fails, you fail."[27] Accountability had to flow through the company all the way to the top, where strategy had to be made based on the interest of the corporation as a whole, not on the sum of the interests of all its parts. Those at the top had the ultimate responsibility for defining effective corporate strategy and then embodying it in both the allocation of capital and the functions assigned to employees.

Regarding the allocation of capital, Rawl and Raymond had lost confidence in the existing system, which relied heavily on financial analyses prepared by the regional companies and affiliates to show whether a particular project could meet a specified "hurdle rate" for return on investment. Jack Bennett was also among those growing increasingly skeptical of the traditional approach, which had made sense in the long era of oil-price stability after World War II. But hurdle rates raised difficult problems in the post-energy-crisis years, since they required dependable projections of oil prices and government policies.[28] Distrusting the financial projections included in many such proposals, Rawl and Raymond fashioned an approach to capital allocation more attuned to the long-term strategic goals of the corporation as a whole.

First came a "capital prioritization exercise" in the late 1980s in which they required each major operating unit to submit a budget based on the possibility of a 20 percent budget cut across the board. This forced each regional company to prepare a prioritized list of projects that would be eliminated under the proposed budget restraints. Top corporate

Rene Dahan upon his election to the Exxon Corporation board of directors, 1997. ExxonMobil Historical Collection, di_06100.

management used the lists to identify both the most attractive and the least attractive projects and to begin to reallocate capital among the companies. That decision made the regions and affiliates compete more aggressively for capital, and gave Rawl and Raymond firmer control of the corporation's destiny. They reinforced the message by filling the top management ranks with executives who had demonstrated their willingness to work for the general corporate interest rather than that of a particular regional company or affiliate.[29]

One such executive, Rene Dahan, played an important role in defining an explicit strategy for the downstream functions. The precise wording of the strategy evolved throughout the 1990s, but the overall direction remained the same and the objectives remained clear. The annual report in 1998, the year of the announcement of the intent to merge with Mobil, listed six key elements of downstream strategy:

Develop a best-in-class cost structure
Increase sales of high-value fuels and specialty products
Capitalize on refining integration with chemicals and specialty
    businesses
Invest selectively in high-return projects
Maximize total retail sales
Rapidly develop and deploy leading-edge technologies[30]

In many ways, the first item on the list subsumed all others: Exxon's key strategic goal was to recapture its historical position as the low-cost refiner. It pursued that objective with a relentless zeal that would have made John D. Rockefeller proud.

UPGRADING DOWNSTREAM OPERATIONS

Successful strategy is, of course, a matter of implementation more than the statement of objectives. The strategy of the 1990s pulled together many initiatives already in progress and introduced other new programs. It became the basis of a sustained drive to make Exxon's downstream operations the benchmark for others in the industry. Several important aspects of the strategy are discussed below, including continuous reductions in costs of labor and fuel and the upgrading of operations with global management systems, technology to increase refinery flexibility and product quality, and the integration of refinery and chemical operations.

CONTINUOUS REDUCTION OF COSTS: LABOR

One primary operating cost downstream was the workforce. In the 1980s, the streamlining of oil-related operations, combined with the divestment of numerous non-oil businesses, dramatically reduced the number of employees at Exxon as a whole. In 1981, the company employed 180,000 people. In early 1986, it employed 135,000 before the wave of reorganizations and divestments cut 33,000 more employees, reducing the total to 102,000 in 1987. After a drop of more than 45 percent from 1981 to 1987, employment stabilized until 1995, when it resumed a slow descent. A big part of the reductions came in refining and chemicals, where automation of operations steadily reduced the number of workers.[31]

Both the magnitude and the pace of the 1986 employee reductions, as well as the human costs, left a lasting impression on top management. Raymond and Rawl agreed about the important lesson learned: "We should never have to do that again. . . . The reality is that change is going to be with us forever, and rather than getting ourselves way behind so we have to do this huge catch-up . . . the only way to do that is to work on that problem every day of every year."[32] Cost control—for labor, fuel, or any other operating expense—had to be continual to be effective.

This was clearest in the refineries and chemical plants, which historically had large workforces. Cliff Garvin remembered his early days after World War II at the Baton Rouge refinery, when "there were six or seven thousand people, and it was less than half the size it is today [2006]."[33] From the 1960s onward, the application of new technology increased the capacity of refineries and the complexity of their products while also greatly reducing their workforces. Large manufacturing plants such as oil refineries and chemical plants applied modern computing to numerous tasks, such as monitoring conditions in the refining process. Control rooms once filled with workers twenty-four hours a day later held banks of computer monitors staffed by a handful of employees. Compared with people, computers monitored processes more efficiently, more closely, and more systematically.

In the years after World War II, the company developed an intensive system of regular employee reviews. After the 1980s, competitive pressures in the review process intensified as Exxon cut back on the number of its employees. In placing individuals into a general category, evaluators were forced to identify the best and worst performers in a group. The top 20 percent could expect good raises; those in the bottom 10 percent found themselves in performance improvement programs, a sort of halfway house from which they were expected to move up or face dismissal.

Acknowledging the reality of ongoing labor reductions, the approach sought to continuously "upgrade" Exxon's workforce, at once reducing its size and improving its efficiency.

CONTINUOUS REDUCTION OF COSTS: FUEL

When oil prices spiked dramatically in the 1970s, Exxon quickly redoubled its commitment to efficiency, since fuel cost was an important component of the total cost of refining and chemical production. As long as oil and natural gas prices remained high, many investments in the more efficient use of energy could be justified, since they promised quick returns that were often large enough to repay capital costs relatively quickly. Even after much lower oil prices returned in the mid-1980s, the company continued to focus on energy-cost reduction as a significant part of its quest to cut all expenses.[34]

The giant scale of Exxon's petroleum refining and chemical operations meant that energy costs directly affected the bottom line in ways too expensive to ignore.[35] The most obvious target was refining; studies in the early 1970s showed that the processing of each ten barrels of product required the consumption of about one barrel of oil equivalent. In the United States alone, this meant that Exxon's five refineries, which had a combined capacity of 1.2 million barrels a day, used about 120,000 BOE as fuel each day. Cutting that figure by 15 percent would produce energy savings of more than 6 million barrels of oil each year. With oil selling at about $15 a barrel, the savings justified new housecleaning initiatives, training programs to alter the habits and attitudes of workers, the redesign of existing equipment, and substantial investments in new equipment.[36]

Making energy efficiency a more important part of Exxon's daily operations required more knowledge of its energy use. Exxon USA led the way by forming a task force to study conservation across all its operations. Surveys of individual plants quickly identified potential investments with high rates of return from cost savings from reduced energy use. Studies of ways to reduce fuel use in shipping led to the preparation of an energy-conservation manual to share the information broadly throughout shipping operations. Exxon Research and Engineering prepared an "energy profile" of a typical refinery in order to identify every point at which energy "enters a refinery, is used and is ultimately discarded." Exxon distributed the results of those and other studies throughout its global organization to assist its affiliates in becoming more energy efficient.[37]

The company's long-term goal was to conserve energy with both money and ingenuity. Cleaning up processes and practices inherited from an era of inexpensive fuel costs was an early priority, and there were plenty of easy changes that could make a difference. Quick dividends came from insulating boilers and pipes, making more systematic and timely repairs of steam leaks, preheating of fuels before their use, adjusting furnaces to be more efficient, replacing oversized pumps and compressors with smaller ones, and using computer controls more rigorously to manage energy use.

The habits of mind and the wasteful practices developed when fuel prices remained low also had to be altered. Management stressed to employees "that saving energy is a top priority." Training programs emphasized the need for an energy-conservation ethic in operations and maintenance, and encouraged employees to take a hard look at traditional practices. Although the most easily identifiable energy savings were in refining and chemical production, substantial savings were also found in tanker operations and oil production. Energy efficiency quickly became an important part of Exxon's daily operations in all regions and all functions, and it gradually became embedded in the company's corporate culture.

Significant long-term gains often required substantial investments. Espousing the benefits of conservation, CEO Cliff Garvin urged in 1977 that it was time "to get on with it." He acknowledged that as a large industrial company with high energy use, "if we're efficient, we'll make a return."[38] Large-scale energy-efficiency investments had to pass the same test required of all major Exxon investments by producing rates of returns better than competing projects. But given high energy prices, the early adoption of new equipment at times quietly paid for itself through savings on energy, even when existing equipment had to be retired from operations earlier than planned.

One important example illustrates the basic technical changes that were central to the more efficient use of fuel. An estimated 75 percent of the energy consumed in refineries in the early 1970s was used as fuel for furnaces that produced the steam required to process crude oil. More efficient furnaces proved to be very good investments. Traditional furnaces had been designed and operated with little concern for the heat content of the flue (waste) gases sent up the stacks and out into the atmosphere at very high temperatures. New designs and heat-recovery equipment could capture much of the previously lost heat, providing substantial energy savings. The "coordinator for refinery energy-saving programs at Exxon USA" noted that the "heat recovery equipment is expensive and we're committing substantial investment to it."[39] Such large investments in capital and management continued throughout the high oil-price years into the mid-1980s. The coming of much lower prices revealed, however, that improvement in energy efficiency had become a permanent part of Exxon's operations.

The focus of energy efficiency at Exxon after 1978 became cogeneration, a good business practice that yielded dramatic energy savings. Cogeneration became more attractive after the Public Utility Holding Company Act of 1978 required U.S. utilities to purchase excess electricity produced "off the grid." The act provided an additional incentive to large manufacturers to expand cogeneration.[40] Cogeneration as practiced by Exxon generally involved the capture of steam from the generation of electricity for "reuse" as heat in refining and chemical manufacturing processes. Before the 1970s, most refineries had purchased electricity from local utility companies and produced steam within the plants, usually using natural gas or even fuel oil as fuel. Exxon estimated in 1989 that by putting those separate functions together, companies could save 10 to 30 percent on energy use.[41] Those savings made cogeneration a logical investment for many large plants, depending on their need for heat, the availability of fuel, and the price of electricity from local utilities.[42]

The impact of cogeneration on costs can be seen in the example of a $65 million project that began operations in 1989 at Exxon Chemical Company's plant in Baytown. At the time, the project was Exxon's largest cogeneration facility in the world. The Baytown Turbine Generator Project featured three newly constructed gas-turbine generators capable of providing more than 110 megawatts (MW) of electricity, enough to supply about 100,000 homes. The turbines were coupled with a heat-recovery generator to capture steam for other uses in the plant. That combination well suited the needs of a plant that required considerable amounts of electricity for mechanical work such as driving motors, as well as large volumes of thermal energy (in the form of steam or dry heat) to

Baytown Cogeneration Plant under construction, 1997.
ExxonMobil Historical Collection, di_06225.

process chemicals. Savings came in two forms. The company generated its own electricity at a lower price than it could purchase power from an outside supplier, and it saved natural gas by recycling it for two uses. Next door in the Baytown refinery, ongoing construction of cogeneration facilities made the plant self-sufficient in the production of both steam and electricity.[43] By reducing fuel use, cogeneration also reduced emissions into the air. As a bonus, cogeneration reduced the company's dependence on outside suppliers of energy, giving it greater control over planning.[44] It is no wonder that cogeneration became the norm as Exxon's global refining and chemical plants grew in scale.

The results were impressive. The company had been investing in cogeneration plants as far back as 1950, and those efforts increased with the high oil prices of the 1970s. By 1980, Exxon had installed slightly more than 500 MW of capacity in its refineries and chemical plants. During the 1980s, capacity grew by another 1,000 MW to reach 1,500 MW. Exxon added another 1,000 MW in the 1990s. By 2000, ExxonMobil had installed in excess of 2,500 MW, a figure that jumped in 2005 to about 3,700 MW of installed capacity, with eighty-five installations at thirty locations. The technology was extended to select petroleum-production facilities, where plant heat was generated to separate crude oil and natural gas.

In 1998, twenty-five years after the 1973 embargo accelerated Exxon's efforts to conserve energy, the company reported that the "refineries and chemical plants of Exxon and its affiliates" had cut their total energy consumption by about 35 percent since 1973. Over a quarter of a century, those efforts produced a total savings of about 1.2 billion BOE, a daily average of more than 130,000 BOE.[45]

In 1999, Exxon embedded its commitment to energy efficiency in a new initiative, the Global Energy Management System (G-EMS). In the tradition of the 1970s surveys of energy use and the energy profiles developed by Exxon Research, G-EMS brought together refining and chemical-plant managers with leaders in research and engineering organizations to develop a sustainable approach for continually reducing energy use worldwide. Under the leadership of Rene Dahan, the team developed manuals for best practices for energy efficiency in key aspects of plant operations. The system developed a common methodology for plants worldwide to identify ways to cut energy use and to evaluate their effectiveness.[46] That systematic, global approach to cost reductions built on previous programs within different parts of Exxon, and it produced long-term results that increased profitability.

UPGRADING THROUGH GLOBAL MANAGEMENT SYSTEMS

G-EMS had numerous forerunners within the company. The Operations Integrity Management System (OIMS) had used a somewhat similar approach to make clear improvements in safety. In the years before the creation of OIMS, Exxon Chemical had developed a forerunner program that was used in the design of OIMS. According to Ray Nesbitt, a president of Exxon Chemical, that program was designed to "improve our safety and our manufacturing performance, plus we wanted to take a whole bunch of cost out of our manufacturing operation."[47] Even before implementing OIMS, the company knew that better safety, energy efficiency, and similar systematic improvements in operations generally lowered costs.

Rene Dahan led the way in creating and applying several such management systems in his years at Exxon Company, International (ECI), where he had a direct impact on the large geographic area under his authority and an indirect effect on the company as a whole. Dahan was a native of Morocco and later a citizen of the Netherlands. He had been educated at the École Nationale des Officiers de la Marine Marchande in Casablanca, Morocco, and he subsequently attended the École d'Hydrographie in Bordeaux, France, where he received a degree in nautical science. After brief service aboard ship, he joined Esso in 1963 as a process technician in the company's Rotterdam refinery. He moved up in the company, becoming the manager of its Refining Department in 1974. Transferred to Esso Europe in London, he became the head of corporate planning in 1977 and took charge of the region's Natural Gas Department in 1978. From 1981 to 1983, he had a two-year stint at Exxon Corporation headquarters as deputy manager of the petroleum products company before returning to Europe from 1983 to 1991 as executive vice president and then president and CEO of Esso B.V., the operating company for all oil and gas operations in Belgium, the Netherlands, and Luxembourg. This included Exxon's major interest in the Groningen gas field as well as several refineries.

In 1991, he was appointed executive vice president of ECI and placed in charge of the company's worldwide downstream operations. Dahan brought to his work an unwavering commitment to the pursuit of operational excellence—and the related quest for competitive advantage through lower costs. His approach reflected his personality: "What I've done throughout my whole career, starting as a young engineer and technician in a refinery . . . has been driven by the same kind of belief. . . . [That] was to . . . very systematically work in the day-to-day performance of the entity you've got in hand." He understood the importance of downstream capacity reductions. But he also felt that Exxon had lost its traditional commitment to "execution, the work we do every day and the quality of that work, both in money terms and in performance terms," and he "worked systematically . . . to reintroduce this dedication to excellence in execution," which he considered the foundation of all that Exxon had done in the last ten years under Raymond: "At the end of the day, there's only one thing that makes a difference between a successful company and a so-so company, and that's how well you execute."[48]

After Dahan became president of ECI in 1992, he made the implementation of OIMS a priority there, explaining it to employees in the company's publication *Voyager* in September 1992. He was drawn to the rigorous use of benchmarking and the aggressive sharing of best practices through OIMS. Believing that approach could improve operational excellence in areas in addition to safety, health, and the environment, he set out to extend OIMS-like management systems to other operational areas and problems. His first effort at ECI came after serious problems in refining. One of ECI's Refining Department coordinators described the problem succinctly: "[The year] 1994 saw an even tighter squeeze on margins than it has seen in a long time, and there doesn't appear to be anything on the horizon to improve the situation. Therefore, we need to find better ways to reduce costs and improve profitability."[49] In response, Dahan spearheaded the creation of the Operating Improvement Program, which initially focused on refining operations. In more than fifty studies in 1994–1995 covering refineries within ECI and its competitors, special teams studied company cost structures and best practices on cost reduction. In addition, they evaluated optimum crude-oil slates, opportunities to reduce maintenance expenses, and the degree to which refineries had adopted the latest process technologies.

The benchmarking from those studies uncovered an uncomfortable reality: best practices found at Exxon facilities generally were applied only at some locations. This was not good enough for Dahan. He wanted an approach similar to OIMS, in which best practices were uncovered and then adopted throughout the company: "This is really a new mindset. It's a way of . . . deciding that we're not going to be satisfied with less than the best. Accepting that, in order to have the best all the time, we'll have to redesign and question. . . . We'll have to make use of all the information we can get our hands on. We'll have to use all the wisdom that is available within the organization."[50]

Determined to improve, ECI created another initiative, World Class 2000, which was aimed at identifying changes that could help Exxon attain industry-leading standards of operations. Its first targets included refinery maintenance, financial processes, terminal rationalization, retail site operations, order fulfillment, and procurement reengineering. The affiliates nominated experts in each of the areas to staff assessment and improvement teams. The members of the improvement team included three managers, eight full-time representatives from refineries in Europe and Japan, observers from Canada and the research company, and a high-level advisory and coordinating group of refinery managers. The groups brought considerable expertise to the task, which was to produce a "standardized, ECI-wide Maintenance and Reliability Management System" that could be applied worldwide. The process was by then familiar: determine best practices inside and outside the company by using detailed studies conducted by experts, spread those practices throughout the organization, create mechanisms to encourage continuous improvement, and systematically monitor the implementation of the standards. Subsequent issues of *Voyager*—and other Exxon publications—detailed the composition and objectives of each of the World Class 2000 teams, sending a loud message to employees that this was a program to be taken seriously and that its goal was to set the standard for the industry as a whole.[51]

As the programs went forward, in 1995, Dahan became a senior vice president of Exxon Corporation while retaining his position as president of ECI. He held that dual responsibility until he moved to Exxon Corporation headquarters in 1997. In late 1996, ECI rolled out another management system modeled after OIMS, the Controls Integrity Management System, which focused on the integrity, thoroughness, and reliability of the company's control procedures. Its work went beyond financial reporting to the reporting of accountability, assessing and managing risks, examining business practices, assessing and training personnel, and the reporting of deficiencies.

With a portfolio of standardized management systems in place, ECI had the tools with which to coordinate and monitor performance in a variety of important, if routine, functions. Although imposed and enforced from the top, the standards were developed by the experts who managed the company's operations. These OIMS-like management systems—along with advances in communications and computing technology—allowed Exxon to conduct its far-flung global business with a comparatively small cadre of senior managers. Dahan, who strongly believed that Exxon made a dramatic improvement in its management quality in the 1990s, summarized the overall impact of the initiatives: "In the second half of the nineties, results from across the board started to flow on a steady basis with broad and convincing messages that excellence in operations was paying off."[52]

Those results fed a growing realization that, according to Dahan, "management processes were effective and well understood throughout the company," and as a result, the company was "better able than ever before to use [its] vast, high-quality central resources to impact performance in the field."[53] The relentless pursuit of operational excellence became a central part of Exxon's overall corporate strategy in the 1990s. It contributed greatly to realizing the top strategic priority of downstream operations— to "develop best-in-class cost structure."[54]

UPGRADING FLEXIBILITY AND PRODUCT QUALITY WITH TECHNOLOGY

One important strategic objective for the downstream was to rapidly develop and deploy leading-edge technologies. The company had a century-long history of leadership in technology, and it had been especially successful in finding new processes for "upgrading" crude oil by removing sulfur. The application of new technology in the 1970s and 1980s introduced a new era of sulfur removal that gave refineries the capacity to convert what had long been considered low-value "residual oil" into cleaner, more valuable products. At the same time, new technology allowed the industry to develop the cleaner-burning motor fuels needed to meet stricter environmental standards. Exxon developed proprietary technologies that made more extensive and more profitable use of the product stream running through its refineries and chemical plants, thereby increasing the value added by refining. In so doing, it increased the profitability of downstream operations by lowering the costs of refining and increasing the proportion of higher-value products produced.

After eliminating smaller, less inefficient plants in the 1970s and 1980s, Exxon could focus more sharply on the construction of refineries and chemical plants large enough to justify investments in the most advanced technical processes. Advanced technology increased the company's flexibility in choosing both the feedstocks and the end products in the refining process. The company was spending billions of dollars around the world in the search for new supplies of crude oil in the years after 1973; at the same time, advanced refining technology allowed it to find a "new" source of oil right under its nose in its refineries. Heavy oil (that is, oil with a high viscosity) and sour oil (that is, oil with high sulfur content) were available at discounts in comparison with the lighter and "sweeter" crudes historically preferred by refiners.

Technology allowed the company to convert heavier and sourer crudes into higher-quality products. In addition, it improved the amount of product a refinery could produce from its total run of oil, converting even "residual" fuel oil—long assumed to be of little value for anything except ship bunker fuel or heavy heating oil—into more valuable products. Technology worked its magic largely unnoticed by those who used motor fuels or other refined products. Indeed, the oil industry's regular reminders that no new refineries had been built from scratch in the United States since the 1970s somewhat obscured the reality of an ongoing refining revolution, since new equipment replaced outmoded technology at existing plants, and incremental expansions raised total refining capacities.

One important part of the upgrading of plants was the adoption of the best available technology on the largest possible scale. In 1976–1977, Exxon's large refinery at Baytown was expanded by almost 50 percent with the addition of 250,000 barrels a day of new capacity. The cost was $500 million, making it, at the time, "one of the largest refinery construction projects in the history of the oil industry." The scale and technical complexity were pathbreaking and required stretching existing technology to its limits. The project gave the Baytown refinery a capacity of 640,000 barrels a day, the largest in the United States.[55]

The giant expansion at Baytown included two technological advances that increased the plant's flexibility to make the most profitable use of crude oil. The first was "the world's largest Powerformer," a unit that increased the production and quality of lead-free high-octane gasoline. That fuel was much in demand as the industry made the painful and expensive transition away from leaded gasoline. The second, the residfiner unit, improved performance at the low end of the refining process by removing sulfur from the heavy residual fuel oil produced during refining. The process had been developed by Exxon Research, which spent much of the 1970s and 1980s looking for ways to obtain usable oil from unconventional sources, including heavy oils, oil sands, and oil shale. In some ways, the new process sought the same result: the production of high quality new products from a decidedly unconventional source, the residual fuel oil that remained at the end of the traditional refining processes.

The proprietary residfiner process had never been used on a commercial scale before the Baytown expansion, and it opened new markets for cleaner products derived from heavy residual oil. The expansion at the plant took place in consultation with the EPA and state environmental regulators to ensure compliance with air- and water-quality standards. The use of advances in energy efficiency made the new units about 50 percent more energy efficient than traditional refineries, producing a savings of about 8,000 barrels of oil equivalent per day. The massive project demonstrated the economies available when new technology was incorporated into large new construction projects. According to an Exxon spokesman, "When you're designing what amounts to a new refinery, you have a golden opportunity to find the most efficient way to join the thing together."[56]

Improvements in residfining technology became an important area for Exxon researchers. One result was an ambitious $635 million Resid Upgrade Project at Baytown in the mid-1980s. The project illustrated both the use of technology to respond to changing market conditions and the ongoing quest to use improved technology to add as much value as possible to crude oil. The Baytown refinery previously had developed the capacity to process many high-sulfur crudes, but as Mobil and ARCO moved ahead quickly in the processing of residual fuel oil, Exxon faced a choice: should it expand its own conversion efforts?

The company was well positioned to compete in this area. It had available high-sulfur crude produced from its Santa Ynez Unit in Southern California, from purchases of Mayan crude from Mexico, and from other sources supplying its European refineries. The goal of the new project was to increase the rate of converting fuel oil to oil that could be refined into "lighter" and cleaner products. Here, the scale of Exxon's operations came into play, since reaching even higher conversion levels required substantial investment, which could be justified only by full use of the large new unit. The desire to use the upgraded Baytown and Baton Rouge refineries more fully was an incentive for Exxon to reduce the amount of crude oil processed at its less efficient and older Bayway refinery in New Jersey before selling it in 1992.[57]

A similar process went forward in Exxon Chemical. In 1979, the "largest capital project the company had ever undertaken," the $500 million construction of a major olefins plant at Baytown, "ushered in a new era" of competitiveness in the manufacture of an important basic chemical product. A point of pride was the unit's computerized control center, an important technical addition in an industry requiring the careful monitoring of manufacturing conditions. The investment secured the company's competitive position for a product that was one of the foundations of Exxon Chemical's success.[58]

Sometimes, a lack of state-of-the-art technology threatened the company's ability to enter or survive in markets where other companies were ahead in the use of larger-scale construction and advanced technology. That was the case for another Exxon Chemical product, polypropylene. In 1981, the company identified key problems at its Baytown chemical plant, where it found "the technology employed" to be "inefficient and outdated." It requested and received permission from the Exxon

A 1986 expansion at Exxon Chemical's olefins plant in Baytown, Texas, significantly increased plant capacity for making high-grade propylene, a key ingredient in many plastics, ca. 1987. ExxonMobil Historical Collection, di_08131.

Management Committee to replace the existing equipment with "modern technology employing our proprietary catalyst technology." Doing so would "provide us with manufacturing costs equal to the lowest in the industry."[59] The existing equipment was replaced not because it was in disrepair; it simply was not competitive with that used by other companies. Investments—large and small—in new technology drove the company's steady upgrading of its refineries and chemical plants.

In chemicals, as in refining, another strong incentive for investments in new technology was to help control long-term costs by making plants more flexible in their use of raw materials. Ed Galante explained the historical importance of this flexibility: "Back in the days . . . [when] gas was inexpensive . . . we, perhaps ahead of our times, built a lot of feed-flexible cracking units in chemical plants. Today . . . you're taking fuel oils and other things that are not valued commodities out in the marketplace as fuel, feeding them through these crackers, and making high-valued chemical products."[60] To gain such cost advantages, a company had to be willing to invest substantial sums in new technology and improved plant facilities. Pursuing that strategy required both the patience and confidence to invest throughout cycles in the chemical industry in pursuit of long-term benefits.

UPGRADING THROUGH THE INTEGRATION OF REFINERY AND CHEMICAL OPERATIONS

From the 1990s onward, one of the most significant sources of greater efficiency, flexibility, and profitability downstream was the integration of the operations of refineries and chemical plants at single large sites. Chemical production had grown within the company's refineries for almost half a century before being pulled out and organized into a separate company in 1965. That independence allowed Exxon Chemical to grow into a major chemical enterprise. Yet according to one experienced downstream executive, Ed Hess, "We still had a lot of interaction with [chemicals]. . . . Chemicals would take a stream, and they worked on it, and then they would send us something back that was different."[61] The two industries intersected at numerous levels, including feedstocks, locations, and manufacturing processes. As cooperation between refining and chemicals within Exxon grew and as the scale of the plants became gigantic, it became clear that more systematic integration of operations could yield significant opportunities for the company as whole.

The consolidation of refining and chemical production at single sites faced barriers built by decades of separate operations. Lee Raymond remembered one "unintended consequence" of the breaking out of chemicals from refining: "We set up two warring tribes" on the shared sites.[62] Memories of the second-class treatment given to chemicals within refineries before the creation of Exxon Chemical made managers of chemical plants reluctant to give up any independence. Yet change came, and its impact was far-reaching. Galante remembered the difference between the times of looser and closer integration. In the mid-1980s, refineries and chemical plants on the same location, as in Baton Rouge, "each had their own lawyer, they each had their own HR [human relations] guy, they each had their own public affairs guy, they each had their own doctor"; since integration, all those "services are now common across the site." One potent symbol of the progress of management integration stood out for him: "In many cases [in the 1980s], the managers sat in different buildings. Today, more and more, the managers are sitting in a common office suite . . . as they try to manage" in ways that maximize the performance of the complex as a whole, not necessarily of their individual plants.[63] Synergies were available in other areas. The major refineries and chemical plants shared support services, facilities investment planning, cogeneration and fuel acquisition and use, and technology development and commercialization, extending all the way to joint research and development. The object, after all, was the long-term profitability of Exxon Corporation as a whole.

Molecules were the heart of the matter. Raw materials flowed into the refinery-chemical complexes and flowed out as products. The key was to find ways to add the most value to the raw material in the manufacturing complex. As Galante described it: "The objective is [when we] bring a molecule in, how do we get the most value out of [it] in what we make coming out of the complex."[64] The choices were complex and ongoing as the raw material moved through the manufacturing process. "Streams" of hydrocarbons flowed back and forth between processing units in the refineries and chemical plants en route to the best use of what remained in each stream. As integration between the refineries and the chemical plants grew, the interfaces during the manufacturing process became more numerous and more technically sophisticated. Mathematical and chemical studies helped determine the best use of each stream; cooperative management at the site helped ensure maximum benefits from the integration of operations.[65]

One long-term benefit of such interchanges came in the development of new products. For example, an early demonstration of the potential benefit of closer operational ties between refineries and chemical plants came in the production of additives for reformulated gasoline in the United States. Here the company found that "synergies with Exxon's adjacent chemical plant facilities have significantly reduced the level of investment required for producing reformulated gasoline."[66] Similar economies were found in the production of additives for cleaner-burning diesel fuel in Europe and Asia.[67] Beyond fuel additives lay a range of other promising synergies between refining and chemical production, including new chemical products, greater conversion capacity in refineries, cleaner production due to the use of more of the hydrocarbon streams, and perhaps eventually even the economic production of a variety of synthetic fuels.

The benefits of closer cooperation between large refineries and chemical plants located on the same sites encouraged Exxon to target such sites for much of its new investments in both areas after the 1990s. Those efforts produced a new generation of world-scale refining-chemical complexes at Baton Rouge and Baytown in the United States; at Antwerp, Port Jerome, Rotterdam, and Fawley in Europe; at Kawasaki in Japan; and at Singapore and Sriracha (Thailand) in Asia. After the Mobil merger, additional complexes in Beaumont, Texas, and Altona, Australia, were added to the list.[68]

The integration of refineries and chemical plants was one part of a movement toward fewer but larger plants, which would employ new conversion technologies. Another significant shift in the years after 1973 was the emphasis on continuous and systematic cost management, which became increasingly important in the 1990s. The cost reductions might be measured in pennies, but an old truth understood by John D. Rockefeller remained: in a continuous-process business handling millions of barrels of oil a day, pennies saved were a competitive advantage earned. That reality made continual reductions in cost a central strategy for success.

ASIA-PACIFIC: EXPANSION INTO
FAST-GROWTH MARKETS

But cost reductions, capacity cutbacks, and better internal management and operational procedures were not the only important downstream initiatives undertaken by Exxon. Another central part of the corporation's strategy marked a final change in the company's operations after 1973: the dramatic shift of downstream operations to the fast-growing markets of the Asia-Pacific region.

The Asia-Pacific region offered ample opportunities for the application of the lessons learned in the United States and Europe from downsizing and upgrading. In booming markets from Singapore to China, the company could construct plants that incorporated the benefits of scale, state-of-the-art technology, and the integration of refining and chemicals.

Exxon was by no means a newcomer to the region. Indeed, Standard's oil lamps had established markets for the company in parts of Asia in the nineteenth century. But in the late twentieth century, Exxon made a series of decisions that decisively expanded its presence in Asia through the construction of regional refining and chemical complexes. This was part of a broad strategy to enter rapidly expanding markets in eastern and southeastern Asia, in part at the expense of the company's historical presence in slower-growing and economically troubled Latin America. Singapore became the focal point of Exxon's Asian strategy, and it steadily grew into an important location in Exxon's global system of manufacturing and distribution.

Exxon expanded in Asia at an exciting time for the region. The company's post–World War II growth there began in Japan, where it played a role in the rebuilding of the nation. It then participated in the "Japanese miracle," when a sustained surge of growth from the 1950s through the 1980s, which had few parallels in modern industrial history, made Japan the third-largest economy in the world. The company also took part during the late twentieth century in the rise of the so-called Asian Tigers—Hong Kong, Singapore, South Korea, and Taiwan. Their economies enjoyed surges of rapid growth under government-guided capitalist systems; the process came to be known as the "Asian model" for development. Both Hong Kong and Singapore played important roles in Exxon's expansion into the region, as did Malaysia.

Underneath much of the drama of Asian development in the years after 1973 was the awakening of the economic giant of the region, China. After the death of Mao Zedong, in 1976, that communist nation's economy was gradually transformed from being largely agrarian and centrally planned to being more open and incentive-driven. Exxon monitored the changing conditions and sought opportunities to reestablish a presence there. Its operations in Hong Kong provided an entrée into the economy of the mainland, and the company had made numerous direct contacts by the 1990s that proved useful in entering China.[69] The nations in the region were marked by different developmental processes and political systems, and Exxon had to adapt to each one. But from the corporation's point of view, one overriding similarity stood out: sustained growth created dynamic markets for both energy and chemicals.

JAPAN: REFINING UNDER MITI

The company entered Japan in 1933 as part of Standard-Vacuum Oil Company (Stanvac), a joint venture with Socony-Vacuum (Mobil's predecessor) in parts of the Far East. It returned after World War II to help develop the refining sector much needed for Japanese recovery. Despite difficulties at times operating in a political economy with very strong governmental direction, the company remained in Japan to take advantage of the growing Asian market. By the early 1980s, Exxon held a large minority interest in two refining companies while also operating a chain of 2,700 service stations, a tanker fleet to transport crude oil—primarily from the Middle East—and a petrochemical plant. It had a major office building in Kawasaki, a large city on the outskirts of Tokyo, and was an established part of the Japanese economy.[70]

The company participated in Japan's sustained growth primarily through partial ownership of two refining companies, Tonen and General Sekiyu (GSK). The Japanese government had created Tonen on the eve of World War II as an all-Japanese refining company. Following the war, Tonen initiated a business relationship with Stanvac in 1948. A year later, the American company purchased 51 percent of Tonen, and it began refining again in 1950. When antitrust officials in the United States split up Stanvac in 1962, Exxon and Socony-Vacuum each retained a little more than a 25 percent interest in the refinery, giving their Japanese partners effective control unless the two American companies voted together.

GSK also emerged in the years of American-directed rebuilding after the war. General Douglas MacArthur had sought to break up the *zaibat-sus*—the giant, distinctive Japanese conglomerates that often contained both industrial and financial holdings. A portion of the old Mitsui zaibatsu set up an independent petroleum-trading operation that formed General Bussan Kaisha, Ltd., which changed its name in 1967 to General Sekiyu and expanded into refining. In 1971, it formed a joint venture with Esso and built a refinery on Okinawa that opened in 1972. That venture was shared half by Esso/Exxon, with the remaining half split between two Japanese partners. A subsequent restructuring under governmental guidance in 1984 combined some of GSK's distribution operations with a wholly owned subsidiary of Exxon, Esso Standard Sekiyu.[71]

Thus, in the late 1980s, Exxon owned 25 percent of Tonen, 49 percent of GSK, 100 percent of Esso Standard Sekiyu, and a 50 percent interest in a refinery on Okinawa. The total refining capacity owned by Exxon in Japan fluctuated over time, although Japan continued to host the company's largest refining capacity in a single Asian nation until the merger with Mobil. In 1998, Exxon's refining capacity in Japan alone was about 40 percent as large as its capacity in the United States. It was almost three times as large as all of Exxon's Latin American refineries combined.

Maurice E. J. O'Loughlin took part in Exxon's early development in Asia as head of Esso Eastern, the regional company with responsibilities for a vast area that stretched from Japan to Australia and included Malaysia and Singapore. When he took charge in 1964, the Japanese refineries and a growing group of offshore properties in Australia were among his primary responsibilities. Management of the refineries introduced him to the realities of business under the direction of MITI, the Japanese Ministry of International Trade and Industry. MITI was the key government agency responsible for guiding the nation's efforts to rebuild itself into an industrial power. Along with other government planning agencies, it

Maurice E. J. O'Loughlin, senior vice president and member of the board of directors, Exxon Corporation, 1979. ExxonMobil Historical Collection, di_06137.

wielded the power to foster the growth of targeted export industries, such as automobiles and electronics, while exerting leadership in much of the remainder of the Japanese economy. A healthy refining sector was important to economic growth in a nation with very little domestic oil or natural gas, and MITI needed the expertise, capital, and access to crude of leading international companies such as Exxon. But it also remained quite protective of domestic markets. The company benefited from its participation in one of the fastest-growing nations in the world, but its long-term prospects for more extensive participation in the Japanese economy were constrained by the government-directed planning system. Japanese-style managed capitalism was unfamiliar and awkward for Exxon, which was accustomed to the freer markets in the United States and much of Europe.[72]

O'Loughlin recalled the close supervision of Exxon by MITI: "You had to practically get permission from them to do almost anything and everything." In the early years, governmental rules dictated that foreign companies participate through joint ventures. The vision of MITI for the refining industry was, according to O'Loughlin, "pretty much" the same as Exxon's vision: "There was never any great struggle over whether you went in here. I think the Japanese . . . were interested in the experience and skills that somebody like Exxon brought to their organization, and they were fast learners."[73] In addition to capital, access to oil and feedstock for chemical plants, and advanced research, Exxon brought state-of-the art refining technology.

One constant source of concern for O'Loughlin, however, was "that the hiring and staffing habits of the Japanese were considerably higher than we were used to."[74] That difference reflected in part MITI's national developmental policy of fostering the expansion of Japan's export industry while using domestic industry and commerce to absorb a substantial portion of the workforce. On such matters, as well as on the nuts and bolts of industry restructuring as occurred in 1984, companies had little power to affect the strategies of MITI, which focused on the national interest of Japan, not the self-interest of individual companies.

The priority given to Japanese interests was particularly clear within the oil-refining sector in the decades after the energy crises of the 1970s. Entering the 1970s, Japan relied on imported oil for more than 50 percent of its energy. The government responded effectively to the dislocations brought about by high oil prices in the years before the mid-1980s with a series of long-term policies designed to reduce the nation's dependence on imported oil and to strongly emphasize energy efficiency.

Meanwhile, Tonen began to experience difficulties in the 1990s after having pursued a strategy of diversification in the prior decade. Nonenergy ventures included research on carbon fibers, genetic engineering, vaccine technology, and a golf club design. The use of Tonen's profits to acquire businesses far beyond its core competencies displeased Exxon, which wanted Tonen to focus on its core business and repatriate more of its profits to its owners.[75] Tonen's management resisted, and the unresponsiveness of its president infuriated Exxon's management. Rene Dahan, at that time the president of ECI, remembered that the president "was running Tonen like his own private company and was essentially confronting us and humiliating us every step of the way."[76] To make changes, however, Exxon needed the support of the other major shareholder of Tonen, Mobil. Although Mobil agreed that Tonen should pay higher dividends to its U.S. owners, it was not willing to take a stronger stance and replace Tonen's top management. Allen Murray was the chairman of Mobil for much of the early 1990s, and Lee Raymond periodically urged him to be more demanding. According to Raymond, representatives from Exxon, Mobil, and Tonen would meet each year, and "Tonen . . . played off Exxon versus Mobil such that Exxon and Mobil kind of came to a standstill and [Tonen] would go off and do what the hell they wanted to do."[77] Things finally changed when Murray decided that he, too, had had enough and was ready for a change. According to Raymond, after one of the annual meetings, Murray said, "That's it. We're going to take them over. . . . I'm done with this kind of thing."[78] In early 1994, Exxon and Mobil replaced the company's president with Tamehiko Tamahori, the head of Tonen's tanker group. Tamahori was on the same page as his joint-venture partners. His new strategy focused on becoming more cost competitive, deploying world-class technology, more fully assessing business risks associated with investing in growth opportunities, and cooperating more closely with both Exxon and Mobil.

As Japan began to deregulate its oil industry in the mid-1990s, the financial pressures on Tonen, GSK, and Esso Standard Sekiyu grew. As a result, the three companies looked for ways to consolidate operations and cut costs. Those efforts accelerated after August 1997, when Exxon increased its share of GSK to 50.1 percent, bringing the company under its control. Now that it owned a majority of GSK as well as all of ESK, Exxon merged some of their administrative functions and their operations. That effort continued and expanded after the Exxon-Mobil merger, since the new firm was the sole owner of both Esso Standard Sekiyu and Mobil Sekiyu, and half owner, approximately, of both Tonen and GSK. In July 2002, GSK and Tonen merged, becoming Japan's largest refiner. The company was renamed Tonen General Sekiyu, with Tamahori as president and GSK's Masayoshi Okai as chairman.[79]

As ExxonMobil congratulated itself on the climax of an often-difficult tenure in Japan, it had already begun to respond to a fact that had become evident at least a decade earlier: Japan, which had been the focus of Western attention during its "miracle," was no longer the undisputed center of Asian growth. Other nations in the region had surged forward as Japan's growth moderated, and China, with about ten times the population of Japan, had made rapid progress toward becoming an economic superpower.

SINGAPORE: BUILDING A STURDY PLATFORM FOR ASIAN EXPANSION

What became one of the three largest refining centers in the world began with the construction of small refineries in Singapore by Mobil Oil in 1966 and then by Esso four years later.[80] Esso's first plant originally had a capacity of 81,000 barrels a day. It refined primarily Middle Eastern oil, and it supplied fuel oil and other products to major markets in Asia, including Esso refineries in Japan and power plants the company owned in Hong Kong. In the years before the Exxon-Mobil merger, Singapore grew into a substantial refining and petrochemical complex for Exxon, Mobil, and other international oil companies.[81]

Given the company's relatively small presence in Asia in the late 1960s, the initial decision to locate a refinery in Singapore could not have seemed particularly important at the corporate level. Maurice O'Loughlin remembered, however, heated discussions within Esso Eastern. He favored Singapore. Others argued just as strongly for Hong Kong. O'Loughlin recalls his winning argument: "We had a market tributary to the Singapore area that basically did consume everything except the heavy fuel oil."[82] By building on Singapore's Pulau Ayer Chawan Island, the company could supply the existing market and then ship the remaining heavy fuel oil to its refineries in Japan. A decade later, an official in Exxon Chemical provided a concise summary of Singapore's geographic advantages: "There could hardly be a better location for a plant which is intended to meet growing demand . . . in the Southeast Asia–Pacific market. . . . Singapore is one of the great crossroads of the world, a major shipping center and near the half-way point on the main tanker route from the Middle East to

Japan."[83] Either Singapore or Hong Kong would have been a reasonably central location from which to serve markets throughout a large section of Asia. Exxon's choice of Singapore helped set the country on the path toward sustained growth centered in part on a petroleum-related cluster of businesses.

Thus was born a long and mutually profitable partnership between Exxon and the government of Singapore. The small city-state grew from a population of about two million in 1970 to more than five million in 2011. It had gained its independence from Great Britain in 1963, and the People's Action Party under Prime Minister Lee Kuan Yew chose a developmental plan that stressed attracting direct foreign investment from international corporations based in the United States and western Europe. The government would invest in the construction of infrastructure needed by specific industries. Assistance to companies interested in moving operations to Singapore often included tax breaks and help in finding suitable sites for facilities.[84] The country also allowed foreign companies to retain 100 percent ownership of their operations. Exxon found Singapore to be a promising political economy in which to build its major platform for growth in Asia, including China. A 1991 report from Esso Eastern's top managers back to Exxon's corporate offices in New York City on the business environment of the nations in their region was forceful and unambiguous: "Singapore's political/business climate remains one of the most attractive for private business in the world."[85]

The expansion of Exxon's investments in Singapore reflected that assessment. The company regularly added more capacity and advanced processes to its refinery. It built a chemical complex alongside the refinery in the 1970s, beginning with a chemical solvent plant and in 1981 adding a $35 million, high-tech paramins plant to produce additives that enhanced the performance of lubricants, a growing market for Exxon Chemical in Asia. By that time, Exxon's refinery capacity had already grown to nearly 200,000 barrels a day, making it similar in size to the company's largest refineries in Europe. The plants of both Exxon and Mobil were among the five large refineries in Singapore that had pushed the country's refining capacity above one million barrels a day in little more than a decade.[86]

Soon after, Exxon faced a decision on the future of its Singapore refinery. As steeply higher oil prices dampened consumer demand for

Catalytic cracker at the Jurong Refinery, Singapore, 2004.
Exxon Mobil Corporation.

refined products in the years from 1973 until the oil-price bust of the mid-1980s, the Singapore plant encountered new competition. Esso Eastern reported, "As government-owned refineries come on-stream in Indonesia and Malaysia post-1985, we will experience a significant reduction in the traditional utilization of our Singapore refinery." Those nearby nations were economic rivals of Singapore. In addition, the company owned refineries in Malaysia and Thailand, and all that capacity could easily become overcapacity unless and until Asian markets rebounded sharply. In fact, Esso Eastern concluded that "deciding how to make the most out of refinery facilities that we own is one of the major questions that we face."[87]

By 1987, Exxon had decided to target investment at the Singapore complex and make it the centerpiece of its downstream activities in Asia. Expansion in both refining and chemicals moved forward with equipment upgrades. A $75 million program in 1987 added equipment to allow the Pulau Ayer Chawan refinery to expand production by 35,000 barrels a day and to refine products such as fuel oil into higher-value and cleaner-burning products, including jet fuel and diesel. To develop new products and provide technical services to customers, affiliates of Exxon

Chemical built a regional technology center in the late 1980s as part of a government-sponsored high-tech complex.[88] Upgrading of the refinery continued in 1993 with the construction of a $237 million hydroprocessing unit to increase its capacity to produce low-sulfur crude and other high-end products.

In addition to its refining, lubricant, and chemical investments, Exxon increased its use of Singapore as a regional operations center. In 1993, the Singapore affiliate was managing the company's marketing activities in Hong Kong, Taiwan, Guam, South Korea, and China. A few years later, the Singapore office took charge of Exxon's lubricant sales throughout the Asia-Pacific region.

Chemical expansion continued apace. By 1993, the company had invested about $90 million in specialty chemical plants adjacent to its Pulau Ayer Chawan refinery, where Exxon Chemical had created "its biggest and most flexible" complex in Asia to produce industrial solvents and other products. At that time, Exxon Chemical went forward with a multimillion-dollar joint venture in Singapore with Amoco Chemical and the China American Petrochemical Company (Taiwan) to build a large aromatics plant to produce paraxylene and benzene.[89] Those basic chemicals were building blocks for a growing array of petrochemical products, and they had a large market in Asia and around the world. The downstream complex in Singapore steadily grew and became more technically advanced. As demand in Asia continued to rise, Exxon directed a growing share of its investment there, and those dollars built some of the most modern refineries and chemical plants in the world. The extensive investments reflected the company's commitment to Singapore as an important new part of its global operations and the center of its Asian strategy.

The process climaxed soon after the Exxon-Mobil merger. The large refineries of Mobil and Exxon in Singapore had the combined capacity to refine 580,000 barrels a day in 2000, a capacity that grew to 605,000 barrels a day in 2005. That made Singapore ExxonMobil's largest refining complex in the world. After the merger and the consolidated management of both companies' plants, ExxonMobil became Singapore's largest foreign investor. The company's total investment then increased sharply with the announcement in early 2002 of plans to build a massive $2 billion chemical complex "fully integrated" with its refinery. The company billed the state-of-the art facility as its "single largest investment in the Asia Pacific region" and its "largest manufacturing complex in Asia."[90] The closer integration of refining and chemical production had become a key means of building competitive advantage for ExxonMobil, and the company aggressively integrated the operations of its refining and chemical complex in Singapore. By the early 2000s, ExxonMobil's Singapore site had come of age as a modern, world-scale manufacturing complex capable of taking full advantage of its location and its special status in Singapore's plans for continued development.

HONG KONG, POWER, AND CHINA

As the company expanded in Asia after World War II, it developed a variety of markets in Hong Kong, whose extraordinary growth in that era created great investment opportunities and expanding markets for petroleum products. By 1981, the crown colony's 400 square miles contained 5.2 million people, and its steady growth and prime location continued to attract international companies active in Asian markets. Hong Kong provided Exxon with a good base of operations for supplying the Asian demand for products ranging from bunkering oil, gasoline and diesel fuel, aviation fuels, and a variety of chemical products.

The company had moved to Hong Kong in 1971 to take advantage of its excellent location, transportation, and communications, which allowed the company to cover a broad region from its central offices.[91] In 1981, the president of Esso Chemical Asia Pacific noted how successful that decision had been: "Hong Kong has served us well as a regional base over the last decade during which our sales revenue has shown an average growth of 23 percent per year." With a majority of its population ethnic Chinese and with strong economic ties to the People's Republic of China, Hong Kong provided useful links to the mainland. Although speculation grew throughout the 1980s and 1990s about the fate of Hong Kong's historical mix of capitalism and personal freedom after it reverted from British to Chinese rule in 1997, Exxon remained confident in Hong Kong's future. It was optimistic that China's early steps in opening to foreign investment eventually would produce much broader opportunities there also. If so, Hong Kong would be a logical gateway to markets on the mainland.

Exxon had substantial fuel-oil markets in Hong Kong. One of these was China Light & Power (CL&P), which grew into the major supplier of electricity for Hong Kong during the city's long economic boom after World War II. From its refinery in Singapore, Esso Eastern supplied fuel oil to CL&P. Jersey Standard and Socony-Vacuum had built a business presence in Hong Kong after World War II through their Stanvac joint venture. But in the court-ordered division of properties after the breakup of Stanvac in 1962, Jersey had few holdings left in Hong Kong. The owners of the tightly held CL&P let it be known that it would welcome Jersey as a partner.[92] The family of Sir Lawrence Kadoorie owned control of the company, and Kadoorie wanted Jersey to take a 60 percent stake in the company at a time when a massive expansion program was needed. CL&P, which would remain as operator, would retain the remaining 40 percent ownership of the generating plants and ownership of the distribution system. The deal was too good for Exxon to refuse, despite the potential future risks posed by the end of British rule. After negotiations that included CL&P, Jersey, and the Hong Kong government, the company acquired a majority share of CL&P in 1964.[93]

Beginning with an initial generating capacity of 350 megawatts (MW), CL&P grew with Hong Kong.[94] The operations of its fuel-oil-powered generating stations supplied approximately half of the region's electricity, and regular expansion was needed to keep pace with growth. In the mid-1980s, the company embarked on an ambitious construction program at its new Castle Peak site, which ultimately included two large units (burning coal and fuel oil) capable of generating more than 2,000 MW of electricity. In the mid-1990s, growing demand required the construction of another large station, one powered by natural gas from an offshore field. By the time of the Exxon-Mobil merger, CL&P was producing almost 7,000 MW of electricity—enough to supply a city of several million. That generating capacity represented a total investment by CL&P of at least $6 billion. By the late 1990s, Exxon could claim to be "the largest independent power provider in the world." Though an unusual investment for a company that had refocused on oil and gas, the appeal of Hong Kong power reflected the happy fact that for several decades beginning in the 1970s, Exxon had enjoyed steady earnings ranging from $100 million to $300 million annually from its power plants there.[95]

Castle Peak Power Plant, Hong Kong. Exxon Mobil Corporation.

THE QUEST FOR THE CHINA MARKET

While Exxon expanded in Hong Kong, it continued to pay close attention to China, following events there from the earliest days of China's gradual movement away from central planning and toward a more incentive-based economy. Most observers date the transition from 1978, when, two years after Mao Zedong's death, a new generation of leaders in the Chinese Communist Party (CCP), led by Deng Xiaoping, decided to explore ways to open the economy to individual initiative and outside companies.[96]

In response to that new direction, Exxon quickly sought more information about opportunities in China. In the summer of 1978, the company sent a group of eleven executives, led by Tom Barrow, on a two-week trip to China that included visits to oil-related sites and discussions with Chinese officials. In the mid-1970s, Barrow had led a similar trip to the Soviet Union, which had likewise seemed on the verge of opening itself to foreign investment. Both nations were beginning to consider a transition from communist-style central planning toward capitalism, without quite grasping what that might be. But once the process had begun, the CCP kept charge of it and moved gradually toward greater economic openness. When Barrow's group returned from China, it urged Exxon to take action: "Exxon has come at the right time because the PRC plans to equal industrialization with developed countries by the end of the century."[97] Over the next few years, the company remained quite confident in the future of China, and it saw an expanding role for itself in the new China that seemed to be emerging from within the communist system.

This trip began a series of small steps that gradually led to the development of commercial opportunities in China. In 1979, Exxon Chemical hosted a group of Chinese chemical engineers, inviting them to explore common interests and commercial possibilities. That same year, the company began a program to acquire seismic data in the South China Sea. An aviation-fuels specialist from Exxon Company, International visited China the following year, and in 1981 the company established an office in Beijing to manage the company's exploration interests. In the early 1980s, exploration took place in the East China Sea. On the fuel-marketing side, Exxon was an early entrant in developing Chinese service stations, which initially were supplied out of Hong Kong. In 1981, following negotiations that involved the Singapore office, Exxon became the first Western oil company to open a service station in the special economic zone created in the Pearl River Delta near both Guangdong province and Hong Kong. In 1982, Esso Eastern's report to New York headquarters on the business environment in its region painted a positive view of China: "For the PRC, we foresee political stability for at least the next decade and a reasonably good climate for resource development. . . . The People's Republic of China appears firmly embarked on a program of economic modernization and development. . . . China will be unable to develop by itself, and will retain Hong Kong in its present function as well as develop a number of Special Economic Zones to serve similar functions."[98]

Exxon's presence in Hong Kong had already opened early access to electricity markets in southern China. In 1979, CL&P signed an agreement to supply excess power to fast-growing Guangdong, which bordered Hong Kong. That connection between CL&P and Guangdong was Exxon's first physical tie to the mainland Chinese economy in thirty years.

A more significant connection to Guangdong came more than a decade later, when Exxon took a 51 percent share in a joint venture with CL&P to help build a pumped-storage plant at Conghua, some 100 miles northeast of Hong Kong. The technology used off-peak power supplied by base-load generating plants at times of low electric demand to pump water up to an elevated reservoir. During peak-load times, the stored water was released to flow back down to the river below, generating power en route. CL&P had a call on half of the power generated by the 1,200 MW plant for distribution in Hong Kong.[99]

One attorney working with Exxon on a variety of initiatives in China said simply, "The Chinese are master negotiators. They have been bargaining with outside cultures for 5,000 years, and they are accomplished at it."[100] That skill was illustrated during bargaining over the pumped-storage facility. Talks began in 1986, and the start-up was in 1994. Even an eight-year lag time was relatively quick in the early years of the opening of China. A ten-year perspective on such negotiations is also useful. That generation of CCP leaders had chosen the difficult path of opening the economy. They had a historic obligation to do the job right, and so they remained skeptical of the foreign companies knocking on their door. For its part, Exxon had always been a careful negotiator of the nuts and bolts of an agreement. To the conservatism of both sides was added a note of caution. Each knew that the other was large enough and powerful enough to be of permanent benefit, and each sought to lay the foundation for a successful long-term relationship.

The need to move cautiously but with long-range goals in mind was clear in the deliberations within Exxon on the pumped-storage project. In 1988, Esso Eastern presented a detailed proposal for discussion with the Exxon Management Committee. One attraction was the "possibility of demonstrating further interest in PRC investments if such investment can be shown to be based on sound principles and attractive economics in its own right." The project presented "the possibility that this can be accomplished for a relatively small Exxon equity interest." But the presentation ended with a warning that if the company moved forward now, it "would require a good reason to back off" in the future.[101] The plant was no ordinary project. It was a demonstration project to show the Chinese

A sign for a Chinese Esso station, 1994. ExxonMobil Historical Collection, di_06219.

the Exxon approach to business and to strengthen the company's relationship with a nation it saw as important to its future.

The Chinese government confined Exxon's activities to the special economic zones until 1992, when it allowed the company to build and operate service stations and a storage terminal outside the zones.[102] In 1985, the chemical company established a representative office in Beijing. Exxon's downstream company in Singapore became a more significant supplier of products to China in the late 1980s. Exploration efforts, however, yielded little. After lengthy negotiations produced an agreement in 1995 for Exxon to explore parts of the promising Tarim Basin desert in western China, the company found no commercial oil there.[103] Also in 1995, a study group began examining the economics of a trans-Asia pipeline to transport natural gas from Turkmenistan across China to Japan.[104]

Exxon also sought refining and chemical-manufacturing opportunities in China, but other companies had beaten it to the punch. Amoco, for example, had negotiated since the late 1980s with the Chinese government to build a chemical plant in the Zhuhai Special Economic Zone near Hong Kong.[105] Other foreign companies had taken steps toward involvement in refining and chemicals by the mid-1990s. Yet despite starting later than many of its competitors, Exxon rapidly made up ground. After discussions with Sinopec, the government-owned company that dominated oil refining, Exxon agreed with Sinopec Guangzhou in 1995 to jointly study the expansion of a major refinery complex and marketing operation in Guangdong.

Years before, in the mid-1980s, it had become evident to Lee Raymond that the company's numerous small steps in China had produced an unwieldy management situation. Several of the company's business groups interacted with the Chinese, but there was little coordination among the businesses. To address a situation that was confusing to both the Chinese and Exxon's employees, Raymond created a new office in Beijing to coordinate the company's activities and named Stephen F. Goldmann to the new position of president of Exxon China. The office opened in September 1985.[106]

Goldmann, a chemical engineering graduate of Lehigh University, joined Exxon in 1970, following his receipt of a doctoral degree from Imperial College, part of the University of London. Before he moved to

China, most of his career had been spent in Exxon USA. He moved up the ladder from the Supply Department to work on the ill-fated Colony oil-shale project, to a time as executive assistant to Randall Meyer in 1986, and finally as head of the Corporate Planning Department in 1993.

The new Beijing office was an organizational anomaly. Each of the leading functional representatives became a vice president of Exxon China, but they reported to their business functions, not to Goldmann, who described his task as "basically a diplomacy job both external and internal."[107] In effect, he became the head of Exxon's government-relations activity in China while also helping coordinate all the functional contacts in China. That structure perhaps cleared up the lines of authority within Exxon, but it also undermined the status, for the Chinese, of the functional heads, whose new titles and new boss seemed to indicate a decline in authority. Yet the functional managers were as influential in the company's management as they had ever been. The resulting tension declined as exploration failed to find few discoveries of long-term interest, but other parts of the company took up the slack with an array of new business ventures.

Shortly after Goldmann moved to Beijing, Sheng Huaren, the head of Sinopec, visited the United States to meet with existing partners, including ARCO in Houston and Phillips in Bartlesville, Oklahoma.[108] Raymond offered to fly to Houston for a meeting, asking only that Exxon be given one evening to explore possibilities for investment in China. The willingness of the head of the leading U.S. oil company to travel to meet him favorably impressed Sheng. At dinner, he met with Raymond and Ray Nesbitt (the head of Exxon Chemical), who had just completed the expansion of the Baytown polyethylene plant. At the time, that project had added more capacity at Baytown than China's entire existing polyethylene capacity.

After Sheng's return to China, Sinopec's planning manager met with Goldmann and invited Exxon to become a partner in a large refinery and chemical project in Fujian province, one designed to increase the capacity of an existing 80,000-barrel-a-day refinery and add a large chemical-manufacturing facility. There was a problem, however. Sinopec had already initiated discussion about the project with Amoco. Goldmann declined the invitation, informing the planning manager that Exxon could not enter into that project without risking a lawsuit for tortious

Raymond B. Nesbitt, president, Exxon Chemical Company, 1991.
ExxonMobil Historical Collection, di_06149.

interference in ongoing negotiations, similar to the one successfully brought by Pennzoil after the Texaco-Getty merger. His logic confused Chinese officials. How could such legal issues be allowed to get in the way of a good business deal? Goldmann believed that after high-levels talks within Sinopec and perhaps the Chinese government, Chinese officials told Amoco—which was engaged also in developing a chemical facility to produce purified terephthalic acid in the Zhuhai Special Economic Zone—that it could not have both the Zhuhai and the Fujian projects.

The Chinese government wanted Amoco to accept the Zhuhai project and Exxon to be its partner in Fujian.[109] The Chinese had their way, and Exxon shortly began conversations with the Chinese on the Fujian project. Its earlier Guangdong refinery-expansion project with Sinopec was put on the back burner.

Exxon continued to build a larger presence in China. It reached an agreement with the Chinese to construct a plant for blending lubrication oils southeast of Shanghai in Nanjiang. Exxon built a second lubricant-blending plant at Tianjin, eighty miles southeast of Beijing. In addition, Exxon Chemical agreed with a Chinese partner to build a Shanghai-area plant to manufacture normal paraffin and linear alkyl benzene. With the marketing activities in Guangdong, the lubricant plants in Nanjiang and Tianjin, chemical manufacturing in Shanghai, and its long-term businesses in power and marketing in Hong Kong, a new Fujian plant would further expand Exxon's already significant presence in China.

Discussions about the Fujian refinery and petrochemical complex continued throughout 1996. In that year, the original two partners invited Saudi Aramco, which owned the largest oil reserves in the world, to participate. Both Saudi Aramco and the government of Saudi Arabia had strong incentives to establish long-term supply relationships in the fastest-growing market for oil in the world. Exxon, the largest and most profitable of the international oil companies, had a strong record of downstream operations and one of the largest chemical companies affiliated with an oil company. It also had an excellent record of building and managing large projects. Sinopec, then the downstream giant of China, badly needed to expand its capacity and to upgrade its downstream facilities in order to meet the nation's fast-growing demand for petroleum products. The fourth partner, the government of Fujian province, looked forward to a major new investment in its rapidly growing special economic zone—with the attendant revenue stream. This joint venture among giants held many complementary advantages.

In 1997, the parties reached agreement to conduct a detailed feasibility study for expanding the refinery and building a large chemical plant in Fujian, with ownership shared by Exxon (25 percent), Aramco Overseas Company B.V. (25 percent), and Sinopec and Fujian Petrochemical Company Limited (50 percent). A decade then passed as the partners studied and negotiated. As in earlier negotiations over the expansion of Hong Kong power, in the Chinese government Exxon had found a negotiator as conservative and detail-oriented as itself.

Caution was not, however, the only thing slowing progress on the venture. The planning for the Exxon-Mobil merger intervened in 1998. In the next year, Sinopec entered a period of reorganization after the Chinese government decided to create greater competition in its domestic oil industry by orchestrating a trade of assets between the largest refiner, Sinopec, and the largest producer of oil, CNPC (Petrochina). Government planners saw this as a way of hastening the emergence of a stronger domestic oil sector, in which vertically integrated national oil companies could grow and quickly become capable of competing internationally. Swapping Sinopec refineries for CNPC production was a quick step in that direction. The asset swap had a dash of U.S. antitrust, a hint of MITI-style industrial planning, and a large dose of old-style communist central planning. It changed the market structure of the Chinese oil industry, providing strong incentives for Sinopec and CNPC to move quickly in the direction indicated by the government.[110]

In addition, the giant Fujian project itself presented several tricky matters for negotiation. Exxon wanted important issues resolved before construction began on the Quanzhou project—now renamed after the city in Fujian where it is located. One set of problems arose because China was not a member of the World Trade Organization when the agreement was approved and had in place restrictions on its wholesale petroleum business. Those restrictions were not resolved satisfactorily until 2006, five years after the Chinese had entered the WTO. Other issues arose because of Exxon's desire to participate in the entire value chain of the project, from refining to chemicals to fuels marketing.[111] Would the company participate in the retail marketing of the venture's products? Under what conditions and terms would it be compensated for its investment in the plant? Could it sell products in the wholesale market? How many service stations would be included and under what brands would they market? What, if any, pricing restrictions would be placed on the petrochemical plant's output? China's long march toward a more open economy was still in progress, and such questions had to be decided before the project could begin.

A final agreement was more than twelve years in the making. It included plans for a $5 billion refining-chemical complex in Quanzhou. An existing and relatively small 80,000-barrel-a-day refinery would be upgraded to 240,000 barrels a day, and a giant chemical facility would be added, with large productive capacities for ethylene, polypropylene, and aromatics. As in all of ExxonMobil's largest refinery-chemical complexes, close integration of the design, operations, and planning for the complex would result in flexibility for maximizing the value of production and managing the desired mix of products. In addition, the plan called for the construction of 750 modern service stations to sell products branded by all three owners.[112] Engineering work and site preparation was underway in 2004, and the facility started up in 2009.

In a blitz of activity after 1986, Exxon had made impressive strides in becoming a major presence in Asia. In seeking the fast-growth markets of the region, the company gradually moved away from its historical commitment to Latin America, where it divested itself of properties and passed on potential investments. To take full advantage of opportunities in Asia, the company leveraged investments in a variety of nations, building a logical and coherent system of facilities that stretched from Australia to Thailand, Malaysia, and Singapore, and then on to Hong Kong, China, and Japan. At the heart of the system were large, high-tech refining-chemical complexes with the operational flexibility and low-cost structure to compete successfully in the region. Indeed, by the first decade of the twenty-first century, ExxonMobil's Asia-Pacific holdings had become major contributors to the global success of the corporation as a whole.

It is worth noting that more than thirty years after the onset of the energy crisis, Exxon Corporation had not matched the refining capacity that it lost in the 1970s and 1980s. In fact, the total refining capacity of Exxon-Mobil in 2005 remained less than that of Exxon alone in 1973. Exxon's long-term adjustments brought sharp reductions in the size of its downstream and a new mentality that made profitability, not volume, the key goal of downstream operations. Refining and chemicals both made impressive strides in adapting to the cost structure, technology, management systems, and commitment to operational excellence needed to remain leading competitors around the world. After struggling for much of the late twentieth century to generate profits commensurate with their size and importance in the company, downstream operations emerged by the turn of the century as a sturdy contributor to the company's bottom line. The transformation of the refining and marketing sectors was a long step toward the transformation of the company as a whole, or at least toward achieving a better balance between its downstream and upstream operations.

CHAPTER NINE

——

MEGAMERGER

INTEGRATING EXXON AND MOBIL

A s the twentieth century came to a close, so did an era in the history
of the international petroleum industry. A wave of megamergers in
the late 1990s fundamentally altered the market structure of the oil
industry, reducing the number of large, privately owned companies while
greatly enhancing the size of those that remained. The largest of those
mergers combined Exxon and Mobil into ExxonMobil. The approval of
the merger in late 1999 was an epochal moment in the long history of
Exxon. The successful consolidation in the following years of two major
companies into one "supermajor" prepared ExxonMobil to prosper in an
industry marked by the growing clout of national oil companies, increasing environmental demands placed on the fossil-fuel industries, and
extreme swings in oil prices. Exxon, the largest international oil company
before the merger wave began, certainly had the capability to remain a
force in its industry without a merger. But the opportunity to combine
its resources with those of Mobil, the fourth-largest international oil company in 1998, proved irresistible.

Important contributions of Mobil to the new company included
extraordinary prospects in oil and natural gas, outstanding petrochemical
facilities, a strong lubricant business, and a pool of experienced executive

talent. In combination with Exxon's strengths, those resources gave the new corporation great potential. But that potential could be fulfilled only by melding the resources of the two companies into a single efficient organization. Those in charge of the consolidation viewed their work through the eyes of engineers, seeking to find the most efficient use of people and resources. They used the merger to accelerate ongoing organizational changes to improve operational excellence while lowering costs. Their handiwork was a well-engineered merger that positioned ExxonMobil for industry leadership in the twenty-first century.

BACKGROUND TO MERGER

The Exxon-Mobil merger was the climax of a quarter century of change propelled by the energy crisis of the early 1970s. The price of oil was one indicator of changing conditions in the industry. The high prices of the 1970s and 1980s shaped an era of expansion and high profits. The price bust of the mid-1980s forced a painful era of cutbacks and reorganizations. Unfortunately for the industry, prices remained relatively low for a decade before beginning to bottom out in the late 1990s at less than $10 a barrel.[1] In real dollars, this meant that oil prices in 1998 were only slightly higher than they had been in 1973. Exxon had adapted to the low-price era by refocusing on its core businesses, tightening its belt, and using new technological and managerial approaches to lower the cost of finding and producing oil. Yet by the late 1990s, Exxon and the petroleum industry as a whole were looking for new ways to prosper as low oil prices lingered.

Although profits did not precisely track prices, they did reflect the ups and downs of the era. According to the U.S. Energy Information Administration, the collective profits of the major U.S. oil companies stood at about $13 billion in 1974, more than doubled to as high as $31 billion in 1980, then plummeted to a low of $9.2 billion in 1986. For the next decade, petroleum industry profits moved up and down with no consistent pattern before a sharp decline in 1998 drove them down to $12 billion, much less in real dollars than the level of 1974. Exxon's profits stayed relatively constant in the 1990s despite swings up and down. From 1990 to 1998, the company's profits rose by more than 25 percent, even as the aggregate profits of other major American oil companies declined by more than 40 percent.[2] This comparison lends credence to an opinion often expressed within Exxon: anyone can make money in an era of high-priced oil, but only the most efficient companies profit when oil prices are low. Exxon maintained profits high enough to place it consistently in the top five companies for profitability in the Fortune 500.[3] Despite relatively high profits, however, its total return to shareholders for the decade of the 1990s was lower than the average of the firms in the Standard & Poor's 500.[4]

By the internal measure of success most trusted by Exxon, rate of return on investments, the company performed better than most other oil companies in the 1990s. In its annual financial and operating reviews, Exxon compared its returns on average capital employed with those of its major international competitors. The company estimated that its return in the 1990s was about 13 percent, some two percentage points higher than the international oil group it chose to use as a comparison.[5] The company's return stayed at that level until about 1994, and then began a slow rise through 1997. It reached about 16 percent before falling back to 12 percent in 1998. Exxon's competitors, by the company's calculations, lagged Exxon's returns throughout those years by as little as two and as much as six percentage points.[6] Such figures did not reflect another important fact. Fifteen years of sustained stock repurchases had given the company a hefty cash reserve that could be used for acquisitions. Its solid financial performance in the depressed conditions of the 1990s placed Exxon in a strong position to respond to opportunities presented by the turmoil of the times.

The company nonetheless faced serious problems common to the industry as a whole. Unpredictable swings in oil prices brought fluctuations in returns from oil production. At the same time, the company's massive investments in refining and marketing produced returns lower in most years than those from upstream operations. That difference mirrored industry experience. An American Petroleum Institute survey indicated that in every year of the 1990s, the return on refining for major petroleum firms trailed the average return of the S&P 500, often by significant amounts. Not once in the decade did average returns on refining reach 10 percent; in two years they were zero.[7] Like all its competitors, Exxon had to examine every option for overcoming these kinds of economic problems and finding ways to improve long-term profitability.

These options included major mergers, which the company had considered and rejected during the sharp downturn of the 1980s. The long period of low oil prices and uncertain profits in the 1980s and 1990s had encouraged an industry-wide movement toward consolidation. The merger movement occurred in two waves, beginning with a flurry of mergers in the early 1980s, then slowed during the oil-price bust of the mid-1980s before returning with a vengeance with the return of low oil prices in the late 1990s (see figure 9.1).

In the years of the first merger wave, low prices did not justify the aggressive frontier-exploration programs common when much higher prices prevailed. That fact made more attractive a second option, acquiring new sources of oil by buying a company whose reserves had a higher "liquidation" value than the total value of the company's stock. Critics scorned the practice as "drilling for oil on Wall Street" and noted that such acquisitions shifted reserves among companies rather than addressing the fundamental need for more oil.[8] With so much of the world's proved reserves located in nations off limits to the international oil companies, however, the old oil adage "oil is where you find it" took on new meaning. In a sense, lower Manhattan became a frontier region.

A quest for the sort of increased efficiency needed to compete in a world of low-priced oil also encouraged consolidation. Mergers presented opportunities for cost cutting through reductions in staff and facilities in the combined companies. Such cuts could be made without the impetus of mergers, but the process of merging two companies allowed managers to eliminate jobs and facilities more quickly and decisively than was common in times of steady-state operations.

A newly permissive legal environment allowed the big mergers in oil to go forward. From the breakup of Standard Oil Company (New Jersey) in 1911 through the early 1980s, the prevailing guidelines on market share enforced by the Federal Trade Commission and the Department of Justice blocked mergers of the largest oil companies. Thus, for almost seventy years, the major oil companies had no reason even to contemplate purchasing other top-ranked oil companies. The primary mergers in the post–World War II era in the U.S. oil industry were between second-tier companies seeking to move into the top tier of competitors. For example, the combination of Atlantic and Richfield created ARCO, greatly

FIGURE 9.1. Major mergers in the petroleum industry, 1981–2001

YEAR	PURCHASER	PURCHASED	PRICE ($ BILLION)
1981	E. I. DuPont de Nemours & Co.	Conoco, Inc.	8.0
	U.S. Steel	Marathon Oil	6.6
	Elf Aquitaine (France)	Texasgulf, Inc.	4.2
1982	Occidental Petroleum	Cities Service Co.	4.1
1984	Chevron Corp.	Gulf Oil Corp.	13.2
	Mobil Corp.	Superior Oil Co.	5.7
	Texaco	Getty	10.1
1985	U.S. Steel	Texas Oil & Gas Corp.	4.1
	Occidental Petroleum	Midcon Corp.	3.1
1987	Amoco Corp.	Dome Petroleum (Canada)	4.2
1989	Exxon Corp.	Texaco Canada, Inc.	4.2
1998	BP	Amoco Corp.	53.0
	Exxon Corp.	Mobil Corp.	75.0
	Total	PetroFina	12.9
1999	BP-Amoco	ARCO	27.0
	TotalFina	Elf Aquitaine	48.8
2000	Chevron	Texaco	45.1
2001	ConocoPhillips	"merger of equals"	35.0*

*Total value of the merger.

Source: *Reinhardt, et al., "BP and the Consolidation of the Oil Industry"; Hargreaves and Hall, "Why Big Oil Has Been Forced to Begin Feeding on Itself."*

increasing the ability of the new company to compete with larger companies such as Exxon and Texaco. Opposition to mergers between major oil companies remained deeply entrenched in public policy until changes in antitrust policies took place in the 1980s.[9]

The election of Ronald Reagan in 1980 brought into the federal antitrust-enforcement agencies officials strongly committed to the deregulation of markets. They believed that the old order in antitrust had emerged to suit the needs of an earlier era, when domestic companies of varied sizes and levels of integration produced the oil needed to fuel the America economy. The rise of producer power in the 1970s, they argued, introduced an era in which U.S.-based companies needed to grow larger in order to compete with the other international oil companies and the national oil companies of the large producing nations. Greater size would help international oil companies retain access to the global supplies that now made up a large and increasing portion of the nation's oil consumption; in that view, outmoded antitrust laws stood in the way of growth through acquisition.[10]

The "Reagan Revolution" marked a distinct change in public policy, particularly regarding antitrust. The FTC's staff began revising guidelines on mergers in September 1981, when the commission quietly dismissed a major antitrust case it had brought in 1973 against Exxon and other oil companies.[11] Then, in 1982, the FTC promulgated new guidelines for assessing the potential effects of mergers on competitiveness. Rather than looking narrowly at the concentration ratios in an industry, the new guidelines focused instead on market efficiencies, barriers to entry, and potential effects on more specifically defined consumer markets.[12] The new approach significantly altered the enforcement of antitrust laws. One result was a green light for mergers of major oil companies.[13]

Before the issuance of the 1982 merger guidelines, the Senate Commerce Committee and Judiciary Committee requested from FTC chairman James Miller a "thorough investigation of the impact of mergers and acquisitions involving large oil companies."[14] The FTC submitted a 300-page study to Congress in September 1982. With numerous caveats, the report concluded, "By and large, recent acquisitions have not had an anticompetitive effect and may have presented opportunities for enhanced efficiency in the industry."[15] The report also stated that the "antitrust laws are sufficient to remedy those acquisitions likely to have anticompetitive effects," and recommended no further statutory action by Congress.[16] In May 1989, an updated version of the 1982 report reached similar conclusions. On the issue of consolidation through acquisition, the 1989 update concluded that "the acquisition activities of the larger petroleum companies are not proportionately greater than those of other large companies."[17] Bolstered by such reports, the FTC and the Antitrust Division of the Department of Justice became more receptive to large-scale mergers in the oil industry.

Just as U.S. antitrust officials opened the gates for megamergers in oil, the European Union began more vigorous reviews of mergers that affected Europe.[18] This meant that global companies active in Europe had to satisfy the concerns of EU officials in Brussels about the competitive effects of proposed combinations. U.S. authorities and EU competition officials established arrangements to coordinate the consideration of mergers, and in most cases, cooperative remedies for potential problems were usually found.[19]

A depressed economic environment combined with a favorable legal one encouraged oil companies to consider the options offered by mergers. Should they acquire? Could they be acquired? If the early-1980s mergers were generally aimed at acquiring reserves at bargain prices, those of the late 1990s were about getting bigger in an increasingly competitive environment. The coming of age of the national oil companies altered the position of the international oil companies, which could not match either the reserves of the largest national oil companies or their favored positions with their governments. The increasing size, cost, and political risks of obtaining substantial new reserves gave the international oil companies strong incentives to use mergers as a way to bulk up their financial and managerial resources.

A new surge in petroleum industry mergers in the mid-1990s continued through the turn of the century. From 1996 to 1998, a series of mergers involving second-tier companies—notably Diamond Shamrock–Ultramar and Ashland Oil–Marathon (also known as USX)—set the stage for what was to come. Then, in 1998, a rapid succession of megamergers between major oil companies fundamentally altered the competitive structure of the international petroleum industry. BP, which had absorbed

Standard Oil Company of Ohio at the beginning of 1989, initiated the new wave of consolidations in August 1998 with the announcement of its intent to merge with Chicago-based Amoco Corporation. At the time, it was the largest oil merger in history, with BP paying approximately $48 billion for Amoco; the combined company had a market value of about $110 billion.[20] Both BP and Amoco had set their sights on growing into a company with the size and global reach to compete with the two existing industry giants, Exxon and Royal Dutch Shell. BP later augmented its size in April 1999 with the announcement of its intent to acquire ARCO for approximately $27 billion.

Other significant mergers went forward throughout 1998. Amerada Hess and Citgo undertook a complicated combination in October 1998. Texaco and Shell combined some operations in January 1998. In that same month, Mobil entered into a joint venture with Citgo at Mobil's refinery in Chalmette, Louisiana. In July 1998 came the creation of a joint Saudi-Texaco venture (Star Enterprise) in downstream operations. In May 1998, Tesoro and BHP Petroleum merged.[21] So powerful was the "urge to merge" in this period that almost all oil companies explored their options. They looked up at larger companies that might be willing to pay a premium for their stock and down at companies they might be able to acquire. Before the unprecedented wave of giant mergers ended, BP had acquired both Amoco and ARCO, Exxon had paired off with Mobil, Total with Elf, Chevron with Texaco, and Conoco with Phillips.[22] Not since John D. Rockefeller consolidated much of the young oil industry in the late nineteenth century had a wave of consolidations had such far-reaching effects on the structure of the petroleum market.

EXXON FINDS MOBIL

Exxon, the largest international oil company, obviously could not look for larger merger partners. It had to look at smaller oil companies or at large companies in related industries. In the late 1990s, it remained relatively strong in a weakened oil industry. It had moderate and generally improving earnings, product sales that appeared to level off, at least temporarily, at about 5.4 million barrels per day, discoveries from exploration sufficient to increase total reserves each year, and surprisingly strong chemical earnings. Debt, never large to begin with, had been halved over the decade. As a consequence, the price of Exxon stock had more than doubled in four years.[23] The corporation had a considerable cash reserve and a "war chest" of repurchased shares that could be reissued at will. Although it could weather the prevailing low oil prices without needing to undergo a major merger, it could not ignore the competitive implications of the merger wave cresting around it.

One of the first possibilities for a big merger came in the form of a feeler put forward by Edward Woolard, the CEO of DuPont. According to Lee Raymond, in late 1997, Woolard suggested to him that DuPont might be willing to consider a deal that in effect traded Conoco (which it owned at the time) to Exxon in exchange for Exxon Chemical. Raymond demurred, but soon after called Ray Nesbitt, the president of Exxon Chemical, to get his opinion. Nesbitt pointed out that the acquisition of Exxon Chemical would fill important gaps in DuPont's product offerings. Raymond said he understood that, but asked how DuPont's offer would benefit Exxon. Nesbitt said that DuPont offered nothing for the chemical side because it wanted to take all of Exxon Chemical, so its value to Exxon rested solely in its petroleum holdings. For his part, Raymond wanted no part of Conoco, which he considered a poor fit for Exxon. He declined Woolard's suggestion but upped the ante by asking whether DuPont would consider being acquired by Exxon. Woolard went back and asked his staff to assess the Exxon counterproposal; DuPont rejected the overture. Upon reflection, Raymond decided that merging with DuPont would not have been a wise move for Exxon, and it probably would have led to the spinning off of a variety of businesses.[24]

The flirtation with DuPont set the wheels turning within Exxon. Raymond and his closest executives began asking basic questions about the company's future. What sort of company did they want Exxon to be? Should it expand its chemical operations? Did it want to become a bigger oil company? Did other choices make sense for the long-term prosperity of the company?

Raymond felt no need for Exxon to acquire another company just to become larger. He held to his view that "eventually return on investment has to win the race," and "you can't win that race on volume." And as for the presumed benefits of gigantic size: "If we haven't found economy of scale by now, we're never going to find it."[25] That said, it galled the Exxon faithful to look up at the end of 1997 and see a large gap between Royal Dutch Shell's proved reserves of more than 19 billion barrels of oil equivalent and its own figure of less than 13.8 BOE. Things became worse in 1998. Upon the completion of the BP-Amoco merger, that combined company would have proved reserves of about 14.8 billion BOE, dropping Exxon to third among large international oil companies in that category.[26] Raymond sought ways to make Exxon both larger and more efficient. To do so, a merger partner would have to add substantial size while also contributing to operating efficiencies and opportunities for profitable expansion.

One possible partner was Mobil Corporation, for which a combination with the right company looked attractive. Although it was the second-largest U.S.-based oil company, Mobil remained below the top tier internationally—a tier that that included Exxon, Shell, and BP after its acquisitions of Amoco and ARCO. The second tier contained giant companies that ranged in size from the remaining American majors— Chevron, Mobil, and Texaco—to the French companies Total and Elf, to somewhat smaller companies such as Phillips and Conoco. As announcements of mergers and the rumors of impending mergers filled the air in the second half of 1998, all those companies looked around to identify both potential partners and potential predators. No company wanted to rush into a bad marriage, but equally strong was the fear of going home alone when the merger party ended.

The challenging task of charting Mobil's path through the uncertainties of this era fell to Lucio A. Noto, its chairman and chief executive officer. He had first worked for that company (then known as Socony Mobil Oil Company) in 1961 as an intern. Upon graduation from Cornell University in 1962 with an MBA, he accepted a permanent job at Stanvac, which had been separated into two parts, one owned by Socony Mobil and the other by Jersey Standard. Noto went to work for the Mobil side beginning in June 1962.

After early orientation assignments, Noto was sent to Italy in 1966, Japan in 1968, and Italy again in 1973, where he stayed through 1976. His next job was in Mobil's New York headquarters working on Middle East matters, and in 1979 he moved to Saudi Arabia as president of Mobil's affiliate there. His long stay in the kingdom and his continuing involvement in the region after he returned to New York in 1985 gave Noto what the *Wall Street Journal* called an "intangible" strength in a world that desperately needed Saudi oil. Back in New York, Noto worked in the Finance Department, where he earned a promotion to chief financial officer for the corporation. He became president of Mobil in 1993. A year later, at age fifty-five, he took the reins as chairman and CEO.[27] One public profile of Noto characterized him as "a street fighter," a hard-driving, effective leader.[28]

As he assessed Mobil's future, Noto identified three areas of concern. First was the company's resource base. Its giant Arun natural gas field in Indonesia, which had been discovered off Sumatra in 1971 and accounted for a significant portion of Mobil's profits, was rapidly declining. Mobil needed new resources to take its place. The company had strong prospects in Kazakhstan's Tengiz field and in Qatar, where Mobil had a 27 percent interest in the ongoing development of massive LNG facilities for one of the largest natural gas fields in the world. Both Tengiz and the Qatar LNG project promised to be quite expensive and technically challenging, and Noto was not confident that Mobil was up to the task. This was the second issue facing Mobil—the need for greater financial and technical resources. The third concern was what to do with Mobil's assets in Europe, where the company held a smaller market share than Exxon and Shell. Noto had struggled to adjust to a prolonged downturn in European markets, but he had found no long-term strategy to make that part of the world more profitable for Mobil.[29]

The company first sought to improve its competitive situation by merging its European downstream assets with those of BP. The two companies announced their intent in February 1996, and the plan received EU approval in August. Under the agreement, BP became the majority owner of a new fuels company that combined Mobil and BP assets, while Mobil was the majority owner of a combined lubricants company. BP promptly rebranded the Mobil stations to BP, a step that Noto considered "a little wacky." Mobil did not rebrand BP lubricants, judging that BP's brand identity had resulted in respected products. Although at times tense, Mobil's European partnership with BP was, in Noto's opinion, a profitable step, and he directed his staff to assess the benefits of a larger corporate merger with BP. After examining the benefits and costs of such a merger, he concluded that "there just wasn't enough . . . beef to it."[30]

One major drawback for Mobil was that the resulting company would have retained its registration in the United Kingdom to avoid a large U.S. tax bill on BP's exploration and production profits. British registration would have required the withdrawal of the merged company's stock from U.S. stock exchanges, leaving Mobil's former shareholders as owners of a foreign stock. Noto believed that his U.S. shareholders would demand a considerable premium to accept that result, and such a premium was not offered by BP. Mobil declined to pursue further a merger with the British company.

Mobil learned several things from that episode: the value of having only a small group involved in merger deliberations, the ability to do without third-party investment bankers, and the need to settle economic terms before focusing on operational matters. Mobil then looked at the possibility of purchasing Conoco and at possible mergers with Chevron and Amoco, which was soon acquired by BP. Mobil did not look at Shell, and it did not initially look seriously at a merger with Exxon.[31]

That position changed in the late spring of 1998 when Noto went to an American Petroleum Institute meeting in Washington, D.C. Raymond, who was then serving as API chairman, was also there. After the meeting, the two men met privately over lunch at Mobil's headquarters in Fairfax, Virginia. Accounts by the two differ somewhat about what was said at the luncheon, but they agree that the primary purpose was to discuss the joint operations of the Exxon and Mobil refining and marketing businesses in Japan. There was the possibility of merging the two marketing companies and making changes in a jointly owned refining company. The discussion provided the opportunity for Noto to ask Raymond, "Is there any reason we should restrict it [the merger discussion] to Japan?" After the meeting, several telephone calls between the two expanded the scope of the discussion to include the possible merger of downstream assets in the United States, and then, at Noto's suggestion, to consider a deal that went beyond the U.S downstream, perhaps even to a worldwide merger.[32]

The two companies were not strangers. In addition to the normal interactions of oil company representatives at the API, the National Petroleum Council, and other industry organizations, Exxon and Mobil had a long history of close cooperation. Both had been parts of John D. Rockefeller's Standard Oil Company until its breakup in 1911. Before that date, Jersey Standard (Exxon) had functioned as a holding company for more than 70 affiliates, including Standard Oil Company of New York (Mobil), and as an operating company primarily involved in administration and refining. Standard Oil Company of New York had focused on marketing and distribution. After the 1911 breakup, both companies grew into vertically integrated international oil companies. From 1931 to 1962, the two companies were fifty-fifty partners in facilities in East Asia under the Stanvac joint venture. Before the nationalizations of the 1970s, both were deeply involved in the post–World War II oil industry in the Middle East as members of consortia in Iran, Iraq, and Saudi Arabia, where they were partners with Chevron and Texaco in Aramco. They both took part in the development of the Trans-Alaska Pipeline System in Alaska and the giant Statfjord project in the Norwegian sector of the North Sea, and they searched for opportunities together in Russia in the 1990s.

At a lunch on June 16, 1998, in Fairfax, Noto acknowledged that Mobil had looked at a variety of merger partners but had found no combination that made good sense. Raymond then asked, "What are your personal ambitions?" In reply, Noto said, "Look, Lee, I have no ambitions. If we ever do anything like this, I understand that I'm the minority company. I'm happy to help with the merger. I'm happy to stay on for a while and help out to get things done, make sure it works well, but that's it."[33] Noto was agreeable to having Raymond as CEO of a merged company. The two men talked also about areas of operations where their two companies were complementary and those where they might overlap.[34]

In follow-up talks the next week, Noto and Raymond identified three key questions. First, could economic terms attractive to both companies be reached? Noto knew that however the matter was publicized, this was a takeover of Mobil, whose shareholders would not agree to it without being given a premium. Second, would regulatory authorities allow the merger? Both men knew that the Mobil-BP arrangement in Europe would need to be undone, and they thought California refining would be a problem because both companies owned large refineries in the state. But those matters did not seem to be insurmountable. Third, could they create a unified, efficient company out of the two organizations? The companies appeared to have complementary strengths, but could they be combined to create a common corporate culture and a unified organization?

After the preliminary conversations, Noto informed Mobil's board of his discussions with Raymond, and the board authorized him to move forward. With that endorsement, Noto and Mobil's general counsel, Samuel H. Gillespie, met with Raymond and Exxon's general counsel, Charles W. Matthews, to explore the relative ownership weighting of a combined company.

Raymond also solicited the opinions of Exxon's senior vice presidents about a possible merger. Under Raymond, a small, cohesive group of top managers made many high-level corporate decisions informally. When a matter of corporate strategy or planning arose, Raymond would call one of his senior vice presidents to discuss the matter and make the appropriate decisions. Formal meetings of the management committee became infrequent. When held, they were used to review routine matters such as a new energy outlook or safety and operational performance data. The small group of senior executives had confidence in one another's judgments, and informal consultations generally produced good results.

To consider the merger, however, Raymond held a formal management committee meeting and solicited the views of its members. Rene Dahan and Harry Longwell were strongly supportive. Bob Wilhelm was not. He felt that Mobil was badly run, and he considered other companies as more promising merger targets.[35] Despite Wilhelm's misgivings, the senior executives encouraged Raymond to continue to explore the prospects of a merger with Mobil.

Top managers of both companies kept their boards apprised of the progress of discussions, and the boards remained supportive. But after Raymond and Noto failed to agree on a mutually acceptable valuation for the merger, they discontinued negotiations on August 5, 1998. Less than a week later, the world of oil changed abruptly when BP announced an agreement to acquire Amoco.[36] The premium of more than 15 percent to be paid by BP for Amoco set a measure by which the Exxon and Mobil boards could assess Exxon's offer to Mobil. Raymond called Noto and said: "One of our neighbors just sold his house. So we now have a lot better idea of what a house is worth. Don't you think we ought to kind of get back together and look at [our] house?"[37] Noto agreed.

Charles W. Matthews, general counsel, Exxon Corporation, 1999.
ExxonMobil Historical Collection, di_06113.

In a series of meetings that quickly followed, a small number of executives from each company discussed potential synergies from a merger. Present at the meetings for Exxon were Dahan and Longwell as well as Matthews and Raymond; Noto brought in a somewhat larger number of executives, including Gillespie and Eugene A. Renna, the president and chief operating officer of Mobil. In addition, Mobil at this stage brought in Goldman Sachs as its investment advisor. Exxon felt no immediate need for investment advice.

The meetings identified enough benefits to justify continued planning. At that point, a complicated series of meetings between the planners, the company boards, and legal counsel sought to determine a mutually acceptable evaluation of the merger. They had to decide what assets might need to be sold, and—in the case of Mobil—what strategic alternatives it might pursue instead of a merger with Exxon. In late September, Noto informed the Mobil board that a deal was progressing with Exxon and that any valuation gap seemed likely to be closed. Goldman Sachs later presented the board with other candidates for a merger, having concluded that Exxon's past skepticism regarding mergers and its reluctance to pay a premium for an acquisition made it an unlikely merger partner. Although the Mobil board was understandably confused by the contradictory advice, it supported the continuation of Noto's negotiations with Exxon. Disappointed with Goldman Sachs's presentation, Noto quietly removed the firm from the role of inside advisor.[38]

The companies held secret meetings with officials from both the U.S. Federal Trade Commission and the European Union's Directorate General for Competition (DG IV) to assess the agencies' attitudes toward a possible merger. The meetings included Robert Pitofsky of the FTC and Karel Van Miert, the head of DG IV and the man who had achieved trans-Atlantic notice for blocking an earlier merger between Boeing and McDonnell Douglas. (The North American units of the companies merged in 1997.) They identified no insurmountable obstacles to an Exxon-Mobil merger, though it was clear that the European BP-Mobil alliance would need to be dissolved and some downstream assets in the United States spun off.[39]

Raymond and Noto agreed that should the FTC formally object to the merger, the companies would resort to the courts to obtain approval of the combination. Both considered this "hell or high water" provision important. They felt that the FTC would not block the merger if it sensed that a negative ruling would be challenged in court.[40] The two executives were confident that any issues with European competition authorities could be managed. Raymond recalled their optimism: "Neither Lou nor I could envision anything that they could reasonably ask us to do that would be a showstopper."[41]

A second essential element from Exxon's perspective was to have the merger considered a "pooling of interests" within the definitions of the U.S. tax code. This meant that the financial accounts of the companies would be combined and the transaction would be considered a tax-free reorganization.[42] Under tax rules at the time, a pooled-interest combination did not have to reflect on its balance sheet any premium—or "goodwill"—that had been paid to shareholders of the acquired company and did not need to amortize that premium against earnings. Considering that in April 1999 the value of the merger was about $115 to a holder of a Mobil share, which at that time sold for about $87, the $28-a-share premium otherwise would have been charged against earnings as an additional expense to the newly merged company. The companies' accounting firms confirmed and certified the merger as a pooling of interests, and it went ahead under that understanding.[43] That proved fortunate, since the Financial Accounting Standards Board soon after changed its accounting standards, and the pooling-of-interest combination was no longer allowed.[44]

Exxon's method of compensating Mobil shareholders also proved advantageous. As described in the later merger proxy, Exxon would exchange 1.32015 shares of ExxonMobil stock for each share of Mobil stock.[45] Based on the companies' stock prices on various comparison dates, this represented a premium of 15 percent to 33 percent. In most giant mergers, the acquiring company issues substantial additional shares to fulfill its commitment to the acquired company. But Exxon could draw from the large block of its own shares it had repurchased since the early 1980s, allowing it to exchange shares held in its treasury account for the majority of the acquired Mobil shares. When Raymond presented the merger to Exxon shareholders in 1999, they authorized the issuance of additional shares needed to complete the transaction and to provide a cushion of authorized shares for future purposes, including executive bonuses. The company's stock prices remained stable after the merger, reflecting the market's judgment that there had been no significant dilution of share value.[46]

From September through November 1998, the two companies hammered out important details of the merger. Those included the relative ownership percentages of the combined company, with Exxon accounting for about 70 percent of the value and Mobil about 30 percent.

Representation on the board reflected that division of ownership, with Mobil receiving six seats on the nineteen-member board. Corporate head-quarters would be in Irving, Texas. Global refining and marketing would be run out of Mobil's former headquarters in Fairfax, Virginia. Headquarters for global production, exploration, development, and chemicals would remain in the Houston area. The chairman and CEO would be Raymond, with Noto, Mobil's chairman, serving as vice chairman. Renna, Mobil's president, would oversee refining and marketing. Exxon's Longwell would head exploration and production; Dahan, chemicals and global services. The two companies set up a transition group for planning the process of consolidation, including the treatment of employees. Finally, to forestall the emergence of a competing deal, the agreement stipulated that if either company pulled out of the merger, it would pay $1.5 billion in fees. Both boards approved the stipulations, and in mid-November the companies prepared the first draft of the merger agreement.[47]

On November 19, Dahan and Longwell met with Renna to discuss Exxon's vision for the newly merged company. At that meeting, the two Exxon executives revealed their plan to create a global company organized along functional lines, a form that copied neither Exxon's nor Mobil's existing organizational structure.

After a briefing by lead executives on the progress of merger negotia-tions, a regularly scheduled meeting of Exxon's board on November 25, 1998, endorsed the merger. That same day, the carefully guarded secrecy surrounding the merger talks began to unravel as several major news out-lets printed speculative reports about merger talks between Exxon and Mobil.[48] The two CEOs publicly confirmed the talks on November 27, which accelerated the resolution of remaining issues. By November 30, both companies were ready to move ahead. Raymond briefed the Exxon board the next day, and the board gave its unanimous approval.[49] Noto convened his board the same day and received its endorsement, though with one dissent. By the end of the day on December 1, 1998, the deal was done. Exxon Corporation and Mobil Corporation agreed to join together as the Exxon Mobil Corporation, or ExxonMobil.

Although rumors of the merger had circulated throughout the previ-ous week, its formal announcement captured the attention of the financial world and the petroleum industry. In what the *Wall Street Journal* called "the largest takeover in history," Exxon disclosed plans to buy Mobil for $75.3 billion, creating the largest industrial corporation in the world. The combined company would produce more than 2.5 million barrels a day of petroleum liquids, making it the leader in global production among the international oil companies. Indeed, that figure exceeded the combined production of the next three largest American companies, Chevron, Texaco, and Amoco. This was a giant undertaking from any perspective. According to one analyst, "Mobil was a monster already, and Exxon was far larger."[50] The new consolidated company would be both the largest oil refiner and the leading marketer of natural gas in the world. It would combine Exxon's proven capacity to finance and manage giant projects with Mobil's healthy list of prospects, along with two well-established chemical companies, ample reserves of both oil and natural gas, and well-developed research capabilities.

The subheading of the *Wall Street Journal* article captured the consensus among media analysts about the root cause of the merger: "Historic Deal, Precipitated by Plunging Oil Prices, Signals Shift in Industry."[51] One New York analyst well summarized that view: "The overriding factor here is that the oil industry is in its worst shape in a decade. . . . This is going to be a very rough ride, and small craft are not going to make it in this storm." A dueling analyst scoffed at that argument: "It is an insult to Exxon and Mobil to say this is happening due to low prices. . . . Companies this size don't base their spending on anything more than $15 oil anyway."[52] But low prices had increased pressures for cost cutting, and a merger provided new opportunities for extensive cuts. When asked about the possibility of further cuts at Mobil, Noto replied simply: "We're at bone."[53] Media reports of estimates from the two companies indicated that the merger would eliminate 9,000 jobs, close duplicative offices and other facilities, and allow for a variety of streamlining measures that would save as much as $2.8 billion for the merged company. A writer for *Newsweek* cut through the numbers and focused on two of the expected short-term results: "The deal is mostly about firing people and goosing the stock price."[54] In the long term, it was also part of a fundamental realignment in an industry searching for the best path forward toward long-term profitability.

Although most analysts seemed optimistic about the economic prospects for the merger, many voiced skepticism about the capacity of Exxon and Mobil to merge cultures. A recurring theme in comments was the difference in the tone of the companies in dealing with the public. The *Wall Street Journal* characterized the cultural difference between the two companies as "tight-lipped Exxon, outspoken Mobil." To illustrate its point, the article repeated a year-old comment from Lee Raymond that a good day was a day when his company stayed out of the news. It also noted that at the press conference to discuss the merger, Noto "joked with reporters," whereas "Raymond caustically responded to a reporter's question on antitrust strategy."[55] A later article in the same newspaper with the headline "Mobil, Exxon like Oil, Water on Air Pollution" noted that both companies had taken public stances skeptical of climate-change legislation such as the Kyoto Protocol. But while Exxon had taken a hard line on the lack of conclusive scientific evidence about the reality of climate change, Noto had "at least twice visited the White House searching for compromise." Spokesmen for environmental groups noted the difference in approach of the two companies, voicing fears that the merger would hinder efforts to reach agreement on climate-change policy. When translated into the language of politics, this became, "We fear the merger will create the Death Star of global warming."[56]

Such observations submerged a grain of truth under a thick layer of caricature. One analyst called Raymond "the mother of all cost cutters." Another called Exxon "conservative to a fault" and observed that Mobil "likes to run things tighter and with fewer people." One contrast made in the media between Exxon and Mobil did have far-reaching implications for the merged company. In the all-important area of exploration, the *Wall Street Journal* asserted that Mobil was "more aggressive," whereas Exxon, by contrast, "isn't a player in some of the more exciting areas of global exploration." A companion article was more explicit: "Mobil also ventured more confidently into politically charged Central Asia, taking advantage of the dissolution of the Soviet Union." The *Journal* reported that Mobil's "five-year reserve-replacement ratio is 147 percent of production, while Exxon's reserves grew by less than 1 percent last year, and its five-year reserve-replacement ratio averages 102 percent."[57] An analyst interviewed by the *New York Times* addressed exploration in stronger language: "From 1988 to 1998, Exxon's exploration and production expenditures rose 8 percent. Mobil's rose 14 percent. . . . They [Mobil] were pushing the envelope, and when prices fell they had to cut back. Exxon has tried to build a very large presence systematically, without paying much attention to month-to-month or even year-to-year fluctuations in oil prices. They are brutally efficient."[58] The comment pointed to a significant factor that made the long-term prospects for the merger so positive. Mobil had a stockpile of interesting prospects in "exciting" areas where Exxon was not active. Moreover, Exxon's financial strengths and its wide experience in completing big projects boded well for the long-term development of the best of those prospects.

As the initial media reactions to the merger announcement waned, in December 1998, far from the popular press, Raymond discussed the potential strengths of the merger at a meeting at the investment firm J. P. Morgan. He stressed three great potential benefits: the larger worldwide portfolio of petroleum and petrochemical operations available to the merged company; its enhanced ability to compete with international majors and government-owned oil companies; and the expanded financial, technological, and human resources that would allow the company to take on new opportunities. While clearly pleased with the resources that the merger provided, Raymond emphasized business synergies, which he characterized as the "unique opportunity for efficiencies not available to the stand-alone companies."[59]

Raymond estimated that after three years, savings from the merger would add $2.3 billion annually to earnings, with growth in such benefits after that time. He expected cost savings from several areas: the elimination of overlapping businesses; more selective exploration; organizational efficiencies; the applications of best operational practices; and improvements in procurement, manufacturing, and supply. Although acknowledging the importance of short-term benefits, Raymond emphasized the long-term benefits from improved capital management. He noted that the broader portfolio of projects within ExxonMobil could be ranked, allowing the company to take better advantage of the opportunities that would arise from its large size and broad presence around the world. Particularly interesting were his comments about return on investment, the central measure of success within Exxon. Raymond acknowledged that Mobil's return had averaged less than Exxon's in the recent past, and that

www.exxon.com

Transition teams plan merger
Page 2

Historic meetings held
Page 4

Minority business award made
Page 6

Power agreement!
Page 3

About the people and the business of Exxon

ExxonToday

Volume 8 • Number 6   June 14, 1999

Exxon, Mobil shareholders: I do, I do

Exxon and Mobil shareholders voted overwhelmingly in favor of the proposed Exxon-Mobil merger. Votes cast by Exxon shareholders were more than 99 percent in favor. Of the votes cast by Mobil shareholders, more than 98 percent were in favor.

Exxon Chairman Lee Raymond and Mobil Chairman Lou Noto said the approvals demonstrated that shareholders of the two companies understood the value of the merger in today's highly competitive marketplace.

"New competitors are emerging in all segments of our business, including the expansion of state-owned oil companies beyond their traditional areas," Raymond said. "The scale of the new firm will help us compete more effectively. The greater financial, technical and human resources provided by this merger will increase our ability to handle large, complex international energy projects."

Noto thanked shareholders for their vote and said, "We're operating in a volatile world economy and in a global industry that is becoming increasingly competitive. As a U.S.-based energy leader, we believe the Exxon Mobil Corporation will be well-positioned in this rigorous, global energy business environment, providing its shareholders with good value, its employ-

Meeting the press: Exxon Chairman Lee Raymond and Mobil Chairman Lou Noto held a joint press conference after the companies' annual meetings.

ees with challenging jobs and its customers with quality products at competitive prices."

The shareholder votes are major steps in creating the new company. The proposed merger is still subject to other conditions, including antitrust review by the U.S. Federal Trade Commission and the European Commission. The companies expect those reviews to be completed by about the end of the third quarter.

What's new

Wealth of info: You'll find the new *Financial and Operating Review* at Exxon's Web site. Many employees and people in the financial community use the well-illustrated 72-page brochure as a reference for statistics and other information about the company.

Station awards: Imperial received honors in 14 out of 26 categories at the annual Canadian service-station awards. The company won first place in seven categories: overall station appearance, pump island appearance, overall station interior merchandising, merchandising of beverages, merchandising of salty snacks, merchandising of motor oils and uniformed personnel. Imperial was the runner-up for convenience-store appearance, interior automotive products display and merchandising of tobacco. The company received honorable mentions for overall customer service, merchandising of confectionery, car-wash appearance and retail gasoline sales incentives campaign.

Baton Rouge earns governor's award

Louisiana Governor Mike Foster presented the Baton Rouge Chemical Plant with an Environmental Leadership Award for using innovative technology to reduce waste.

The site's Ceramic Membrane Filtration Project uses cutting-edge methods to

Clean, clear water: Teresa Jurgens-Kowal (left), Joel Parrott and Steve Beadle of the Baton Rouge Chemical Plant check the red sight-glass of the innovative water filter.

remove particulates from process water. Fewer particulates in the process water require fewer additive chemicals that later have to be biologically destroyed in the site wastewater treatment unit. According to Bruce Barbre, environmental coordinator, the new process decreases the amount of organic waste discharged to surface waters and helps Exxon easily meet permit limits.

"The process is typically used in making food products such as cranberry juice," says Bruce Wickert, manufacturing engineer. "Ceramic membrane filtration makes the juice a clear red. This project is unique because we tried a technology that hadn't been used in this type of setting. It is a technical and economic success."

Process operations at the chemical plant tested the

University recruiting takes team effort

University recruiting supports Exxon's strategy of "continually improving an already high-quality work force." With this article, Exxon Today continues its series examining long-term business strategies listed in Exxon's annual Financial and Operating Review.

By Deborah Heath

Exxon's Coordinated University Recruiting Team looks for hundreds of good people.

The team of nearly 350 employees, from Human Resources staff members to individuals who volunteer their time, is committed to finding the best-qualified graduates to join Exxon's work force.

To hire about 600 new employees during the 1998-1999 recruiting season, Exxon held about 175 campus recruiting trips throughout the United States. About 75 percent of the new hires will have been recent university graduates.

See **Strategies**, page 3

See **Water**, page 3

QuickPix

Statistics about our business and our people

Powering up

An average American household uses about 10,600 kilowatt-hours of electricity a year. It takes about 3.5 tons of coal to provide that much electricity.

Exxon's 1998 worldwide coal production share of 15.5 million tons could power more than 4.4 million U.S. homes.

Source: Exxon Coal and Minerals   Juan Thomassie

Children find ways to help tigers

By Deborah Heath

You can do a lot with spare lunch change and a few pickles. Just ask the hundreds of children who have raised money for the Save the Tiger Fund and discovered new ways to link science and concern for the environment with positive action.

► At Hamilton Junior High in Cypress, Texas, Exxon employee Wayne Lewoczko, a Junior Achievement volunteer, encouraged students to raise money to help save the tiger — the school's mascot. Students and teachers put their spare

See **Tigers**, page 7

International effort: Students at Xiamen International School in China made tiger-shaped beanbags, tiger cookies, postcards and fact books and sold them to raise money for tiger conservation.

Front page of ExxonToday, *Exxon's monthly employee newspaper, announcing the shareholders' approval of the Exxon and Mobil merger, June 14, 1999. ExxonMobil Historical Collection, di_08133.*

a weighted average for the two companies might suggest ExxonMobil's returns would be lower than that of Exxon alone. But he estimated that by the third year after the merger, near-term synergies and capital-productivity improvements would raise the combined return above Exxon's stand-alone return. He predicted that by the fifth year, the combined return would be at least three percentage points better than that of Exxon alone.[60] Raymond's forecast proved to be conservative.

Assessments of the prospective benefits of the merger were all well and good, but they were not yet reality. For them to be realized, the companies had to navigate the difficult process of completing the merger. That required obtaining legal approvals, fulfilling regulatory requirements, designing an organizational structure, selecting management personnel, deciding on policies and procedures to use, and designing an appropriate strategy. All that had to be done while continuing the ongoing business operations of the two still-separate companies without any damaging loss of focus.

Obtaining legal approval was complicated and time-consuming.[61] The Exxon-Mobil merger was a major test of cooperation between the European Commission (the executive body of the European Union) and the FTC.[62] Exxon and Mobil began the process of obtaining legal approval shortly after the official announcement of the merger. They supplied a large number of documents, and hoped for relatively rapid reactions. In fact, the review process took longer than expected.

The first official response came from the European Commission in September 1999, when it approved the merger subject to a series of compliance steps, almost all of which the two companies had anticipated.[63] The commission understandably demanded that Mobil sell its 30 percent interest in the recently completed BP-Mobil joint-marketing venture in Europe. It also required the sale of some retail gasoline-marketing assets Mobil operated jointly in Germany with the firm Aral. In addition, Mobil had to find a buyer for some lubricant-manufacturing operations, and Exxon had to sell some assets associated with its lubrication business for commercial airlines. The European Commission also required Mobil to divest itself of the Dutch gas-trading company Megas, and Exxon to withdraw from its 25 percent interest in the German gas-distribution company Thyssengas. A Mobil pipeline serving Gatwick Airport, outside London, had to be sold. All in all, these were minor changes, with no impact on upstream oil and gas production.

The FTC's investigation of the merger took eleven months, with results announced in late November 1999. The FTC reviewed numerous local markets to assess the competitive impact of the merger, and it brought state officials into its deliberations. The commission found potential competitive problems in the marketing of gasoline in the Northeast and mid-Atlantic areas of the United States and in Arizona, California, and five metropolitan areas in Texas. In those areas, it required the companies to dispose of 2,431 gas stations. At the time, Exxon alone supplied about 6,500 stations in the United States and 32,000 worldwide.[64] Mobil had about a third as many. The merged company would be left with more than 45,000 worldwide.[65] The FTC also saw the need for an array of divestments, including the marketing of specially formulated gasoline in California, the refining of jet fuel for the navy on the West Coast, several terminals for petroleum products, the refining and marketing of paraffinic lubricant base oils, Mobil's interest in the Trans-Alaska Pipeline, and Exxon's operations in Guam.

Several of the FTC's requirements were particularly unwelcome. Either Exxon or Mobil had to leave one of the two major interstate pipelines in the United States (Colonial or Plantation). Exxon had to exit the profitable jet-turbine-lubricant business, in which Exxon and Mobil held about a 90 percent market share. Exxon had to sell service stations in the Northeast.[66] Exxon officials deeply regretted the demand that it dispose of its refinery in Benicia, California, and exit all gasoline marketing in California. The recently modernized refinery was highly efficient and prized by Exxon. That demand was included at the request of the State of California, which believed that gasoline refining was concentrated in the hands of too few companies in the state and did not want any further concentration. In any event, the new company would still own a large Mobil refinery in Torrance, near Los Angeles.

The headline of the FTC press release about its provisional approval of the merger proclaimed, "Exxon/Mobil Agree to Largest FTC Divestiture Ever in Order to Settle FTC Antitrust Charges; Settlement Requires Extensive Restructuring and Prevents Merger of Significant Competing U.S. Assets."[67] From the point of view of the companies, the actions demanded by the FTC seemed far less significant. To be fair to the FTC, the commission faced a series of difficult calculations about all the big oil mergers of the era, and so of necessity fell back on traditional mea-surements of the impact of each merger on the level of concentration in specific and narrowly defined markets. Ultimately, it approved all the megamergers of the era while requiring only relatively minor divestments. Raymond briefly considered challenging the FTC on the disposition of the Benicia refinery, but he concluded that the companies should comply with the FTC's quite limited requirements and move on.

ENGINEERING INTEGRATION

While antitrust officials deliberated, planning for consolidation went for-ward. In choosing the basic organizational structure for ExxonMobil, the leaders of the new company made the bold decision to consolidate the companies within a functionally organized global structure. This meant completing a process Exxon had started in the 1980s, and it required a leap of faith that the new company could simultaneously integrate the operations of the merged companies and create an effective new global structure. In the years just before the merger, Exxon had made signifi-cant steps toward creating a global company organized by function. The chemical company, exploration, production, and computing and some other support activities were globally organized. But Exxon still employed a mixture of organizational structures in other parts of its operations. Exxon USA and Imperial Oil, in Canada, were major country-based divisions without exploration functions. Exxon operated conventional petroleum operations outside North America through the multinational Exxon Company, International (ECI). But ECI nevertheless maintained national affiliates as well as some broader support units, such as tanker supply. Despite some variance in the corporation's organizational struc-ture, a trend was clear: as Exxon grew and as new communications tech-nologies made global operations possible, it had moved from national or regional management toward global management. The massive scale of the Mobil merger accelerated the pace of organizational changes already in motion at Exxon.

Skillful handling of the consolidation process was crucial, since the choices made would shape the future prospects for ExxonMobil. There was also a clear imperative to move quickly in order to avoid an extended period of confusion and poor financial results. The situation called for the application of basic principles of engineering efficiency to the complex task of fashioning one company from two. In the year between the announcement and the approval of the merger, planning for integration went smoothly enough to allow ExxonMobil to hit the ground running.

The merger focused attention on the need to translate general discussions of consolidation into a concrete structure. In the months following the merger announcement, a rough division of labor emerged within Exxon. Dahan became the key merger planner, with the lead role in the overarching design of the new company. Longwell fleshed out the specifics in the upstream operations, and Wilhelm had the task of organizing the support functions. On the Mobil side, Renna led the effort to structure the downstream.

Dahan and Longwell saw both the need and the opportunity to adopt a global functional structure, that is, one that managed critical functions within a unified structure capable of coordinating activities worldwide. Months before the merger was initiated, they had speculated about the value of reorganizing Exxon along global functional lines. After the merger talks began, they became convinced that Mobil also was not optimally organized. According to Dahan, "Mobil didn't know clearly where to go. . . . It had partly a highly localized organization. . . . [The] U.S. was run almost totally separate from the rest of it. It had partly worldwide things on certain types of functions, but there was no kind of big picture, and it was very opportunistically done. . . . And this is where Mobil was. They were a little bit of everything."[68] Dahan and Longwell agreed that in a company the size of ExxonMobil, "the time and the era of affiliates and big, independent, powerful affiliates had to come to an end." That view proved acceptable to Mobil.[69]

Both Dahan and Longwell had held senior positions in ECI, where they had observed firsthand the benefits of functional global organization. They had seen how well Exxon Exploration and Exxon Chemical assessed global opportunities, and they were clearly convinced of the value of a company in which the business functions had global scope and responsibility. They had urged that view upon Raymond on a number of occasions, but he had been reluctant to move entirely away from national and regional structures.[70] Later, when discussing the new organization, Raymond acknowledged his unease: "It's inconvenient for a functional organization to have to recognize that there are countries that exist. And when you're doing business in a country, you have a lot of legal obligations just because of that country and you clearly have tax obligations. So there was a lot of discussion about how . . . we deal with that."[71] Despite his initial skepticism, Raymond ultimately accepted the need to step outside traditional ways of doing business. He also understood that the integration of two companies provided an opportune time to introduce bold changes.

Dahan and Longwell addressed Raymond's concerns by designating a "lead country manager" in those nations where more than one function operated. The lead country manager, generally chosen from the function with the most significant business operations in the country, would be the overall representative of ExxonMobil to the government. On issues that affected other businesses, the lead country manager would accompany the appropriate business manager when dealing with the government. Raymond agreed that this proposal appeared to be workable. That managerial designation was, in Longwell's view, the "final linchpin" to the decision to move forward with the global functional structure.[72] When Dahan and Longwell, with Renna's endorsement, presented the detailed organizational plans for the global structure, neither Raymond nor Noto objected.[73] All realized that their decision would greatly affect the success or failure of the merger.

Within months, Dahan had set up a merger transition group and embarked on turning the global functional concept into a concrete organizational proposal. At its largest, transition planning involved somewhat more than 2,000 people, an indication of both the complexity of the planning and the thoroughness of the effort.[74] As planned, Exxon-Mobil employed functional divisions with worldwide responsibilities (see figure 9.2).

One special case was Imperial Oil Limited. Although Exxon Corporation owned almost 70 percent of Imperial, that company's management had often used the 30 percent share held by other shareholders to argue that it had an obligation to its non-Exxon shareholders to operate with a degree of independence. Exxon's management differed, feeling that its

FIGURE 9.2. The organization of Exxon Mobil Corporation

UPSTREAM	DOWNSTREAM	OTHER
Exploration	Refining and supply	Chemical company
Development	Fuels marketing	Coal and minerals
Production	Lubricants and specialties	Imperial Oil Ltd.
Gas marketing	Downstream research	Global services
Upstream research		

Source: *Exxon Mobil Corporation*

70 percent ownership of Imperial gave it the authority to call the shots.[75] Imperial had made a number of moves that had not found favor with Exxon.[76] But Exxon's management and shareholders had been unwilling to bring the matter to a head, in part because Canadian law made the buyout of remaining shares difficult and in part because of the expense of purchasing the minority shares.

The merger, however, offered an opportunity to address this lingering problem. ExxonMobil decided to use Mobil's former holdings in that country to create a wholly owned subsidiary, ExxonMobil Canada, to operate all its non-Imperial properties in Canada. The arrangement irritated Imperial, but Raymond was unyielding. He knew that the establishment of a parallel company operating in Canada and not under the control of Imperial was an embarrassing and perhaps inefficient arrangement, but he believed it communicated a strong message: "If [Imperial] had run your business better for the last twenty years, you wouldn't have to be embarrassed."[77]

Exxon named contact executives on the corporation's management committee for the major groups early in the transition. In general, Raymond and Noto became the contact executives for select headquarters departments; Longwell took responsibility for the upstream businesses; Renna, for the downstream companies; Dahan, for chemicals; and Wilhelm, for global services. With that structure in place, the transition teams next turned to deciding who would lead the major units and who would be

Lee Raymond, chairman (left), and Lucio Noto, vice chairman, of the newly formed Exxon Mobil Corporation, 1999. ExxonMobil Historical Collection, di_06253.

their primary subordinates. They knew that most merged companies gave preference to employees and managers of the acquiring merger partner, but they looked for ways to find the best people regardless of company.

For decades, Exxon had rank-ordered all employees after detailed personal evaluations, placing each person in a limited number of categories that reflected his manager's judgment of his relative performance and potential. To attempt to avoid special treatment of Exxon employees, appraisals had included the views of several managers. Those evaluations affected compensation and promotions and reflected the employee's potential to assume greater responsibilities. Mobil's performance-appraisal system was less formal and less systematic than that of Exxon. The differences made it difficult to determine how best to ensure that Mobil employees would be evaluated fairly in comparison with Exxon employees.

Exxon's top management had watched acquiring firms in other mergers discard able employees of the acquired firms, and they felt that the practice was inefficient and not in the long-term interest of the consolidated company. They had been particularly shocked at the ruthlessness of BP's purge of Amoco employees in what had been initially called a "marriage of equals." In Longwell's words: "BP just basically wiped out Amoco, no bones about it. 'Here's your pink slip.... We'll take it over. We don't need you.' Whereas that never entered our mind in terms of doing it that way because . . . we had respect . . . for Mobil going in and their people and their organization."[78] The Exxon management group wanted the best employees, regardless of their company of origin.[79] They wanted employees to have responsibilities that took full advantage of their abilities, and they wanted employees to emerge from the process of job integration with a sense that they worked for a fair company interested in results.

Raymond, Longwell, and Dahan—in close cooperation with Noto and Renna—chose the presidents, executive vice presidents, and vice presidents of the new operating companies early in 1999.[80] Then the process moved on to the evaluation of employees for lower-level positions. By the fall of 1999, the company had determined which employees it wished to keep and which jobs they would be offered, and they had communicated those decisions to the employees. Those who lost their jobs received severance packages.[81]

In the end, a greater percentage of former Mobil employees than Exxon employees lost their jobs in the merger. Before the merger, the two companies combined had 3,194 employees classified as executives, 1,731 with Exxon (54.2 percent) and 1,463 with Mobil (45.8 percent).[82] Shortly after the merger, the total number of executives had fallen to 2,290, and the percentage of Mobil executives had fallen to 33.8 percent of the total.[83] That percentage remained steady through 2005, indicating that the retained Mobil employees tended to stay. The total number of executives had fallen to 1,821 by 2005, only 5 percent more than the number working for Exxon alone before the merger, even though by 2005 ExxonMobil's revenues were triple those of Exxon in 1998.[84]

Among the most senior executives chosen for similarly high-level positions in the new company, those from Mobil (in addition to Noto and Renna) included H. R. (Hal) Cramer, the president of ExxonMobil Fuels Marketing Company; Steve Pryor, named to head up ExxonMobil Lubricants & Petroleum Specialties Company; and Gerry Kohlenberger, the new president of ExxonMobil Global Services Company. Mobil's downstream executives fared better than their upstream counterparts. But Exxon managers filled the large majority of the senior executive positions in ExxonMobil.[85]

The Exxon system for employee-performance evaluation and promotion became the policy of the merged company. Adapting the system to the influx of tens of thousands of former Mobil employees posed challenges. The new Mobil employees were by and large unknown to Exxon evaluators. At the same time, former Mobil supervisors and managers who remained at ExxonMobil were unfamiliar with the workings of the Exxon evaluation system and unfamiliar with heritage Exxon employees. A breaking-in period allowed the traditional Exxon system to recalibrate itself. During the transition period, personnel assessments and assignments had to be done with the realization that only after employees worked in the new company for a while could they be fairly compared with others. In the interim, personnel assessments based on best efforts and the judgments of prior supervisors were used. As offers were accepted and declined, staffing gradually moved forward and the evaluation system became more firmly reestablished.

Not all decisions resulted in the adoption of Exxon's approach. Company computing and communications systems needed to be harmonized to enable ExxonMobil employees to communicate effectively. In the case of the office-document system, the new company adopted Mobil's traditional system, a decision based on its greater internal networking capabilities but also influenced by the quality of the Mobil executive in charge of that area.[86]

Two objectives guided the creation of the legal structure of the new corporation: capture all of the potential legal and tax benefits from a new structure, and minimize problems from national laws under which the corporation and its numerous affiliates were organized. A Corporate Structure Task Force, with representation from law, tax, the controller, and other functions, worked with financial consultants to consider the possibility of using tax-favorable holding companies, with care taken to avoid reopening production-concession agreements or incurring excessive costs from the reregistration of properties already held.[87]

Differences in the cultures of the two companies raised difficult issues. One was the extension of benefits to same-sex partners of employees. Mobil paid such benefits; Exxon generally did not. The merged company adopted Exxon's policy except in states or nations that required such benefits by law. This decision proved controversial, sparking heated debate at ExxonMobil's annual meeting of shareholders.[88] The transition team realized that the adoption of the Exxon policy could alienate former Mobil employees from their new employer. Dahan, who was worried that employees might feel that the new company was hostile to them, wanted to be "very, very cautious to avoid or prevent any such attitude [of hostility] developing in the organization."[89] Nevertheless, the merged company adopted the Exxon policy.

That issue raised a fundamental question: how well could the corporate cultures of the two companies be merged? Dahan recalled concerns that Mobil personnel might "identify with our business principles" but "remain concerned about our way of thinking, our philosophical . . . background," which could "end up being offensive to them." There was no easy answer to the question. Dahan felt that "we did our very best to marry the two [companies] such that we didn't give up [our] basic philosophical point of view."[90]

The language of this statement, as well as the policies ultimately adopted, reflected a practical reality of business. In almost every merger, one company is dominant. Although the Exxon members of the transition team were conscious of the challenge they faced and worked hard to be as fair and objective as possible, they also represented the values and traditions of the acquirer, not the acquired. Exxon had no doubts about its ability to impose its will when necessary, but it tried to remain focused on the overall goal of using the merger to build a stronger, more profitable company.

Lucio Noto's leadership helped make the transition successful. According to Longwell, Noto was "outgoing, upbeat, positive, [and] optimistic. . . . He was instrumental . . . in bringing his organization into the merger and convincing them that this was best for the company."[91] Leadership was a key ingredient in integrating two giant, global companies into a single new concern. The people managing that process for ExxonMobil took a systematic approach to the undertaking, and they succeeded about as well as possible. When the company celebrated the official merger date of November 30, 1999, it had made considerable progress toward the goal of operating ExxonMobil from day one as a global company organized along functional lines.

Once the merger became official, the new ExxonMobil was understandably ebullient. In an op-ed written for the *New York Times*, it declared the merger a "once-in-a-lifetime opportunity . . . to create the world's premier petroleum and petrochemical company." And it noted that "the whole point [is] not to be bigger, but better."[92]

As top management molded two organizations into one, the company went about the business of complying with the conditions of approval by the antitrust authorities. By May 2000, ExxonMobil had worked out the details for dissolving the BP-Mobil fuels and lubricants joint venture in Europe, completed the sale of northeastern and mid-Atlantic service stations to Tosco, and sold the Benicia refinery to Valero Energy Corporation. Those divestments generated revenues that added to the near-term returns of the merger. In a later summary of the divestments, the company estimated that it had gained after-tax proceeds of $4.3 billion from the divested properties, which had a combined annual earnings potential of about $1.7 billion.[93] With the formal merger process competed, ExxonMobil could now focus on the task of integrating its operations.

INTEGRATING OPERATIONS

ExxonMobil's major challenge during and after consolidation was to find the best use for the assets brought into the merged company. Integration was vital in upstream operations. Here, ExxonMobil faced the dilemma of all international oil companies in the era of producer control: how could it find, develop, and produce enough oil and natural gas to continue to expand its reserves? Integration was more complicated in the downstream operations, where the two companies had vast investments in refineries, chemical plants, retail outlets, and transportation. In corporate services ranging from research to public affairs, the people and the approaches of the two companies had to be efficiently combined.

UPSTREAM: DEVELOPMENT AND PRODUCTION

Morris Foster, who became the first head of ExxonMobil Development Company, had a demanding but enjoyable job just after the merger. Born into a poor family in Central Texas, he had worked his way through Texas A&M and then worked his way up the ladder at Exxon. In his distinguished upstream career, Foster had traveled the world from the North Slope to the North Sea to Malaysia developing new reserves for Exxon. While at ECI in the early 1990s, he was among a group of senior executives who had approached Larry Rawl with the idea of forming a worldwide development company. In 1998, that idea became a reality with the creation of Exxon Development Company, with Foster as its first president. The company's global organization was similar to that previously created for both exploration and production. By separating development from exploration and production, Exxon could gain greater competitive advantage from its well-developed expertise in building giant projects on budget and on time. That important organizational innovation increased the company's capacity to draw experts from around the world to complete the work of bringing new reserves into production as efficiently, inexpensively, and quickly as possible. The larger the project, the more important development became. At the time of the merger announcement, Foster, who was still taking preliminary steps to get the recently created Exxon Development up and running, began to plan for a global development organization for the combined companies.[94]

Foster could not contain his excitement when he first examined the portfolio of prospects that Mobil brought into the company. He recalled that at the time, "the [Exxon] development company . . . had four big projects." When he finally could look at the Mobil books, he was astonished at the size and quality of the Mobil projects. The next morning, he said to Harry Longwell: "You're not going to believe this. I feel like a kid in a candy store—[Mobil has] a hundred and forty billion dollars worth of projects . . . they haven't executed. . . . And Harry said, 'I don't want to hear you talk about that, because what it [is] saying is Mobil's in better shape than we are.' [But] they were."[95] The merger greatly increased the

Morris E. Foster, president, ExxonMobil Development Company, 1999.
ExxonMobil Historical Collection, di_06124.

inventory of promising large projects. Mobil had appealing prospects but had lacked the financial and technical resources to develop them quickly. Exxon had those skills but lacked as full a portfolio of attractive projects. This was the sort of synergy that proponents of mergers dream about.

Three Mobil prospects were particularly noteworthy: the Tengiz and Kashagan oil fields in Kazakhstan and the RasGas natural gas project in Qatar. Combined with Exxon's ongoing work on deepwater projects in Angola and the Gulf of Mexico, the Sakhalin-I development in Russia (then about to begin construction), and other projects around the world, the list was a full plate for ExxonMobil and Foster's new organization. But the innovative concept of a separate global development function quickly proved its worth with the mobilization of the people, money, and expertise needed for the projects.

The ExxonMobil Production Company, based in downtown Houston in the old Exxon USA building, had the extremely important job of ensuring the efficient and low-cost operation of the company's many existing producing properties.[96] Terry Koonce returned from his position as head of Exxon Ventures in the former Soviet Union to lead the new organization in its formative years. Koonce inherited a huge production portfolio, and his company generated the solid majority of ExxonMobil's profits. The merged company produced oil and natural gas in more than twenty-five countries, and about one-third of those were new to Koonce and other former Exxon managers.[97] Before the merger, Exxon had begun to improve slowly in the critical area of reserve replacement. From 1990 to 1994, it had replaced just 81 percent of its production (including the effects of reserves it had sold to others); from 1994 to 1998, after the worldwide exploration company had been fully operational for several years, the figure rose to 110 percent. The increase in reserves, however, was not matched by an increase in production, which declined slightly in the five years before the merger. After the merger, daily production jumped from 2.6 million to 4.2 million barrels of oil equivalent per day. At the same time, and even with increased production, ExxonMobil replaced 106 percent of its now-higher production. In 1998 before the merger, Exxon had identified thirty-three major new projects that would come onstream after 1999. In the first postmerger report in 1999, the figure had almost doubled, to sixty-five.[98]

To maintain key relationships with national governments and to help smoothly integrate producing operations, Koonce made trips to more than twenty countries in the year after the merger; Longwell, Noto, Jon Thompson, or Morris Foster often accompanied him. Production was a vital area in which ExxonMobil could not afford to falter, and it did not. Koonce and others succeeded in cementing good relationships with producing nations while holding down production costs.[99] Upon Koonce's retirement in 2004, Foster became the president of ExxonMobil

Production Company. In his work in the development company, Foster had focused on bringing in big projects on time and on budget. He now moved over to manage the operations of those projects and all the other production brought into the merged company.

DOWNSTREAM: REFINING AND CHEMICALS

As ExxonMobil worked quickly to integrate and expand production, it also combined its downstream assets. Eugene Renna managed the process of unifying Exxon and Mobil's downstream assets. A postmerger article in the *Lamp* boasted, "If it were a separate company, ExxonMobil's downstream business would be bigger . . . than General Electric. In fact, it would be one of the top 10 companies in the Fortune Global 500 list."[100] J. Steven Simon, a former Exxon executive, took charge of ExxonMobil Refining & Supply Company under Renna. Upon Renna's retirement in 2000, Simon became the head of the downstream business and a senior vice president of Exxon Mobil Corporation. Long experience in downstream operations made Simon closely attuned to the principles behind the merger, and he rapidly embarked on efforts to absorb the Mobil properties and to optimize long-run profits from the downstream businesses.

Exxon's refinery runs before the merger were about 3.9 million barrels a day. This figure grew by more than 50 percent to almost 6 million b/d for ExxonMobil. Sales of petroleum products went from roughly 5.4 million b/d to nearly 8.9 million b/d (up 65 percent). The combined company owned forty-four refineries in twenty-two countries; 43 percent of its capacity was in the Western Hemisphere, 33 percent in Europe, and 25 percent in the Asia-Pacific region. After the merger, Exxon sold or manufactured petroleum products in 194 countries. It had an impressive geographic balance in international sales: 37 percent in North America, 25 percent in Europe, 23 percent in the Asia-Pacific area, 11 percent in Latin America, and 4 percent in Africa and the Middle East.[101] The new company sold fuels at 700 airports in 80 countries, had more than 40,000 branded stations in 118 nations, and owned and operated 13,000 miles of petroleum pipelines and 350 product terminals.

ExxonMobil had a pressing need to consolidate its refining capacity.[102] Rather than large-scale expansion, downstream investment after the merger focused on increasing the efficiency of existing plants and reducing costs. Those moves were needed, for downstream earnings in 1999 were down two-thirds from the prior year, and industry-wide margins had been declining for one to three years, depending upon the region of the world.[103] The consolidation and integration of refinery and chemical plant operations had been underway at Exxon for some time, as were efforts to reduce energy consumption costs. By the time of the merger, Exxon had integrated a major refining complex with a nearby chemical plant at thirteen sites.[104]

ExxonMobil kept both the Exxon and the Mobil brand names. In doing so, it took into account problems previously experienced by BP, which had rebranded its assets each time it had merged, eliminating the Sohio and Amoco brands in retail marketing. ExxonMobil believed that BP had eliminated brands with established market presence and value, created an unnecessary expense for rebranding its stations and products, and substituted for well-known acquired brands a new brand that required extensive advertising to become broadly known. Exxon's leadership did not believe those sorts of decisions made good business sense.[105]

Immediately following the merger, the number of Exxon- and Mobil-branded service stations remained level with figures from the prior two years, despite a reduction of $1.3 billion in capital investments for marketing facilities. After the merger, the company took a hard look at the profitability of its service station chain, and resumed closing stations. By 2005, their number had dropped to about 35,500. Although the number of stations in 2005 was only about 10 percent greater than the number for Exxon alone in 1998, overall gasoline sales had more than doubled from 1.8 million b/d for Exxon in 1998 to 3.8 million b/d for ExxonMobil in 2005.[106] By most measures, ExxonMobil led its competitors, who had generally done less to reduce expenses, energy use, personnel levels, and had lower average refinery utilization.[107]

Other steps encouraged the continued decline of the break-even point at which the company could make a profit on fuel sales.[108] The company's refineries became better able to produce clean petroleum products from heavier crude oils, which, although more difficult to refine, were less expensive than higher-quality crudes. In 2004 and 2005, the company completed eleven projects to produce low-sulfur diesel fuel, with an equal number scheduled for 2006. Those programs also improved returns from refining and marketing. Return on average capital employed had been a historically high 15.4 percent for Exxon just before the merger. It sank to as low as 5 percent in 2002 before rebounding to 21 percent in 2004 and a robust 32 percent the next year. The measures to improve refining operations, increase service-station returns, and produce a higher-value product slate made significant contributions to the corporation's overall earnings.[109]

Combining the chemical businesses of the two companies proved to be relatively straightforward. ExxonMobil Chemical operated eighty plants in twenty-four countries, with major integrated complexes on the U.S. Gulf Coast and in Belgium, the Netherlands, France, the United Kingdom, Singapore, and Saudi Arabia.[110] With the chemical operations added by the merger, ExxonMobil's chemical sales were about 30 percent greater than those of Exxon before the merger.[111] Yet that percentage understates the importance of the merger to ExxonMobil Chemical. Prime-product chemical sales for Exxon before the merger were about 17 million metric tons; after, they were about 25 million tons. By 2005, sales had grown to almost 27 million metric tons (up 44 percent over the pre-merger Exxon figure).

The new company catapulted into a position as the world's largest producer of olefins, polyethylene, polypropylene, paraxylene, and benzene. It also had a strong position in a variety of other products. Ninety percent of the company's assets were in businesses where its sales ranked number one or two worldwide.[112] The newly merged company undertook significant expansion, starting sixteen major projects within a year. It built or expanded two new facilities in Beaumont, Texas; six in Baton Rouge; and others in Italy, Thailand, Brazil, Shanghai, Guangdong province (in China), Singapore, and Saudi Arabia. In total, ExxonMobil Chemical had fifty-four manufacturing locations around the world, with strong representation in North America, Europe, Asia, and the Middle East.[113] The worldwide market for chemicals was in a slump at the time of the merger, but recovery was underway by 2002, and ExxonMobil Chemical's earnings accelerated rapidly. By 2005, they had risen to $3.94 billion from a postmerger low of $830 million in 2002. Return on capital employed, which had been as high as 35 percent in premerger 1995 and as low as 6.1 percent in 2002, recovered to 28 percent in 2005. With the abundance of

FIGURE 9.3. ExxonMobil Chemical sales rankings, 2005

PRODUCT	GLOBAL SALES RANK
Commodity chemicals	
Paraxylene	1
Olefins	2
Polyethylene	2
Polypropylene	5
Specialty chemicals	
Butyl polymers	1
Fluids	1
Plasticizers/oxo	1
Synthetics	1
Oriented polypropylene films	1
Adhesive polymers	1
Etylene elastomers	2
Petroleum additives	2

Source: *Exxon Mobil Corporation.*

new capacity that ExxonMobil had added by 2005, the company's chemical sales maintained strong market positions in a variety of products, as detailed in figure 9.3.

With strong earnings, a return on capital that rivaled that of petroleum, and leading market positions in a large number of its business segments, ExxonMobil Chemical was the most successful chemical company affiliated with a petroleum company. In returns and size, it had become a strong chemical company in its own right by 2005, mentioned in the same breath as BASF, DuPont, Dow, and other major chemical enterprises.[114]

RESEARCH AND SERVICES

When ExxonMobil turned to the technologies available for development, it was particularly pleased with the choices offered by the combination of the research programs of Exxon and Mobil. The array of technologies that each company contributed was repeatedly cited as one of the synergies that exceeded premerger expectations. Raymond recalled: "Research turned out to be a very pleasant surprise. Like when you open up . . . the box under the Christmas tree. You don't know if there's going to be coal in there or what [is] going to be in there. And on the technology side it was sound technology, and in most cases it was very complementary. We had feared [there] would be a lot of overlap, and it turned out that wasn't the case."[115]

The combined areas of research had considerable application to the central functions of a vertically integrated oil company. For the upstream, those included advances in underground basin modeling, three-dimensional seismic imaging, drilling technology, reservoir characterization and management, materials design, and gas commercialization. In the downstream, the company cited lubrication science and application, solvent-refining technology, hydroprocessing, dewaxing and gas-to-liquid research. The chemical company identified catalysis technology and polypropylene film advances.[116]

In some areas, new insights arose from research programs coming at the same problem from different directions. For example, Mobil's "compositional modeling" of refinery operations used mathematical models to predict how various categories of petroleum molecules would behave during refining. That technology allowed refineries to choose the crude best suited for their equipment, optimizing refining efficiency. After the merger, it allowed scientists at ExxonMobil to "fingerprint" the molecules in individual crude oils, leading to operational modifications that maximized the production of products from specific crudes.

THE DIFFICULT PROBLEMS OF PUBLIC AFFAIRS

The integration of the companies' public affairs departments raised difficult problems that demanded quick solutions as the merged company sought to introduce itself to the public. Indeed, as Raymond, Noto, and other executives pushed through the completion of the merger, critics stepped up their attacks on ExxonMobil's stances on a variety of social and political issues. Some of the controversies, in particular the debate over climate change, came into the merged company primarily through Exxon.

Others came with Mobil, including criticisms of the company for alleged human rights abuses by the Indonesian army near the ExxonMobil natural gas plant in Aceh (the northwestern part of Sumatra). The company's relations with local peoples near its oil-production facilities in Nigeria and Chad, along with human rights abuses in Equatorial Guinea, created similar problems.[117] The Public Affairs Department had to respond to such criticism while also representing the company to a broader public.

Exxon's uncompromising stance on climate change in the 1990s and into the 2000s did not make the job of public affairs at ExxonMobil any easier. By the early 1990s, a growing consensus began to emerge that rising temperatures caused by the accumulation of greenhouse gases in the atmosphere posed a long-term threat to the global environment. Big questions remained. To what extent were greenhouse gases the result of human activities, especially the burning of fossil fuels? Did concern for the Earth's future call for reductions in carbon emissions from human activities? How should this be done and at what cost? As public and political debate over global climate change heightened, Exxon (and later ExxonMobil) became a prominent skeptic of the science of global warming and the public policies proposed to reduce it.[118]

A number of nations, including the United States, met under United Nations auspices in June 1992 in Rio de Janeiro to discuss ways to stabilize and ultimately reduce greenhouse-gas emissions. This gathering produced the United Nations Framework Convention on Climate Change, a voluntary commitment by signatory nations to explore the reductions of emissions. Under the provisions of the framework, some 160 nations reconvened at Kyoto, Japan, in the fall of 1997 to seek a binding agreement. Before the Kyoto meetings convened, however, the United States Senate passed by a 95–0 vote a resolution that it would not look favorably on an agreement that did "serious harm" to the U.S. economy or did not require reductions by all major emitters, including developing nations such as China. Although U.S representatives at Kyoto supported the protocol, the agreement took the form of a treaty, which meant that it had to be approved by a two-thirds vote of the Senate. Political realities dictated that the Kyoto Protocol was not submitted to the Senate for approval. It entered into force in 2004, with the United States as the most significant developed nation that was not a signatory.[119]

In these years, Lee Raymond became an outspoken critic of the Kyoto Protocol and its approach to reducing greenhouse-gas emissions. He laid out his basic objections in an article entitled "Climate Change: Don't Ignore the Facts" in the fall of 1996 in Exxon's shareholder magazine. He argued that the "scientific evidence remains inconclusive as to whether human activities affect global climate" and cautioned that "those who argue otherwise are drawing on bad science, faulty logic or unrealistic assumptions" before concluding that "we must reject policies that will clearly impose a heavy burden of costs but offer benefits that are largely speculative and undefined." Strongly opposed to mandatory government regulations to reduce fossil fuel use, Raymond advocated "voluntary, market-based steps along with a better understanding of how humans and ecosystems can adapt to climate change" as the best approach to policies that are "rational, scientifically sound and cost effective."[120]

Raymond gave a more highly publicized speech with many of the same arguments at the fifteenth World Petroleum Conference in Beijing in October 1997, just before the vote on a binding agreement at Kyoto. The timing and location of the presentation amplified the voice of the CEO of Exxon. Raymond spoke bluntly: "Only four percent of the carbon dioxide entering the atmosphere is due to human activities. . . . Leaping to radically cut this tiny sliver of the greenhouse pie on the premise that it will affect climate defies common sense."[121] He said "With no readily available economic alternatives on the horizon, fossil fuels will continue to supply most of the world's . . . energy needs for the foreseeable future." After observing that "the most pressing environmental problems of the developing nations are related to poverty, not global climate change," he told the audience that "addressing these problems will require economic growth, and that will entail increasing, not curtailing, the use of fossil fuels."[122]

The well-publicized speech in Beijing made Raymond a ready target for those who supported strong public policies to reduce greenhouse-gas emissions. In an interview soon after he spoke, a *Wall Street Journal* reporter asked if a "low-profile [stance on public issues] is the Exxon way, why are you taking on the greenhouse issue just at a time when the *Valdez* has sort of drifted away?" "Somebody's got to speak up," Raymond responded. "Somebody's got to come forth and say, wait a minute, do we really understand what we're doing here?" He felt a responsibility to oppose what he considered ill-conceived public policy that would have high costs and uncertain benefits given the limits of scientific knowledge about climate change.[123]

In the earlier stages of the public-policy debate on climate change, many within the petroleum industry had taken positions on climate change similar to those of Raymond. Other major energy companies previously had joined Exxon to form the Global Climate Coalition (GCC) in 1989 under the auspices of the National Association of Manufacturers. The GCC, whose members included petroleum, automobile, and mineral-extraction companies, as well as several industry associations, argued for caution in adopting new climate policies. But as climate change became more controversial, a number of petroleum companies, including BP and Shell, withdrew from the organization, and it disbanded in 2002. As time passed and scientific opinion shifted toward greater concern for the impact of the growing use of fossil fuels on global warming, ExxonMobil grew increasingly isolated in its position on climate change.

On the controversial issues raised by the debate over climate change, effective communication with the public proved difficult. Beginning in the 1970s, Mobil had used advocacy advertising to state its positions in national magazines and newspapers on key issues.[124] Using opinion essays on oil-related matters of public interest, the company had practiced "creative confrontation" to engage the public. In adopting an approach earlier taken by Mobil, ExxonMobil took a significant step away from Exxon's traditional public relations posture. It employed advocacy ads to recommend "moving past Kyoto" toward "a sounder climate policy."[125] Concrete proposals put forward by the company included encouragement of voluntary actions, promotion of carbon storage, additional scientific research, the realistic appraisal of renewable energy sources, and research on promising long-term technological options for reducing greenhouse gases. These proposals, of course, received much less attention than the reputation of the company's CEO as "one of the most outspoken executives in the nation against regulation to curtail global warming."[126]

Concerned that the company's traditional stance on climate was too rigid, Frank Sprow, the vice president of Safety, Health and Environment at ExxonMobil, met in early 2002 with Raymond, Dahan, and Renna

Frank B. Sprow, vice president of Safety, Health and Environment, 1999.
ExxonMobil Historical Collection, di_06129.

to discuss further modifications of the company's approach to climate change. Rather than maintain that the company was "not going to do anything until the science is one hundred percent clear," Sprow proposed a risk-based approach that assessed what cost-effective actions should be taken when there was a high risk of adverse effects of warming. He wanted to spend resources where "they are likely to do the most good, and that is on step-out technology to mitigate the risk."[127] Raymond agreed, and

Sprow put together a project along the lines the group had discussed. He found a partner in Stanford University. Sprow approached other companies about participating in order to give the project the legitimacy that it might lack if ExxonMobil were the only supporter. Eventually, General Electric, Schlumberger, and Toyota agreed to join the effort.

The new Global Climate and Energy Project was led by Franklin M. Orr Jr., the dean of the School of Earth Sciences at Stanford University, and funded with $225 million over ten years. The funding supported research to identify and develop low-emission, high-efficiency energy technologies and share the results with a broad audience. Even before the public announcement of the project on November 20, 2002, the company had funded several academic efforts at leading universities to study climate change and ways to address it. Sponsorship of academic research, however, was undermined by media reports of the company's support for think tanks that published materials disputing the reality of global warming and opposing initiatives to limit the emissions of greenhouse gases.[128]

After Raymond's retirement at the end of 2005, the tone of ExxonMobil's public pronouncements gradually became less combative. The company placed more emphasis on the practical problems of implementing effective and cost-efficient public policies regarding climate change. It had also ended its support of public-policy think tanks that remained highly skeptical of climate change. It addition, the company continued to take steps to reduce its energy use and atmospheric emissions.[129] With rising oil prices, the debate about alternatives to oil and natural gas heated up in the first decade of the new millennium and became a more prominent part of the debate on climate change. As some form of climate-change legislation in the United States appeared imminent in 2009, the company used the op-ed approach inherited from Mobil to argue that if the United States were preparing to act on climate change, it might do better to consider a tax on carbon rather than a cap-and-trade system of the kind put forth by Kyoto. In practice, the company's approach had evolved from acting as an outside critic of climate change to offering its views on policy choices designed to reduce carbon emissions.[130]

Kenneth Cohen led the Public Affairs Department in the decade after the merger. A graduate of Northwestern University, with an L.L.M. from Yale Law School and a J.D. from Baylor School of Law, Cohen had moved

Kenneth P. Cohen, vice president, ExxonMobil Public Affairs, ca. 2005.
ExxonMobil Historical Collection, di_06114.

up the ranks in the corporate legal departments in Exxon. He had also been a manager in Exxon USA's Public Affairs Department in the early 1980s. He inherited the unenviable task of creating a more positive public image for ExxonMobil. Doing so would require more effective ways of communicating with a skeptical public. The company had often felt misunderstood by the public. Could more effective public affairs change that perception?

Sprow's Safety, Health and Environment Department joined Cohen in the effort to find more effective ways to communicate the company's positions to the public. Cohen believed that the merger had created a new imperative to address the public-policy issues the company faced. Exxon-Mobil was now much larger. It was involved in more issues around the world and was a far more visible participant in the public arena.[131] Cohen had the support and encouragement of Dahan, who acknowledged: "It took us quite some time to really understand the meaning of public affairs in a scientific, professional way, [and] it took some people a lot of time to accept that active management of those issues and what it takes to do so in terms of resources were necessarily justified."[132] A first effort was to pinpoint public perceptions of the company. That was done through a series of public-opinion studies and conversations with outside groups. Cohen concluded from those meetings that there was "a disconnect between the reality of what we do and how we do it versus the public perception of who we are and how we do what we do." He came to believe that "if we don't approach things through that [public] perception, we may not get them to start listening to us."[133]

Sprow's department published "Environment, Health and Safety: A Progress Report" in 1991, 1996, 2000, and 2001. In 2000, the Public Affairs Department issued a short report entitled "Caring Neighbors" about the corporation's social responsibility activities. In 2002, those two reports were merged into the company's first comprehensive corporate-responsibility reporting effort.[134] The new omnibus report joined the corporation's annual report and the financial and operating review as a yearly publication and signaled an important departure in the company's communications with the public.[135]

Public-image advertising was the most visible symbol of the new approach to public affairs. The image advertisements were shorter than the opinion essays, more visually stylized, and more widely distributed. They sought to enhance public understanding of the company by explaining its operations and values. The ads were placed in mass-circulation publications and developed for television broadcasting. They conveyed messages of technical competence in providing energy and social responsibility in company operations and charitable corporate programs. Not since the 1970s had the company devoted so much attention to corporate-image advertising.

Outside the Public Affairs Department, the company's philanthropic programs indirectly contributed to its image as a good corporate citizen. Since 1975, the company had published a list of Exxon Education Foundation philanthropic contributions in its *Dimensions* publication. It had not, however, routinely published the amounts of other, nonfoundation grants, nor had it attempted to publicize other socially significant expenditures.

Historically, the bulk of Exxon's contributions had been directed through the Exxon Education Foundation, which initially targeted improvements in higher education. Over time, however, it began to focus more on secondary and primary educational experiments. Moreover, Exxon had a generous three-to-one matching-grant program under which employees and annuitants could direct their gifts and the company's match to specific colleges and universities.[136] Within an overall limit set by corporate management on the level of funding for the foundation, the sheer number and size of the employee gifts began to squeeze the discretionary funds of the foundation, and its special initiatives gradually declined.

To make the most effective use of its funds, the Exxon Education Foundation began to target areas closely aligned with the company's business operations. In addition, ExxonMobil expanded the range and size of the charitable or socially beneficial programs that it funded outside the foundation, often in direct support of company projects. One point of emphasis, for example, was programs to reduce malaria in western Africa (these efforts are detailed in chapter 7). Such funding was of special importance for a company engaged around the world in the production of oil and natural gas. In the developing nations in which ExxonMobil operated, grants at times had a dramatic impact on education, health, and the quality of life. This "strategic philanthropy" generally reinforced the corporation's business objectives, at least indirectly. A representative list of such grants is shown in figure 9.4. The variety is unified by an overall strategy focused on education (especially of minority and disadvantaged groups), public health in areas where ExxonMobil had production operations, women's issues, and environmental preservation. Not all the company's efforts fit neatly into those categories, of course, but even the apparent outliers usually had some tie-in with overarching company objectives.[137]

FIGURE 9.4. Representative ExxonMobil charitable programs, 1995–2005

Save the Tiger Fund (1995)
A joint effort with the (U.S.) National Fish and Wildlife Foundation,
later joined by facilitating partners such as the World Wildlife Fund and
Conservation International, to save tigers in the wild. The company's
sustained support for this effort of $15.7 million from 1995 to 2007 was,
according to the National Fish and Wildlife Foundation, the largest single
corporate contribution to saving a species.

Africa Health Initiative (2000)
ExxonMobil gave more than $40 million from 2000 to 2008 in support of
efforts to increase awareness and access to malaria treatment, prevention,
added health care capacity, malaria drug and vaccine research and development, and international advocacy for additional actions.

Educating Women and Girls Initiative (2005)
Designed to improve the education opportunities for girls in the developing
world, this effort, directed through local non-governmental organizations,
was premised on the view that education of females is one of the best ways
to reduce poverty, slow the spread of HIV/AIDS, and improve local health.

Project Next (ca. 2004)
New Experiences in Teaching provided support for Ph.D. mathematicians in
preparing them for teaching undergraduate mathematics classes.

Support for minority education (traditional)
The company maintained a variety of grant efforts to organizations such
as the United Negro College Fund and the Society of Women Engineers
directed toward improving the career opportunities for women and minori-
ties, particularly in science, technology, engineering and mathematics.

Source: *Exxon Mobil Corporation*

In addition to these activities, the Exxon Education Foundation's staff assisted the operating organizations in planning and executing programs that targeted social benefits to people directly affected by the company's development projects. This was particularly the case in Chad, Cameroon, Angola, Sakhalin Island, Kazakhstan, and Nigeria.[138]

MANAGEMENT SUCCESSION

In the years after the completion of the merger, several senior executives who had been active in the merger process retired. Their departure underscored a problem that had been recognized by Exxon's board as early as 1998: most of the senior Exxon executives were about the same age, and their mandatory retirement at sixty-five posed a challenging problem of management continuity in the first decade of the twenty-first century. The merger with Mobil did not materially improve the situation. During the Exxon board meeting in July 1998 to discuss the merger, outside director William R. Howell, the chairman emeritus of J. C. Penney, addressed the problem. According to Peter Townsend, the secretary of Exxon, Howell argued: "If we're going to do this, I want to make sure we maintain the continuity of our management. If you're going to have a big merger . . . the worst thing you can do is if you can't be comfortable with the continuity of management. As long as all this team is going to be around, fine. I'm happy with it."[139] The team to which Howell referred did not stay long after the merger, and planning for succession became a priority in the immediate aftermath of the merger.

The first postmerger retirement of a senior Exxon executive came at the end of 1999 with the departure at age fifty-eight of Robert Wilhelm, who had voiced early skepticism about the merger. After helping get the merger off to a smooth start, Lou Noto retired a little more than a year later, at the end of January 2001. Gene Renna presided over the setup and early operations of the downstream functions before his retirement in January 2002. That year Rene Dahan, a key architect of the new company, left at age sixty. Harry Longwell, another stalwart in merger planning, retired in 2004 at sixty-two.

Even before that wave of retirements by senior executives, the company had begun early in 2001 to focus on finding a successor to Raymond.

Experienced executives such as Dahan and Longwell were of an age at which their elevation to CEO could be only an interim step. With Raymond moving toward the mandatory retirement age of sixty-five in 2004, the board broke tradition by asking Raymond to stay beyond the normal retirement age. In late July 2001, the company announced that Raymond had agreed to the board's request to stay beyond his scheduled retirement to allow more time to find a successor.

The company then moved decisively. In 2001, Ed Galante, the executive vice president of ExxonMobil Chemical Company, was made an Exxon Mobil Corporation senior vice president at the age of fifty-one, though he was not elected to the board. Rex Tillerson, the vice president of ExxonMobil Development Company, became a senior vice president in August 2001 at age forty-nine, and also was not immediately elevated to the board. Those two candidates were both exceptionally able, but neither was a long-term veteran of Exxon Mobil Corporation's senior management. Their promotions, combined with the extension of Raymond's tenure, gave the board options for the future.

Speculation about Raymond's successor effectively ended in March 2004 with the selection of Tillerson to the newly reconstituted position of president of ExxonMobil and his placement on the board. Galante, who remained a senior vice president, retired later in 2004. Tillerson then served as president of the corporation until Raymond retired at the end of 2005. Tillerson assumed both positions held by his predecessor, chairman of the board and chief executive officer.

Rex Tillerson was raised in Wichita Falls, Texas, and then went to the University of Texas at Austin, where he earned a degree in civil engineering. He went to work at Exxon USA in 1975, starting as a production engineer in Katy, an outlying suburb of Houston that was then the company's smallest district. He steadily took on greater responsibilities in production-engineering jobs in Texas, including work at the King Ranch and in East Texas. A tour in Houston at Exxon USA's upstream planning group brought him in contact with Sid Reso, Harry Longwell, and Mel Harrison. As he progressed through numerous positions, he gained considerable experience in natural gas production and regulation, even spending a stint planning aspects of the proposed gas pipeline from Prudhoe Bay to the lower forty-eight states.

Rex Tillerson, chairman and CEO, Exxon Mobil Corporation, 2005.
Exxon Mobil Corporation.

In 1992 he moved to corporate headquarters as a production advisor under Don MacGyver, at the time a member of the Exxon Management Committee. In discussing Tillerson's responsibilities, Larry Rawl, CEO at the time, told him that he would be a troubleshooter responsible for analyzing proposals concerning production that came to the management committee from around the world. That position gave him exposure to Lee Raymond and other top officials in Irving.[140]

In 1994 he took on a series of challenging assignments that proved

critical in his career. In Yemen, he spent more than two years negotiating a new contract for a natural gas concession to replace a disputed
contract. As head of gas sales to affiliates in Thailand, he gained experience in international natural-gas marketing. In 1997 he became the vice
president of engineering at Exxon Ventures (CIS), where he became
deeply involved in the Sakhalin-I project. He recalled that the "time I
spent in Russia got a lot of people's attention."[141] He stayed there until the
merger transition had been completed and then returned to the United
States as executive vice president under Morris Foster in the ExxonMobil
Development Company.

His career trajectory exposed him to people and places that prepared
him to lead ExxonMobil in the early twenty-first century. He was a production specialist with a broad background in natural gas as well as oil.
He had handled himself well in a series of nations characterized by high
political risks, and in the United States and abroad he had worked closely
with the company's best production specialists of the previous generation.
A lifetime of experience within the Exxon system shaped his approach to
problems and his knowledge of the company and its people. Along with
his broad experience, he brought to his new position a sturdy and unifying presence and a comfortable touch with people outside the company.

Raymond's retirement marked the passing of an era in leadership. He
had served the company for forty-two years, from 1963 through 2005. For
the last thirteen of those years, he had been its chief executive officer and
the chairman of its board of directors. From an early age, he had taken on
difficult challenges. He had played a central role in the process of organizational change that had begun in earnest in the mid-1980s, and he led the
planning and implementation of the Mobil merger, the culmination of
that change. The company that emerged gradually in the years after 1986
had Raymond's fingerprints all over it. With other leaders, he had pushed
hard to refocus the company on core functions and to reinforce its commitment to traditional operating values, especially its concern with long-
term profitability built on engineering efficiency and financial discipline.

To the end of his career, Raymond remained a blunt, outspoken
defender of the company. Never shy about taking unpopular stances, at
times he seemed to invite controversy. His retirement brought one more
controversy. His long service in high positions had been remunerative,

and he had earned cumulative benefits in excess of $100 million at the time of his retirement, and more than that in unexercised stock options. The *New York Times* added together his pay and benefits from 1993 to 2005 and calculated that he had been paid $144,573 a day over that period.[142] Public outrage followed, influencing the creation of a new SEC standard on compensation disclosure.[143]

But the *Times* article noted also the success of the company during the years of Raymond's most senior leadership, when its share price had risen an average of 13 percent a year, faster than the value of the Dow Jones Industrial Average.[144] Dividends had provided a further $67 billion to Exxon and ExxonMobil shareholders. The company's net income had risen from $4.8 billion in 1992 to a record $36.1 billion in 2005. In very turbulent times and in a lengthy period of depressed oil prices, Exxon under Raymond's chairmanship had consistently remained among the largest private industrial corporations by sales. For much of that era, it was the most profitable corporation in the United States and one of the most profitable private corporations in the world.

Raymond's leadership of the company over nearly two decades placed him in the company of John D. Rockefeller as one of the most successful leaders in the firm's history. Indeed, his success reflected his strong and systematic commitment to the values that Rockefeller had originally built into Standard Oil's corporate culture a century earlier. His leadership was a central factor in Exxon's emergence from the market crises it faced in the 1980s and 1990s. His vision guided the transformation of the company by taking it back to its roots as the low-cost producer and the benchmark for operational excellence in its industry.

He had made his mark as one of the most successful problem solvers yet produced by Exxon. At a young age he cut the Gordian knot represented by the giant Aruba refinery, and he unraveled the problems raised by Exxon's excursion into the nuclear business. He was irascible and could be rude in his public appearances, but there was no mistaking the rare, high quality of his intellect. A confidant and loyal deputy of Larry Rawl, Raymond was on point for all major phases of Exxon's response to the *Valdez* accident. But what made Raymond unusually able was his vision of the solutions to the company's weaknesses, and what made him an extraordinary leader was his determination to pursue his evolving, reformist ideas—for decades if necessary—until he achieved what he had intended. In sum, Raymond was a forceful leader, a master of detail, and a keen identifier of executive abilities. Indeed, the extraordinary success of ExxonMobil at the turn of the century owed much to the group of outstanding executives working with him—and to the ExxonMobil training and evaluation system that groomed this cohort for top management.

Rex Tillerson inherited a company well positioned for further success. It was big enough to compete around the world in diverse areas with extreme political, economic, and technical risks. It had access to the technology, capital, and markets needed to find and develop new sources of energy and to remain an attractive joint-venture partner with other international oil companies and with the major national oil companies. Its financial discipline had produced profits and stock value that made it attractive to investors. History's most successful petroleum company, Exxon, could look forward to continued success as ExxonMobil. But in the future as in the past, Tillerson and a new generation of leaders at ExxonMobil would have to earn their success in a world fraught with uncertainties.

TRANSFORMATION

FROM THE PAST TO THE FUTURE

I n the decades after 1973, Exxon, and then ExxonMobil, had to adapt to what amounted to the emergence of a new global oil industry shaped by three powerful forces. The rise of producer power forced the company to find new sources of crude to replace easy oil from Venezuela and the Middle East. It did so by developing technology adapted for harsher environments, more efficient systems of management, and new political and diplomatic skills. A second set of challenges was presented by the return of extreme swings in oil prices, which made long-term planning very difficult. The company responded by planning for a low-price future, taking steps to become a low-cost producer and refiner, honing its organization so that it would be a more efficient competitor, adopting innovative management systems, and using its financial strengths near the bottom of price swings to seize opportunities, most notably the chance to merge with Mobil. A final driver of change was the coming of much stricter environmental regulations. Exxon met that challenge by developing technology designed to increase fuel efficiency, ensure cleaner operations, and produce the greener products required by regulations.

Over thirty years of responding to those and other changes, ExxonMobil emerged with new sources of crude and natural gas; basic alterations in the balance between its oil, natural gas, and chemical businesses; a global functional organization; and an overriding commitment to operational excellence as a basic strategy. One thing did not change. It remained one of the most profitable oil companies in the world, although it generated its profits via new sources of strength.

STRATEGY AND STRUCTURE

The company's strategy during this era reflected the chaotic conditions in its industry. The tenfold increase in oil prices in the 1970s convinced Exxon and most of its competitors that the industry had entered an era of growing shortages of oil despite ever-rising oil prices. Diversification out of oil seemed a logical response, but when oil prices slammed to earth in the mid-1980s, Exxon refocused on its core businesses and operating values. After a quick round of divestments, the company entered a sustained period of eliminating inefficient plants, upgrading the size and technology of those that remained, and systematically cutting costs in operations and employment.

Lee Raymond's description of the process of "downsizing while upgrading" in employment used refining terms to capture the brutal efficiency of the process: "We put them [managers] through a big distillation column. The top of the column stays here."[1] Just as the most valuable "cuts" of oil move to the top of the distillation tower during refining, high-value executives emerged from the rigors of the company's annual evaluation process and from rotations through increasingly challenging positions. Raymond's comment could just as well describe other key aspects of the transformation of Exxon, including the rationing of capital within the company, the global prioritization of exploration prospects, and the determination of the best use of feedstock streams for the giant refining-chemical complexes. The systematic search for the most efficient use of resources was matched by a near-obsession with operational excellence after the *Exxon Valdez* accident. In effect, Exxon made safe, efficient, and low-cost operations at all levels a fundamental part of its corporate strategy.

The company fashioned an innovative structure within which to pursue its strategy. From the sprawling, multilayered organizational structure with which Exxon entered the 1970s, a much different, globally function-alized structure evolved from the mid-1980s onward. Starting with Exxon Chemical and then the reorganization of global exploration, the company built a structure that took advantage of modern communications and advanced information systems to group together the management of key functions around the world. Upstream, that reorganization meant separate global management for exploration, development, and production; downstream, for refining, marketing, and chemicals.

The heart of the transformation of ExxonMobil after the mid-1980s was the creation of institutions and attitudes that strengthened the pursuit of a global, corporate interest over regional interests. A small cadre of top managers defined corporate strategy and allocated capital based on the priorities of the entire organization. A renewed commitment to operational performance accompanied that global perspective. Management tools similar to the Operations Integrity Management System defined and enforced best practices worldwide, monitoring the continual improvement of operating standards in order to improve performance on everything from fuel efficiency to routine maintenance. The systems gave those with operational responsibilities clear guidelines within which to exercise their managerial authority, and helped return the company to its historical focus on the strict management of costs.

TRANSFORMATION IN UPSTREAM, DOWNSTREAM, AND CHEMICALS

The transformation of Exxon is best seen in the organization and operation of its major businesses—oil, natural gas, and chemicals. Each faced different challenges in the years after 1973, but better management and a more systematic approach to operational excellence improved performance in all three. The key force in allowing the company to adapt to its new competitive environment was the systematic application of new technologies. That can be illustrated by snapshots of oil, natural gas, and chemicals at four points: 1973, the year before the rise of producer power; 1986, the year the bottom fell out of oil prices; 1998, the year of the announcement of the Mobil merger; and 2005, a date chosen to symbolize the completion of the first stage of the integration of Exxon and Mobil.

UPSTREAM: OIL AND SYNCRUDES

One statistic regarding ExxonMobil's upstream operations from 1973 to 2005 stands out starkly. In 1973, Exxon produced about 6.7 million barrels of "crude oil and natural gas liquids" each day, or more than 12 percent of the world's production. In 2005, ExxonMobil produced only 2.5 million barrels per day, or about 3 percent of world production in that year.[2] Consider the implications of those numbers. After thirty-two years and billions of dollars in investments around the world in exploration and production, Exxon and Mobil combined produced less than 40 percent as much oil as Exxon alone had produced on the eve of the energy crisis. That sharp decline represents the lasting legacy of the nationalizations of the 1970s. It occurred despite the company's development of new technology for use in Arctic conditions and deep water, the revolution in seismic technology that allowed oil companies to "see" oil deposits under the earth's surface, and Exxon's efforts around the world to find and produce more oil and gas in politically volatile regions.

A more detailed look at oil-production statistics gives a clearer sense of the fundamental shifts in oil production at Exxon after 1973. Before the wave of nationalizations, 70 percent (about 4.7 million barrels a day) of Exxon's total oil production (6.7 million b/d) came from Venezuela and the Middle East. Soon that figure was zero, although Exxon continues to purchase oil from Venezuela and Saudi Arabia. Without that relatively inexpensive crude oil, Exxon's oil production in 1973 totaled only about 2 million b/d, more than half of which (1.1 million b/d) came from the United States. By 1986, even with the addition of new Alaskan production, which accounted for 200,000–300,000 b/d of oil to Exxon during the 1980s and much of the 1990s, the company's U.S. production had fallen to about three-fourths of the 1973 total; by 1998, it stood at roughly half the 1973 total, or 500,000 b/d. This figure had risen only slightly by 2005, even after the Mobil merger. As Exxon explored for non-OPEC oil to replace nationalized reserves, it sought oil also to replace declining production in the United States, where overall oil production peaked in 1972.

Filling the gap was oil from the North Sea, which grew in the 1970s and 1980s within Exxon to a peak of about 500,000 b/d before increasing slightly with the Mobil merger. On the eve of the Mobil merger in 1998, Exxon's production statistics were disturbing. Not only was the overall figure, about 1.6 million b/d, low, but the geographic mix was quite limited also, with about 500,000 b/d from both the United States and Europe and about half that much from Australia and Malaysia combined. The company had no significant oil production in the Middle East, Latin America, Africa, most of Asia, or the newly formed republics of the former Soviet Union.

Regarding potential production, however, 2005 gave reason for optimism. The development of new fields was a long-term endeavor, and Exxon's efforts in Africa, Russia, and Azerbaijan had begun to show substantial results by that year; the addition of Mobil's ongoing projects in Nigeria, Equatorial Guinea, the Republic of Congo, Indonesia, Abu Dhabi, Qatar, Kazakhstan, Newfoundland, and Canada added reserves, production, and geographic diversity. The most impressive number from the 2005 statistics is the astonishing surge of production for ExxonMobil from Africa, where total production of about 660,000 b/d exceeded Exxon's total for either the United States or Europe. Only Canada was higher; including oil sands and heavy oil, its production within Exxon exceeded 800,000 b/d.

Examining these statistics in more detail illustrates the impact of new technology and innovative management systems. The figures for most regions of the world include substantial offshore production that increasingly originated in deepwater projects. The figures for Canada embody the swift growth of syncrude from both heavy oil and oil sands. Deepwater production and synfuels required concentrated, systematic research and the application of new technology before they became cost competitive with conventional crude oil.

The Hoover-Diana project in the Gulf of Mexico at the turn of the twenty-first century illustrated how the company took part in the technical developments underlying a new generation of deepwater production in depths beyond 3,000 feet. Exxon and Mobil were pioneers in the early years of offshore development in the Gulf of Mexico after World War II. Both took part in the technological revolution in offshore operations spawned by the rapid development of the North Sea in the 1970s and 1980s. Both explored around the world for promising offshore prospects.

FIGURE E.1: Exxon Offshore Structures Through Time

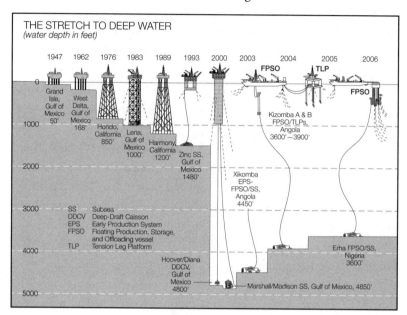

Source: *ExxonMobil,* 2005 Financial and Operating Review, *p. 35.*

As discussed in chapters 3 and 7, Exxon Production Research Company made major technical contributions to the offshore industry's "tool kit," and the company applied the lessons it had learned in the discovery, development, and production of oil in deep water off Angola. Throughout the 1970s and early 1980s, Exxon remained committed to exploration in the Gulf of Mexico. Its innovative Lena guyed tower platform pushed the company beyond 1,000 feet in the early 1980s. But Exxon hesitated to take the next step, into still-deeper waters in the Gulf, passing on lease sales for the region in 1985 and 1988. Larry Rawl could not envision the technology needed to develop those leases, and the company temporarily left that frontier to others.

After a string of impressive discoveries by other companies redefined deepwater operations in the Gulf, Exxon bought its way back in through a series of joint ventures with three of the leaders in the region: Shell, BP, and Amoco. It participated in two pathbreaking projects led by Shell in the 1990s that resulted in tension-legged platforms to develop Ram-

Hoover-Diana Deep-Draft Caisson Vessel, 1999. Exxon Mobil Corporation.

Powell (at 3,214 feet, with first production in 1997) and Ursa (at more than 4,000 feet, with first production in 1998). In addition, Exxon took part in projects that built the first two "deep-draft caisson vessels," both in the Gulf of Mexico.[3]

When Exxon became the operator of a major project in the Gulf's deep water, it embraced the relatively new deep-draft technology for the development of the Hoover and Diana fields off Texas in 4,800 feet of water. The approach required the construction and launch of a structure eighty-three stories high, which looked like a giant grain silo floating upright in the ocean. Mooring lines held it fast to the ocean floor, making it extremely stable even in rough waters. A crew of more than 300, including Exxon employees from around the world and contractors, designed the caisson to sit vertically in the water, with about 90 percent of it floating below the waterline. Oil could be produced into the caisson, providing flexibility in operations. As with Lena earlier, the project served a dual purpose: to produce oil from the Hoover-Diana fields as economically as possible and to develop a new technology that

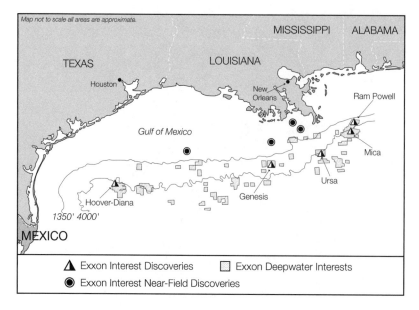

MAP E.1: Source: *ExxonMobil,* 2005 Financial and Operating Review, *p. 43.*

seemed promising for fields in even deeper waters.[4] As had been the case with Lena and earlier developments in the North Sea, the Hoover-Diana platform became the centerpiece for production from a variety of other smaller, nearby fields.

The company began planning the deep-draft caisson in June 1997, started construction in 1998, and produced its first oil in May 2000. It was the operator and majority owner, with BP sharing one-third ownership. The total cost to the partners was about $1 billion, but others in the deepwater industry indirectly absorbed additional costs of the joint effort. The drilling contractor, for example, built a new $250 million offshore drilling rig for the project; another contractor built a giant tower with which to lay pipeline, assuming that its $200 million investment would place it in a leadership position in the industry.[5] As always in ventures into deeper waters, the offshore fraternity of drillers, construction companies, oil companies, transportation specialists, and service and supply companies moved out together.

At the time of first production from Hoover-Diana, ExxonMobil had become a leading leaseholder in the deep water of both Africa and the

*The Hibernia platform about 200 miles off the coast of St. John's,
Newfoundland, 2003. Exxon Mobil Corporation.*

Gulf of Mexico. In 2000, it held "shared interests" in almost 600 deepwater blocks in the Gulf of Mexico, totaling about 3.6 million acres.[6] It had also signed on as a 25 percent joint-venture partner in one of the largest offshore projects of the era, BP's Thunder Horse project in 6,000 feet of water about seventy miles south of New Orleans. The ambitious project pushed the limits of existing technology as it sought to recover an estimated one billion barrels of oil equivalent from the largest deepwater field yet found in the Gulf of Mexico. Despite long delays after serious damage from a hurricane, Thunder Horse illustrated the continuing attraction of the Gulf of Mexico. Here was a region where expensive, technically demanding projects could be justified in part because they involved relatively large fields located in U.S. waters, where the rules were known and the political risks were ordinarily predictable and manageable.

The Mobil merger brought into ExxonMobil added strengths in offshore technology and substantial geographic diversity. Mobil had a large presence off Newfoundland in the northern Atlantic, where it held a one-third interest in the large Hibernia project, which made use of a concrete platform similar to those first developed in the North Sea. Its other large offshore projects around the world—from Nigeria to Indonesia to the North Sea—brought into ExxonMobil significant offshore production, experience, and technology.

Mobil also strengthened ExxonMobil's presence in a technologically advanced undertaking in Canada: the production of syncrudes from oil sands and heavy-oil deposits in Alberta. There, ExxonMobil's wholly owned affiliate (built around Mobil's former holdings in Canada) operated along with Imperial Oil. Considered together, the two were both the largest crude producer in Canada and a leading natural gas producer.

Both affiliates had taken part in the syncrude boom in Alberta in the 1970s and early 1980s. Imperial's syncrude production came from technical processes applied to two different resources. The first was oil produced by injecting steam into deposits of heavy oil near Cold Lake, Alberta. The heated petroleum became less viscous and more easily pumped from 1,500 feet underground. Imperial had begun its efforts to produce bitumen from heavy oil at Cold Lake in the mid-1960s. Gradual improvements in technology led to lower costs and helped increase production to 25,000 b/d by 1985. The collapse of oil prices led Exxon to limit further growth in the expensive production process until the early 1990s, when a new wave of expansion began. By 1995, production had grown to 97,000 b/d of bitumen, which had to be diluted with natural gas condensate before it would flow through pipelines. More than 130,000 barrels a day of the bitumen-condensate mixture was then pumped to refineries in Canada and the United States for further processing.[7] By 2007, production of bitumen at Cold Lake had increased to more than 150,000 b/d.[8]

Meanwhile, technology for extracting heavy oil had improved field-recovery percentages from about 13 percent in the early days of the project to 30 percent by 2008. The importance of the ongoing use of technology to enhance the recovery of bitumen at Cold Lake was underlined by ExxonMobil's heavy-oil reserves there having been estimated to be as high as 40 billion barrels.[9] A quick calculation yields striking evidence of the past and potential impact of enhanced recovery: 13 percent of 40 billion equals 5.2 billion; 30 percent of 40 billion equals 12 billion. A field

Bitumen heated by injection of steam is pumped from multiple wells at Cold Lake, Alberta, where Imperial Oil is extracting the heavy oil from deposits of sand some 1,500 feet below the surface, ca. 1988. ExxonMobil Historical Collection, di_08129.

containing a billion barrels of recoverable oil is considered a "giant." As with enhanced recovery on the North Slope in Alaska, the application of sustained research efforts in recovering greater percentages of bitumen at Cold Lake had a potential payoff as large as discovering and developing several giant oil fields.

The other syncrude Exxon produced in Alberta was from the Syncrude Canada oil sands project. As discussed in chapter 4, that venture—located north of Cold Lake near Fort McMurray—strip-mined shallow, bitumen-laden sands, then used steam processes to separate out the oil. Imperial held the largest share (25 percent) of Syncrude Canada. In 1978, the government-backed project produced its first synthetic oil, an excellent product that earned a premium price. In 1995, it sold for about $17 per barrel at a time when its production costs were slightly more than $10 per barrel. Production reached about 205,000 b/d in 1995, when Imperial's share was approximately 50,000 b/d. After Alberta's provincial government extended the Syncrude Canada operating license from 2018 to 2025, Exxon and its co-venturers expanded the project's capacity. Production reached 214,000 b/d by 2005, when rising oil prices set off a renewed boom in Canadian oil sands.[10] Developments there were reflected in the *Oil and Gas Journal*'s decision in the early 2000s to begin to include oil sands as proved reserves in its annual estimates of the proved oil reserves of Canada. With that change, Canada shot up near Saudi Arabia at the top of the list of nations with the highest proved oil reserves in the world.

By 1995, Imperial was deriving about half its crude-oil production from the Cold Lake and Syncrude Canada oil ventures. Their reserves were so large that they were capable of sustaining substantial production over long periods of time.[11] Realization of their potential production will be determined by a complex array of economic, environmental, and technical considerations. In 2005, the company assessed those issues as it considered the large investment needed to undertake a major tar-sands project at Kearl Lake, due north of Fort McMurray in eastern Alberta.[12]

ExxonMobil's long experience with syncrude projects in Alberta illustrates how new technologies, combined with safeguards for emissions and the resolution of concerns about fresh water, might continue to expand the definition of "oil reserves." Synthetic fuels have been viewed as a possible supplement to conventional oil since at least the 1920s. In the past, discoveries of additional sources of conventional oil have suspended most development of synfuels. In the future, economic competiveness and environmental impact will determine whether this old standby for conventional oil will make the sort of strides suggested by ExxonMobil's energy outlook in 2009, which projected a potential production from oil sands of four million b/d by 2030.[13]

UPSTREAM: NATURAL GAS

In 2001, ExxonMobil's natural gas production stood poised for expansion. As with oil, the company's production of natural gas for sale had not reached its 1973 level (9.7 billion cubic feet per day) by 2005. But unlike oil production, natural gas production grew between 1986 and 1998 to a level of about two-thirds that of 1973 (6.3 bcf/d). Production levels then pushed upward toward 1973 levels with the addition of Mobil's large natural gas production, which brought production up to 9.3 bcf/d in 2005.

The company's natural gas reserves were found around the world. Exxon and Mobil had found and produced natural gas associated with oil for more than a century before their merger. For decades, the flaring of gas around the world removed what was then considered a waste product and a hindrance to oil production. Gas sales to local markets grew in the United States before the Great Depression, and then bulk sales to cross-country pipelines became common after World War II. Exxon and other major oil companies generally remained willing to sell natural gas not needed for reinjection into oil fields or for use as fuel and as feedstock in chemical production in their operations. By 1973, natural gas remained subject to price regulation in the United States, and shortages caused in part by regulation helped convince policy makers that gas was a scarce commodity not to be used for such purposes as the generation of electricity. Yet around the world, Exxon and Mobil kept finding large deposits of natural gas and then creating new markets for the product. The big breakthrough came at Groningen in the 1960s, where giant reserves near large European markets pulled the company and its partner, Royal Dutch Shell, more deeply into the natural gas business. Big gas fields in the North Sea reinforced the company's growing involvement in natural gas. So did a string of discoveries that greatly increased the company's known reserves of natural gas in such far-flung places as Libya, the North Slope, Malaysia, Australia, and Mobile Bay in the United States.

Nationalization in Libya in the early 1980s killed an early LNG project that could have made Exxon a leader in the first wave of construction in the new industry. In retrospect, that development appears more important than it did at the time. Liquefaction held the promise of creating a more global market for natural gas, removing the most significant limitation on its use. As long as pipeline technology defined the limits of markets for specific supplies of natural gas, expansion of those markets remained constrained. But LNG could loosen that constraint and begin to create an international market for natural gas, at least to the extent that it could compete with local sources of natural gas despite the high

LNG (liquefied natural gas) tanker at night, Ras Laffin, Qatar, 1999.
Exxon Mobil Corporation.

costs of liquefaction and shipment in special tankers. After its departure from Libya, Exxon did not reestablish a strong presence in LNG. Indeed, according to Rene Dahan, by the mid-1990s, "Access to the profitable LNG business, which had been neglected by the corporation . . . was proving an uphill struggle."[14]

That condition changed dramatically with the Mobil merger. Mobil held a leading position in the largest ongoing LNG project in the world—the massive development of Qatar's North Field. After the discovery of the field in 1970, it gradually became evident that it was the among the largest nonassociated gas fields in the world, with about 900 trillion cubic feet of reserves.[15] Beginning in the 1970s, Exxon made several futile efforts to establish a strong presence in Qatar. In the 1990s, Qatar approached several companies about developing LNG projects for the North Field, and it ultimately chose Mobil, not Exxon, to lead the first project, within a consortium containing its national oil and gas companies and Japanese industrial conglomerates. LNG from the first two of the world-class liquefaction facilities shipped from Qatar to Spain in 1997. Thus, when Mobil and Exxon merged in 1999, the development of the North Field project was well along.

With the assistance of Mobil's former CEO, Lou Noto, ExxonMobil retained a close relationship with the government of Qatar, which facilitated the construction of additional large-scale LNG projects. By 2005, three LNG plants (or "trains") operated under a joint venture agreement called Qatargas, supplying markets primarily in Japan and Spain. Two more plants were under construction in 2008 and 2009 for markets in the UK. The second joint venture, RasGas, had four plants operating by 2005, with markets in Korea, India, and Europe. An additional three plants under construction were targeted for startup in 2007, 2008, and 2009. In 2006, Qatar surpassed Indonesia as the world leader in LNG exports.[16] As originally planned, the twelve joint-venture facilities would have produced more than 61 million tons of LNG a year by 2010; however, declining demand for LNG during the economic downturn of the era resulted in delays in construction.[17] Despite those postponements, ExxonMobil's LNG operations in Qatar set new global standards for size and efficiency. Little more than a decade before, Exxon had been viewed as a company that missed the boat on LNG.

Another joint initiative sought to use natural gas to produce liquid fuels. Agreements to commercialize the technology to turn natural gas into a liquid (gas-to-liquid or GTL technology) using natural gas from Qatar began in July 2004, but cost and design problems proved more difficult than expected. In February 2007, the partners announced the cancellation of the project after estimates of final costs far exceeded the original estimate of $7 billion. In its place, ExxonMobil agreed to undertake a project designed to deliver more natural gas to Qatar's domestic market.[18] The rapid rise and demise of that project recalled Exxon's experience with synfuels in the early 1980s. In both cases, dramatic declines in oil prices called into question the economics of innovative efforts to produce new products from fossil fuels. In both cases, however, new technology offered the tantalizing prospect of adding vast amounts of oil and gas to world reserves when, or if, prices rose for conventional oil or prices for the new fuels declined as production grew in scale.

The increasing importance of natural gas within Exxon and Exxon-Mobil from the 1990s forward is evident in the surge in the company's gas reserves from the 1990s to 2005 and in the growing percentage of the company's reserves and production accounted for by natural gas instead of oil. As the world searches for alternatives to conventional coal or oil, natural gas presents one realistic alternative as a "bridge fuel" in the long transition away from fossil fuels and toward energy supplies that have a reduced carbon impact. As with synfuels, the idea of natural gas as an alternative to conventional oil draws criticism from environmental groups because gas is a fossil fuel. But as a fuel that has significantly less environmental impact than coal and less than oil and poses none of the cost and safety concerns of nuclear energy, natural gas has a place in the ongoing adjustment of the global mix of fuel, especially since it is an abundant, proven fuel that can take advantage of well-established infrastructure. And ExxonMobil has managed to position itself as a leader in access to natural gas reserves.[19]

Changes in technology have the capacity to address one central reality of the post-1973 international oil industry—the location and control of oil reserves. Some 70 percent of known reserves of conventional oil are owned by OPEC nations. That means proved reserves for the large national oil companies dwarf those of ExxonMobil. ExxonMobil, the largest of the international oil companies, ranked only twelfth in proved reserves in 2005, trailing the national oil company of every major producing nation. The company's best hope for keeping pace with national oil companies is to use technology to "create" new reserves from "static" reserves identified earlier but not recoverable with existing technology at current prices.[20]

Technology can transform unconventional oil and natural gas into conventional oil and gas by bringing those reserves to market. In the late twentieth century, new technology added to proved reserves on the North Slope of Alaska, in enhanced-recovery projects in numerous locations, in the deep water of the Gulf of Mexico, from "stranded" gas fields (that is, isolated fields far removed from markets), and from Canadian oil sands. The early twenty-first century witnessed the advent of a revolution in gas supply through the old technology of hydraulic fracturing applied on a massive scale with the use of advanced horizontal drilling techniques. Price—of conventional oil and gas and the would-be new sources of conventional oil and gas—has shaped the possibilities for such change. Technology has been the agent of change.

DOWNSTREAM: REFINING

Statistics on refining tell a story of far-reaching adjustments in the size, location, and technological complexity of Exxon's refineries. The most obvious change from 1973 through 2005 was a sharp drop in refining capacity, from 6.7 million b/d in 1973 to 4.1 million b/d in 1986, followed by a measure of growth before 1998 (4.4 million b/d) and a surge in capacity after the Mobil merger—up to 6.4 million b/d by 2005. Measures of capacity, however, are deceptive, since one of the thrusts of company policy in the years after the mid-1980s was to reorganize refining in order to increase the utilization of existing facilities and enhance economies of scale. Utilization of capacity fell from 80 percent in 1973 to around 75 percent in 1986 before rebounding to almost 90 percent in 1998 and 2005.

Fundamental changes in the geographic distribution of Exxon's refining marked another dramatic point of transformation. Although the company cut almost one-third of its European refining capacity between 1973 and 1986, the region, with roughly 40 percent of Exxon's refining capacity for most of the period before 1998, remained the company's leading refining area until the Mobil merger, which pushed the United States to the top of the list. The most visible, and perhaps the most important, geographic change in downstream operations was the dramatic rise of both production and sales in Asia-Pacific markets from the 1980s onward. Although Japan remained an important refining center for Exxon in those years, the sustained expansion of downstream operations in Singapore best symbolized the rise of Asia within ExxonMobil. In 2005, Singapore became the location of ExxonMobil's largest single refinery. More growth could be expected in a nation well situated to serve growing markets in Asia and willing to allow foreign corporations full ownership of facilities there.

As discussed in chapter 8, downsizing and upgrading were the order of the day from the 1980s onward. Exxon and then ExxonMobil marched relentlessly toward the closing of smaller, inefficient plants, the expansion of the largest refineries, and the application of new technologies that could increase the flexibility and profitability of those that remained. Flexibility of operations came also from the integration of refining and chemical operations on shared sites. By 2005, twelve of ExxonMobil's largest refineries worldwide practiced such integration. The company often called that package of changes the "rationalization" of refining, which generally referred to reorganization to increase operational efficiency.

The same process went forward in other parts of the downstream operations. The most extreme example was in shipping. In 1973, Exxon had a fleet of 326 vessels ranging from very large crude carriers the length of several football fields to supply boats, totaling about 12 million deadweight tons in all. Deadweight tonnage rose to more than 16 million in 1977 before very low returns, with no prospect of early improvement, convinced the company to begin a steady reduction in its fleet. By 1986, it had only 74 vessels, with a total capacity of about 10 million deadweight tons. Divestment of the fleet accelerated after the *Exxon Valdez* oil spill and the growing realization that tanker transportation was not a major profit center, entailed serious economic and political risks, and could be purchased from outside companies, thereby allowing Exxon to focus more sharply on its core functions. By 2005, ExxonMobil had nothing that could be called a fleet. That dramatic reduction was important for the company's bottom line in downstream operations, where consistent profits were hard to come by for much of the period after 1973.

As in oil and gas production, the key to improving downstream profitability was the introduction of new technology. A variety of research organizations, led by Exxon Research and Engineering, developed new techniques for processing crude oil, altering the choices available to refiners. Steady advances in sulfur removal allowed them to create a more environmentally benign manufacturing process while expanding the variety of higher-end products offered. Processes for removing sulfur and refining heavy oils gave Exxon's refineries greater flexibility in using varieties of crude that were both "sour" (high in sulfur content) and heavy (of thicker consistency)—and less expensive. Within the plants, improved technology gave refiners the flexibility to make more complete use of "bottom of the barrel" residuals left over from the making of gasoline; similar changes in technology made the company's operations more fuel-efficient and less polluting. Innovations in refining enabled the company to meet regulatory requirements for cleaner-burning gasoline, first with the removal of lead and later with the introduction of reformulated gasoline to meet the mandates in the United States of the Clean Air Act amendments of 1990.

While improving its refineries, the company did not neglect its marketing and supply businesses. The number of service stations was reduced significantly, but the remaining ones were more modern, had greater throughput, and were more efficient than their predecessors. The company's product terminals were rationalized. And research on making better consumer products in both fuels and lubricants continued throughout the period.

The scale of ExxonMobil's operations presented opportunities for carrying best practices around the globe. In 2005, the company had forty-two refineries. Twenty-two had capacities of more than 100,000 b/d, and all but two of those had cogeneration equipment to lower fuel costs. All but one of its twelve largest refineries had integrated operations with nearby chemical plants. The overall "conversion capacity" of the company's refineries was 41 percent, which meant a substantial portion of the refineries had sophisticated equipment to upgrade raw materials for the production of higher-value products. Systemic efforts to downsize and upgrade downstream operations after the mid-1980s produced a dramatic change in the company's cost structure and its competitive position.

DOWNSTREAM: CHEMICALS

In many ways, the evolution of chemicals within Exxon after 1973 mirrored that of refining. Both witnessed the steady elimination of smaller, inefficient plants inherited from an era of haphazard expansion, especially in Europe. Both underwent systematic upgrading in scale and technological capacities. Both shared advantages derived from the increasing integration of large refineries and large chemical plants on the same site. Yet several key differences existed. Changes in chemicals went forward in an atmosphere of long-term, sustained growth. Those in refining occurred as a part of an ongoing effort to shrink refining capacity in light of new market conditions in oil, and to gradually modernize and expand existing facilities. Additionally, Exxon Chemical faced a highly competitive and cyclical market for its products. In short, chemicals sought to gain a secure place both within Exxon and within a rapidly expanding industry; refining sought to defend its traditional position in a section of the oil industry that experienced hard times for much of the era after 1973.

Statistics on the growth of Exxon Chemical in this era capture the changing position of the company within Exxon. Sales surged from $3.3 billion in 1973 to $17.7 billion in 1998 and then to $26.8 billion in 2005. More importantly to those who sought to make chemicals an accepted and important part of Exxon, earnings reflected that growth. An early president of Exxon Chemical observed that "we had to be profitable if we were going to survive in Exxon."[21] That was accomplished after the 1970s. Earnings rose from $205 million in 1973, to $470 million in 1986, to $1.2 billion in 1998, to $3.9 billion in 2005. Because of volatile changes in demand in chemical markets, those figures at times fluctuated sharply within the span of three to four years, but the overall trend clearly was upward. At the same time, the chemical company's percentage of total earnings within Exxon (and then ExxonMobil) also moved upward, from about 8 percent in 1973 to as high as 19 percent in 1998. One key goal of Exxon Chemical in the 1980s was to maintain a return on investment at least as high as that achieved by Exxon's petroleum business, and it met that goal through much of the period. Profits from chemicals were somewhat countercyclical to oil prices, providing some balance for the corporation in times of decreasing oil profits. Once Exxon Chemical was separated from refining in the 1960s, many in the company wondered whether it could become a permanent, profitable part of Exxon. By the 1990s, that question had been answered strongly in the affirmative.

Indeed, ExxonMobil Chemical grew steadily into an increasingly potent competitor in the global chemical industry. In 2005, it was one of the world's largest producers of olefins, a basic building block for chemical products. It was the largest producer of several important chemicals, notably paraxylene (a raw material used in fibers) and benzene (used in the production of nylon and other products). It successfully pursued a strategy that took advantage of its ties to a major oil company by maintaining leadership in the production of basic chemicals while also establishing strong market positions in a variety of specialty chemicals. That strategy allowed it to profit through cycles of production in both areas, with the two providing a measure of balance. In both markets, ExxonMobil Chemical built competitive advantages from low-cost feedstocks, the application of technology, an emphasis on operational excellence, and synergies with refining. The company also benefited from its increasing presence in fast-growing markets in the Asia-Pacific region and from its flexible manufacturing capabilities, both at its older sites in the United States and Europe and at its newer facilities in Saudi Arabia, Singapore, and Japan.

Those associated with chemicals saw the separation from refining in the 1960s as the key change needed to build a global company that could compete in a market then dominated by well-established giants such as DuPont. After a quarter of a century of independence, chemicals and refining moved toward greater coordination of operations in the 1990s.

Both benefited. Cooperation in the management of technically advanced refining and chemical complexes on a single site added value to the raw materials used to make both refined products and chemicals. The successful diversification into chemicals and then the reintegration of chemical and refining processes marked sharp departures in both the organization and performance of the two manufacturing functions. The resulting improvement in the performance of each strengthened the corporation as a whole.

FROM EXXON TO EXXONMOBIL

To many who work in the oil industry, invest in it, or study it, the corporation as a whole—now ExxonMobil—appears to be a moneymaking machine. Oil and natural gas go in; money comes out in the form of profits and steady stock dividends. Statistically, that view holds much truth. The section above, for example, reports that chemicals contributed an impressive $3.9 billion in profit in 2005. But that represented only 12 percent of the corporation's record $33.8 billion in profits that year. Indeed, in the period of relatively high oil prices after 2004, announcements of record profits at ExxonMobil became almost an annual occurrence. That was not a new phenomenon. Exxon and then ExxonMobil regularly posted record profits in the volatile and competitive oil industry in the period from 1973 to 2005.

The company did so by adapting to the changes brought about by producer power. It reorganized sooner and more thoroughly than most of its competitors. It was the first to adopt a truly global structure, and its introduction of common accounting procedures, global computer networks, and a worldwide operational integrity and safety program became a model within the petroleum industry. It built on its traditional strengths—its size and financial resources, technical expertise, managerial capacities, and access to markets—to develop new sources of oil outside of OPEC. It improved the political and diplomatic skills needed to work with national oil companies and their governments and to gain and maintain entry to nations undergoing political turmoil. In pursuing profits, it worked on the understanding that long-term profitability could be enhanced by developing mutually beneficial relationships with producing nations.

After the payment of taxes and other costs, the bulk of the company's profits came from the spread between the price of oil and its production costs. A systematic focus on cutting costs and finding efficiencies through operational excellence helped increase that spread. Before 1973, Exxon had produced easy oil from giant fields in Venezuela and the Middle East at a level it has since struggled to regain. But it learned to produce oil from much harsher and demanding regions at increasingly lower cost. Thus, despite the fact that ExxonMobil in 2005 produced "only" 2.5 million b/d instead of the 6.7 million b/d by Exxon alone in 1973, it must be remembered that even the lower level of production yields a total of almost one billion barrels a year (and the daily production figure has moved up significantly in the years since 2005). Figures measuring "profits per barrel" quickly become very large numbers when multiplied by one billion. ExxonMobil has succeeded by increasing the number of barrels produced and decreasing the parts of the cost per barrel that it controls. Add to that its systematic effort to improve operations in downstream areas and chemicals, and the results have been record profits.

Unless a person works for the company or owns a part of it, of course, profitability might at times seem more like a vice than a virtue. The company's key societal function within the global economy is to supply energy. Over the long term, it has done so as efficiently and effectively as any oil company in the history of the petroleum industry. From Rockefeller's Standard Oil to Exxon to ExxonMobil, the company generally has remained a model for effective management and, in particular, for innovative organizational structures. Rockefeller was a master of both strategy and management systems, and he created a corporate culture committed to systematic attention to detail and the application of good engineering principles, a legacy that remains embedded in ExxonMobil's DNA. Those who followed his path to the top of ExxonMobil in the late twentieth century confronted different problems, which called on all their management skills. A key challenge facing corporate managers after 1973 was the protection of the company's core operating values, originally instilled by Rockefeller to ensure efficient internal operations, as they responded to a wide range of political, social, environmental issues that emerged in the late twentieth century.

Like Standard Oil (New Jersey), the modern company often has faced harsh criticism. When criticism peaked after the *Exxon Valdez* oil spill, the company had great difficulty in finding an effective voice with which to address the public. Although much attention has been paid to public affairs since the spill, the key response by Exxon was that of good engineers—the Operations Integrity Management System, which was designed and operated to reduce accidents in the future. Mobil brought into the company a more direct and more visible approach to public affairs, and the melding of the two approaches may alter both the content and the tone of the company's public outreach efforts.

In December 1999, the *Wall Street Journal* mulled over the source of the company's often-noted problems with its public image. Discussing a major public-opinion survey by a leading polling company, the article noted the survey's conclusion that "Exxon has one of the worst reputations among multinationals," with respondents supporting their poor opinions of the company by citing "ill will from the *Valdez* spill and a perception of corporate arrogance." The *Journal* itself referred to the company's "insular culture," which "frowns on publicity," as a possible cause of Exxon's public-image problems.[22] The *New York Times* returned to that theme in 2007, pondering the question of how Exxon could be "so utterly competent at its core mission—finding, producing, refining and delivering oil and gas" while being "so utterly incompetent when it comes to making the case that it is not the devil incarnate when it comes to the environment."[23]

ExxonMobil's history suggests that what critics perceive as arrogance is a short step across a thin line from what might be called "earned confidence," an attribute in great supply within a proud engineering company that has for more than a century been the leader in one of the most important industries in the world economy. What some see as the company's "insular culture" reflects two keys to its success: its tradition of training and promoting its own and its inculcation of widely shared core values based on engineering efficiency—or, put another way, a commitment to being utterly competent in its core mission.

No assessment of the corporation's recent history would be complete without evaluating its remarkable ability to produce talented and visionary managers. Clearly, John D. Rockefeller was of this genus. Later, the extraordinary Walter C. Teagle led Jersey Standard for twenty-five years.[24] Subsequent senior managers of Standard and Exxon held themselves to the high standards set by the company's earlier leaders. Cliff Garvin struggled to guide the company out of an exceptionally chaotic period, and had the courage to reverse course when Exxon's early endeavors were disappointing. Jack Bennett created some of the most innovative financial initiatives in American business. Jon Thompson led a resurgence of exploration success. In the years after 1986, Larry Rawl and Lee Raymond worked closely together to revitalize the company. Then Lee Raymond, Harry Longwell, Rene Dahan, and others worked with an uncommon unity of purpose that produced unprecedented financial results.

There can be no mistaking the foundational importance of the quality of senior management in guiding a corporation through turbulent events. Garvin faced an unprecedented loss of crude-oil ownership as producer power crested, and he was compelled to adjust to significant fluctuations in the energy market. Rawl, who endured a near collapse of oil prices, understood that success for Exxon meant refocusing on its traditional businesses but with a much lower cost structure. Raymond worked through a series of business crises or mistakes and came to be a crusading supporter of operational excellence. He also developed a vision for the company that he worked for decades to achieve. Though each of these men had different skills and faced different challenges, they were of such quality that Exxon was able to navigate shoals that could have sunk the company. It is well to remember that many companies, responding to an identical business environment, were unable to adjust as successfully, and are no longer in business. ExxonMobil is, in large measure because over many decades it has nurtured and selected for leadership unusually able executives.

As in prior periods in its history, tectonic forces since 1973 have compelled the company to adapt. It has done so by expanding on its historical strengths and adding additional capacities to work in joint ventures, including those with national oil companies. It has become adept at bargaining from weakness with the governments of major producing nations. It has absorbed regulatory demands for improved environmental performance. It has learned to prosper despite swings in oil prices. The message of its recent past is simple: ExxonMobil is still a work in progress, constantly adapting to a changing and demanding world within the framework of its core operating values, its inherited institutions, and its corporate culture.

It has a stubborn belief in its approach to business and a thick skin for deflecting public criticism. And why not? ExxonMobil is one of the few major corporations in the world that has remained a leader in its industry for more than 130 years. The company's history since 1973 argues strongly that it will continue to find state-of-the-art means to profit from the production and sale of oil and natural gas for as long as those energy sources remain essential to the global economy. After that, it will adapt.

NOTES

INTRODUCTION: TRANSFORMATION

1   The corporate name of ExxonMobil has changed over time. The Standard Oil
    Company of New Jersey and the Standard Oil Company of New York were
    original members of what was known in the late nineteenth century as the
    "Standard Oil Trust" or "Rockefeller's Standard Oil." In 1892, the Standard Oil
    Company of New Jersey became a holding company, and its name was changed
    to Standard Oil Company (New Jersey). In 1899, the company became the
    parent and central holding organization for all Standard Oil interests, includ-
    ing the Standard Oil Company of New York. After the United States Supreme
    Court dissolved this holding company in 1911, the two became separate compa-
    nies. Standard Oil Company (New Jersey), or Jersey Standard, became known
    as "Esso" in much of the world. Its primary U.S. company, the majority-owned
    Humble Oil & Refining Company, was headquartered in Houston. One of its
    major foreign subsidiaries after the 1930s was the Creole Petroleum Company
    in Venezuela. The Standard Oil Company of New York (Socony) merged with
    the Vacuum Oil Company, another former Standard Oil company, in 1931 and
    became the Socony-Vacuum Corporation and, later, the Socony-Vacuum Oil
    Company. The company changed its name to the Socony Mobil Oil Company,
    Inc. in 1955 and to the Mobil Oil Corporation in 1966. In 1948, Jersey Standard
    and Socony-Vacuum joined with the Standard Oil Company of California
    (which became Chevron) and the Texas Company (which became Texaco) to
    form the Arabian American Oil Company (Aramco)—the consortium that

developed oil reserves in Saudi Arabia into the 1970s. In 1972, Standard Oil Company (New Jersey) was renamed Exxon Corporation and its major U.S. affiliate, Humble Oil & Refining, became Exxon Company USA. In 1999, Exxon and Mobil merged, taking the new name ExxonMobil. The most popular account of the rise and fall of the Seven Sisters is Anthony Sampson, *The Seven Sisters: The Great Oil Companies and the World They Shaped* (New York, 1975).

2   The distinction between privately owned, globally active companies such as Exxon and the state-owned oil companies—such as Statoil in Norway and PDVSA in Venezuela—created by the major producing nations to manage their reserves became blurred once numerous national oil companies began expanding operations outside their home nations. For a more extensive discussion of national oil companies, see Christopher E. H. Ross and Lane Sloan, *Terra Incognita: A Navigation Aid for Energy Leaders* (Tulsa, 2007), 51–91.

3   This is a somewhat different approach than that taken in previous volumes on the history of Exxon, which are longer and more comprehensive books. See Ralph W. Hidy and Muriel E. Hidy, *Pioneering in Big Business, 1882–1911: History of Standard Oil Company (New Jersey)* (New York: 1955); George S. Gibb and Evelyn H. Knowlton, *The Resurgent Years, 1911–1927: History of Standard Oil Company (New Jersey)* (New York 1956); Henrietta M. Larson, Evelyn H. Knowlton, and Charles S. Popple, *New Horizons, 1927–1950: History of Standard Oil Company (New Jersey)* (New York, 1971); and Bennett H. Wall, *Growth in a Changing Environment: A History of Standard Oil Company (New Jersey), 1950–1972 and Exxon Corporation, 1972–1975* (New York, 1988). See also Henrietta M. Larson and Kenneth Wiggins Porter, *History of Humble Oil & Refining Company: A Study in Industrial Growth* (New York, 1959). For an account of ExxonMobil's recent history, see Steve Coll, *Private Empire: Exxon-Mobil and American Power* (New York, 2012). For a recently published history of Royal Dutch Shell since the 1970s, see Keetie Sluyterman, *Keeping Competitive in Turbulent Markets, 1973–2007: A History of Royal Dutch Shell, Volume 3* (Oxford, 2007); see also Tyler Priest, *The Offshore Imperative: Shell Oil's Search for Petroleum in Postwar America* (College Station, Texas, 2007). For the history of British Petroleum, see James Bamberg, *British Petroleum and Global Oil, 1950–1975: The Challenge of Nationalism* (Cambridge, 2000). For Amoco, which was absorbed by BP in 1998, see Joseph A. Pratt, *Prelude to Merger: A History of Amoco Corporation, 1973–1998* (Houston, 2000).

4   Exxon Corporation, *1973 Annual Report*, 1; Exxon Corporation, *1986 Annual Report*, 1.

5   For an overview of the international petroleum industry before the energy crises of the 1970s, see Peter Odell, *Oil and World Power*, 2nd ed. (New York, 1972). For overviews of the oil crisis of 1973, see Fiona Venn, *The Oil Crisis* (London, 2002) and Karen R. Merrill, *The Oil Crisis of 1973–1974: A Brief*

History with Documents (Boston, 2007). An excellent view of the energy crisis of 1973 from inside a major oil company active in the Middle East is Bamberg, *British Petroleum and Global Oil.* For contemporary and detailed discussion of the coming of producer power, see Sampson, *The Seven Sisters.* A broader historical account is included in two books by Daniel Yergin, *The Prize: The Epic Quest for Oil, Money, and Power* (New York, 1991) and *The Quest: Energy, Security, and the Remaking of the Modern World* (New York, 2011). See also Tom Bower, *Oil: Money, Politics, and Power in the 21st Century* (New York, 2009).

6 Leslie E. Grayson, *National Oil Companies* (New York, 1981).

7 For the history of energy policies during this era, see Richard H. K. Vietor, *Energy Policy in America since 1945: A Study of Business-Government Relations* (Cambridge, Mass., 1984); Craufurd D. Goodwin, ed., *Energy Policy in Perspective: Today's Problems, Yesterday's Solutions* (Washington, D.C., 1981); and Jay Hakes, *A Declaration of Energy Independence* (Hoboken, N.J., 2008).

8 For historical overviews of oil-pollution control in the United States, see Hugh S. Gorman, *Redefining Efficiency: Pollution Concerns, Regulatory Mechanisms, and Technological Change in the U.S. Petroleum Industry* (Akron, Ohio, 2001) and Joseph A. Pratt, *Black Waters: Responses to America's First Oil Pollution Crisis* (Kansas City, 2008). See also Richard N. L. Andrews, *Managing the Environment, Managing Ourselves: A History of American Environmental Policy* (New Haven, Conn., 1999); Michael E. Kraft and Sheldon Kamieniecki, eds., *Business and Environmental Policy* (Cambridge, Mass., 2007); and Andrew J. Hoffman, *From Heresy to Dogma* (San Francisco, 1997).

9 John D. Rockefeller, *Random Reminiscences of Men and Events* (New York, 1908), 74. The most recent biography of Rockefeller is Ron Chernow, *Titan: The Life of John D. Rockefeller, Sr.* (New York, 1998). For the company's corporate history under Rockefeller, see Hidy and Hidy, *Pioneering in Big Business.*

10 Rockefeller, *Random Reminiscences*, 88.

11 Alfred D. Chandler and Richard S. Tedlow, "The Standard Oil Company—Combination, Consolidation, and Integration," in *The Coming of Managerial Capitalism: A Casebook on the History of American Economic Institutions*, ed. Chandler and Tedlow (Homewood, Ill., 1985), 343–371.

12 Rockefeller, *Random Reminiscences*, 86–87.

13 Ibid., 66–69. A glaring exception to the quest for efficiency in this formative era of the petroleum industry was the rampant waste of oil, which led to serious environmental damage to the land, air, and water in the producing and refining regions. See Brian Black, *Petrolia: The Landscape of America's First Oil Boom* (Baltimore, 2000).

14 Rockefeller, *Random Reminiscences*, 86.

15 For a good overview of the criticism of Standard Oil, see Hidy and Hidy, *Pioneering in Big Business*, 639–670.

16   Quoted in Peter Collier and David Horowitz, *The Rockefellers: An American Dynasty* (New York, 1976), 38.

17   Hidy and Hidy, *Pioneering in Big Business*, 639–670; Ida M. Tarbell, *The History of the Standard Oil Company* (1904; rept., New York, 1969), 196–208.

18   Quoted in Collier and Horowitz, *Rockefellers*, 28. See also Allan Nevins, *Study in Power* (2 vols.; New York, 1953), 2:467–476; Tarbell, *History of Standard Oil*, 144–153.

19   Quoted in Hidy and Hidy, *Pioneering in Big Business*, 648.

20   Bruce Bringhurst, *Antitrust and the Oil Monopoly: The Standard Oil Cases, 1890–1911* (Westport, Conn., 1979).

21   The case was *Standard Oil Co. of New Jersey v. United States*, 221 U.S. 1 (1911); the decision was unanimous.

22   Black, *Petrolia*.

23   These observations are based on more than a hundred interviews with Exxon employees conducted by Joseph Pratt and William Hale during the research for this book. For a list of these interviews, see Appendix B.

24   This overview of the company's management system in the early 1970s draws heavily on a detailed description in Exxon Corporation, *1976 Annual Report*, 6–11.

25   These are my own reflections on this management system, which are based on my reading of the corporate management committee's records from 1970 through the early 1990s.

26   See, for example, "Gross Production of Oil and Gas Liquids," in the Five-Year Operating Summary presented in Standard Oil Company (New Jersey), *1970 Annual Report*, 30.

27   Clifton Garvin, interview by Joseph Pratt, November 16, 2006, Jupiter, Florida, ExxonMobil Oral History Project, ExxonMobil Historical Collection, Dolph Briscoe Center for American History, University of Texas at Austin (hereafter cited as ExxonMobil Oral History).

28   The general background on the spill is covered in Peter Coates, *The Trans-Alaska Pipeline Controversy: Technology, Conservation, and the Frontier* (Fairbanks, 1993). For a view from the perspective of an Alaskan harmed by the spill, see Riki Ott, *Not One Drop: Betrayal and Courage in the Wake of the Exxon Valdez Oil Spill* (White River Junction, Vt., 2008).

29   Lee Raymond, interviews by Joseph Pratt and William Hale, February 20, 2007, Irving, Texas; May 17, 2007, Irving; June 14, 2007, Dallas, Texas; June 25, 2007, Irving; August 2, 2007, Irving; September 11, 2007, Dallas; November 1, 2007, Dallas; December 12, 2007, Irving; January 21, 2008, Irving; ExxonMobil Oral History.

30   For overviews of the major mergers in oil in this era, see Forest Reinhardt, Ramon Casedesus-Mansanell, and David J. Hanson, "BP and the

Consolidation of the Oil Industry, 1998–2002," Harvard Business School Case # 9-702-012, and Yergin, *The Quest*, 83–105. For a study of the BP-Amoco merger, see Pratt, *Prelude to Merger,* 1–16, 285–294.

CHAPTER ONE: DOWNSIDE UP

1 Jack Clarke, interview by Joseph Pratt, January 3, 2007, Orlando, Florida, 13, ExxonMobil Oral History.

2 Garvin interview.

3 "Jack G. Clarke, New Director," *Lamp* 58, no. 1 (Spring 1976): 13.

4 Larson, Knowlton, and Popple, *New Horizons,* 134; for a general history of the company's early years in Venezuela, see 132–144.

5 Wall, *Growth in a Changing Environment,* 396.

6 Rómulo Betancourt, *Venezuela's Oil,* trans. Donald Peck (London, 1978); Betancourt, *Venezuela: Oil and Politics,* trans. Everett Bauman (Boston, 1979); Edwin Lieuwin, *Petroleum in Venezuela: A History* (Berkeley and Los Angeles, 1954); Yergin, *The Prize,* 232–237, 433–437, 648–649; Wayne Chatfield Taylor, *The Creole Petroleum Corporation in Venezuela* (Washington, D.C., 1955).

7 "Venezuela's Pérez Inaugurated; Calls Take-Over a 'Certainty,'" *Oil and Gas Journal,* March 18, 1974, 38–39.

8 Yergin, *The Prize,* 648–650.

9 "1973 Creole/Lago Environmental Outlook—Executive Summary," April 11, 1973, Records of the Exxon Management Committee, Exxon Mobil Corporation, Irving, Texas (hereafter, Exxon Corporate Archives).

10 Robert Dolph, report to Exxon Management Committee, April 2, 1973, 9, Exxon Corporate Archives.

11 "Venezuela's Pérez Promises Take-Over of Oil in 2 Years," *Oil and Gas Journal,* February 25, 1974, 29.

12 William D. Smith, "Venezuela Reviews Role in Oil Balance," *New York Times,* November 12, 1973.

13 Dolph to Exxon Management Committee, April 24, 1974, 6, Exxon Corporate Archives.

14 "Venezuela's Pérez Inaugurated," *Oil and Gas Journal,* March 18, 1974, 38–39. For works that put these changes in perspective, see Gustavo Coronel, *The Nationalization of the Venezuelan Oil Industry: From Technocratic Success to Political Failure* (Lexington, Mass., 1983); Terry Lynn Karl, *The Paradox of Plenty: Oil Booms and Petro-States* (Berkeley and Los Angeles, 1997); Franklin Tugwell, *The Politics of Venezuelan Oil* (Stanford, Calif., 1975); and Laura Randall, *The Political Economy of Venezuelan Oil* (New York, 1988).

15 Creole Petroleum, report to Exxon Management Committee, September 26, 1974, 1–2, "Fall 1974 CEOs Letters," Exxon Corporate Archives.

16 Creole Petroleum, report to Exxon Management Committee, April 25, 1974, 3, Exxon Corporate Archives; "Venezuela Starts Down Road to Nationalization," *Oil and Gas Journal*, May 27, 1974, 33.

17 Creole Petroleum, report to Exxon Management Committee, April 25, 1974, 6, Exxon Corporate Archives.

18 "Exxon to Buy All Creole Shares," *New York Times*, June 24, 1975, 43.

19 Yergin, *The Prize*, 649.

20 Howard Kauffmann, interview by Joseph Pratt, November 27, 2007, Atlanta, 21–23, ExxonMobil Oral History.

21 "Terms of Venezuelan Oil Nationalization Aired," *Oil and Gas Journal*, August 26, 1974, 63–64; Guillermo Eraso to Exxon Management Committee, September 26, 1974, 2, Exxon Corporate Archives.

22 Dolph to Exxon Management Committee, January 28, 1975, 2, Exxon Corporate Archives.

23 Emma Brossard, *Petroleum Research and Venezuela's Intevep: The Clash of the Giants* (Houston, 1993), 108–114. For more on the reorganization of the Venezuelan oil industry after nationalization, see Norman Gall, "The Challenge of Venezuelan Oil," *Foreign Policy* 18 (Spring 1975): 44–67; Vegard Bye, "Nationalization of Oil in Venezuela: Re-Defined Dependence and Legitimization of Imperialism," *Journal of Peace Research* 16, no. 1 (1979): 57–78; "Venezuela Nationalizes Her Petroleum Industry," *New York Times*, August 30, 1975; "New Petroleum State Firm Will Run Petroleum Industry," *Oil and Gas Journal*, July 14, 1975, 45; Eduardo Acosta-Hermosa, "Venezuelan Oil Exports Decline," *Oil and Gas Journal*, March 29, 1976, 95–98.

24 "Venezuela Take-Over Set Jan. 1 for 21 Private Oil Companies," *Oil and Gas Journal*, September 8, 1975, 25; "Exxon in Contract with Venezuela," *New York Times*, January 7, 1976; C. O. Peyton to Exxon Management Committee, December 15, 1975, 1, Exxon Corporate Archives.

25 "Creole Petroleum in Venezuelan Pact," *New York Times*, November 13, 1975.

26 A. L. Monroe to J. F. Bennett, September 22, 1978, "CEO Letters 1978," 6, Exxon Corporate Archives; Esso Inter-America, "1983 Corporate Plan," 9, "CEO Letters 1983," Exxon Corporate Archives; Robert Wilhelm, interview by William Hale, April 26, 2007, Dallas, ExxonMobil Oral History, 28.

27 Creole to Exxon Management Committee, September 26, 1974, 3–6, Exxon Corporate Archives.

28 "The Middle East Oil Squeeze on the Oil Giants," *BusinessWeek*, July 29, 1972, 57; Exxon Corporation, *1972 Annual Report*, 18.

29 John Blair, *The Control of Oil* (New York, 1976) provides the most thorough statement of these practices, which are also central to Anthony Sampson's description in *The Seven Sisters* of the control over price exercised by the major international oil companies well into the 1960s.

30 Allen T. Demure, "Aramco Is a Lesson in the Management of Chaos," *Fortune*, February 1974, 57–65, 160–163.

31 Ibid., 65.

32 President of Esso Middle East to Exxon Management Committee, October 2, 1973, 1–6, Exxon Corporate Archives; Steffen Hertog, *Princes, Brokers, and Bureaucrats: Oil and State in Saudi Arabia* (Ithaca, 2011).

33 President of Esso Middle East to Exxon Management Committee, October 2, 1973, 6; Robert Vitalis, *America's Kingdom* (Stanford, 2007).

34 President of Esso Middle East to Exxon Management Committee, October 2, 1973, 5–8.

35 Gas flaring is generally defined as releasing excess and unmarketable gas from an oil field through a flare and burning it. It was widely practiced in the oil industry in the early to mid-twentieth century to dispose of natural gas that hindered the production of oil from a field and was not near enough to a market for natural gas to be sold.

36 President of Esso Middle East to Exxon Management Committee, October 2, 1973, 2.

37 Yergin, *The Prize*, 671–672, 746–750; Garvin interview, 54; Ian Skeet, *OPEC: Twenty-five Years of Prices and Politics* (Cambridge, 1988).

38 "Terms of Reference for Meeting with Yamani in Early June 1974," May 31, 1974 and June 11, 1974, 2, Exxon Corporate Archives.

39 Quoted in Leonard Mosley, "The Richest Oil Company in the World," *New York Times Magazine*, March 10, 1974.

40 John Tagliabue, "Man in the News; Pacesetter of OPEC: Sheik Ahmed Zaki Yamani," *New York Times*, October 30, 1986; Tagliabue, "Yamani Caught in a Crossfire," *New York Times*, October 31, 1986. Pamela Sherrid is quoted in "Ahmed Zaki Yamani Biography" at http://www.bookrags.com/biography /ahmed-zaki-yamani/.

41 Jeffrey Robinson, *Yamani: The Inside Story* (London, 1989); Garvin interview, 10–16.

42 Esso Middle East, report to Exxon Management Committee, October 17, 1974, 1–11, Exxon Corporate Archives.

43 Mosley, "Richest Oil Company in the World," 30.

44 Esso Middle East, report to Exxon Management Committee, October 14, 1974, 9, Exxon Corporate Archives. Mobil, Dow Chemical, and Royal Dutch Shell also entered into talks with the Saudi government about participating in similar ventures, which appeared to offer a way to gain favor with the Saudis while also taking part in major industrial developments.

45 Ibid., 10–11.

46 Quoted in William D. Smith, "Exxon's New Top Two: Big Challenges Facing Garvin and Kauffmann," *New York Times*, July 13, 1975.

47 Mosley, "Richest Oil Company in the World," 36.

48 "The Role of State Oil Companies—Saudi Arabia," *Oil and Gas Journal*, August 16, 1993, 38–47; see also Amy Myers Jaffe and Jareer Elass, "Saudi Aramco: National Flagship with Global Responsibilities," a paper presented at the James A. Baker Institute, Rice University, Houston, 2007, 43.

49 Esso Middle East to Exxon Management Committee, January 31, 1975, 2, Exxon Corporate Archives.

50 Esso Middle East to Exxon Management Committee, "Guidelines for Iran, Abu Dhabi, and Qatar Negotiations," May 7, 1975, 1, Exxon Corporate Archives.

51 Ibid., 2.

52 Esso Middle East to Exxon, "Aramco Negotiations: Approach on May 20," May 7, 1975, 2, Exxon Corporate Archives.

53 Esso Middle East to Exxon Management Committee, "1976 Planning and Budget Review," September 27, 1976, 6, Exxon Corporate Archives.

54 Ibid., 5–7.

55 Esso Middle East to Exxon Management Committee, February 13, 1976, Exxon Corporate Archives.

56 Esso Middle East to Exxon Management Committee, September 27, 1976, 8, Exxon Corporate Archives.

57 Esso Middle East to Exxon Management Committee, September 26, 1978, 5–6, "CEO Letters 1978," Exxon Corporate Archives.

58 Ibid., 3.

59 Ibid., 2–3.

60 Ibid., 1–2.

61 Robert Stobaugh, "The Evolution of Iranian Oil Policy, 1925-1975," in *Iran Under the Pahlavis*, ed. George Lenczowski (Stanford, Calif., 1978). For a general overview of Iran's evolution, see Don Peretz, *The Middle East Today*, 5th ed. (New York, 1988), 498–528. Anthony Sampson's *The Seven Sisters* contains a useful chapter entitled "Iran and Democracy." The three volumes of British Petroleum history are very useful in understanding the place of oil in modern Iranian history: R. W. Ferrier, *The History of the British Petroleum Company: The Developing Years, 1901–1932* (Cambridge, 1982); James Bamberg, *The History of the British Petroleum Company: The Anglo-Iranian Years, 1928–1954* (Cambridge, 1994); and Bamberg, *British Petroleum and Global Oil, 1950–1975: The Challenge of Nationalism* (Cambridge, 2000).

62 This description of the Consortium Agreement is taken from a case decided in 1987 by the Iran–United States Claims Tribunal, which resolved claims against the Iranian government arising out of the expropriation of properties during and after the Iranian Revolution; see case nos. 74, 76, 81, and 150, Chamber Three, award no. 311-74/76/81/150-3, Iran–United States Claims Tribunal,

signed and filed July 14, 1987, 2. The case files of the tribunal are available at http://www.iusct.org, with a finding aid for cases at http://www.iusct.org/lists/list-04.html.

63 Bamberg, *British Petroleum and Global Oil*, 45.

64 "Preferential lifting" was a term used to describe the shah's persistent pressure on the international oil companies to give Iran favored status on the amount of oil produced from their system of interconnected production in the various nations in the Middle East. Exxon regularly faced such demands as a part of the Iranian consortium; see, for example, Esso Middle East to Exxon Management Committee, "1976 Financial and Operating Report," February 13, 1976, 9, Exxon Corporate Archives.

65 This rivalry reflected numerous factors, including their proximity, their embrace of different forms of Islam (Shiism in Iran, Sunni Islam in Saudi Arabia), their different ethnicities (Persian Iranians, Arab Saudis), and their competitiveness as two of the largest oil producers in the world. The tensions between the two nations were played out within OPEC, where Iran generally pushed for higher prices and greater production in order to increase the revenues needed by its large population, whereas Saudi Arabia (which had a much smaller population and larger reserves) generally supported gradual price increases in order to prevent a decline in the growth of demand for oil and the rise of alternatives to oil. See Abbas Milani, *The Shah* (New York, 2011).

66 Esso Middle East to Exxon Management Committee, "Tehran Negotiations," January 5, 1973, 1, Exxon Corporate Archives.

67 Esso Middle East to Exxon Management Committee, "Tehran Negotiations," February 9, 1973, 1–7, Exxon Corporate Archives.

68 Ibid., 2.

69 For an excellent overview of these negotiations in the 1970s, see Bamberg, *British Petroleum and Global Oil*, 445–489. For a look at the ongoing negotiations between the Iranian consortium and the government, see Esso Middle East to Exxon Executive Committee, March 26, 1976, and Esso Middle East to Exxon Executive Committee, April 29, 1976, both in Exxon Corporate Archives.

70 Award no. 311-74/76/81/150-3, Iran–United States Tribunal, 8.

71 For details on this sparring, see award no. 311-74/76/81/150-3, Iran–United States Tribunal.

72 See, for example, Esso Middle East to Exxon, "Proposal for R&D Collaboration with NIOC," September 15, 1975, Exxon Corporate Archives. The assumptions here were much like those employed by Esso Middle East in Saudi Arabia. Exxon foresaw an extended period of uncertainty in its dealings with the shah, and the company sought to build a stronger and, it hoped, longer-lasting relationship with the Iranian government through mutually beneficial joint ventures with the National Iranian Oil Company. As in Saudi Arabia, one goal was to retain access to as much oil as possible for as long as possible.

73 Case no. 155, Chamber Three, award no. 308-155-3, Iran–United States Tribunal, signed and filed June 9, 1987.

74 Yergin, *The Prize*, 660.

75 For the workers, see case no. 155, Chamber Three, award no. 308-155-3, Iran–United States Claims Tribunal. For the quotation on the shah's departure, see Esso Middle East to Exxon Management Committee, "1980 Planning Report," October 6, 1980, 2, "CEO Letters 1980," Exxon Corporate Archives. For the shah's departure, see Abbas Milani, *The Shah*.

76 Yergin, *The Prize*, 450–478, and 674–714; Mostafa Elm, *Oil, Power, and Principle: Iran's Oil Nationalization and Its Aftermath* (Syracuse, N.Y., 1994).

77 For a useful overview of modern Libyan history, see Dirk Vandewalle, *A History of Modern Libya* (Cambridge, 2006). For its oil history, see Vandewalle, *Libya since Independence: Oil and State-Building* (Ithaca, N.Y., 1998); Frank C. Waddams, *The Libyan Oil Industry* (Baltimore, 1980); and Judith Gurney, *Libya: The Political Economy of Oil* (Oxford, 1996).

78 Dan Snook, "The History of Esso Standard Libya," *Exxon Manhattan*, September 21, 1973, 5, copy in box 2.207/D24, ExxonMobil Historical Collection, Dolph Briscoe Center for American History, University of Texas at Austin (hereafter cited as ExxonMobil Historical Collection).

79 Extended accounts of the oil industry under King Idris can be found in Waddams, *Libyan Oil Industry,* 57–228; also, J. A. Allan, *Libya: The Experience of Oil* (Boulder, Colo., 1981).

80 Anthony Sampson emphasizes Libya's central role in extracting concessions from the international oil companies, which were also then demanded and received by other producing nations in the chapter entitled "Libyan Ultimatum," in *The Seven Sisters*.

81 "Oil Companies Protest Nationalization in Libya," *Exxon Manhattan*, September 21, 1973, 4.

82 Esso Middle East to Exxon Management Committee, September 27, 1976, 8, "CEO Letters," Exxon Corporate Archives.

83 Ibid.

84 Gurney, *Libya*, 178–194.

85 Waddams, *Libyan Oil Industry*, 199–200, 288–292.

86 *Frozen Energy from Libya to Europe*, pamphlet from Esso Middle East, box 2.207/G199, ExxonMobil Historical Collection.

87 For a brief history of the early development of LNG in this era, see George D. Carameros Jr., "LNG to Play Role in the Natural-Gas Industry's Future," *Oil and Gas Journal*, August 1977, 466–471.

88 Waddams, *Libyan Oil Industry*, 288.

89 Exxon Management Committee to C. J. Hedlund, president of Esso Middle East, June 14, 1974, 1–2 "Chrono File," Exxon Corporate Archives.

90 Esso Middle East, report to Exxon Management Committee, October 14, 1974, "CEO Letters 1974," Exxon Corporate Archives; Waddams, *Libyan Oil Industry*, 288.

91 Exxon Management Committee to Esso Middle East, December 2, 1975, 1, Exxon Corporate Archives.

92 Esso Middle East to Exxon Management Committee, "1980 Planning and Budget Report," 4, 9–12, "CEO Letters," Exxon Corporate Archives.

93 Vandewalle, *History of Modern Libya*, 130–138.

94 Esso Middle East to Exxon Management Committee, "1981 Corporate Plan Report," 11–13, "CEO Letters," Exxon Corporate Archives.

95 Mel Harrison, interview by Joseph Pratt, April 20, 2007, Houston, 11, Exxon-Mobil Oral History; Jerry Ackerman, "Exxon Withdrawal from Libya Has Shadow of Reagan Pressure," *Houston Chronicle*, November 23, 1981. Libya officially announced that it had acquired all of Exxon's remaining properties as of December 1, 1981, with a payment for the properties and their transfer to the Libyan National Oil Company.

96 Garvin interview, 23.

97 Esso Middle East to Exxon Management Committee, October 8, 1979, 7, Exxon Corporate Archives.

98 Downs Matthews, "Saudi Arabia: A Profile in Energy," *Lamp* 83, no. 2 (Summer 2001): 15–22.

99 Stephen Fidler, "PDVSA and the Economy: A Rare Case of Well-Oiled Efficiency," *Financial Times*, October 21, 1997. Three case studies with special relevance for this chapter were produced by the James A. Baker Institute for Public Policy at Rice University for a conference titled "The Changing Role of National Oil Companies in International Markets," held March 1–2, 2007: David R. Mares and Nelson Altamirano, "Venezuela's PDVSA and World Energy Markets: Corporate Strategies and Political Factors Determining Behavior and Influence"; Amy Myers Jaffe and Jareer Elass, "Saudi Aramco: National Flagship with Global Responsibilities"; and Daniel Brumberg and Ariel I. Ahram, "The National Iranian Oil Company in Iranian Politics."

100 Garvin interview, 52–53.

CHAPTER TWO: UNDER SIEGE

1 Public Affairs, memorandum to Management Committee, July 12, 1979, Exxon Corporate Archives.

2 General histories of energy policy in the United States in the 1970s include Goodwin, *Energy Policy in Perspective*; Vietor, *Energy Policy in America Since 1945*; and Hakes, *A Declaration of Energy Independence*.

3 For a useful analysis of business influence on politics, see Neil Gunningham,

Robert Kagan, and Dorothy Thompson, *Shades of Green: Business, Regulation, and Environment* (Stanford, Calif., 2003); also, Kraft and Kamieniecki, *Business and Environmental Policy*.

4   Joseph A. Pratt, William Becker, and William McClenahan Jr., *Voice of the Marketplace: A History of the National Petroleum Council* (College Station, Tex., 2002).

5   William D. Smith, "Exxon's New Top Two: Big Challenge Facing Garvin and Kauffmann Is Oil's Image," *New York Times*, July 13, 1975 (ProQuest Historical Newspapers, *New York Times, 1851–2003*, 121); Yergin, *The Prize*, 692; Anthony J. Parisi, "Exxon Chief Adds New Role," *New York Times*, July 4, 1980.

6   See, for example, the following articles by C. C. Garvin Jr.: "Who Needs Multinational Oil Companies?" *Lamp* 58, no. 1 (Spring 1976): i–1; "Business Ethics," *Lamp* 59, no. 3 (Fall 1976): i–1; and "Let's Work Together," *Lamp* 58, no. 2 (Summer 1976): 2–3.

7   Roy A. Baze, "The Energy Future," speech delivered at Georgia Institute of Technology, November 24, 1975, Speech Files, Exxon Corporate Archives.

8   "National Tax and Price Policies," memorandum to Exxon Management Committee, January 23, 1964, Exxon Corporate Archives. The federal oil depletion allowance, in force beginning in the 1920s, provided a substantial tax break for oil producers by permitting them to shelter 27.5 percent of the sales of oil from a well. The rationale was that oil is a depleting resource, and the depletion allowance accounts for the decline in resources in the operation of producing property.

9   Goodwin, *Energy Policy in Perspective*, 456–458, 467–473, 497–502.

10 A good source for analysis of the price controls and the allocations system is Vietor, *Energy Policy in America since 1945*, 236–272; for a chart summarizing changes over time in the oil-price control system, see 237. See also Joseph P. Kalt, *The Economics and Politics of Price Regulation* (Cambridge, Mass., 1981). A comparative perspective is found in Edward R. Fried and Charles L. Schultze, eds., *Higher Oil Prices and the World Economy: The Adjustment Problem* (Washington, D.C., 1975).

11 Vietor, *Energy Policy in America*, 248.

12 Randall Meyer, interview by Joseph Pratt, December 6, 2006, Houston, 43; Kenneth Roberts, interview by Joseph Pratt, September 21, 2007, Houston, 9; both in ExxonMobil Oral History.

13 Goodwin, *Energy Policy in Perspective*, 487.

14 Ibid., 612–631; Vietor, *Energy Policy in America*, 258–271.

15 George A. Reigeluth and Douglas Thompson, eds., *Capitalism and Competition: Oil Industry Divestiture and the Public Interest; Proceedings of the Johns Hopkins University Conference on Divestiture, Washington, D.C., May 27, 1976* (Baltimore,

1976); David J. Teece, *Vertical Integration and Vertical Divestiture in the U.S. Oil Industry* (Stanford, Calif., 1976); Exxon Corporation, *Competition in the Petroleum Industry* (New York, 1975), 11, ExxonMobil Historical Collection.

16 For an impassioned overview of antitrust in oil in this era, see John Blair, *The Control of Oil* (New York, 1976); Standard of California, "Standard of California's Oil Divestiture Manual" (1986; copy in author's possession).

17 "Exxon Wins Price-Fixing Case; Other Oil Giants Settle for $320 Million," Associated Press, May 8, 1992.

18 Exxon Corporation, *Competition in the Petroleum Industry*, 41, 42.

19 "Dismemberment as Economic Malpractice," *Exxon USA*, no. 2, 1976, 8–11; Baze, "The Energy Future."

20 For discussion of the numerous bills in Congress for horizontal and vertical divestiture, see Standard of California, "Divestiture Manual," April 1976, I:1–3.

21 Les Gapay, "Oil Firms Fear Moves to Bar Their Owning Other Energy Sources," *Wall Street Journal*, May 25, 1977.

22 "The Case for Diversification," *Exxon USA*, no. 2, 1977, 26–31; William A. Johnson, "The Divestiture Debate," *Lamp* 58, no. 3 (Fall 1976): 2–5.

23 "Response to Attack on Industrial Structure," planning memorandum to Exxon Executive Committee, dated January 14, 1976, Exxon Corporate Archives.

24 Exxon Corporation, *Competition in the Petroleum Industry*, 11, 18.

25 Ibid., 41, 42.

26 Gapay, "Oil Firms Fear Moves."

27 Ibid.

28 Louis Galambos and Joseph Pratt, *The Rise of the Corporate Commonwealth* (New York, 1988), 201–226.

29 Goodwin, *Energy Policy in Perspective*, 395–636.

30 C. C. Garvin, "Facing Energy Realities," *Lamp* 58, no. 4 (Winter 1976): i–1. For an excellent study of the rise and fall of nuclear power, see J. Samuel Walker, *Three Mile Island: A Nuclear Crisis in Historical Perspective* (Berkeley and Los Angeles, 2004); see also Daniel Pope, *Nuclear Implosions: The Rise and Fall of the Washington Public Power Supply System* (Cambridge, 2008).

31 C. C. Garvin, "Facing Hard Choices," *Lamp* 61, no. 1 (Spring 1979): 1.

32 For a good overview of governmental policies toward synthetic fuels in the 1970s, see Vietor, *Energy Policy in America since 1945*, 163–192. Garvin is quoted in William A. Smith, "Exxon's New Top Two," *New York Times*, July 13, 1975.

33 M. Elizabeth Sanders, *The History of Natural Gas Regulation, 1938–1978* (Philadelphia, 1982); Arlon R. Tussing and Bob Tippee, *The Natural Gas Industry: Evolution, Structure, and Economics*, 2nd ed. (Tulsa, 1995), 185–266.

34 C. C. Garvin, "The Continuing Need for Conservation," *Lamp* 58, no. 1 (Spring 1976): 1.

35 Edward L. Lublin and Marvin G. Pickholz, "Introduction to the Powerplant and Industrial Fuel Use Act of 1978: Securing Exemptions for Utilities and Industrial Users," *American University Law Review* 29:485–513. The pace of change was rapid in this era of energy price swings. By 1987, most of these restrictions on natural gas use had been lifted.

36 C. C. Garvin Jr., "The Continuing Need for Conservation," 1.

37 Ibid.

38 Richard Rutter, "How Exxon Saves Energy," *Lamp* 57, no. 1 (Spring 1975): 14–19.

39 Charles Berg, "Conservation in Industry," *Science* 184, no. 4131 (April 19, 1974): 264–270; for an excellent overview of the prospects for energy conservation in 1979, see Daniel Yergin, "Conservation: The Key Energy Source," in Roger Stobaugh and Daniel Yergin, eds., *Energy Future* (New York, 1979), 136–182.

40 C. C. Garvin, "We're Running Out of Time," *Lamp* 59, no. 3 (Fall 1977): i.

41 For examples, see "Energy Savers, Take Heart! Help Is on the Way," *Exxon USA*, no. 4, 1977, 16–21; Jack Long, "Sweden and Germany: Living with Costlier Energy," *Lamp* 60, no. 4 (Winter 1978): 19–25.

42 C. C. Garvin, "Looking Ahead in Energy," *Lamp* 60, no. 1 (Spring 1978): 1.

43 "Conserving Today's Energy for Tomorrow's Needs," *Exxon USA*, 1977, no. 4, 27–31.

44 Randall Meyer, interview by Joseph Pratt, December 6, 2006, Houston, 40, ExxonMobil Oral History.

45 For two useful overviews of post–World War II environmental policies in the United States, see Andrews, *Managing the Environment*, and Samuel P. Hays, *Environmental Politics Since 1945* (Pittsburgh, 2000). For Exxon's take on the EIS, see "What on Earth Is an EEE-Eye-ESS?" *Exxon USA*, 1976, no. 1, 12–15.

46 Two books on the pipeline system are particularly useful: Coates, *The Trans-Alaska Pipeline Controversy*, and James P. Roscow, *800 Miles to Valdez: The Building of the Alaska Pipeline* (Englewood Cliffs, N.J., 1977). Also useful is "Toward the Energy Frontiers," *Lamp* 59, no. 4 (Winter 1977): 2–3. See also Charles J. Cicchetti, *Alaskan Oil: Alternative Routes and Markets* (Washington, D.C., 1972); ARCO Alaska, *Industry Pioneers: ARCO in Alaska, 1955–1999* (Anchorage, 1999).

47 Walter K. Wilson, "TAPS Revisited," *Lamp* 63, no. 3 (Fall 1984): 2–11; Edward J. Fortier, "The Impossible Challenge," *Lamp* 59, no. 4 (Winter 1977): 13–25.

48 "Trans-Alaska Line Effects Under Study," *Oil and Gas Journal*, June 23, 1969, 80, 82; Wilson, "Impossible Challenge," 14.

49 "Delay Clouds Trans-Alaska Line Future," *Oil and Gas Journal*, March 8, 1971, 31–33; Milton L. Alberstadt, "Ten Years of TAPS," *Lamp* 69, no. 3 (Fall 1987): 17.

50 Gene T. Kinney, "The Environmental Craze: Will It Strangle Energy?" *Oil and*

Gas Journal, March 15, 1971, 23–28; "Environmentalists Forcing Energy Crisis on Nation," *Oil and Gas Journal,* March 15, 1971, 21.

51 Roscow, *800 Miles to Valdez,* 87–91.

52 Morris Foster, interview by Joseph Pratt, August 22, 2007, Houston, 89, Exxon-Mobil Oral History.

53 Roscow, *800 Miles to Valdez,* 92–94.

54 Harrison interview, 23.

55 Website of Alyeska, http://www.alyeska-pipe.com/TAPS/PipelineFacts, accessed February 18, 2013. For a good discussion of the pipeline design, see Ulrich Luscher, William T. Black, and Keshavan Nair, "Geotechnical Aspects of Trans-Alaska Pipeline," *Transportation Engineering Journal* 101, no. 4 (November 1975): 669–680.

56 C. C. Garvin, "Toward Energy Frontiers," *Lamp* 59, no. 4 (Winter 1977): 3.

57 "The Oil Industry and the Environment," reprinted in Exxon Corporation, *Exxon and the Environment* (New York, 1975), 6.

58 Quoted in James Krier and Edmund Ursin, *Pollution and Policy: A Case Essay on California and Federal Experience with Motor Vehicle Air Pollution, 1940–1975* (Berkeley and Los Angeles, 1977), 204.

59 Joseph A. Pratt, "Letting the Grandchildren Do It," *Public Historian* 2, no. 4 (Summer 1980): 28–61; Gerald Markowitz and David Rosner, *Deceit and Denial: The Deadly Politics of Industrial Pollution* (Berkeley and Los Angeles, 2003), 109–138.

60 Exxon Corporation, "Oil Industry and the Environment," 7.

61 "API, NPRA Blast Lead Removal Plans," *Oil and Gas Journal,* July 26, 1972, 26–27.

62 Wilhelm interview, April 26, 2007, 10.

63 Myron G. Harrison, interview by William Hale, January 29, 2008, Irving, Texas, 16, ExxonMobil Oral History; V. M. Thomas, "The Elimination of Lead in Gasoline," *Annual Review of Energy and the Environment* 20 (November 1995): 301–324; Pratt, "Letting the Grandchildren Do It."

64 "Exxon Urges Easing of Fuel Specs," *Oil and Gas Journal,* May 14, 1973, 55.

65 "EPA Sees Possible Demise of Converter," *Oil and Gas Journal,* March 10, 1975, 46; "EPA Warned of Gasoline Desulfurization Costs," *Oil and Gas Journal,* March 3, 1975, 61.

66 "Catalytic Systems Called Key to Cutting Sulfate Emissions," *Oil and Gas Journal,* October 25, 1976, 55; *Implementation of the Clean Air Act, 1975: Hearings before the Senate Subcommittee on Environmental Pollution of the Committee on Public Works,* 94th Cong., 1st sess., May 20–21, 1975, 1285–1313 (statement of Frederick Dennstedt).

67 "Exxon Urges Easing of Fuel Specs," 55.

68 "EPA: Oil Pays Big Pollution Control Cost Share," *Oil and Gas Journal,*

October 15, 1979, 89. For a different view, see Joan Norris Booth, *Cleaning Up: The Cost of Refinery Pollution Control* (New York, 1975), and Gregg Kerlin and Daniel Rabovsky, *Cracking Down: Oil Refining and Pollution Control* (New York, 1975).

69 Lee R. Aalund, "Refining Trends Are Submerged by a Flood of Uncertainties," *Oil and Gas Journal*, March 27, 1972, 108–126.

70 Lee R. Aalund, "Big Refining Riddle: What Kind, How Much Gasoline," *Oil and Gas Journal*, August 26, 1974, 41–44.

71 "Summary of EUSA Octane Strategy," report to Exxon Management Committee, March 15, 1978, Exxon Corporate Archives; "Low Lead Mogas Facilities," May 15, 1974, Consolidated Correspondence, Exxon Corporate Archives; Gary Yerkey, "Europe Stalls on Move to Switch to Lead-Free Gasoline," *Christian Science Monitor*, November 10, 1982.

72 "API Seeks Overhaul of Air Quality Regs," *Oil and Gas Journal*, December 20, 1975, 36; for the quotation, see "EPA Rejects API Bid for Review of Air Quality Standards," *Oil and Gas Journal*, February 7, 1977, 34–35.

73 "EPA Pushing Air Emissions Trade Off Policy," *Oil and Gas Journal*, November 22, 1976, 72; for the quotation, from an unidentified "top executive" of a large petrochemical company, see "Regulatory Overkill Could Stall Petrochemical Growth," *Oil and Gas Journal*, March 21, 1977, 55.

74 "EPA: Anti-Pollution Plant $5.9 Billion by 1983," *Oil and Gas Journal*, June 14, 1976, 49; "EPA: Oil Pays Big Pollution Control Cost Share."

75 "The Hondo Chronicles," *Exxon USA*, 1979, no. 3, 16–23; Teresa Sabol Spezio, "Rising Tide: The Santa Barbara Oil Spill and Its Aftermath" (Ph.D. diss., University of California, Davis, March 2011).

76 Tom Quinn to Howard Kauffmann, August 27, 1976; Kauffmann to Quinn, September 1, 1976, both in file dated November 4, 1976, Exxon Corporate Archives.

77 "Stiff Environmental Regs Slow U.S. Energy Plans," *Oil and Gas Journal*, February 6, 1978, 23.

78 *Exxon USA*, "Hondo Chronicles," 16.

79 Congressional Research Service, *Outer Continental Shelf: Debate over Oil and Gas Leasing and Revenue Sharing*, CRS Issue Brief for Congress, Library of Congress, Washington, D.C., updated October 27, 2005, 5; Robert Gramling, *Oil on the Edge: Offshore Development, Conflict, Gridlock* (Albany, 1996).

80 Exxon USA, "1980 Company Plan Narrative: Exploration, Production, and Natural Gas Departments: 1980 Company Plan," October 22, 1980, 13, Exxon Corporate Archives.

81 For a history of the era before the new laws of the 1960s and of the transition to these laws, see Gorman, *Redefining Efficiency*.

82 Esso Eastern, report to Exxon Management Committee, January 29, 1973; in folder dated April 11, 1973, Exxon Corporate Archives.

83   Winston Harrington, Richard D. Morganstern, and Thomas Sterner, eds., *Choosing Environmental Policy* (Washington, D.C., 2004).

CHAPTER THREE: COLDER AND DEEPER

1   Exxon Corporation, "Review of Operations," *1975 Annual Report*, 4.
2   Foster interview, 12.
3   Harry Longwell, interview by William Hale, July 7, 2007, Irving, Texas, 7–9, ExxonMobil Oral History.
4   William Rintoul, "Looking for Oil in Alaska," *Lamp* 68, no. 4 (Winter 1986): 18–23. For more on Arctic exploration, see National Petroleum Council, *U.S. Arctic Oil and Gas* (Washington, D.C., 1981), 36–46.
5   Exxon USA Exploration Department, "Prudhoe Bay: An Exploration Epoch," *Search* 2, no. 2 (1986); see also ARCO Alaska, *Industry Pioneers*.
6   Harry Longwell, interview by William Hale, July 27, 2007, Irving, 5–12, Exxon-Mobil Oral History.
7   Mel Harrison interview, 23–24; Mark Albers, interview by William Hale, January 9, 2008, Irving, 12, ExxonMobil Oral History.
8   Earle Gray, "Study Will Answer Arctic Gas-Pipeline Questions," *Oil and Gas Journal*, October 25, 1971, 92–96.
9   For an excellent short discussion of these options, see Zaheer Jan, "Alaska Natural Gas Pipeline Project Needs Thinking Outside the Box," *Pipeline and Gas Journal*, March 2007, 42-45.
10   See, for example, Exxon Corporation, *1973 Annual Report*, 14.
11   Meyer interview, February 7, 2008, 46-47.
12   "Gas: Summary of Plans and 1978 Budgets," report prepared for the Exxon Management Committee, November 31, 1977, 2, Exxon Corporate Archives. For a summary of events, see Betty Galbraith, "Alaska Natural Gas Pipeline Proposals (North Slope to Market): Chronology of Events, 1981," July 15, 2009, http://library.state.ak.us/pdf/gasline/ANGTS_1981.pdf. See also Robert J. Johnson, "Carter's Bogged-Down Energy Policy: Alcan Pipeline Wallows in Sea of Doubt," *Ottawa Citizen*, May 4, 1978.
13   "Executive Summary: Supplemental Gas Supplies," report prepared for Exxon Management Committee, March 12, 1979, Exxon Corporate Archives; Exxon USA, "1979 Company Plan," memorandum to Exxon Management Committee, October 5, 1979, 6, Exxon Corporate Archives; Exxon Company USA, "Exxon Negotiates Last North Slope Gas Contract," memorandum for Exxon Management Committee and news release dated February 12, 1979, Exxon Corporate Archives.
14   Exxon USA, "1980 Company Plan Narrative: Exploration, Production, and Natural Departments," report to Exxon Management Committee, October 22, 1980, 24–25, Exxon Corporate Archives; Exxon USA, "1980 Company

Plan—Exxon U.S.A.," report to Exxon Management Committee, October 10, 1980, 11–12, Exxon Corporate Archives.

15 Exxon USA, "1981 Company Plan Narrative: Exploration, Production and Natural Gas," report to Exxon Management Committee, October 1981, 32–34, Exxon Corporate Archives.

16 Exxon USA, "1982 Corporate Plan," report to Exxon Management Committee, September 30, 1982, 3, Exxon Corporate Archives.

17 Exxon USA, "1982 Financial and Operating Report, Exxon, U.S.A.: Business Summary—Business Climate," report to Exxon Management Committee, February 14, 1983, 4, Exxon Corporate Archives; Exxon USA CEO to Exxon Management Committee, November 3, 1983, 4, Exxon Corporate Archives.

18 Longwell interview, July 27, 2007, 15.

19 Exxon USA, "Expansion of the Trans-Alaska Pipeline System," memorandum to Exxon Management Committee, February 22, 1977, Exxon Corporate Archives.

20 "Exxon USA: Proposed Advance Commitment for Prudhoe Bay Low Pressure Gas Separation Project," memorandum to Exxon Management Committee, November 6, 1979, Exxon Corporate Archives.

21 "Exxon USA: Prudhoe Bay Unit—Produced Water Injection Project—$256 million," Exxon USA to Exxon Management Committee, memorandum dated March 26, 1981, Exxon Corporate Archives.

22 Exxon USA, "Exxon USA: Prudhoe Bay Unit—Miscible Gas Flood Enhanced Recovery Project—$34.7M," memorandum to Exxon Management Committee, May 14, 1981, Exxon Corporate Archives.

23 National Petroleum Council, *U.S. Arctic Oil & Gas*; "The Great Arctic Energy Rush," *BusinessWeek*, January 24, 1983, 52.

24 Exxon USA, "1979 Company Plan," 12.

25 Priest, *Offshore Imperative*, 213–215.

26 Arthur C. Banet Jr., *Oil and Gas Development on Alaska's North Slope: Past Results and Future Prospects*, BLM-Alaska Open File Report 34, March 1991; Pratt, *Prelude to Merger*, 112–116.

27 Exxon USA, "Lisburne Development Project: Advance Commitment," memorandum to Exxon Management Committee, November 30, 1983, Exxon Corporate Archives; "Digging Deeper at Prudhoe Bay," *Lamp* 67, no. 1 (Spring 1985): 23.

28 "Offshore Alaska Production Begins," *Lamp* 69, no. 3 (Fall 1987): 19.

29 Downs Matthews, "New Vigor on Alaska's North Slope," *Lamp* 75, no. 4 (Winter 1993): 17–24.

30 "The Alaska Arctic: A Technological Frontier," *Lamp* 59, no. 4 (Winter 1977; special issue on Alaska): 26; Imperial Oil, *The Story of Imperial Oil* (Toronto, 1991), 20–23; "CIDS: Island in the Ice," *Exxon USA*, 1985, no. 3, 10–15;

"A Concrete Answer for Arctic Exploration," *Lamp* 66, no. 3, (Fall 1984): 22; "Exploring the Arctic for Oil," *Exxon USA*, 1980, no. 2, 4. For a good overview of Arctic exploration, see Karin Clark, Cory Hetherington, Chris O'Neil, and Jana Zavitz, *Breaking Ice with Finesse: Oil and Gas Exploration in the Canadian Arctic* (Calgary, 1997).

31 Albers interview, 12–16.

32 Longwell interview, July 27, 2007, 9–10.

33 For general histories of offshore development, see F. Jay Schempf, *Pioneering Offshore: The Early Years* (Houston, 2007); Hans Veldman and George Lagers, *Fifty Years Offshore* (Delft, 1997); and *Fifty Years of Offshore Oil and Gas Development* (Houston, 1997).

34 Joseph A. Pratt, Tyler Priest, and Christopher J. Castaneda, *Offshore Pioneers: Brown & Root and the History of Offshore Oil and Gas* (Houston, 1997); Priest, *Offshore Imperative*; and William R. Freudenburg and Robert Grambling, *Oil in Troubled Waters: Perceptions, Politics, and the Battle over Offshore Drilling* (Albany, 1994).

35 "Humble Test Cracks 600-ft Deepwater Mark off California," *Oil and Gas Journal*, August 2, 1965, 68.

36 Robert Lindsey, "Exxon Nears Completion of Deepest Offshore Rig," *New York Times*, November 10, 1976. In the interest of clarity, it should be noted that Hondo was not a drilling "rig" in the common parlance of the offshore industry, but rather a production platform.

37 Ibid.

38 M. L. Delflache, et al., "Design of the Hondo Platform for 850-Feet Water Depth in the Santa Barbara Channel," Offshore Technology Conference Proceedings, Paper OTC 2960, 1977, 17–26; Dixon Fiske, "Hondo Means Deep," *Lamp* 59, no. 1 (Spring 1977): 21; *Exxon USA*, "The Hondo Chronicles"; Exxon USA, "Exxon USA: Santa Barbara Channel (Hondo Field): Budget Supplement for Offshore Storage and Treating Project," letter to Exxon Management Committee, November 30, 1979, 1–3, Exxon Corporate Archives; "Temblor Time," *Exxon USA*, 1984, first quarter, 9–11.

39 Joseph A. Pratt, "The Bold and the Foolhardy: Hurricanes and the Early Offshore Oil Industry," in *The Challenge of Remaining Innovative: Insights from Twentieth-Century Business History*, ed. Sally H. Clarke, Naomi R. Lamoreaux, and Steven W. Usselman (Stanford, Calif., 2009), 191–218.

40 Richard K. Miller and Stephen F. Felszeghy, *Engineering Features of the Santa Barbara Earthquake of August 13, 1978*, report no. UCSB-ME-78-2 (Berkeley, 1978); R. M. Hamilton, et al., "Seismicity and Associated Effects, Santa Barbara Region," Geological Survey Professional Paper 679-D, U.S. Department of Interior, 1969.

41 Anthony Wolff, "New Mood in Malaysia," *Lamp* 60, no. 1 (Summer 1982): 2–13.

42 Richard Kruizenga, interview by William Hale, October 10, 2006, Dallas, 1, ExxonMobil Oral History.

43 Ed Flint, interview by Joseph Pratt, September 6, 2007, Houston, Texas, 21, ExxonMobil Oral History.

44 Ed Flint, "Presentation to Exxon Board: An Overview of Esso's Exploration and Production Business," June 20, 1997, 4.

45 M. E. J. O'Loughlin (Esso Eastern) to Exxon Management Committee, "Malaysia Budget Proposal," January 27, 1977, 1, 3, Exxon Corporate Archives.

46 As quoted in Downs Matthews, "A Century of Progress in Malaysia," *Lamp* 75, no. 1 (Spring 1993): 8.

47 Flint interview, 22. For a brief history of Petronas, see Fred R. von der Mehden and Al Troner, "Petronas: A National Oil Company with an International Vision" (James Baker III Institute for Public Policy, Rice University, Houston, March 2007).

48 Quoted in Matthews, "A Century of Progress in Malaysia," 5.

49 Sandford Brown, "The Pioneers of Terengganu," *Lamp* 70, no. 3 (Fall 1988): 6–11.

50 Charles Roxburgh, interview by Joseph Pratt, August 6, 2007, Houston, Texas, 21, ExxonMobil Oral History.

51 Flint, "Presentation to Exxon Board," 21–22.

52 Ibid., 18–20.

53 Joep Schenk, *Groningen's Gas Field: The First Fifty Years; Beating Heart of the Dutch Natural Gas Industry*, trans. Petra Timmer (Amsterdam, 2009).

54 Wall, *Growth in a Changing Environment*, 251.

55 Schenk, *Groningen's Gas Field*, 23; Stephen Howarth and Joost Jonker, *Powering the Hydrocarbon Revolution, 1939–1973: A History of Royal Dutch Shell* (Oxford, 2007), 2:209.

56 Schenk, *Groningen's Gas Field*, 205–206.

57 Ibid., 93–151.

58 Schenk, *Groningen's Gas Field*; Juliet A. McGhie, "Natural Gas Leads the Way," *Lamp* 76, no. 1 (Spring 1994): 13–18; Shelley Moore, "The Greatness of Groningen," *Lamp* 84, no. 1 (Spring 2002): 1–6.

59 Bjorn Vidar Lerøen, "Fredrik Hagemann Looks Back on 25 Years in the Oil Business: A Norwegian Oil Saga with International Beginnings," *Esso Perspecktiv* (Esso Norway), 1997, 76–79; Pratt, Priest, and Castaneda, *Offshore Pioneers*, 202–204: Walter Gibbs, *North Sea Saga: The Oil Age in Norway* (Oslo, 1999).

60 As quoted in Veldman and Lagers, *Fifty Years Offshore*, 105.

61 Pratt, Priest, and Castaneda, *Offshore Pioneers*, 199–221.

62 Flint interview, 14.

63 Longwell interview, July 7, 2007, 32.

64 Flint interview, 14.

65 Esso Europe, "Esso Europe: U.K. Northern North Sea Project Review and

Budget Supplement," memorandum to Exxon Management Committee, September 24, 1976, Exxon Corporate Archives.

66 One of the clearest and most controversial disputes between the partners came at a very bad time for Shell, when it was under heavy fire in 1995 for its announced plans to dispose of the massive Brent Spar floating oil storage terminal by sinking it in the North Sea instead of towing it ashore and scrapping it. Exxon, Shell, and the British government all agreed that this was reasonable; environmental groups did not, however, and intense protests led by Greenpeace erupted in Europe. As Shell fought a very public battle with the protestors, it also faced the anger of the British government, which still favored the original plan to dump the structure at sea. According to a history of the offshore industry, Exxon, throughout the episode, although "being equally involved, remained dead silent and escaped the public's anger," leaving "the Operator" alone to fight the partners' fight (Veldman and Lagers, *Fifty Years Offshore*, 165–167). In fact, according to the memories of Exxon executives, the company took the hard line that if Shell decided to abandon the original agreement and instead to tow the structure to Norway for dismantling, then it would have to absorb the added expense. This must have reinforced Shell's image of Exxon as a company obsessively concerned with profits; even insiders at Exxon admitted in retrospect that "we could have handled that whole thing a lot better" and that "it may have poisoned things a bit with Shell" (Robert Wilhelm, interview by William Hale, December 6, 2007, Dallas, 23, ExxonMobil Oral History).

67 Andrew Neil, "Too Big a Maybe," *Economist*, July 26, 1975.

68 The *Economist* thoroughly reported on the debates on industrial policy and oil in the mid-1970s. See, for example, the following articles, all from that publication: "North Sea Guillotine: The Parliamentary Bill to Control Britain's North Sea Oil Development is Imperfect, but Continued Uncertainty would be Worse," July 12, 1975; Andrew Neil, "The Gifthorse Gallops By," July 26, 1975; "Government and Industry," May 10, 1975; Andrew Neil, "Some are More Marginal than Others," July 26, 1975; and Andrew Neil, "Slow Learner," July 26, 1975.

69 "North Sea Oil: £2.5 Billion Sticking Point," *Economist*, January 11, 1975.

70 "North Sea: Statesmen and Oilmen," *Economist*, November 20, 1976; "North Sea Oil: It's British," *Economist*, March 6, 1976; "North Sea Oil: Less License," *Economist*, February 14, 1976.

71 "North Sea Oil's Secret Laissez-Faire Policy," *Economist*, November 25, 1978.

72 Earlier speculation had assumed that Margaret Thatcher would have difficulty altering the policies put in place by the Labour Party. The *Economist* had written in 1978 that the outgoing energy secretary and the chairman of BNOC "are both keen to make it difficult for an incoming Conservative energy minister to dismantle the corporation's burgeoning activities" ("North Sea Is Slipping Through Mrs. Thatcher's Grasp," *Economist*, April 22, 1978).

73 Esso Europe, "1979 CEO Letter," memorandum to Exxon Management Committee, October 4, 1979, 1, 5, 6, Exxon Corporate Archives.

74 Jim Hedberg, interview by Joseph Pratt, August 1, 2007, Houston, 24, Exxon-Mobil Oral History Project; Esso Europe, memorandum to Exxon Management Committee, August 2, 1979, 2, Exxon Corporate Archives.

75 Hedberg interview, 23.

76 "The New Vikings," *Economist*, July 26, 1975, 34.

77 Esso Europe to Exxon Management Committee, January 30, 1981, 1, Exxon Corporate Archives.

78 Esso Europe, "Esso Exploration and Production Norway—Balder Field Development Project," memorandum to Exxon Management Committee, November 24, 1980, 2, Exxon Corporate Archives.

79 Vidar Lerøen, "Fredrik Hagemann," 76–79.

80 Svein Andersen, *The Struggle over North Sea Oil and Gas: Government Strategies in Denmark and Norway* (Oslo, 1993), 97; Oystein Noreng, *The Oil Industry and Government Strategy in the North Sea* (London, 1980); Brent F. Nelson, *The State Offshore: Petroleum, Politics, and State Intervention on the British and Norwegian Continental Shelves* (Madison, 1989).

81 Howard Kauffmann, interview by Joseph Pratt, November 27, 2007, Atlanta, 12–13, ExxonMobil Oral History.

82 Ernest Dunbar, "Norway's New Era," *Lamp* 58, no. 4 (Winter 1976): 11; for the history of Statoil, see Richard Gordon and Thomas Stenvoil, "Statoil: A Study in Political Entrepreneurship," paper delivered at The Changing Role of National Oil Companies in International Energy Markets, a conference held March 2007, James A. Baker Institute for Public Policy, Rice University, Houston; Leslie E. Grayson, *National Oil Companies* (New York, 1981), 197–225; T. Lind and G. A. MacKay, *Norwegian Oil Policies* (Montreal, 1979), 98–116.

83 Norwegian Ministry of Petroleum and Energy, *Facts 2000: The Norwegian Petroleum Sector* (2000), 88–89.

84 Lance Lamberton, "Developing Oil and Gas Worldwide," *Lamp* 74, no. 3 (Fall 1992): 1–5.

85 Sandford Brown, "North Sea Venture," *Lamp* 57, no. 1 (Winter 1975): 6–13.

86 Hedberg interview, 28.

87 Fred S. Ellers, "Advanced Offshore Oil Platforms," *Scientific American*, April 1982, 39–42, 45–50, 162.

88 Ibid., 49.

89 Ibid., 43, 45, 48.

90 "Building a Deepwater Platform," *Lamp* 57, no. 4 (Winter 1975): 14–15.

91 Flint interview, 11–16.

92 Sluyterman, *Competitive in Turbulent Markets*, 143–146. See also Ove T. Eide, Leif G. Larsen, and O. Mo, "Installation of the Shell/Esso Brent B Condeep

Production Platform," OTC Paper 2434, *Proceedings of the Eighth Annual Offshore Technology Conference*, Houston, May 3–6, 1976.

93   Ellers, "Advanced Offshore Platforms," 48; Russ Banham, *Conoco: 125 Years of Energy* (Lyme, Conn., 2000), 169.

94   Pratt, Priest, and Castaneda, *Offshore Pioneers*, 84.

95   Exxon USA (Randall Meyer), "Development of Lena Prospect," memorandum to Howard Kauffmann, February 18, 1981, Exxon Corporate Archives.

96   "Exxon's Guyed Tower Earns an Award," *Lamp* 66, no. 2 (Summer 1984): 26; L. D. Finn, "A Deepwater Offshore Platform: The Guyed Tower," OTC Paper 2688, *Proceedings of the Eighth Annual Offshore Technology Conference*, Houston, May 3–6, 1976.

97   Dean Guttormson, interview by Joseph Pratt, July 20, 2007, Houston, 13–18, ExxonMobil Oral History.

98   "Global Deepwater Search Entering Critical Phase," *Oil and Gas Journal*, February 13, 1978, 23; R. H. Gunderson, "Production Riser Technology Moves into Deeper Water," *Oil and Gas Journal*, March 19, 1979, 79; "Subsea Production Systems Outlook," *Oil and Gas Journal*, September 17, 1979, 97.

99   Sandford Brown, "Pioneering and Producing on the Ocean Floor," *Lamp* 64, no. 3 (Fall 1982): 16–21; see also memorandum, July 6, 1981, Management Committee Minutes, 1981, Exxon Corporate Archives.

100   Brown, "Pioneering and Producing on the Ocean Floor," 19.

101   Exxon's submerged (or subsea) production system frequently appeared in technical papers presented at the annual Offshore Technology Conference in Houston. See, for example, J. A. Burkhardt and T. W. Michie (Exxon), "Submerged Production System: A Final Report," OTC 3450, *Proceedings of the Offshore Technology Conference 1979*, 801–805. This paper has references to numerous other OTC papers that had been presented by other Exxon employees on the development of the submerged production system.

102   Brown, "Pioneering and Producing," 19.

103   Esso Europe, "Snorre Development Plan," report to Exxon Management Committee, July 28, 1987, Exxon Corporate Archives; Sandford Brown, "Producing Oil and Gas from SubSea Wells," *Lamp* 74, no. 1 (Spring 1992): 8–11.

104   Don Dedera, "On the Move in Australia," *Lamp* 76, no. 2 (Summer 1994): 1–10; "A Concrete Solution: Islands of Bass Strait," *Lamp* 79, no. 1 (Spring 1997): 16–21.

105   Brown, "Oil and Gas from Subsea Wells," 9–11.

CHAPTER FOUR: OUT OF OIL

1   Garvin interview, 69.

2   The history of the oil-price bust of the 1980s and its impact has yet to be

written. For an overview of its impact on Shell, see Sluyterman, *Competitive in Turbulent Markets*, 54–56. For a description of Exxon's reaction, see C. C. Garvin Jr., "The Challenge of Adjustment," *Lamp* 68, no. 2 (Summer 1986): 1.

3 Robert Wilhelm, interview by William Hale, April 4, 1007, Dallas, 4, Exxon-Mobil Oral History; Lee Raymond, interview by William Hale, June 25, 2007, Irving, 21, ExxonMobil Oral History.

4 Frank Howard, one of the giants of research in this era of Exxon's history, quoted in Wall, *Growth in a Changing Environment*, 175.

5 George Rizzo, interview by Joseph Pratt, November 26, 2007, Houston, 3, ExxonMobil Oral History.

6 Exxon Chemical Company, *Leadership in Petrochemicals: The Story of Exxon Chemical Company* (Houston, 1998); Wall, *Growth in a Changing Environment*, 170–246. For a good international perspective on the chemical industry, see Louis Galambos, Takashi Hikino, and Vera Zamagni, eds., *The Global Chemical Industry in the Age of the Petrochemical Revolution* (Cambridge, 2006).

7 Gene McBrayer, telephone interview by William Hale, March 26, 2009, Mercer Island, Washington, 4–6, 35, ExxonMobil Oral History.

8 Lee Raymond interview, June 25, 2007, 7.

9 George McCullough, interview by Joseph Pratt, July 30, 2007, Houston, 4–8, ExxonMobil Oral History; Edwin Hess, interview by Joseph Pratt, January 8, 2007, Houston, 10, ExxonMobil Oral History; Lee Raymond interview, June 25, 2007, 6; Robert Winslow, interview by Joseph Pratt, November 11, 2007, Houston, 13–14, ExxonMobil Oral History; McBrayer interview, 14.

10 McCullough interview, 7.

11 Lee Raymond interview, June 25, 2007, 10.

12 The material in this paragraph encompasses views expressed in several interviews. See Ed Galante, interview by William Hale and Joseph Pratt, October 4, 2006, Irving, 26–29, ExxonMobil Oral History; McBrayer interview, 14–19.

13 "Interview with Edwin C. Holmer: How Exxon Chemicals Prepares for the '90s," *Chemical Week*, July 30, 1980, 38–43.

14 Frank Risch, interview by William Hale, April 9, 2007, Irving, 18, ExxonMobil Oral History.

15 The data on earnings are taken from Exxon's annual "Financial and Statistical Supplement to the Annual Report"; Exxon Chemical Company, "1982 Corporate Plan," report to Exxon Executive Committee, October 1, 1982, 1, Exxon Corporate Archives.

16 McBrayer interview, 35.

17 The word "synfuels" refers to any of a number of liquid and gaseous fuels created from hydrocarbons but not originally found as a liquid or a gas. At times, this word also is applied to biomass-derived fuels such as ethanol. The primary synfuels are manufactured from coal, oil shale, oil sands, and heavy oils.

18 For a summary of oil companies' acquisitions outside of energy, see "How U.S. Oil Companies Are Making Non-Energy Acquisitions," *BusinessWeek*, April 24, 1978, 77. Gulf did not acquire Ringling Bros. Circus.

19 "Will Tenneco's Harvester Deal Turn Out to Be 'The Corporate Equivalent of Vietnam?'" *BusinessWeek*, February 4, 1985, 80–81; David Raley, "Out of Gas: Tenneco in the Era of Natural Gas Regulation, 1938–1978," Ph.D. diss., University of Houston, May 2011.

20 The best discussion of the evolution of Exxon Enterprises is found in the annual planning and budget reviews submitted each fall by the regional companies to the corporate management committee. These files, generally labeled "CEO Letters," are stored in the ExxonMobil Historical Collection. For the origins of Exxon Enterprises (originally Jersey Enterprises), see Wall, *Growth in a Changing Environment*, 47–59.

21 A good discussion of the vision of Exxon and Exxon Enterprises in the quest for diversification is in Allen Kaufman and Gordon Walker, "The Strategy-History Connection: The Case of Exxon," *Public Historian* 8, no. 2 (Spring, 1986): 23–39.

22 H. E. McBride to G. T. Piercy, "1973 Planning and Budget Review—Exxon Enterprises," October 1, 1973, ExxonMobil Historical Collection.

23 A long-term perspective on these initiatives is found in the annual reports submitted by the head of Exxon Enterprises to the Exxon Management Committee. For a useful insider's view of the process, see the Winslow interview. Winslow was one of the last presidents of Exxon Enterprises.

24 Winslow interview, 30–35; see also CEO Letters, ExxonMobil Historical Collection; Charles E. Petty, "Automating the Office," *Lamp* 63, no. 3 (Fall 1981): 26–33; "Introducing QXY, the Intelligent Typewriter," *Exxon Manhattan*, May 12, 1978, 1–3, box 2.207/H19, ExxonMobil Historical Collection.

25 Garvin interview, 66–70.

26 Winslow interview, 31.

27 For an overview of Friendswood Development's first twenty-five years, see *A Houston Landmark for Twenty-five Years*, Friendswood Development Company brochure, 1983.

28 Muriel Scott, "Exxon's Friendswood: Showcase Community Developer," *Lamp* 70, no. 3 (Fall 1988): 12–17; B. W. Massey to R. W. Kimball, December 31, 1974, 1, ExxonMobil Historical Collection.

29 "The New Oil Game: Diversification," *BusinessWeek*, April 24, 1978, 76–88.

30 Although Crandon's zinc and copper reserves remained attractive to Exxon for almost twenty years, problems with obtaining permits to develop the properties blocked their development. In 1986, Exxon withdrew its permit application. When it tried again in 1994, the new attempt proved no more successful, and Exxon sold its interests at Crandon in 1993.

31   J. T. Burgess to M. E. J. O'Loughlin, "Esso Eastern: Disputada," memorandum, December 29, 1978, ExxonMobil Historical Collection.

32   W. M. McCardell to M. E. J. O'Loughlin, memorandum, October 6, 1980, Exxon Minerals, ExxonMobil Historical Collection.

33   "Objectives, Strategies and Assumptions," memorandum, October 1981, Exxon Minerals, ExxonMobil Historical Collection.

34   W. M. McCardell to M. E. J. O'Loughlin, memorandum, October 1, 1982, Exxon Minerals, ExxonMobil Historical Collection.

35   The figures for profitability are taken from Exxon, *Financial and Operating Review*, 1998, 71, ExxonMobil Historical Collection.

36   C. C. Garvin, "Exxon and the Fuels of the Future," *Lamp* 59, no. 1 (Spring 1977): i.

37   Stephen Stamas to R. W. Kimball, memorandum, October 7, 1974, Exxon-Mobil Historical Collection. This memo is attached to a copy of a lengthy submittal from Emilio Collado (Exxon) to Robert B. Krueger (a partner in the law firm of Nossaman, Waters, Scot, Krueger, and Riordan) that provides answers to a questionnaire from the Federal Energy Administration on the role of the U.S. government in the international oil industry. The material on uranium is in the answer to question 16, part 2; see also Garvin interview, 58.

38   H. E. McBrayer to G. T. Piercy, memorandum, March 25, 1974, ExxonMobil Historical Collection.

39   Ibid.

40   Goodwin, *Energy Policy in Perspective*, 523–525; Exxon Corporation, *1975 Annual Report*, 13–14, ExxonMobil Historical Collection; Garvin interview, 58. The reasons for President Ford's support are given in a White House press release of June 26, 1975. The legislation submitted to Congress that month was intended to facilitate the transition to private competition in uranium enrichment. The website of the Gerald R. Ford Presidential Library and Museum includes copies of all the president's press releases.

41   T. A. Kirkley to G. T. Piercy, memorandum, October 20, 1978, 6, ExxonMobil Historical Collection.

42   R. A. Winslow to G. T. Piercy, memorandum, October 5, 1979, 7–10, Exxon-Mobil Historical Collection.

43   Joseph Stromberg, "Atomic Cowboys: The South Texas Project and the Decline of Nuclear Power" (Ph.D. diss., University of Houston, 2012).

44   For a historian's overview of the opposition to nuclear power in the 1970s, including criticism of its rising costs, see Walker, *Three Mile Island*, 7–17; for a contemporary discussion of the rising costs of nuclear power, see "Nuclear Dilemma," *BusinessWeek*, March 25, 1978, 54–68.

45   The long-term uranium contracts Exxon had negotiated exposed the company to costs in excess of $10 billion. They were renegotiated with great difficulty; see Lee Raymond, interview by William Hale, Irving, January 21, 2008.

46 Exxon Corporation, *1986 Annual Report*, 19, ExxonMobil Historical Collection.

47 *Solar Power Corporation: Capabilities* (pamphlet), no date, copy in box 2.207/
    H19B, ExxonMobil Historical Collection; "Building for a Solar Future," *Lamp*
    61, no. 3 (Fall 1979): 31–33.

48 The CEO letters from Exxon Enterprises to the Exxon Management Committee
    for the annual planning and budget review provide good overviews of the evo-
    lution of Exxon's solar-cell activities; see, for example, R. A. Winslow to G. T.
    Piercy, memorandum, October 5, 1979, 6–7, and R. A. Winslow to G. T. Piercy,
    memorandum, October 3, 1980, 8, both in ExxonMobil Historical Collection.

49 "Exxon Flees Photovoltaics," *Energy Daily* 12, no. 75 (April 17, 1984): 1.

50 Exxon Corporation, *1979 Annual Report*, 21–22, ExxonMobil Historical
    Collection.

51 The figures for the sales are reported in a memorandum of October 25, 1982,
    ExxonMobil Historical Collection. It lists figures of $372 million for "good-
    will" and $104 million more for "identified intangibles," suggesting a premium
    of more than $475 million.

52 Exxon Corporation, *1979 Annual Report*, 21.

53 Exxon Corporation, *1980 Annual Report*, 17, ExxonMobil Historical Collection.

54 Lewis Beman, "Exxon's $600 Million Mistake," *Fortune*, October 19, 1981;
    Kaufman and Walker, "Strategy-History Connection."

55 "What's Wrong at Exxon Enterprises," *BusinessWeek*, August 24, 1981, 90.

56 Exxon Corporation, *1986 Annual Report*, 19.

57 "The Majors Bet on Coal," *BusinessWeek*, September 24, 1979, 104; Exxon
    Corporation, *1983 Annual Report*, 14, ExxonMobil Historical Collection.

58 Goodwin, *Energy Policy in Perspective*, 584–587; Walker, *Three Mile Island*.

59 "Summary of Discussions," memorandum, February 2, 1977, Management
    Committee Coal Review, ExxonMobil Historical Collection.

60 Exxon Corporation, *1976 Annual Report*, 16.

61 Charles N. Barnard, "Colombia: History, Mystery, and Promise," *Lamp* 63,
    no. 4 (Winter 1981): 3–13; Downs Matthews, "Remembering the Forgotten
    Land," *Lamp* 73, no. 1 (Spring 1991): 1–7; Walter K. Wilson, "El Cerrejón:
    Power for the World," *Lamp* 78, no. 1 (Spring 1996): 11–18; Harvey F. Kline,
    The Coal of Cerrejón (University Park, Pa., 1987).

62 Exxon, *1998 Financial and Operating Review*, 72, ExxonMobil Historical
    Collection.

63 The historical literature on synfuels in the United States is slight but growing.
    See, for example, Vietor, *Energy Policy in America since 1945*, 44–63, 163–189;
    Richard H. K. Vietor, *Environmental Politics and the Coal Coalition* (College
    Station, Tex., 1980); Lee Scamehorn, *High Altitude Energy: A History of
    Fossil Fuels in Colorado* (Boulder, 2002): 143–164; Goodwin, *Energy Policy in
    Perspective*; Andrew Gulliford, *Boomtown Blues: Colorado Oil Shale* (Boulder,
    2003); James T. Bartis, et al., *Oil Shale Development in the U.S.: Prospects and*

Policy Issues (Santa Monica, Calif., 2005); Victor Clifton Alderson, *The Oil Shale Industry* (1920; various reprints); Paul L. Russell, *History of Western Oil Shale* (East Brunswick, N.J., 1980); and Chris Welles, *The Elusive Business* (New York, 1970). For the Canadian oil sands, see Paul Chastko, *Developing Alberta's Oil Sands from Karl Clark to Kyoto* (Calgary, 2004).

64 Walter Teagle (president, Standard Oil of New Jersey) to Federal Oil Conservation Board, July, 15, 1925, "Correspondence, R-2," Records of Federal Oil Conservation Board, National Archives, College Park, Maryland.

65 "Test Piloting for Coal Process," *Chemical Week*, February 6, 1980, 35.

66 Exxon constructed the plant and the Department of Energy helped finance its operation; see "DOE, Exxon Plan Start-up of Coal-Conversion Test Plant," *Oil and Gas Journal*, November 6, 1978, 21.

67 Ibid. The five other participants were the Electric Power Research Institute (12.2%), Japan Coal Liquefaction Development Co. (8.3%), Phillips Petroleum (2.1%), Atlantic Richfield (2.1%), Ruhrkohle A.G. (2.1%). Japan Coal Liquefaction Development was a consortium of twelve Japanese companies, with participation by the government. Ruhrkohle's commitment was supported by the German government.

68 Paul Van Slambrouck, "Synfuel Pilot Projects Sprout, but Technology Risks High," *Christian Science Monitor*, February 29, 1980; "Exxon Donor Solvent Process Demonstrated," *Oil and Gas Journal*, February 8, 1982, 61.

69 "Exxon Completes a Coal-Liquefaction Project," *Chemical Week*, August 25, 1982, 54.

70 "Exxon Calls 2 Year Coal Liquefaction Pilot Test a Success," *Oil and Gas Journal*, August 30, 1982, 47.

71 "Exxon Coal Process Held Too Costly," *Journal of Commerce*, September 6, 1983, n.p., copy in ExxonMobil Historical Collection.

72 *Oil and Gas Journal*, December 20, 1982, 5.

73 "Synthetic Fuels: The Processes, Problems and Potential," *Lamp* 62, no. 2 (Summer 1980): 2–11.

74 Ibid., 4; Wynne Thomas, "Sweet Oil from Syncrude," *Lamp* 74, no. 4 (Winter 1995–1996): 21–25.

75 Paul Grescoe, "Syncrude: New Energy for Canada," *Lamp* 60, no. 3 (Fall 1978): 2–9.

76 Ibid.

77 For annual reports on the Syncrude Project and Cold Lake, see annual CEO Letter (Report on Planning and Budgets) from Imperial Oil to Exxon Management Committee, ExxonMobil Historical Collection.

78 Sandford Brown, "Wringing Oil from Sand," *Lamp* 67, no. 1 (Spring 1985): 17–21; "Expansion at Cold Lake," *Lamp* 69, no. 3 (Fall 1987): 18.

79 J. K. Jamieson and C. C. Garvin Jr., "Energy Questions and Answers," *Lamp* 57, no. 2 (Summer 1975): 3.

80 Randall Meyer, "Planning a Synthetic Fuels Industry," *Exxon USA*, 1981, no. 2, 22–26; C. C. Garvin Jr., "The Need for Synthetic Fuels," *Lamp* 61, no. 4 (Winter 1979): 1; "Synthetic Fuels: The Processes, Problems, and Potential," *Lamp* 62, no. 2 (Summer 1980): 5. Exxon's stance is reported in John M. Berry, "U.S. Set to Spend Billions Devising Synthetic Fuels," *Washington Post*, June 8, 1980.

81 This public enthusiasm in 1980 would come back to haunt Exxon two years later, when it withdrew abruptly from the Colony project.

82 J. D. Baker, "World Oil Shale Resources and Development History," in *Synthetic Fuels from Oil Shale: Symposium Papers presented December 3–6, 1979, Atlanta, Georgia* (Chicago: Institute of Gas Technology), 5.

83 Paul Rothberg, "Synthetic Fuels Corporation and National Synfuels Policy," issue brief no. IB81139, Congressional Research Service, August 17, 1981, updated February 18, 1983, 3.

84 C. C. Garvin, "Toward the Age of Energy Diversity," *Lamp* 62, no. 1 (Spring 1980): 1.

85 W. M. McCardell, "Colorado Shale Oil Project," report, January 24, 1980, ExxonMobil Historical Collection.

86 "Five Active U.S. Oil-Shale Projects Are Advancing," *Oil and Gas Journal*, June 29, 1981: 76; "Shale Oil Is Coming of Age," *New York Times*, November 6, 1981; "As the Synfuels Industry Picks Up Steam," *U.S. News & World Report*, December 7, 1981, 66.

87 "Synfuels Offer Challenging Future," *Oil and Gas Journal*, June 29, 1981, 71.

88 J. D. Lyons, "The Colony Shale Oil Project in Colorado," *Alternative Energy Sources* 6, no. 3 (1980): 427–444.

89 Robert D. Hershey Jr., "Tosco's Shale Oil Plan Gets Another U.S. Loan," *New York Times*, March 31, 1982, copy in box 2.207/G185, ExxonMobil Historical Collection; "Exxon to Discontinue Funding of Present Colony Shale Oil Project," Exxon news release, May 2, 1982, box 2.207/G185, ExxonMobil Historical Collection.

90 Hershey, "Tosco Shale Oil Plan Gets Another Loan."

91 Douglas Martin, "Exxon Abandons Shale Oil Project," *New York Times*, May 3, 1982.

92 "Garvin Addresses Shareholders Today," copy of address dated May 13, 1982, box 2.207/G185, ExxonMobil Historical Collection.

93 "Tosco Elects to Sell Entire Colony Interest to Exxon," Tosco news release, undated, box 2.207/G185, ExxonMobil Historical Collection.

94 "Exxon Abandons Oil Shale Project," *New York Times*, May 3, 1982; "The Death of Synfuels," *Newsweek*, May 17, 1982, 75–76; "Setback for Synfuels," *Time*, May 17, 1982, 58–59.

95 Victor Schroeder to Clifton Garvin, October 22, 1982, Circular Correspondence Files, 1982, ExxonMobil Historical Collection.

96 Clifton Garvin to Victor Schroeder, November 22, 1982, Circular Correspondence Files, 1982, ExxonMobil Historical Collection.

97 J. R. Riley to A. H. Wolford, memorandum, August 17, 1982, box 2.207/G185, ExxonMobil Historical Collection. Attached to this memo are letters between Cliff Garvin and Rawleigh Warner Jr.: Warner to Garvin, June 3, 1982, and Garvin to Warner, June 28, 1982. Also attached is a clipping from the *New York Times*, July 17, 1982: Robert D. Hershey Jr., "Oil Shale Consortium Suggested: Mobil Plan for Synthetic Fuels."

98 R. H. Beresford to B. W. Massey, memorandum, September 20, 1983, ExxonMobil Historical Collection.

99 Exxon's presentations on oil shale's future were based on the work of its *World Energy Outlook*, which the company published annually in the late 1970s and early 1980s "as a communication vehicle for broad dissemination of our views on America's energy future." Along with most such efforts by business and government to predict the nation's energy future in an era of extreme volatility in the price of oil, Exxon's projections proved badly off when basic economic conditions in the oil industry changed in the 1980s. Several broader studies of energy in America in this era remain useful and interesting; see Robert Stobaugh and Daniel Yergin, eds., *Energy Future: Report of the Energy Project at the Harvard Business School* (New York, 1979); Sam Schurr, et al., eds., *Energy in America's Future: The Choices Before Us* (Baltimore, 1979).

100 Garvin interview, 61.

101 R. A. Winslow to G. T. Piercy, memorandum, October 5, 1979, 11, ExxonMobil Historical Collection.

102 "Exxon Enterprises: Summary and Key Strategic Issues," memorandum, 2, November 10, 1982, ExxonMobil Historical Collection.

CHAPTER FIVE: REVIVAL

1 An overview of events that led to the oil bust of the 1980s can be found in Yergin, *The Prize*, 699–768; see also Charles Alexander, "Tough Times for the Tiger," *Time*, August 2, 1982; "Belt-Tightening Hits Major Oil Firms," *Toronto Globe and Mail*, August 9, 1982; C. C. Garvin Jr., "Exxon Today," *Lamp* 65, no. 4 (Winter 1983), i–1.

2 Exxon Corporation, *1986 Annual Report*, 1; "Oil After the Crash," *Oil and Gas Journal*, November 10, 1986, 54; Thomas C. Hayes, "Big Oil Firms Returning to Basics," *Oklahoma City Journal Record*, May 9, 1985; C. C. Garvin Jr., "The Challenge of Adjustment," *Lamp* 68, no. 2 (Summer 1986), i–1; "Exxon Restructures," *Lamp* 68, no. 2 (Summer 1986), 18.

3 Exxon Corporation, *1985 Annual Report*, 3, Exxon Corporate Archives.

4 Richard Kruizenga, interview by William Hale, October 10, 2006, Dallas, 7, ExxonMobil Oral History.

5   Lee Raymond, interview by William Hale, May 17, 2007, Dallas, 16, ExxonMobil Oral History.

6   Ibid., 17.

7   Colin Leinster and Cynthia Hutton, "Exxon's Axman Cometh," *Fortune*, April 14, 1986.

8   Ibid.

9   Garvin, like many others interviewed, had a highly favorable opinion of Kauff-mann: "I found Howard to be an exceptional man in running this operation. He had more experience than any of us in more aspects of the world, but the fact that he was only a couple of years younger than I was made it clear that either I had to retire early or he was going to have to retire early in order for me to get somebody else ready. And after some consideration with the Exxon board, he decided to take early retirement" (Garvin interview, 62).

10   Kruizenga interview, 17.

11   Leinster and Hutton, "Exxon's Axman Cometh."

12   Rene Dahan, interview by William Hale and Joseph Pratt, January 7, 2007, Dallas, 4.

13   The quotation and much of the material on Raymond's boyhood is from an unpublished interview with Allanna Sullivan of the *Wall Street Journal*, November 24, 1997, transcript in ExxonMobil Historical Collection.

14   Interviews with Lee Raymond, April 17, 2007, June 26, 2007, and January 21, 2008. For information about Raymond's stay at Exxon Nuclear, see Risch interview, April 9, 2007, 7–9; for Aruba, see Lee Raymond, interview by William Hale, June 14, 2007, Irving, 23–24, ExxonMobil Oral History.

15   Raymond interview, May 17, 2007, 18.

16   Foster interview, 14.

17   Anthony Parisi, "Inside Exxon," *New York Times Magazine*, August 3, 1980, 5.

18   Dahan interview, 2–5.

19   "The Rebel Shaking Up Exxon: Larry Rawl Has Smashed a Bureaucratic Culture and Pumped Up Profits," *BusinessWeek*, July 18, 1988, 107, 110.

20   Raymond interview, May 17, 2007, 20.

21   McBrayer interview, 16.

22   For broad changes on the reorganization of Exxon Chemical, see Risch interview, April 9, 2007, 18–20; Raymond interview, June 25, 2007; and Kathleen Failla, "The New Exxon Chemical," *Chemical Week*, December 10, 1986, 38–41.

23   McBrayer interview, 38–39.

24   Ibid., 18.

25   Ibid., 19–20.

26   Approximately 60 percent of earnings were in the United States; see Exxon Corporation, *1989 Financial and Statistical Supplement to the Annual Report*, 10, and *1990 Financial and Operating Statistical Supplement to the Annual Report*, 10, both in Exxon Corporate Archives.

27 Exxon in many cases retained a number of its prior groups as legal entities, even though they were no longer true operating companies—often for tax purposes.

28 Lee Raymond, interview by William Hale, April 23, 2009, Dallas, ExxonMobil Oral History.

29 Ibid.

30 Jon Thompson, interview by William Hale, August 16, 2007, Dallas, 33–56; Jon Thompson, interview by William Hale, November 15, 2007, Irving, 27–32; Robert Wilhelm, interview, October 11, 2007, 3–28; Wilhelm interview, December 6, 2007, 7–12; Walter Schroth, interview by Joseph Pratt, November 19, 2007, Stewart, Florida, 18–29; all in ExxonMobil Oral History.

31 Raymond interview, May 17, 2007, 5–6.

32 Raymond interview, January 21, 2008.

33 Exxon Corporation, *1986 Annual Report*, 3.

34 Ibid., 26.

35 Ibid.

36 Exxon Corporation, *1989 Annual Report*, 10.

37 Data is from Exxon Corporation, *Financial and Statistical Supplement to the Annual Report*, for the years 1985–1990, in Exxon Corporate Archives.

38 The company moved the natural gas from net proved reserves because the gas, in order to be sold, would need to be transported to markets at a cost that at the time did not appear to be realistically attainable (Exxon Corporation, *1988 Annual Report*, 39).

39 Rawl's and Raymond's "Letter to the Shareholders" in the *1988 Annual Report* noted that the company had been able to "replace with proved reserves more hydrocarbons than we produced," but just barely, at 101 percent.

40 Raymond interview, June 14, 2007, 14.

41 Peter Nulty and Frederick H. Katayama, "Exxon's Problem: Not What You Think," *Fortune*, April 23, 1990.

42 Raymond interview, June 14, 2007, 5.

43 Raymond interview, April 23, 2009.

44 Thompson interview, August 16, 2007; Thompson interview, November 15, 2007. In addition, see Jon Thompson, interview by Julian Pleasants, June 15, 2005, Gainesville, Florida, Florida Business Leaders, Samuel Proctor Oral History Program.

45 Thompson interview, August 16, 2007, 3.

46 Ibid., 25.

47 Ibid., 26.

48 Ibid., 28.

49 Ibid., 35.

50 Ibid., 41. Thompson described the relationship thus: "Perkins was this . . . entrepreneur in engineering clothing. . . . He was kind of a traffic cop, Rawl's traffic cop."

51 Mike Forrest, "'Bright' Investments Paid Off," *Explorer* (American Association of Petroleum Geologists), July 2000. Of course, oil prices declined significantly after the 1985 sale took place.

52 Thompson interview, August 16, 2007, 42.

53 Ibid.

54 Ibid., 44.

55 Ibid. Exxon would later acquire a far larger number of leases in a 1988 sale, and then fewer numbers of them in 1989 and 1990.

56 Thompson interview, November 15, 2007, 34–35.

57 The reserve replacement ratios exclude sales of assets. See Exxon Corporation, *1991 Financial and Statistical Supplement to the Annual Report*, 32–33.

58 Larson and Porter, *Humble Oil & Refining Company*.

59 Raymond interview, June 14, 2007, 8–9.

60 Ibid.

61 Raymond interview, January 21, 2008, 5.

62 Quoted in Seamus McGraw, "Envy: The Kidnapping and Murder of Sidney Reso," Seamus McGraw on TruTV, www.trutv.com/library/crime/gangsters _outlaws/sidney_reso_kidnap/index.html.

63 A second major strengthening of corporate executive security occurred as a result of an invasion of the company's Irving headquarters on May 27, 2003—the day before the annual shareholders meeting. A group of Greenpeace activists that had camped in a remote wooded area of the headquarters site used ladders to get over the main gate and entered the building—some dressed in tiger suits. The audacity and the success of the Greenpeace move generated several changes in facility security and in how the company managed its security operations.

64 Raymond interview, January 21, 2008.

65 Harry Longwell, interview by William Hale, May 16, 2007, Dallas, 17, Exxon-Mobil Oral History.

66 Harry Longwell, interview by William Hale, April 4, 2007, Dallas, 1–26, ExxonMobil Oral History.

67 Ibid., 22.

68 These statistics are taken from Exxon Corporation, *1990 Financial and Statistical Supplement to the Annual Report*, 34–35; *1994 Supplement*, 42–43; *1998 Supplement*, 14, 20, 43–44.

69 The categories were defined as follows: "proved" reserves were those that could be economically produced from known reservoirs with existing technology; "probable" reserves were those that had a good chance of being recovered with further drilling or improved recovery methods; "static resources" included those that had been discovered but whose production awaited further field delineation, market development, new technology, or some combination of lower development costs and higher prices. In an era of rapid technological change and intense price swings, such distinctions were significant.

70 Exxon Corporation, *1990 Financial and Statistical Supplement to the Annual Report*, 36.

71 The Shell official history for this period indicates that Shell passed Exxon in oil product sales in 1983, and that Shell's petroleum production began to exceed that of Exxon at about the same time. Shell retained higher sales and production levels until the Exxon merger with Mobil in 1999 (Sluyterman, *Keeping Competitive in Turbulent Markets*, 449–463). Sluyterman's volume contains charts comparing Shell, BP, and Exxon on various measures of growth; see 198–99, 204, 236, 382–83. The public remained interested in such comparisons; see the lengthy headline on an interesting, useful comparison of the two companies: James Tanner and Allanna Sullivan, "Rival Goliaths: Two Giant Oil Firms Battle for Supremacy with Differing Tactics, Exxon Emphasizes Earnings But Shell Seeks Growth; Both See Industry Upturn; Wildcatter vs. Cambridge," *Wall Street Journal*, July 8, 1987. See also Corporate Planning Department, "Competitor Strategy Analyses," memorandum to Exxon management Committee, October 16, 1981, ExxonMobil Historical Collection.

72 Raymond interview, May 17, 2007, 2–4.

73 Raymond interview, June 14, 2007, 27.

74 Jack F. Bennett, interview by Joseph Pratt, January 3, 2007, Vero Beach, Florida, 1, ExxonMobil Oral History.

75 Frank Risch, interview by William Hale, June 12, 2007, Irving, 17–18.

76 For an overview of oil mergers of the low-oil-price era, see Yergin, *The Quest*, 83–105. For a contemporary discussion of the mid-1980s merger waves, see Leonard Silk, "The Peril Behind the Takeover Boom," *New York Times*, December 29, 1985.

77 Exxon Corporation, *1994 Annual Report*, 3.

78 Steven P. Rosenfeld, "Exxon Spends $1.9 Billion to Purchase Own Stock," *Washington Post*, June 22, 1984.

79 J. F. Bennett, remarks to the Exxon Research Club, October 26, 1988, 8, Bennett File, ExxonMobil Historical Collection.

80 Lawrence J. Tell, "Tiger in Its Tank: How Exxon's Huge Cash Flow May Fuel Its Stock," *Barron's National and Financial Weekly*, December 24, 1984, 14.

81 Bennett interview, 4.

82 Bennett, remarks to Exxon Research Club, 9.

83 Bennett interview, 4.

84 Ibid., 5.

85 Carol J. Loomis, "Beating the Stock Market by Buying Back Stock," *Fortune*, April 29, 1985, 42.

86 Risch interview, April 9, 2007, 12; Neil Osborn, "The Furor over Shelf Registration," *Institutional Investor*, June 1982, 19; Anne L. Adams, "Exxon's Done It All," *Investment Dealers' Digest*, February 22, 1983, 8–10.

87 Risch interview, June 12, 2007, 13.

88   Bennett interview, 3; John Thackray, "The Rise of Do-It-Yourself Corporate Finance," *Institutional Investor*, June 1982, 194–196; Adams, "Exxon's Done It All."

89   For example, Exxon was required to post a performance bond to ensure payment after the adverse *Exxon Valdez* judgment.

90   Lee Raymond commented that in 1984, research "was an absolute shambles" (Lee Raymond, interview by William Hale, February 20, 2007, Irving, 7).

91   John Walsh, "Exxon Builds on Basic Research," *Science*, New Series, vol. 225, no. 4666 (Sept. 7, 1984): 1001-08. The quotation is from Richard D. Lyons, "Science Advisor to Nixon Leaving for Industry Job," *New York Times*, January 3, 1973.

92   Raymond interview, February 20, 2007, 7. Exxon Chemical had had a separate research organization since the early 1960s. Though Exxon Chemical was a branch of Exxon Research and Engineering, its research was done by a separate research group in the latter's New Jersey headquarters as well as in facilities in Baytown, Texas, and later, in Europe.

93   Frank B. Sprow, interview by William Hale, January 16, 2007, Dallas, 5, Exxon-Mobil Oral History.

94   Ibid., 4.

95   Raymond interview, February 20, 2007, 7.

96   This narrative owes much to chapter 4, "Realignment and Readjustment, 1984–1987," of Exxon Research and Engineering Company, *Thirty Years of Advantage Through Science* (1998). See also Exxon Research and Engineering, *Seventy-Five Years of Technological Opportunity & Advantage* (Florham Park, N.J., 1994).

97   Sprow interview, 9.

98   *Thirty Years of Advantage Through Science*, 35. Examples of such "step-out" innovations discussed in this book include the development of tension-leg platforms and subsea production systems.

99   Exxon Corporation, *1988 Annual Report*, 16–17.

100 The Corporate Research Advisory Council's design and early activities are described in *Thirty Years of Advantage Through Science*, 42–43.

101 Raymond interview, April 23, 2009, 25.

102 Roderick Seeman, "Real Estate—Japanese Money Inflates the World," October 1987, http://www.japanlaw.info/lawletter/oct87/gpj.htm, accessed February 18, 2013.

103 The Mitsui buyer is also known as Mitsui Fudoson.

104 In August 1987, Mobil Corporation sold its headquarters building on New York's 42nd Street to Hiro Real Estate Company for $260 million.

105 The Standard Oil Trust moved its headquarters to New York City from Cleveland, Ohio, in 1883. The founders of Exxon, the Rockefellers, had been particularly generous to New York. To them, the city owed Rockefeller Center,

Riverside Church, the Cathedral of St. John the Divine, the Rockefeller Institute for Medical Research, the Cloisters, Fort Tryon Park, the land upon which the United Nations and the Museum of Modern Art were built, Lincoln Center for the Performing Arts, Palisades Park, and more. The company continued to make significant gifts to the local area and its cultural organizations, though its grants to local arts and cultural organizations dropped sharply beginning in 1987. All contributions of this nature were summarized each year in the company's publication *Dimensions*.

106 Raymond interview, April 23, 2009, 25.

CHAPTER SIX: *EXXON VALDEZ*

1 Dahan interview, 9.

2 A readable and detailed account of these events is included in John Keeble, *Out of the Channel: The Exxon Valdez Oil Spill in Prince William Sound*, 10th anniv. ed. (Cheney, Wash., 1999), 32–54. The official report on the accident by the National Transportation Safety Board was not released until July 31, 1990. It ruled that drinking by the ship's captain, a fatigued and undermanned crew, and inadequate vessel traffic control all contributed to the grounding. It attributed the severity of the damages to inadequate oil-spill contingency planning and an insufficient initial response; see National Transportation Safety Board, "Marine Accident Report: Grounding of U.S. Tankship *Exxon Valdez* on Bligh Reef, Prince William Sound Near Valdez, AK, March 24, 1989," NTSB report no. MAR-90-04.

3 Later, in dry dock in San Diego, it was said that one could stand underneath the ship and see seventy feet to the main deck above (comment by Fred Hallett, vice president and chief financial officer, National Steel and Shipbuilding Company, quoted in AP report by Dennis Georgatos, March 19, 1990).

4 Interview with Bob Nicholas by Jason Theriot, November 21, 2006, and December 4, 2006, Houston, UH Oral History of Houston Project, UH Houston History Archives, University of Houston.

5 This quote by Fred Hallett of the National Steel and Shipbuilding Company in San Diego is from the *New York Times*, October 22, 1989.

6 Bryan Hodgson, "Alaska's Big Spill: Can the Wilderness Heal?" *National Geographic*, January 1990, 32–33. Two other ships, the *Exxon San Francisco* and the *Exxon Baytown*, were eventually used also for the lightering.

7 Nicholas interview.

8 Thomas A. Lewis, "Tragedy in Alaska," *National Wildlife*, June–July 1989, 6–7.

9 Much information about the early spill response is contained in Exxon Production Research Company, "Valdez Oil Spill Technology: 1989 Operations" (1990), and in Samuel K. Skinner and William K. Reilly, *A Report to the President: The* Exxon Valdez *Oil Spill* (Washington: GPO, May 1989).

10 Gerry Yemen, "The *Exxon Valdez* Revisited: The Untold Story (A)," 18–19; this is a case study used at the Darden School of Business, University of Virginia, Charlottesville.

11 Ibid., 5, 10, 16–21; "Smothering the Waters," *Newsweek*, April 10, 1989, 55–56; Jerry Adler, "Alaska after Exxon," *Newsweek*, September 18, 1989, 50–60; "Steering a Course to Doom," *Houston Post*, April 9, 1989.

12 *Exxon Valdez* Oil Spill Trustee Council, "Map of the *Exxon Valdez* Oil Spill," http://www.evostc.state.ak.us/facts/spillmap.cfm, accessed July 15, 2012.

13 Hodgson, "Alaska's Big Spill," 5–43; Exxon Company USA, *Two Years After: Conditions in Prince William Sound and the Gulf of Alaska* (Houston, 1991).

14 The best history of TAPS (Coates, *Trans-Alaskan Pipeline Controversy*) emphasizes the importance of Alaska as "the last frontier" and the tensions between the engineers who built TAPS and the environmentalists who opposed them.

15 Quoted in Keeble, *Out of the Channel*, 101.

16 *Exxon Valdez* Oil Spill Trustee Council, "*Exxon Valdez* Oil Spill Restoration Plan," November 1994, appendix A. This council of Alaskans was created to monitor restoration efforts in the settlement of cases against Exxon by the state and federal governments, and was supported by funds from fines paid by the company; see Downs Matthews, "Saving Oiled Animals," *Lamp* 71, no.2 (Summer 1989): 17.

17 Ott, *Not One Drop*.

18 For all quotations, see Charles McCoy, "Broken Promises: Alyeska Record Shows How Big Oil Neglected Alaskan Environment," *Wall Street Journal*, July 6, 1989; Adler, "Alaska after Exxon," 55. For a good general account of oil and the Alaska economy, see John Strohmeyer, *Extreme Conditions: Big Oil and the Transformation of Alaska* (Anchorage, 2003); see especially 223–268 for a discussion of the contingency plans for *Valdez* and the spill in general.

19 Quoted in Lewis, "Tragedy in Alaska," 7–8.

20 Quoted in Hodgson, "Alaska's Big Spill," 36.

21 Claudia H. Deutsch, "The Giant With a Black Eye," *New York Times*, April 2, 1989.

22 Adler, "Alaska after Exxon," 50–62; *Newsweek*, "Smothering the Waters," 54.

23 For the transportation secretary and Senator Chafee, see "Preparedness Hit in Oil Spill Hearing," *Houston Chronicle*, April 20, 1989. For ADEC, see McCoy, "Broken Promises."

24 Skinner and Reilly, *The* Exxon Valdez *Oil Spill*, ES-1.

25 The most visible such case came out soon after the spill; see Anne K. Delehunt and Kenneth E. Goodpaster, "Exxon Corporation: Trouble at Valdez," Harvard Business School Case #9-390-024, October 1989.

26 Lee Raymond, interview by William Hale, November 1, 2007, Dallas, 19, ExxonMobil Oral History.

27 Art Davidson, *In the Wake of the "Exxon Valdez"* (San Francisco, 1990), 309.

28 "Exxon's Future," *BusinessWeek*, April 2, 1990, 72–73.

29 Allanna Sullivan, "Exxon's Holders Assail Chairman Rawl Over Firm's Handling of Alaska Oil Spill," *Wall Street Journal*, May 19, 1989.

30 John Keeble's account of the response to the spill finds Exxon guilty of not telling "the fuller truth" in what he judged to be incomplete statements about conditions in Alaska (Keeble, *Out of the Channel*, 254, 291).

31 For the "totally irrational" quotation, see Adler, "Alaska after Exxon," 54; for the Harrison quotation, *Houston Chronicle*, May 9, 1991; for the Raymond quotation, Deutsch, "Giant With a Black Eye." In an article in *National Wildlife*, the magazine of the National Wildlife Federation, Thomas A. Lewis, after a long discussion of the broad and devastating impact of the oil spill on wildlife, quotes an unidentified "Exxon environmental biologist" as saying this was "the cost of civilization" ("Tragedy in Alaska," 8).

32 Committee on Commerce, Science and Transportation of the United States Senate, April 6, 1989, Washington, D.C. (statement of L. G. Rawl), as reported in *Employee Information Bulletin*, Exxon USA.

33 Allanna Sullivan, "Rawl Wishes He'd Visited Valdez Sooner," *Wall Street Journal*, June 30, 1989.

34 "Exxon's Future: What Has Larry Rawl Wrought?" *BusinessWeek*, April 2, 1990, 76.

35 "Exxon Should Live Up to Its World Stature," *BusinessWeek*, April 2, 1990, 128.

36 *BusinessWeek*, "Exxon's Future," 73.

37 Ibid., 76.

38 Longwell interview, April 4, 2007, 26.

39 Larry Rawl to editor, *BusinessWeek*, March 27, 1990; copy in ExxonMobil Historical Collection.

40 Ibid.

41 Lawrence Rawl, "Alaska Update," *Lamp* 71, no. 3 (Fall 1989), 1.

42 Rawl to shareholders, March 15, 1990, Exxon Corporate and Public Affairs records, ExxonMobil Historical Collection.

43 Skinner and Reilly observe that the state's cleanup activities became largely independent of the federal response organization (*The* Exxon Valdez *Oil Spill*, 16). FEMA took no role in emergency operations after the spill, since it interpreted its function as responding to natural disasters.

44 Raymond interview, November 1, 2007, 14. For example, by April 12, four coast guard cutters and nine aircraft were on the scene, as well as 208 people. By the same date, the U.S. Navy had contributed 20 skimmers and 94 people. Later equipment from the navy included larger landing ships, such as the USS *Duluth*.

45 Quoted in Keeble, *Out of the Channel*, 152.

46 Mel Harrison interview, 27–28.

47 Otto V. Harrison, interview by Joseph Pratt, October 9, 2007, New Braunfels, Texas, 15–16, ExxonMobil Oral History.

48 Otto Harrison, quoted in Yemen, "*Exxon Valdez* Revisited: The Untold Story (A)," 9.

49 The loss of the *Atlantic Empress* in 1979 off Tobago spilled more than 2 million barrels; the breakup of the *Amoco Cadiz* spilled about 1.6 million barrels off Brittany in 1978, affecting only 240 miles of coastline. The *Exxon Valdez's* loss of 260,000 barrels makes it only the thirty-fifth-largest spill since 1975, yet it affected far more shoreline than much larger spills. A list of the largest spills can be found in the statistics section of the International Tanker Owners Pollution Federation Limited website, http://www.itopf.com.

50 Quoted in Yemen, "*Exxon Valdez* Revisited: The Untold Story (A)," 8.

51 The title of a book by one of Exxon's most determined critics captures the tension of the time: Riki Ott, *Sound Truth and Corporate Myth$: The Legacy of the "Exxon Valdez" Oil Spill* (Cordova, Alaska, 2005).

52 Mel Harrison interview, 27–28.

53 Exxon Corporation, *1999 Update: Prince William Sound, Alaska*, 1.

54 An extensive discussion of such techniques and technology is in Exxon Production Research Company, "Valdez Oil Spill Technology" (1990).

55 Terry Koonce, interview by Joseph Pratt, November 5, 2007, Houston, 41, ExxonMobil Oral History.

56 Remarks by Admiral Yost at hearing before Senate Commerce Committee; reported in John H. Cushman Jr., "Alaska Cleanup May Drag Into '90, U.S. Says," *New York Times*, May 11, 1990.

57 Scott Nauman, interview by William Hale, November 16, 2006, Dallas, 6, ExxonMobil Oral History.

58 Ibid., 8, 12.

59 Exxon Production Research Company, "Valdez Oil Spill Technology," 79.

60 Exxon produced numerous special publications on conditions over time in Prince William Sound and the Gulf of Alaska. The first, by Edward H. Owens of Woodward-Clyde Consultants, was presented at the 14th Annual Arctic and Marine Oil Spill Program Technical Seminar, Vancouver, British Columbia, June 1991. The company published "Prince William Sound, Alaska: One Year After" in 1991; it followed up with "Two Years After: Conditions in Prince William Sound and the Gulf of Alaska" (October 1991), and "Three Years After: Conditions in Prince William Sound and the Gulf of Alaska" (October 1992); all in ExxonMobil Historical Collection.

61 Shortly after the accident, in 1990, Art Davidson published a critical, detailed account of the spill and its immediate effects on Alaskans (*In the Wake of the "Exxon Valdez"*).

62 Hodgson, "Alaska's Big Oil Spill"; John G. Mitchell, "In the Wake of the Spill: Ten Years after *Exxon Valdez*," *National Geographic*, March 1999, 94–117.

63 Downs Matthews, "The Remarkable Recovery of Prince William Sound," *Lamp* 75, no. 3 (Fall 1993): 4–13; Shelley Moore, "Prince William Sound Revisited," *Lamp* 81, no. 1 (Spring 1999): 24–25.

64 Quoted in "Oil Plagues Sound 20 Years after *Exxon Valdez*," msnbc.com, updated March 24, 2009, http://www.msnbc.msn.com/id/29838444/ns /us_news-environment/t/oil-plagues-sound-years-after-exxon-valdez /#.UBRiGULaiAI, accessed June 3, 2012.

65 Hal Bernton, "*Exxon Valdez* Oil Spill Recovery Still Is Work in Progress, 20 Years Later," SeattleTimes.com, October 5, 2009, http://seattletimes.nwsource .com/html/localnews/2008912109_exxonherring24m.html.

66 Ed Ahnert, interview by William Hale, February 7, 2007, Dallas, 36, Exxon-Mobil Oral History.

67 Otto Harrison interview, 18.

68 Lou Noto, interview by William Hale, April 10, 2008, New York, 31, Exxon-Mobil Oral History.

69 U.S Environmental Protection Agency, Emergency Management, "Oil Pollution Act Overview," http://epa.gov/osweroe1/content/lawsregs/opaover.htm, accessed January 9, 2012.

70 Jane Baird, "A Cleanup Boom," *Houston Chronicle*, August 22, 1993.

71 The National Academy of Sciences assessed double-hull tanker designs and reported its conclusions in *Double-Hull Tanker Legislation: An Assessment of the Oil Pollution Act of 1990* (Washington, D.C., 1998). One of its conclusions stated: "Recent research . . . has revealed intact stability and oil outflow problems with certain double-hull designs" (145).

72 The court ruled that since, by 2002, a few other ships might be affected, the provision was valid.

73 The measures are listed in "Spill Forced Oil Shippers, Coast Guard To Change," *Anchorage Daily News*, April 16, 1995. The *Exxon Valdez* Oil Spill Trustee Council maintains a current summary of "Spill Prevention and Response" data for Prince William Sound.

74 "One Worker Killed and Several Hurt in Blast in Louisiana," *New York Times*, December 25, 1989; Randall Rothenberg, "Refinery Fire Could Raise Heating-Oil Costs," *New York Times*, December 26, 1989.

75 Robert Wilhelm, interview by William Hale, December 6, 2007, Dallas, 11, ExxonMobil Oral History.

76 Craig Wolff, "Federal Officials Order Exxon to Explain Leak in Arthur Kill," *New York Times*, January 12, 1990.

77 Matthew L. Wald, "Exxon Adopts Preventive Measures in $10 Million Project to Avoid Spills," *New York Times*, September 29, 1991.

78 "Corporate Error—And Arrogance," *New York Times*, February 14, 1990; Robert Hanley, "Florio Appoints a Prosecutor for Environmental Concerns," *New*

York Times, January 25, 1990; Craig Wolff, "E.P.A. Officials Condemn Exxon for Staten Island Spill," *New York Times*, January 20, 1990; Leo H. Carney, "Gaps Found in Rules on Preventing Oil Spills," *New York Times*, January 21, 1990; Barbara Rudolph, "Exxon's Attitude Problem," *Time*, January 23, 1990; Craig Wolff, "Exxon Admits a Year of Breakdowns in S.I. Oil Spill," *New York Times*, January 10, 1990.

79 Allan R. Grob, "Exxon Said to Offer Millions to Erase 1990 Harbor Spill," *New York Times*, March 15, 1991.

80 Dahan interview, 6.

81 Raymond interview, February 20, 2007, 5.

82 Hess interview, 12.

83 In September 1989, a meeting of environmental groups and institutional investors issued what was at that time called the Valdez Principles. These ten principles, or statements of environmental responsibility, later became known as the CERES (Coalition for Environmentally Responsible Economies) Principles. The initiative sought to take advantage of the intense concern over environmental issues generated by the *Valdez* oil spill to convince major companies to enlist in a crusade for greater responsibility and environmental accountability. The principles put forward embodied basic ideas of corporate citizenship and greater transparency.

84 "Exxon Names Executive on the Environment," *New York Times*, January 11, 1990; Wald, "Exxon Avoids Preventive Measures in $10 Million Project."

85 Hess interview, 15.

86 Raymond interview, February 20, 2007, 7.

87 For the history of self-regulation of oil pollution, see Gorman, *Redefining Efficiency*, and Pratt, *Black Waters*.

88 Hess interview, 17.

89 Ed Glab, interview by Joseph Pratt, April 4, 2007, Miami, 27, ExxonMobil Oral History.

90 Hess interview, 14.

91 Statistics are from Exxon Corporation, "Exxon Environment, Health and Safety Progress Report" (1996).

92 Moore, "Prince William Sound Revisited," 24–25.

93 Ott, *Not One Drop*, ix–x, 46–47.

94 Don Hunter, "Hazelwood Cleared on Three Counts," *Anchorage Daily News*, March 23, 1990. Even before the verdict, Exxon had fired Hazelwood for leaving the bridge during a critical maneuver, a violation of company policy.

95 Raymond interview, November 1, 2007.

96 Ibid., 22. The *Anchorage Daily News* (March 13, 1991) would later report that Charlie Cole recalled that Hickel had originally proposed $1.2 billion. In any event, the final agreement was for $1 billion over a number of years.

97   Raymond interview, November 1, 2007, 22–23.

98   Reported in the *Anchorage Daily News*, March 13, 1991.

99   Sharon Begley, "One Deal That Was Too Good for Exxon," *Newsweek*, May 6, 1991, 54.

100 Bill Mintz, "Settlement in Valdez Spill OK'd," *Houston Chronicle*, October 9, 1991.

101 For details, see Strohmeyer, *Extreme Conditions*, 237–243.

102 One of the private parties that agreed to drop any suits was Exxon, which could have sued by arguing contributory negligence on the part of the state and federal governments.

103 Mintz, "Settlement in Valdez Spill OK'd"; *Anchorage Daily News*, October 10, 1991.

104 Majority leader Max Gruenberg of Anchorage, quoted in the *Anchorage Daily News*, October 10, 1991; "Judge Accepts Exxon Pact, Ending Suits on Valdez Spill," *New York Times*, October 9, 1991.

105 "Pipeline Owner to Pay $98 Million in Valdez Spill," *New York Times*, July 15, 1993.

106 "Exxon Wins Insurance Case," *Anchorage Daily News*, June 11, 1996.

107 "With Insurers' Payment, Exxon Says Valdez Case Is Ended," *New York Times*, November 1, 1996.

108 "Exxon Spill Payment Sliced," *Anchorage Daily News*, September 8, 1995.

109 The company's net income had ranged from a low of $3.52 billion in 1990 to $5.28 billion in 1993.

110 The jury deliberations were reported in the *Anchorage Daily News*, September 18, 1994; see also Keeble, *Out of the Channel*, 50, 325.

111 The companies were ADF, Icicle Seafoods, North Coast Seafood Processors, North Pacific Processors, Ocean Beauty Seafoods, Trident Seafoods, and Wards Cove Packing Company.

112 *Anchorage Daily News*, June 13, 1996.

113 Raymond interview, November 1, 2007, 4.

114 In his first term on the court, in 2007, he generally aligned himself with the more conservative justices.

115 The decision also allowed the Seattle Seven to assess the wisdom of their 1991 settlement. After the phase 3 jury verdict, the agreement they had made with Exxon looked to be a very bad decision on their part, but in the end, the Seattle Seven's arrangement was not adverse: their share of the final award would have been $76 million, slightly higher than the $63.75 million they received in 1991, but would have been paid much later.

116 For a detailed analysis of the events and issues raised by the Macondo oil spill, see National Commission on the BP Deepwater Horizon Oil Spill and Offshore Drilling, *Deep Water: The Gulf Oil Disaster and the Future of Offshore*

Drilling; Report to the President (Washington, D.C., 2011), available at http://www.oilspillcommission.gov/final-report.

117 Reilly repeated this comment in an interview (Jeffrey Ball, "Lessons from the Gulf," *Wall Street Journal*, March 7, 2011). The company had good reason to celebrate this public acknowledgment of the success of OIMS, but a much-publicized spill, estimated at 1,000 barrels of oil, several months later from one of its pipelines near Missoula, Montana, brought intense criticism, reminding the company of the need for vigilance.

118 Nauman interview, 26.

CHAPTER SEVEN: NEW FRONTIERS

1 The literature on the promise and pitfalls of democratic capitalism and prosperity in the global economy of the 1990s includes numerous points of view. See, for example, Daniel Yergin and Joseph Stanislaw, *The Commanding Heights: The Battle Between Government and the Marketplace That Is Remaking the Modern World* (New York, 1998); Joseph E. Stiglitz, *Globalization and Its Discontents* (New York, 2002); Stiglitz, *Making Globalization Work* (New York, 2006); Jagdish Bhagwati, *In Defense of Globalization* (Oxford, 2007); Thomas Friedman, *The World Is Flat: A Brief History of the Twenty-First Century* (New York, 2005); and Dani Rodrik, *The Globalization Paradox: Democracy and the Future of the World Economy* (New York, 2011).

2 Exxon Corporation, *1997 Financial and Operating Review*, 3, ExxonMobil Historical Collection.

3 David E. Hoffman, *The Oligarchs: Wealth and Power in the New Russia* (New York, 2002); Thane Gustafson, *Capitalism Russian-Style* (Cambridge, 1999); Thane Gustafson, *Wheel of Fortune: The Battle for Oil and Power in Russia* (Cambridge, Mass., 2012).

4 A useful timeline of Exxon's entry into the former Soviet Union can be found in "Exxon Ventures (CIS), Inc., C.I.S. Milestones," ExxonMobil Historical Collection. For a more personal view, see Koonce interview, 2–20.

5 For a good overview of the oil sector in Russia in the 1990s, see Oksan Bayulgen, *Foreign Investment and Political Regimes: The Oil Sector in Azerbaijan, Russia, and Norway* (Cambridge, 2010). For a history of one major oil company's adventures in the former Soviet Union, see Pratt, *Prelude to Merger*, 170–190.

6 Koonce interview, 4.

7 Ibid., 8.

8 Quoted in Gibb and Knowlton, *Resurgent Years*, 331–332.

9 Tom Barrow, interview by Joseph Pratt, April 4, 2007, Houston, 23–32, ExxonMobil Oral History.

10 Downs Matthews, "Russia: A Great Petroleum Frontier," *Lamp* 75, no. 1 (Spring 1993): 20–21.

11 Ibid., 19–23. For more on the company's early office in the region, see "Exxon Establishes Operating Affiliate in the Former Soviet Union," *Lamp* 75, no. 3 (Fall 1993): 14.

12 Koonce interview, 38–39.

13 Ibid., 4.

14 Exxon Corporation, *Sakhalin-1: A New Frontier* (Tulsa).

15 The discussion of the Sakhalin negotiations is based on the Koonce interview, 7–10; Harry Longwell, interview by William Hale, October 3, 2007, Dallas, 15–25, ExxonMobil Oral History; Rex W. Tillerson, interview by William Hale, July 3, 2007, Dallas, 31–39, ExxonMobil Oral History.

16 Koonce interview, 3.

17 Longwell interview, October 3, 2007, 17–18. Governor Farkhutdinov died in a helicopter crash in 2003.

18 Exxon Corporation, *1993 Annual Report*, 3.

19 John D. Grace, *Russian Oil Supply: Performance and Prospects* (Oxford, 2005), 80. In his detailed study of Russian oil, Grace indicates that the year 1994 is "generally considered the low point of the Russian oil industry." The production-sharing agreements negotiated by Exxon and Royal Dutch Shell reflected the weakness of the Russian government and the sharp decline in the nation's petroleum industry after the fall of communism.

20 Koonce interview, 14–15.

21 For the quotation, see Koonce interview, 15; for related information, see Longwell interview, October 3, 2007, 18–19; Lee Raymond, interview by William Hale, October 22, 2007, Dallas, 23, ExxonMobil Oral History.

22 Koonce interview, 15. For a good discussion of the evolution of PSAs in Russia in the 1990s, see Bayulgen, *Foreign Investment and Political Regimes*, 125–140; Shell Oil had executed its PSA on the Sakhalin-II project, which had a large LNG component, in 1994.

23 For a detailed overview of the process of privatizing oil in Russia, see Li-Chen Sim, *The Rise and Fall of Privatization in the Russian Oil Industry* (New York, 2008); see also Grace, *Russian Oil Supply*, 89, 104–161.

24 A good description of this process is found in Grace, *Russian Oil Supply*, 104–177; see also Sim, *Privatization in the Russian Oil Industry*. The general process of privatization in Russian has been the topic of numerous popular books. See, for example, Hoffman, *The Oligarchs*.

25 Yergin and Stanislaw, *Commanding Heights*, 270–308.

26 "Project Capitalism: It's the IMF's Biggest Challenge; Helping Russia Restructure Its Economy," *BusinessWeek*, September 28, 1992, 104–108; "Economic Transformation in the Fifteen Republics of the Former U.S.S.R: A Challenge or Opportunity for the World?" address by Michel Camdessus, managing director

of the International Monetary Fund, Georgetown University School of Foreign Affairs, April 15, 1992.

27 For a highly critical evaluation of the performance of the international lending institutions' performance in Russia and other nations in the 1990s, see Stiglitz, *Globalization and Its Discontents.* For a good overview of the Russian economy in those years, see Richard H. K. Vietor, *How Countries Compete: Strategy, Structure, and Government in the Global Economy* (Boston, 2007), 169–192.

28 Koonce interview, 26-27.

29 Tillerson interview, 31, 39.

30 Mike Long, "Can a Civil Engineer Succeed at ExxonMobil?" *Lamp* 86, no. 1 (2004), 6.

31 Exxon Corporation, *1998 Annual Report*, 11.

32 Ibid.; ExxonMobil, *1999 Annual Report*, 13–14; ExxonMobil, *2000 Annual Report*, 13; ExxonMobil, *2001 Annual Report*, 13–14.

33 Material on the early planning for Sakhalin-I is found in "Exxon Establishes Operating Affiliate in the Former Soviet Union," *Lamp* 75, no. 3 (Fall 1993): 14; Henry Beathard, "From Russia with Oil," *Lamp* 79, no. 4 (Winter 1997–1998): 4–11.

34 Longwell interview, October 3, 2007, 14–15.

35 Ibid., 21–24; Albers interview, 19–26.

36 ExxonMobil, *2004 Annual Report*, 17.

37 Denise Allen Zecker, "Massive Development to Turn Spotlight on Russian Far East," *Lamp* 83, no. 4 (Winter 2001–2002): 13–18; ExxonMobil, *Corporate Citizenship Report, 2004*, 41.

38 Quote from Vladimir Astafyev, in Amanda Coyne, "Unlocking Russia's Vast Energy Resources," *Lamp* 87, no. 3 (2005): 12.

39 Fred Weir, "Kremlin Reasserts Control of Oil, Gas," *Christian Science Monitor*, December 28, 2005. For a more detailed discussion, see Rawi Abdelal, "Journey to Sakhalin: Royal Dutch Shell in Russia (A)," Case #9-704-040 (Boston: Harvard Business School Publishing, 2005). Additions B and C to this case were made by Rawi Abdelal and Irina Tarsis (Case #9-706-013, 2006), and Rawi Abdelal and Marina N. Vandamme, (Case #9-707-038, 2007). See also Alex Turkeltaub and Stephen Bailey, "Sakhalin-2 Deal Will Alter Business Climate, Markets," *Oil and Gas Journal*, January 15, 2007, 34–35.

40 For the Exxon-Yukos negotiations and Raymond's meeting with Putin, see Gustafson, *Wheel of Fortune*, 272–318. Also, Tom Brower, *Oil: Money, Politics, and Power in the 21st Century* (New York, 2009), 253–264; and Martin Sixsmith, *Putin's Oil: The Yukos Affair and the Struggle for Russia* (New York, 2010), 123–132. For the Yergin quotation, see *The Quest*, 39.

41 Seth Mydans and Erin E. Arvedlund, "Police in Russia Seize Oil Tycoon," *New York Times*, October 26, 2003; Michael Davis and David Ivanovich, "Russian Oil Tycoon's Arrest Sends Stocks into Free Fall," *Houston Chronicle*, October

25, 2003; Steven Lee Myers, "Verdict in Russian Court: Guilty Until Proven Guilty," *New York Times*, June 20, 2004; "Business in Russia: After Yukos," *Economist*, May 12, 2007, 67–68; "Yukos Revisited," *Economist*, September 23, 2006, 13; Guy Chazan, "Russia's Courts Go on Trial," *Wall Street Journal*, May 23, 2005. For a profile of a younger Khodorkovsky, see Paul Klebnikov, "Russia's Robber Barons," *Forbes*, November 21, 1994, 74–84.

42   Greg Walters, "Russia Cancels Shell Permit, May Seek Better Deal," *Wall Street Journal*, September 19, 2006; "Shell Addresses Sakhalin Complaints," *Wall Street Journal*, October 17, 2006; Bower, *Oil*, 387. Useful background in understanding the changing role of the Russian oil and gas companies include three case studies by Rawi Abdelal, Sogomon Tarontsi, and Alexander Jorov: "Gazprom (A): Energy and Strategy in Russian History," Case #9-709-008 (Boston: Harvard Business School Publishing, 2009); "Gazprom (B): Energy and Strategy in a New Era," Case #9-709-009, 2009; and "Gazprom (C): The Ukranian Crisis and Its Aftermath, Case #9-709-010, 2009. For Rosneft, see Nina Poussenkova, "Lord of the Rigs: Rosneft as a Mirror of Russia's Evolution," paper presented at the Conference on the Changing Role of National Oil Companies in International Energy Markets, 2007, James A. Baker III Institute for Public Policy, Rice University. From the same conference, see Isabel Gorst, "Lukoil: Russia's Largest Oil Company"; see also Malcolm S. Salter, "OAO Yukos Oil Company," Case #9-902-021 (Boston, 2002).

43   Akkady Ostrovsky, "Energy of the State: How Gazprom Acts as Lever in Putin's Power Play," *Financial Times*, March 14, 2006; Daniel Yergin and Thane Gustafson, *Russia 2010 and What It Means for the World* (New York, 1993); Andrew Hurst, "Production Begins at Russia's Enormous Sakhalin-1 Field," *Houston Chronicle*, October 4, 2005.

44   Koonce interview, 24.

45   ExxonMobil's experience at Sakhalin-I laid the foundation for future projects in Russia. See Andrew W. Kramer, "Exxon Reaches Arctic Oil Deal with Russians," *New York Times*, August 30, 2011. This potential giant joint venture with Rosneft was part of a broader initiative by the Russian government to develop oil fields in promising areas of the Russian Arctic.

46   Pratt, *Prelude to Merger*, 180–190; see also Bayulgen, *Foreign Investments and Political Regimes*, 87–121.

47   ExxonMobil Corporation, *2002 Annual Report*, 11–12; Thomas L. Torget, "The Soul of Kazakhstan," *Lamp* 84, no. 2 (Summer 2002): 15–22.

48   Ron Stodghill, "Oil, Cash and Corruption: How Influence Flowed Through Political Pipelines," *New York Times*, November 5, 2006; Guy Chazan, "Kazakh Oil-Field Tensions Rise," *Wall Street Journal*, August 8, 2007; "Vapour Trials," *Economist*, July 3, 2010, 59–60.

49   Koonce interview, 24, 35.

50 Juan Carlos Boué, *Venezuela: The Political Economy of Oil* (Oxford, 1993); Terry Lynn Karl, *The Paradox of Plenty*; Jorge Salazar-Carrillo and Bernadette West, *Oil and Development in Venezuela during the Twentieth Century* (Westport, Conn., 2004).

51 James Tanner, "Change of Heart: Venezuela Now Woos Oil Firms It Booted in '70s Nationalization," *Wall Street Journal*, October 2, 1991.

52 Agis Salpukas, "A Go-Slow Strategy for Exxon," *New York Times*, September 19, 1994; David R. Mares and Nelson Altamirano, "Venezuela's PDVSA and World Energy Markets: Corporate Strategies and Political Factors Determining Its Behavior and Influence," 7–9, 67–70, paper presented at the conference Changing Role of National Oil Companies in International Energy Markets, March 2007, James A. Baker III Institute for Public Policy, Rice University. For a useful overview of events in Venezuela in this era, see Yergin, *The Quest*, 107–224.

53 Thi Chang, "Upgrading and Refining Essential Parts of Orinoco Development," *Oil and Gas Journal*, October 19, 1998, 67; Richard Cunningham, "Faja," *Lamp* 82, no. 2 (Summer 2000): 15–19.

54 For detailed accounts of Hugo Chávez's early days in office, see Mares and Altamirano, "Venezuela's PDVSA and World Energy Markets"; see also Tina Rosenberg, "The New Nationalization: Where Hugo Chávez's 'Oil Socialism' Could Be Taking the Developing World," *New York Times Magazine*, November 4, 2007, 42–49, 78–80.

55 Rosenberg, "The New Nationalization," 45.

56 Gustavo Coronel, "PDVSA's Crisis a Tragedy for Venezuela," *Oil and Gas Journal*, March 3, 2003, 20; "Chávez Fires a Third of Oil Monopoly's Staff," *Houston Chronicle*, February 13, 2003, 31; see also Yergin, *The Quest*, 129–132.

57 Yergin, *The Quest*, 257–259; Brian Ellsworth, "Chávez Views 90s Oil Deals as Criminal," *Houston Chronicle*, April 19, 2006; Bower, *Oil*, 337–341.

58 "Exxon Mobil Pays Price for Balking," *Houston Chronicle*, February 8, 2006.

59 Yergin, *The Quest*, 258.

60 "Venezuela Takes on ExxonMobil," Associated Press, March 30, 2006.

61 Russell Gold, "Exxon, Conoco Exit Venezuela under Pressure," *Wall Street Journal*, June 27, 2007; Kristen Hats and John Otis, "Two Oil Giants Defy Chávez," *Houston Chronicle*, June 27, 2007; Peter Howard Wertheim, "Venezuela to Nationalize Orinoco Oil Operations," *Oil and Gas Journal*, January 15, 2007, 41. After ExxonMobil left Venezuela, the struggle with the Chávez government moved into the slow-moving world of international tribunals; see Russell Gold, Raul Gallegos, and Chad Bray, "Exxon Steps Up Fight against Venezuelan Powers," *Wall Street Journal*, February 8, 2008; Raul Gallegos and Chad Bray, "ExxonMobil Wins Ruling in Venezuelan Dispute," *Houston Chronicle*, February 8, 2008; and Russell Gold and Erica Herrero-Martinez, "Exxon Suffers

Blow in PDVSA Battle," *Wall Street Journal*, March 18, 2008. In December 2011, the arbitration to determine the amount of money to be received by Exxon for its Venezuelan properties remained unresolved. For recent developments, see "ExxonMobil Wins $908 Million in Dispute with Venezuela," *Houston Chronicle*, January 2, 2012; Fabiola Sanchez, "Venezuela Says It Only Owes Exxon $255 Million," *Houston Chronicle*, January 2, 2012.

62 Overviews of events in Chad can be found in Carrie Ferman and Benjamin C. Esty, "The Chad-Cameroon Petroleum Development and Pipeline Project (A) and (B)," Cases #9-202-010 and #9-202-012 (Boston, 2001); Jerry Useem, "Exxon's African Adventure," *Fortune*, April 15, 2002, 102–111; African Development Bank and the African Union, *Oil and Gas in Africa* (Oxford, 2009).

63 Hedberg interview, 5. For an earlier incident in Nigeria in which Exxon severed "immediately and permanently" its ties to "consultants" who had made "unacceptable unethical demands," see Exxon Management Committee, "Nigerian Bid Proposal, August 17, 1979," memorandum to file, August 21, 1979, Exxon Corporate Archives.

64 Ferman and Esty, "Chad-Cameroon Petroleum Development (A)," 5.

65 Richard Cunningham, "Roads of Hope," *Lamp* 84, no. 3 (Fall 2002): 1–3.

66 André Madec, interview by William Hale, May 28, 2009, Dallas, 1–6, ExxonMobil Oral History.

67 Ibid., 12.

68 Ferman and Esty, "Chad-Cameroon Petroleum Development (A)," 5.

69 For historical background on the World Bank, see Jochen Kraske, et al., *Bankers with a Mission: The Presidents of the World Bank, 1946–1991* (Oxford, 1996); Devesh Kapur, John Prior Lewis, and Richard Charles Webb, *The World Bank: Its First Half Century* (Washington, D.C., 1997); Michelle Miller Adams, *The World Bank: New Agenda in a Changing World* (London, 1999); and Katherine Marshall, *The World Bank: From Reconstruction to Development to Equity* (London, 2008). For a much-read critique of the World Bank and the IMF, see Stiglitz, *Globalization and Its Discontents*.

70 Quoted in Ferman and Esty, "Chad-Cameroon Petroleum Development (A)," 5.

71 *Chad-Cameroon Petroleum Development and Pipeline Project: Overview*, Report No. 36569-TD, Document of the World Bank and International Finance Corporation, December 2006, ii. The company's and the World Bank's rationales are both well explained in this document.

72 When the bank agreed to help provide support for the project, both ELF and Shell were still involved, yet even with the bank's role, the project was clearly seen as involving unusual political and economic risk.

73 Stephen Arbogast, "Project Financing and Political Risk Mitigation: The Singular Case of the Chad-Cameroon Pipeline," *Texas Journal of Oil, Gas, and*

Energy Law 4, no. 2 (2008–2009): 269–298. The full details are contained in World Bank, *Chad-Cameroon Petroleum Development and Pipeline Project: Overview*, 6–8.

74 Ferman and Esty, "Chad-Cameroon Petroleum Development (A)," 14; Arbogast, "Project Financing," 8–9.

75 The staff of the World Bank had earlier produced a paper supporting World Bank guarantees for oil and gas projects: Scott Sinclair, "World Bank Guarantees for Oil and Gas Projects," *Public Policy for the Private Sector*, note no. 157 (November 1998). For a good general overview of the agreement, see "The Resource Curse Anew: Why a Grand World Bank Project Has Run into the Sand," *Financial Times*, January 23, 2006.

76 For a discussion of this "unprecedented experiment," see Ricardo Soares de Oliveira, *Oil and Politics in the Gulf of Guinea* (New York, 2007), 269–327.

77 Kenneth Walsh, "World Bank Funding of Chad/Cameroon Oil Project," Environmental Defense Fund, March 17, 1997; Genoveva Hernandez Uriz, "To Lend or Not to Lend: Oil, Human Rights, and the World Bank's Internal Contradictions," *Harvard Human Rights Journal* 14 (Spring 2001); Korinna Horta, "The Chad/Cameroon Oil & Pipeline Project: Reaching a Critical Milestone," *Environmental Defense*, January 2003. A good summary of opposition to the project is in Ferman and Esty, "Chad-Cameroon Petroleum Development (A)," 9–10.

78 Antoine Lawson, "Chad-Cameroon Pipeline: A Chance for Africa," *Le Monde*, May 30, 2000.

79 Quoted in Ferman and Esty, "Chad-Cameroon Petroleum Development (A)," 11.

80 Madec interview, 2-6. For more discussion, see Soares de Oliveira, *Oil in the Gulf of Guinea*, 279.

81 Dean Guttormson, interview by Joseph Pratt, July 20, 2007, Houston, 42–51, ExxonMobil Oral History.

82 Ibid., 48.

83 Ibid., 49.

84 See, for example, the discussion in Center for Energy Economics, "Chad-Cameroon Oil Pipeline," a case study from the Bureau of Economic Geology, University of Texas at Austin, 9–10.

85 Useem, "Exxon's African Adventure"; "Key Chad-Cameroon Project Under Way," *Lamp* 82, no. 3 (Fall 2000): 30; Cunningham, "Roads of Hope"; and Don Dedera, "The New Bridge at Baro," *Lamp* 73, no. 1 (Spring 1991): 16–23.

86 Madec interview, 19.

87 "African Pipeline Born of Promise to Spread Wealth," *Houston Chronicle*, October 5, 2003.

88 Cunningham, "Roads of Hope," 9–10.

89 *Profile: Chad/Cameroon–Doba Basin*, ExxonMobil, May 2008, ExxonMobil Historical Collection.

90 World Bank, *Chad-Cameroon Petroleum Development and Pipeline Project: Overview*, 28.

91 "African Pipeline Born of Promise," *Houston Chronicle*.

92 The events leading up to the rewriting of the original agreement made headlines: David White, "The 'Resource Curse' Anew: Why a Grand World Bank Oil Project Has Fast Run into the Sand," *Financial Times*, January 23, 2006; Chip Cummins, "Exxon Faces a Dilemma on Chad Project," *Wall Street Journal*, February 28, 2006; "The Chadian Experiment," *Oil and Gas Journal*, February 13, 2006, 19.

93 "World Bank Announces Withdrawal from Chad-Cameroon Pipeline after Early Repayment," Bank Information Center, September 12, 2008.

94 For responses to the World Bank's withdrawal, see Artur Colom Jaen, "Lessons from the Failure of Chad's Oil Revenue Management Model," Real Instituto Elcano, December 3, 2010; "Chad's Resource Curse," *Oil and Gas Journal*, December 21, 2009, 16; Audrey C. Cash, "Corporate Social Responsibility and Petroleum Development in Sub-Saharan Africa: The Case of Chad," *Resources Policy* 37 (2012): 144–151.

95 Thomas L. Torget, "Africa Emerging as a Key Global Producer," *Lamp*, 2009, no. 1, 25–27.

96 Patrick Chabal, ed., *Angola: The Weight of History* (New York, 2008).

97 For background on modern Angola and its oil history, see Aldo Musacchio, Eric Werker, and Jonathan Schlefer, "Angola and the Resource Curse," Case #N9-711-016, (Boston: Harvard Business School Publishing, 2010); Margaret Ross, "Africa's Elephants of the Deep," *Lamp* 80, no. 4 (Winter 1998–1999): 4–11.

98 Tony Hodges, *Angola: Anatomy of an Oil State* (Bloomington, 2004).

99 U.S. Energy Information Administration, "Angola," updated August 2011, http://www.eia.gov/countries/cab.cfm?fips=AO, accessed January 15, 2012; Larry Karasevich, *Angola Entry*, DVD, ExxonMobil Exploration Company.

100 Thompson interview, August 16, 2007, 42–43.

101 Kevin Gault, "Angola Block 15 at 15: A National Success," *Lamp*, 2009 no. 4: 13–15; S. Anne Reeckmann, D. K. S. Wilkin, and J. W. Flannery, "Kizomba: A Deep-Water Giant Field, Block 15 Angola," in *Giant Oil and Gas Fields of the Decade 1990–1999*, ed. Michel T. Halbouty (Tulsa, 2003), 227–236.

102 Much of the information in the next several paragraphs comes from the video *Angola Entry* by Karasevich.

103 Thomas L. Torget, "Production in the Fast Lane," *Lamp* 84, no. 4 (Winter 2002–2003): 1–4.

104 Morris Foster, quoted in Torget, "Production in the Fast Lane," 3.

105 Lisa Walters, quoted in Richard Cunningham, "Production Grows in West

Africa's Largest Deepwater Development," *Lamp* 86, no. 3 (Fall 2004): 8; ExxonMobil, "Profile Angola," n.d.

106 Guttormson interview, 48; U.S. Energy Information Administration, "Angola," 6–7.

107 Arne Wiig and Madalena Ramilho, "Corporate Social Responsibility in the Angolan Oil Industry," Bergen, Norway, Chr. Michelsen Institute, CMI Working Papers, WP 2005:8, 10–136; Soares de Oliveira, *Oil in the Gulf of Guinea*, 87–92.

108 Wiig and Ramalho, "Angolan Oil Industry," 14–15.

109 Hedberg interview, 22.

110 "West Africa's Largest Deepwater Development," 9–10.

111 Sonangol, Produzir Para Traansformar, Gabinete Juridico, Decree 20/82, "Mandatory Hiring and Training of Angolans by Foreign Companies Operating in the Angolan Oil Industry," Council of Ministers, Decree no. 20/82 of April 17, 1982 as Amended by: Decree 20/94 of 27 May 1994; Sonangol, "Sonangol's Experience on Promoting Local Content," AL Local Content Summit for Oil and Gas, UK 2006, copy in ExxonMobil Historical Collection; Wiig and Ramallho, "Angolan Oil Industry," 14–15; Gault, "Angola Block 15 at 15," 18; Bill Corporon, "Angolan Deepwater Success Continues," *Lamp*, 2007, no. 4: 3–4; Corporon, "Angolan Project Brings Gains in Oil Production, Use of Local Resources and Worker Safety," *Lamp*, 2008, no. 3: 1–16.

112 Harry Longwell, interview by William Hale, October 24, 2007, Irving, Texas, 27–28, ExxonMobil Oral History.

113 ExxonMobil reported its activities in corporate citizenship reports. See, for example, ExxonMobil, "Good Works in Africa," *Corporate Citizenship in a Changing World*, May 2002, 18–21. At times, the company faced criticism for not doing enough; see Jeffrey Ball, "Digging Deep: As Exxon Pursues African Oil, Charity Becomes Political Issue," *Wall Street Journal*, January 10, 2006. See also Salley Shannon, "Beyond the Fence," *Lamp* 82, no. 1 (Spring 2000): 15–19.

114 Ahnert interview, 26.

115 Many of the company's efforts are described in Salley Shannon, "Malaria: Stopping a Killer," *Lamp* 83, no. 8 (Winter 2001–2002): 9–12; Shelly Moore, "Joining the Fight against Malaria," *Lamp*, no. 1 (2007): 11–13.

116 Bonnie Campbell, "Corporate Social Responsibility and Development in Africa: Redefining the Roles and Responsibilities of Public and Private Actors in the Mining Sector," *Resources Policy* 37, no. 2 (2012): 138–143; ExxonMobil, *Chad/Cameroon Oil Development Project, Fact Sheet—August 2007*. This ongoing fact sheet has data from throughout the development of the pipeline. It is posted on the Esso Chad website (http://www.essochad.com), where Project Progress Reports are available in the Library section.

117 U.S. Energy Information Administration, "Angola," 4.

118 Thompson interview, August 16, 2007, 54.

CHAPTER EIGHT: UPGRADING DOWNSTREAM

1 For 1950, see Larson, Knowlton, and Popple, *New Horizons*, 769; for 1973, see Exxon Corporation, *1973 Annual Report*, 1.

2 Wall, *Growth in a Changing Environment*, 266.

3 Ibid., 275. Exxon Corporation, *1981 Financial and Statistical Supplement to the Annual Report*, 32.

4 Exxon Corporation, *1992 Financial and Operating Review*, 48.

5 Exxon Corporation, *1982 Annual Report*, 10; *1992 Annual Report*, 15.

6 The initial purchase information is from Exxon Corporation, *1989 Annual Report*, 9. The update is from U.S. Energy Information Administration, "Canada Natural Gas," July 2009. The administration's report estimated that Imperial's Taglu field held three trillion cubic feet, and the company held a share of Niglintgak Field, which had reserves of one trillion cubic feet.

7 "Imperial Cleared for Texaco Deal," *New York Times*, February 7, 1990.

8 Imperial lost $42 million in its petroleum-products segment in 1990, and earned only $24 million in chemicals. Its petroleum production and other earnings were, however, robust at $431 million, in part because of the sale of other assets. As a result, the company was profitable overall in 1990. This result was helped by the rise in prices during the Gulf War in 1990: oil prices in 1990 had been about $15 a barrel, then spiked to almost $40 a barrel after the start of the war. They dropped sharply back to the high $20s a barrel until 1996, when they declined precipitously.

9 Wilhelm interview, December 6, 2007, 14–15.

10 Ibid., 15.

11 Lee Raymond, interview by William Hale, September 11, 2007, Dallas, 8, ExxonMobil Oral History.

12 McBrayer interview, 28.

13 Raymond interview, June 25, 2007, 19.

14 Wall, *Growth in a Changing Environment*, 416–430.

15 Ibid., 398.

16 Raymond subsequently became president of Exxon in 1986.

17 Robert Wilhelm, interview by William Hale, April 26, 2007, Dallas, 27, Exxon-Mobil Oral History.

18 Ibid.

19 Ibid., 22–23.

20 These statistics are taken from Exxon's annual *Financial and Operating Reviews*. For the report on the twenty-year pattern of reductions, see Exxon Corporation, *1996 Financial and Operating Review*, 51.

21 Exxon's tanker capacity is summarized in figure 8.3. For a general discussion of trends in the tanker industry as a whole, see Richard Rawlin and Michael E.

Porter, "The Tanker Shipping Industry in 1983," Harvard Business School Case 9-384-034, revised February 6, 1989 (Boston).

22 Exxon Corporation, *1988 Annual Report*, 11.

23 Ibid.

24 Exxon Corporation, *1990 Annual Report*, 19.

25 These statistics and summaries are taken from Exxon's annual reports for the years 1980–1990. See in particular Exxon Corporation, *1984 Annual Report*, 3, 14; *1990 Annual Report*, 14–15.

26 Lee Raymond, interview by William Hale, December 3, 2009, Irving, Exxon-Mobil Oral History.

27 Ibid.

28 Bennett interview, 6.

29 Stephen Arbogast, interview by Joseph Pratt, February 29, 2007, Houston, 12, ExxonMobil Oral History.

30 Exxon Corporation, *1998 Annual Report*, 13.

31 Exxon Corporation, *Financial and Statistical Supplement to the Annual Report* for the years 1981, 1986, and 1987; see also Exxon Corporation, *1995 Financial and Operating Review*. The format and content of this supplement changed, as did its title, in the early 1990s.

32 Raymond interview, June 14, 2007, 34.

33 Garvin interview, 28.

34 Richard Rutter, "How Exxon Saves Energy," *Lamp* 57, no. 1 (Spring 1975): 14–19.

35 Berg, "Conservation in Industry"; "Energy Conservation: Spawning a Billion-Dollar Industry," *BusinessWeek*, April 1981, 58–70; National Petroleum Council, *Potential for Energy Conservation in the United States, 1974–1978: Industrial* (Washington: National Petroleum Council, 1974).

36 "Using Energy Efficiently," *Exxon USA*, 1974, no. 1, 10–15; Charles A. Berg, "Conservation in Industry," *Science* 184 (April 19, 1974): 264–270.

37 Rutter, "How Exxon Saves Energy," 14–19.

38 C. C. Garvin, "We're Running Out of Time," *Lamp* 51, no. 3 (Fall 1977): i.

39 Rutter, "How Exxon Saves Energy," 17.

40 Richard T. Hirsh, *Technology and Transformation in the American Utility Industry* (Cambridge, 2003); Hirsh, *Power Loss: The Origins of Deregulation and Restructuring in the American Utility System* (Cambridge, Mass.: MIT Press, 1999); and Hirsh, "PURPA: The Spur to Competition and Utility Restructuring," *Electricity Journal* 12, no. 7 (1999): 60–72.

41 Denise Allen Zwicker, "Cogeneration Gains Momentum," *Lamp* 71, no. 3 (Fall 1989): 14–19; for a discussion of Exxon's global use of cogeneration, see "Spinning Off Power to Spare," *Lamp* 78, no. 4 (Winter 1996–1997): 3–8.

42 A description of various cogeneration options, along with considerations

related to their economic attraction, is contained in a briefing given by Paul Dillon, planning executive, ExxonMobil Refining and Supply, before the COGEN Europe Annual Conference 2005, March 10–11, 2005, ExxonMobil Historical Collection.

43 Zwicker, "Cogeneration Gains Momentum," 14–15.

44 For example, the environmental benefit was emphasized in Bill Corporan, "High-Efficiency Cogeneration Plants Create Cost and Environmental Benefits," *Lamp*, 2008 no. 2, (2008), 13–14, as well as in the presentation by Paul Dillon cited above in note 42. It was featured in all of Exxon's and ExxonMobil's environmental and corporate citizenship reports from 1990 onward, in opinion editorials placed in the *New York Times*, and in television advertisements. Typical was the coverage of the subject in "Tapping a Powerful Resource," opinion editorial, *New York Times*, July 24, 2008.

45 "Saving 80 Million Barrels of Oil . . . Every Year," *Lamp* 80, no. 3 (Fall 1998): 13.

46 Thomas A. Torget, "Saving Energy Makes a Lot of Sense," *Lamp* 83, no. 4 (Winter 2001–2002): 2–3.

47 Ray Nesbitt, interview by Joseph Pratt, December 13, 2007, Houston, 25, ExxonMobil Oral History.

48 Dahan interview, 6, 9.

49 Quoted in Exxon Company, International, "ECI Refining Fights Back Against Low Industry Margins," *Voyager*, May 5, 1995.

50 Rene Dahan, "World Class 2000: What and Why?" *Voyager*, September 22, 1995, 2.

51 The World Class 2000 materials were published in *Voyager* in September 22, 1995; October 6, 1995; October 30, 1995; November 3, 1995; November 17, 1995; and December 16, 1995.

52 Rene Dahan to William Hale, email, July 15, 2007, Rene Dahan file, ExxonMobil Oral History.

53 Dahan interview, 11–14.

54 Exxon Corporation, *1998 Financial and Operating Review*, 49.

55 Exxon Corporation, *1976 Annual Report*, 16; *1977 Annual Report*, 17–18;

56 Dixon Fiske, "The Biggest Thing at Baytown," *Lamp* 58, no. 3 (Fall 1976): 24–27.

57 This investment is discussed at length in Exxon USA, "Baytown Resid Upgrade Project," report to Exxon Management Committee, September 16, 1983, 1–3.

58 Exxon Corporation, *1976 Annual Report*, 20.

59 Exxon Chemical Company, *Leadership in Petrochemicals*, 40-42; Exxon Chemical Company, *1981 Corporate Plan*, report to Exxon Management Committee, October 6, 1981, 4.

60 Ed Galante, interview by William Hale, January 7, 2007, Irving, 28, ExxonMobil Oral History.

61 Hess interview, 10.

62 Raymond interview, June 25, 2007, 14.

63 Galante interview, January 7, 2007, 28.

64 Ibid.

65 For basic information about integration, see Exxon Corporation, *Financial and Operation Review* for the following years: 1991, 43; 1993, 56; 1994, 60–62; 1997, 58–59.

66 Exxon Corporation, *1992 Annual Report Supplement*, 45; Exxon Corporation, *1994 Financial and Operating Review*, 53.

67 In the case of methyl tertiary butyl ether (MTBE), the advantages proved short-lived. Almost as soon as MTBE became widely used, rumblings began about the health hazards posed by the leakage of gasoline containing the additive from underground storage tanks at service stations into groundwater. Lawsuits soon began. In 1999, the EPA backed back away from its earlier approval of MTBE, recommending that its use be reduced and that Congress lower the oxygen requirement for reformulated gasoline. Other additives were substituted, and Congress did reduce the percentage of oxygen required in reformulated gasoline in 2005. In what one environmental lawyer called a "precautionary tale," the rapid introduction and then withdrawal of MTBE as the additive of choice for cleaner-burning gasoline illustrated the regulatory risks for refiners as they sought to adapt to societal demands affecting the manufacture of their products; see Thomas O. McGarity, "MTBE: A Precautionary Tale," *Harvard Environmental Law Review* 28 (2004): 281–342; and McGarity, *Reinventing Rationality: The Role of Regulatory Analysis in the Federal Bureaucracy* (Cambridge, 1991).

68 The refineries "integrated with a chemical complex" are listed in the "Downstream Operating Statistics" each year in Exxon Corporation, *Financial and Operating Review*.

69 A good introduction to Japan, Singapore, and China is Vietor, *How Countries Compete*.

70 Norman Richards, "Okinawa," *Lamp* 57, no. 3 (Fall 1975): 33; Sandford Brown, "Japan: The Fast-Track Country," *Lamp* 65, no. 1 (Spring 1983): 7.

71 Brown, "Japan," 7–11.

72 A logical starting point for the study of MITI remains Chalmers Johnson, *MITI and the Japanese Miracle* (Palo Alto, Calif., 1982); see also Thomas K. McCraw, ed., *America Versus Japan* (Boston, 1986); Takatoshi Ito, *The Japanese Economy* (Cambridge, Mass., 1992).

73 Maurice E. J. O'Loughlin, interview by Joseph Pratt, November 28, 2007, Indian River Shores, Florida, 10, ExxonMobil Oral History.

74 Ibid.

75 Tonen did repatriate an increasing share of its profits as dividends in the late

1980s and early 1990s, but the amount was still deemed insufficient by Exxon, especially in light of the other uses to which Tonen's profits were being devoted.

76 Dahan interview, 33.

77 Lee Raymond, interview by William Hale, August 2, 2007, Irving, 6, Exxon-Mobil Oral History.

78 Ibid., 6–7.

79 Ibid., 8–9.

80 Walter K. Wilson, "An Esso Century in Singapore," *Lamp* 75, no. 4 (Winter 1993): 1–8; Tilak Doshi, *Houston of Asia: The Singapore Petroleum Industry* (Singapore, 1980).

81 "Ready in Singapore," *Lamp* 84, no. 1 (Spring 2002): 15–20.

82 O'Loughlin interview, 15.

83 "A Paramins Plant for Singapore," *Lamp* 63, no. 2 (Summer 1981): 23.

84 Vietor, *How Countries Compete,* 39–56; Lee Kuan Yew, *From Third World to First World: The Singapore Story, 1965–2000* (New York: Harper Collins, 2000).

85 Esso Eastern, "Report on Business Environment," memorandum, October 1981, Management Committee Minutes, ExxonMobil Historical Collection.

86 *Lamp,* "A Paramins Plant for Singapore," 23.

87 Esso Eastern, *Plan for 1983,* report to Exxon Management Committee, September 29, 1982, 5, ExxonMobil Historical Collection.

88 Walter K. Wilson, "Singapore," *Lamp* 69, no. 3 (Fall 1987): i–9.

89 Wilson, "Esso Century in Singapore," 1–8.

90 *Lamp,* "Ready in Singapore," 15–20.

91 Ernest Dunbar, "Hong Kong," *Lamp* 63, no. 3 (Fall 1981): 10.

92 O'Loughlin interview, 11–14; Exxon Corporation, *1988 Annual Report,* 15.

93 "Dedication at Castle Peak," *Lamp* 68, no. 4 (Winter 1986): 12–13.

94 Yeo Toon Joo, "New Energy for an Asian Tiger," *Lamp* 73, no. 3 (Fall 1991): i–9.

95 Yeo Toon Joo, "Lighting the Pearl of the Orient," *Lamp* 78, no. 3 (Fall 1996): 27–31. The estimated annual profits for Hong Kong Electric are taken from Esso Eastern's reports to the Exxon Management Committee over time.

96 Vietor, *How Countries Compete,* 57–80; Michael B. McElroy, Chris Nielson, and Peter Lyndon, eds., *Energizing China: Reconciling Environmental Protection and Economic Growth* (Cambridge, Mass., 1998); George Zhibin Gu, *China's Global Reach: Markets, Multinationals, and Globalization* (Palo Alto, Calif., 2006).

97 T. D. Barrow to H. C. Kauffmann, "Summary Trip Report," Exxon delegation visit to PRC, July 30–August 13, 1978, 1, Exxon Management Committee, Exxon Corporate Archives; Sandford Brown, "Visit to China," *Lamp* 62 (Summer 1980): 24–27.

98 Esso Eastern, "Summary Trip Report," memorandum, August 24, 1978, 1; Esso

Eastern, "Business Environment," memorandum, November 3, 1982, 3–4; both in ExxonMobil Historical Collection.

99   For details about this project, see Esso Eastern, "Packet on Pumped Storage," memorandum to Exxon Management Committee, July 27, 1987, Exxon Management Committee Minutes, ExxonMobil Historical Collection.

100   Downs Matthews, "Exxon in China," *Lamp* 76, no. 1 (Spring 1994): 1–10.

101   Presentation to Exxon Management Committee, material dated May 16, 1988, Exxon Management Committee Minutes, ExxonMobil Historical Collection.

102   Wilson, "An Esso Century in Singapore," 8.

103   Exxon would not discover commercial quantities of petroleum in the Tarim Basin or elsewhere onshore.

104   The economics proved unattractive, and the project was never pursued.

105   Amoco's attempts to enter the Chinese market are described in Pratt, *Prelude to Merger*, 238–239.

106   Steven F. Goldmann, interview by William Hale, February 12, 2007, Dallas, 42, ExxonMobil Oral History.

107   Ibid., 45.

108   Ibid., 44–48.

109   Amoco pursued the Zhuhai purified terephthalic acid project for a decade but lost interest in the late 1990s, when economic conditions were no longer favorable; see Pratt, *Prelude to Merger*, 238–239.

110   Richard Vietor and Julia Galef, "Sinopec: Refining Its Strategy," August 13, 2007 (Boston); see also Ka-Fu Wong, "Oil Refining in China," Case HK 0631, 2006, Asian Case Research Centre, University of Hong Kong.

111   This matter is described in general terms in Pam Kevelson, "A Journey of a Thousand Miles: Historic Investment in China," *Lamp*, 2007, no. 2: 7–9.

112   Ibid., 9.

CHAPTER NINE: MEGAMERGER

1   Jad Mouawad, "Saudi Officials Seek to Temper the Price of Oil," *New York Times* on the Web, January 28, 2007: http//www.susris.com/articles/2007 /ioi/070129-oil-policy.html, accessed September 14, 2012.

2   Exxon's earnings in 1990 may have been affected by expenditures for the cleanup of the *Exxon Valdez* oil spill, but the primary financial provision for that incident ($1.68 billion) was charged against 1989 earnings.

3   *Fortune* magazine. Exxon fell to number five in 1990 as a result of the expenses associated with the *Exxon Valdez* mishap. It was ranked fourth in 1999 and 2000. For the thirty-one years from 1975 to 2005, Exxon and ExxonMobil ranked number one in profits in the *Fortune* list fifteen times.

4   Exxon Corporation, *1998 Financial and Operating Review*, 13. Exxon's

calculation of return on capital employed (ROCE) included the effects of stock repurchases as well as dividends and stock prices. It showed that the total return to Exxon shareholders was about 17.5 percent a year versus a return greater than 19 percent for the S&P 500.

5 The companies changed as mergers took effect, but usually included BP, Shell, Chevron, Total, and other major international oil companies.

6 These calculations are displayed in each of Exxon Corporation's annual *Financial and Operating Reviews*. The ROCE calculation is a complex one, and other companies' methodologies might yield different results. Nevertheless, there is little doubt about the general validity of the claim that Exxon earned higher returns than its competitors.

7 A comparison of the return on investment for U.S. refiners and S&P returns is shown in American Petroleum Institute, *The Facts About Oil Industry Mergers, Market Power, and Fuel Prices: An API Primer* (August 2008), 7.

8 Ian Hargreaves and William Hall, "Why Big Oil Has Been Forced to Begin Feeding on Itself," *Houston Chronicle*, February 6, 1984 (reprinted from the *Financial Times*).

9 For the evolution of antitrust through key cases in the twentieth century, see William E. Kovacic and Carl Shapiro, "Antitrust Policy: A Century of Economic and Legal Thinking," *Journal of Economic Perspectives*, Vol. 14, no. 1 (Winter 2000): 43–60. For the evolution of the structure of the American petroleum industry under traditional antitrust law into the 1950s, see John McLean and Robert Haigh, *The Growth of Integrated Oil Companies* (Boston, 1954).

10 Changes in the enforcement of antitrust in the 1970s and 1980s were controversial and much discussed. See, for example, Marc Allen Eisner, *Antitrust and the Triumph of Economics: Institutions, Expertise, and Policy Change* (Chapel Hill, 1991); Robert Bork, *The Antitrust Paradox* (New York, 1978); Walter Adams and James W. Brock, "The New Learning and the Euthanasia of Antitrust," 74 Cal. L. Rev. 1515 (1986); and Walter Mead and James W. Brock, *Antitrust Economics on Trial* (Princeton, 1991).

11 The official name is *FTC v. Exxon, et al.*, and it was filed by the FTC on July 18, 1973.

12 Descriptions of the changes in FTC thinking are discussed in a variety of sources: David Scheffman, Malcolm Coate, and Louis Silva, "Twenty Years of Merger Guidelines Enforcement at the FTC: An Economic Perspective," U.S. Department of Justice; James Langenfeld and David Sheffman, "The FTC in the 1980s," *Review of Industrial Organizations* 5, no. 2 (June 1990).

13 Trends and thinking in U.S. antitrust activity are described at length by Robert E. Litan and Carl Shapiro, "Antitrust Policy During the Clinton Administration" (July 1, 2001), Center for Competition Policy, Working Paper CPC01-022, University of California, Berkeley.

14 Bob Packwood, Howard Cannon, Strom Thurmond, and Joseph Biden to the Honorable James C. Miller III, January 15, 1982, 1. Packwood was chairman of the Committee on Commerce, Science, & Transportation, Cannon was ranking minority member, Thurmond was chairman of the Judiciary Committee, and Biden was the ranking minority member.

15 Federal Trade Commission, "Mergers in the Petroleum Industry: Report of the Federal Trade Commission," September 1982, 7.

16 Ibid.

17 Jay S. Creswell Jr., Scott M. Harvey, and Louis Silvia, "Mergers in the U.S. Petroleum Industry, 1971–1984: An Updated Comparative Analysis," Report to Bureau of Economics of the Federal Trade Commission, May 1989, 13. http://www.ftc.gov/be/econrpt/232168.pdf, accessed June 21, 2012.

18 At the time, the European Directorate was DG IV. It has subsequently become the Directorate General for Competition.

19 The first formal agreement between the authorities was the 1991 EC/US Competition Cooperation Agreement. Later modified, it was clarified in 1999 by a memorandum of understanding between the enforcement authorities; see Alexandr Svetlicinii, "Cooperation between Merger Control Authorities of the EU and the U.S.: A Viable Solution for Transatlantic Mergers?" *University of California Davis Business Law Journal* 7, no. 1 (2006): 171–198.

20 Pratt, *Prelude to Merger*.

21 Ibid., 15–18.

22 Forest Reinhart, Ramon Casasesus Masanell, and David J. Hanson, "BP and the Consolidation of the Oil Industry, 1998–2002," Case #9-702-012 (Boston, 2003); Yergin, *The Quest*, 83–105.

23 The year-end price in 1998 was $73.13 a share versus $30.38 a share at the end of 1994 (Exxon Corporation, *1998 Financial and Operating Review*, 13). The rise took place from 1995, as the year-end price from 1991 to 1994 was only a little more than $30 a share.

24 Raymond interview, August 2, 2007, 11–17.

25 Ibid., 17.

26 Steve Liesman, Christopher Cooper, and Allanna Sullivan, "Sinking Oil Prices Prod Exxon, Mobil to Meet at Negotiating Table," *Wall Street Journal*, November 27, 1998.

27 Noto interview, 10.

28 Christopher Cooper and Steve Liesman, "Exxon Agrees to Buy Mobil for $75.3 Billion," *Wall Street Journal*, December 2, 1998.

29 Noto interview, 5–6.

30 Ibid.

31 Kenneth N. Gilpin, "What's Behind the Gush of Oil Deals?" *New York Times*, November 29, 1998.

32 Yergin, *The Quest*, 94–97.

33 Ibid. This account was verified in its main particulars in Raymond interview, August 2, 2007.

34 The sequence of events for the period during which the merger was negotiated and reviewed with Exxon's and Mobil's boards is detailed in the "Proxy Statement/Prospectus" distributed at the 1999 annual meeting in Dallas, Texas, I-14 to I-19.

35 Wilhelm interview, December 6, 2007, 31.

36 "BP and Amoco in Oil Mega-Merger," BBC News, August 11, 1998.

37 Raymond interview, August 2, 2007, 21.

38 Noto interview, 16.

39 Ibid., 13.

40 Raymond interview, August 2, 2007, 27–28.

41 Ibid., 30.

42 This element was identified as a central factor by Raymond; see also Donald F. Humphrey (at the time of the merger, Exxon's controller), interview by William Hale, December 13, 2007, Dallas, ExxonMobil Oral History.

43 This was certified in the merger proxy.

44 The new FASB rules relevant to this were *Statement of Financial Accounting Standards No. 141, Business Combinations,* and *No. 142, Goodwill and Other Intangible Assets.*

45 Annual meeting; Exxon & Mobil Merger, *Proxy Statement/Prospectus,* April 5, 1999. Based on prices for Exxon and Mobil on the day the merger proxy was printed, a Mobil shareholder who owned one share of Mobil stock worth $87.375 could receive shares of ExxonMobil stock worth $115.35, a 32 percent premium, if the stock of the combined company remained at the value that Exxon had experienced.

46 Prices in the first quarter of 1999 ranged from $64.31 to $76.37 a share, while the postmerger fourth-quarter price range was $70.06 to $86.56 (ExxonMobil Corporation, *1991 Annual Report,* F38).

47 Christopher Cooper and Steve Liesman, "Exxon Agrees to Buy Mobil for $75.3 Billion," *Wall Street Journal,* December 2, 1998.

48 These media outlets were mentioned as sources in Agis Salpukas's *New York Times* article (November 26, 1998) on the merger talks.

49 By this time, Robert Wilhelm's skepticism of the value of the merger had not abated, but seeing the writing on the wall, he offered to help put the two companies together (Wilhelm interview, December 6, 2007, 32).

50 Cooper and Liesman, "Exxon Agrees to Buy Mobil."

51 Ibid.

52 Michael Davis, "Exxon, Mobil Confirm Deal," *Houston Chronicle,* December 2, 1998.

53 Noto quoted in Allan Sloan, "A Real Lump of Coal: Cost-Cutting Companies Hand Out Pink Slips," *Newsweek,* December 14, 1998, 50.

54   Ibid.

55   Steve Liesman and Allanna Sullivan, "Tight-Lipped Exxon, Outspoken Mobil Face Major Image, Culture Differences," *Wall Street Journal*, December 2, 1998.

56   As quoted in Steve Liesman, "Mobil, Exxon Like Oil, Water on Air Pollution," *Wall Street Journal*, May 24, 1999.

57   Liesman, et al., "Sinking Prices Prod Exxon, Mobil to Meet at Negotiating Table." See also Liesman and Sullivan, "Tight-Lipped Exxon."

58   Gilpin, "What's Behind the Gush of Oil Deals?"

59   Lee Raymond, presentation to J. P. Morgan, December 1998, ExxonMobil Historical Collection.

60   A study by McKinsey & Company in 2004 found that 70 percent of 160 mergers studied failed to achieve expected revenue synergies; see Scott A. Christofferson, Robert S. McNish, and Diane L. Sias, "Where Mergers Go Wrong," *McKinsey Quarterly*, 2004, no. 2: 1–6.

61   As mentioned, the most important reviews were by the FTC and DG IV, but the merger also faced review by U.S. state attorneys general as well as by other national competition authorities, none of whom raised consequential issues.

62   Svetlicinii, "Cooperation Between Merger Control Authorities."

63   The commission's requirements for approval were described in Agis Salpukas, "European Commission Clears Exxon-Mobil Merger," *New York Times*, September 30, 1999. The same day, the commission gave provisional clearance to the merger of BP Amoco and Atlantic Richfield.

64   Exxon Corporation, *1998 Financial and Operating Review*, 58.

65   ExxonMobil Corporation, *1999 Annual Report*, 20.

66   Noto interview, 15, 25.

67   "Exxon/Mobil Agree to Largest FTC Divestiture Ever in Order to Settle FTC Antitrust Charges; Settlement Requires Extensive Restructuring and Prevents Merger of Significant Competing U.S. Assets," FTC press release, November 30, 1999.

68   Dahan interview, 58.

69   Ibid.

70   Ibid., 57.

71   Raymond interview, September 11, 2007, 1.

72   Harry Longwell, interview by William Hale, September 12, 2007, Irving, 13, ExxonMobil Oral History.

73   Dahan interview, 74.

74   ExxonMobil Corporation, *1999 Financial and Operating Review*, 3.

75   Raymond interview, September 11, 2007, 6–8.

76   The 1989 purchase of Texaco Canada was one. Imperial paid $3.24 billion for Texaco, and then was required by Canadian competition authorities to sell a Texaco refinery in Nova Scotia and to dispose of a tenth of the combined

companies' service stations in Canada. The acquisition turned out to be a very poor investment.

77   Raymond interview, September 11, 2007, 6.

78   Longwell interview, September 12, 2007, 29–30.

79   This was a key point made emphatically by Raymond in his instructions to his transition managers.

80   Longwell interview, September 12, 2007, 17–22.

81   Generally, this was one week of severance pay for every year of service.

82   Data taken from a presentation to the board, "ExxonMobil Merger Retrospective," given by D. D. Humphreys, vice president and treasurer, June 28, 2005.

83   The number of executives was 72 percent of the premerger level. For the percentage of Mobil executives in the merged corporations, see Humphreys, "ExxonMobil Merger Retrospective." Two hundred fifteen Exxon executives left, while 689 Mobil executives were severed. That result had been expected. Mobil was more liberal in qualifying employees for separation if they would be required to move or change jobs, and Mobil's severance benefits were considerably more generous than Exxon's.

84   Humphreys, "ExxonMobil Merger Retrospective"; data were taken also from the company's *Financial and Operating Reviews* for 1998 and 2005.

85   Of the twenty-three corporate officers in the merged company in 1999, all but five were from Exxon (Exxon Corporation, *1999 Annual Report*, F41).

86   Lotus Notes was selected for most office applications, in place of or in addition to Microsoft Windows. The former Mobil executive was G. L. Kohlenberger.

87   Talbert J. Fox, interview with William Hale, January 1, 2009, Dallas, ExxonMobil Oral History. Fox was the Law Department representative on the Corporate Structure Task Force and later general corporate counsel for ExxonMobil.

88   The issue was presented in ExxonMobil shareholder resolutions at every annual meeting through 2008. Company critics wanted ExxonMobil to adopt an explicit statement barring discrimination based on sexual orientation or gender identity. ExxonMobil maintained that since it prohibited discrimination of all forms, including those based on sexual orientation and gender identity, an explicit policy focused specifically on sexual orientation was not needed (*Proxy Statement*, April 10, 2008, 32). It also resisted extending company-supplied benefits to same-sex partners except where required by law.

89   Dahan interview, 55.

90   Ibid.

91   Longwell interview, September 12, 2007, 31.

92   ExxonMobil, editorial, *New York Times*, December 2, 1999.

93   Benicia had been generating earnings for Exxon of more than $200 million, and the Tosco-acquired properties about $275 million. The BP-Mobil joint venture had experienced earnings of about $200 million for Mobil.

94   Foster interview, 23–32.

95   Ibid.

96   Exploration was the responsibility of the exploration company; getting new projects built and on-stream was the job of the development company, and the other upstream groups were focused on gas sales, computing, and research and development.

97   Koonce interview, 52.

98   These figures, which include natural gas, are on an oil-equivalent basis (Exxon Corporation, *Financial and Operating Review*, 1994 and 1998).

99   Koonce interview, 51–52.

100   Martha Spalding, "Petroleum Products Leader Extends Global Reach," *Lamp* 81, no. 3 (Fall 1999): 17.

101   Ibid., 18.

102   An indicator of the relative intensity of change in the upstream versus the downstream can be seen in the *1999 Financial and Operating Review*, in which upstream projects and data occupy thirty-four pages and downstream activities and data only fourteen pages.

103   In the *1999 Financial and Operating Review*, the Benicia refinery's results were still reported. This refinery was sold, in keeping with antitrust requirements, shortly thereafter.

104   This number dropped to twelve in the *2005 Financial and Operating Review* only because the Mobil and the Exxon refineries in one country were now operating as a coordinated unit and were listed as one refinery in 2005.

105   Exxon- and Mobil-branded service stations continued to serve motorists in the United States, and motor lubricants continued to be marketed under two brands. Outside the country, the company retained the Mobil and Esso brand names for service stations and lubricants, but switched to ExxonMobil for selected products, such as aviation fuel.

106   Sources are Exxon and ExxonMobil *Financial and Operating Reviews* for the period.

107   ExxonMobil, *2005 Financial and Operating Review*, 65–75.

108   Ibid.

109   Earnings in 2005 for the downstream were $7.992 billion, 650 percent higher than in the year following the merger; even compared to earnings during the (better) years that immediately preceded the merger, earnings in the downstream had still more than doubled by 2005. ExxonMobil, *2005 Financial and Operating Review*, 66; *2001 Financial and Operating Review*, 65; *1996 Financial and Operating Review*, 48.

110   Ibid., 22.

111   Total market and supply sales for ExxonMobil were 63.6 percent larger, and oil-equivalent production was 60.9 percent larger, than for premerger Exxon alone.

112   ExxonMobil Corporation, *1999 Financial and Operating Review*, 72.

113   Ibid., 74–79.

114 For example, net income reported in 2005 for the companies mentioned was as follows: BASF, $3.559 billion (using a year-end exchange rate of $1.861 to 1 euro); DuPont, $2.053 billion; Dow, $4.5158 billion; Exxon Mobil Chemical, $3.94 billion.

115 Raymond interview, September 11, 2007, 16–17.

116 ExxonMobil, *1999 Financial and Operating Review*, 26–27, 63, 76–77.

117 These matters were referred to in shareholder resolutions in 2000, 2002, 2003, 2004, and 2005. The Aceh issue was raised by the Washington, D.C.–based International Labor Rights Fund suit in 2001 under the Alien Torts Claims Act, which charged ExxonMobil with complicity in the Indonesian government's suppression of civil unrest in Aceh.

118 Spencer R. Weart, *The Discovery of Global Warming* (Cambridge, Mass., 2003); Mark Maslin, *Global Warming: A Very Short Introduction* (Oxford, 2004); David Archer and Stefan Rahmstorf, *The Climate Crisis: An Introductory Guide to Climate Change* (Cambridge, 2010); Bert Bolin, *A History of the Science and Politics of Climate Change: The Role of the Intergovernmental Panel on Climate Change* (Cambridge, 2008); Yergin, *The Quest*, 419–520.

119 Yergin, *The Quest*, 464–487.

120 Lee R. Raymond, "Climate Change: Don't Ignore the Facts," *Lamp* 78, no. 3 (Fall 1996): 2–3.

121 Remarks by Lee R. Raymond to World Petroleum Congress, October 13, 1997, copy in Lee Raymond folder, 9, ExxonMobil Oral History.

122 Ibid., 12.

123 Lee Raymond, unpublished interview, Allanna Sullivan of the *Wall Street Journal*, November 24, 1997, 74–76, transcript in ExxonMobil Historical Collection.

124 Paula Spann, "Era of 'Creative Confrontation' Ends as Schmertz Leaves Mobil," *Washington Post*, May 8, 1988.

125 For copies of advocacy ads on climate change, see ExxonMobil, "Moving Past Kyoto" and "To a Sounder Climate Policy," 2001, Folder, "Advocacy Ads," ExxonMobil Historical Collection.

126 Thaddeus Herrick, "CEO's Controversial Views Lead to Tough Summer for ExxonMobil," *Wall Street Journal*, August 29, 2001, B1, B6; Jeffrey Ball, "Digging In: Exxon Chief Makes a Cold Calculation on Global Warming," *New York Times*, June 14, 2005, A1, A10; Joe Nocera, "Exxon Just Wants to Be Loved," *New York Times*, February 10, 2007.

127 Sprow interview, 19.

128 Sheldon Kamieniecki, *Corporate America and Environmental Policy: How Often Does Business Get Its Way?* (Stanford, 2006); Andrew C. Revkin, "Skeptics Dispute Climate Worries and Each Other," *New York Times*, March 9, 2009.

129 Jeffrey Ball, "Exxon Shifts 'Green' Policy," *Wall Street Journal*, January 11, 2007; Steven Mufson, "ExxonMobil Warming Up to Global Climate Issue,"

APPENDIX A

THE EXXONMOBIL HISTORICAL COLLECTION AT THE DOLPH BRISCOE CENTER FOR AMERICAN HISTORY

By far the largest energy industry collection at the Briscoe Center, the ExxonMobil Historical Collection (EMHC) documents the long history of Exxon Mobil Corporation, highlighting four major corporate entities—Standard Oil Company, Mobil Corporation, Exxon Corporation, and Exxon Mobil Corporation—as well as various predecessor, affiliate, and subsidiary companies, notably Texas-based Humble Oil & Refining Company and Magnolia Petroleum Company. Comprised of an estimated 4 million documents, 1.5 million photographs, 3,000 artifacts, and nearly 20,000 moving image and sound recordings, the EMHC is understood to be the largest publicly available collection documenting the history of a single petroleum company.

The EMHC offers insight into the early activities of the Standard Oil Company and charts the growth of Exxon's and Mobil's core business activities—namely the exploration, production, refining and marketing of petroleum products and chemicals, and the industry's development and societal impact throughout the last century. In addition, the collection includes diverse material that can support research on related topics such as advertising and brand identity, management and corporate culture, the environment, architecture, graphic design, and corporate philanthropy.

washingtonpost.com, February 10, 2007, at http://www.washingtonpost.com/wp-dyn/content/article/2007/02/09/AR2007020902081; Marc Gunther, "ExxonMobil Greens Up Its Act," CNNMoney.com, January 26, 2007, http://money.conn.com/2007/01/25/magazines/fortune/pluggedin-gunther-exxonmobil.fortune. The article was originally published in *Fortune* magazine. For a broad description of ExxonMobil's ongoing adaptation to climate change within its own operations, see its annual corporate citizenship reports: http://www.exxonmobil.com/Corporate/community_ccr.aspx.

130 Ball, "Exxon Shifts 'Green' Policy."

131 Kenneth P. Cohen, interview by William Hale, January 8, 2008, Irving, 27–30, 54–55, ExxonMobil Oral History.

132 Dahan interview, 44.

133 Cohen interview, 3.

134 The company's long-standing report on charitable contributions, *Dimensions*, was discontinued at this time, although data on ExxonMobil's contributions was separately listed elsewhere.

135 Perhaps it would be more accurate to say that this was a return to an earlier though less robust Exxon Corporation practice. From the early 1970s through 1984, Exxon published the "Exxon Background Series" on key issues related to the petroleum industry, and one of these, published in March 1973, was entitled "Social Responsibility."

136 The company's match had been increased in the 1970s to three-to-one from two-to-one, and groups other than institutions of higher education were added.

137 For example, the company began to sponsor the Masters Golf Tournament in 2004, but in doing so provided monies to the professional golfer Phil Mickelson, who used the support on behalf of a charitable educational foundation he and his wife had created.

138 The experience of the company in Chad is described in more detail in chapter 7.

139 T. Peter Townsend, interview by William Hale, February 14, 2007, Dallas, 33, ExxonMobil Oral History.

140 The material for this profile is taken from Tillerson interview, 20–39; Mike Long, "Can a Civil Engineer Succeed at ExxonMobil?" *Lamp* 86, no. 1 (2004): 6; and Jeffrey Ball, "The New Face at Exxon: CEO Tillerson, Prototype of Texas Oilman, Must Focus on Delicate Global Balance," *Wall Street Journal*, March 8, 2006.

141 Tillerson interview, 32.

142 Jad Mouawad, "Exxon's CEO Paid Like a Rockefeller," *New York Times*, April 15, 2006.

143 The Securities and Exchange Commission adopted a rule on July 26, 2006, under which companies had to disclose additional information on deferred pay and retirement benefits awarded to senior executives. The SEC chairman,

Christopher Cox, said that "no issue" in the agency's seventy-two-year history had "generated such interest" as disclosure of executive pay (*USA Today*, July 27, 2006).

144 From 1993 to the end of 2005, ExxonMobil stock quadrupled in value. The Dow Jones Industrial Average tripled.

EPILOGUE: TRANSFORMATION

1 Jeffrey Ball, "Mighty Profit Maker: Under CEO Lee Raymond, ExxonMobil Gushes Money," *Wall Street Journal*, April 8, 2005.

2 The statistics on Exxon's production are taken from the company's annual reports in 1973 and 2005. World oil-production figures come from the U.S. Energy Information Agency. The figure for 1973 reflects the convention of the time used to designate production in regions still in transition to full nationalization. It lists 5.525 million b/d "of crude oil and natural gas liquids" and an additional 1.193 million b/d as "crude oil offtake under special arrangements."

3 "Into the Deep: Exxon Advances Deepwater Frontier," *Lamp* 80, no. 3 (Fall 1998): 4–9; Michael Davis, "Launch Pad into the Deep," *Houston Chronicle*, August 17, 1997; Amanda Coyne and Richard Cunningham, "Technology Leads the Way to Deepwater Success," *Lamp* 87, no. 3 (2005): 17–20.

4 Richard Cunningham, "Hoover-Diana: One Team, No Surprises," *Lamp* 82, no. 3 (Fall 2000): 15–20.

5 Ibid., 18.

6 ExxonMobil, *2000 Financial and Operating Review*, 30.

7 The Cold Lake process is described in Ted Bower, "Heating Up Cold Lake," *Lamp* 77, no. 3 (Fall 1995): 25–26.

8 Amanda Coyne, "Steaming for Oil in Canada," *Lamp*, 2008, no. 1: 20.

9 Bower, "Heating Up Cold Lake," 26.

10 The 1994 agreement with Alberta contained permission to expand capacity to 217,000 barrels a day (Exxon Corporation, *1994 Financial and Operating Review*, 35).

11 The Syncrude Canada reserves were expected to last beyond 2025.

12 According to Timothy J. Hearn, Imperial's chairman from 2001 to 2008, this resource could contain four billion to five billion barrels of oil. Timothy J. Hearn, interview by William Hale, Irving, May 15, 2008, 38, ExxonMobil Oral History.

13 Exxon Mobil Corporation, *The Outlook for Energy: A View to 2030* (2009), data and projections to be found in the section "Global Liquids Supply and Demand."

14 Rene Dahan to William Hale, February 22, 2010, 3.

15 The size of Qatar's gas deposits is enormous. The *Oil and Gas Journal* (January 1, 2007) estimated its reserves of gas as exceeding 900 trillion cubic feet,

third behind Russia and Iran, and far ahead of the 200 trillion cubic feet estimated for the United States. This estimate has been endorsed by the U.S. Energy Information Administration, which includes the figure on its website under "Qatar: Country Analysis Brief."

16 U.S. Energy Information Administration, "Qatar: Country Analysis Brief."

17 ExxonMobil, *2005 Financial and Operating Review*, 52–53.

18 This was the Barzan gas project. An earlier project with the same objective was the Al Khaleej gas project.

19 In June 2010, ExxonMobil strengthened its commitment to be a future leader in natural gas with the completion of its $41 billion merger with XTO Energy, a leader in shale-gas production using advances in both hydraulic fracturing and horizontal drilling. The merger created an organization focused on the global development and production of unconventional natural gas resources, including tight-sands gas. Like other energy companies, ExxonMobil-XTO is looking throughout North America and around the globe for promising fracking opportunities. See Mike Long, "ExxonMobil-XTO Merger Takes Unconventional Oil and Gas to a New Level," *Lamp*, no. 2 (2010): 2–8.

20 For information on the changing role of national oil companies compared to privately-owned companies, see Ross and Sloan, *Terra Incognita*, 51–91; also, Robert Pirog, CRS Report for Congress, "The Role of National Oil Companies in the International Oil Market," Washington, D.C., Congressional Research Service, August 21, 2007.

21 McBrayer interview, 35.

22 Steve Liesman and Allanna Sullivan, "Mystery Man: Exxon-Mobil Merger Positions an Enigma at Oil Giant's Helm," *Wall Street Journal*, December 1, 1999.

23 Joe Nocera, "Exxon Mobil Just Wants to Be Loved," *New York Times*, February 10, 2007.

24 Teagle was the company's youngest director when he was named to the board in 1909, at age thirty-one. He served as Jersey's president (1917–1937), and then as chairman (1937–1942). At that point, he took a central position on the U.S. Petroleum War Service Committee. One of the founders of the American Petroleum Institute, he was named by President Roosevelt to an advisory position on the National Recovery Administration.

The oldest items in the collection are corporate charters, contracts, correspondence, and agreements dating back to the 1870s, documenting how John D. Rockefeller and his associates founded the Standard Oil Company of Ohio and operated the company for more than forty-one years. These materials record Standard Oil's aggressive acquisition of refineries, land, stock, and property throughout Ohio, Pennsylvania, and New York. They also include agreements forging exclusive relationships with pipeline and refining companies, one of the keys to Standard Oil's success.

Beyond these foundational materials, the EMHC's greater significance lies in its documentation of two of the strongest companies to emerge from the 1911 breakup of Standard Oil: Standard Oil Company of New York, known as Socony, and Standard Oil Company (New Jersey), commonly called Jersey Standard. Socony, which became Mobil Corporation, and Jersey Standard, later renamed Exxon, spent the better part of ninety years as tough competitors, forging individual identities and distancing themselves from their origins as sister companies.

The EMHC's extensive series of corporate newspapers, magazines, newsletters, and other periodicals—more than five hundred unique titles spanning over one hundred years—documents all aspects of the corporations' domestic and foreign operations, from changes in corporate administration to the work occurring at individual facilities. As a resource for historical inquiry, these titles offer specific information about exploration, production and refining, and chemicals in various regions over time. Focusing on places as diverse as Torrance, California, New Zealand, and Brazil, the publications document how Mobil, Exxon, and their subsidiaries positioned themselves globally and the impact they have had on economies and communities.

One of the cornerstones of Mobil and Exxon's success throughout the twentieth century was the expert use of marketing and advertising, making these companies a visible fixture in America and around the world. By acquiring consistent, well-placed ad space in prominent national and local publications, by filling the airwaves with radio spots and television commercials, and by dotting the roadways with signs and billboards, Mobil and Exxon battled to lure drivers to the pumps. The collection's advertising component—artwork, full-page advertisements, customer brochures and booklets, and several decades of television commercials for numerous products and services—provides a concentrated resource for tracing the changing trends in the advertising industry.

Throughout the collection, one can see evidence of the fusion of brand and corporate identities when Socony Mobil Oil Company changed its name to Mobil Oil Corporation in 1966, and Standard Oil Company (New Jersey) became Exxon Corporation in 1972. Researchers can see the Pegasus trademark emerge as Mobil's icon of speed and power, and the transformation of Esso and Humble's mascot from animated oil drop to the whimsical tiger of its "Put a Tiger in Your Tank" campaign to the more symbolic live tiger of the mid-1970s and beyond. Some of the twentieth century's most recognizable graphic design is represented in famed industrial designer Raymond Loewy's sleek Exxon logo and the work of Chermayeff & Geismar, creators of Mobil's complete identity package that informed every graphic element from the company's familiar "red 'O'" logo to all of Mobil's print and broadcast materials.

A detailed inventory of the ExxonMobil Historical Collection is available online at the following URL: http://www.lib.utexas.edu/taro /utcah/00352/cah-00352.html.

APPENDIX B

INTERVIEWS

NAME	INTERVIEW DATES
Ahnert, E. F.	2/7/2007
Albers, M. W.	1/9/2008
Arbogast, S.	2/28/2007
Atkiss, A. W.	1/23/2007
Barfield, E. C.	10/29/2007
Barrow, T. D.	4/25/2007
Bennett, J. F.	1/3/2007
Boatwright, J. B.	7/19/2007
Cassiani, S.	7/25/2007
Cattarulla, E. R.	10/5/2006
Clarke Sr., J. G.	1/3/2007
Cohen, K. P.	12/5/2007; 1/8/2008
Dahan, R.	1/8/2007; 10/17/2009; 2/22/2010
DiCorcia, E. T.	4/16/2007
Flannery, B. P.	1/30/2008
Foster, M. E.	8/22/2007
Galante, E. G.	10/4/2006

NAME	INTERVIEW DATES
Garvin, C. C.	11/16/2006
Glab, E. F.	4/4/2007
Goldmann, S. F.	2/8/2007
Guttormson, D. L.	7/20/2007
Harrison, O. R.	10/19/2007
Harrison, C. M.	4/20/2007
Harrison, M. G.	1/29/2008
Hay, J. T.	6/5/2007
Hearn, T. J.	5/15/2008
Hedburg, J. D.	8/1/2007
Henderek, M. F.	3/5/2008
Hess, E. J.	1/9/2007
Houghton, J. R.	10/30/2007
Hubble, H. H.	2/9/2007
Humphreys, D. D.	12/12/2007
Kauffmann, H. C.	11/30/2007
Koonce, K. T.	11/5/2007
Kruizenga, R. J.	10/20/2006
Lartigue Jr., H. J.	12/12/2007
Longmire, R. A.	11/16/2007
Longwell, H. J.	10/4/2006; 4/4/2007; 4/18/2007; 5/16/2007; 6/28/2007; 7/27/2007; 8/28/2007; 9/12/2007; 10/3/2007; 10/24/2007; 3/1/2010
Luby Jr., J. O.	2/18/2008
Madec, A.	5/28/2009
Matthews, C. W.	1/22/2007
McBrayer, H. E.	3/26/2009
McCullough, G. B.	7/30/2007
McGill, S. R.	11/17/2006; 3/14/2007; 3/18/2007
McIvor, D. K.	4/26/2008

washingtonpost.com, February 10, 2007, at http://www.washingtonpost.com
/wp-dyn/content/article/2007/02/09/AR2007020902081; Marc Gunther,
"ExxonMobil Greens Up Its Act," CNNMoney.com, January 26, 2007, http://
money.conn.com/2007/01/25/magazines/fortune/pluggedin-gunther
-exxonmobil.fortune. The article was originally published in *Fortune* magazine.
For a broad description of ExxonMobil's ongoing adaptation to climate change
within its own operations, see its annual corporate citizenship reports: http://
www.exxonmobil.com/Corporate/community_ccr.aspx.

130 Ball, "Exxon Shifts 'Green' Policy."

131 Kenneth P. Cohen, interview by William Hale, January 8, 2008, Irving, 27–30,
54–55, ExxonMobil Oral History.

132 Dahan interview, 44.

133 Cohen interview, 3.

134 The company's long-standing report on charitable contributions, *Dimensions*,
was discontinued at this time, although data on ExxonMobil's contributions
was separately listed elsewhere.

135 Perhaps it would be more accurate to say that this was a return to an earlier
though less robust Exxon Corporation practice. From the early 1970s through
1984, Exxon published the "Exxon Background Series" on key issues related
to the petroleum industry, and one of these, published in March 1973, was
entitled "Social Responsibility."

136 The company's match had been increased in the 1970s to three-to-one from
two-to-one, and groups other than institutions of higher education were
added.

137 For example, the company began to sponsor the Masters Golf Tournament in
2004, but in doing so provided monies to the professional golfer Phil Mickelson, who used the support on behalf of a charitable educational foundation he
and his wife had created.

138 The experience of the company in Chad is described in more detail in chapter 7.

139 T. Peter Townsend, interview by William Hale, February 14, 2007, Dallas, 33,
ExxonMobil Oral History.

140 The material for this profile is taken from Tillerson interview, 20–39; Mike
Long, "Can a Civil Engineer Succeed at ExxonMobil?" *Lamp* 86, no. 1 (2004):
6; and Jeffrey Ball, "The New Face at Exxon: CEO Tillerson, Prototype of
Texas Oilman, Must Focus on Delicate Global Balance," *Wall Street Journal*,
March 8, 2006.

141 Tillerson interview, 32.

142 Jad Mouawad, "Exxon's CEO Paid Like a Rockefeller," *New York Times*,
April 15, 2006.

143 The Securities and Exchange Commission adopted a rule on July 26, 2006,
under which companies had to disclose additional information on deferred
pay and retirement benefits awarded to senior executives. The SEC chairman,

Christopher Cox, said that "no issue" in the agency's seventy-two-year history had "generated such interest" as disclosure of executive pay (*USA Today*, July 27, 2006).

144 From 1993 to the end of 2005, ExxonMobil stock quadrupled in value. The Dow Jones Industrial Average tripled.

EPILOGUE: TRANSFORMATION

1 Jeffrey Ball, "Mighty Profit Maker: Under CEO Lee Raymond, ExxonMobil Gushes Money," *Wall Street Journal*, April 8, 2005.

2 The statistics on Exxon's production are taken from the company's annual reports in 1973 and 2005. World oil-production figures come from the U.S. Energy Information Agency. The figure for 1973 reflects the convention of the time used to designate production in regions still in transition to full nationalization. It lists 5.525 million b/d "of crude oil and natural gas liquids" and an additional 1.193 million b/d as "crude oil offtake under special arrangements."

3 "Into the Deep: Exxon Advances Deepwater Frontier," *Lamp* 80, no. 3 (Fall 1998): 4-9; Michael Davis, "Launch Pad into the Deep," *Houston Chronicle*, August 17, 1997; Amanda Coyne and Richard Cunningham, "Technology Leads the Way to Deepwater Success," *Lamp* 87, no. 3 (2005): 17-20.

4 Richard Cunningham, "Hoover-Diana: One Team, No Surprises," *Lamp* 82, no. 3 (Fall 2000): 15-20.

5 Ibid., 18.

6 ExxonMobil, *2000 Financial and Operating Review*, 30.

7 The Cold Lake process is described in Ted Bower, "Heating Up Cold Lake," *Lamp* 77, no. 3 (Fall 1995): 25-26.

8 Amanda Coyne, "Steaming for Oil in Canada," *Lamp*, 2008, no. 1: 20.

9 Bower, "Heating Up Cold Lake," 26.

10 The 1994 agreement with Alberta contained permission to expand capacity to 217,000 barrels a day (Exxon Corporation, *1994 Financial and Operating Review*, 35).

11 The Syncrude Canada reserves were expected to last beyond 2025.

12 According to Timothy J. Hearn, Imperial's chairman from 2001 to 2008, this resource could contain four billion to five billion barrels of oil. Timothy J. Hearn, interview by William Hale, Irving, May 15, 2008, 38, ExxonMobil Oral History.

13 Exxon Mobil Corporation, *The Outlook for Energy: A View to 2030* (2009), data and projections to be found in the section "Global Liquids Supply and Demand."

14 Rene Dahan to William Hale, February 22, 2010, 3.

15 The size of Qatar's gas deposits is enormous. The *Oil and Gas Journal* (January 1, 2007) estimated its reserves of gas as exceeding 900 trillion cubic feet,

third behind Russia and Iran, and far ahead of the 200 trillion cubic feet estimated for the United States. This estimate has been endorsed by the U.S. Energy Information Administration, which includes the figure on its website under "Qatar: Country Analysis Brief."

16 U.S. Energy Information Administration, "Qatar: Country Analysis Brief."

17 ExxonMobil, *2005 Financial and Operating Review*, 52–53.

18 This was the Barzan gas project. An earlier project with the same objective was the Al Khaleej gas project.

19 In June 2010, ExxonMobil strengthened its commitment to be a future leader in natural gas with the completion of its $41 billion merger with XTO Energy, a leader in shale-gas production using advances in both hydraulic fracturing and horizontal drilling. The merger created an organization focused on the global development and production of unconventional natural gas resources, including tight-sands gas. Like other energy companies, ExxonMobil-XTO is looking throughout North America and around the globe for promising fracking opportunities. See Mike Long, "ExxonMobil-XTO Merger Takes Unconventional Oil and Gas to a New Level," *Lamp*, no. 2 (2010): 2–8.

20 For information on the changing role of national oil companies compared to privately-owned companies, see Ross and Sloan, *Terra Incognita*, 51–91; also, Robert Pirog, CRS Report for Congress, "The Role of National Oil Companies in the International Oil Market," Washington, D.C., Congressional Research Service, August 21, 2007.

21 McBrayer interview, 35.

22 Steve Liesman and Allanna Sullivan, "Mystery Man: Exxon-Mobil Merger Positions an Enigma at Oil Giant's Helm," *Wall Street Journal*, December 1, 1999.

23 Joe Nocera, "Exxon Mobil Just Wants to Be Loved," *New York Times*, February 10, 2007.

24 Teagle was the company's youngest director when he was named to the board in 1909, at age thirty-one. He served as Jersey's president (1917–1937), and then as chairman (1937–1942). At that point, he took a central position on the U.S. Petroleum War Service Committee. One of the founders of the American Petroleum Institute, he was named by President Roosevelt to an advisory position on the National Recovery Administration.

APPENDIX A

THE EXXONMOBIL HISTORICAL COLLECTION AT THE
DOLPH BRISCOE CENTER FOR AMERICAN HISTORY

By far the largest energy industry collection at the Briscoe Center, the ExxonMobil Historical Collection (EMHC) documents the long history of Exxon Mobil Corporation, highlighting four major corporate entities—Standard Oil Company, Mobil Corporation, Exxon Corporation, and Exxon Mobil Corporation—as well as various predecessor, affiliate, and subsidiary companies, notably Texas-based Humble Oil & Refining Company and Magnolia Petroleum Company. Comprised of an estimated 4 million documents, 1.5 million photographs, 3,000 artifacts, and nearly 20,000 moving image and sound recordings, the EMHC is understood to be the largest publicly available collection documenting the history of a single petroleum company.

The EMHC offers insight into the early activities of the Standard Oil Company and charts the growth of Exxon's and Mobil's core business activities—namely the exploration, production, refining and marketing of petroleum products and chemicals, and the industry's development and societal impact throughout the last century. In addition, the collection includes diverse material that can support research on related topics such as advertising and brand identity, management and corporate culture, the environment, architecture, graphic design, and corporate philanthropy.

NAME	INTERVIEW DATES
McMillan, J. T.	8/8/2007
Meyer, R.	12/6/2007
Michalski, J. J.	5/6/2008
Nauman, S. A.	11/16/2006
Nelson, R. D.	9/25/2007
Nelson, M. C.	1/30/2008
Nesbitt, R. B.	12/13/2007
Norton, A. S. H.	3/15/2007
Noto, L. A.	4/10/2008
O'Loughlin, M. E. J.	11/28/2007
Phillips, S. C.	11/19/2009
Pramuk, F. S.	4/11/2008
Raymond, L. R.	2/19/2007; 5/17/2007; 6/14/2007; 6/25/2007; 8/2/2007; 8/21/2007; 9/11/2007; 10/22/2007; 1/21/2008; 4/23/2009; 12/3/2009; 3/22/2010
Risch, F. A.	4/9/2007; 4/17/2007; 4/25/2007
Rizzo, G. A.	11/26/2007
Roberts, C. K.	9/19/2007
Rouse, J. J.	6/22/2007
Roxburgh, C. D.	8/6/2007
Salvador, A.	8/20/2007
Schroth, W. G.	11/29/2007
Seddelmeyer, J. E.	3/28/2007; 4/27/2007
Simon, J. S.	11/17/2006
Slick, W. T.	9/19/2007
Spivey, R. J.	10/18/2007
Sprow, F. B.	1/16/2007
Stamas, S.	4/11/2008
Taylor, J. G.	9/21/2009
Thompson, J. L.	8/16/2007; 11/15/2007

NAME	INTERVIEW DATES
Tillerson, R. W.	6/5/2007; 7/3/2007
Townsend, T. P.	2/14/2007
VanBiber Jr., R. C.	8/10/2007
Vastola Jr., S. J.	10/20/2006
Vela III, A. N.	4/4/2007
Wilhelm, R. E.	4/26/2007; 10/11/2007; 12/6/2007
Winslow, R. A.	11/13/2007
Wood, P. W. J.	9/19/2007

NOTE:

The interviews with Exxon employees were conducted by Joseph A. Pratt and William E. Hale during the research for this book. The tapes and transcripts of these interviews comprise the ExxonMobil Oral History Project, part of the ExxonMobil Historical Collection at the Dolph Briscoe Center for American History at the University of Texas at Austin. As of press time, the interviews are closed to the public with plans to make the material available to researchers in the future.

APPENDIX C

EXXONMOBIL DIRECTORS AND OFFICERS,
DECEMBER 1975–JUNE 2012

EXXONMOBIL DIRECTORS AND OFFICERS:
DEC. 1975–JUNE 2012

LEGEND

Co:	EC (Exxon Corporation) or EMC (Exxon Mobil Corporation)
M	Merger
Title	A Director or Officer may have held various titles during tenure
	Current Directors and Officers are highlighted

DIRECTORS

PERSON NAME	EFFECTIVE DATE	END DATE
Piercy, G. T.	05/18/66	11/30/80
Franklin, W. H.	05/14/69	05/16/79
Long, F. A.	10/30/69	05/14/81
MacNaughton, D. S.	05/13/70	05/19/88
Campbell, N. J., Jr.	01/01/71	11/30/76
Cox, D. M.	05/12/71	05/16/85
von Amerongen, W. O.	10/27/71	01/25/89
Barrow, T. D.	05/18/72	11/15/78
Wright, M. A.	01/01/73	03/31/76
Kauffmann, H. C.	01/01/74	05/16/85
Peterson, M.	05/16/74	05/21/87
Dobson, R. P.	05/15/75	05/17/84
Harness, E. G.	05/15/75	11/15/84
Jamieson, J. K.	07/31/75	05/14/81
Garvin, C. C., Jr.	08/01/75	12/31/86
Bennett, J. F.	08/01/75	01/31/89
Clarke, J. G.	12/01/75	08/31/92
Gray, H. J.	01/26/77	05/14/80
Bromery, R. W.	10/26/77	04/24/96
Dean, J. F.	09/01/78	08/31/83
Shaub, H. A.	05/17/79	05/15/86

CO./ORG.	TITLE
Exxon Corporation	Senior Vice President
Caterpillar Tractor Company	Director
Cornell University	Professor of Chemistry
Hospital Corporation of America; Prudential Insurance Company	Chairman and CEO (HCA); Chairman (PIC)
Exxon Corporation	Senior Vice President
Exxon Corporation	Senior Vice President
Otto Wolff AG	Chairman and CEO; President; Chairman of the Management Board
Exxon Corporation	Senior Vice President
Exxon Company, U.S.A.	Chairman and CEO
Exxon Corporation	President
Beloit College	President; President Emeritus
British American Tobacco Company Ltd.; British Leyland Ltd.	Chairman; Chairman (British Leyland); President; President (retired)
The Proctor & Gamble Company	Chairman and CEO; Chairman of the Executive Committee; Chairman (retired)
Exxon Corporation	Chairman (retired)
Exxon Corporation	Chairman and CEO
Exxon Corporation	Senior Vice President
Exxon Corporation	Senior Vice President
United Technologies Corporation	Chairman and President; Chairman and CEO
University of Massachusetts Amherst	Executive Vice President and Chancellor; Commonwealth Professor of Geophysics; President
Exxon Corporation	Senior Vice President
Campbell Soup Company	President and CEO; President and CEO (retired)

PERSON NAME	EFFECTIVE DATE	END DATE
O'Loughlin, M. E. J.	05/17/79	05/21/87
Phillips, B. E.	05/17/79	05/18/89
Richman, J. M.	05/15/80	05/19/83
Rawl, L. G.	12/01/80	04/28/93
Andres, W. A.	05/14/81	04/24/91
Hay, J. T.	05/14/81	05/30/01
Howell, W. R.	07/28/82	05/28/08
Laing, H., Baron Laing of Dunphail	05/17/84	04/27/94
Raymond, L. R.	09/01/84	05/31/05
MacVicar, M. L.	05/16/85	09/30/91
McIvor, D. K.	05/16/85	12/31/92
Sitter, C. R.	05/16/85	01/31/96
Lippincott, P. E.	01/29/86	05/28/08
Williams, J. D.	10/26/88	04/30/97
Calloway, D. W.	12/21/88	07/09/98
Steele, J. H.	08/03/89	04/30/97
Nelson, M. C.	04/24/91	05/31/12
Wilhelm, R. E.	09/01/92	01/01/00
Houghton, J. R.	06/29/94	05/27/09

CO./ORG.	TITLE
Exxon Corporation	Senior Vice President
Clark Equipment Company	Chairman and President; Chairman (retired)
Dart & Kraft Inc.	Chairman and CEO
Exxon Corporation	Senior Vice President; President; Chairman and CEO
Dayton Hudson Corporation	Chairman; Chairman and CEO; Chairman (retired)
Texas Foundation for High Education; Lomas & Nettleton Financial Corporation	Chairman (TFHE); Chairman and CEO (L&NFC); CEO (L&NFC; retired)
J. C. Penney Company, Inc.	Chairman and CEO; Chairman Emeritus
United Biscuits, plc	Chairman and Life President
Exxon Corporation and Exxon Mobil Corporation	Senior Vice President; President; Chairman and CEO
Massachusetts Institute of Technology	Dean for Undergraduate Education; Professor of Physical Science and Cecil and Ida Green Professor of Education
Exxon Corporation	Senior Vice President
Exxon Corporation	Senior Vice President; President
Scott Paper Company; Campbell Soup Company	Chairman and CEO (SPC); Chairman (CSC)
Warner-Lambert Company	Chairman and CEO; Chairman and CEO (retired)
PepsiCo Inc.	Chairman and CEO; Chairman and CEO (retired)
Corporation of Woods Hole Oceanographic Institution	Senior Scientist; President Emeritus
Carlson Companies, Inc.	Chairman and CEO
Exxon Corporation and Exxon Mobil Corporation	Senior Vice President
Corning Incorporated	Chairman and CEO; Chairman of the Board Emeritus

PERSON NAME	EFFECTIVE DATE	END DATE
Longwell, H. J.	10/25/95	12/30/04
Boskin, M. J.	01/31/96	
King, R. C.	06/24/97	05/26/10
Dahan, R.	01/01/98	06/30/02
Shipley, W. V.	04/29/98	05/27/09
Esrey, W. T.	07/30/98	05/28/03
Noto, L. A.	11/30/99	01/31/01
Munro, J. R.	11/30/99	05/30/01
Heimbold, C. A., Jr.	11/30/99	08/31/01
Renna, E. A.	11/30/99	01/31/02
Fites, D. V.	11/30/99	05/26/04
Kaplan, H. L.	11/30/99	05/26/04
McKinnell, H. A., Jr.	10/29/02	05/30/07
Tillerson, R. W.	03/01/04	
George, W. W.	05/25/05	
Simon, J. S.	01/25/06	05/28/08
Palmisano, S. J.	01/25/06	
Reinemund, S. S.	05/30/07	
Faulkner, L. R.	01/30/08	
Whitacre, E. E., Jr.	05/28/08	
Frazier, K. C.	05/27/09	
Brabeck-Letmathe, P.	05/26/10	
Fishman, J. S.	05/26/10	
Fore, H. H.	02/29/12	

CO./ORG.	TITLE
Exxon Corporation and Exxon Mobil Corporation	Senior Vice President; Executive Vice President
Stanford University	T. M. Friedman Professor of Economics and Hoover Institution Senior Fellow
General Mills Foundation; General Mills, Inc.	President and Executive Director; Vice President
Exxon Corporation and Exxon Mobil Corporation	Senior Vice President; Executive Vice President
The Chase Manhattan Corporation	Chairman and CEO; Chairman and CEO (retired)
Sprint Corporationo	Chairman and CEO
Exxon Mobil Corporation	Vice Chairman
Time Inc.	Former Chairman and CEO
Bristol-Myers Squibb Company	Chairman and CEO
Exxon Mobil Corporation	Senior Vice President
Caterpillar Inc.	Chairman and CEO (retired)
Skadden, Arps, Slate, Meagher & Flom LLP	Of Counsel
Pfizer, Inc.	Chairman and CEO
Exxon Mobil Corporation	President; Chairman and CEO
Harvard University	Professor of Management Practice
Exxon Mobil Corporation	Senior Vice President
IBM Corporation	Chairman
Wake Forest University	Dean of Business
The University of Texas at Austin	President Emeritus
General Motors; AT&T Inc.	Former Chairman (GM); Chairman Emeritus (AT&T)
Merck & Co., Inc.	Chairman, President and CEO
Nestle	Chairman
The Travelers Companies	Chairman and CEO
Holsman International	Chairman

PERSON NAME	EFFECTIVE DATE	END DATE	TITLE
CHAIRMEN			
Jamieson, J. K.	07/31/75	05/14/81	Chairman
Garvin, C. C., Jr.	08/01/75	12/31/86	Chairman & CEO
Rawl, L. G.	01/01/87	04/28/93	Chairman & CEO
Raymond, L. R.	04/28/93	12/31/05	Chairman & CEO
Noto, L. A.	11/30/99	01/31/01	Vice Chairman
Tillerson, R. W.	01/01/06		Chairman & CEO
PRESIDENTS			
Garvin, C. C., Jr.	11/01/72	07/31/75	President
Kauffmann, H. C.	08/01/75	05/16/85	President
Rawl, L. G.	05/16/85	12/31/86	President
Raymond, L. R.	01/01/87	04/28/93	President
Sitter, C. R.	04/28/93	01/31/96	President
Tillerson, R. W.	03/01/04	12/31/05	President
SENIOR AND EXECUTIVE VICE PRESIDENTS			
Barrow, T. D.	05/18/72	11/15/78	Senior Vice President
Bennett, J. F.	08/01/75	01/31/89	Senior Vice President
Campbell, N. J., Jr.	01/01/71	11/30/76	Senior Vice President
Clarke, J. G.	12/01/75	08/31/92	Senior Vice President
Cox, D. M.	05/12/71	05/16/85	Senior Vice President
Dahan, R.	10/25/95	08/01/01	Senior Vice President
Dahan, R.	08/01/01	06/30/02	Executive Vice President
Dean, J. F.	09/01/78	08/31/83	Senior Vice President
Galante, E. G.	08/01/01	01/31/06	Senior Vice President
Harrison, C. M.	09/01/92	12/31/94	Senior Vice President
Hess, E. J.	02/01/93	01/31/98	Senior Vice President
Humphreys, D. D.	01/25/06	04/30/11	Senior Vice President and Treasurer

PERSON NAME	EFFECTIVE DATE	END DATE	TITLE
Longwell, H. J.	01/01/95	08/01/01	Senior Vice President
Longwell, H. J.	08/01/01	12/30/04	Executive Vice President
McGill, S. R.	10/01/04	07/31/07	Senior Vice President
McIvor, D. K.	04/23/85	12/31/92	Senior Vice President
O'Loughlin, M. E. J.	05/17/79	05/21/87	Senior Vice President
Piercy, G. T.	05/13/70	11/30/80	Senior Vice President
Rawl, L. G.	12/01/80	05/16/85	Senior Vice President
Raymond, L. R.	09/01/84	12/31/86	Senior Vice President
Renna, E. A.	11/30/99	08/01/01	Senior Vice President
Renna, E. A.	08/01/01	01/31/02	Executive Vice President
Simon, J. S.	01/25/06	05/28/08	Senior Vice President
Sitter, C. R.	05/16/85	04/28/93	Senior Vice President
Tillerson, R. W.	08/01/01	03/01/04	Senior Vice President
Wilhelm, R. E.	09/01/92	01/01/00	Senior Vice President
Wright, M. A.	01/01/73	04/01/76	Executive Vice President
Albers, M. W.	04/01/07		Senior Vice President
Dolan, M. J.	04/01/08		Senior Vice President
Swiger, A. P.	04/01/09		Senior Vice President
Humphreys, D. D.	04/30/11		Senior Vice President and Principal Financial Officer

TREASURERS

Hamilton, A. C.	05/13/70	05/15/80	Treasurer
Hamilton, A. C.	05/15/80	05/31/83	Treasurer and Vice President
Robinson, E. A.	06/01/83	12/31/98	Treasurer and Vice President
Risch, F. A.	01/01/99	06/30/04	Treasurer and Vice President

PERSON NAME	EFFECTIVE DATE	END DATE	TITLE
Humphreys, D. D.	07/01/04	01/25/06	Treasurer and Vice President
Humphreys, D. D.	01/25/06	04/30/11	Treasurer and Senior Vice President
Schleckser, R. N.	05/01/11		Treasurer and Vice President

SECRETARIES AND INVESTOR RELATIONS

PERSON NAME	EFFECTIVE DATE	END DATE	TITLE
Anderson, R. E.	11/01/72	09/01/77	Secretary
Faggioli, R. E.	10/01/77	09/01/85	Secretary
Cattarulla, E. R.	09/01/85	08/01/90	Secretary and Vice President
Baird, D. L., Jr.	08/01/90	02/22/95	Secretary
Townsend, T. P.	07/01/90	01/31/02	Vice President, Investor Relations
Townsend, T. P.	02/22/95	01/31/02	Vice President, Investor Relations and Secretary
Mulva, P. T.	02/01/02	06/30/04	Vice President, Investor Relations and Secretary
Hubble, H. H.	07/01/04	10/01/08	Vice President, Investor Relations and Secretary
Rosenthal, D. S.	10/01/08		Vice President, Investor Relations and Secretary

GENERAL COUNSEL

PERSON NAME	EFFECTIVE DATE	END DATE	TITLE
Lombard, R. S.	09/17/73	05/15/80	General Counsel
Lombard, R. S.	05/15/80	01/31/93	General Counsel and Vice President
Roberts, C. K.	02/01/93	12/31/94	General Counsel and Vice President

PERSON NAME	EFFECTIVE DATE	END DATE	TITLE
Matthews, C. W.	01/01/95	02/28/10	General Counsel and Vice President
Balagia, S. J.	03/01/10		General Counsel and Vice President

TAX COUNSEL

PERSON NAME	EFFECTIVE DATE	END DATE	TITLE
Hayes, A. M.	07/28/76	06/30/80	General Tax Counsel
Schroder, R. A.	07/01/80	12/31/88	General Tax Counsel and Vice President
O'Brien, W. D.	01/01/89	12/31/94	General Tax Counsel and Vice President
Sullivan, P. E.	01/01/95	03/31/07	General Tax Counsel and Vice President
LaSala, S. R.	04/01/07	02/28/10	General Tax Counsel and Vice President
Spellings, J. M.	03/01/10		General Tax Counsel and Vice President

CONTROLLERS

PERSON NAME	EFFECTIVE DATE	END DATE	TITLE
Monroe, A. L.	7/1/73	5/31/77	Controller
LeGrange, U. J.	06/01/77	05/15/80	Controller
LeGrange, U. J.	05/15/80	05/31/83	Controller and Vice President
Monroe, A. L.	06/01/83	08/31/86	Controller and Vice President
Steine, D.	09/01/86	12/31/93	Controller and Vice President
Cook, W. B.	01/01/94	06/30/97	Controller and Vice President
Humphreys, D. D.	07/01/97	06/30/04	Controller and Vice President
Mulva, P. T.	07/01/04		Controller and Vice President

PERSON NAME	EFFECTIVE DATE	END DATE	TITLE
CORPORATE PLANNING			
Belknap, N.	04/01/73	05/31/79	Vice President, Corporate Planning
Sitter, C. R.	06/01/79	01/31/81	Vice President, Corporate Planning
Kruizenga, R. J.	02/01/81	12/31/92	Vice President, Corporate Planning
Goldmann, S. F.	01/01/93	10/01/95	General Manager, Corporate Planning
Harris, J. P.	10/01/95	04/01/97	General Manager, Corporate Planning
Brenneman, R. A.	04/30/97	11/30/99	General Manager, Corporate Planning
Tan, P. C.	11/30/99	04/01/01	General Manager, Corporate Planning
Glass, S. J., Jr.	05/30/01	12/31/01	General Manager, Corporate Planning
Genova, J. V.	04/24/02	08/18/03	General Manager, Corporate Planning
Kelly, A. J.	09/24/03	01/31/05	General Manager, Corporate Planning
Spellings, J. M.	02/01/05	03/31/07	General Manager, Corporate Planning
Luxbacher, R. A.	04/01/07	02/01/09	General Manager, Corporate Planning
Colton, W. M.	02/01/09		Vice President, Corporate Strategic Planning
VICE PRESIDENTS			
Hedlund, C. J.	02/01/68	10/31/79	Vice President
Peyton, C. O.	05/13/70	12/15/76	Vice President
Holmer, E. C.	01/01/73	03/01/86	Vice President
Meyer, R.	01/01/73	05/19/88	Vice President

PERSON NAME	EFFECTIVE DATE	END DATE	TITLE
Swan, D. O.	01/01/73	04/26/76	Vice President
Winslow, R. A.	08/28/74	05/14/79	Vice President
Dolph, R. N.	12/15/76	06/30/86	Vice President
Kirkley, T. A.	11/01/79	02/28/81	Vice President
Faggioli, R. E.	05/15/80	09/01/85	Vice President
McCardell, W. M.	05/15/80	09/01/83	Vice President
Winslow, R. A.	01/01/81	04/01/85	Vice President
Kruger, W. D.	04/01/81	05/16/85	Vice President
Ingram, R. M.	09/01/83	06/30/86	Vice President
Strohl, L. K.	04/01/85	11/18/87	Vice President
Crutchfield, J. D.	05/16/85	06/30/86	Vice President
McBrayer, H. E.	03/01/86	12/31/91	Vice President
Kirkley, T. A.	05/01/86	05/31/90	Vice President
Reid, R. G.	05/01/86	01/01/88	Vice President
Reso, S. J.	01/01/88	05/03/92	Vice President
Stevens, W. D.	01/31/88	01/31/92	Vice President
Larkins, R. P.	06/01/90	03/01/95	Vice President
Thompson, J. L.	10/01/91	05/31/04	Vice President
Nesbitt, R. B.	01/01/92	12/31/98	Vice President
Longwell, H. J.	02/01/92	12/31/94	Vice President
Dahan, R.	09/01/92	10/25/95	Vice President
Condray, A. L.	01/01/95	11/30/99	Vice President
Roxburgh, C. D.	03/01/95	05/31/97	Vice President
McMillan, J. T.	06/01/97	06/30/02	Vice President
McGill, S. R.	01/01/98	09/30/04	Vice President
Sanders, D. S.	01/01/99	08/31/04	Vice President
Cramer, H. R.	11/30/99	12/31/11	Vice President
Koonce, K. T.	11/30/99	06/30/03	Vice President
Pryor, S. D.	11/30/99	12/31/01	Vice President
Simon, J. S.	11/30/99	11/30/04	Vice President
Kohlenberger, G. L.	01/01/02	11/30/07	Vice President

PERSON NAME	EFFECTIVE DATE	END DATE	TITLE
Dingle, P. J.	07/01/03	09/19/06	Vice President
Cejka, A. T.	06/01/04	08/31/10	Vice President
Dolan, M. J.	09/01/04	03/31/08	Vice President
Foster, M. E.	10/01/04	03/31/08	Vice President
Pryor, S. D.	12/01/04		Vice President
Swiger, A. P.	10/01/06	04/01/09	Vice President
Kelly, A. J.	12/01/07		Vice President
Glass, Jr., S. J.	04/01/08	07/31/12	Vice President
Kruger, R. M.	04/01/08		Vice President
Owen, O. K.	02/01/09	06/30/11	Vice President
Walters, T. R.	04/01/09		Vice President
Franklin, R. S.	05/01/09		Vice President
Greenlee, S. M.	09/01/10		Vice President
Jones D. J.	05/13/70	12/08/76	Vice President, Finance
Bonn, R. T.	05/13/70	06/30/76	Vice President, Gas
Hoglund, F. E.	07/01/76	11/07/77	Vice President, Gas
Stevens, W. D.	01/01/78	07/31/78	Vice President, Gas
Reso, S. J.	08/01/78	06/30/80	Vice President, Gas
Perkins, F. M.	07/01/80	05/16/85	Vice President, Gas
Kruger, W. D.	05/16/85	06/30/86	Vice President, Gas
Kirkley, T. A.	10/01/75	07/14/78	Vice President, Logistics
Beresford, R. H.	07/15/78	05/17/79	Vice President, Logistics
Herman, R. H.	10/01/75	05/16/79	Vice President, Marketing
McCardell, W. M.	08/01/77	08/31/80	Vice President, Mining and Synthetic Fuels
Beresford, R. H.	05/17/79	06/30/86	Vice President, Petroleum Products

PERSON NAME	EFFECTIVE DATE	END DATE	TITLE
Patterson, C. R.	07/01/74	07/31/77	Vice President, Producing
McIvor, D. K.	08/01/77	06/30/81	Vice President, Producing
Wheeler, C. B.	07/01/81	09/30/83	Vice President, Producing
Harrison, C. M.	10/01/83	05/16/85	Vice President, Producing
Perkins, F. M.	05/16/85	06/30/86	Vice President, Producing
Holloway, F. A. L.	04/01/73	10/31/78	Vice President, Science and Technology
David, E. E.	11/01/78	07/31/80	Vice President, Science and Technology
Mathis, J. F.	08/01/80	04/01/84	Vice President, Science and Technology
Harvey, R. H.	05/14/81	07/31/83	Vice President, Communication and Computer Science
Nobles, W. B.	08/01/83	06/30/86	Vice President, Communication and Computer Science
Nobles, W. B.	07/01/86	12/31/90	Vice President, Information Systems and Central Services
McCullough, G. B.	05/15/80	06/30/86	Vice President, Employee Relations
Tiedemann, T. H., Jr.	07/01/86	08/31/90	Vice President, Human Resources
Gillis, M. E.	09/01/90	12/31/93	Vice President, Human Resources
Sanders, D. S.	01/01/94	02/28/98	Vice President, Human Resources

PERSON NAME	EFFECTIVE DATE	END DATE	TITLE
Hearn, T. J.	03/01/98	12/31/01	Vice President, Human Resources
Cavanaugh, L. J.	01/01/02	03/31/12	Vice President, Human Resources
Farrant, M. A.	04/01/12		Vice President, Human Resources
Stamas, S.	06/01/73	06/30/86	Vice President, Public Affairs
Cattarulla, E. R.	07/01/86	08/01/90	Vice President, Corporate and Public Affairs
Cattarulla, E. R.	08/01/90	12/31/94	Vice President, Public Affairs
Atkiss, A. W.	01/01/95	11/30/99	Vice President, Public Affairs
Cohen, K. P.	11/30/99	01/09/09	Vice President, Public Affairs
Cohen, K. P.	01/09/09		Vice President, Public and Government Affairs
Smiley, D. E.	02/22/78	07/31/96	Vice President, Washington Office
Rouse, J. J.	08/01/96	05/31/04	Vice President, Washington Office
Nelson, R. D.	06/01/04	03/31/09	Vice President, Washington Office
Fariello, T. M.	02/01/09		Vice President. Washington Office
Roberts, N. J.	05/14/81	6/31/81	Vice President, Medicine & Environmental Health
McDonagh, T. J.	07/01/81	01/31/97	Vice President, Medicine and Occupational Health
Hess, E. J.	01/15/90	01/31/93	Vice President, Environment and Safety

PERSON NAME	EFFECTIVE DATE	END DATE	TITLE
Graves, G. L.	02/01/93	11/30/95	Vice President, Environmental and Safety
Sprow, F. B.	12/01/95	11/30/04	Vice President, Safety, Health and Environment
Stuewer, S. K.	12/01/04	12/31/11	Vice President, Environmental Policy and Planning
Woodbury, J. J.	07/01/11		Vice President, Safety, Security, Health and Environment

APPENDIX D

EXXONMOBIL OPERATING STATISTICS, 1975–2009

FINANCIAL DATA

YEAR	SALES AND OTHER OPERATING REVENUE (M$)	TOTAL ASSETS AT YEAR END (M$)	DEBT TO CAPITAL (%)	NET INCOME CORP (M$)	UPSTREAM E&P (M$)	DOWN-STREAM R&M (MARINE) (M$)	CHEMICAL (M$)
2009	301,500	233,323	7.7	19,280	17,107	1,781	2,309
2008	459,579	228,052	7.4	45,220	35,402	8,151	2,957
2007	390,328	242,082	7.1	40,610	26,497	9,573	4,563
2006	365,467	219,015	6.6	39,500	26,230	8,454	4,382
2005	358,955	208,335	6.5	36,130	24,349	7,992	3,943
2004	291,252	195,256	7.3	25,330	16,675	5,706	3,428
2003	237,054	174,278	9.3	21,510	14,502	3,516	1,432
2002	200,949	152,644	12.2	11,460	9,598	1,300	830
2001	208,715	143,174	12.4	15,320	10,736	4,227	707
2000	227,596	149,000	15.4	17,720	12,685	3,418	1,161
1999	181,759	144,521	22.0	7,910	6,244	1,227	1,354
1998	115,417	92,630	16.2	6,370	2,708	2,458	1,213
1997	135,142	96,064	17.8	8,460	4,693	2,063	1,368
1996	131,543	95,527	17.7	7,510	5,058	885	1,199

OTHER (M$)	NET INCOME (U.S. GAAP) E&P, R&M, CHEMICAL US (M$)	NON-US (M$)	OTHER (M$)	ROCE CORP (%)	UPS (%)	DOWN (%)	CHEM (%)
(1,917)	3,509	17,688	(1,917)	16.3	23.4	7.1	13.9
(1,290)	8,616	37,894	(1,290)	34.2	53.6	31.8	20.4
(23)	10,171	30,462	(23)	31.8	41.7	37.8	34.0
434	10,778	28,288	434	32.2	45.3	35.8	33.2
(154)	11,297	24,987	(154)	31.3	45.7	32.4	28.0
(479)	8,154	17,655	(479)	23.8	32.9	21.0	23.5
2,060	5,634	13,816	2,060	20.9	30.4	13.0	10.2
(268)	3,601	8,127	(268)	13.5	22.3	5.0	6.1
(350)	6,155	9,515	(350)	17.8	26.8	16.1	6.4
456	6,747	10,517	456	20.6	30.8	12.3	8.4
(915)	3,188	5,637	(915)	10.3	15.2	4.4	10.9
(9)	2,186	4,193	(9)	12.2	11.8	15.4	14.6
336	3,052	5,072	336	16.5	21.3	13.2	17.4
368	2,651	4,491	368	14.7	23.0	5.6	16.1

FINANCIAL DATA, CONT'D

YEAR	SALES AND OTHER OPERATING REVENUE (M$)	TOTAL ASSETS AT YEAR END (M$)	DEBT TO CAPITAL (%)	NET INCOME CORP (M$)	UPSTREAM E&P (M$)	DOWN-STREAM R&M (MARINE) (M$)	CHEMICAL (M$)
1995	121,804	91,296	19.0	6,470	3,412	1,272	2,018
1994	112,128	87,862	24.3	5,100	2,782	1,389	954
1993	109,532	84,145	25.3	5,280	3,313	2,015	411
1992	115,672	85,030	26.8	4,770	3,374	1,574	451
1991	115,068	87,560	25.6	5,600	3,128	2,555	512
1990	115,794	87,707	27.7	5,010	4,038	1,315	522
1989	95,173	83,219	32.6	3,510	3,058	1,098	1,082
1988	87,252	74,293	22.1	5,260	2,591	1,812	1,306
1987	82,083	74,042	18.2	4,840	3,767	509	750
1986	74,987	69,484	19.0	5,360	3,060	1,934	470
1985	91,620	69,160	20.6	4,870	4,937	807	249
1984	95,873	63,278	17.5	5,528	4,789	345	430
1983	93,447	62,963	15.3	4,978	4,079	1,055	270
1982	102,059	62,289	19.8	4,186	3,431	1,065	93
1981	113,220	61,575	22.0	4,826	4,117	1,161	238
1980	108,412	57,854	18.3	5,350	3,797	1,825	345
1979	83,555	49,490	20.7	4,295	3,017	1,612	456
1978	63,896	41,531	19.6	2,763	2,484	826	268
1977	57,529	38,437	20.9	2,443	2,169	749	222
1976	51,626	36,280	22.8	2,615	2,063	600	251
1975	47,796	32,813	16.6	2,456	1,937	445	199

OTHER (M$)	NET INCOME (U.S. GAAP) E&P, R&M, CHEMICAL US (M$)	NON-US (M$)	OTHER (M$)	ROCE CORP (%)	UPS (%)	DOWN (%)	CHEM (%)
(232)	2,307	4,395	(232)	13.8	15.4	8.2	29.6
(25)	1,560	3,565	(25)	11.2	12.5	9.4	14.7
(459)	1,667	4,072	(459)	12.0	15.0	14.0	6.4
(629)	1,192	4,207	(629)	11.0	15.1	10.7	7.0
(595)	1,478	4,717	(595)	12.8	13.8	16.8	8.2
(865)	1,691	4,184	(865)	12.8	17.4	9.1	9.3
(1,728)	2,185	3,053	(1,728)	9.7	13.6	8.7	22.4
(449)	2,227	3,482	(449)	14.0	12.1	15.0	29.8
(186)	1,725	3,301	(186)	11.9	18.2	4.5	19.0
(104)	1,423	4,041	(104)	14.2	16.3	19.2	12.9
(1,123)	2,463	3,530	(1,123)	14.2	28.8	8.5	6.9
(36)	2,377	3,187	(36)	15.4	29.3	4.0	11.5
(426)	2,440	2,964	(426)	14.5	24.9	10.9	7.1
(403)	2,341	2,248	(403)	11.7	21.3	9.4	2.6
(690)	2,480	3,036	(690)	14.8	28.7	9.7	7.3
(617)	2,406	3,561	(617)	17.3	30.0	15.6	11.8
(790)	1,748	3,337	(790)	16.6	26.1	15.4	18.2
(815)	1,650	1,928	(815)	12.5	22.9	8.5	12.1
(697)	1,488	1,652	(697)	11.9	22.7	7.8	11.5
(299)	1,428	1,486	(299)	12.0	26.2	6.3	15.3
(125)	1,263	1,318	(125)	11.2	34.1	5.2	13.9

NOTES:

Sales and operating revenue includes sales-based taxes of $25,936 million for 2009, $34,508 million for 2008, $31,728 million for 2007, $30,381 million in 2006, and $30,742 million for 2005.

Sales and operating revenue includes $30,810 million for 2005 purchases/sales contracts with the same counterparty. Associated costs were included in crude oil and product purchases. Effective January 1, 2006, these purchases/sales were recorded on a net basis with no resulting impact on net imcome.

OPERATING DATA—UPSTREAM / SHAREHOLDER

YEAR	CRUDE OIL AND NATURAL GAS LIQUIDS PRODUCTION (KBD)	NATURAL GAS PRODUCTION AVAILABLE FOR SALE (MCFD)	OIL-EQUIVALENT PRODUCTION (KOEBD)	PROVED RESERVES REPLACEMENT RATIO[1,2] (%)
2009	2,387	9,273	3,932	134
2008	2,405	9,095	3,921	110
2007	2,616	9,384	4,180	132
2006	2,681	9,334	4,237	129
2005	2,523	9,251	4,065	129
2004	2,571	9,864	4,215	125
2003	2,516	10,119	4,203	107
2002	2,496	10,452	4,238	118
2001	2,542	10,279	4,255	111
2000	2,553	10,343	4,277	112
1999	2,517	10,308	4,235	106
1998	1,567	6,322	2,621	106
1997	1,599	6,339	2,656	121
1996	1,615	6,577	2,711	108
1995	1,726	6,013	2,728	110
1994	1,709	5,978	2,705	106
1993	1,667	5,825	2,638	96
1992	1,705	5,661	2,649	65
1991	1,715	5,497	2,631	91
1990	1,712	5,318	2,598	98
1989	1,804	5,385	2,702	153
1988	1,919	5,192	2,784	102
1987	1,835	5,227	2,706	114
1986	1,796	5,329	2,684	not in F&O
1985	1,720	5,661	2,664	
1984	1,678	5,918	2,664	
1983	1,607	5,628	2,545	
1982	1,439	5,749	2,397	

RESERVES REPLACEMENT COST[3] ($/B)	REGULAR EMPLOYEES AT YEAR END (K)	YEAR-END SHARE PRICE[4] ($/SH)	DIVIDENDS PER SHARE[4] ($/SH)	TOTAL SHAREHOLDER RETURN[5] (%)
10.83	80.7	68.19	1.66	(12.6)
10.76	79.9	79.83	1.55	(13.2)
6.50	80.8	93.69	1.37	24.3
7.00	82.1	76.63	1.28	39.2
6.25	83.7	56.17	1.14	11.7
5.29	85.9	51.26	1.06	27.9
6.53	88.3	41.00	0.98	20.5
4.97	92.5	34.94	0.92	(8.9)
4.45	97.9	39.30	0.91	(7.6)
3.39	99.6	86.94	1.76	10.2
4.62	107	80.56	1.69	12.5
5.22	79	73.13	1.64	22.4
4.02	80	61.19	1.63	28.3
4.02	79	98.00	3.12	26.3
3.85	82	80.50	3.00	38.1
3.44	86	60.75	2.91	0.8
4.30	91	63.13	2.88	7.9
7.10	95	61.13	2.83	5.2
5.38	101	60.88	2.68	23.3
4.59	104	51.75	2.47	8.9
4.41	104	50.00	2.30	19.5
4.33	101	44.00	2.15	21.1
4.17	100	38.13	1.90	13.7
not in F&O	135	70.13	3.60	34.8
	146	55.13	3.45	31.1
	150	45.00	3.35	30.3
	156	37.38	3.10	37.1
	173	29.75	3.00	5.5

OPERATING DATA—UPSTREAM / SHAREHOLDER, CONT'D

YEAR	CRUDE OIL AND NATURAL GAS LIQUIDS PRODUCTION (KBD)	NATURAL GAS PRODUCTION AVAILABLE FOR SALE (MCFD)	OIL- EQUIVALENT PRODUCTION (KOEBD)	PROVED RESERVES REPLACEMENT RATIO[1,2] (%)
1981	1,405	6,620	2,508	
1980	1,758	7,033	2,930	
1979	2,601	7,860	3,911	
1978	2,454	7,882	3,768	
1977	2,512	8,422	3,916	
1976	2,380	8,849	3,855	
1975	3,151	9,092	4,666	

RESERVES REPLACEMENT COST[3] ($/B)	REGULAR EMPLOYEES AT YEAR END (K)	YEAR-END SHARE PRICE[4] ($/SH)	DIVIDENDS PER SHARE[4] ($/SH)	TOTAL SHAREHOLDER RETURN[5] (%)
180	31.25	3.00	(15.3)
177	80.60	5.40	57.9
169	55.13	3.90	20.4
130	49.13	3.30	9.2
127	48.13	3.00	(4.7)
126	53.60	2.73	27.5
137	88.75	5.00	45.7

NOTES:

(1) Reserves determined on ExxonMobil's basis
(2) Excluding asset sales and the 2007 Venezuela expropriation, includes Syncrude Oil Sands operations
(3) Includes Syncryde Oil Sands operations
(4) Not split adjusted
(5) Share price appreciation plus reinvested dividends

CAPITAL EXPENDITURES

YEAR	CAPEX CORP (M$)	UPSTREAM (EXPL, PROD, COAL, POWER) (M$)	DOWNSTREAM (REF, MKT, PIPELINE, MARINE) (M$)	CHEMICAL (M$)	OTHER (M$)	UNITED STATES (M$)	CANADA/ LATIN AMERICA (M$)	CANADA (M$)
2009	27,092	20,704	3,196	3,148	44	5,459	3,448	
2008	26,143	19,734	3,529	2,819	61	5,472	1,926	
2007	20,853	15,724	3,303	1,782	44	3,744	1,522	
2006	19,855	16,231	2,729	756	139	3,720	1,862	
2005	17,699	14,470	2,495	654	80	3,218	1,940	
2004	14,885	11,715	2,405	690	75	3,025	1,867	
2003	15,525	11,988	2,781	692	64	3,766	1,826	
2002	13,955	10,394	2,450	954	157	3,957		1,513
2001	12,311	8,816	2,322	872	301	3,942		1,262
2000	11,168	6,933	2,618	1,468	149	3,338		1,004
1999	13,307	8,428	2,401	2,243	235	3,402		1,204
1998	10,035	6,157	2,019	1,742	117	2,868		470
1997	8,811	5,610	1,987	1,049	165	2,619		517
1996	9,226	5,419	2,004	1,615	188	2,456		438
1995	8,966	5,538	2,112	1,087	229	2,139		438
1994	7,834	4,692	2,238	598	306	2,023		421
1993	8,167	5,077	2,250	580	260	2,395		410
1992	8,758	5,454	2,191	661	452	2,559		401
1991	8,823	5,757	1,883	677	506	3,055		505
1990	8,333	4,958	1,813	1,105	457	2,780		569
1989	11,784	7,539	3,117	766	362	3,147		4,630
1988	7,508	5,028	1,594	571	315	2,860		1,184
1987	7,136	5,380	1,258	298	200	2,374		1,113
1986	7,219	5,168	1,545	277	229	3,040		514
1985	10,793	8,274	1,934	333	252	5,569		904
1984	9,755	7,748	1,409	322	276	4,958		605
1983	9,030	6,799	1,195	545	491	4,426		630
1982	11,412	7,844	1,621	917	1,030	5,837		974
1981	11,092	7,886	1,622	892	692	5,688		943

OTHER WESTERN HEMISPHERE (M$)	LATIN AMERICA (M$)	EUROPE (M$)	AFRICA (M$)	ASIA/ PACIFIC MID EAST (M$)	RUSSIA/ CASPIAN (M$)	OTHER (M$)	OTHER EASTERN HEMISPHERE (M$)	INT'L MARINE (M$)
		3,251	6,182	6,722	2,030			
		3,727	5,422	7,669	1,927			
		4,042	3,639	6,156	1,750			
		3,721	4,019	4,601	1,932			
		2,829	3,815	3,241	2,656			
		2,845	3,330	2,168	1,650			
		3,046	3,657	2,046	1,184			
		2,919	2,405	1,863	893	405		
		2,564	1,585	1,681	553	724		
	677	2,255	981	2,362			551	
	744	3,255		2,498			2,204	
	415	3,570		2,027			685	
	375	3,331		1,591			378	
	321	3,691		1,907			413	
	276	3,321		2,459			333	
	284	2,686		2,161			259	
	256	2,812		2,028			266	
	339	3,647		1,566			246	
	410	3,230		1,458			165	
	347	3,103					1,534	
289		2,152					1,566	
203		2,148					1,113	
269		1,731					1,649	
423		2,058					1,184	
479		2,223					1,618	
517		2,435					1,240	
561		1,967					1,446	
512		2,476					1,613	
424		2,499					1,538	

CAPITAL EXPENDITURES, CONT'D

YEAR	CAPEX CORP (M$)	UPSTREAM (EXPL, PROD, COAL, POWER) (M$)	DOWNSTREAM (REF, MKT, PIPELINE, MARINE) (M$)	CHEMICAL (M$)	OTHER (M$)	UNITED STATES (M$)	CANADA/ LATIN AMERICA (M$)	CANADA (M$)
1980	8,041	5,541	1,262	415	823	3,537		768
1979	7,396	5,021	1,111	433	831	3,619		762
1978	5,303	3,541	925	470	367	2,369		486
1977	4,599	3,167	964	311	157	2,030		400
1976	5,077	3,703	876	386	112	2,668		441
1975	4,526	2,941	1,214	263	108	2,117		379

OTHER WESTERN HEMI- SPHERE (M$)	LATIN AMERICA (M$)	EUROPE (M$)	AFRICA (M$)	ASIA/ PACIFIC MID EAST (M$)	RUSSIA/ CASPIAN (M$)	OTHER (M$)	OTHER EASTERN HEMI- SPHERE (M$)	INT'L MARINE (M$)
273		2,338					1,125	
225		1,822					968	
336		1,516					596	
82		1,279					483	325
36		1,257					424	251
23		1,139					605	263

OPERATING DATA—DOWNSTREAM/CHEMICAL

YEAR	REFINERY THROUGHPUT (KBD)	REFINERY CAPACITY UTILIZATION (%)	U.S. (%)	EUROPE (%)	REST OF WORLD (%)	PETROLEUM PRODUCT SALES (KBD)
2009	5,350	86	90	89	81	6,428
2008	5,416	87	87	92	84	6,761
2007	5,571	88	89	93	84	7,099
2006	5,603	88	90	92	84	7,247
2005	5,723	90	92	93	87	7,519
2004	5,713	90	95	93	84	7,511
2003	5,510	88	94	89	82	7,270
2002	5,443	87	97	88	79	7,075
2001	5,542	89	96	90	83	7,971
2000	5,642	90	96	91	84	7,993
1999	5,977	90	98	87	86	8,887
1998	3,928	90	95	88	88	5,433
1997	4,011	92	100	87	91	5,430
1996	3,792	89	95	84	90	5,211
1995	3,659	86	98	79	86	5,076
1994	3,680	88	97	84	87	5,028
1993	3,616	88	95	86	86	4,925
1992	3,619	87	91	86	84	4,909
1991	3,585	87	89	87	85	4,869
1990	3,546	85	83	85	88	4,755
1989	3,624	85	88	83	86	4,720
1988	3,370	82	85	80	83	4,396
1987	3,208	77	84	71	79	4,043
1986	3,032	74	90	62	78	4,043
1985	2,903	68	88	52	75	4,082

CHEMICAL PRIME PRODUCT SALES[1] (KTONS)	NUMBER OF SERVICE STATIONS OWNED (#)	ALL (#)	U.S.—ALL (#)	EUROPE ALL (#)	REST OF WORLD ALL (#)
24,825	9,965	27,720	10,216	6,827	10,677
24,982	10,516	28,674	10,451	6,927	11,296
27,480	11,446	32,386	10,904	7,092	14,390
27,350	12,151	33,848	11,117	7,394	15,337
26,777	12,856	35,432	11,536	7,591	16,305
27,788	13,659	37,374	12,119	7,881	17,374
26,567	14,377	39,488	12,473	8,399	18,616
26,606	15,084	41,786	13,133	8,768	19,885
25,780	15,516	42,853	13,306	9,039	20,508
25,637	15,850	45,001	14,038	9,282	21,681
25,283	16,565	48,233	16,520	9,572	22,141
17,204	11,310	32,311	8,524	9,340	14,447
17,301	11,920	33,021	8,416	9,772	14,833
15,712	11,516	31,369	8,334	10,173	12,862
14,377	11,520	31,721	8,215	10,355	13,151
13,969	11,727	32,935	8,593	10,645	13,697
13,393	12,077	33,849	9,029	10,989	13,831
13,463	12,488	35,368	9,809	11,338	14,221
11,790	13,126	37,165	10,727	11,839	14,599
11,693	13,255	38,826	11,560	Not publicly reported	27,266
Not publicly reported	13,952	41,066	11,984		29,082
	13,396	40,342	12,342		28,000

DATA IN THESE COLUMNS NOT PUBLICLY REPORTED PRIOR TO 1988.

OPERATING DATA—DOWNSTREAM/CHEMICAL, CONT'D

YEAR	REFINERY THROUGHPUT (KBD)	REFINERY CAPACITY UTILIZATION (%)	U.S. (%)	EUROPE (%)	REST OF WORLD (%)	PETROLEUM PRODUCT SALES (KBD)
1984	3,220	70	85	58	75	4,192
1983	3,266	69	80	57	75	4,085
1982	3,496	65	70	58	70	4,310
1981	3,878	70	73	62	77	4,601
1980	4,149	71	79	63	75	4,953
1979	4,354	73	84	67	72	5,319
1978	4,427	71	90	61	70	5,390
1977	4,348	70	92	60	66	5,266
1976	4,359	72	101	61	69	5,353
1975	4,331	65	95	56	59	4,990

(1) Prime Product Sales include ExxonMobil's share of equity company volumes and finished product transfers to the downsrtream. Carbon black oil and sulfur are excluded.

Source: *Exxon Mobil Corporation*

INDEX

Page numbers followed by *f* refer to figures. Notes are indicated by n and note
number following the page number, e.g.,
504n1. Initial articles (the, el-) are ignored
in sorting of titles and personal names.

A

Abu Dhabi, 65
Acción Democrática (Venezuela), 27
ACS (alternating current synthesis),
    191–192
ADEC (Alaska Department of Environ-
    mental Conservation), 265, 274
Africa Health Initiative, 357, 358*f*, 470
Agnew, Spiro, 92
Ahnert, Edward, 357
air quality standards. *See* Clean Air Act
    Amendments of 1970
Al Khaleej gas project (Qatar), 569n18
Alaska: as the last frontier, 539n14
Alaska Department of Environmental
    Conservation (ADEC), 265, 274
Alaska Natural Gas Transportation System
    (ANGTS), 117–120

Albers, Mark, 116, 126–127
Alito, Samuel, 306, 544n114
Aliyev, Heydar, 327
Almaty, Kazakhstan: Exxon Ventures
    office in, 316
alternating current synthesis (ACS),
    191–192
alternative energy: conservation as, 86–87;
    diversification into, 80, 185–196; elec-
    tric motors, 190–192; energy policy
    and, 84–85; Meyer on oil companies'
    role in, 79–80; solar power, 80–81, 81*f*,
    189–190. *See also* nuclear power
Alyeska (consortium), 90
Alyeska Pipeline Service Company: civil
    lawsuits against, 303; criticized for lack
    of preparedness for *Exxon Valdez*, 268–
    269; formation of, 90; responsibility for
    Exxon Valdez cleanup, 264
ambient air standards, 96, 102
American Petroleum Institute (API), 70,
    97, 432
Amoco: joint venture with Union Oil for
    Beaufort Sea drilling, 124; operations

in Azerbaijan, 327; Zhuhai refinery and chemical project, 414, 415–417, 559n109

Amoco Cadiz oil spill (1978), 541n49

Amoco Chemical, 407

Amuay (Venezuela) refinery, 370

Andrus, Cecil, 80

Anglo-American Polar Expedition, 113

Anglo-Persian Oil Company. *See* BP (British Petroleum)

Angola, 346–360; as Africa's largest oil producer, 359; Block 15 oil production, 350–351, 350*f*, 359; Chad vs., in oil production, 346–347; civil war, 347; as Cold War battlefield, 347, 349; deepwater potential of, 346; deepwater technology and Exxon performance, 352–353; early offshore oil production, 349; economic challenges, 346–347; establishing strong relations with, 351; ExxonMobil philanthropic contributions, 357–359; fast production system, 353; legal and regulatory framework encouraging oil industry development, 354–355; as member of OPEC, 355; Ministry of Petroleum, 355; mutual self-interest as key to success in, 351–352; negotiations for drilling rights, 349–350, 354; oil exploration in, 244; oil fields, map, 348*f*; political risk management by Exxon, 346, 353, 359–360; recoverable offshore oil reserves, 349, 350, 352; reserving ownership of hydrocarbon resources for nation, 355; tradition of oil production, 346–347; training and hiring of local workers by Exxon, 355–357

ANGTS (Alaska Natural Gas Transportation System), 117–120

anti-Americanism: in Middle East, 56

anti-oil policies, U.S.: Buy-Sell Program, 73–74; debate over windfall profits, 75; domestic oil price controls, 72–73; high oil prices and, 71–82; hostility toward oil industry, 72

antitrust laws and actions: breakup of Standard Oil of New Jersey, 9; Clayton Act of 1914, 9; Exxon as target of, 75–82; "Exxon Case" (FTC), 76; horizontal divestment proposals, 78–82; limiting capacity of American companies to compete in international markets, 76; new economies of oil undermining effectiveness of, 76–77; price fixing cases against oil companies, 76; revised guidelines on mergers, 426; Sherman Antitrust Act of 1890, 9; vertical divestment encouraging competition, 77–78

Aramco of Saudi Arabia: accommodation strategy, 37; American owners, prenationalization, 25–26, 36; as center of global oil production, 36–37; challenges to operations in 1970s, 40; Exxon interest in, 25, 36; limiting impact on Saudi culture, 37; management procedures, 37; oil policy conflicts with government as part-owner, 38–39; producer power impacts on, 37–38; profit-sharing policies, 37; Saudi government as part owner, 37–38. *See also* Saudi Aramco

Aramco Overseas Company B.V., 417

ARCO. *See* Atlantic Richfield Company (ARCO)

Arctic regions: Exxon/Imperial Oil cooperation in new technology development, 126; managerial and technical challenges for oil production, 112–127; permafrost as technical challenge, 93–94

Arkutun-Dagi oil field (Russia), 317

Arthur Kill oil spill (1990), 288–290

Aruba (Venezuela) refinery, 370–371

Ashland Oil–Marathon (USX) merger, 427

Asian Tigers, 398

Asia–Pacific region: Exxon expansion into, 398–399; ExxonMobil holdings, 419; post–World War II economic expansion, 398–399. *See also* names of *individual countries*

Atlantic Empress oil spill (1979), 541n49

Atlantic Richfield Company (ARCO): acquisition by BP, 126, 428; joint venture with Humble in Prudhoe Bay, 114; in Libya, 58; Lisburne oil field joint venture with Exxon, 124; merger increasing competitiveness of company, 58; as partner in Trans-Alaska Pipeline System, 90; Phillips Petroleum purchase of holdings on North Slope, 126

auto emissions: leaded gasoline and, 96–99; sulfates from catalytic converters, 99–100

auto industry: inability to meet EPA deadlines for unleaded gas in cars, 100

Azerbaijan: international oil company operations in, 327

B

Baku, Azerbaijan: Exxon Ventures office in, 316

Bamberg, James, 51–52

Bardgette, John, 130–131

barrels of oil equivalent (BOE): Bass Strait oil fields, 165; energy conservation and savings in, 386, 392; ExxonMobil reserves replacement, post-merger, 456; Groningen oil field, 138; North Sea oil production, 151; offshore Angola, 349; recoverable from U.S. Arctic, 122; Shell vs. Exxon oil reserves, 430; syncrude projects, 201–202, 204; Thunder Horse project, Gulf of Mexico, 485; use as fuel by Exxon's U.S. refineries, 382

Barrow, Tom, 315, 410–411

Barzan gas project (Qatar), 569n18

Bass Strait, Australia: Exxon oil production, 165; offshore drilling and operations, 163–164

Baton Rouge refinery explosion, 287–288

Baytown refinery: expansion and technological upgrades, 391–392

Baytown Turbine Generator Project, 384, 385f, 386, 556n44

Baze, Roy, 71

Beaufort Sea: ice island exploration platform model, 123f; Mukluk tract drilling, 123; offshore drilling projects, 124–125

Benicia refinery (California): divestment required for ExxonMobil merger, 368, 444, 445, 564n93; sale to Valero Energy Corporation, 453

Bennett, Jack, 247f; as deputy undersecretary of the treasury, 246; Exxon stock buyback initiative and, 248–250, 250f; financial innovation as chief financial officer, 248–252, 500; as mentor to financial executives, 247–248; shelf registration initiative, 250–251

Bering Sea: oil exploration, 125

Betancourt, Rómulo, 27

Biden, Joseph, 561n14

Big Oil: costs of breaking up, 77; criticism of price manipulation by, 71; evils of, as Rockefeller legacy, 10; horizontal divestment, 78–82; political challenges for, 69–110; public skepticism of, 69; vertical divestment encouraging competition, 77–78

Blair, John, 508n29

BNOC (British National Oil Company), 144–145, 148

BOE. *See* barrels of oil equivalent (BOE)

BP (British Petroleum): as co-owner of Hoover-Diana project, 484; dominance in Iranian oil industry, 50; elimination of Sohio and Amoco brands in retail marketing, 458; European partnership with Mobil, 431–432; investment in TNK (Russian oil company), 325;

joint venture with Sohio in Prudhoe Bay, 114; Macondo drilling rig blowout, 307–308; as member of "Seven Sisters," 1; merger with Amoco, 428, 434; merger with ARCO, 126, 428; Noto rejecting Mobil merger with, 432; operations in Azerbaijan, 327; as partner in Trans-Alaska Pipeline System, 90; Thunder Horse project, 485

Brent oil field (North Sea), 140, 150, 155, 165. *See also under* North Sea

British Gas Council, 143

British National Oil Company (BNOC), 144–145, 148

British Petroleum. *See* BP (British Petroleum)

Britoil, 145

Bureau of Competition Policy (Canada), 368

Business Roundtable, 70

Buy-Sell Program, 73–74

C

CAFE (Corporate Average Fuel Economy) standards, 84

California Air Resources Board, 105

Cameroon: oil pipeline from Chad, 336–342; treaty with Chad for oil project construction, 338. *See also* Chad

Canada: oil and gas reserves, 481; restructuring of downstream operations, 368–370. *See also* Imperial Oil Limited of Canada

Cannon, Howard, 561n14

capital allocations process, 378–379

capital prioritization exercise, 378–379

capitalist nationalization, 19, 24

"Caring Neighbors," 468

Carter Administration: energy policy, 82; pressure for horizontal divestiture of oil companies, 78, 80

Caspian Sea: oil exploration and production, 327–328

catalytic converters: sulfate emissions from, 99–100

Cejka, Tim, 316, 321

CERES (Coalition for Environmentally Responsible Economies) Principles, 543n83

Cerrejón coal mine (Colombia), 194–195, 195f, 196

Cerro Negro project (Mobil), 330

Chad: agreement with World Bank on use of oil revenues, 338; avoiding "oil curse" in, 345–346; changes in pipeline routing protecting settlements and environment, 343; Chevron and Petronas investments in, 341; compensation for use of land, 343; construction projects, 342; Déby government rewriting petroleum law and agreement with World Bank, 344; employment of local workers for oil project, 342; Exxon meetings with local communities, 342–343; joint ventures for oil field development in Doba Basin, 335–336; oil-led development and risk mitigation in, 334–346; Petroleum Revenue Management Law (1999), 338; pipeline from Doba Basin to Cameroon, 342; political upheaval in, 335; road construction in, 335f; socioeconomics of, 334–345; suspension of World Bank payments to, 344; treaty with Cameroon for oil project construction, 338; withdrawal of Shell and Elf from Chad oil joint venture, 338; World Bank loans for oil development, 337–340, 550n72

Chafee, John, 268–269

charitable activities. *See* philanthropic programs

Chávez, Hugo: failed military coup attempt, 329; policies and Exxon departure from Venezuela, 66; showdown with PDVSA, 331; social reforms and oil industry takeover, 330–331 chemicals: as byproducts of refining, 168–169; consolidation of Exxon and Mobil chemical businesses, 459–460, 565n111; diversification and, 168–175; integration of production with refining, 395–398, 458, 483; proximity of refining and chemicals in Exxon, 171; as separate industry from petroleum, 171–172; separation from refining operations, 170–171; transformation following ExxonMobil merger, 495–497. *See also* Exxon Chemical Company

Chevron: acquisition of Gulf Oil Corporation, 1, 248; investment in Chad oil development project, 341; merger with Texaco, 1, 428; sale of Chad oil fields to Elf, 336

China: Exxon operations in special economic zone near Guangdon province, 411; Exxon service stations allowed outside special economic zones, 414, 415f; Fujian refinery and chemical project, 415–417; incentive-based economy, movement toward, 410; oil exploration in, 411; pumped-storage facility negotiations, 412, 414; Quanzhou project negotiations, 418–419; Tarim Basin oil exploration, 414, 559n103; trans-Asia pipeline, 414, 559n104; unwieldy management situation for Exxon, 414; Zhuhai refinery and chemical project, 414, 415–417, 559n109

China American Petrochemical Company (Taiwan), 407

China Light & Power (CL&P): Castle Peak Power Plant, 409, 410f; as fuel-oil market for Exxon, 409; supplying power to Guangdong in mainland China, 411–412

China Sea: offshore drilling projects, 133, 134

Chinese Communist Party (CCP), 410, 411

Chukchi Sea: oil exploration, 125

Cirigliano, Tom, 277

CIS (Exxon Ventures), 315, 316

Clarke, Jack C., 300f; advising on legal strategy in *Exxon Valdez* lawsuits, 300–301; as advisor to Exxon top management, 26; on inevitability of producer power, 23; relocation of Exxon headquarters to Texas, 258; role in *Exxon Valdez* cleanup, 276

Clayton Act of 1914, 9

Clean Air Act Amendments of 1970: ambient air standards, 96, 102; costs to industry of compliance, 95, 96, 99, 100, 103; leaded gasoline as target, 96–99; timeline for meeting auto emissions standards, 96, 98

Clean Water Act Amendments of 1972, 95

"cleaned beach," definition, 278

Clear Lake City (planned development, Houston), 179–180

climate change: debate as public relations problem for ExxonMobil, 461–472; Exxon as skeptic on global warming, 462; ExxonMobil funding of research projects, 466; ExxonMobil supporting policy choices reducing carbon emissions, 466; Exxon's skepticism about in 1990s, 462–463; Kyoto Protocol, 462–463; public stances of Exxon and Mobil on, 440

CL&P. *See* China Light & Power (CL&P)

coal: gasification of lignite, 199; liquefaction of, 198

coal industry: affinity with oil industry, 80, 84; government policies supporting, 193; oil company diversification into, 180, 192–196

Coalition for Environmentally Responsible Economies (CERES) Principles, 543n83

cogeneration: Baytown Turbine Generator

Project, 384, 385*f*, 386, 556n44; energy efficiency and, 384–396, 556n44

Cohen, Kenneth, 466–468, 467*f*

Cold War: political risks and end of, 310

Cole, Charlie, 301

Colony project: Exxon investment in, 203, 204–205, 531n81; Exxon suspension of funding for, 208–209; history of, 203–204; participating partners, 203–204; rejection of government subsidies for commercial plant, 206; surface mining methods, 206–207, 207*f*; TOSCO as creator of, 203–204

Commonwealth of Independent States, 311–312

communism: globalization and collapse of, 310

Competition in the Petroleum Industry (brochure), 79

concrete deepwater (Condeep) platforms, 153, 154–155

Conoco: joint ventures for Doba Basin oil field development, 335–336; merger with Phillips, 428; withdrawal from Venezuela after Chávez election, 332–333

contract sanctity: producer power and erosion of, 39

Controls Integrity Management System, 390

copper mining: in Chile, 182; copper reserves in Crandon Wisconsin, 181, 527n30; oil company diversification into, 180

Cormorant oil field (North Sea), 140, 141, 150, 150*f*, 162–163

Corporate Average Fuel Economy (CAFE) standards, 84

corporate culture: Exxon, as legacy of Rockefeller, 5, 6–12, 498; ExxonMobil merger and conflicts in, 452; technical leadership, 7–8

corporate management committee (Exxon), 223–224

Corporate Research, Exxon, 254–256

Corporate Research Advisory Committee (CRAC), 255

Corproven (oil company), 32

cost controls: Rockefeller and, 6

Council on Environmental Quality, 90

Cousins, Gregory, 261

Cowper, Steve, 274

CRAC (Corporate Research Advisory Committee), 255

Cramer, H. R. (Hal), 451

Crandon, Wisconsin: zinc and copper reserves, 181, 527n30

Creole Petroleum Corporation (Venezuela): as Exxon affiliate, 15, 503n1; government suit over disputed taxes, 34; reduction in natural-gas flaring, 27; response to nationalization, 30–31; retaining control of petroleum production and oil prices, 27; supply and distribution obligations to CVP, 30–31; "welfare capitalism" of, 26

Cristobal Colon LNG project, 34, 330

CVP (Corporación Venezolana del Petróleo), 30

D

Dahan, Rene, 379*f*; career, 388–388; as contact executive for chemicals, 446–447; on corporate management committee, 224; defining strategy for downstream functions, 379–380; on *Exxon Valdez* oil spill, 261, 290; as head of chemical and global services at Exxon-Mobil, 438; on impact of management quality initiatives, 390; implementing management systems at ECI, 386–387; as key merger planner, 446–447; managerial success of, 500; OIMS implementation worldwide, 388; responsibility for worldwide downstream operations, 388;

retirement of, 471; succeeding Reso at ECI, 241; support for ExxonMobil merger, 434, 435

David, Edward E., Jr., 252–253, 254

Davidson, Art, 270–271

Daystar, 189, 190

Dean, James, 231

Déby, Idriss, 335, 340–341

deep-draft caisson vessels, 350, 483*f*, 484

deepwater operations. *See* offshore drilling and operations

Del Webb Corporation, 179–180

Deng Xiaoping, 410

Dennstedt, Frederic, 99–100

Department of the Interior Appropriations Act (U.S.), 106–108

derrick barge, dynamically positioned, 158

Diamond Shamrock–Ultramar merger, 427

Directorate General for Competition (EU) (DG IV): divestments required for ExxonMobil merger, 443–444, 561n18; Exxon–Mobil assessment of attitude toward merger, 436

diversification beyond oil and gas, 167–214; alternative energy, 185–196 (*See also* alternative energy); chemicals, 168–175 (*See also* chemicals); coal, 80, 84, 180, 192–196; conglomerate mergers, 175; factors in success of, 173–175; lessons learned from, 211–214; minerals, 180–184; nonenergy businesses, 176–184; office equipment, 177–179; as opportunity for long-term growth, 167; outside core competencies, 20, 175–176; real estate development, 179–180; synthetic fuels, 196–211

Doba Basin (Chad): oil field development in, 335–336

Dolph Briscoe Center for American History: ExxonMobil Historical Collection, 570–572

Dolph, Robert: on negotiations over

nationalization, 31; as president of Creole, 29–31; as president of Esso Middle East, 29*f*; on relationship between Creole and Venezuelan government, 28, 29–30

domestic energy subsidies: as policy of national oil companies, 30

Dos Santos, José Eduardo, 347, 349, 354

downstream operations, 362–420; adjustments in Canada, 368–370; allocation of capital, 378–379; Asia–Pacific region, 398–399; in China, 410–419; clarifying lines of responsibility for, 377; closure of service stations, 458, 494, 565n105; comprehensive strategy for, 376–380; Controls Integrity Management System, 390; Dahan's responsibilities, 388; drop in oil demand devastating, 364; earnings following merger, 459, 565n109, 565n111; elements of strategy, 380; energy efficiency in, 382–387; fuel cost reductions, 382–387; global management systems, 387–390; goal-based strategies, 377–378; in Hong Kong, 408–409; idle capacity as drag on performance, 364; integrating refining and chemical operations, 395–398; integration following ExxonMobil merger, 457–460; labor cost reductions, 380–382; large minority shareholders and, 369; low-sulfur diesel fuel production, 458; Maintenance and Reliability Management System, 389; Mobil merger and integration of chemical businesses, 459–460, 460*f*, 565n111; operating cost reductions in Europe, 367; Operating Improvement Program, 388; Operations Integrity Management System (OIMS), 387–389; post–World War II expansion, 363–364; profitability as goal of, 419–420; retention of Exxon and Mobil brand names following merger, 458; tanker fleet, 373–376, 493–494;

technological upgrades, 390–395, 494; upgrading of, 377, 380–387; in Venezuela, 370–372; World Class 2000 initiative, 389. *See also* refining and refineries

E

ECI. *See* Exxon Company, International (ECI)

economies of scale, 7

EC/US Competition Cooperation Agreement, 427, 561n19

EDS (Exxon donor solvent process), 198–199, 530nn66–67

Educating Women and Girls Initiative, 470

Egypt: Exxon operations in, 65

Eidt, Clarence, 255

EIS. *See* environmental impact statements (EIS)

Ekofisk oil field (North Sea), 140

electric motors, 190–192

Elf (French oil company), 336, 340, 428

EMPI (Esso Malaysia Production, Inc.), 134

Endicott oil field (Alaska), 124–125

energy efficiency: cogeneration and, 384–396, 556n44; as continuous cost reduction, 382–387; in downstream operations, 382–387, 493; Global Energy Management System, 386–387; reducing greenhouse-gas emissions, 297

energy policy: alternative energies and, 84–85, 508n29; changing approaches to, 82–83; conservation as alternative energy, 86–87; domestic oil price controls, 72–73; energy independence, 83; Energy Policy and Conservation Act of 1975, 83–84; enhanced domestic oil production, 86; environmental policy conflicts, 88–108; in Europe, 109–110; Exxon and, 82–88; gasoline shortage impacts on, 72; incentive-based recommendations for, 84; in Japan, 108–109;

natural gas and, 85–86, 516n35; oil depletion allowance, elimination of, 72, 86; piecemeal regulations by type of fuel, 83; political debates on, 70; subsidies and, 84, 85

Energy Policy and Conservation Act of 1975, 83–84

Energy Security Act of 1980, 204, 209

Enjay Chemical Company, 169

"Environment, Health and Safety: A Progress Report," 468

"The Environmental Craze: Will It Strangle Energy?" (Kinney), 91

environmental disasters: Arthur Kill oil spill, 288–290; Baton Rouge refinery explosion, 287–288; cost justification for preventive measures, 298; *Exxon Valdez* oil spill as comparison benchmark for other oil spills, 307; Exxon's settlement of Arthur Kill claims, 289–290; failures in Exxon operating procedures causing, 287–288; Operations Integrity Management System as outcome of, 293–298; public criticism of Exxon for causing, 289. *See also Exxon Valdez* oil spill

environmental impact statements (EIS): altering planning for construction in America, 89–90; Hondo project, 103, 104; for Trans-Alaska Pipeline System, 89–90

Environmental Protection Agency (EPA): ambient air standards, extension of target date for, 102; auto emissions standards timeline, 98; automobile industry's inability to meet unleaded gas deadlines, 100; costs of lead removal from gasoline, 100–101; creation of, 97; on health hazards of leaded gas, 97; industry complaints about, 98–99; lead removal from gasoline, timeline for, 98–99; rejecting API petition for revision of air-quality standards, 102 environmental regulations: accommodation between business and government, 108; air and water quality standards (U.S.), 95; Clean Water Amendments of 1972 (U.S.), 95; conflict with energy policy, 88–108; Council on Environmental Quality, 90; Exxon resistance to, 110; impact on drilling, 108; in Japan, 108–110; National Environmental Planning Act of 1969 (U.S.), 89; offshore drilling and operations, 103–108 (*See also* Hondo project); as political challenge for oil industry, 5, 19; reduction in automobile emissions, 96; shaping global oil industry, 477; TAPS Authorization Act and, 92–93. *See also* Clean Air Act Amendments of 1970

EPA. *See* Environmental Protection Agency (EPA)

Epperly, Robert, 254

Esso Atlantic (tanker), 376*f*

Esso Chemical Company, 169

Esso Eastern, 13

Esso Europe, 13

Esso Exploration, 13

Esso Exploration Angola, 356

Esso Inter-America, 13, 221

Esso Libya, 58–59, 63

Esso Malaysia, 223

Esso Malaysia Production, Inc. (EMPI), 134

Esso Middle East, 13; challenges for, 39; concern about corporate structure in Libya, 58–59; on economic perils of Aramco full nationalization, 45; Libya and, 56; objectives and challenges, 44; politics and setting of production rates, 49; reporting dangers of operations in Libya, 59

Esso Standard Sekiyu, 400

ETAG (Exploration Technical Assessment Group), 236–237, 346

Ethyl Corporation, 96–97

European Bank for Reconstruction and Development, 341

European Commission, 443–445

European Economic Community, 102

European Investment Bank, 338

European Union: review of mergers affecting Europe, 426, 427, 561nn18–19

executive security, strengthening of, 241, 535n63

Exploration Technical Assessment Group (ETAG), 236–237, 346

Exxon Baton Rouge (tanker), 264

Exxon Chemical Company, 13; computerized control center, 392–393; earnings and status within Exxon, 172, 173, 495–596; joint venture in Singapore with Amoco Chemical and China American Petrochemical Company, 407; operating outside ECI, 228; petrochemicals production, 16–17; product groups following reorganization, 227; reorganization of, 225–228; responsibility for chemical operations in Canada, 370; selective divestments, 172; separate research organization within, 170, 253, 537n92; separation of chemicals from refining, 170–171; simplified geographic structure, 227, 228; specialty chemicals, 172–173; transformation following ExxonMobil merger, 485–497

Exxon Company, International (ECI): creation of, 228–231; exploration group, 231, 237; management structure, 229; operating improvement initiatives, 388–389; organizational structure, 445; organizational tensions from creation of, 229–230; regional companies merged into, 228, 533n27

Exxon Company USA: central role in history of Exxon, 239–240; ECI overshadowing importance of, 229–230, 239*f*; Humble Oil & Refining Company renamed to, 16; independence

from ECI, 228; as largest producer
and refiner in system, 223; maintaining
separate exploration group, 239; organizational structure, 445; planning for
ANGST project, 117–120; price control
problems, 74; as regional company, 13;
responsibility for *Exxon Valdez* cleanup,
262; responsibility for major environmental disasters, 290

Exxon Corporation (1973–1998): adaptation to industry changes, 24; challenges
and Rockefeller legacy, 11; Compensation and Executive Development Committee, 12; corporate culture, 5, 6–12,
341; diversification (*See* diversification
beyond oil and gas); divisions and affiliated companies, 13–14; endorsement
of ExxonMobil merger by board, 438;
environmental objectives, 95–96 (*See
also* environmental regulations); headquarters building, New York City, 256,
257*f*; Investment Advisory Committee,
14, 102, 121 (*See also* Exxon Enterprises); as largest international oil company, 15; lobbying by, 70; management
structure, 12–15, 17–18, 223–224, 449
(*See also* organizational innovation); as
member of "Seven Sisters," 1; nationalization impacts (*See* nationalization
of oil production); natural gas production (*See* natural gas); oil production
decline, 3, 480–481, 568n2 (*See also* oil
bust of 1986); oil-refining operations
(*See* refining and refineries); operating
statistics, 1975–2009, 594–608; pressure to invest in producing nations, 46;
profits during 1990s, 559nn2–4; public
relations, 70 (*See also* public affairs,
ExxonMobil); rate of return on investments, 423, 560nn5–6; refocus on core
business after 1986, 216–217, 478, 498;
relocation of corporate headquarters to
Texas, 256–259; size of, vs. Royal Dutch
Shell, 245, 536n71; Standard Oil Company (New Jersey) as predecessor, 2–3;
strengths of, 5, 12–17; strict budgetary
controls emphasized by, 39; weaknesses
of, 5, 17–18, 56

Exxon Development Company, 454

Exxon donor solvent process (EDS),
198–199, 530nn66–67

Exxon Education Foundation, 469

Exxon Enterprises, 13; investments in
office systems, 177–179; nuclear power,
185–189, 528n37; Reliance Electric and
electric motors, 190–192; resources
on evolution of, 527n20; solar power,
189–190; as successor to Jersey Enterprises, 176–177

Exxon Exploration Company: as consolidated worldwide exploration group
within Exxon, 240; early results in
exploration, 243–245

Exxon International Company, 13, 228

Exxon Minerals Company, 182–184

Exxon Mobil Corporation (ExxonMobil):
charitable activities (*See* philanthropic
programs); climate change research
funding, 465–466; corporate name
changes, 503n1; corporate strategy and
structure, 478–479; development integration, 453–471; directors and officers,
December 1975–June 2012, 577–593;
functional divisions, 447, 448*f*; Global
Climate and Energy Project funding,
465–466; as global company organized along functional lines, 437–438,
478–479, 497; integration of operations
following merger, 453–471; isolated
position on climate change, 464; as
largest international oil company, 1; as
largest private investor in Saudi Arabia,
66; lead country managers as representatives to governments, 447; management
succession, 471–476; merger expanding research resources and technology

expertise, 256; merger with XTO Energy, 569n19; official merger date, 453; oil and gas reserves (2005), 453; operating statistics, 1975–2009, 594–608; personnel evaluation system, 449, 451, 478; production integration, 456–477; profitability of, 497–498; public affairs (*See* public affairs, ExxonMobil); retention of both Exxon and Mobil brand names, 458, 565n105; Rockefeller's approach to operations influencing, 10–11, 498–499; transformation from Exxon to ExxonMobil, 1–22, 497–501; transformation from past to future, 477–501; as work in progress, 500–501. *See also* Exxon–Mobil merger process

Exxon–Mobil merger process: accelerating organizational changes at Exxon, 444; adoption of Mobil office-document system, 451, 564n86; background, 422–428; benefits for same-sex partners of employees, 452, 564n88; compensation of Mobil shareholders, 437, 562nn45–46; completion of merger, 443–445; consolidation as global company with functional organization, 437–438, 445; contact executives designated for major groups, 448; Corporate Structure Task Force, 451–452; designation of lead country managers, 447; divestments required by regulators, 443–445, 453, 564n93; employee selection for merged company, 449–451, 564n85; engineering integration, 445–453; Exxon identification of Mobil as merger partner, 430; Exxon senior executives supporting, 434; Exxon's flirtation with DuPont, 429; Exxon's strengths for merger, 428–429, 561n23; history of cooperation between firms, 432–433; jobs lost in merger, 450, 564n83; media reaction to merger, 438–441, 442f; merger of corporate cultures, 452,

564n88; merger transition group, 447; Mobil contributions to, 421–422; Mobil's board authorizing negotiations with Exxon, 284, 434, 436; as pooling of interests, 436–437; potential synergies from merger, 435–436; preliminary talks between Raymond and Noto, 432, 433–434; Raymond overseeing, 21; reallocation of responsibilities, 437–438; relative ownership percentages of combined company, 437–438; review process, 563n61; secret meetings with regulatory agencies, 436; Senate Commerce and Judiciary Committees requesting FTC investigation of oil company mergers, 426, 561n14; Standard Oil Company as ancestor of both companies, 433

Exxon Neftegas Limited, 322

Exxon Nuclear, 176, 185–189

Exxon Production Research Company (EPR): exploration technology development by, 238, 352; guyed tower technology and, 156, 157, 160; realignment with business objectives, 254; succeeded by ExxonMobil Upstream Research Company, 352; technical contributions to offshore industry, 482; technology development for Endicott field project, 124

Exxon Research and Engineering (ER&E), 14; contract with NIOC for refinery research, 54; energy profile of typical refinery, 382; guyed tower technology development, 156, 157; realignment with business objectives, 254; reorganization of, 252; technology development for Endicott field project, 124; transition to applied research, 253

Exxon Santa Ynez (vessel), 132

Exxon Shipping, 262

Exxon Valdez oil spill
  as benchmark for other oil spills,

307; comparative size of, 541n49;
Macondo drilling blowout, 307–308

cleanup: apportionment of blame for
delays, 265; controversy over success
of, 281–282; definition of "cleaned
beach," 278; disagreement over use
of chemical dispersants, 265; divided
authority for cleanup, 264; early
cleanup efforts, 540n43; lack of adequate equipment for, 264; LeGrange
and management of, 247; manpower
for, 279, 281–282; natural biodegradation of oil, 281; offloading of oil,
263f, 264; as regional problem, 265–
267, 266f; responsibility for, 274–278,
540n43, 540n44; technology and
equipment, 278, 280–281, 281f

contributing causes for, 538n2; grounding of tanker, 260; Hazelwood's role,
261–262

criminal and civil lawsuits, 298–307;
acceptance of revised settlement by
judge, 303; appeal to Supreme Court,
306–307; appeals to Ninth Circuit
Court of Appeals, 305–306; compensatory damages awarded, 304;
countersuit by Exxon against State
of Alaska, 301; criminal fines and
civil settlements paid by Exxon, 303;
against Exxon insurers, 303; federal
and state criminal charges against
Exxon, 299–300; federal civil lawsuit
against Exxon, 303–305; against
Hazelwood, 299; punitive damages awarded, 304–305, 544n109;
rejection of settlement by judge,
302; secret agreement with "Seattle
Seven" fish-processing companies,
305, 544n115; settlement negotiations, 301–303, 543n96; against
Trans-Alaska Pipeline owners, 301

criticism of failed contingency plans for
oil spill containment, 268–269

damages from: impact on company
morale, 273; long-term effects on
Exxon public image, 307; to ship
from grounding, 262, 538n3; to wildlife, 267–268

Exxon's response to: criticism of,
269–270; incomplete statements
about conditions in Alaska, 540n30;
prompt payment of claims for damages, 278; stock buybacks, 250

outcomes: oil spill contingency planning, 286; performance bond
required of Exxon following, 537n89;
political environment in New
York, 256; public policy responses,
284–286; self-insurance strategies,
252, 537n89

as synonymous with environmental
disaster, 260

Exxon Valdez Oil Spill Trustee Council,
267, 283, 539n16

Exxon Ventures (CIS), 315, 316

ExxonMobil. *See* Exxon Mobil Corporation (ExxonMobil)

ExxonMobil Canada, 448

ExxonMobil Chemical: outcome of
merger, 450–460, 496–497, 566n114;
sales rankings, 2005, 460f, 566n114

ExxonMobil Development Company,
454–456

ExxonMobil Fuels Marketing Company,
451

ExxonMobil Global Services Company,
451

ExxonMobil Historical Collection,
570–572; advertising and marketing
materials, 571–572; document types,
571; scope of, 570

ExxonMobil Lubricants & Petroleum
Specialties Company, 451

ExxonMobil Production Company: production integration, 456–457, 565n96;
research and services integration,

460–461; reserves replacement, 456; Terry Koonce as first head of, 456

ExxonMobil Refining & Supply Company, 457

ExxonMobil Upstream Research Company, 352. *See also* Exxon Production Research Company

F

Faisal, King of Saudi Arabia, 39

Farkhutdinov, Igor, 317

fast production system, 353

Federal Oil Conservation Board, 196

Federal Trade Commission (FTC): antitrust case against Exxon, 76; divestments required for ExxonMobil merger, 444–445; Exxon–Mobil assessment of attitude toward merger, 436; focus on market efficiencies as green light for mergers, 426; revised guidelines on mergers, 426

first mover advantages, 351

Fischer-Topsch process, 198

floating production storage and offloading (FPSO) vessels, 352, 353*f*, 354

Florio, Jim, 289

foreign policy, U.S.: unconditional support for Israel, 39

Foster, Morris: on fast production system, 353; as head of Esso Malaysia, 223; as president of ExxonMobil Development Company, 454, 455*f*; on search for non-OPEC oil, 112; succeeding Koonce as president of ExxonMobil Production Company, 456

FPSO (floating production storage and offloading) vessels, 352, 353*f*, 354

Friendswood Development Company, 179–180

FTC. *See* Federal Trade Commission (FTC)

fuel costs, continuous reduction of, 382–387

Fujian Petrochemical Company Ltd., 417

Fujian refinery and chemical project (China), 415–417

Fulmar oil field (North Sea), 140, 150

G

Galante, Ed, 395, 396, 472

Garvin, Clifton C., Jr., 25*f*, 216*f*; career of, 24–25; on diversification by Exxon, 167, 185; energy crises of 1973 and 1979 shaping career of, 19; on energy efficiency, 382–387; as Exxon Chairman/CEO during high-price era, 18–20; on Exxon withdrawal from Colony project, 208–210; on Exxon withdrawal from Libya, 64; on horizontal divestment, 78; Jack Clarke as advisor to, 26; managerial qualities, 500; managing Exxon response to nationalization, 19; on national energy policy, 84–86; negotiations with OPEC, 23; relationship with Yamani, 42–43, 67; reorganization of chemical operations, 169; response to oil bust of 1986, 216; responsibility for Middle East portfolio, 25–26; retirement of, 19, 216; on search for non-OPEC energy sources, 113; on slowness of Saudi nationalization, 45; as spokesman for oil industry, 19, 70–71; on TAPS construction delays, 95; on vertical divestment, 77; on workforce reductions, 381

gas, miscible, 121

gas flaring, 27, 40, 509n35

Gasgebouw (gas structure), 137

gasoline, leaded. *See* leaded gasoline

gasoline shortages, U.S. (1973-1974), 72

gas-to-liquid (GTL) technology, 491

Gazprom (natural gas company), 319; economic and political power of, 325; Shell's loss of Sakhalin-II project control to Gazprom, 325–326

GCC (Global Climate Coalition), 464

G-EMS (Global Energy Management System), 386–387

General Seikyu (GSK), 399, 400, 403

geopolitics: shaping outcome of events, 360–361

Getty Oil: acquisition by Texaco, 248

Gillespie, Samuel H., 434, 435

Global Climate and Energy Project, 465–466

Global Climate Coalition (GCC), 464

Global Energy Management System (G-EMS), 386–387

global warming. *See* climate change

globalization: collapse of communism and, 310

Goldmann, Stephen F., 414–415

Goldmann Sachs: as investment advisor to Mobil, 435, 436

Gómez, Juan Vicente, 26

Govoroff, Nicholas, 315

Grace, John D., 546n19

Grand Isle oil field (offshore Louisiana), 129

Grant Baker et al. vs. Exxon Corporation, 303–307

Great Britain: policy conflicts with Shell/Exxon over North Sea oil and gas, 141–145, 523n66; push for partial nationalization of North Sea oil, 143–144

greenhouse gases: contribution to global warming, 462; energy efficiency at Exxon facilities reducing emissions, 297; Raymond's opposition policies reducing emissions, 463–464. *See also* climate change

Greenpeace: invasion of ExxonMobil headquarters, 535n63

Groningen oil field (Netherlands): Exxon oil production, 165; as Exxon's doorway to North Sea, 136–138; as Exxon's turning point from oil company to oil and natural gas, 138

GTL (gas-to-liquid) technology, 491

Gulf of Mexico: Exxon projects in, 484–485, 484*f*; Hoover-Diana project, 481–484, 483*f*; Lena field guyed tower, 156–160, 157*f*, 482, 483–484; oil exploration in, 244

Gulf Oil: Angola offshore production, 349; as member of "Seven Sisters," 1; purchase by Chevron, 248

Guttormson, Dean, 159, 160, 336

guyed tower platform, 153, 156–160, 157*f*

H

Hagemann, Fredrik, 139, 148

Haider, Mike, 219

Hamaca Este project, 330

Harrison, Melvin (Mel), 275*f*; on benefits of TAPS construction delays, 93–94; career of, 276; on Exxon withdrawal from Libya, 64; as manager of upstream portfolio, 241; on Prudhoe Bay management negotiations, 116; on rapid payment of *Exxon Valdez* claims, 278

Harrison, Myron, 98

Harrison, Otto V.: on aftermath of *Exxon Valdez* cleanup, 283–284; managing *Exxon Valdez* cleanup, 271, 276–277

Harrison, W. Allen, 247

Hart, Gary, 81

Harvard Malaria Initiative, 358

Hazelwood, Joseph (ship captain), 260, 261–262, 299

heavy oil, 391

Hedlund, Charles J., 38–39

Hellmuth, Obata, and Kassabaum (architects), 258

Hess, Edwin J.: career of, 291–292; as corporate vice president for environment and safety, 291; creation and enforcement of OIMS, 293–298; as executive assistant to Raymond, 291; on integration of refining with chemical production, 395; on interaction between chemicals and refining, 395

Hibernia oil field (offshore Newfoundland), 164, 486
Hickel, Walter, 301, 302, 543n96
Holland, H. Russel, 302, 305–306
Holmer, Ed: on chemicals as different
industry from petroleum, 171; reorganization of Exxon Chemical, 225–226,
227; retirement as president of Exxon
Chemical, 226
Hondo project, 103–108; as deepwater
project, 128, 130; earthquake risk
to platform, 131; EIS hearings and
approval, 103, 104; environmental
regulation-related delays, 104; Exxon
response to environmentalist opposition, 131–132; forecasting future of
offshore drilling, 106; offshore oil treating facility, 105; oil production, 165;
permitting process, 104–105; platform
design and construction, 107f, 130–131,
153; platform in operation, 129f; regulatory delays in oil production, 106
Hong Kong: Exxon as majority shareholder in CL&P, 409; Exxon move
into, 408; links to mainland China,
398–399; post–World War II markets
in, 398–399
Hoover-Diana project (Gulf of Mexico),
481–484, 483f
horizontal divestment of oil companies,
78–82
Howell, William R., 471
Humble Oil & Refining Company: corporate name changes, 503n1; diversification into real estate development, 179–
180; exploration in southern Alaska,
114; Grand Isle offshore project, 129;
Hondo offshore project, 104, 128–133;
joint venture with Richfield for North
Slope exploration, 114; management of
chemicals in U.S., 169; offshore projects
in Gulf of Mexico, 128–129; oil production in early 1970s, 16; as partner

in Trans-Alaska Pipeline System, 90.
See also Exxon Company USA
Hutton oil field (North Sea): platform
design, 153, 156

I

Iarossi, Frank, 262
Idris, King of Libya (1949–1969): oil
industry under, 57–58
IMF (International Monetary Fund):
loans to Russia, 312, 320
Imperial Oil Limited of Canada: acquisition of 78 percent of Texaco Canada,
368–369, 554n6; Cold Lake heavy-oil
project, 201–202, 486–487, 487f;
earnings in 1990, 554n8; Endicott field
development, 124; as exception to
ExxonMobil functional organization,
447–448, 564n79; as Exxon affiliate, 13;
ExxonMobil creation of Canadian affiliate independent of Imperial, 370; independent status within Exxon, 223, 228;
maintaining separate exploration group,
239; oil production, 16; organizational
structure, 445; purchase of land for new
headquarters building in Toronto, 369;
Syncrude Canada Ltd. and, 200–292,
291f, 487–488, 568nn10–12
In the Wake of the "Exxon Valdez"
(Davidson), 271
International Convention for the
Prevention of Pollution from Ships
(MARPOL), 284
International Maritime Organization, 284
International Monetary Fund (IMF):
loans to Russia, 312, 320
Iran: BP dominance in, 50; Consortium
Agreement (1954), 50–51, 510n62;
Exxon concessions in, 54; Exxon hold-
ings in Iranian consortium, 49; funda-
mentalist nationalization in, 19, 49–56;
oil nationalization under shah, 50–54;
profitable relationship between shah

and Exxon, 54, 511n72; resource nationalism in, 50; rivalry with Saudi Arabia, 51, 511n65; U.S. ban of companies dealing with Iran, 55–56. *See also* Iranian Revolution
Iranian National Oil Company, 66
Iranian Oil Participants (IOP): accepting demands of shah, 53; as consortium of international oil companies, 50; fear of NIOC takeover, 53; nonnegotiable demands by shah, 51–53; Sales and Purchase Agreement, 53–54
Iranian Revolution: expulsion of consortium, 55; freezing of Iranian assets in West, 55; global oil supplies and, 4, 55–56; withdrawal of Consortium workers, 54–55
Iraq: limited Exxon presence in, 65
Iraq Petroleum Company, 36
Israel: King Faisal's demands for U.S. policy changes, 39; OPEC embargo on oil shipments to supporters of, 3, 29; unconditional U.S. support for, 39

J
Jamieson, J. Kenneth, 18, 25, 202–203
Japan: deregulation of oil industry, 403; Exxon's post–World War II growth beginning in, 398; Exxon's refining capacity in, 400; Ministry of International Trade and Industry (MITI), 109, 400–402; Standard Oil entry into, 399
Japanese National Oil Company (JAPEX), 317
Jersey Enterprises, 175, 176. *See also* Exxon Enterprises
Jersey Nuclear Company, 176
Joint Underwater Development Team, Shell/Exxon, 161–162
Jungers, Frank, 38

K
Kadoorie, Lawrence, 409

Kashagan oil field (Caspian Sea), 328, 455
Kauffmann, Howard: on Exxon's association with Statoil, 149–150; on Hondo project, 105; retirement as Exxon president, 219, 533n9
Kazakhstan: ExxonMobil investment in Tengiz and Kashagan fields, 328
Keeble, John, 538n2
Khodorkovsky, Mikhail, 319–320, 325
Kizomba oil field, 352
Kohlenberger, Gerry, 451
Koonce, K. Terry, 314f; on cultural differences in dealing with Russians, 313–314; as first president of ExxonMobil Production Company, 456; as head of Exxon Research, 255; on lack of Russian plan for petroleum industry, 320; on legal hurdles for PSAs in Russia, 318–319; on oil business in former Soviet Union, 328; on political risks for ExxonMobil in Russia, 326; as president of Exxon Ventures, 315–316, 456
Kraftwerk Union, 189
Kribi, Cameroon, 342
Kruizenga, Richard, 133, 217
Kuparak River oil field (Alaska), 124
Kyoto Protocol on climate change, 462

L
labor costs: continuous reduction of, 380–382
Lagoven (oil company, Venezuela), 32
Lamp (magazine), 84
Lamp, Jack, 268–269
Las Flores Canyon (California), 164
Latin America: Exxon investments in, 372
Lawit Gas Field (offshore Malaysia), 134f
leaded gasoline: costs of lead removal for refining industry, 100–101; debate over health effects of, 96–98; emissions as health hazard, 97–98; harmful effects on catalytic converters, 97; lead

reduction in different nations, 101–102; timeline for lead removal, 98–99

Leffingwell, Earnest de Koven, 113–114

LeGrange, Ulysses, 247

Lena oil field (offshore Louisiana): guyed tower, 156–160, 157*f*, 482, 483–484

Libya: burning of American embassy in Tripoli, 63; confiscation of Exxon's gasoline distribution system, 58; Exxon withdrawal from, 63–64; Exxon-operated LGN plant and nationalization, 56; management committees for international oil companies, 58; oil company dependents evacuated from (1979), 63; oil concession system, 57; oil explorations by Exxon, 56; as oil price hawk, 58, 512n80; oil production in 1960s, 56–57; partial nationalization in early 1970s, 58–59; production-sharing agreements under Qaddafi, 58; revolutionary nationalization of oil production, 1, 19, 56–68; U.S. sanctions against Qaddafi regime, 63; Zelten oil field, 56

Libyan National Oil Company, 57, 58, 64

liquefied natural gas (LNG) projects: creating global market for natural gas, 489; Cristobal Colon (Venezuela), 34, 35; Marsa el-Brega (Libya), 59–62, 489; neglect by Exxon before merger., 490; RasGas project, 491; tankers, 490, 490*f*

Lisburne oil field (Alaska), 124

Lisburne Processing Center, 125

Lloyd, Henry Demarest, 9

LNG projects. *See* liquefied natural gas (LNG) projects

lobbying and lobbyists, 70

long-distance drilling, 352

Longwell, Harry J., 235*f*; career of, 242–243; on deferment of ANGST project, 120; on *Exxon Valdez* disaster, 273; as head of ExxonMobil exploration and production, 438; on importance of Prudhoe Bay to Exxon, 113; on Japanese

exploration of Sakhalin Island, 317; managerial success of, 500; negotiations for Angola drilling rights, 349–350; organizing consolidation of Exxon-Mobil upstream operations, 446–447, 448; as president of Exxon USA, 241, 242*f*, 243, 290–291; on Prudhoe Bay management negotiations, 115–116; retirement of, 471; support for merger with Mobil, 434, 435

Lucchesi, Peter, 253, 254

Lukoil (international oil company), 320, 327

Lurgi-Ruhrgas process, 199

M

Macondo oil spill (Gulf of Mexico), 307–308

Madec, André, 336, 337

Magnus field platform, 153–154, 154*f*

Maintenance and Reliability Management System, 389

malaria: ExxonMobil antimalarial funding, 357–358, 469

Malaysia: demanding new contracts with Exxon after OPEC revolution, 133–134; education of workforce, 135–136; government demands on Exxon, 135; offshore drilling projects, 133–136

Manufacturing Chemists' Association, 103

Maraven (oil company, Venezuela), 32

Marine Preservation Association, 284

Marine Spill Response Corporation, 284

MARPOL (International Convention for the Prevention of Pollution from Ships), 284

Marsa el-Brega LNG project, 57*f*, 59–62; LNG shipments via tanker to Europe, 60, 61*f*; negotiated sale of facility to Libyan government, 62; pipeline from Zelten oil field to, 56

Matthews, Charles W., 434, 435*f*

McBrayer, Eugene, 171, 174*f*, 226–227

"megamajor" oil companies, 1

methyl tertiary butyl ether (MTBE), 557n67

Mexico: expropriation of properties of foreign oil companies, 26

Meyer, Randall: on ANGST project planning, 117; on oil price controls and allocation process, 73–74; on potential for oil shale and other synfuels, 203; on role for oil companies in alternative energy development, 79–80; on Trans-Alaska Pipeline System, 89

Mickelson, Phil, 567n137

Middle East: anti-Americanism in, 56; Exxon oil production, 1972-1977, 40; Exxon oil reserves in, 36; nationalization of oil production, 19; nationalization vs. Venezuela, 35–36; U.S. foreign policy, 39–40

Miller, James, 426

minerals production, 180–184; Chilean copper mines, 182, 184f; as diversification strategy, 180–181; divestment by Exxon, 183–184; Exxon holdings, 181–182, 181f, 527n30

Ministry of International Trade and Industry (MITI) (Japan), 109, 400–402

minority education, ExxonMobil support for, 470

miscible gas, 121

Mitchell Energy & Development, 241

Mitsubishi, 317

Mitsui Real Estate Development (Mitsui Fudoson), 256, 537n103

Mobil Oil Corporation: as Aramco co-owner, 25, 36; Cerro Negro heavy-oil project, 330; contributions to Exxon–Mobil merger, 421–422; corporate name changes, 503n1; endorsement of merger by Board, 438; European partnership with BP, 431–432; in Libya, 58; as localized organization, 446; as member of "Seven Sisters," 1; position on climate change, 464; purchase of Montgomery Ward, 175; purchase of Superior Oil Company, 248; reorganization (1966), 13; resource base pre-merger, 431; as second largest U.S.-based oil company, 430; as second-tier international oil company, 430; shortage of financial and technical resources, 431. *See also* Exxon Mobil Corporation (ExxonMobil); Exxon–Mobil merger process

Moody-Stewart, Mark, 340

Mosbacher, Robert, 301

MTBE (methyl tertiary butyl ether), 557n67

Mukluk tract (Beaufort Sea), 123

Murray, Allen, 402–403

Muskie, Edmund, 96

N

NAM (Nederlandse Aardolie Maatschappij, B.V.), 137

National Association of Manufacturers: Global Climate Coalition, 464

National Commission on BP Deepwater Horizon Oil Spill and Offshore Drilling, 308

National Contingency Plan, 274

National Environmental Planning Act of 1969: environmental impact statements and, 89; impeding development of oil on public lands, 91; TAPS Authorization Act as exemption to further environmental review, 91–92

National Iranian Oil Company (NIOC): contract with ER&E for refinery research, 54; control of Oil Service Company of Iran, 53; created by revolutionary government, 50; managing domestic oil market, 51; oil reserves, 1; as overseer of consortium, 53

national oil companies: privately owned global oil companies distinguished from, 504n2; producer power of, 66–67. *See also* names of *individual countries*

National Petroleum Council (NPC), 70, 122

nationalization of oil production: advantages of full nationalization for Exxon, 46; capitalist, 19, 24, 65 (*See also* Saudi Arabia; Venezuela); as Exxon challenge in 1970s, 24; fundamentalist, in Iran, 49–56; loss of Exxon oil reserves and, 19, 64–66; major uncertainties and loss of control under, 66; negotiation of technical service contract fees in Saudi Arabia, 47–48; outcomes of, 65–68; partial, in Saudi Arabia, 43–44; producer power and, 3–4; reducing global production of oil, 1; revolutionary, 19, 24, 65–66 (*See also* Iran; Libya); search for non-OPEC oil and gas, 113–166; Venezuela vs. Middle East, 35–36

Natural Energy Board of Canada, 118

natural gas: as "bridge fuel" from fossil fuels, 491–492; British government encouraging use of, 142–143; deregulation of, 84; energy policy and, 85–86, 516n35; estimated reserves in Russia, 315; ExxonMobil production 2005, 312; ExxonMobil reserves, 489, 491; ExxonMobil–XTO merger, 569n19; flaring, defined, 509n35; flaring, reduction in, 27, 40; gas-to-liquid (GTL) technology, 491; Netherlands energy policy based on, 137–138; North Sea fields, 489; planning for ANGST pipeline from Prudhoe Bay field, 116–120; prices linked to oil price by producing nations, 61, 489; Prudhoe Bay supplies, 113; removal from net proved reserves, 534n38; reserves in former Soviet Union, 312; as scarce resource, 489; transformations following ExxonMobil merger, 488–492; U.S. legislation addressing, 84. *See also* liquefied natural gas (LNG) projects

Natural Gas Policy Act of 1978, 85–86

Nauman, Scott, 279–280

Nazarbayev, Nursultan, 328

Nederlandse Aardolie Maatschappij, B.V. (NAM), 137

Nesbitt, Raymond B., 387, 416*f*

Netherlands: energy policy based on natural gas, 137–138; Groningen natural gas field, 136–138

New Ventures, 237

New York World (newspaper): on Standard Oil, 9

Newfoundland: Hibernia oil field, 164, 486

Niakuk oil field (Alaska), 124

Nicholas, Bob, 264

Nigeria: "oil curse" in, 334

NIOC. *See* National Iranian Oil Company (NIOC)

Nixon Administration: energy policy, 83

North Sea: Brent field, 140, 150, 165; British sector offshore projects, 140–145, 150–151; Cormorant field, 140, 141, 150, 150*f*, 165; division of territorial rights to, 138–139; Ekofisk field, 140; environmental challenges for offshore exploration, 139; Exxon investments in offshore fields, 140, 150–151; Fulmar field, 140, 150; natural gas fields, 489; Norwegian sector offshore projects, 145–151; Odin gas field, 151; oil and gas fields, map, 152*f*; platform design for, 151, 153–156; recoverable oil reserves, 150; Shell/Esso Brent Spar oil storage buoy, 142*f*, 523n66; Shell/Exxon conflicts with British government, 141–145, 523n66; Statfjord field, 148–149, 150; technological innovations in, 151, 153–156, 163–164

North Slope (Alaska): early exploration of, 113–114; oil reserves, 16. *See also* Prudhoe Bay oil field

Norway: concrete platform design, 155; economic and educational strengths, 147; Exxon's relationship with government, 145; institutional framework for oil industry, 147–148; offshore oil production projects, 145–151; oil licensing terms, 146–147; Snorre field, 163; State's Direct Financial Interest (SDFI), 149; Statoil as national oil company, 148–150

Norwegian Petroleum Directorate (NPD), 148

Not One Drop: Betrayal and Courage in the Wake of the Exxon Valdez Oil Spill (Ott), 299

Noto, Lucio A.: career at Mobil, 430–431; as ExxonMobil vice chairman, 438, 449*f*; as Mobil chairman and CEO, 430; rejecting merger with BP, 432; retirement of, 471; role in successful transition to ExxonMobil, 452–453

nuclear fuel processing, 20, 186, 528n40

nuclear power: as alternative energy, 85; Exxon diversification into, 185–189, 528n37; Exxon divestment of, 189, 528n45; public policy changes and industry decline, 187–188

O

Odin gas field (North Sea), 151

offshore drilling and operations: Angola, 349–354; Bass Strait, Australia, 163–164; Beaufort Sea, 124–125; bidding for offshore Alaska leases, 122–123; concrete island drilling systems, 126; deepwater drilling, 128, 130–131; Exxon offshore structures, 482*f*; ExxonMobil strengths from merger, 485–486; Hondo project, 103–108; Hoover-Diana project (Gulf of Mexico), 481–484, 483*f*; Lena guyed tower, 156–160, 157*f*, 482, 483–484; Malaysia, 133–136; moratoriums on, 106–108;

new technologies, 126, 481–486; as oil frontier, 128; oilfield explorations, 125; organized opposition to, 104–105; platform design for deepwater drilling, 130–131, 151, 153–156; Ram-Powell project, 482–483; regulatory authority for, 105; Santa Ynez Unit, 132, 153; subsea production systems (SPS), 160–165; technological innovation, 163, 164–165, 481; Thunder Horse project (Gulf of Mexico), 485; underwater manifold center (UMC), 161–163; Ursa project, 483. *See also* North Sea

Offshore Technology Conference (1984), 159

Oil and Gas Journal (trade magazine), 91

oil and gas reserves: Africa, 481; Angola, 349, 350, 352; Canada, 481; categories of, 535n69; ExxonMobil (2005), 481; Exxon's top ten fields (1985), 165; natural gas in former Soviet Union, 312, 315; net proved, 244, 535n69; North Slope (Alaska), 16; OPEC, 492; Prudhoe Bay oil field, 113, 150, 165; Qatar natural gas reserves, 568n15; Sakhalin Island (Russia), 321–322; static reserves, 245; technology and increase in, 492; Venezuela, 329

oil bust of 1986: encouraging consolidation of oil companies, 424; impact on oil industry, 215; organizational innovations following, 215–259; transformation of Exxon and, 18–19

"oil curse," 333–334

oil depletion allowance, 72, 86, 514n8

oil embargo, OPEC (1973-1974): easing of, 29; effects on Venezuela, 29; gasoline shortages in U.S., 72; high U.S. gasoline prices resulting from, 71; Trans-Alaska Pipeline authorization and, 92; against U.S. and other supporters of Israel, 3, 29; Yamani as architect of, 42

"Oil Firms Fear Moves to Bar Their

Owning Other Energy Sources"
(Gapay), 80
oil industry
elimination of industry tax breaks, 86
fall of communism and, 311–327
forces shaping, 477
on health impacts of leaded gasoline,
97–98
lobbying by, 70
mergers: EU review of mergers affecting
Europe, 426, 427, 561nn18–19; megamergers in late 1990s, 421; in 1980s,
424–427, 425*f*; reasons for failures,
425*f*, 427–428, 563n60; regulatory
changes encouraging, 426–427 (*See
also* Exxon–Mobil merger process)
parallels between late 19th and late 20th
centuries, 10–11
political challenges for, 69–110 (*See also*
politics and oil industry)
price volatility and changes in, 17–18
(*See also* oil bust of 1986)
privatization in Russia in 1990s,
319–320
quest for efficiency vs. waste of oil,
505n13
search for non-OPEC oil and gas
reserves, 113–166
second-tier international companies,
430
Oil Pollution Act of 1990 (OPA 90),
284–285
oil prices: corporate change and, 18; crash
of 1986 (*See* oil bust of 1986); deregulation, 75; high prices and antitrust
actions against oil companies, 75–82;
high prices and calls for regulation,
69–70; "old" vs. "new" crude oil, 73;
political events affecting, 3–4; price
controls, domestic, 72–75, 84; producer
power and, 3–4, 71; relative stability
following World War II, 4, 4*f*; volatility
since 1973, 4–5, 17–18, 477

oil sands processing, 197, 199–203, 486–
488, 487*f*, 568nn10–12
Oil Service Company of Iran, 53, 54
oil shale processing: Colony project, 203–
204, 205–210; end of industry in U.S.,
210–211; Exxon diversification into,
20, 197, 199–200; potential reserves in
North America, 197, 199–200
Oil Spill Liability Trust Fund, 92, 284
oil spills: *Amoco Cadiz* (1978), 541n49;
Arthur Kill (1990), 288–290; *Atlantic Empress* (1979), 541n49; largest,
541n49; Macondo (Gulf of Mexico),
307–308; pipeline, near Missoula,
Montana, 545n117; Santa Barbara, California (1969), 104, 131. *See also Exxon
Valdez* oil spill
oil tankers: charter capacity vs. fleet maintenance, 376; double-hull, 284, 542n71;
Exxon's reduction in deadweight tonnage, 374, 375*f*, 493–494; rise and fall
of Exxon's fleet, 373–376, 554n21; rules
and safeguards following *Exxon Valdez*
spill, 285–286, 542n72; ultra-large crude
carriers, 375, 376*f*. *See also Exxon Valdez*
oil spill, 374
OIMS. *See* Operations Integrity Management System (OIMS)
Okai, Masayoshi, 403
O'Leary, John, 80
olefins plant (Baytown, Texas), 393, 394*f*
O'Loughlin, Maurice E. J.: as head of Esso
Eastern, 400, 401*f*; on Japanese hiring
and staffing patterns, 402; on market
tributary to Singapore area, 404; on
supervision of Exxon by MITI, 402
Omnibus Energy Act (1975), 83–84
ONG Videsh Limited, 322
OPA 90 (Oil Pollution Act of 1990),
284–285
OPEC. *See* Organization of Petroleum
Exporting Countries (OPEC)
Operating Improvement Program, 388

Operations Integrity Management System (OIMS), 293–298; addressing safety and environmental issues, 293; as disciplined approach to emergency planning, 298, 387–389, 499; elements of, 294, 295f; employees accountable for, 294, 296; enforcement of principles, 294, 296; global nature of safety programs, 298; as internal self-regulatory system, 20; operational excellence central to, 298, 478; reflecting core operating values of Exxon, 293–294, 308, 545n117; reliability of information, 297; repairing public image following *Exxon Valdez*, 309; safety and environmental measures, 297; working environment fostered by, 296–297

Organization of Petroleum Exporting Countries (OPEC): control over oil prices and national production, 3–4, 74; conventional oil reserves, 492; embargo on oil shipments to U.S. (1973), 3, 29; Libya membership in, 57; Yamani as architect of embargo, 42

organizational innovation, 215–259; addressing structural barriers to efficiency, 222–225; cost reductions by streamlined operations, 230–231; ECI creation, 228–231, 533n27; executive development, 243, 478, 499–500; exploration outside North America, 231–243; Exxon Chemical reorganization, 225–228; in finance, 246–252; oil bust of 1986 as mandate for action, 18–19, 215, 217–222; oil exploration and, 240, 243–245; Rawl and, 20; recognizing future of Exxon as outside U.S., 229–230; refocus on research, 252–256; relocation of corporate headquarters to Irving, Texas, 256–259; reserves replacement and, 232–233, 534n38; self-insurance, 251–252, 537n89; shelf registration innovation, 250–251;

systematic repurchases of Exxon shares, 246–252, 250f

Orinoco, Venezuela, 329

Orinoco Basin heavy oil, 34

Orr, Franklin M., Jr., 466

Ott, Riki, 299

Out of the Channel: The Exxon Valdez Oil Spill in Prince William Sound (Keeble), 538n2

Outer Continental Shelf: air quality regulatory authority on, 106; moratoriums on drilling and oil leases, 106–108

P

Packwood, Robert, 561n14

Page, Howard, 23

Pahlavi, Mohammad Reza (Shah of Iran), 50–54

Patton, Edward, 91

PEMEX (Petróleos Mexicanos), 30

Pennzoil, 327

Pérez, Carlos Andrés: nationalization of oil production, 28, 30, 328–329; reelection and reentry of Exxon into Venezuela, 329

Perkins, Fred, 238, 254, 534n50

permafrost and oil pipelines, 93–94

personnel management: executive development, 12–13, 243, 478, 499–500; personnel evaluation system, 449, 451, 478

Peterson, Robert, 369

petrochemicals, 16–17, 21, 169. *See also* chemicals

Petróleos de Venezuela, SA (PDVSA), 1, 32, 331

Petroleum Revenue Management Law (Chad, 1999), 338

Petromin (Saudi agency), 41

Petronas (oil company), 133–136, 341

philanthropic programs: in Angola, 357–359; for areas affected by development projects, 471; education programs, 469,

567n136; Exxon Education Foundation, 469; representative programs, 469, 470*f*; scope of, 311; sponsorship of Masters Golf Tournament, 567n137; strategic philanthropy, 469, 567n137

Phillips Petroleum, 126, 428

pipelines: Selten oil field to Marsa el-Brega (Libya), 56. *See also* Trans-Alaska Pipeline System (TAPS)

platform design, 130–131, 151, 153–156, 154*f*

political action committees, 69

politics and oil industry, 69–110; anti-oil policies and high prices, 71–82; collapse of communism and globalization, 310; compliance with air quality standards, 95–103; energy/environmental policy conflicts, 88–108; Exxon and energy policy, 82–88; geopolitics shaping outcome of events, 360–361; industry resistance to political attacks and policy limitations, 110; offshore drilling and operations, 103–108; political action committees, 69; producer power, post-Cold War, 311; in Venezuela, 330–333. *See also* energy policy; environmental regulations

polypropylene, 392–393

Port McIntyre oil field, 125

Powerformer, 391

Powerplant and Industrial Fuel Use Act of 1978, 86, 193

Pratt, Wallace, 239

preferential lifting, 51, 511n64

Prince William Sound (Alaska), 20, 274. *See also Exxon Valdez* oil spill

producer power, 23–68; emergence after 1973, 3; erosion of contract sanctity, 39; global oil industry shaped by, 477; international companies as contractors under, 67–68, 133–136; of national oil companies, 66; of non-OPEC nations, 133–136; oil economics and, 71; oil prices and, 3–4, 71, 74; politics and

setting of production rates, 49; Russia and transition from Communism, 311–327; self-interest and accommodation with governments, 311. *See also* nationalization of oil production

production-sharing agreements (PSAs), 317–319

Project Independence (1973), 83

Project Next, 470

Prudhoe Bay oil field, 115*f*; discovery of, 113; expansion of recovered oil, 120–122; exploratory wells, 114; joint ventures for exploration and development, 114; management negotiations, 114–116; natural gas pipeline project planning, 116–120; oil and natural gas reserves, 113, 165; operational impact on Exxon management, 127; ownership of, 90; reapportionment of oil among partners, 120; renegotiation of oil and gas valuations, 126–127; satellite fields, 124. *See also* Trans-Alaska Pipeline System (TAPS)

Pryor, Steve, 451

PSAs (production-sharing agreements), 317–319

public affairs, ExxonMobil: advocacy campaign opposing climate change, 464; charges of human rights abuses near Indonesian facilities, 462, 566n117; climate change stance as issue following merger, 461–466; corporate responsibility reports, 468, 567nn134–135; Global Climate and Energy Project, 465–466; integration of departments following merger, 461–471; publications on corporate responsibility activities, 464

Public Utility Holding Company Act of 1978 (U.S.), 384

Pulau Ayer Chawan Island, Singapore, 404

Putin, Vladimir, 320, 324–325

Q

el-Qaddafi, Muammar: ascent to power in Libya, 56; building oil industry on foundation created by King Idris, 57–58; seeking support from Soviet Union, 59; tying natural gas prices to oil prices, 59

Qatar: Exxon's lack of success in, before merger, 65; natural gas reserves, 568n15; North Field LNG projects with Mobil and ExxonMobil, 490–491; as world leader in LNG exports, 491

Quanzhou project negotiations, 418–419

The Quest (Yergin), 325

Quinn, Tom, 105

R

RasGas LNG project, 491

Ravard, Rafael Alfonzo, 31

Rawl, Lawrence G., 216*f*; career of, 218–220; establishing safety as top corporate priority, 290; as Exxon chairman/CEO during low-price era, 18, 20, 216–217, 219*f*; on Exxon's decision-making system, 224–225; on future energy needs, 87–88; on importance of accountability, 377; innovation and reserves replacement, 234; management approach of, 222; on oil and gas exploration, 231–232; organizational innovation of, 20, 216–217; personality of, 220; reaction to *Exxon Valdez* oil spill, 20, 270–273, 275, 302; refocusing Exxon on core business after 1986, 216–217; relocation of Exxon headquarters to Texas, 256–259; on reserves replacement, 234n39; restructuring managerial responsibility, 377; revitalizing company, 500; Thompson on, 236

Raymond, Lee R., 233*f*; on benefits of merger, 441, 443, 563n60; career of, 220–222, 474–476; as chairman/CEO of Exxon during low-price era, 18,

20–21; as chairman/CEO of Exxon-Mobil, 438, 449*f*; on chemical operations, 170; on company focus on return vs. volume, 371–372; compensation of, 1993–2005, 475; on competition between refining and chemical production, 396; criticism of Kyoto Protocol and greenhouse-gas emissions policies, 463–464; declining Woolard's offer to trade Conoco for Exxon Chemical, 429; dissatisfaction with Exxon research programs, 252–253; on diversification as excursions, 168; encouraging change in refining and petrochemicals operations, 21; endorsing closure of Aruba refinery, 371; on importance of accountability, 377; on Koffmann, 533n9; on lack of process for assessing responsibility, 377; management approach of, 222; managerial success of, 500; overseeing ExxonMobil merger, 21; as President of Exxon, 216; relocation of Exxon headquarters to Texas, 258; on reserves replacements, 232–233, 534n38; role in *Exxon Valdez* cleanup, 274, 276; search for successor to, 472; on synergy of research following merger, 461; unease with functional organization, 447; on Venezuelan tax dispute with Creole, 34

Reagan, Ronald, 63, 426

refining and refineries
 conversion capacity, 495
 as core downstream function, 376–377
 energy efficiency, 382–387, 493; cogeneration and, 384–386, 556n44; OIMS operations and, 388
 European strategy post–World War II, 366–367
 integration with chemical production, 395–398, 457–458, 495
 in Japan, 399–404
 lead removal from gasoline, 100–103
 (*See also* leaded gasoline)

post–World War II expansion of, 363–364

rationalization of, 493

Raymond encouraging changes in, 21

refinery runs: decline in, 1973–1986, 364, 365*f*; regional distribution of, 366*f*

refining capacity: consolidation following merger, 457–458, 565nn103–104; ExxonMobil (2005), 419, 493; idle capacity as drag on performance, 364; Latin America vs. Asia-Pacific, 372–373; nationalization and reduction in Venezuela, 370–371; overcapacity by region, 363–366; reductions after 1973, 362–363, 367–368, 492–493

regional adjustments in, 366–373

in Singapore, 404–408

sulfur removal from residual oil, 391–393, 494

technological upgrades, 390–395, 481, 494

transformations since ExxonMobil merger, 492–495

Reid, Richard G., 229, 241

Reliance Electric Company, 190–192

renewable energy: subsidies for, 84

Renna, Eugene A.: organizing consolidation of downstream operations, 446, 448, 457; as president and CEO of Mobil, 435; responsibility for refining and marketing at ExxonMobil, 438; retirement of, 471

residifiner technology, 392–393

Reso, Sidney J., 229, 237, 240, 241

resource nationalism, 27

"Response to Attack on Industrial Structure" (Exxon), 78–79

return on capital employed (ROCE), 559n4, 560n6

Reversion Commission (Venezuela), 30, 32

revolutionary nationalization: in Iran, 54–56; in Libya, 56–68

Richfield Oil Company. *See* Atlantic Richfield Company (ARCO)

Risch, Frank B., 247–248

Rizzo, George, 169

RN-Astra (oil company), 322

Robbins, Clyde E., 274

Robinson, Edward A., 247

Rockefeller, John D.: cost controls, 6; on criticism of Standard Oil as monopoly, 9–10; dual legacy of, 10; efficiency as passion, 6; financing Anglo-American Polar Expedition, 113; predatory business practices, 8; Standard Oil corporate culture and, 6–12; trust as holding company, 7; vertical integration as organizational tactic, 7; as visionary manager, 499

Rockefeller family: contributions to New York City, 537n105

Roll Back Malaria, 357

Roosevelt, Theodore: on Standard Oil, 9

Royal Dutch Shell: as Exxon partner in British sector of North Sea, 140–141; joint exploration agreement with Standard Oil (New Jersey), 136–137; joint operations with Texaco, 428; joint venture for oil field development in Doba Basin, 336; in Libya, 58; as member of "Seven Sisters," 1; renegotiation of PSA for Sakhalin-II project, 325–326; size of, vs. Exxon, 245, 536n71; withdrawal from Chad oil joint venture, 340

Russia: chaos following end of communism, 312; lack of political/administrative authority after fall of Communism, 313; low point of oil industry, 546n19; privatization of oil industry in 1990s, 319–320; Putin and formal petroleum policy, 324–325; transition to capitalist economy, 313–314; Yeltsin government allowing foreign investment, 312, 320

Russian Oil Supply: Performance and Prospects (Grace), 546n19

S

Sacony-Vacuum, 399, 400

Sadlerochit formation (Alaska), 114

Sakhalin Island (Russia): Barrow on, 315; bidding for offshore drilling rights, 317; extended-reach drilling schematic, 322*f*, 323; Exxon Ventures office in, 316; ExxonMobil training of local workers, 323–324; facilities and equipment, 322; first phase of development, 321–323; geography, 316; Japanese exploration of, 317; modular construction used for, 322–323; oil exploration in, 244; partnerships in, 322; permitting process delays, 321; production-sharing agreement for Sakhalin-I, 317–318; recoverable oil reserves, 321–322; Sakhalin-II project, 325–326; Sakhalin-III development rights loss to Gazprom and Rosneft, 326; use of regional contractors, 324

Sakhalin Island Oil & Gas Development Company, 317, 322

Sakhalinmorneftegas (oil company), 317

Sakhalinmorneftegas-Shelf, 322

Sampson, Anthony, 512n80

Santa Barbara Channel: earthquake risk and drilling platform, 131; Hondo project, 128, 130

Saudi Arabia: ExxonMobil investments in, 66; joint ventures between oil companies and Saudis, 509n44; as largest oil producer in Middle East, 36; as linchpin of Exxon's oil supply in Middle East, 65; nationalization of oil production, 36–49; rivalry with Iran, 51, 511n65; technical service contract fees, 47–49. *See also* Aramco of Saudi Arabia

Saudi Aramco: ExxonMobil as largest foreign purchaser of crude oil and hydrocarbons, 66; full nationalization agreement and creation of, 45; as national oil company, 1, 67

Save the Tiger Fund, 470

Savimbi, Jonas, 347, 350

Schroeder, Victor, 209

SDFI (State's Direct Financial Interest), Norway, 149

SeaRiver Mediterranean (formerly *Exxon Valdez*), 285

Securities and Exchange Commission (SEC): Rule 415 and self registration, 250–251; standard on compensation disclosure, 475, 567n143

semisubmersible platforms, 155

Senate Judiciary Subcommittee on Antitrust and Monopoly: testimony opposing Industrial Reorganization Act, 79

"Seven Sisters," 1

Shah of Iran (Mohammad Reza Pahlavi), 50–54; relationship with Exxon, 54, 511n72; removal from power, 54, 55

shale oil. *See* oil shale processing

shale-gas production, 569n19

Shell Oil. *See* Royal Dutch Shell

Sheng Huaren, 415

Sherman Antitrust Act of 1890, 9

significant incident rates, 297

Simon, J. Steven, 457

Singapore, 404–408; catalytic cracker at Jurong Refinery, 406*f*; as centerpiece of downstream activities in Asia, 406–407; chemical expansion in, 407; development plan stressing foreign investment, 405; Exxon expansion in Asia–Pacific region and, 398; as Exxon regional operations center, 407; ExxonMobil as largest foreign investor in, 407–408; geographic advantages for Exxon, 404; partnership between government and Exxon, 405; as refining and petrochemical complex, 404

Sinopec (oil company), 414, 415, 417

Skinner, Samuel K., 274, 301

Slick, W. T. (Bill), Jr., 79, 80, 81

SOCAR (Azerbaijan national oil company), 327

solar energy: Exxon investments in, 80–81, 81*f*, 189–190

Solar Power Corporation (Exxon), 189

Sonagol (Angola national oil company), 346, 355

sour oil, 391

South China Sea: offshore drilling projects, 133, 134

Sprow, Frank B.: on cost effectiveness of oil spill prevention, 298; as director of Corporate Research, 254–255; on reorganization of research programs, 253; of success of *Exxon Valdez* cleanup, 281–282; as vice president of Safety, Health and Environment at Exxon-Mobil, 464, 465*f*

Standard Oil Company (New Jersey): breakup of company as monopoly, 9–10; corporate culture, 6–12; corporate name changes, 503n1; dissolution decree (1911), 10; diversification by, 169; as low-cost oil producer, 6; oil and natural gas production (1970), 15; partnership with Shell in Groningen natural gas field, 136–138; on potentials of oil exploration in Soviet Union, 314–315; as predecessor to Exxon, 2–3, 96, 433; as predecessor to Mobil, 433; recruitment and promotion of managers, 8; technical leadership as corporate value, 7–8; tribal culture of managers, 9; vertical integration, 7. *See also* Rockefeller, John D.

Standard Oil Company of New York (Socony), 503n1

Standard Oil of California: as Aramco co-owner, 25, 36; in Libya, 58; as member of "Seven Sisters," 1. *See also* Chevron

Standard Oil of Ohio (Sohio), 114, 123

Standard Oil Trust, 503n1, 537n105

Standard-Vacuum Oil Company (Stanvac), 399, 400

Star Enterprise (Saudi-Texaco joint venture), 428

State's Direct Financial Interest (SDFI), Norway, 149

Statfjord oil field (North Sea), 148–149, 150; platform design, 153, 154–155

Statoil (Norwegian national oil company), 148–150, 327

steel-jacket platform, 153, 155

step-out innovations, scientific research on, 255, 537n98

Stevens, William, 240, 241; Longwell replacing as head of Exxon USAA, 290

Stevens, William (Bill), 275–276

stock buybacks, 246–252

Strategic Petroleum Reserve, 84

subsea production systems (SPS), 160–165; generic designs for general conditions, 354; long-distance drilling, 352–353; presentations at Offshore Technology Conference in London, 162, 525n101; Shell/Exxon Joint Underwater Development Team, 161–162; underwater manifold center (UMC), 161–162

sulfates: catalytic converter emissions of, 99–100

Superior Oil Company, 248

supertankers. *See* oil tankers

Syncrude Canada Ltd., 200–202, 201*f*, 487–499

syncrudes. *See* synthetic fuels

synfuels, definition, 426n17

synthetic fuels: coal liquefaction, 198; Cold Lake heavy-oil project, 201–202, 486–487, 487*f*; Colony project, 203–204, 205–210, 531n81; commercial viability of, 205–206; cost disadvantages vs. oil, 197; diversification into, 175; Exxon donor solvent process, 198–199,

530nn66–67; Fischer-Topsch process, 198; government subsidies for, 84, 204, 209, 211; irrational exuberance for, 205; oil sands processing, 197, 199–203, 486–488, 487f, 568nn10–12; oil shale processing, 20, 197, 199–200, 203–210; production processes, 197–198; as supplement to conventional oil, 488; synfuels, definition, 526n17

Synthetic Fuels Corporation, 204, 209, 211

T

Tamahori, Tamchiko, 402–403

tanker fleet. *See* oil tankers

TAPS. *See* Trans-Alaska Pipeline System (TAPS)

tar sands. *See* oil sands processing

Tarbell, Ida, 9

Teagle, Walter C., 196, 499, 569n24

Tehran: storming of U.S. Embassy in, 55

Tengiz oil field (Caspian Sea), 328, 455

Tenneco, 175

Tennessee Valley Authority, 85

tension-leg platform, 153, 156, 482

Terengganu, Malaysia, 135

Tesoro–BHP Petroleum merger, 428

tetraethyl lead (TEL), 97

Texaco (oil company): acquisition of Getty Oil, 248; as Aramco co-owner, 25, 36; joint operations with Shell, 428; in Libya, 58; as member of "Seven Sisters," 1

Texaco Canada: purchase by Imperial, 563n76

Thatcher, Margaret: favoring privatization of oil, 145, 523n72

Thompson, Jon: career of, 234–236; exploratory success of, 500; on Exxon's prospects in West Africa, 361; as head of Exploration Technical Assessment Group (ETAG), 236–237; as head of Exxon Exploration Company, 240; negotiations for Angola drilling rights,

349–350; as president of ExxonMobil Exploration Company, 235f; prioritizing exploration program, 239; on Rawl, 236; urging focus on deepwater exploration, 238–239; as vice president of exploration, 236–237

Thornburgh, Richard, 301

Thunder Horse project (Gulf of Mexico), 485

Thurmond, Strom, 561n14

Tillerson, Rex: career of, 472–474; as chairman and CEO of ExxonMobil, 472, 473f; inheriting company positioned for success, 476; on keeping Sakhalin-I project moving, 321; Koonce on, 316

Tomas Ranch (South Texas), 240

Tonen (refining company), 399, 402–403, 557n75

Tonen General Sekiyu, 403

TOSCO (The Oil Shale Company): Colony project cost projections, 206, 207; creation of Colony project, 203–204; on Exxon's withdrawal from Colony project, 209

Townsend, Peter, 471

Train, Russell, 99–100, 103

Trans-Alaska Pipeline Authorization Act (1973), 92–93

Trans-Alaska Pipeline System (TAPS), 89–95; benefits of delays in construction, 92–94; challenges of working in the Arctic, 93–94; under construction, 94f; costs to oil industry of construction delays, 94–95; environmental regulations delaying construction, 19, 86, 91–92, 539n14; feasibility study ("Gold Book"), 90–91; government monitoring of construction, 92; legislation authorizing construction as exemption to environmental challenges, 92; map of, 93f; planning and design of, 90–91; scope of project, 89

Turkish State Oil Company, 327

U

Udall, Morris, 80
underwater manifold center (UMC),
  161–163
Union of Soviet Socialist Republics,
  311–312. *See also* Russia
Union Oil, 124, 209
United Nations Framework Convention
  on Climate Change, 462
Unocal: operations in Azerbaijan, 327
upstream operations: integration following ExxonMobil merger, 454–457,
  565n102; natural gas transformations,
  488–492; oil and syncrudes transformation, 480–488
uranium mining: Exxon and, 185, 528n37;
  oil company diversification into, 180,
  183

V

Valdez Principles, 543n83
Valero Energy Corporation, 453
Vanderbilt, William, 9
Venezuela: Chávez rewriting contracts for
  oil projects, 331–332; early reversion of
  1943 oil leases, 28, 30, 32; Exxon/Con-
  oco withdrawal after Chávez election,
  332–333; Exxon reentry into (1990s),
  66, 328–333; government observers of
  international oil companies, 31–32;
  heavy-oil deposits in Orinoco region,
  329, 330; heavy-oil processing contracts,
  330, 331–332; importance to Exxon as
  oil producer, 15, 26; law of reversion for
  oil leases (1971), 27–28; nationalization of oil production, 1, 19, 24, 26–36;
  nationalization vs. Middle East, 35–36;
  oil export permits, 32; oil-dominated
  economy of, 27, 329–330; original petroleum laws drafted by Exxon lawyers,
  26; petroleum law of 1943, 27; political

opposition to foreign oil companies, 27,
  330–331; post-OPEC embargo tensions
  affecting, 29; profit-sharing agreements
  with oil companies, 26; recoverable oil
  reserves, 329; reorganization of oil companies under reversion, 32; suit against
  Creole for disputed taxes, 34; technical
  assistance contracts with oil companies,
  33. *See also* Creole Petroleum Corporation (Venezuela)
Venezuela's Oil (Betancourt), 27
vertical divestment of oil companies,
  77–78
vertical integration: as Rockefeller strategy, 7
Voorhess, Henry, 25

W

Warner, Rawleigh, Jr., 210
Washington Consensus, 320
Waters, Lisa, 354
Welch, L. W., Jr., 254
West Africa: "oil curse" in, 333–334
Wilhelm, Robert, 287*f*; on Baton Rouge
  refinery explosion, 287–288; as contact
  executive for global services, 446; on
  Exxon's defense of leaded gasoline, 98;
  on Imperial's acquisition of Texaco
  Canada, 368; misgivings about merger
  with Mobil, 434, 562n49; organizing
  consolidation of support functions,
  446, 562n49; recommending disposal
  of Aruba refinery, 371; retirement of,
  471; on Venezuela reversion process, 34
windfall profits: oil price debates over, 75;
  tax legislation, 84; tax proposals preventing realization of, 72
Winslow, Bob, 178, 179, 213
Wolfensohn, James D., 337–338
Woolard, Edward, 429
workforce reductions, 380–382
World Bank: loans assisting transition
  from communism in Russia, 312, 320;

loans to Chad for oil field development, 337–340, 550n72

World Class 2000 initiative, 389

World Energy Outlook (1980), 203, 212, 532n99

X

XTO Energy, 569n19

Y

Yamani, Zaki: as architect of OPEC oil embargo, 42; on Exxon as agent of change in Saudi Arabia, 43; influence on Aramco, 41–43; influence on international oil industry, 41–43; as key to

full nationalization, 46–47; relationship with Garvin, 42–43, 67; as Saudi oil minister, 26

Yastreb offshore drilling rig, 322*f*, 323

Yeltsin, Boris, 312, 316

Yergin, Daniel, 325

Yom Kippur War, 39

Yost, Paul A., 274

Yukos (oil company), 319–320

Z

Zelten oil field (Libya), 56, 59

Zhuhai refinery and chemical project, 414, 415–417, 559n109

Zhuhai Special Economic Zone, 414